38th Annual International Logistics Conference and Exhibition (SOLE 2003)

Melding Defense and Commercial Logistics

Huntsville, Alabama, USA
12 - 14 August 2003

ISBN: 978-1-5108-3839-0

Printed from e-media with permission by:

Curran Associates, Inc.
57 Morehouse Lane
Red Hook, NY 12571

Some format issues inherent in the e-media version may also appear in this print version.

Printed by Curran Associates, Inc. (2017)

For permission requests, please contact SOLE – The International Society of Logistics at the address below.

SOLE – The International Society of Logistics
14625 Baltimore Avenue, Suite 303
Laurel, Maryland 20707-4902
USA

Phone: (301) 459-8446
Fax: (301) 459-1522

solehq@erols.com

Additional copies of this publication are available from:

Curran Associates, Inc.
57 Morehouse Lane
Red Hook, NY 12571 USA
Phone: 845-758-0400
Fax: 845-758-2633
Email: curran@proceedings.com
Web: www.proceedings.com

TABLE OF CONTENTS

EXECUTIVE PLENARY SESSION – BRIDGING DEFENSE AND INDUSTRY

CONFIGURATION MANAGEMENT / DATA MANAGEMENT

ACQUISITION SUPPORT IN AN E-BUSINESS ENVIRONMENT

TRACK 1 – COTS APPLICATIONS

TRACK 2 – LOGISTICS PLANS AND CALS

MANAGEMENT AND STRATEGY PANEL

SPACE PLENARY

HOMELAND SECURITY PLENARY SESSION

SPACE PANEL

HOMELAND SECURITY PANEL

INDUSTRY PANEL – DEFENSE LOGISTICS CHALLENGES WITH INTEGRATING COMMERCIAL ELECTRONICS TECHNOLOGY

TRACK 1 – PERFORMANCE BASED LOGISTICS

TRACK 2 – LOGISTICS DATA AND DATA ANALYSIS

TRACK 3 – OBSOLESCENCE AND WARRANTIES

TRACK 4 – LOGISTICS MANAGEMENT AND LIFE CYCLE COSTS

ADDITIONAL PAPER

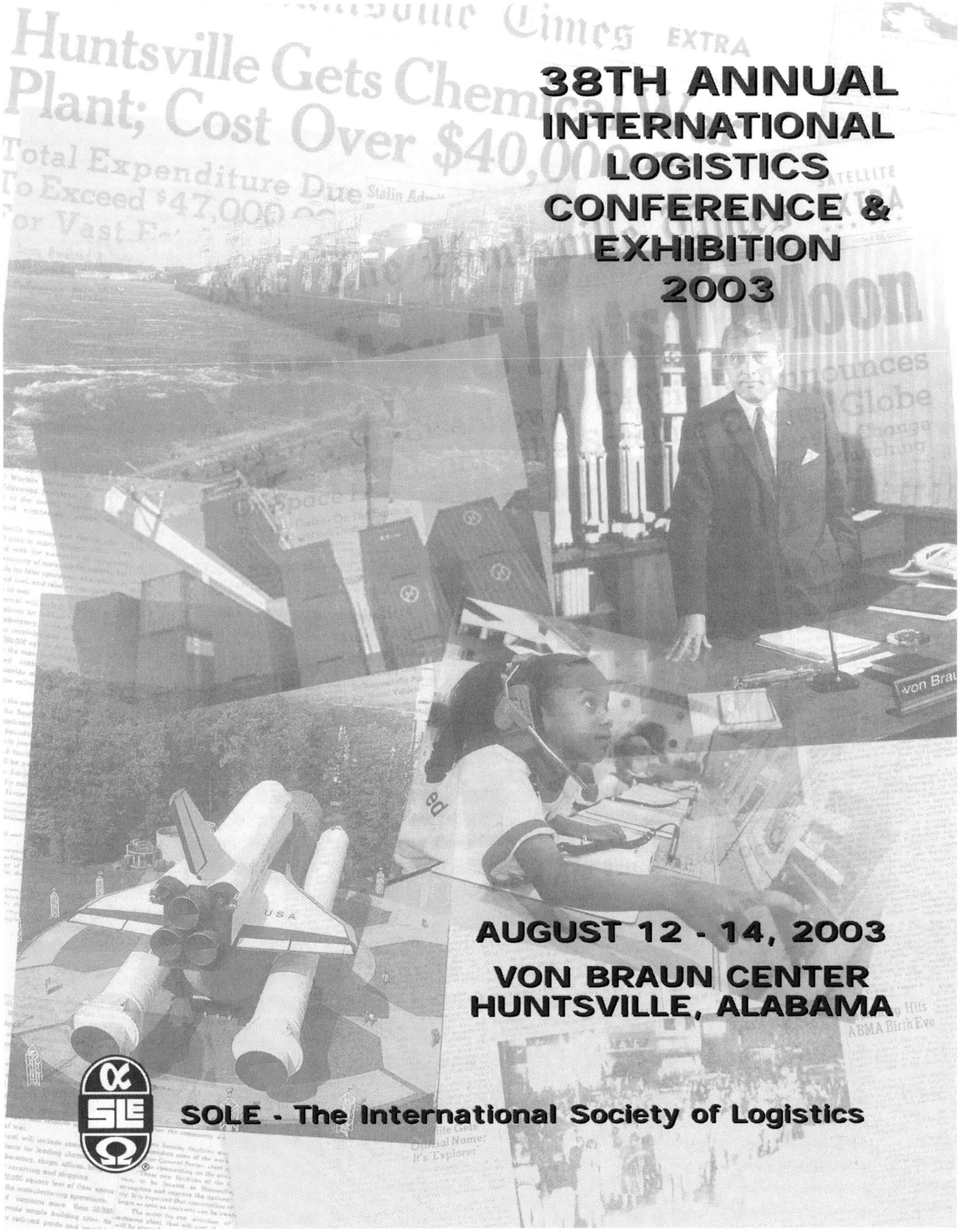

38TH ANNUAL INTERNATIONAL LOGISTICS CONFERENCE & EXHIBITION 2003

AUGUST 12 - 14, 2003
VON BRAUN CENTER
HUNTSVILLE, ALABAMA

SOLE - The International Society of Logistics

Welcome to SOLE 2003

Welcome to SOLE's 38th International Conference and Exposition.

This year's conference theme – "Melding Defense & Commercial Logistics" – provides the forum for a shift in the focus of the Society's symposia. The program lays a foundation for ongoing dialogue during the coming year on both the future of logistics and the education of logisticians, each with a developing emphasis on the evolution of acquisition and support processes. The Society has brought together critical decision-makers in the Government and Industry as keynote speakers, plenary panel members, and presenters for this year's event. In addition, we have an added feature for this year's conference in the demonstration and application of logistics in four key centers in the region.

I trust that the conference will be personally fulfilling for all attendees and those whom you will work with when you return home. Sharing experiences will provide the broadest benefit to you and to you co-workers in the field of logistics.

One element of success in any conference is the location. The location this year provides a foundation for two historical benchmarks in the Society. Huntsville plays a key role in our history as a Society, since it was here in the early 1960s that Dr. Wernher von Braun first identified the need for a professional society for logisticians. It is also the home of Redstone Arsenal and NASA's Marshall Space Flight Center, both representing the opportunities of the future.

I hope that you, your family and your guests will take time during the week to enjoy the many attractions in the Huntsville area. The Port of Huntsville provides a new vision for a regional intermodal port; while local - museums and historical sites provide a historical perspective for the state, the nation and the region. The Space and Rocket Center is a family oriented view of our history in space, and the local golf experience and variety of courses is unparalleled in appeal.

Welcome to the conference and enjoy the experience.

Anthony E. Trovato, CPL
President
SOLE – The International Society of Logistics

OFFICE OF THE GOVERNOR

BOB RILEY
GOVERNOR

STATE CAPITOL
MONTGOMERY, ALABAMA 36130

(334) 242-7100
FAX: (334) 242-0937

STATE OF ALABAMA

August 11, 2003

Greetings:

On behalf of the people of Alabama, welcome to Huntsville for the International Society of Logistics 38th Annual International Symposium and Exhibition. I know you will enjoy your stay.

If time permits, stay an extra day or two to enjoy additional attractions in the Huntsville area. Return to our beautiful state in the future to experience the variety of cultures, food and friendly residents.

Again, thanks for visiting Alabama. Come back any time.

Sincerely,

Bob Riley
Governor

BR/ls/sf

MADISON COUNTY

Mike Gillespie, Chairman
Roger Jones, District 1
Faye Dyer, District 2
Jerry Craig, District 3
Dale W. Strong, District 4
Mo Brooks, District 5
Prince Preyer, Jr., District 6

SOLE – The International Society of Logistics

Dear Attendees:

On behalf of the Madison County Commission, I am pleased to welcome you to our city. We thank you for choosing Huntsville as the host city for SOLE 2003, your 38th Annual International Symposium and Exhibition.

We think our city has a personality similar to that of its people—enthusiastic, warm and hospitable. We have become not only a county that reinforces its rich heritage, but also an international community on the leading edge of technology. We have excellent meeting facilities, an abundance of guest rooms, many attractions and points of interest and a convention bureau that enjoys assisting groups such as yours.

We hope you have an enjoyable stay in Huntsville.

Sincerely,

Mike Gillespie, Chairman
MADISON COUNTY COMMISSION

MG:sh

Madison County Courthouse
100 Northside Square
Huntsville, AL
35801-4820
256-532-3492
Fax 256-532-6994
www.co.madison.al.us

Loretta Spencer
Mayor

"The Space to be in the 21st Century"

SOLE – The International Society of Logistics

GREETINGS AND WELCOME TO THE CITY OF HUNTSVILLE!

As Mayor and on behalf of the citizens of the city of Huntsville, I would like to welcome you to our fine city. I want to take this opportunity to express our appreciation for being chosen host city for SOLE 2003, your 38th Annual International Symposium and Exhibition.

We invite you to spend some time visiting the many points of interest in and around Huntsville. Our attractions and recreational facilities will provide you with a variety of interesting things to do.

You will find the hospitality of the citizens of the city of Huntsville to be second to none in the state of Alabama. If there is anything that we in the Mayor's office can do to assist you during your visit, please contact us.

Sincerely yours,

Loretta Spencer
Mayor

P. O. Box 308 • Huntsville, AL 35804-0308 • Phone (256) 427-5000 • FAX (256) 427-5257
www.hsvcity.com

OFFICE OF THE MAYOR

Mayor Jan Wells

August 12, 2003

SOLE – The International Society of Logistics

Greetings!

Thank you for allowing the city of Madison the opportunity to extend greetings and congratulations as you celebrate the 38th Annual International Symposium and Exhibition of SOLE – The International Society of Logistics.

From Dr. Wernher von Braun to the International Space Station, Marshall Space Flight Center continues to play an important role in our Space initiatives. I am grateful to your recognition of the role northern Alabama has played in the history of the Society by "returning to its roots".

Welcome to each guest! Congratulations and a heartfelt "thank you" to all volunteers who worked tirelessly to make this event successful.

Sincerely,

Jan Wells
Mayor

100 Hughes Road • Madison, AL 35758
(256) 772-5603 • 1-800-337-1631 • Fax (256) 772-3828

LOCATION AND TIMES

MEETINGS

Day	Start	End	Event	Room
Sat, 8/9/03	AM 8:00	5:00	Executive Board	Heritage 1 (Hilton)
Sun, 8/10/03	AM 8:00	5:00	Board of Directors	Heritage 1 (Hilton)
	8:00	5:00	Chapter Chair Select Committee	Von Braun (Hilton)
	8:00	5:00	LEF Board of Governors	Twickenham (Hilton)
Mon, 8/11/03	AM 7:30	5:30	CPL Exam #62	Twickenham (Hilton)
	8:00	4:00	Board of Directors	Heritage 1 (Hilton)
	8:00	5:00	Chapter Chair Select Committee	Von Braun (Hilton)
	PM 4:00	5:00	LEF Board of Trustees Election	Heritage 1 & 2 (Hilton)
	5:00	5:30	Annual Meeting	Heritage 1 & 2 (Hilton)
Tues, 8/12/03	PM 1:00	5:00	Board of Advisors	Twickenham (Hilton)

MEALS AND RECEPTIONS

Day	Start	End	Event	Room
Mon, 8/11/03	PM 6:00	7:30	Exhibitors Reception	North Hall 1 & 2 (VBC)
Tue, 8/12/03	AM 7:00	8:00	Continental Breakfast	North Hall Gallery (VBC)
	noon	1:30	Lunch	North Hall 1 & 2 (VBC)
	PM 6:30	8:30	Opening Reception	Space & Rocket Center
Wed, 8/13/03	AM 7:00	8:00	Continental Breakfast	North Hall Gallery (VBC)
	AM 11:30	1:00	Lunch	North Hall 1 & 2 (VBC)
	PM 6:30	7:30	CPLs, Fellows and Past Presidents Reception	Milltown (Hilton)
Thu, 8/14/03	AM 7:00	8:00	Continental Breakfast	North Hall Gallery (VBC)
	AM 11:30	1:30	President's Luncheon	North Hall 1 (VBC)
	PM 5:30	6:00	Award Winner's Reception	Twickenham (Hilton)
	5:30	6:00	Awards Reception	Grand Salon Pre-Function Area
	6:00	9:00	Awards Banquet	Grand Salon (Hilton)

CONFERENCE AT A GLANCE

Date	Start	End	Description	Room
Sat, 8/9/03	noon	5:00	Registration Desk Open	Hotel Lobby (Hilton)
	AM 8:00	5:00	Executive Board	Heritage 1 (Hilton)
Sun, 8/10/03	noon	5:00	Registration	Hotel Lobby (Hilton)
	AM 8:00	5:00	Board of Directors	Heritage 1 (Hilton)
	8:00	5:00	Chapter Chair Select Committee	Von Braun (Hilton)
	8:00	5:00	LEF Board of Governors	Twickenham (Hilton)
	8:00	12:00	Workshop: **SOLE and You**	Hunt (Hilton)
	8:00	5:00	Workshop: **Performance Based Logistics**	Milltown (Hilton)
	PM 1:00	5:00	Workshop: **Logistics: The Totality of Quality**	Hunt (Hilton)
Mon, 8/11/03	AM 6:30	12:00	Registration (AM)	Hotel Lobby (Hilton)
	12:30	6:00	Registration (PM)	North Hall Gallery (VBC)
	7:30	5:30	CPL Exam #62	Twickenham (Hilton)
	8:00	12:00	Workshop: **Quantitative Measures of Logistics**	Milltown (Hilton)
	8:00	4:00	Board of Directors	Heritage 1 (Hilton)
	8:00	4:00	Exhibitor Move-In	North Hall 1 & 2 (Hilton)
	8:00	5:00	Chapter Chair Select Committee	Von Braun (Hilton)
	PM 1:00	5:00	Workshop: **Logistics in the Integrated Enterpirse - 400 Easy Lessons**	Hunt (Hilton)
	1:00	5:00	Workshop: **PowerLOG/COMPASS**	Milltown (Hilton)
	4:00	5:00	LEF Board of Trustees Election	Heritage 1 & 2 (Hilton)
	5:00	5:30	Annual Meeting	Heritage 1 & 2 (Hilton)
	6:00	7:30	Exhibitors Reception	North Hall 1 & 2 (VBC)
Tue, 8/12/03	AM 7:00	5:30	Registration	North Hall Gallery (VBC)
	7:00	8:00	Continental Breakfast	North Hall Gallery (VBC)
	8:00	9:00	Opening Session	North Hall 3 (VBC)
	9:00	10:00	Break	North Hall 1 & 2 (VBC)
	10:00	12:00	**Executive Plenary Session**	North Hall 3 (VBC)
	PM noon	1:30	Lunch	North Hall 1 & 2 (VBC)
	1:00	5:00	Board of Advisors	Twickenham (Hilton)
	1:30	3:00	**CM/DM Panel**	Orchestra Rehearsal (VBC)
	1:30	3:00	**E-Business Panel**	North Hall Salon 1 (VBC)
	3:00	4:00	Break	North Hall 1 & 2 (VBC)
	4:00	5:00	**Track 1: COTS Applications**	Orchestra Rehearsal (VBC)
	4:00	5:00	**Track 2: Logisitics Plans and CALS**	North Hall Salon 2 (VBC)
	4:00	5:00	**Track 3: Maintenance and Maintainability**	North Hall Salon 1 (VBC)
	4:00	5:00	**Track 4: Inventory Data**	North Hall Salon 4 (VBC)
	6:30	8:30	Opening Reception	Space & Rocket Center

Continued on next page

CONFERENCE AT A GLANCE *con't.*

Date	Start	End	Description	Room
Wed, 8/13/03	AM 7:00	6:00	Registration	North Hall Gallery (VBC)
	7:00	8:00	Continental Breakfast	North Hall Gallery (VBC)
	8:00	9:30	**Industry Plenary Session**	North Hall 3 (VBC)
	9:30	10:30	Break	North Hall 1 & 2 (VBC)
	10:30	11:30	**Defense Plenary Session**	North Hall 3 (VBC)
	11:30	1:00	Lunch	North Hall 1 & 2 (VBC)
	PM 1:00	2:15	**Defense Panel**	North Hall 3 (VBC)
	1:00	2:15	**Transportation & Distribution Panel**	Orchestra Rehearsal (VBC)
	1:00	2:15	**Management & Strategy Panel**	North Hall Salon 1 (VBC)
	2:15	3:15	Break	North Hall 1 & 2 (VBC)
	3:15	6:00	Logistics Operational Demos	Off Site
	6:30	7:30	CPLs, Fellows and Past Presidents Reception	Milltown (Hilton)
Thurs, 8/14/03	AM 7:00	12:00	Registration	North Hall Gallery (VBC)
	7:00	8:00	Continental Breakfast	North Hall Gallery (VBC)
	8:00	9:30	**Space Plenary Session**	North Hall 3 (VBC)
	9:30	10:00	Break	North Hall Gallery (VBC)
	10:00	11:30	**Homeland Defense Plenary Session**	North Hall 3 (VBC)
	11:30	1:30	**President's Luncheon**	North Hall 1 (VBC)
	PM 1:30	3:00	**Space Panel**	Orchestra Rehearsal (VBC)
	1:30	3:00	**Homeland Security Panel**	North Hall Salon 1 (VBC)
	1:30	3:00	**Industry Panel**	North Hall 3 (VBC)
	3:00	3:30	Break	North Hall Gallery (VBC)
	3:30	5:00	**Track 1: Performance Based Logistics**	Orchestra Rehearsal (VBC)
	3:30	5:00	**Track 2: Logistics Data and Data Analysis**	North Hall Salon 2 (VBC)
	3:30	5:00	**Track 3: Obsolescence and Warranties**	North Hall Salon 1 B (VBC)
	3:30	5:00	**Track 4: Logistics Management and Life Cycle Costs**	North Hall Salon 4 (VBC)
	5:30	6:00	Award Winner's Reception	Twickenham (Hilton)
	5:30	6:00	**Awards Reception**	Grand Salon Pre-Function Area (Hilton)
	6:00	9:00	**Awards Banquet**	Grand Salon (Hilton)

WORKSHOP SUMMARIES

SUNDAY

SOLE and You

Mr. Kenneth H. Brockel, Defense Application Division Director

This workshop is FREE to all attendees. It is designed for both new and old members of SOLE, as well as those non-members interested in establishing their credentials as professional logisticians, or those who are simply curious about the resources available from our international Society. The workshop will explore the benefits of SOLE membership, as well as the activities available for the individual to contribute to both his/her own growth as a logistician and to the furtherance of Society objectives within the global logistics community.

Performance Based Logistics

Mr. W. Erich Hausner, Supportability Engineering Application Division Director; and Michael J. Osborne, CPL

For the logistician desiring to achieve enhanced levels of knowledge in Performance Based Logistics (PBL) linked to development of discrete Supportability Design-to Requirements (SDTRs) conveyed via CAD, this workshop will provide a methodical, rigorous, and participative process to achieve those objectives. The participants will view examples of SDTRs, generate SDTRs for three case studies, and will be instructed on Simultaneous Design for Producibility and Supportability Focused on Cost Containment. At the detailed level, the participant will focus on:

- Considering the possibility of seamless "design reviews"
- Examining the Work Breakdown Structure (WBS) as an information node for requirements and features tracking
- Rigorously identifying Supportability cost drivers
- Tracking contractor's degree of Producibility and Supportability design progress
- Reducing risk by minimizing transition impact between design, production and support
- Providing critical communication links with designers to achieve information "design fusion" and effective feedback to production and support IPTs

Participants will receive a copy of the U.S. Army Materiel Command Logistics Support Activity's Cost Analysis Strategy Assessment (CASA) decision support software to assist in the calculation of the total cost of ownership, Trade-off Analysis, Support Concept Analysis, Production Rate and Quantity Analysis, Warranty Analysis, Spares Provisioning, Reliability Growth Analysis, and Operational Availability Analysis.

Approved for CEUs.

Logistics: The Totality of Quality

Brig Gen (Ret) Frank R. Steer, MBE, President, European Organization for Quality and Director General, Institute of Quality Assurance

The Business Excellence Model developed by the European Foundation for Quality Management establishes an iterative approach to achieving excellence in the pursuit of logistics management. The model positions leadership as the starting point for an enabling mechanism channeled through the organization's people, strategy, and resources by means of organizational processes. The subsequent results impact upon customers, people within the organization, and upon society as a whole. These results can be quantitatively and qualitatively measured as performance indicators. Attendees at this workshop will "write their own script" for logistics process improvements, using this self-reinforcing innovation and learning model.

Approved for CEUs.

MONDAY

Quantitative Measures of Logistics

Mr. Philip T. Frohne, CPL, The Boeing Company

This workshop will present basic and advanced logistics mathematics. It is applicable to logistics students, CPL candidates, and experienced logisticians. It includes both business and military mathematics applications. A "four function" level of mathematical knowledge is sufficient to benefit from this workshop. Participants are encouraged to bring simple scientific and/or financial calculators to take part in the exercises. The instructor has a light, informal, discussion-style approach to presenting this material. Participants will receive a copy of a new SOLE-published logistics mathematics reference book written by the instructor (278 pages). This book provides examples and solutions of over 350 formulas used in the logistics profession. The appendices contain additional definitions including categorizing failures, maintenance, and supportability. Many charts, graphs, logistics quotes, and thought provoking "notes" are included.

Approved for CEUs.

WORKSHOP SUMMARIES con't.

Logistics in the Integrated Enterprise: 400 Easy Lessons

Mr. Gary A. Landis, CPIM, CIRM; APICS

We've heard the expression before: "what goes around – comes around." Well, it's happening again. In the early days of the space program, the military was the first to recognize the need for "materiel" management – ensuring all materials were identified and available to come together for final assembly. From those early days, the private sector learned from the military the need to manage the overwhelming quantity of materials within their organizations. Through this progression, an immense body of knowledge devoted to understanding the complete supply chain – from your supplier's supplier to your customer's customer – was identified and developed. In today's world, logistics is the largest section of that supply chain, and plays an integral role in the success of companies around the world. Companies – and the military – are continuously looking at ways to maximize efforts in the total supply chain, utilizing technologies such as ERP, LEAN, and Supply Chain Management. Organizations are identifying methods to move materials from supplier to customer at rapid speeds – some using warehouses only to stage subassemblies before going to assembly destinations – and clearing the warehouse daily. Some are even having materials shipped directly from the supplier to the customer, eliminating the warehouse all together. Before this all works, however, organizations – and the military – will have to understand every aspect of the entire enterprise. The enterprise will have to be fully integrated, and logistics will play its most important role since the early days of the space program. This workshop will provide in-depth education on the need for integrated enterprise management, and the role logistics plays in that effort. Logistics in the Integrated Enterprise – 400 Easy Lessons.

Approved for CEUs.

PowerLOG/COMPASS

Mr. Nicholas Giordano and Mr. Louis Sciaroni, U.S. Army Materiel Command Logistics Support Activity

This workshop will provide an overview of PowerLOG and COMPASS. PowerLOG is an acquisition logistics data management tool that satisfies requirements for the Logistics Management Information (LMI) and Logistics Support Analysis Record (LSAR). It can be used to develop, evaluate, review, and integrate logistics data for materiel systems and generate logistics support summaries such as the Repair Parts and Special Tools Lists (RPSTL), Maintenance Allocation Charts (MAC), Task Analysis (LSA-019), Provisioning Technical Documentation, Bill of Materials, and more! Technical Manual Reports meet MIL-STD-40051 formats and have XML, and HTML outputs. It can also convert legacy data formats such as MIL-STD-1552, MIL-STD-1388-2A LSA-036, and MIL-STD-1388-2B LSA-036. The Computerized Optimization Model for Predicting and Analyzing Support Structures (COMPASS) is a computer model designed to assist in conducting a Level of Repair Analysis (LORA) study. The objective of COMPASS is to simultaneously optimize both the maintenance concept and supply support. COMPASS simultaneously considers up to four levels of maintenance and supply support plus contractor support. It will identify the most economical maintenance level to either repair or discard the end item and all line replaceable units (LRU) and shop replaceable units (SRU). COMPASS can also evaluate logistics life cycle maintenance and support costs associated with a user defined maintenance concept. The COMPASS output report includes: Cost and allocation of manpower and support equipment required to repair all items; Economics of TPS development, contractor versus organic repair, and screening items before repair; Cost of initial and replenishment spares; and other overall logistics related cost data (i.e., transportation, cataloging, etc.).

Approved for CEUs.

LOCATION OF WORKSHOPS

SUNDAY	Room	Start Time	End Time
SOLE and You	Hunt (Hilton)	8:00 AM	noon
Performance Based Logistics	Milltown (Hilton)	8:00 AM	5:00 PM
Logistics: The Totality of Quality	Hunt (Hilton)	1:00 PM	5:00 PM
MONDAY			
Quantitative Measures of Logistics	Milltown (Hilton)	8:00 AM	noon
Logistics in the Integrated Enterprise - 400 Easy Lessons	Hunt (Hilton)	1:00 PM	5:00 PM
PowerLOG/COMPASS	Milltown (Hilton)	1:00 PM	5:00 PM

TUESDAY SCHEDULE

7:00 - 5:30	**Registration**
7:00 - 8:00	**Continental Breakfast** (North Hall Gallery)
8:00 - 8:30	**Welcome and Opening Remarks** Mr. Anthony E. Trovato, CPL, President, SOLE – The International Society of Logistics; LTG (Ret) James M. Link, SOLE 2003 General Chair, President & CEO, Teledyne-Brown Engineering; Honorable Loretta Spencer, Mayor, Huntsville; Honorable Jan Wells, Mayor, Madison; MG Larry J. Dodgen, Commanding General, US Army Aviation & Missile Command; Mr. James H. Carter, Deputy Director, Center Operations Directorate, Marshall Space Flight Center
8:30 - 9:00	**Keynote Address** **Congressman Curt Weldon (R-PA) [Invited]**
9:00 - 10:00	**Break** (Exhibit Hall)
10:00 - 12:00	**Executive Plenary Session: "Bridging Defense and Industry"** *Moderator: Mr. Charles (Chuck) Huber, CPL, President, HCI* Mr. Allen W. Beckett, Principal Assistant Deputy Undersecretary of Defense for Logistics and Material Readiness; LTG Richard L. Kelly, Deputy Commandant, Installations and Logistics, Headquarters USMC; LTG Charles F. Mahan, Jr., G-4, Headquarters, Department of the Army; VADM Charles W. Moore, Jr., N-4, Headquarters, Department of the Navy; VADM Gordon S. Holder, J-4, Joint Chiefs of Staff; MG Hawthorne L. (Peete) Proctor, Director, -Logistics Operations, Defense Logistics Agency
12:00 - 1:30	**Lunch** (Exhibit Hall)

	Panel Orchestra Rehearsal	Panel North Hall Salon 2
1:30 - 3:00	**"Configuration Management/Data Management"** *Moderator: Dr. Richard M. Davis, Director, Defense Programs Office,* Oak Ridge National Laboratory COL Mike Ivy, Director, Combat Support Battle Laboratory, U.S. Army Combined Arms Support Command; Mr. Dan Dannermueller, Vice President, Knowledge Management Solutions, Inc.; Mr. Robert Kuper, Program Director, Army Transformation Reliability Improvement Program, U.S. Army TACOM-ARDEC; Mr. Greg Peters, Program Manager, U.S. Army TACOM-ARDEC; Mr. Paul Skalny, Deputy Director, U.S. Army TACOM National Automotive Center	**"Acquisition Support in an E-Business Environment"** *Moderator: Colonel Joseph Cassel, Commander, Defense Logistics Information Service* Mr. Peter Benson, Chief Technical Officer, Electronic Code Commerce Management Association (ECCMA); Ms. Gabrielle Zimmerman, Deputy Program Manager, DOD Electronic Commerce Mall (EMALL), Headquarters Defense Logistics Agency; Mr. Richard (Brett) Andrews, Professor of Logistics, Defense Acquisition University
3:00 - 4:00	**Break** (Exhibit Hall)	

	Track 1 Orchestra Rehearsal	Track 2 North Hall Salon 2	Track 3 North Hall Salon 1	Track 4 North Hall Salon 4
4:00 - 5:00	**Paper Presentations:** "COTS Applications" *Moderator: Mr. Marty Martin, CPL* • "Integration of Commercial Products into the Military Search and Rescue Personnel Recovery (SARPR) System," Kenneth H. Brockel, Michael D. Fredrickson, Harry G. Ivory Jr. and Douglas Howe. • "A Case Study of a Dual-Use Embedded Vehicle Computer," Mark Haslim and Thomas White • "Application of Commercial Information Technology Tools to Support Defense Logistics Analysis and the Logistics of Field Defense Systems," Michael Davis, Jean Ann Davis, and Michael Gibbons • "Information Technology: Expediting Intermodal Military Logistics," US Merchant Marine Midshipmen Cornelio, Perri and Chrosniak	**Paper Presentations:** "Logistics Plans and CALS" *Moderator: Mr. Richard (Rick) Turner* • "Defense Procurement Under the New DOD 5000 Series," Dr. Ralph Harper • "Implementation of CALS Strategy at Public Enterprise of PTT Traffic in Serbia," Rados Popadic • "China's Logistics Industry and the World Trade Organization: A Trend of Globalization," Daiheng Ni and Chunx Feng • "Linking Supportability Analysis Data and Support Publications for Full Service Life of Complex Assets," Patrick Read and Frank Hallam	**Paper Presentations:** "Maintenance and Maintainability *Moderator: Mr. Mel Waters* • "Product Support Logistics Based on Product Design Characteristics and Operating Environment," Behzad Ghodrati and Uday Kumar • "Impact of RCM on Performance and Customer Perception," Melkote Ramaswamy, Ph.D. • "Operability in Space: Commonality and Interchangeability – An Approch to Cost Reduction," Michael F. Baran • "Data Modeling Change Detection of Inventory Flow and Instrument Calibration," Holger M. Jaenisch, Ph.D; James W. Handley, and Louis A. Bonhams	**Paper Presentations:** "Inventory Data" *Moderator: Mr. Artro Whitman* • "Secondary Item Management," John T. LaFalce • "Melding Defense and Commercial Logistics to Optimize Key Performance Indicator Using Porters Value Chain Secondary Activities," Paul Wilcox • "Applying Trend analysis Techniques to Logistics Needs," J.R. Miller • "A Review of Logistics Management Information," Joe Ketron
6:30 - 8:30	**Opening Reception** (Space and Rocket Center)			

TUESDAY TRACK DETAILS

TRACK 1

4:00 - 5:00 **Paper Presentations: "COTS Applications"**

Moderator: Mr. Marty Martin, CPL

- "Integration of Commercial Products into the Military Search and Rescue Personnel Recovery (SARPR) System," Kenneth H. Brockel, Michael D. Fredrickson, Harry G. Ivory Jr. and Douglas Howe.
- "A Case Study of a Dual-Use Embedded Vehicle Computer," Mark Haslim and Thomas White
- "Application of Commercial Information Technology Tools to Support Defense Logistics Analysis and the Logistics of Field Defense Systems," Michael Davis, Jean Ann Davis, and Michael Gibbons
- "Information Technology: Expediting Intermodal Military Logistics," US Merchant Marine Midshipmen Cornelio, Perri and Chrosniak

TRACK 2

4:00 - 5:00 **Paper Presentations: "Logistics Plans and CALS"**

Moderator: Mr. Richard (Rick) Turner

- "Defense Procurement Under the New DOD 5000 Series," Dr. Ralph Harper
- "Implementation of CALS Strategy at Public Enterprise of PTT Traffic in Serbia," Rados Popadic
- "China's Logistics Industry and the World Trade Organization: A Trend of Globalization," Daiheng Ni and Chunx Feng
- "Linking Supportability Analysis Data and Support Publications for Full Service Life of Complex Assets," Patrick Read and Frank Hallam

TRACK 3

4:00 - 5:00 **Paper Presentations: "Maintenance and Maintainability**

Moderator: Mr. Mel Waters

- "Product Support Logistics Based on Product Design Characteristics and Operating Environment," Behzad Ghodrati and Uday Kumar
- "Impact of RCM on Performance and Customer Perception," Melkote Ramaswamy, Ph.D.
- "Operability in Space: Commonality and Interchangeability – An Approch to Cost Reduction," Michael F. Baran
- "Data Modeling Change Detection of Inventory Flow and Instrument Calibration," Holger M. Jaenisch, Ph.D; James W. Handley, and Louis A. Bonhams

TRACK 4

4:00 - 5:00 **Paper Presentations: "Inventory Data"**

Moderator: Mr. Artro Whitman

- "Secondary Item Management," John T. LaFalce
- "Melding Defense and Commercial Logistics to Optimize Key Performance Indicator Using Porters Value Chain Secondary Activities," Paul Wilcox
- "Applying Trend analysis Techniques to Logistics Needs," J.R. Miller
- "A Review of Logistics Management Information," Joe Ketron

Acknowledgements

The Society would like to thank the following for their support to SOLE 2003:

- **LTG (Ret) James M. Link**, General Chairman; **Douglas R. Baker, CPL**, Deputy Chairman; the members of the Conference Committee; and all the SOLE members that have volunteered countless hours, both before and during the symposium, to make this year's program a success.
- **Mr. Charles (Chuck) Huber, CPL**, and **Dr. Russell E. Vacante**, members of SOLE's Board of Advisors, for coordinating and orchestrating the Plenary Sessions.
- **Marshall Space Flight Center, Port of Huntsville, Target Distribution Center** and **Nektar Therapeutics** for generously hosting Wednesday's Operational Logistics Demonstrations.
- **Raytheon Technical Services Company** (Reston, Virginia) for providing the symposium pocket guides and the symposium signage.
- **All the companies and organizations** that generously provided material for inclusion in the conference bags.

and, last but certainly not least, the

- **Citizens and companies of Madison County** for their gracious "welcome home" to SOLE.

WEDNESDAY SCHEDULE

7:00 - 6:00	**Registration**
7:00 - 8:00	**Continental Breakfast** (North Hall Gallery)
8:00 - 9:30	**Industry Plenary Session** *Moderator: Mr. Charles (Chuck) Huber, CPL, President, HCI* Mr. Thomas J. Burlin, Vice President, Federal Government Industry, IBM Business Consulting (Invited); Mr. Thomas J. Edwards, Deputy to the Commander, U.S. Army Combined Arms Support Command; Mr. Jeffery L. Holmes, Executive Vice President and President, Government, Aerospace & Defense, Manugistics; Mr. Brian Manty, General Manager, Information Technology, CTC; LTG (Ret) John M. McDuffie, Vice President, Defense Programs and Systems, Anteon Corporation; Mr. John Messmore, Vice President and General Manager, Logistics Services Division, Electronic Systems, Northrop Grumman Electronic Systems; Mr. John F. Phillips, Vice President, Government Services, Defense & Space, Honeywell; Mr. Eric S. Stange, Managing Partner, Defense Programs, Accenture; Mr. R. Kenneth Trammell, Executive Director, Marine Corps Logistics Command
9:30 - 10:30	**Break** (Exhibit Hall)
10:30 - 11:30	**Defense Plenary Session: "The Future Logistics Workforce"** *Brig Gen Frank J. Anderson, Jr., President, Defense Acquisition University – Moderator* Mr. Allen W. Beckett, Principal Assistant Deputy Undersecretary of Defense for Logistics and Material Readiness; LTG (Ret) Roy E. Beauchamp, Senior Vice President, Defense Infrastructure Services, Washington Group International; Mr. William T. Powell, Jr., Executive Director, Institute for Defense & Business
11:30 - 1:00	**Lunch** (Exhibit Hall)

	Panel North Hall Salon 3	Panel Orchestra Rehearsal	Panel North Hall Salon 1
1:00 - 2:15	**Defense Panel: "Lean Thinking Applications to the Military"** *Moderator: Mr. Kenneth H. Brockel, Chief, Airborne Mission Division, U.S. Army Communications and Electronics Command* Mr. James Miller, Program Manager, PMTO SPAWAR Logistics Contract, C-Cubed Corporation; Dr. Mel Adams, Senior Business Advisor, Alabama Technology Network, University of Alabama in Huntsville; Mr. Larry P. Dessureault, Director, Supportability And CM/DM Engineering, BAE Systems; Professor Robert A. Miller, CPIM, George College & State University	**Transportation & Distribution Panel: "The Role of Transportation in Logistics Chain Management"** *Moderator: Mr. Clifford G. Geiger, President, Geiger & Associates* Mr. Roy Bowman, Vice President, Government Affairs, APL Ltd.; Ms. Susan C. Kinney, Deputy Director, Logistics Plans, Policies & Strategic Mobility Division Headquarters, U.S. Marine Corps; Mr. William R. Lucas, Deputy to the Commander Military Traffic Management Command	**Management & Strategy Panel** *Moderator: Dr. Ralph L. Harper, Director, Management & Strategy Application Division, SOLE – The International Society of Logistics* LTG (Ret) John M. McDuffie, Vice President, Defense Programs and Systems, Anteon Corporation; Mr. Thomas J. Edwards, Deputy to the Commander, US Army Combined Arms Support Command; Mr. Paul Bogosian, Army Deputy Program Executive Officer, Aviation; Mr. Dick O'Neil, Executive Director, Technology Programs, Concurrent Technologies Corporation

2:15 - 3:15	**Break** (Exhibit Hall)
3:15 - 6:00	**Operational Logistics Demonstrations** • Marshall Space Flight Center • Port of Huntsville Intermodal Center • Target Distribution Center • Nektar Therapeutics

The society extends its sincerest thanks to the following corporate and individual sponsors:

SILVER SPONSOR
SOLE 2003 & Space & Rocket Center Reception

TELEDYNE BROWN ENGINEERING, INC.
A Teledyne Technologies Company

BRONZE SPONSOR
Space & Rocket Center Reception

Raytheon
Integrated Defense Systems

BRONZE SPONSOR
President's Luncheon

Anthony E. Trovato, CPL, President

Space & Rocket Center Reception

CAS inc. SYSTEM SOLUTIONS

LESCO

SAIC Science Applications International Corporation
An Employee-Owned Company

SPARTA

OPERATIONAL LOGISTICS DEMOS

Marshall Space Flight Center (one of the following)

The Payload Operations Integration Control Center (POIC) is the science command post for the International Space Station. It is the focal point for American and international science activities aboard the Space Station. The POIC's unique capabilities allow science experts and researchers around the world to perform cutting-edge science in the unique micro-gravity environment of space. The center coordinates the payload activities of NASA's International partners.

The National Center for Advanced Manufacturing (NCAM) addresses the manufacturing requirements of space transportation systems. Through the NCAM, partnerships between NASA and other government agencies, industry, and academia leverage assets and successfully meet the requirements for future systems; systems that will ultimately provide safe, low-cost, access to space.

Port of Huntsville Intermodal Center

The Port of Huntsville comprises Huntsville International Airport, the International Intermodal Center, and the Jetplex Industrial Park. The port is designed to serve, through one central multimodal facility, the cargo needs of the Tennessee Valley Region with quality service and competitively priced transportation alternatives that combine the efficiencies of air, rail, and highway distribution. The air cargo area comprises two 100,000 sq. ft. warehouse buildings. The international Air Cargo Center is a multi-use facility housing the air freight operations of six major all-cargo air carriers: Airborne Express, DHL, Eagle, Global Logistics, Emery, FedEx and UPS. There are 30 steamship lines that also use the intermodal center, serving the transportation needs of industry located in the Tennessee Valley.

Target Distribution Center

The Huntsville Target Stores Distribution Center services 73 stores in Alabama, Florida, Georgia, Kentucky, Mississippi and Tennessee. The site is on 132 acres and the building is 25 football fields in size. The parking lot handles almost 1,000 tractor-trailer units. The inbound materials area operates 105 docking bays. The warehouse includes stocking, order processing, and inventory management departments. The outbound materials area comprises 130 docking bays and operates on a minimum of a door per store served. This allows separate trailers to be loaded for each store. The logistics team serves as the liaison between marketing, distribution, and the carrier network in serving the individual Target store. Target possesses one of the most modern and highly automated warehousing systems in the United States.

Nektar Therapeutics

Nektar is the leader in polyethelene glycol-based (PEG) drug delivery and development. Nektar-Huntsville operates two facilities to provide manufacturing and technical support to customers desiring Nektar's Advanced PEGylation, Hydrogels, and Solubilizing Agents. The facility at 1112 Church Street is the primary manufacturing site and it is the one that houses the compliant GMP (Good Manufacturing Practices) manufacturing operations. The facility is currently used to manufacture thirty-seven different PEG reagents for its pharmaceutical industry partners. These different reagents are produced for drug products or devices that are either in clinical trials or on the market.

The Society is pleased to thank Silver Sponsor

NORTHROP GRUMMAN

Electronic Systems

for their generous underwriting of the production and distribution of the *SOLE 2003 Proceedings.*

A CD-ROM of the plenary session, panel, and technical paper presentations will be distributed to all symposium registrants after the conference, in order to enable the fullest coverage of this year's sessions.

Please stop at the Registration Desk to verify your mailing address so as to ensure your receipt.

THURSDAY SCHEDULE

7:00 - 12:00	**Registration**
7:00 - 8:00	**Continental Breakfast** (North Hall Gallery)
8:00 - 9:30	**Space Plenary Session** *Moderator: Mr. William A. (Andy) Evans, ISS Manager, Logistics and Maintenance, Johnson Space Center (United Space Alliance)* Mr. Arthur Stephenson, Special Assistant to the Associate Administrator for Education, NASA; Mr. Gordon Porter, Deputy Director, Logistics Directorate, Ground-Based Midcourse Defense, National Missile Defense Joint Program Office (JPO), Marshall Space Flight Center; Mr. Charles Murphy, Logistics Process Director, United Space Alliance, Kennedy Space Center
9:30 - 10:00	**Break** (Exhibit Hall)
10:00 - 11:30	**Homeland Security Plenary Session** *Moderator: Dr. Russell A. Vacante, Defense Acquisition University* Mr. Steven Cooperman, Vice President, Homeland Security Solutions, Oracle Corporation; Captain Jon Helmick, Director, Logistics and Inter-Modal Transportation Program, United States Merchant Marine Academy; Mr. Gerald F. (Jerry) Woolever, Senior Vice President for Field Operations, Innovative Logistics Techniques, Inc. (INNOLOG); Mr. Steven Lambright, Vice President, Savi Technology
11:30 - 1:30	**President's Lunch**

	Panel Orchestra Rehearsal	Panel North Hall Salon 2	Panel North Hall Salon 1 B
1:30 - 3:00	**Space Panel** *Moderator: Ms. Janlyn A. Hall, Director, Space Application Division, SOLE – The International Society of Logistics* Mr. Ronald Burns, Director of Logistics, Marshall Space Flight Center; Mr. William A. (Andy) Evans, ISS Manager, Logistics and Maintenance, Johnson Space Center (United Space Alliance); Mr. David P. Martin, II, CPL, Ground-Based Mid-Course Defense System Joint Program Office, Sparta, Inc.; Mr. Tim Welton, Logistics, Lockheed Martin (Denver)	**Homeland Security Panel: "The Devil's In the Details"** *Moderator: Dr. Russell A. Vacante, Defense Acquisition University* Captain James Bamberger, Deputy, Maritime Passenger Security Branch, Transportation Security Administration; Dr. Linda S. Brandt, Director, Acquisition Logistics, Industrial College of the Armed Forces, National Defense University; Mr. Michael D. Krause, Vice President, Strategic Planning, Orion International Technologies; Mr. Gerald F. (Jerry) Woolever, Senior Vice President for Field Operations, Innovative Logistics Techniques, Inc. (INNOLOG)	**Industry Panel: "Defense Logistics Challenges with Integrating Commercial Electronics Technology"** *Moderator: Mr. Michael Frederickson, Program Director, American Competitiveness Institute* Mr. James Robles, Senior Program Manager, Boeing; Mr. Jack Harris, Director, Rockwell Collins; Space Flight Center; Mr. Jay Heath, Director, Honeywell (Invited)
3:00 - 3:30	**Break** (North Hall Gallery)		

	Track 1 Orchestra Rehearsal	Track 2 North Hall Salon 2	Track 3 North Hall Salon 1 B	Track 4 North Hall Salon 4
3:30 - 5:00	**Paper Presentations:** **"Performance Based Logistics"** *Moderator: Mr. Marty Martin, CPL* • "Emerging Opportunities for Fourth-Party Logistics Service Providers in the U.S. Defense Industry," Michael D. Connor • "Performance Based Logistics: What Does it Take?" Charles O. Coogan, CPL, Fellow • "COTS Fixed Wing Aircraft and Life Cycle Contractor Support," Joseph J. Vins, CPL • "Zen Tao Logistics," Dale K. Starr, CPL • "Performance Based Logistics: What it is & How we do it," William T. Baylis, Ph.D. • "Maritime Security, Legislation and Initiatives: The Effects on the Global Supply Chain," US Merchant Marine Midshipmen Brendan Smith, Aaron Lewis, and Ryan Melogy	**Paper Presentations:** **"Logistics Data and Data Analysis"** *Moderator: Mr. Richard (Rick) Turner* • "Technical Data Knowledge Management: Transforming the Delivery and Use of Logistics Technical Data," William J. Rumschlag • "Logistics Data Integration," Louis Sciaroni, CPL • "Kibbles and Bits: Logistics Analysis for Critical Infrastructure Protection, Factory to Foxhole," Larry W. Ground, CPL and Robert L. Smith, PMP • "Application of Logistics Support for a Management Tool Development," Kongkiti Phusavat, Ph.D.	**Paper Presentations:** **"Obsolescence and Warranties"** *Moderator: Mr. Mel Waters* • "How do you deal with Unplanned Obsolescence in a Military Environment?" Laura E. King • "Mimosa and Army Metrology," Carl M. Powe, Ph.D. • "The Logistics of Aircraft Survivability: Protection against Hostile Threats, Critical to Mission Success/Battle Space Supremacy," Kenneth H. Brockel, Harry G. Ivory, Jr. and Cliff S. Vermont • "Increased Profitability Through Warranty Assessment," G. Stephen Brunner • "The 'Just in Time' Process and the Objective Force: A Perfect Match?" Clifton Officer, Jr.	**Paper Presentations:** **"Logistics Management and Life Cycle Costs"** *Moderator: Mr. Artro Whitman* • "The Teaming Toolset: An Effective Merging of Government and Commercial Project Team Practices," Conna Condon • "Integrated Logistics Support as a Conductor," Hilmi Ozdemir • "Through Life Costing Requirements in the Norwegian Defence Forces," Thomas L. Halvorssen
5:30 - 6:00	**Awards Reception** (Hilton Hotel)			
6:00 - 9:00	**Awards Banquet** (Hilton Hotel)			

THURSDAY TRACK DETAILS

TRACK 1

3:30 - 5:00

Paper Presentations: "Performance Based Logistics"
Moderator: Mr. Marty Martin, CPL

- "Emerging Opportunities for Fourth-Party Logistics Service Providers in the U.S. Defense Industry," Michael D. Connor
- "Performance Based Logistics: What Does it Take?" Charles O. Coogan, CPL, Fellow
- "COTS Fixed Wing Aircraft and Life Cycle Contractor Support," Joseph J. Vins, CPL
- "Zen Tao Logistics," Dale K. Starr, CPL
- "Performance Based Logistics: What it is & How we do it," William T. Baylis, Ph.D.
- "Maritime Security, Legislation and Initiatives: The Effects on the Global Supply Chain," US Merchant Marine Midshipmen Brendan Smith, Aaron Lewis, and Ryan Melogy

3:30 - 5:00 **TRACK 2**

Paper Presentations: "Logistics Data and Data Analysis"
Moderator: Mr. Richard (Rick) Turner

- "Technical Data Knowledge Management: Transforming the Delivery and Use of Logistics Technical Data," William J. Rumschlag
- "Logistics Data Integration," Louis Sciaroni, CPL
- "Kibbles and Bits: Logistics Analysis for Critical Infrastructure Protection, Factory to Foxhole," Larry W. Ground, CPL and Robert L. Smith, PMP
- "Application of Logistics Support for a Management Tool Development," Kongkiti Phusavat, Ph.D.

3:30 - 5:00 **TRACK 3**

Paper Presentations: "Obsolescence and Warranties"
Moderator: Mr. Mel Waters

- "How do you deal with Unplanned Obsolescence in a Military Environment?" Laura E. King
- "Mimosa and Army Metrology," Carl M. Powe, Ph.D.
- "The Logistics of Aircraft Survivability: Protection against Hostile Threats, Critical to Mission Success/Battle Space Supremacy," Kenneth H. Brockel, Harry G. Ivory, Jr. and Cliff S. Vermont
- "Increased Profitability Through Warranty Assessment," G. Stephen Brunner
- "The 'Just in Time' Process and the Objective Force: A Perfect Match?" Clifton Officer, Jr.

TRACK 4

Paper Presentations: "Logistics Management and Life Cycle Costs"
Moderator: Mr. Artro Whitman

- "The Teaming Toolset: An Effective Merging of Government and Commercial Project Team Practices," Conna Condon
- "Integrated Logistics Support as a Conductor," Hilmi Ozdemir
- "Through Life Costing Requirements in the Norwegian Defence Forces," Thomas L. Halvorssen

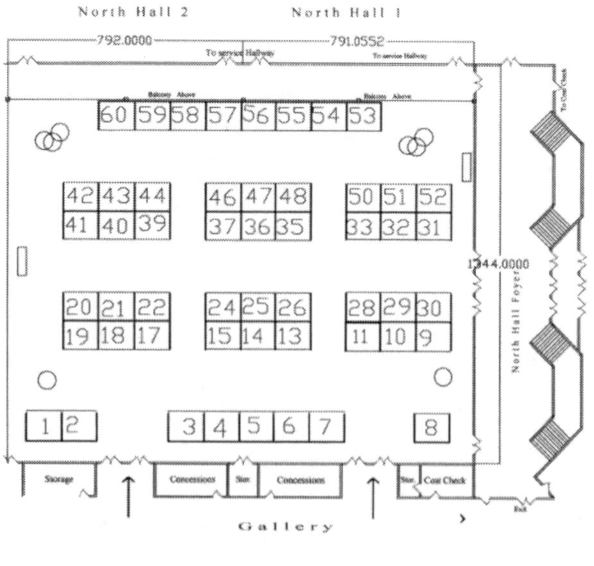

Exhibit Hall Floor Plan

EXHIBIT HALL EVENTS

Monday, August 11		Tuesday, August 12		Wednesday, August 13	
Exhibitors Reception	6:00 pm – 7:30 pm	Morning Break	9:00 am – 10:00 am	Morning Break	9:30 am – 10:30 am
		Lunch	12:00 pm – 1:30 pm	Lunch	11:30 am – 1:00 pm
		Afternoon Break	3:00 pm – 4:00 pm	Afternoon Break	2:15 pm – 3:15 pm

SOLE 2003 EXHIBITOR LISTING

Company **Booth #**

All Points Logistics, Inc. **3**

2567 Athens Highway
Gainesville, Georgia 30507-7457
Ph: 770-503-7474 / Fax: 770-503-9941
www.allpointslogistics.com

All Points Logistics (Logistics and Transportation Division) is a full-service contract logistics division specializing in cost-effective design and management of product transportation, storage, distribution and integrated logistics services. Special services include consulting, package engineering, merge-in-transit, product returns and mass customization. All Points Logistics managers, consultants and affiliates excel with experience and expertise in computer hardware, software and data services, electronic parts and distribution, the Internet and telephone technology, project management and management consulting, chemicals and construction.

American Competitiveness Institute **51 & 52**

1 International Plaza, Suite 600
Philadelphia, Pennsylvania 19113-1510
Ph: 610-362-1200 / Fax: 610-362-1290
www.aciusa.org

The American Competitiveness Institute (ACI) was established in 1992 as a scientific research corporation dedicated to the advancement and integration of leading edge technologies in electronics manufacturing and related engineering applications. ACI is uniquely qualified to address research and development activities, including applied research, product and process development, prototype demonstration, product evaluation, reverse engineering and obsolescence mitigation, technology transfer and commercialization activities for both military and industrial-driven technologies. ACI has design, development, analysis, and prototyping capabilities and maintains a staff of highly experienced technical personnel whose expertise covers the entire spectrum of the electronics industry. ACI's facility is located in an office campus adjacent to the Philadelphia International Airport. The facility houses a 10,000 square foot demonstration factory, fully equipped classrooms with multimedia training aids, an analytical laboratory for materials and environmental testing, conference and lecture rooms with video conferencing capabilities, and a fully functional technical library.

Company **Booth #**

APICS Bookstore **25, 26, 35 & 36**

5301 Shawnee Road
Alexandria, Virginia 22312-2317
Ph: 703-354-8996 / Fax: 703-354-8662
www.apics.org

As the leading provider of high-quality, cutting edge educational materials, the APICS Bookstore supplies industry professionals with the knowledge and expertise to advance their organizational success in a changing and competitive marketplace.

Avion, Inc. **32**

5000 Bradford Drive
Building 3, Suite B
Huntsville, Alabama 35805-1937
Ph: 256-721-7006 / Fax: 256-721-7007
http://huntsville.avioninc.com

Avion, developer and manufacture of the Universal Static Balance Fixture (USBF), not only has grown steadily since its inception a decade ago but has increased staff selectively creating a full service engineering support, and engineering development, rapid prototyping and manufacturing activity. Avion maintains a close tie with Army Aviation through an engineering support contract with the Army Aviation and Missile Command. A dedicated staff of engineering personnel play a key role in the management of Flight Safety Parts; engineering support in the definition of critical parts, engineering testing requirements, and performance and evaluation of tests performed; and engineering oversight of the 500 vendors who manufacture critical aircraft components. Receiving the AAAA Materiel Readiness Award in 1997, Avion is still to this point the developer and manufacture that produces the only approved field tool for rotor blade balancing.

Belzon, Inc. **15**

6767 Old Madison Pike NW, Suite 135
Huntsville, Alabama 35806-2186
Ph: 256-461-6039 / Fax: 256-461-6067
http://www.belzon.com

Belzon was incorporated on October 1, 1994: from late 1994 through the summer of 1998 the company was predominantly a one-man consulting effort in support of Army aviation clients. On July 1, 1998 they received their first information technology contract. From there, they have continued to grow by providing premier professional outsourced services to Department of Defense agencies. Their customer base includes PEO Aviation, PM Aviation Electronic Systems (AES), PM Aircrew Integrated Systems (ACIS), and the United States Army.

Company	Booth #

CACI — 59

1100 North Glebe Road
Arlington, Virginia 22201
Ph: 703-841-7800 / Fax: 703-528-4196
www.caci.com

CACI, as a leading international information technology products and services corporation, helps clients apply information technology that enables their enterprises to work more efficiently and maintain their competitive advantage. With a strength in preserving legacy system value while enabling organizations to leverage the potential of the future without the risk of having to start over, their solutions offer superior functionality backed by more than 41 years of technology experience. By capturing unique, mission-critical requirements and implementing solutions to position enterprises for both immediate and long-term gains, clients can keep pace with technology advancements while protecting existing investments.

Command and Control Systems/Avionics Directorate — 50

U.S. Army Communications Electronics Command (CECOM)
ATTN: AMSEL-LC-CCS-A
Fort Monmouth, New Jersey 07703-5043
Ph: 732-532-2898 / Fax: 732-532-2935

The Command and Control Systems/Avionics Directorate (CCS/A) is one of the three premier commodity directorates within the Logistics and Readiness Center (LRC) at CECOM providing full life-cycle production for superior information technologies and integrated systems to the warfighter. The CCS/A Directorate has four divisions providing acquisition and logistics support for Defense Acquisition Category I, II, and III equipment and systems. These include Airborne Navigation, Airborne Mission, Command and Control, and Power/Environmental. Some of the equipment includes: platform unique avionics, common avionics-navigation, avionics communication, air traffic control, aircraft survivability, and survival radios. They continue to be the Army's premier performing weapon system directorate in providing logistics and sustainment support to America's warfighters and allies.

Defense Acquisition University (DAU) — 9 & 10

9820 Belvoir Road
Fort Belvoir, Virginia 22060-5565
Ph: 800-845-7606 / Fax: 703-805-2639
www.dau.mil

The DAU coordinates the DoD acquisition education and training program to meet the training requirements of more than 145,000 personnel serving in acquisition positions. Through its campuses, the DAU sponsors acquisition curriculum and instructor training to provide a full range of basic, intermediate, and advanced courses to support the career goals and professional development of the acquisition workforce. Through its member institutions, DAU fosters research, publications, symposia, and consulting in areas related to the acquisition functional areas. DAU is a corporate university providing mandatory, assignment specific, and continuing education courses for military and civilian personnel serving in 11 acquisition career fields. Its mission is to educate and train professionals for effective service in the Defense acquisition system. The Chief Executive Officer of the University is the President, who reports to the USD(A&T). A Board of Visitors, individuals selected for their preeminence in academia, business, and industry, advises the President and the USD(A&T) on matters related to organizational management, curricula, methods of instruction, facilities, and other matters of interest to the University. Visit them at their booth during SOLE 2003 to learn about the changes taking place in their logistics curriculum in support of the warfighter in the 21st Century.

Company	Booth #

Defense Logistics Information Service (DLIS) — 47 & 48

74 Washington Avenue N, Suite 7
Battle Creek, Michigan 49017-3084
Ph: 1-877-352-2255 / Fax: 269-961-4715
www.dla.mil/dlis

The Defense Logistics Information Service is a field activity for the Defense Logistics Agency (DLA), in support of logistics information operations. Partnering with global customers, DLIS creates, obtains, manages and integrates logistics data from a variety of sources for dissemination as user-friendly information to meet or exceed the needs of the Department of Defense (DoD), Federal and international logisticians. Recognized as the premier DoD logistics information broker, their customer base includes the Commanders-In-Chief of the U.S. armed forces and all military services; other DoD, Federal, State, local, non-profit agencies, private industry, the international community; and the general public. They provide exceptional value by using best business practices and merging technologies. Complete product and services information is available at their website.

GSA/FSS Management Services Center — 17 & 18

400 15th Street, SW
Auburn, Washington 98001-6599
Ph: 1-800-241-7246 / Fax: 253 931-7544
www.gsa.gov

GSA Federal Supply Schedules offer commercial solutions to meet a multiple of logistics needs. Logistics Worldwide (LOGWORLD) can help agencies reduce procurement costs and lead times, while increasing operational capabilities. They offer world-class contractors, the latest technology, best value solutions, and provide an acquisition strategy the customer controls.

Information Handling Services (IHS) — 20 & 21

15 Inverness Way East
Englewood, Colorado 80112-5710
Ph: 303-397-7956 / Fax: 303-397-2740
www.ihs.com

IHS services are the result of more than 40 years experience managing technical information. IHS consultants have a deep understanding of client processes, a history of successful enterprise solutions, and a synergistic combination of partners, leaders and acquisitions to help you succeed. For many clients, IHS is a critical process partner, enabling them to increase productivity, decrease time-to-market, and improve quality. Services include Parts Management Solutions, Information Strategy, Information Capture, Information Integration, training on IHS tools and content, as well as customized training on implemented solutions, industry issues, and Managed Services give you the opportunity to outsource anything from personnel or hosting to entire information management processes, allowing you to focus on your core competencies.

Innovative Logistics Techniques, Inc. (INNOLOG) — 37

2010 Corporate Ridge, 9th Floor
McLean, Virginia 22102-7857
Ph: 703-506-1555 / Fax: 703-506-4559
www.innolog.com

As a leading logistics solutions firm, INNOLOG provides a wide range of services to both public and private sector clients in the areas of supply chain logistics, enterprise asset management, information engineering, acquisition management and weapons systems engineering. Founded in 1989, INNOLOG is one of a few logistics and process-focused solutions firms with a truly global focus, with 40 service centers in addition to its headquarters in McLean, Virginia.

Company	Booth #

Institute for Defense and Business 58

300 Meadowmount Village Circle, Suite 336
Chapel Hill, North Carolina 25717-7518
Ph: 919-969-8008 / Fax: 919-969-1619
www.theidb.org

The Institute for Defense and Business (IDB), a North Carolina nonprofit foundation, focuses attention on the imperative need to increase and sustain the interchange of information between the U.S. military and the private sector. The U.S. Army selected the Kenan-Flagler Business School at the University of North Carolina at Chapel Hill to establish the Center of Excellence in Logistics and Technology. The Institute for Defense & Business, which was established by, and is affiliated with, the University of North Carolina, conceptualized and manages the program. The U.S. Army Materiel Command serves as the DoD executive agent for this project that includes the services and the joint commands as well as the DoD. The Center of Excellence in Logistics and Technology (LOGTECH) is a dynamic program that conducts research, provides executive education courses, holds forums, and delivers a specialized distance and in-residence MBA program focused on logistics and technology. It is dedicated to furthering its goals through a unique approach combining the functional and operational areas of scholarly research and education.

Instrumented Sensor Technology, Inc. (IST) 2

4704 Moore Street
Okemos, Michigan 48864-1722
Ph: 517-349-8487 / Fax: 517-349-8469
www.isthq.com

IST is one of the leading developers and manufacturers of portable shock and vibration measurement and data recording systems for shipment and logistics monitoring. Their product line ranges from recorders with from one to nine channels; reusable, battery powered, solid state data storage; PC interface for data debriefing and analysis. All of their recorders are intrinsically safe and RFI flight certified. New products include ShockTimerTM, a low cost, biaxial electronic shock detector for shipment monitoring; and MotionMasterTM, six DOF recorder also measures roll, pitch, and yaw. All of their recording systems are available for short-term rental as well as purchase.

Interactive Authoring and Display System (IADS) 24

U.S. Army Missile Command (AMCOM)
AMSAM-MMC-MA-NP
Building 5301, Room 1128
Redstone Arsenal, Alabama 35898
Ph: 256-955-7123 / Fax: 256-842-6546
www.iads.redstone.army.mil

Interactive Authoring and Display System (IADS) was developed as a U.S. Army Missile Command initiative to reduce paper documentation. IADS uses Standard Generalized Markup Language to manipulate the text and graphics. The author can choose to display graphics within the text and/or in separate windows. While IADS was originally developed to eliminate the need for paper technical manuals in the field, it also eliminates the need for paper documentation in the office. IADS eliminates paper storage problems, increases speed and accuracy for updates, reduces print costs, and enhances search and retrieval times. Combine all this with its intuitive user interface, and IADS is a winner in the Electronic Documentation arena. The IADS Team is part of a larger group called the Publications Services Management Team. The Pubs Team supports publications, U.S. and foreign military, worldwide. Ranging from conversion specialists, trainers and programmers to publications specialists, team IADS is the response to the military's need for tools to ensure support for the paperless future.

Company	Booth #

Jacobs Sverdrup, Inc. (Team ITSS) 54

6703 Odyssey Drive, Suite 304
Huntsville, Alabama 35806-3308
Ph: 256-971-5558 / Fax: 256-971-0413
www.sverdrup.com

The Jacobs Sverdrup Team ITSS specializes in information technology areas such as project management, network management support, enterprise management – systems technology, web, database and applications development, diverse pool of resources, and competitive cost structure. With a record of demonstrated excellence in the government contracting environment, their customer base includes Department of Defense (all services) and commercial projects.

MacSema, Inc. 31

62971 Plateau Drive, Suite 400
Bend, Oregon 97701-5890
Ph: 541-389-1122 / Fax: 541-389-1888
www.macsema.com

MacSema, Inc. manufactures survivable Automated Data Collection (ADC) hardware proven in harsh operating environments, to include ButtonMemory® read/write contact memory buttons (CMB) with up to 8 megabytes of capacity. This versatile product's uses include configuration management, electronic maintenance log book, life cycle asset tracking and life-limited component management. Capable of storing technical manuals and schematics as well as cradle to grave history, it can also act as a barrier to unauthorized parts and has a proven track record of success in harsh military environments with demanding operational specifications. MacSema also manufactures metal cased, rugged bar code and button readers whose systems are Internet compatible and support open architecture, data compression and encryption.

Manugistics 13 & 14

9715 Key West Avenue
Rockville, Maryland 20850-3915
Ph: 301-255-5000 / Fax: 301-255-5370
www.manugistics.com

Manugistics is a leader in delivering innovative supply and demand chain software solutions. With over 20 years experience, their innovative solutions help commercial organizations make their supply chains more efficient and cost effective. That commercial expertise has also made Manugistics a top solution provider to the military and government agencies. Manugistics solutions can automate and improve processes to optimize forecasting, source materials, collaborate with suppliers and customers, manage transportation and delivery, and help ensure emergency preparedness planning. For more information, go to www.manugistics.com.

Marine Corps Logistics Command 41

814 Radford Boulevard
Albany, Georgia 31704-1128
Ph: 229-639-6777 / Fax: 229-639-5111
www.logcom.usmc.mil

The Marine Corps Logistics Command provides worldwide, integrated logistics/supply chain and distribution management; depot level maintenance management; and strategic prepositioning capability in support of the operating forces and other supported units to maximize their readiness and sustainability and to support enterprise and program level Total Life Cycle Management. Their newest software initiative, MERIT, uses a state of the art Graphical User Interface (GUI) that transforms existing legacy data into valuable information, providing a dynamic, adaptable view of Equipment Readiness for the Marine Corps. Featuring a user-friendly graphical analysis tool as a front end for USMC data, MERIT allows for complex assessment of current and historical readiness trends with "drill-down" capabilities. The resulting Readiness Maps have drastically reduced the overall information gathering process, focusing the efforts of readiness experts away from making charts and towards solving and preventing mission critical readiness problems.

Company	Booth #

The M&T Company — 19

Government Services Group
6196 Lake Gray Boulevard, Suite 114
Jacksonville, Florida 32244-5687
Ph: 904-771-8914 / Fax: 904-771-6321
www.cdi-gs.com/mt.shtm

M&T specializes in providing engineering and technical services for airborne avionics systems, support equipment and aircraft launch and recovery equipment. They provide a full spectrum of acquisition and life cycle management services that includes Independent Logistics Assessments (ILA) and the development of Logistics Management Information (LMI) such as logistics support plans, maintenance plans, logistics support analysis, support material lists, paper and electronic technical manuals, provisioning support, supportability analyses, reliability and maintainability studies, level of repair analysis, and failure mode effects and criticality analysis. They also provide computer based training development and support, the demilitarization of equipment and a variety of program management services relating to system acquisition management and foreign military sales. In addition, they have the capability to provide prototype and manufacturing of electronic equipment such as circuit card assemblies, cables and test sets.

Naval Surface Warfare Center (NSWC) – Crane — 11

Code 80224EW, Building 3330S
300 Highway 361, NSWC
Crane, Indiana 47522-5001
Ph: 812-854-1815 / Fax: 812-854-4900
https://c802tdc2.crane.navy.mil/TDC/main.cfm

Crane Division, Naval Surface Warfare Center is well known for its high-quality products and work ethic in supporting the Fleet Operating Forces. In response to the changing needs of the warfighter, NSWC Crane has evolved from its Ordnance roots into a high-tech Acquisition, Engineering, Logistics and Fleet Support organization focused on Ordnance, Electronics, and Electronic Warfare. Crane prides itself on teaming with industry and DOD Government Activities to maintain and improve systems, subsystems, components and support equipment across all warfare areas throughout their life cycles. Their broad customer base includes the Navy, Marine Corps, Army, Air Force, United States Special Operations Command (USSOCOM), Coast Guard, NASA, and many other military, civilian, and foreign military organizations.

Parker AeroSpace — 22

14300 Alton Parkway, MS208
Irvine, California 92618-1898
Ph: 818-225-8558 / Fax: 818-225-8558
www.parkeraerospace.com

Parker Aerospace is a group of the Parker Hannifin Corporation, a world leader in motion and control technologies. Parker Aerospace designs, manufactures, and services hydraulic, fuel, and pneumatic components; designs and integrates complete systems; and designs and manufactures related electronic controls for aerospace and other high-technology markets. Enhanced operational readiness is a matter of working harder, smarter, and faster on the support side. Because they repair their components to OEM spec, using OEM parts and processes, they can provide higher levels of reliability, maintainability, and sustainability. Their Performance-Based Logistics, technology insertions, reliability improvement programs, field and tech support, and customization options offer flexibility in reducing cost of ownership.

Pennant Information Services, Inc. — 39 & 40

1400 Blair Place, Suite 707
Ottowa, Ontario K1J 9B8
Canada
Ph: 613-745-3811 / Fax: 613-745-4206
www.pennantcanada.com/www.pennantusa.com

Pennant Information Services supplies government and industrial activities worldwide with superior, state-of-the-art software products and consulting services to meet their logistics planning and operations needs. Pennant's Logistics support Analysis (LSA) software, known as OmegaPS, manages data to provide users with powerful Product Support solutions. Their solutions apply throughout a product's or system's life cycle. This includes early product design, configuration management and maintenance management. OmegaPS Analyzer (formerly known as LOGAN) provides life cycle costing (LCC), level of repair analysis (LORA), and a sparing module. OmegaPS Publisher integrates an SGML and XML authoring environment with the core OmegaPS LSA software to generate and maintain Integrated Electronic Technical Manuals (IETMs). Pennant Information Services Inc, with offices in Ottawa, Ontario, Canada and Placentia, California, USA is a subsidiary of a UK based company, Pennant International Group Plc. In addition to information services, Pennant International Group Plc provides Computer Based Training (CBT), simulation and emulation training systems and electronic technical documentation solutions, to governments and aerospace and defense industries worldwide.

Radian Inc. — 4 & 5

5845 Richmond Highway, Suite 725
Alexandria, Virginia 22303-1873
Ph: 703-329-9300 / Fax: 703-229-9510
www.radianinc.com

As a full service engineering, logistics and technical service provider, Radian Inc. has developed an in-depth level of diversified and multi-functional capabilities that support a wide spectrum of DoD, civilian agencies, and commercial clients worldwide. Each of their business areas, including the Engineering, Logistics and Training Services, Advanced Technology Services, Asset Protection Systems, and System Integration Services, are all dedicated to delivery of consistently superior products and services through the application of advanced technology, sound engineering principles, and practical solutions. For more information, visit their website at www.radianinc.com.

Raytheon Technical Services Company — 6 & 7

1665 Hughes Way
Long Beach, California 90810-1835
Ph: 866-773-0557 / Fax: 310-952-4441
www.raytheon.com/businesses/rts

Raytheon Technical Services Company offers a wide array of Military Management Products including: EAGLE (Enhanced Automated Graphical Logistics Environment), an integrated collection of Raytheon-developed and commercial off-the-shelf (COTS) tools optimized for the Windows operating environment; AIMSS (Advanced Integrated Maintenance Support Systems), a class 4 and 5 IETM authoring system that provides all the tools needed to create, maintain, and distribute powerful ITEMs; ASENT (Advanced Specialty Engineering Networked Toolkit) on (generalized Automated Maintenance Environment), a collection of innovative and fully integrated-configuration/asset management and maintenance automation tools designed to meet the information needs of personnel responsible for maintaining a broad range of military and commercial systems.

Company	Booth #

Science Applications International Corporation (SAIC) 28 & 29

6726 Odyssey Drive NW
Huntsville, Alabama 35806-3302
Ph: 256-971-6400 / Fax: 256-864-8200
www.saic.com

A diversified High-Technology research and engineering company, Science Applications International Corporation (SAIC) offers a broad range of experience in technology development and analysis, eSolutions, computer systems development and integration, technical support services, and computer hardware and software products. SAIC engineers and scientists work to solve complex technical problems in national and homeland security, energy, environment, space, telecommunications, health care, transportation and logistics. The company is using state-of-the-art technology to help commercial and government clients secure data and conduct business on the Internet. SAIC is implementing e-procurement systems, improving the quality of health care through automated patient care systems and telemedicine, and providing outsourcing services and information technology to oil companies and utilities to improve efficiency and competitiveness. Founded in 1969, SAIC ranks as the largest employee-owned research and engineering firm in the nation. SAIC and its subsidiaries have more than 40,000 employees with offices in more than 150 cities worldwide.

Shockwatch 44

7929 Brookriver Drive, Suite 200
Dallas, Texas 75247-4945
Ph: 214-630-9625 / Fax: 214-638-4512
www.shockwatch.com

Shockwatch develops, manufactures and markets a broad range of impact, tilt and environmental monitoring products built to prevent damage and enhance safety standards. Recognized for their high quality, excellent reliability and forward-thinking technology, Shockwatch products are distributed worldwide by a network of strategic partners and resellers. Founded in 1974, the company is headquartered in Dallas, Texas.

SOLE – The International Society of Logistics 46

8100 Professional Place, Suite 111
Hyattsville, Maryland 20785-2229
Ph: 301-459-8446 / Fax: 301-458-1522
www.sole.org

SOLE - The International Society of Logistics is a non-profit, international professional society devoted to scientific, educational and literary endeavors to enhance the art and science of logistics technology, education and management. Membership is open to all individuals and companies working, studying or interested in the career fields of logistics technology, management, engineering, education, product support and physical distribution.

Teledyne Brown Engineering, Inc. 42 & 43

300 Sparkman Drive NW
Huntsville, Alabama 35805-1912
Ph: 256-726-5624 / Fax: 256-726-6286
www.tbe.com

This year Teledyne Brown Engineering, Inc. (TBE) celebrates 50 years of success in systems engineering and logistics. TBE has been a key contractor supporting our nation's space programs and providing engineering support and manufacturing for Department of Defense and the U.S. Army missile defense programs. Today, TBE is a major team member in the testing and deployment of the Ground Based Midcourse Defense system. TBE provide a full range of systems engineering, logistics analyses and support and on-site services throughout the DoD and to international customers. Teledyne Brown's proven logistics expertise spans system life cycle beginning with requirements analysis, product design, trade studies, RAM, equipment documentation, LSA/LSAR, provisioning and PHS&T. TBE expertise continues through deployment, operation, maintenance, inventory and configuration management to system life extension and disposal. TBE serves commercial as well as government customers worldwide in research, modeling and simulation, systems integration, advanced manufacturing, environmental services, emergency management, Homeland Security and information technology.

Company	Booth #

Tools For Decision (TFD) Group 57

70 Garden Court, Suite 300
Monterey, California 93940-5302
Ph: 831-649-3800 / Fax: 831-649-3866
www.tfdg.com

Tools for Decision Group is a world leader in the development of analytical methods and software tools to support economic and strategic decisions that the designers, manufacturers, owners and maintainers of hardware systems, both military and nonmilitary, are called upon to make. TFD tools are being used in support of ship, aircraft, tank, missile and C3I programs by defense departments and companies engaged in aerospace and defense business in more than 15 countries. TFD tools are finding application in commercial aviation, urban transit and automotive manufacturing. Numbered among TFD's clients are a variety of military establishments, virtually all the significant aerospace and defense companies in the world, and a growing list of organizations in the commercial sphere. Notable clients include Lockheed Martin, Northrop Grumman, BAE Systems, General Electric, General Motors, Parker Hannifin, the Royal Air Force, and the US Coast Guard. There are more than 600 separate TFD software installations.

University of Tennessee Center for Executive Education 53

708 Stokely Management Center
Knoxville, Tennessee 37996-0575
Ph: 865-974-5001 / Fax: 865-974-4989
http://thecenter.utk.edu

The Center has an award-winning portfolio of management development, custom training and executive MBA programs. Their leading position in Supply Chain Management and Logistics, Sales Forecasting Management, Process Improvement, Lean Enterprise, and Leadership Development is reflected through open enrollment and custom executive development programming and our four Executive MBA programs.

US Army G-4 55 & 56

5001 Eisenhower Avenue
Alexandria, Virginia 22333-0001
Ph: 703-617-7044 / Fax: 703-617-5080
https://lta.army.mil; www.hqda.army.mil/logweb/sitemap/sitemap.htm

The Office of the Deputy Chief of Staff, G4 (ODCS, G4), Headquarters Department of the Army, establishes policies, develops logistics programs, and provides guidance that ensures responsive, flexible and effective logistics support to the Army. It resources programs that support the Army in Readiness, Supply Maintenance, Strategic Mobility, Munitions, Transportation/Distribution, War Reserves/Propositioning, and Integrated Logistics Support.

US Army Materiel Command Logistics Support Activity (LOGSA) 33

Building 5307, Sparkman Complex
Redstone Arsenal, Alabama 35868
Ph: 256-313-6693 / Fax: 256-955-0659
www.logsa.army.mil

The USAMC LOGSA serves as the Army and DoD champion for the integrity and integration of logistics data and performs analysis of weapon systems maintenance; readiness; supply; transportation; equipment authorizations, asset and in-transit visibility. Additionally, LOGSA is the responsible organization for numerous key Army and DoD missions that reach across the logistics disciplines to include Army acquisition policy and procedures.

CONFERENCE DETAILS

Dress Code

Dress for the Thursday night dinner is business. All other functions are business casual.

Messages

You can be contacted at The Von Braun Center at (256) 533-1953. Your caller should ask for the **SOLE 2003** registration desk. Messages will be taken and posted to the Message Board at the Registration Desk. Please check the board during breaks for messages in your name.

Registration

Your full paid registration includes participation in the following events Monday through Thursday: unlimited attendance to plenary sessions and Exhibit Hall; track sessions, Monday night's Exhibitor's Reception in the Von Braun Center, Tuesday night's Opening Reception at the Space & Rocket Center, all continental breakfasts, luncheons, and refreshment breaks, and the Thursday evening Awards Reception and Awards Banquet. Tickets can be purchased for guests at the Registration Desk for the Monday and Tuesday receptions, all luncheons and the Thursday Awards Banquet.

Gain Certified Professional Logistician (CPL) Recertification Points

You earn three recertification points for attending the conference and conference presenters earn five points. Those who teach a workshop earn three and those who attend workshops earn one. For more information concerning these points, refer to the Recertification Guidelines Table, Sections 5 and 9.

Continuing Education Units (CEUs)

Several of this year's symposium sessions will offer Continuing Education Units (CEUs) for individuals who wish to obtain them. The cost to the individual is $1 per certificate (unless the individual is also a member of the National Management Association). There will be a form available in the rooms where CEUs have been approved for the session: the completed form and $1 is to be turned in to the session facilitator/instructor. A certificate will be awarded for each approved session.

The Continuing Education Unit (CEU) is nationally recognized as a uniform unit of educational accomplishment by colleges, universities, and other adult education organizations. CEUs are awarded to individuals who satisfactorily complete educational opportunities that meet stated criteria. The National Management Association (NMA) can award CEU credit to both NMA members and even non-members.

SOLE – The International Society of Logistics
8100 Professional Place, Suite 111
Hyattsville, MD 20785-2229
www.sole.org
solehq@erols.com

CORPORATE MEMBERS

We'd like to thank the Society's Corporate Members for their support during the past year.

AAI Engineering Support, Inc.
Hunt Valley, MD

Accenture
St. Louis, MO

APL Limited
Bethesda, MD

Air Logistics Department,
Republic of Singapore Air Force
SINGAPORE

ARINC, Incorporated
Annapolis, MD

The Boeing Company
St. Louis, MO

C-Cubed Corporation
San Diego, CA

Computer Systems Technology, Inc.
Huntsville, AL

Concurrent Technologies Corporation
Johnstown, PA

Defense Acquisition University
Fort Belvoir, VA

Defense Logistics Information Service
Battlecreek, MI

Defense Science Technology Agency
SINGAPORE

Defense Technology Resource Office
(MINDEF)
SINGAPORE

EXP Pharmaceutical Services Corporation
Union City, CA

General Services Administration
Management Services Center
Auburn, WA

i2 Technologies Taiwan, Inc.
TAIWAN

IBM Business Consulting Services
Bethesda, MD

Information Handling Services Group
Englewood, CO

Innovative Logistics
Techniques, Inc.
McLean, VA

Jacobs Sverdrup (Team ITSS)
Huntsville, AL

Lockheed Martin
Technology Services, Inc.
Alexandria, VA

ManTech Systems Engineering Corporation
Lexington Park, MD

Manugistics, Inc.
Rockville, MD

Naval Logistics Department,
Republic of Singapore Navy
SINGAPORE

Naval Air Warfare Center (Aircraft Division)
Lakehurst, NJ

Pennant Information Services, Inc.
Placentia, CA

Pratt and Whitney
East Hartford, CT

Radian Inc.
Alexandria, VA

Raytheon Technical Services Company
Burlington, MA

SAIC/AMSEC
Huntsville, AL/
Hampton, VA

Savi Technology
San Francisco, CA

SembCorp Logistics
SINGAPORE

Singapore Technologies Marine, Limited
SINGAPORE

Stevens Institute of Technology
Hoboken, NJ

Tele-Consultants, Inc.
San Diego, CA

United Defense, L.P.
Arlington, VA

Veridian Engineering
Lexington Park, MD

World-Logi Co., Ltd.
San Francisco, CA

SOLE 2003 Floor Plans

North Hall Upper Level

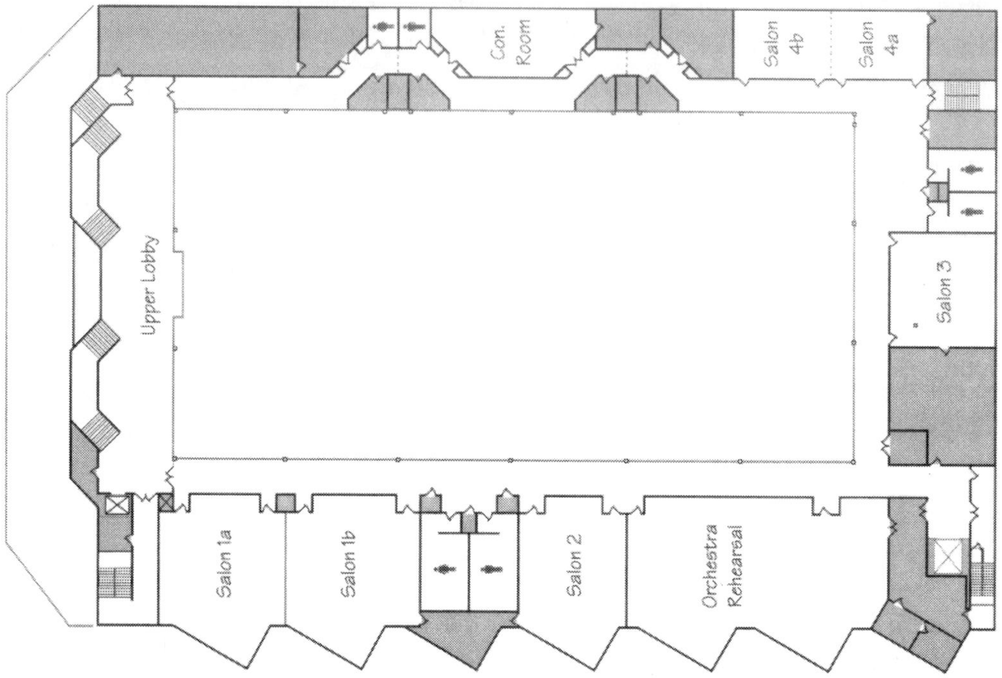

North Hall Lower Level

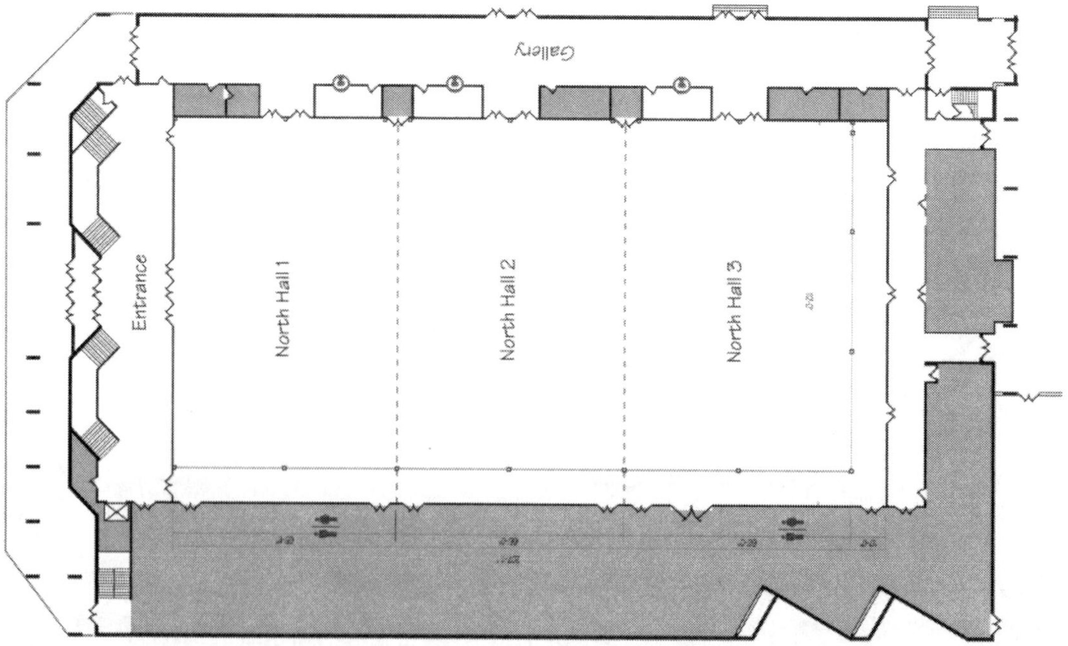

Bridging Defense and Industry

Col R. M. Nixon
HQMC/LPV
August 2003

Why?

- GCSS-MC - IT needs
- SEABASING - Distribution needs
- LOGISTICS MODERNIZATION AND EDUCATION
  Equipment and people
- ENCROACHMENT - Training

How?

- COT vs. GOTS - IT needs
- Process Adoption - Distribution needs
- Existing Equipment and Academia partnerships - Equipment and people
- Business Approach - Training

Knockdown TEU's

- Reduce Space
- Move 6 in 1
- ISO Certified

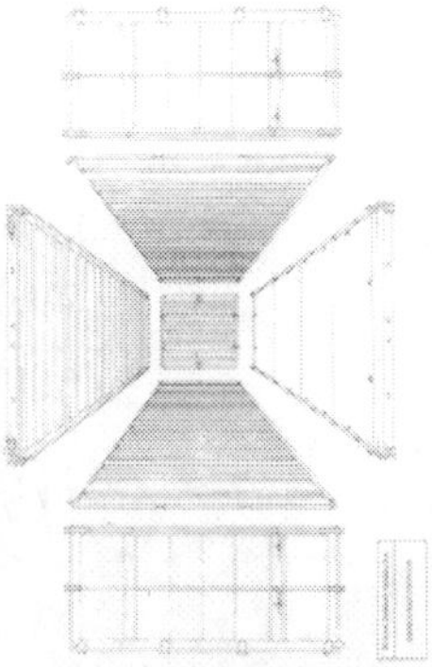

It can be done Better....

Standardized Family of Modular and Streamlined"Big Boxes"

ıdcons: Four connected together make one 20-ft container

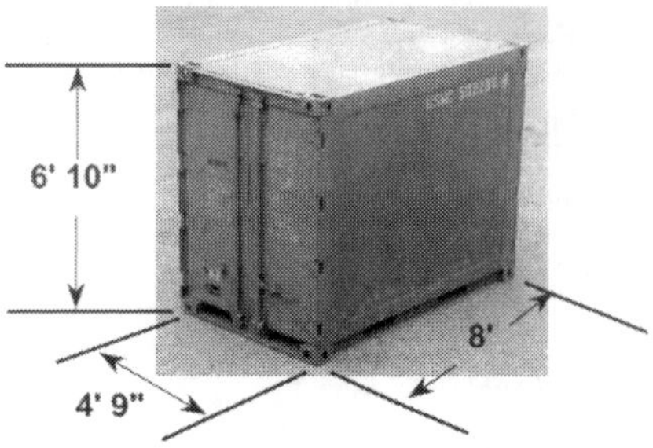

- DD(X) big box = ½ Quadcon
  - Two stackable (each is 4'9" x 8' x 3'5")
- Same package from depot origin to combatant

From this... ⟶ ...to this

(Current) (Future Modular Container)

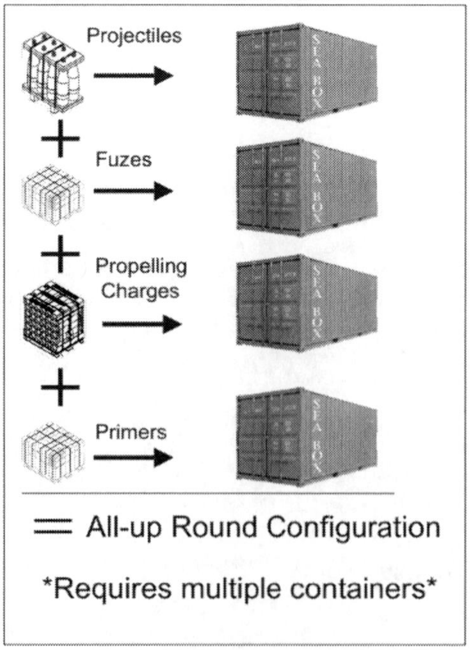

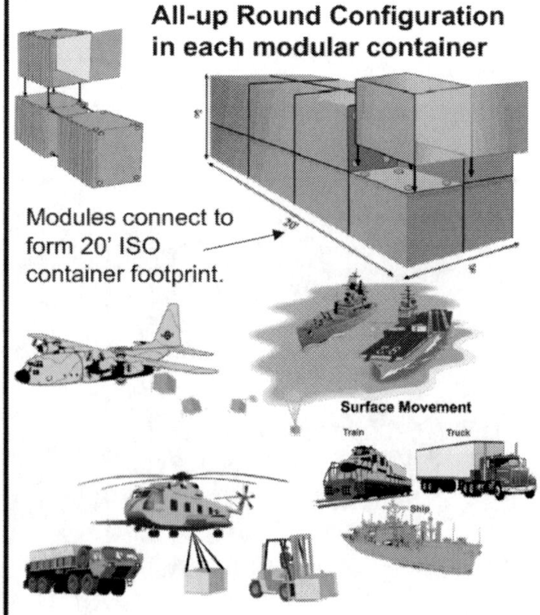

SOLE
BOARD OF ADVISORS
12 Aug 03

"21st Century Logistics: The Global Bridge"

LTG Charles S. Mahan Jr.
United States Army
Deputy Chief of Staff, G-4

Sustaining The Transforming Army

Current Activities

- ***Responsible Official for Sustainment.*** Reliability as a KPP; sustainment in requirements development and acquisition)
- ***Fast Sealift.*** Theater Support Vessel

- ***Pre-positioning of equipment***
- ***AP3 (Army Power Projection Program)*** Enhanced strategic mobility and deployability

- ***Force Provider and Quality of Life initiatives***
- ***Recapitalization***
- ***Single Stock Fund***
- ***National Maintenance Program***

Sustaining The Transforming Army

Current Activities
Automation

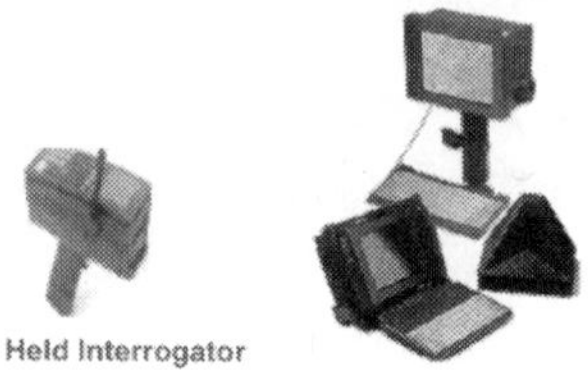

Hand Held Interrogator

- ***Enterprise Resource Planning***
- ***Strategic Readiness System***
- ***Intransit Visibility.*** Hand-held interrogator, Radio frequency tags, Movement tracking system
- ***TC-AIMS II*** (Transportation Coordinators Automated Information for Movements System)
- ***FBCB2*** (Force XXI Battle Command Battalion/Brigade and Below)

Sustaining The Transforming Army

Future Activities

- ***Future Technologies.*** Fuel efficiency through reduced consumption (i.e. fuel cells); water production, distribution and storage improvements

- ***Standardized Parts.*** Common component sets and standardized markings
- ***Condition-based Maintenance Plus.*** Diagnostics / Prognostics
- ***Configured Loads.*** Sustainment modules, platform embedded materiel handling
- ***Advanced Wireless Technologies / Nanotechnology.*** Wireless networks, personnel monitoring, machinery health monitoring
- ***LCOP***
(Logistics Common Operating Picture)

A vision without resources is a hallucination.

Sustaining The Transforming Army

THE ARMY –
AT WAR AND
TRANSFORMING

The Joint Staff
Directorate of Logistics (J4)

Brig Gen Henry L. Taylor, USAF
Vice Director for Logistics (VJ4)

SOLE 38th International Conference
Defense Plenary Session
Huntsville, AL
12 August 2003

UNCLASSIFIED

Defense Strategy Goals

- Assuring Allies and Friends
- Dissuading Opponents
- Deterring Threats and Coercion Against US Interests
- If Deterrence Fails, Decisively Defeat the Enemy

2

UNCLASSIFIED

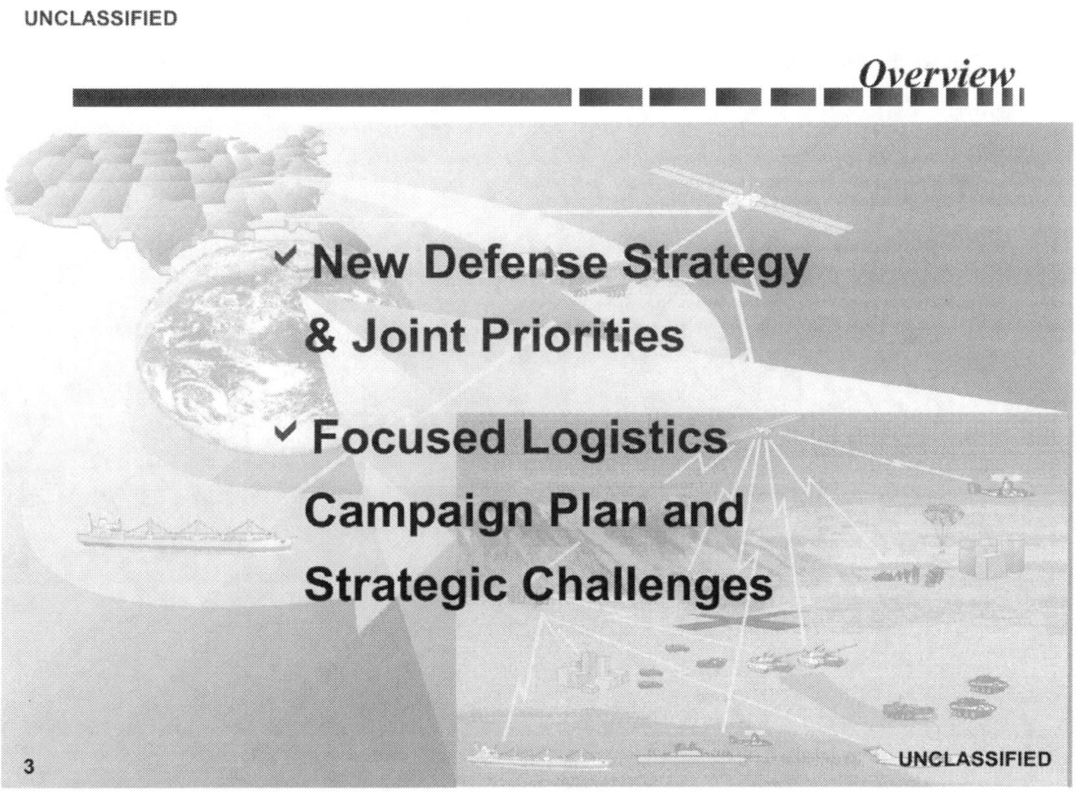
UNCLASSIFIED
Overview
New Defense Strategy
& Joint Priorities
Focused Logistics
Campaign Plan and
Strategic Challenges
3
UNCLASSIFIED

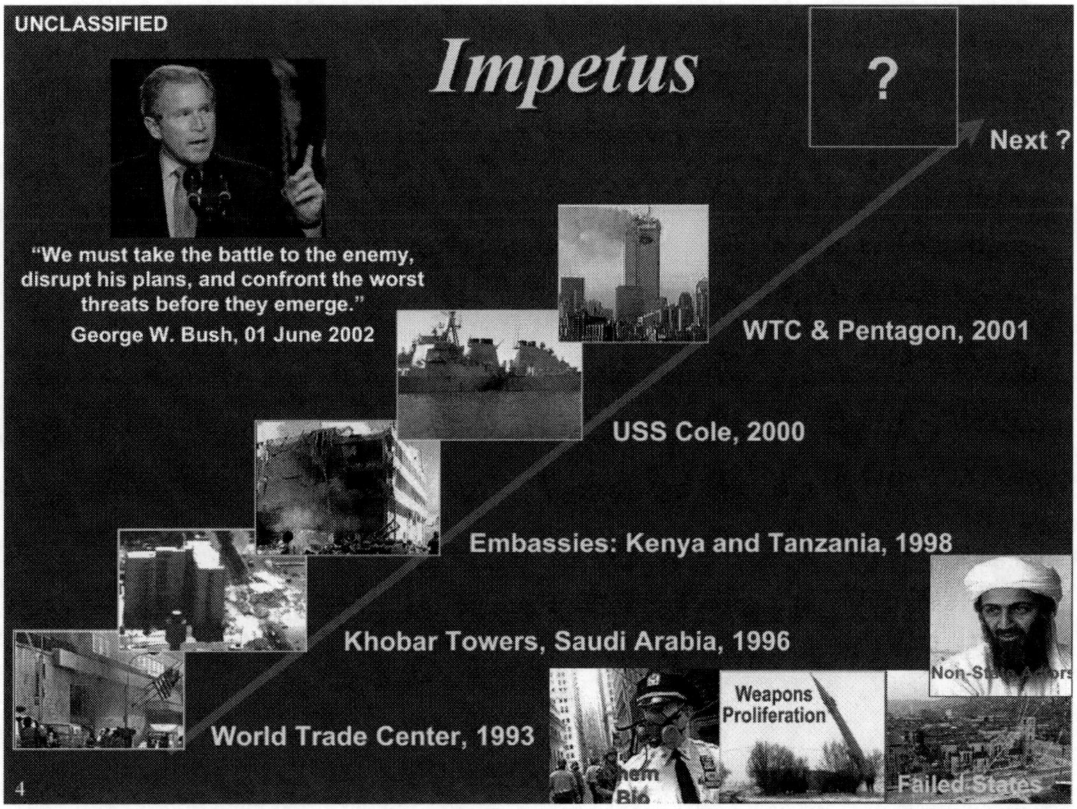
UNCLASSIFIED
Impetus
?
Next ?
"We must take the battle to the enemy, disrupt his plans, and confront the worst threats before they emerge."
George W. Bush, 01 June 2002
WTC & Pentagon, 2001
USS Cole, 2000
Embassies: Kenya and Tanzania, 1998
Khobar Towers, Saudi Arabia, 1996
World Trade Center, 1993
Weapons Proliferation
Failed States
4

UNCLASSIFIED

Joint Priorities

UNCLASSIFIED

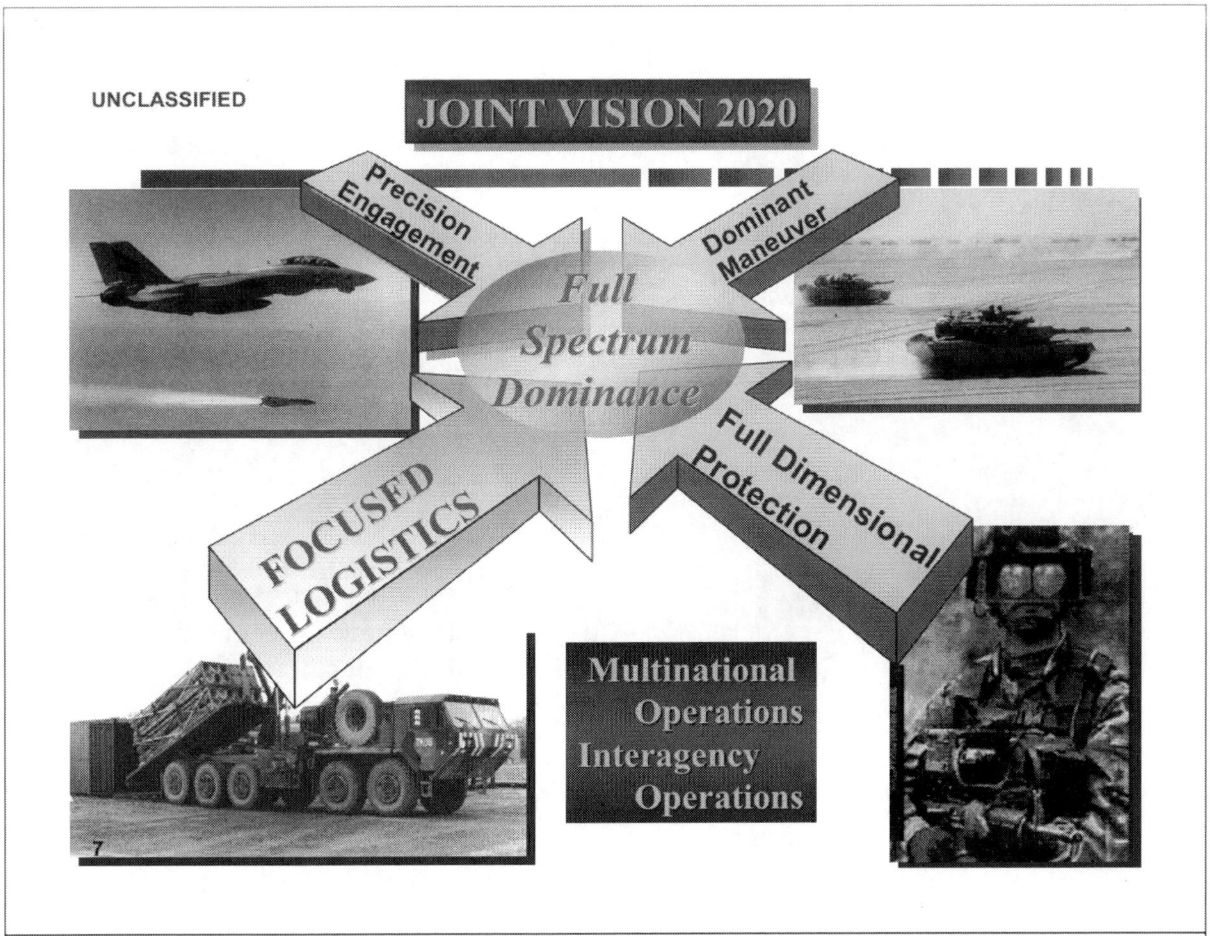
UNCLASSIFIED
JOINT VISION 2020
Precision Engagement
Dominant Maneuver
Full Spectrum Dominance
FOCUSED LOGISTICS
Full Dimensional Protection
Multinational Operations
Interagency Operations
7

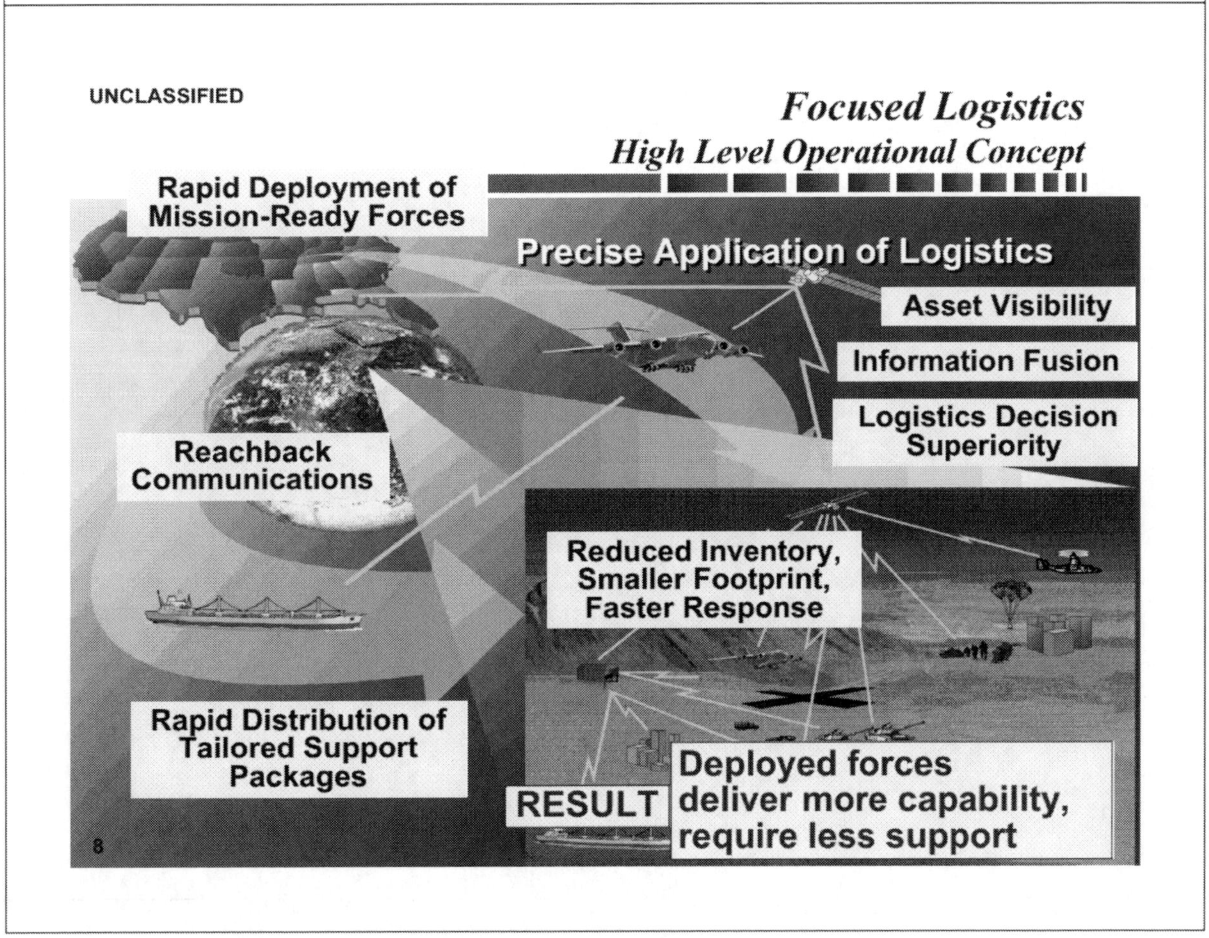
UNCLASSIFIED
Focused Logistics
High Level Operational Concept
Rapid Deployment of Mission-Ready Forces
Precise Application of Logistics
Asset Visibility
Information Fusion
Logistics Decision Superiority
Reachback Communications
Reduced Inventory, Smaller Footprint, Faster Response
Rapid Distribution of Tailored Support Packages
RESULT
Deployed forces deliver more capability, require less support
8

UNCLASSIFIED

Focused Logistics Campaign Plan

Published Aug '02

Comprehensive, integrated approach for achieving full spectrum support for the future joint warfighter

Major Sections

- Building Blocks
  - Logistics Transformation
  - Future Logistics Enterprise
- Challenges
  - Joint Deployment/Rapid Distribution
  - Joint Theater Logistics Management
  - Agile Sustainment
  - Operational Engineering
  - Information Fusion
  - Multinational Logistics
  - Force Health Protection
- Joint Logistics Experimentation
- Keeping Focused Logistics on Track

http://www.dtic.mil/jcs/j4/projects/foclog/foclog.htm

9

UNCLASSIFIED

UNCLASSIFIED

Joint Deployment / Rapid Distribution

What's Our Challenge?

We must rapidly deliver combat forces to the joint force commander and link operating forces with viable sustainment systems.

What's Our Vision?

We will provide a fully enabled mobility system to optimize rapid projection, delivery, and handoff of joint forces and sustainment assets worldwide; distribute the required forces and sustainment at the place and time required; support rapid force maneuver within the joint operations area; and return those forces to home station for regeneration and reconstitution.

10

UNCLASSIFIED

UNCLASSIFIED

Joint Deployment Process
Get There to Fight and Win

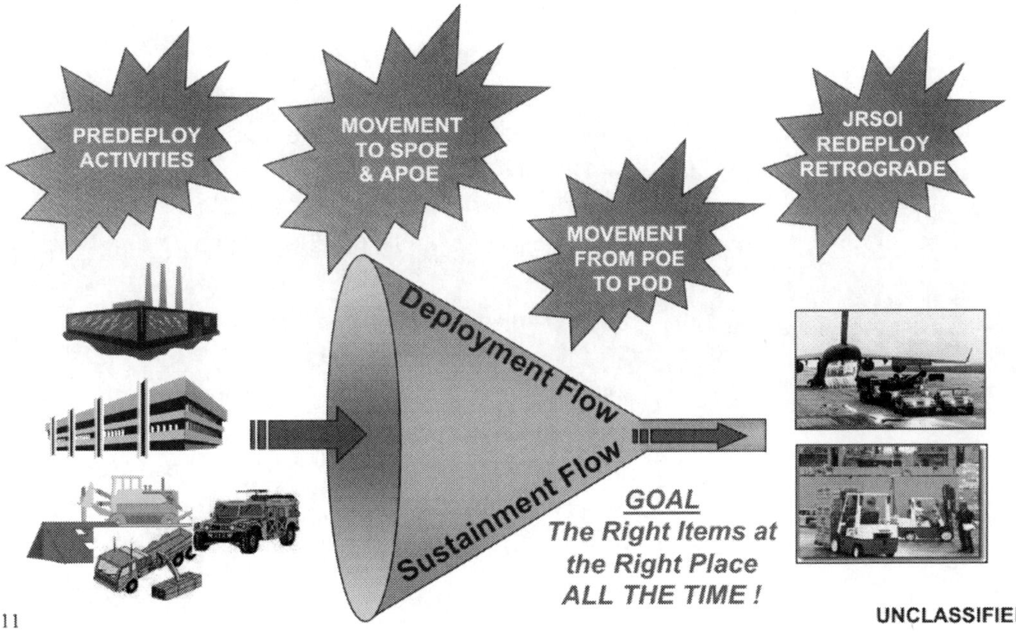

11

UNCLASSIFIED

UNCLASSIFIED

Strategic Mobility Requirements
Global Mobility for a Global Campaign

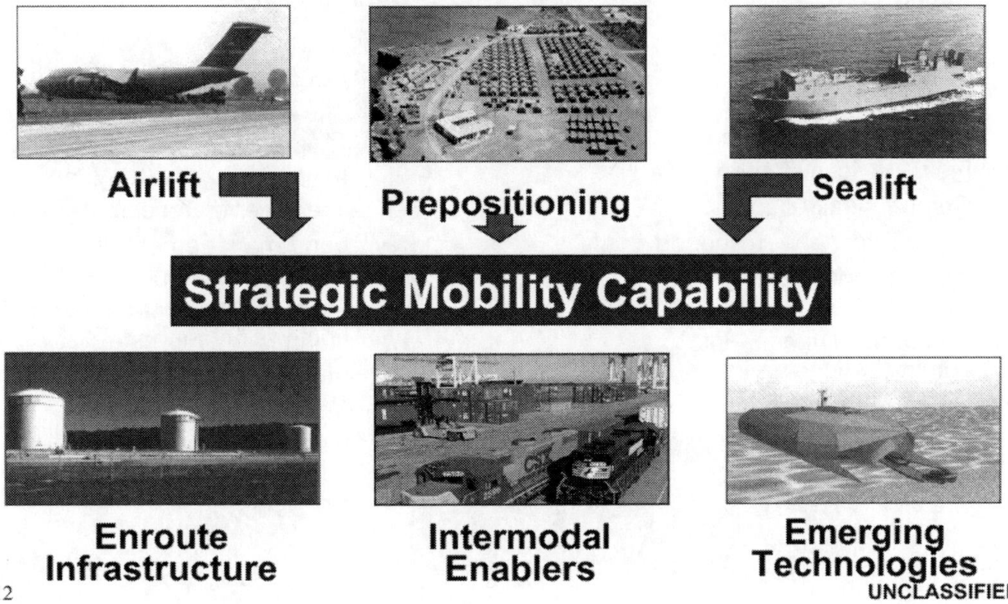

12

UNCLASSIFIED

UNCLASSIFIED

Joint Theater Logistics Management

What's Our Challenge?

We must develop tools that give the joint force commander the capability to effectively oversee the management of logistics throughout the range of full spectrum dominance operations.

What's Our Vision?

We will give the joint force commander the ability to synchronize, prioritize, direct, integrate, and coordinate common-user and cross-service logistics functions.

13 UNCLASSIFIED

UNCLASSIFIED

Typical Theater Logistics Functions

- Reception and onward movement of forces and units
- Supply
- Procurement and property disposal support
- Maintenance support
- Transportation support
- Field services support
- Combat health support
- Civil-military affairs support
- Construction and engineer support
- Personnel, finance, and administration services support
- Rear area security

- EPW custody, control, internment, and disposition
- Land management (in concert with host nation)
- Local procurement, contracting, host nation support
- Materiel management
- Movement control
- Retrograde and redeployment operations
- NBC support

What are the minimum essential critical C2 functions?

14 UNCLASSIFIED

UNCLASSIFIED

Agile Sustainment

What's Our Challenge?

We must transform sustainment policies, processes, and capabilities to improve the flexibility, agility, and precision with which we sustain the warfighter.

What's Our Vision?

We will create an effective, efficient, and responsive sustainment capability that enables the warfighter to achieve full spectrum dominance through application of decisive force, power projection, overseas presence, and strategic agility.

15

UNCLASSIFIED

UNCLASSIFIED

Agile Sustainment

Projecting Power & Sustaining the Fight

Deployment ⟷ **Sustainment**

Mobilization

Critical Commodities Oversight

Prepo/Bare Base Assets

Combat Support/Combat Service Support

Contractor Logistics Support/Host Nation Support/ Coalition Support

Chemical, Biological, Radiological and Nuclear Defense

16

UNCLASSIFIED

UNCLASSIFIED

Operational Engineering

What's Our Challenge?

We must improve engineer response. This includes developing tools for rapid engineer assessments and contingency planning, enabling combat service support forces to be tailored to reduce strategic lift requirements, and minimizing footprint in the joint operations area.

What's Our Vision?

We will provide effective, efficient, responsive, tailored engineer support to meet combatant commander and warfighter operational requirements and timeframes.

17

UNCLASSIFIED

UNCLASSIFIED

Operational Engineering...

... identifies, assesses, and overcomes physical constraints and limitations on operations to maximize operational capability while limiting or constraining that of the enemy.

18

UNCLASSIFIED

UNCLASSIFIED

Information Fusion

What's Our Challenge?

We must provide logisticians and operators a common operational picture that offers reliable asset visibility and access to logistics resources.

What's Our Vision?

We will provide timely and accurate enhanced asset visibility, control, and management through unimpeded access to operational and logistics information for all who need it.

19 UNCLASSIFIED

UNCLASSIFIED

End State…
Logistics Collaboration as Force Multiplier

Provide Warfighter real-time operations & logistics collaborative capability to support planning and execution

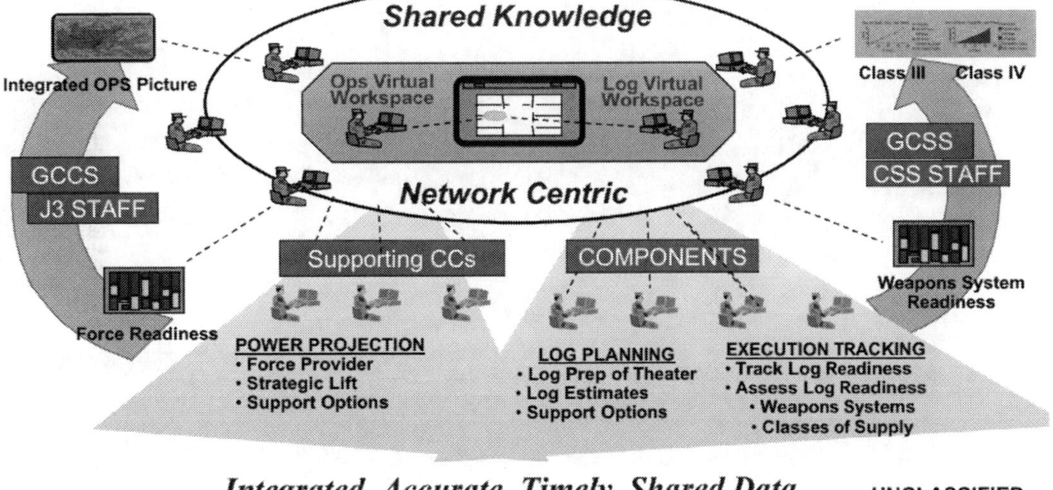

Integrated, Accurate, Timely, Shared Data

20 UNCLASSIFIED

UNCLASSIFIED

Multinational Logistics

What's Our Challenge?

We must strengthen the support relationship between the United States and its allied and coalition partners.

What's Our Vision?

We will optimize logistics operations across and between all echelons, coalitions, and host nations.

21

UNCLASSIFIED

UNCLASSIFIED

Multi-National Interoperability

Building The Team To Win

<u>Our Challenge</u>: Improve the level of Multi-National Logistics Cooperation

Acquisition Cross Servicing Agreements in Place

Doctrine Established   Wargames/Exercises

Be Prepared for Multi-National Logistics Cooperation BEFORE the Crisis

22

UNCLASSIFIED

UNCLASSIFIED

ACSAs by Combatant Commander

65 Agreements In-place
10 pending signature

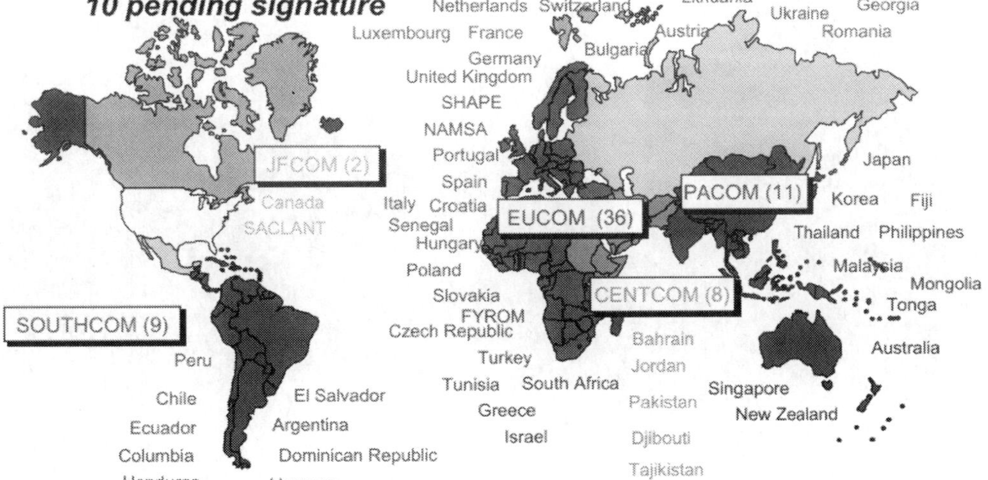

65 Other Nations Eligible (15 in negotiations)

Updated: 20 Jun 03

UNCLASSIFIED

23

UNCLASSIFIED

Force Health Protection

What's Our Challenge?

We must protect service members from all health and environmental hazards associated with military service.

What's Our Vision?

We will protect forces from all health threats across the full spectrum of conflict and tailor standardized joint medical systems to provide essential care in theater and enhanced care during evacuation to definitive care.

24

UNCLASSIFIED

UNCLASSIFIED

Joint Health Service Support

... responds to warfighter requirements for a deployable, lighter, more mobile medical capability ensuring full implementation of force health strategy throughout the spectrum of conflict.

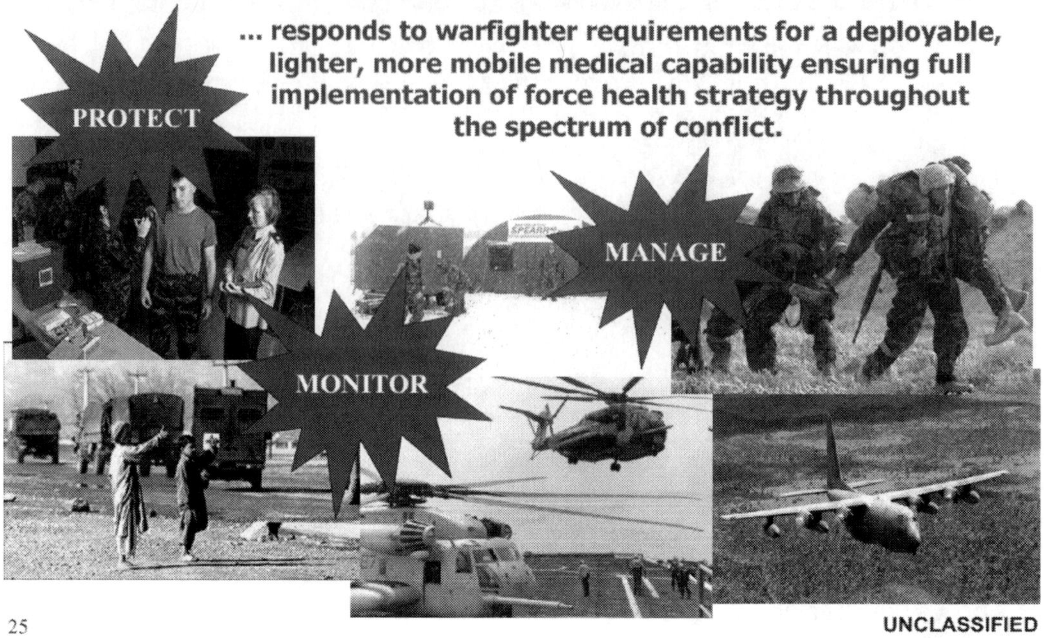

25

UNCLASSIFIED

UNCLASSIFIED

Joint Logistics Strategy for Global Operations

26

UNCLASSIFIED

UNCLASSIFIED
JOINT
CHIEFS OF STAFF
UNCLASSIFIED

"Bridging Defense and Industry"

Transforming our Business for Improved Support to the Warfighter while Partnering with Industry

Presented by
MG Hawthorne L. Proctor, USA
to
Society of Logistics Engineers
August 12, 2003

1

"Bridging Defense and Industry"

Roadmap for Today's Presentation

- Supporting the Warfighter – Operation Iraqi Freedom (OIF)
- Public/Private Competition (A-76)
- Strategic Material Sourcing (SMS)
- Business Systems Modernization (BSM)

2

What We Are About...

Giving The Warfighter's What They Need...

Reduced Inventories

Faster, Reliable Service

Better Quality

Lower Costs

From Manager of Supplies To Manager of <u>Suppliers</u>

What We Did Differently in OIF

- Identified Requirements and Funding:
- $500M in FY02 and $424M in FY03
  - Invested $241M for 1.2M Surge Production of Joint Service Lightweight Integrated Suit Technology (JSLIST).
- Executed Support :
  - Forward stocking
  - Prime Vendor (Food, Medical, Construction)
  - Deployed DLA Contingency Support Teams

4

Leveraging Subsistence Prime Vendors in OIF

Prime Vendor Contracts worked…

Meals Ready To Eat

Total Meals – 54.7M
Total Cost - $370.3M

Bottled Water

- 38M Liters of Water
- Dollar Value - $7.9M
- Approved Source Vendors
  - BMMI (Bahrain)
  - Seven Seas (UAE)
  - DSCP-Europe Contracting
    - Greece

5

Forward Stocking Barrier and Construction Material (DDZZ) in OIF

What Worked…

Forward Stocking…made sense for 23 items of Barrier and Construction Material

- 23 NSNs
- 2,415 containers
- $9.7 million total value
- Equates to 1,208 C-17 Sorties

Contractor Support Provided By:

Danish Camp Supply

Contract Dollar Value: $6.6M

6

We All Benefit From Our Partnerships With Industry

Since 1990, we have had a variety of programs for Partnering with Industry – Corporate Contracts, Performance-Based Logistics, Strategic Supplier Alliances, Competitive Sourcing, . . .

Savings = $2B

- Public/Private Competition (A-76)
- Strategic Materiel Sourcing (SMS)

7

A-76 Competitive Sourcing Shift To Commercial Practices

Average Net Savings Of 29 Percent

- Competitions Completed –
  - 11 in areas of Distribution, Disposal Sites, Document Automation
  - 2,599 Full Time Equivalents Saved
- Competition Results
  - 4 Most Efficient Organizations
  - 7 Private Sector
    - ➢Resource Consultants, Inc
    - ➢EG&G
    - ➢MANCON
    - ➢ LABAT-Anderson

8

A-76 Competitive Sourcing
Shift To Commercial Practices

- Competitions in Progress
  - 8 in areas of Distribution and Disposal/Reutilization
  - 2 solicitations closed
  - 4 solicitations to be released
- Future Competitions include installation support and a re-solicitation of two distribution depots
- New Office of Management and Budget Rules
  - Working with Office of Secretary of Defense to implement
  - Building our plan to transition

9

Strategic Materiel Sourcing
Benefits and Costs

- SMS is focused on developing long-term agreements with suppliers on a target item population
  - Population consists of DLA-managed Hardware items that account for 80% (or 85%) of sales and demand and an additional group that affects readiness
- $87.2M in estimated Savings attributable to SMS and SSAs from 1QFY98 to 2QFY03
- SMS LTC obligations were $210M in FY02; currently $157M in FY03

10

Strategic Materiel Sourcing Contract Toolbox

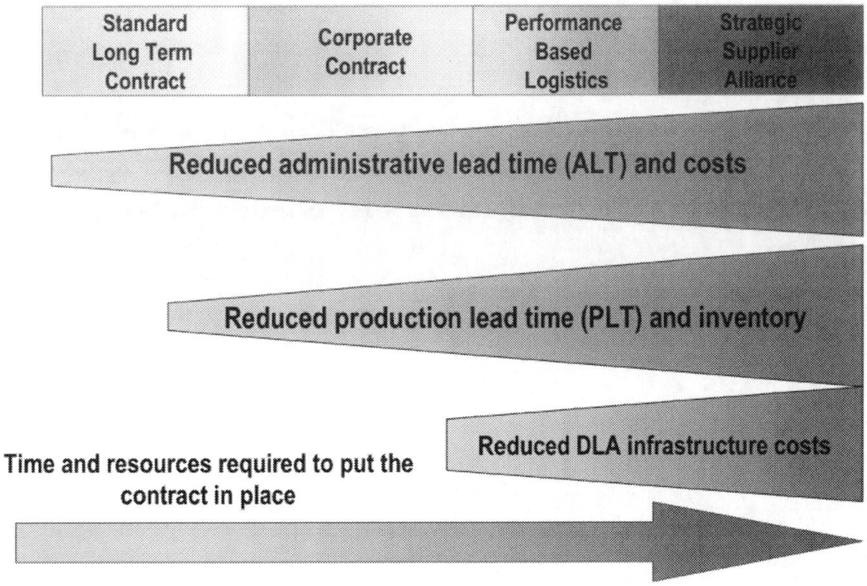

11

Strategic Supplier Alliance Execution Plan August 2003

FY02	FY03	FY04	FY05
Completed	**Completed**	**Proposed**	**Proposed**
Boeing	Avibank	Hamilton Sundstrand	Aircraft Breaking Systems
Pratt & Whitney*	Canadian Commercial Corporation	Stewart & Stevenson	Unison Industries
General Electric*	**Proposed**	Bell Helicopter/Textron	
Parker Hannifin*	Eaton	Raytheon	
Northrop Gruman	Osh Kosh	United Defense LP	
Dresser Rand**	Goodrich	Rosemont	
BAE Systems	Rolls Royce	Moog, Inc.	
Honeywell*	SPS Technology	GDLS & GD Defense	
	AM General	Fairchild	
	Sikorsky		
	Lockheed Martin		

* Air Force

** Navy

12

Transforming Our Business

BSM business systems modernization

delivering 21st century logistics

13

BSM Will Enable DLA To:

- Replace Legacy Systems with COTS software
- Re-Engineer by fielding Best Practices
- Improve customer service by collaborating with customers
- Provide Best Value Solutions
- Provide the training, experience, and opportunity to succeed

An "Agile Infrastructure"...

"The adoption, within the DoD, of the best practices of the commercial market place, resulting in continuously improving logistics operations, cost savings/avoidance, and process cycle reductions."

--JV 2020 Focused Logistics

The BSM Vision

DLA's mission-critical legacy systems are replaced with a new enterprise IT environment based on commercial-off-the-shelf (COTS) software and best practices

14

The BSM Strategy...

- BSM Program: Supply (Less Energy)
  - Class I (Subsistence)
  - Class II (Clothing and Textiles)
  - Class IV (Construction)
  - Class VIII (Medical)
  - Class IX (Repair Parts)
- Beyond the BSM Program:
  - Customer Relationship Management
  - Distribution Planning Management System
- Other Major Related Efforts
  - Catalog Reengineered System (CRS)
  - Fuels Automated System (FAS)

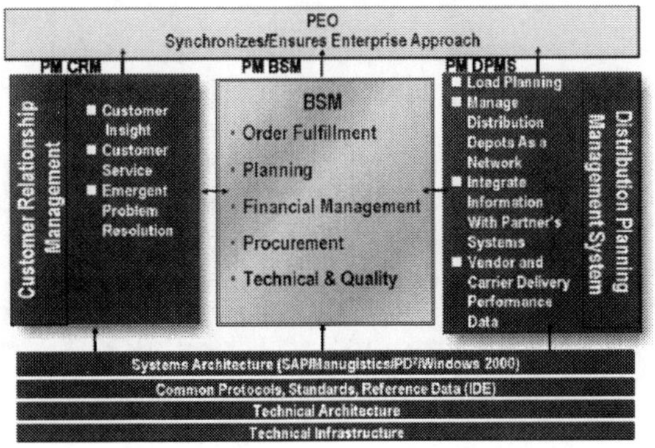

15

The Process: Reengineer by Fielding Best Practices

Order Fulfillment

- Enables quick order turnaround
- Provides timely information
- Tracks & traces orders

Planning

Demand Planning

- Identifies future needs through collaboration
- Improves demand plan accuracy

Supply Planning

- Ensures inventory is available when & where needed
- Optimizes inventory levels, inventory turns, and assist in reducing leadtimes

Procurement

- Provides for payment based on receipt
- Is a single contract writing application
- Uses single integrated master data
- Provides visibility of long term contracts across the enterprise

Financial

- Enables better planning; better budgets
- Provides better cost visibility
- Enables CFO compliance
- Provides near real-time data

Technical & Quality

- Streamlines item introduction
- Enables comprehensive product lifecycle management
- Improves product quality assurance

16

What we Delivered in Release One

- Delivered a fully operational, tested system and trained workforce
- Fully supported existing customer commitments
- Delivered 73% of the Functional Requirement in the ORD ... for about 5% of the line items
- Risk mitigation plans were in place

Concept Demonstration

- Maritime Carrier and Sub Surface teams
  - LM-2500
- Terminal Lugs and Insulation Sleeving
- Fleet Prime Vendor
- Garrison Feeding (Prime Vendor Southeast Region, Food Service Equipment)
- Helicopter systems (UH-1, H-3, H-46, and H-53)

#	NSNs	Customer Orders	Sales	Users	Customers	Suppliers
TOTAL	170K	2.5M	$600M	380	17K	2.5K

Broad enough to demonstrate ... small enough to manage risk

17

BSM Continues to Add Value to Our Business

Order Fulfillment
- Over 300K Customer Orders Processed
- $ 310M sales
- Over 37K depot receipts posted

Procurement
- Over 164K PRs awarded

Planning
- Stable Demand Planning Process
- Beginning to Work Collaborative Planning

Finance
- Over 16,000 Vendor Payments Made
- Over $ 234M Paid

What we did
After Our 1st Year
July '02 – July '03

18

Lessons Learned from Rel 1 and Adjustments made Going Forward

- Change in Planning Process – "Hub & Spoke"
- Customer facing portion of Standard Organization tweaked to Incorporate "CRM Cells" and New Planning scheme
- Changing Procurement Tool

PD² / AcquiLine → DPACS → SAP

- Maintain integrity of "Design-Build-Test-Train" Plan

19

BSM Timeline

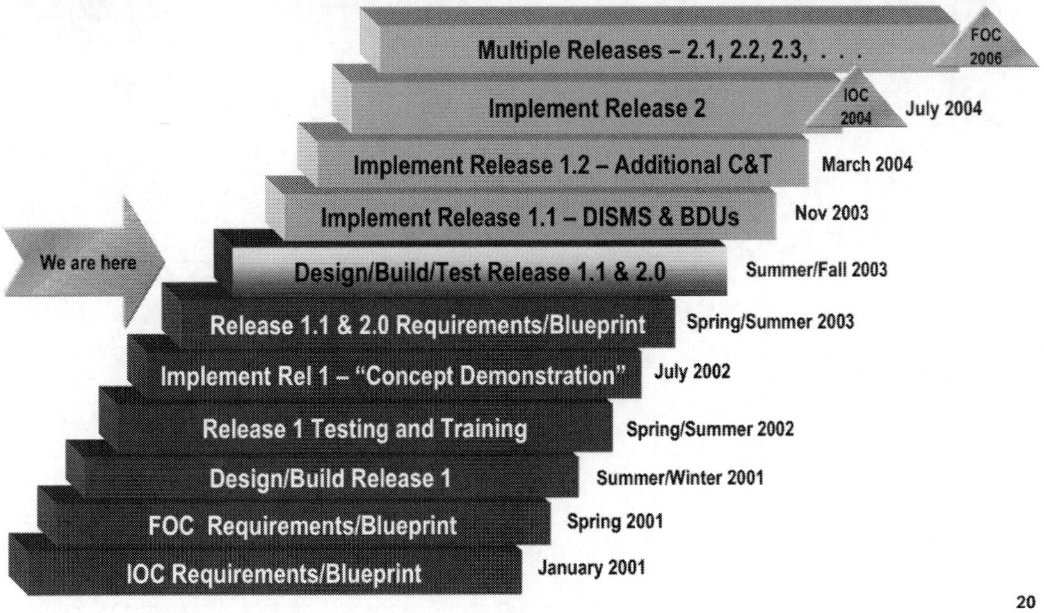

20

DWCF
Cost Recovery Rate Over Time

(Operating Costs as a Percentage of Total Sales)

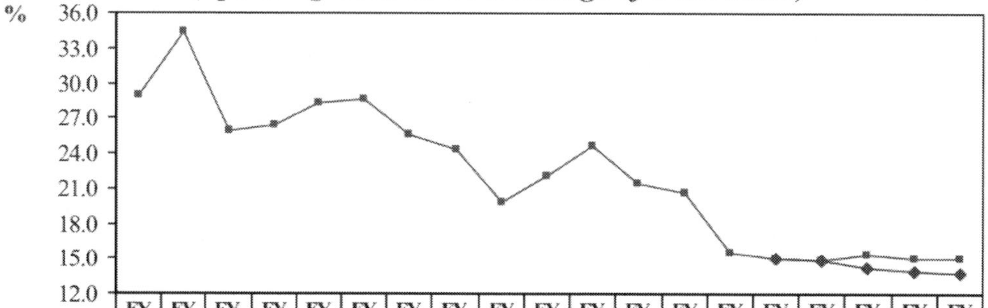

	FY 91	FY 92	FY 93	FY 94	FY 95	FY 96	FY 97	FY 98	FY 99	FY 00	FY 01	FY 02	FY 03	FY 04	FY 05	FY 06	FY 07	FY 08	FY 09
PB/POM 04	29.0	34.4	25.9	26.4	28.4	28.7	25.6	24.4	19.8	22.1	24.7	21.5	20.7	15.5	15.1	14.9	15.3	15.1	15.1
POM 05 Proposal															15.0	14.9	14.3	14.0	13.8

Lowest Cost Recovery Rate in DLA History

Savings Returned to Warfighter

21

The Role of Future Combat System (FCS) Reliability, Availability, and Maintainability on Objective Force Organizational Design

COL Mike Ivy
Vice-Director
Combat Service Support
Battle Lab
Fort Lee, Virginia

The UA Battlespace

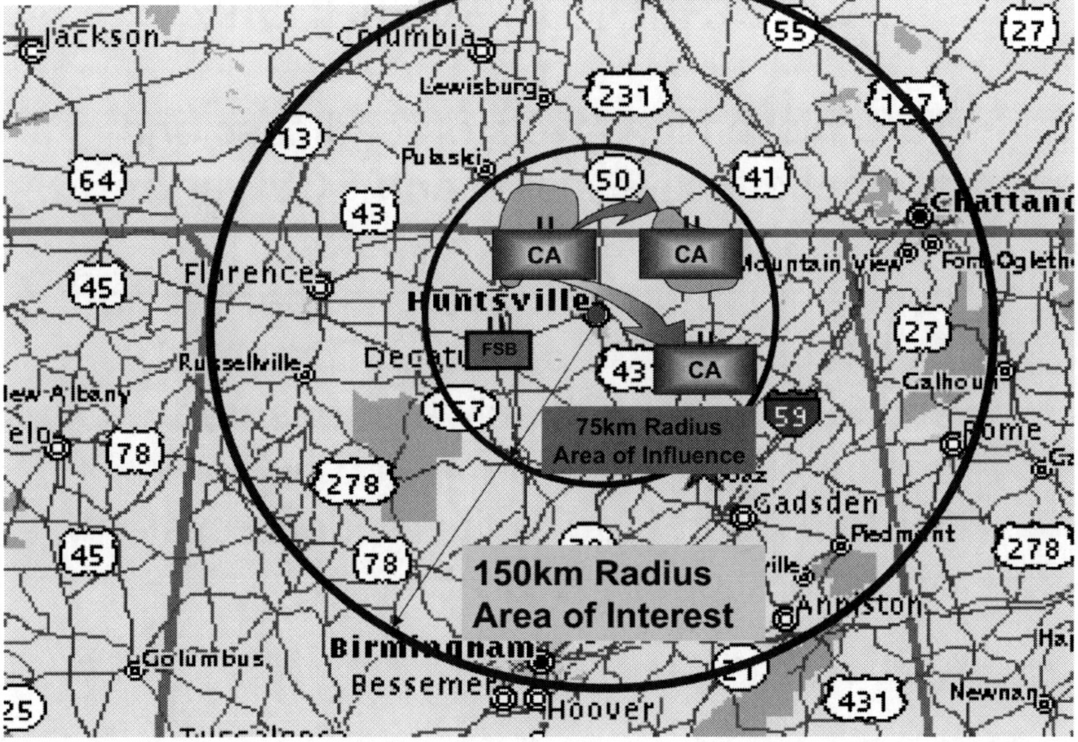

FCS Major Supportability Requirements

CSA Mandates:
Improve Deployability
Decrease Log Footprint
Decrease O&S Costs

- Transportability
- **Availability**
- **Reliability**
- **Maintainability to include "pit stop" engineering, diagnostics/prognostics, minimal tools, minimal services, crew chief repair, etc.**
- Fuel efficiency and self-refuel
- On-board water generation
- Automated resupply to the platform
- Many others

Operational Availability

- To achieve high levels of readiness and combat effectiveness, **each FCS variant within a unit** (battalion/separate company) **must achieve an Operational Availability of 95 percent** (Threshold) and 99 percent (Objective) measured continuously during a mission pulse. System Abort (SA) faults render a system not Operationally Available.

Source JROC ORD 1239

Future Combat System

Operational Availability

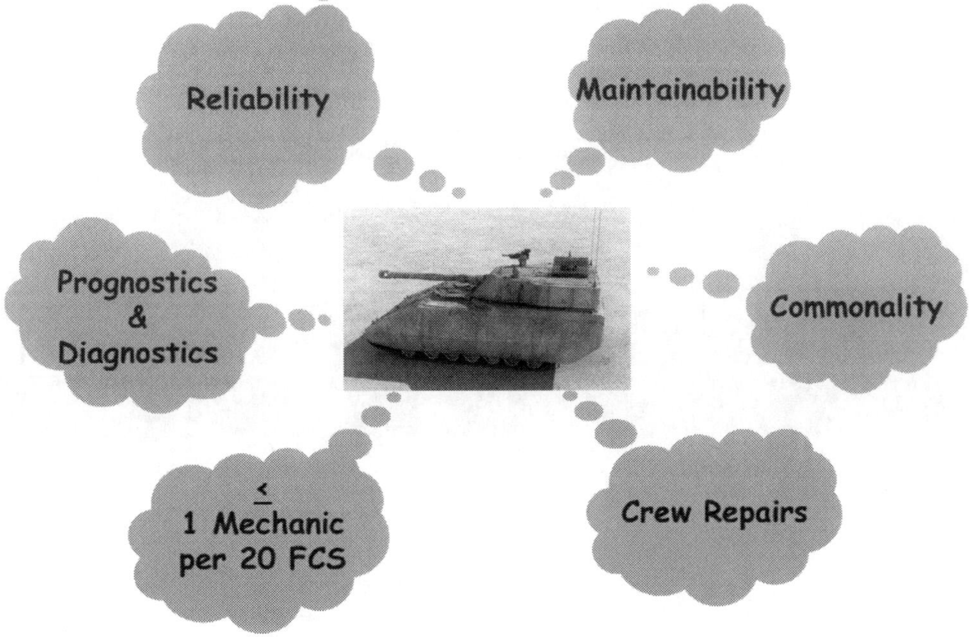

Operational Availability (Ao) - Impact on Combat Power -

UA CAB	
ICV	25
MCS	18
C2V	20
NLOS Mort	8
RSV	9
MV	7
UAV LS	3
RMV	2
NLOS Bn (slice)	
NLOS Cannon	6
NLOS LS	20

72 hr Pulse

92.8% Combat Power

Each FCS Ao ≥ 95%

Platform Type	Qty Down
ICV	1
MCS	2
C2V	1
NLOS Mortar	1
RSV	1
MV	1
UAV LS	0
RMV	0
NLOS Cannon	1
NLOS LS	1
Total	14

82.5% Combat Power

Each FCS Ao ≥ 90%

Platform Type	Qty Down
ICV	3
MCS	4
C2V	3
NLOS Mortar	2
RSV	2
MV	1
UAV LS	1
RMV	1
NLOS Can	2
NLOS LS	3
Total	34

Based on 100 simulation runs

72 hr Pulse

Potential for 2.4 x the losses!

Data based on a single 72 hour pulse and does not include combat damage/losses!

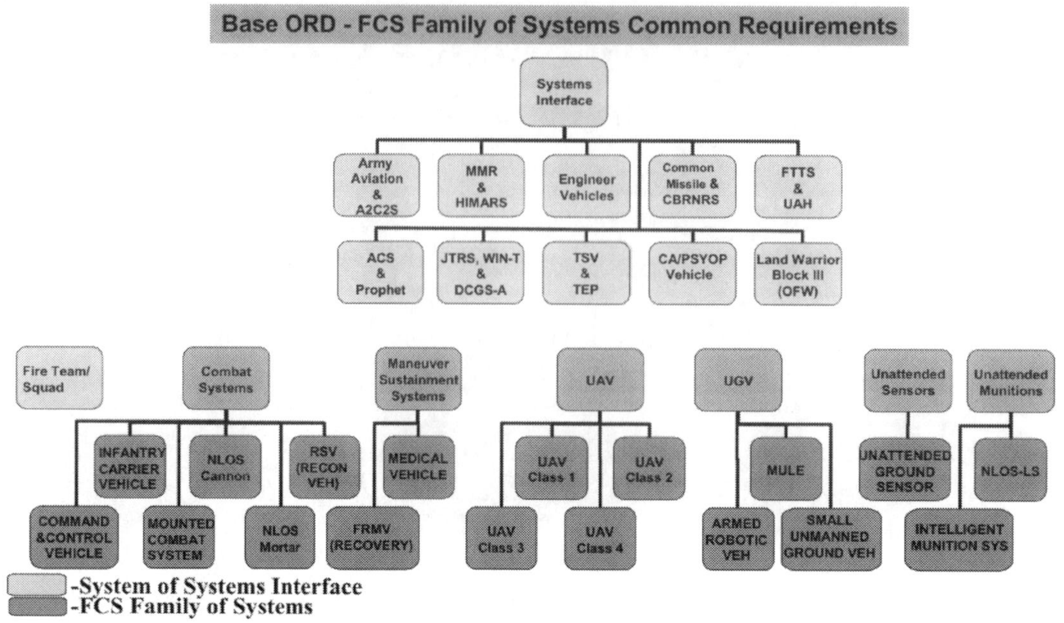

JROC Approved FCS ORD, 14 April 03

MTBSA Reliability Comparisons

Current		Stryker[1]		FCS		Improvement .	
Platform	MTBSA[2]	Platform	MTBSA[2]	Platform	MTBSA[2]	Stryker	Current
C2V	250	CV	500	C2V	2600	5.2 x	10.4 x
FSCS	290	RV	420	RSV	1100	2.6 x	3.8 x
LAV Mortar[3]	180	Mortar Carrier[4]	740	NLOS Mortar	1000	1.4 x	5.6 x
M1A2	90	MGS	480	MCS	1100	2.3 x	12.2 x
M2A2	160	ATGM	610	ARV	1100	1.8 x	6.9 x
M113A3	200	ICV	480	ICV	2400	5 x	12 x
M113A3	200	MEV	280	MEV/TV	2700	9.6 x	13.5 x
M88	?	NA	-	FRMV	1400	NA	?
Crusader	62	NA	-	NLOS Can	740	NA	11.9 x

1. *Stryker MTBSA values based on ORD requirements and OMS/MP conversions*
2. *MTBSA values rounded to 2 significant digits for easy comparion*
3. *LAV Mortar data based on Saudi test using OMFs (a turreted system)*
4. *Stryker Mortar Carrier does not include the mortar and is not a turreted system*

Source: HQ TRADOC, RID

Maintainability

- Maintenance Ratio (MR) will not exceed 0.05 Maintenance Man-Hours/Operating Hour (MMH/OH).
- Platform Crew Chief must be able to repair/replace at least 80% of system aborts, 80% Essential Functional Failures (EFF), and 80% of NEFF unscheduled field maintenance requirements.
- Diagnostics & Prognostics

Source: JROC ORD 3635

Platform to Mechanic Ratios

- Current
  - AOE Hvy Div 317 Abrams tanks
  - 176 10/20 level 63A maintenance personnel
  - 1.8 to 1 ratio tanks per mechanic
- Stryker
  - 308 Strykers in the SBCT
  - 30 mechanics
  - 10.3 to 1 ratio Strykers per mechanic
- FCS (Unit of Action)
  - Approximately 525 systems in the UA
  - 21 maintenance personnel
  - 25 to 1 ratio FCS per mechanic

As of 8 July 2003

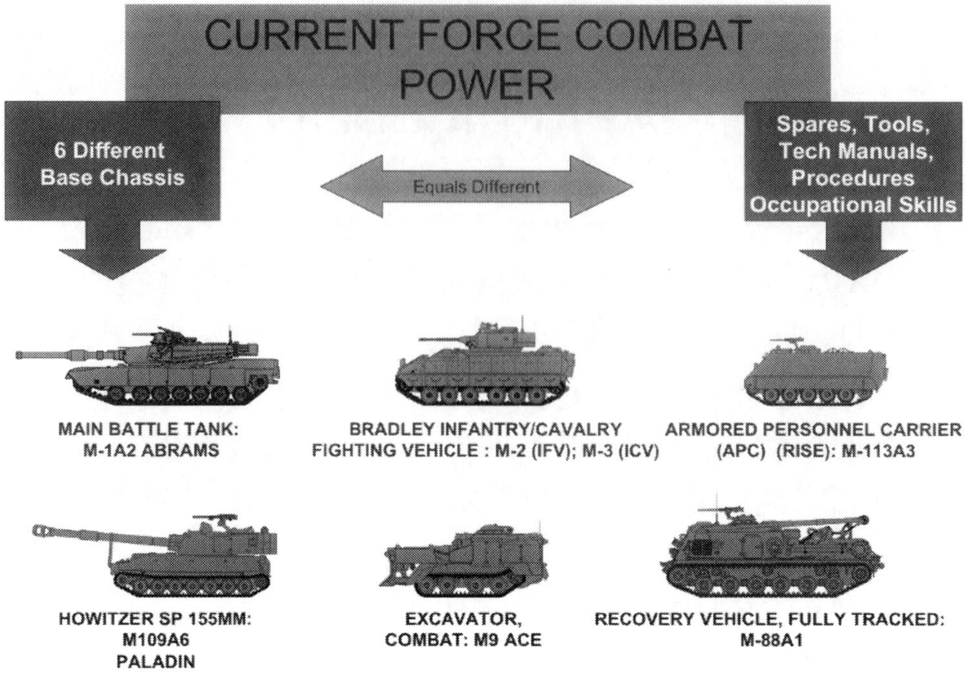

Commonality

- The FCS FoS will maximize platform and component commonality within each system (manned/unmanned) class (70% Threshold/90% Objective) to simplify and reduce total spare part support requirements.

Source JROC ORD 3622

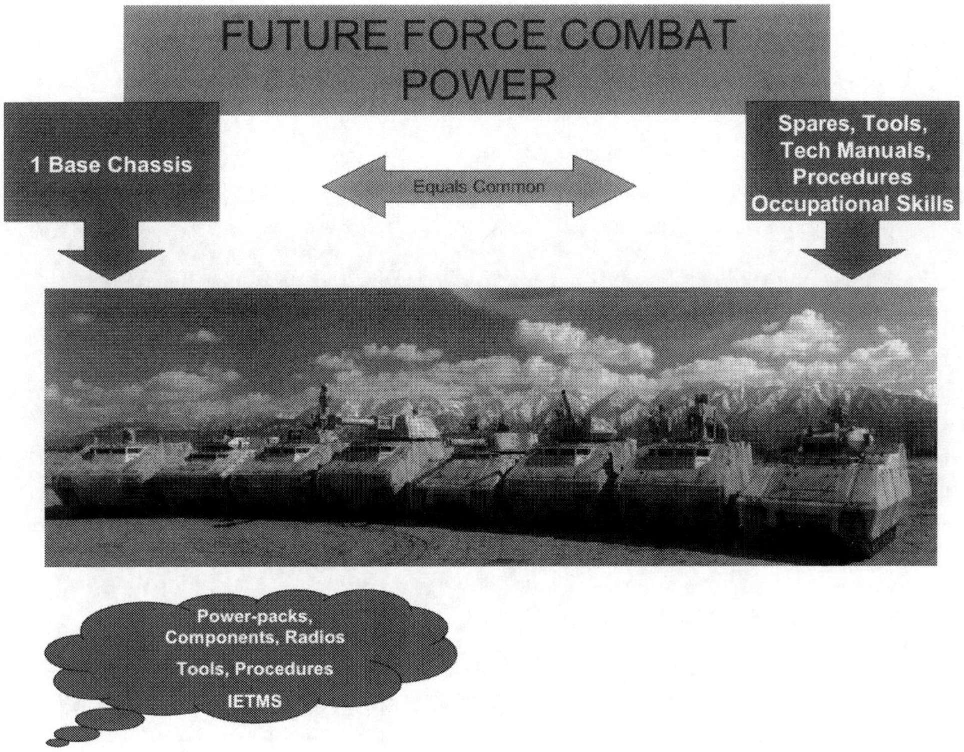

Tools

- On-board tools common to each FCS platform will not exceed 10 common tools.
- Those carried on the FRMV will not exceed 20 common tools and at a minimum will include those common tools found on each FCS platform.

Source JROC ORD 3623

FCS C2 Variant

Incredible agility, aerodynamic, crew protection, fuel efficient, 5600 MTBSA-M, 8692 MTBSA, 76 MPG, 3998 LBS, .006 MR, MaxTTR of .13

State-of-the-art crew stations with embedded video IETM

On board water Generation

Featuring Ergonomic Modular design, Light Weight Materials, All plug-N-play and installed by a crew in under 12.5 minutes

Commander Station with LDSS, Voice recognition, embedded diagnostic/prognostics

Holographic 2nd Generation Tele-Maintenance/CLS Support

USA TACOM-ARDEC/ASCO
Logistics R&D Activity
Picatinny Arsenal, NJ
Enabling a Transformation in Logistics
International Logistics Conference
12 Aug 03
GREGG PETERS
AMCOM Field Office
DSN 746-3686, (256) 876-3686
"Providing America Advanced Armaments for Peace and War"
Tank-automotive & Armaments COMmand

Logistics R&D Activity Thrust Areas
Battlefield Rearm
Reduced Weapons System Rearm Times
50% Faster Rearm of Apache Longbow
Explosives Safety & Insensitive Munitions
Improved Munitions Survivability
Stops Explosive Propagation - Ammo stack separation reduced from 163 ft to 15 ft
Ammunition Packaging
Rapid Access & Reduced Weight and Cube
36 % Reduced Cube, 10% lighter and 61% faster rearm
Logistics C4
Munitions Information Technology & Ultrareliability
Visibility of each munition's health - ensuring the warfighter only receives good ammo
Logistics Analysis
Real-time Analysis of Logistics Issues
"What-if" analysis to optimize the ammunition logistics system
Combat Service Support
Improved Strategic & Battlefield Ammo Distribution
PLS CROP and PLS Container Handling Unit (CHU)

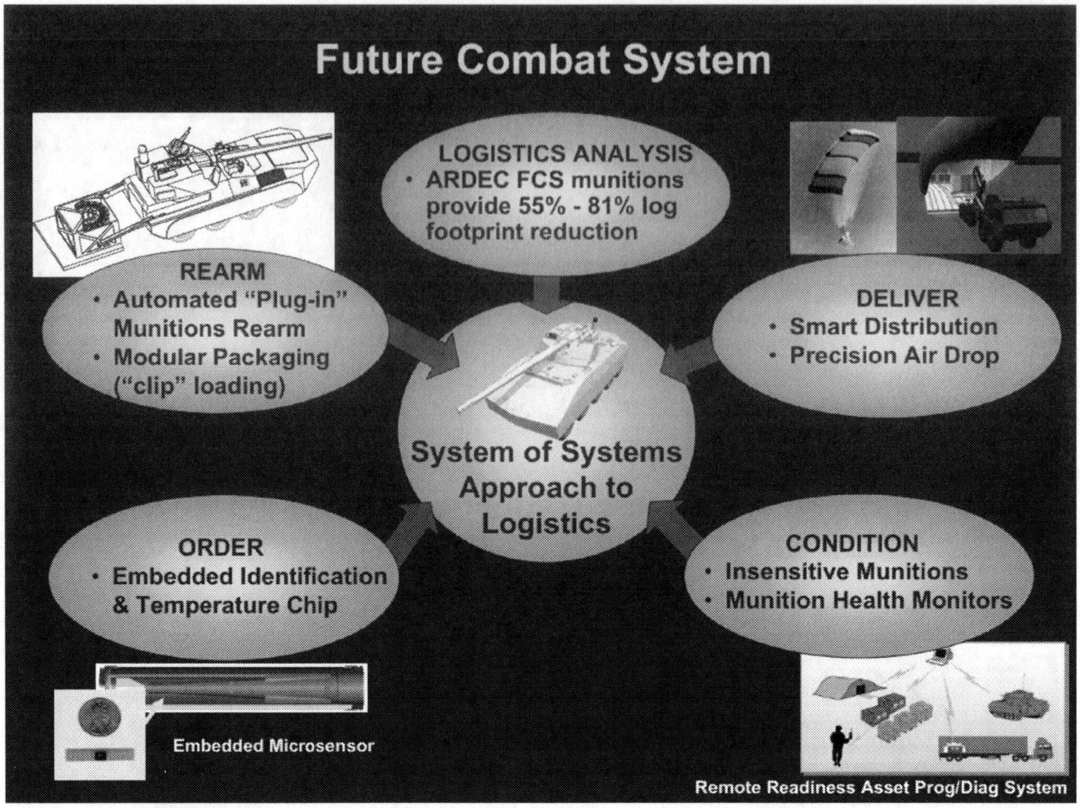
Future Combat System
LOGISTICS ANALYSIS
• ARDEC FCS munitions provide 55% - 81% log footprint reduction
REARM
• Automated "Plug-in" Munitions Rearm
• Modular Packaging ("clip" loading)
DELIVER
• Smart Distribution
• Precision Air Drop
System of Systems Approach to Logistics
ORDER
• Embedded Identification & Temperature Chip
CONDITION
• Insensitive Munitions
• Munition Health Monitors
Embedded Microsensor
Remote Readiness Asset Prog/Diag System

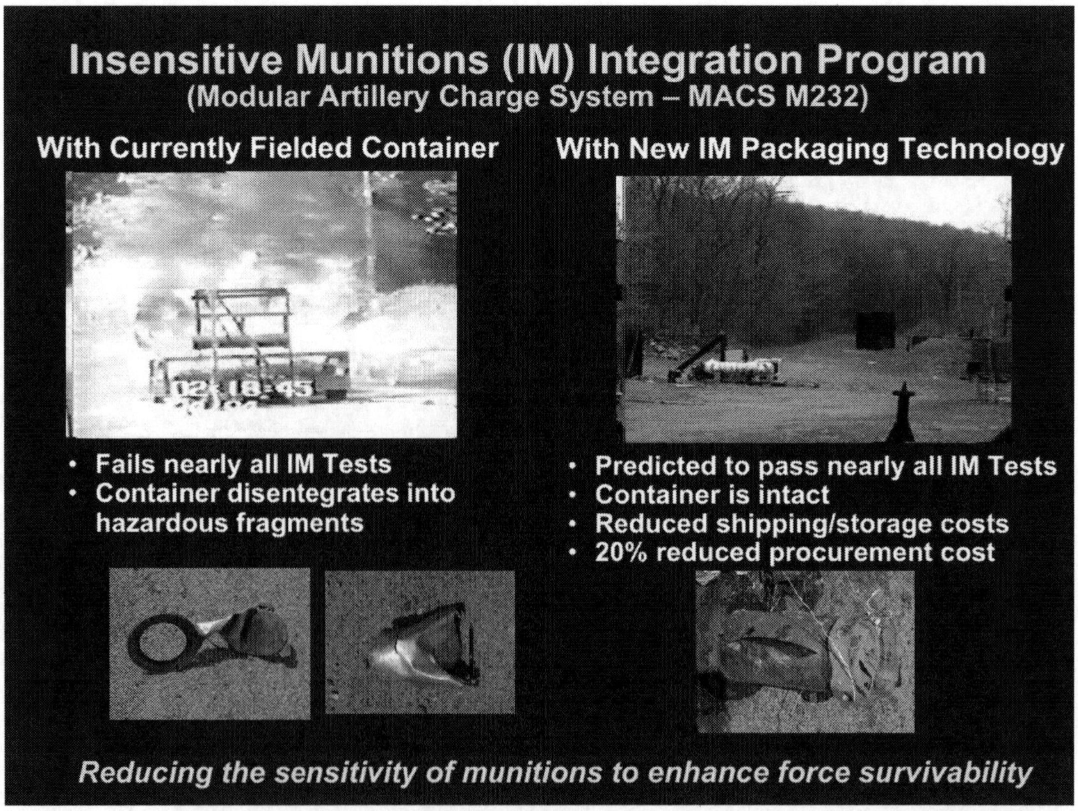
Insensitive Munitions (IM) Integration Program
(Modular Artillery Charge System – MACS M232)
With Currently Fielded Container
With New IM Packaging Technology
• Fails nearly all IM Tests
• Container disentegrates into hazardous fragments
• Predicted to pass nearly all IM Tests
• Container is intact
• Reduced shipping/storage costs
• 20% reduced procurement cost
Reducing the sensitivity of munitions to enhance force survivability

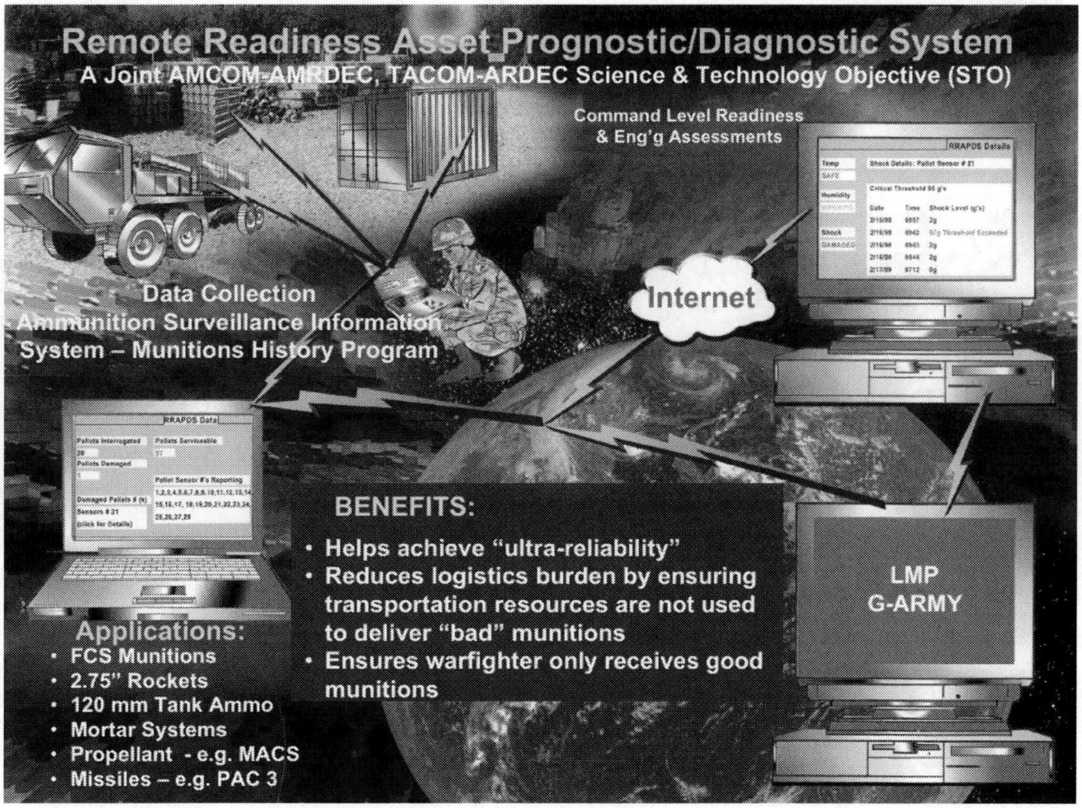

Remote Readiness Asset Prognostic/Diagnostic System
A Joint AMCOM-AMRDEC, TACOM-ARDEC Science & Technology Objective (STO)
Command Level Readiness
& Eng'g Assessments
Data Collection
Ammunition Surveillance Information
System – Munitions History Program
Internet
BENEFITS:
• Helps achieve "ultra-reliability"
• Reduces logistics burden by ensuring transportation resources are not used to deliver "bad" munitions
• Ensures warfighter only receives good munitions
LMP
G-ARMY
Applications:
• FCS Munitions
• 2.75" Rockets
• 120 mm Tank Ammo
• Mortar Systems
• Propellant - e.g. MACS
• Missiles – e.g. PAC 3

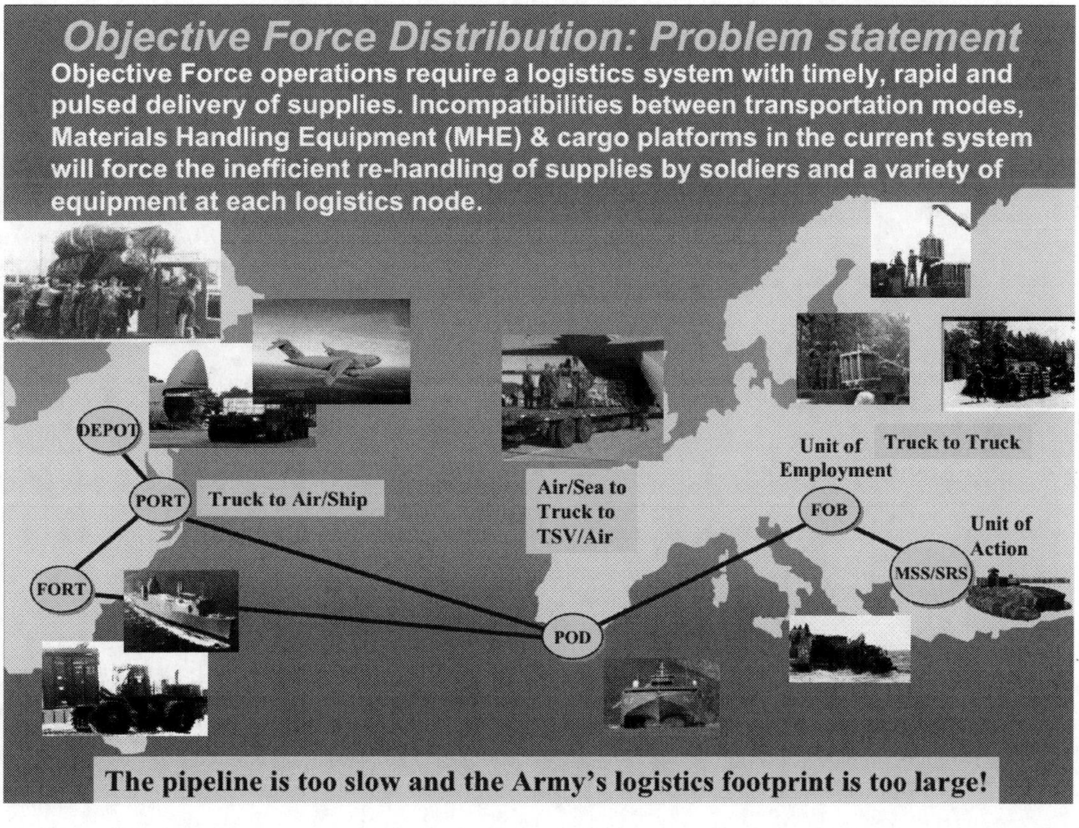

Objective Force Distribution: Problem statement
Objective Force operations require a logistics system with timely, rapid and pulsed delivery of supplies. Incompatibilities between transportation modes, Materials Handling Equipment (MHE) & cargo platforms in the current system will force the inefficient re-handling of supplies by soldiers and a variety of equipment at each logistics node.
DEPOT
PORT
Truck to Air/Ship
FORT
POD
Air/Sea to
Truck to
TSV/Air
Unit of
Employment
Truck to Truck
FOB
MSS/SRS
Unit of
Action
The pipeline is too slow and the Army's logistics footprint is too large!

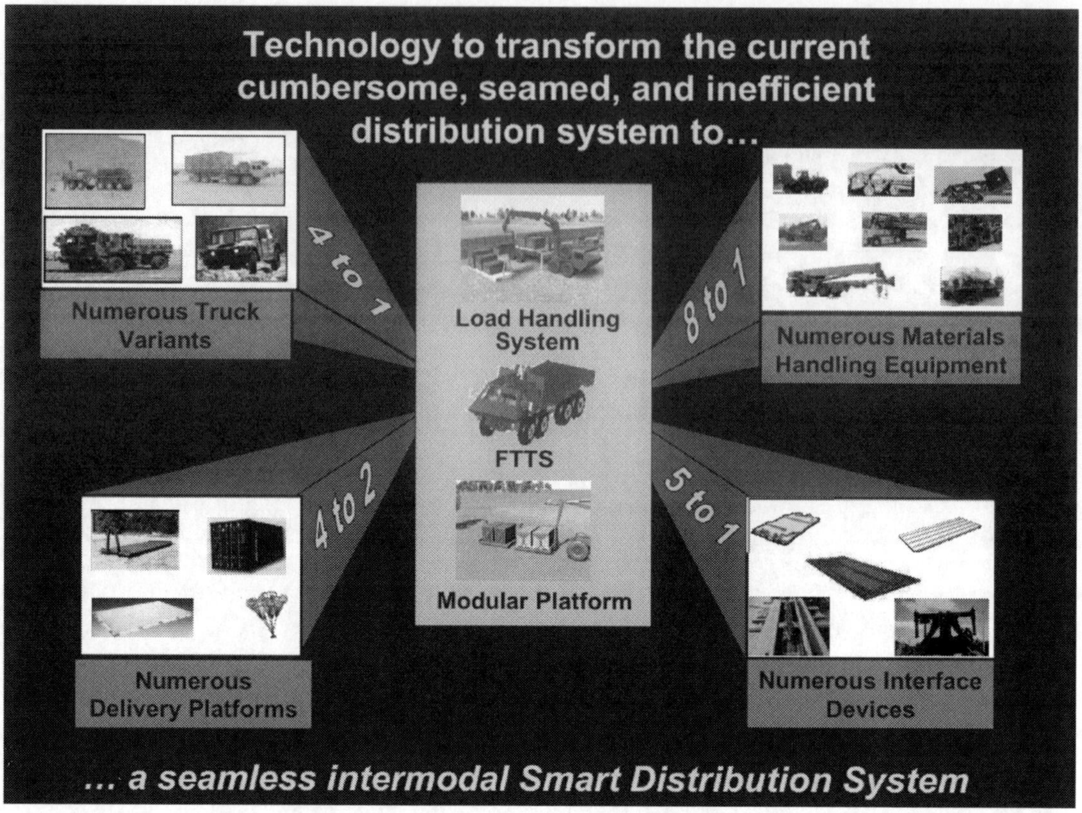

Smart Distribution System Video

Video Presentation in Original e-media

Smart Distribution Benefits

	Baseline	Smart	Change
Clock Hours	38.5	17.9	-54%
Equipment Hours	311.0	96.8	-69%
Personnel Hours	515.3	151.2	-71%
Pallet Positions	120	80	-33%

- **Lethality - increased combat power through reduced FCS resupply time - 60% quicker "Pit-Stop" at the Sustainment Replenishment Site (SRS)**
- **Agility - able to respond to changing unit needs to maintain battle rhythm - 70% quicker reconfigure**
- **Deployability - reduction in MHE reduces deployment footprint by 100 tons/brigade or over 5 C-130J lifts**

Support for Smart Distribution

- **MG Juskowiak (CG CASCOM)**
  - **"I fully support this concept" – 9 May**
- **MG Dail (Chief of Transportation)**
  - **"The potential impact is enormous" – 15 May**
- **GEN Kern (CG AMC)**
  - **"You've got some good ideas. Now make them happen." – 30 June**
- **COL(P) Cannon (ASAALT)**
  - **"Smart Distribution saves battlefield time"- 7 Oct**
- **GEN Abrams (CG TRADOC)**
  - **(To the LSI) "Need to track this and make it a reality" – 9 Oct**
- **BG Waterman (Army G-4)**
  - **" This is a key link - without it we can't achieve what we have to with the SBCT and Objective Force" - 10 December**
- **MG Stevenson (Chief of Ordnance)**
  - **"These are precisely the things we ought to be doing to revolutionize logistics" – 12 Feb**

Enabling the Logistics Transformation

- Our FCS Modular rearm clip concept has led to a new requirement in the FCS ORD and has been been chosen by PM FCS Lethality
- Received funding from HQ AMC G-3 / Army G-4 for 19 new logistics transformation projects
- Received funding from Army G-4 LTA, and AMC G-3 to develop Configured Load Building Tool for the SBCT
- Received funding from PM Force Projection and demo'd a modular platform at May 03 Force Projection Conference
- Received funding from Army G-4 LTA to execute 4 new logistics transformation projects

Program Funding has more than doubled in last the last two years - from 6.6M to 15.6M!

Summary: ARDEC is developing innovative solutions to achieve the logistics transformation

- Smart Distribution is identified by TRADOC as a key enabler to the Army's Maneuver Sustainment Concept
- Program support and funding are growing rapidly
- "Biggest bang for the buck of any program I fund" – Army G-8 Focused Logistics Division (May 02)
- Working with all the AMC RDECs/Labs, other services, DOE labs, industry, and academia to leverage and integrate technologies into collaborative programs

Innovative solutions to assure the right stuff is in the right place, at the right time

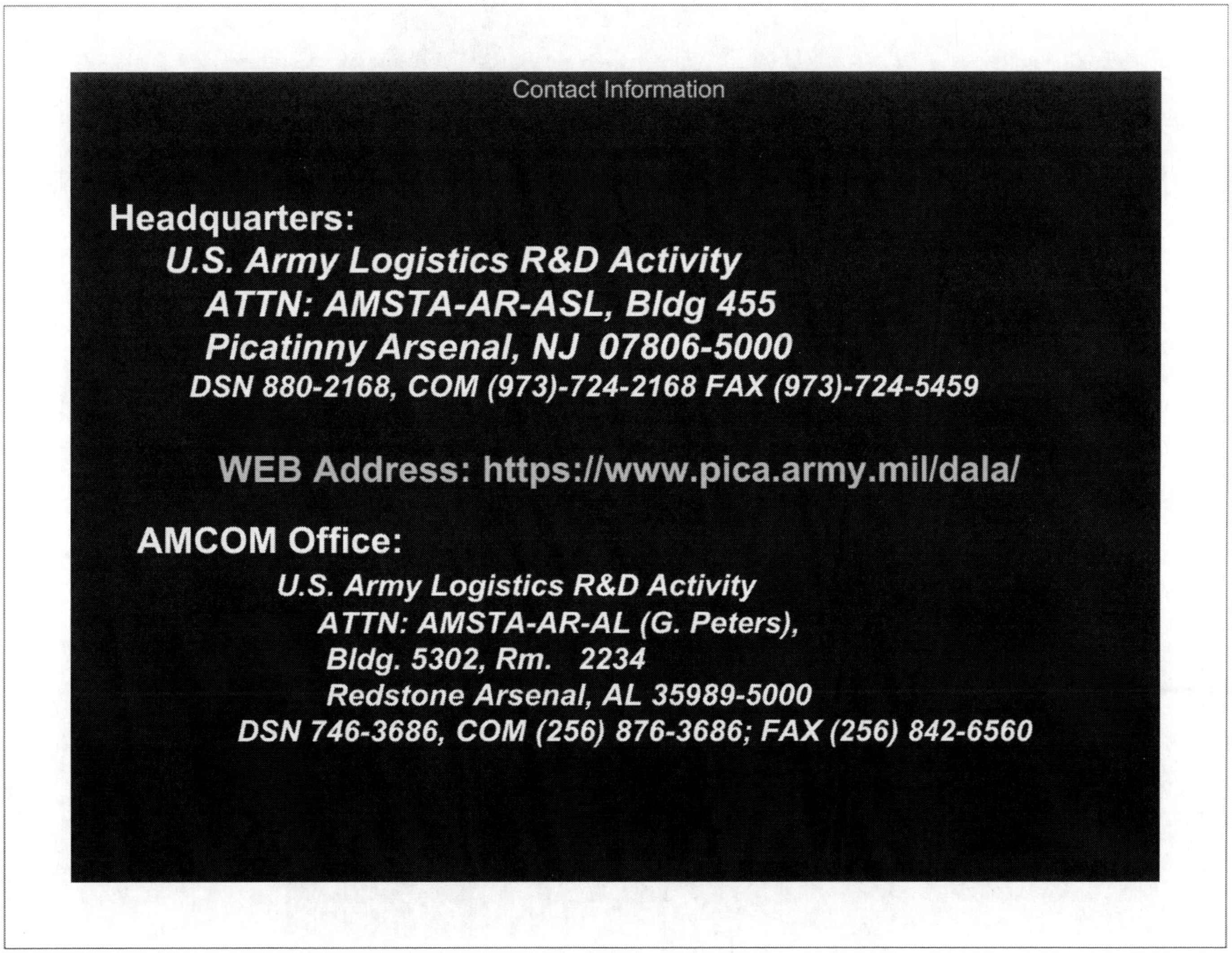
Contact Information
Headquarters:
U.S. Army Logistics R&D Activity
ATTN: AMSTA-AR-ASL, Bldg 455
Picatinny Arsenal, NJ 07806-5000
DSN 880-2168, COM (973)-724-2168 FAX (973)-724-5459
WEB Address: https://www.pica.army.mil/dala/
AMCOM Office:
U.S. Army Logistics R&D Activity
ATTN: AMSTA-AR-AL (G. Peters),
Bldg. 5302, Rm. 2234
Redstone Arsenal, AL 35989-5000
DSN 746-3686, COM (256) 876-3686; FAX (256) 842-6560

MELDING DEFENSE AND COMMERCIAL LOGISTICS

ACQUISITION SUPPORT IN AN e-BUSINESS ENVIRONMENT

DLIS -- Information Brokers
Defense Logistics Information Service
"A Defense Logistics Agency Activity"
COLONEL JOSEPH D. CASSEL, JR.
Commander CPL
Federal Center
74 Washington Ave N. Suite 7
Battle Creek, MI 49017-3084
E-mail joseph.cassel@dia.mil
www.dia.mil/dlis
269-961-4989
DSN 932-4989
FAX 269-961-7383
Customer Service 1-888-352-9333

The Need for Speed ... Agility ... and Precision ...

DOD Transformation

'Acquisition in an e-Business Environment' brings new and increasing demands for information…

to support enduring requirements for weapon system sustainment, cost effectiveness, and streamlined support to the warfighter

Future Logistics Enterprise

- **Depot partnering**
- **Condition based maintenance**
- **Total Life Cycle Systems Management**
- **Executive agents**
- **End–to–end distribution**
- **Enterprise Integration –** the enabler of the other 5 initiatives with a modern integrated information approach supporting the entire-community

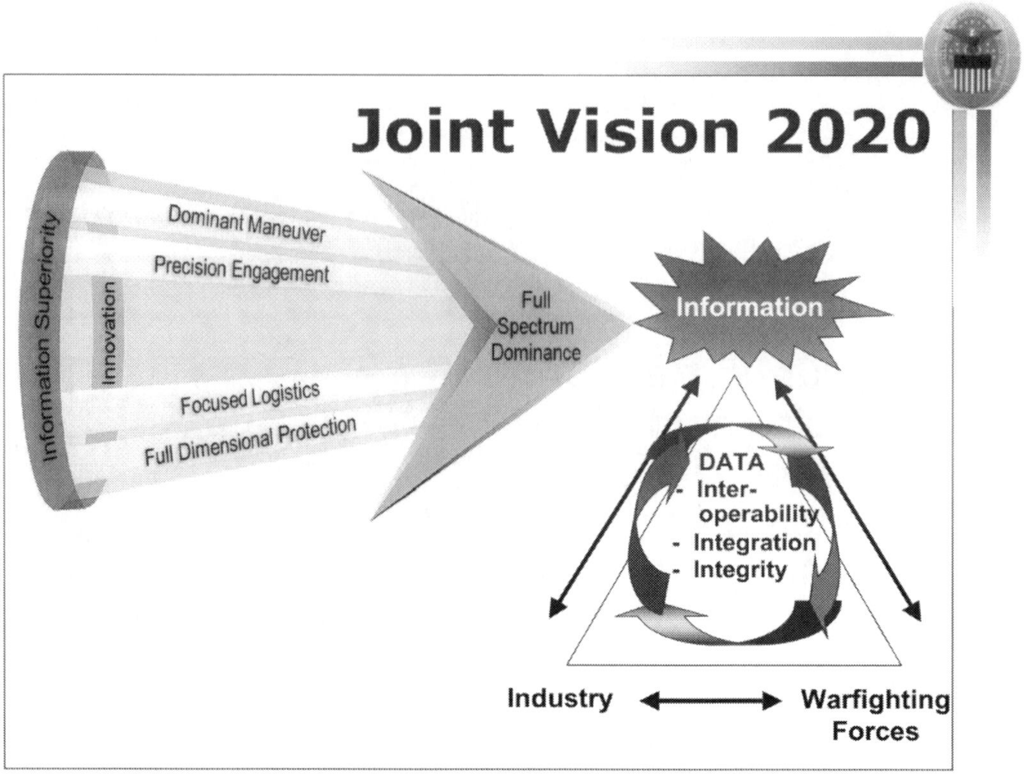
Joint Vision 2020
Information Superiority
Innovation
Dominant Maneuver
Precision Engagement
Focused Logistics
Full Dimensional Protection
Full Spectrum Dominance
Information
DATA
- Inter-operability
- Integration
- Integrity
Industry
Warfighting Forces

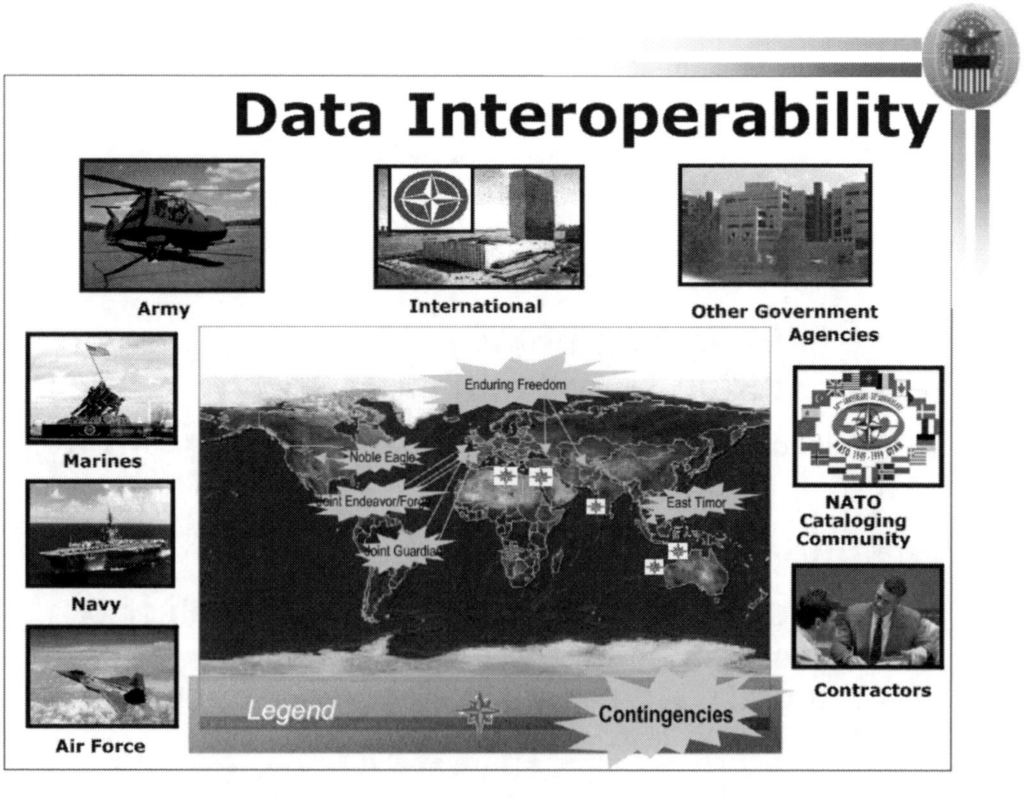
Data Interoperability
Army
International
Other Government Agencies
Marines
Navy
Air Force
Enduring Freedom
Noble Eagle
East Timor
Legend
Contingencies
NATO Cataloging Community
Contractors

SYSTEM AND DATA INTEGRATION

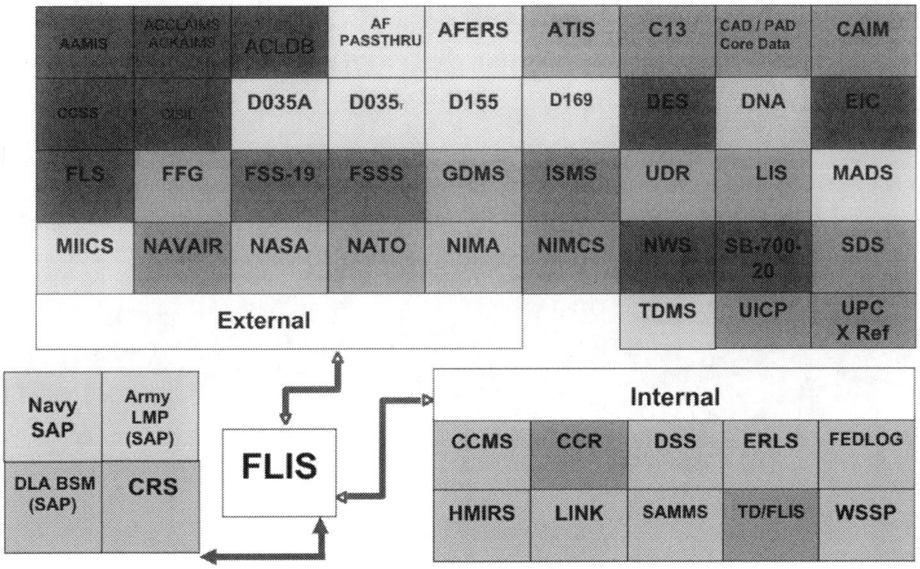

Enterprise Resource Planning

Data Integrity

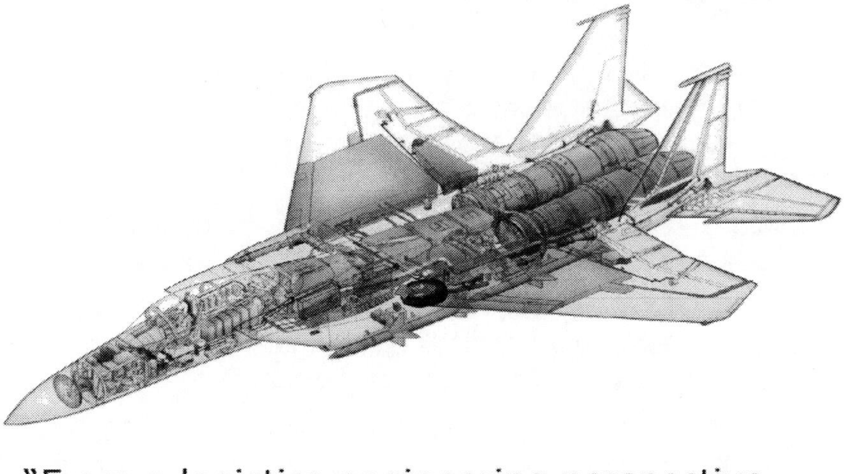

"From a logistics engineering perspective…
an F-15 is just 171,000 parts flying
in close formation"

DOD Supply Chain
Data is the DNA

Identification → Procurement → Distribution → Disposal

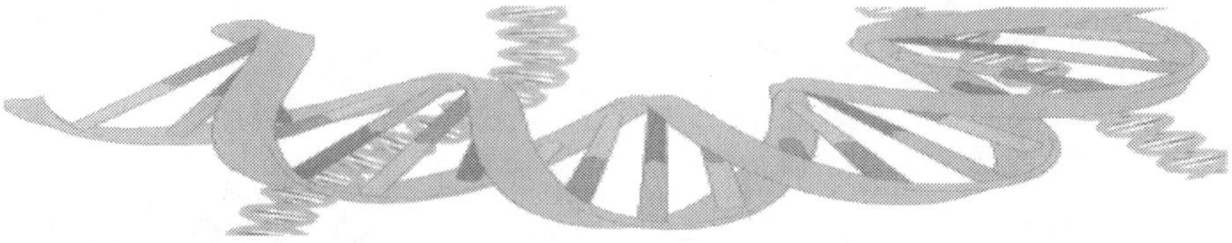

Logistics Information

Weapon Systems

Disposal

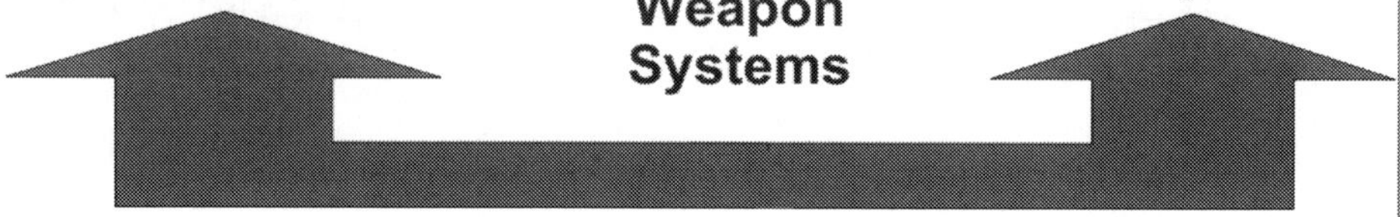

IT & Systems Integration

Questions ?

1. What alternatives are available for data standardization to provide customized information to warfighting forces?
2. How do flying squadrons, combatant ships, Army and Marine Corps fighting battalions receive the right data to maximize weapon system readiness and sustainability and minimize logistics footprint?
3. What are the unifying imperatives to fully meld the efforts of acquisition professionals, logisticians and IT/Data experts to fully realize the promise of DOD Transformation?
4. How best to navigate “islands of information” and the “alphabet soup of data” in joint and coalition operations?
5. How, if at all, will unique weapons system supportability efforts and multiple supply/distribution chains be integrated in the DOD or theater supply chain?

Questions ?

6. What data sharing initiatives, e-business applications, standards, web tools and so on can best meld defense and commercial logistics?
7. What "red tape" can be eliminated to streamline support to warfighting forces?
8. If we contract for "Logistics on Demand" during peacetime, can it be delivered during wartime and what are the risks?
9. Will DOD meet its efficiency and interoperability requirements if it allows multiple "supply chains" to emerge with each new acquisition?
10. How has the evolution in e-Commerce influenced the evolution in defense acquisition?
11. If information is treated as a critical commodity, can it be effectively integrated and used to create a data environment that will fulfill critical needs?

Panel Members

Brett Andrews
Defense Acquisition University (DAU)
Richard.Andrews@dau.mil

Peter Benson
Electronic Commerce Code Management Assn. (ECCMA)
Peter.Benson@ECCMA.org

Gabrielle Zimmerman
DOD eBusiness Program Office
Gabrielle.Zimmerman@dla.mil

Glenn Holmwall
Defense Logistics Information Service
Glenn.Holmwall@dla.mil

Acquisition Support in an e-Business Environment

eccma
electronic commerce
code management association

Peter Benson
Chief Technical Officer
2980 Linden Street, Suite E2
Bethlehem, PA 18017
Tel: +1 610 861 5990
Peter.Benson@ECCMA.org

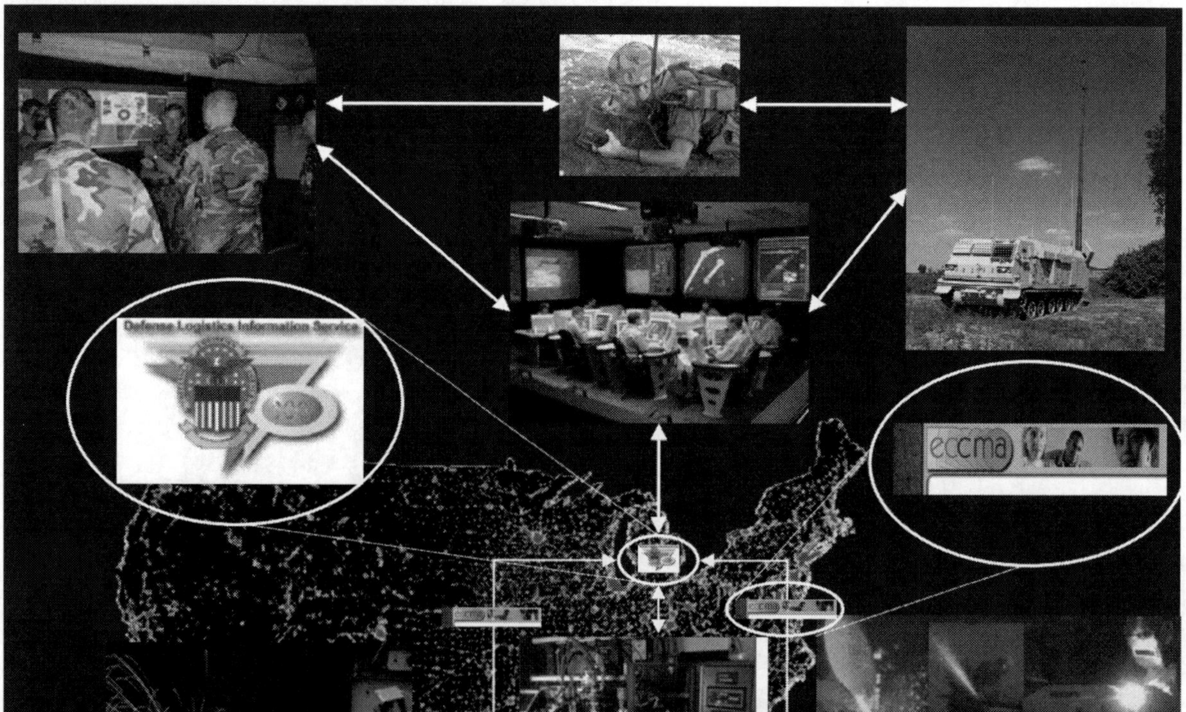

Who is ECCMA?

Not for profit Membership Association based in Bethlehem, Pennsylvania;

- **16 staff supporting 500+ member companies from 42 countries.**
  - Buyers, suppliers, application providers and consultants
  - Public and private sector
- **ECCMA Research Laboratory at Lehigh University**
  - Data integration
  - Data mining
  - Query processing
  - Content delivery

eOTD

ECCMA'S MISSION

- **Applied Cooperative Research**
  - To lower member's cost of implementing content standardization within their existing systems
  - By managing an accessible, open and democratic process for achieving rapid consensus in the development of Open Technical Dictionaries
- **Practical solutions to real immediate problems**
  - Standardized catalogs – Inventory Visibility
  - Inventory Rationalization
  - Spend Analysis

eOTD

What is the eOTD?

The ECCMA Open Technical Dictionary

- A global standard for the identification, description and *differentiation* of individuals, organizations, locations, goods and services.
- A classification neutral and language independent dictionary of Standard Item Names and Standard Attribute Names
- A leading standard in cataloging, inventory management, procurement and spend analysis

Use of Coded Reply Tables accommodates multi-lingual and multi-classification environments

eOTD

What is the eOTD?

The ECCMA Open Technical Dictionary

- Based on the U.S. Federal Catalog System (FCS) and the NATO Codification System (NCS)
- The U.S. and NATO use the same system of item identification based on Standard NATO Agreements (STANAGs)
- The eOTD is designed to support the NSN as a global inventory item identification number

Everything can be described using simple Attribute-Value pairs!

eOTD

ECCMA Open Technical Dictionary (eOTD)

Used to build Standard Specifications

Item → EGIS Standard Item Name

↓

EGAS Standard Attribute Names

eOTD

#3225020037 Hexagonal Bolt; Nominal thread diameter: 1/4 in; Width across flats: 0.425 inches; Width across corners: 0.484 inches; Head height: 0.150 inches; Count per pack: 10; Pack price: $0.80

Rendered

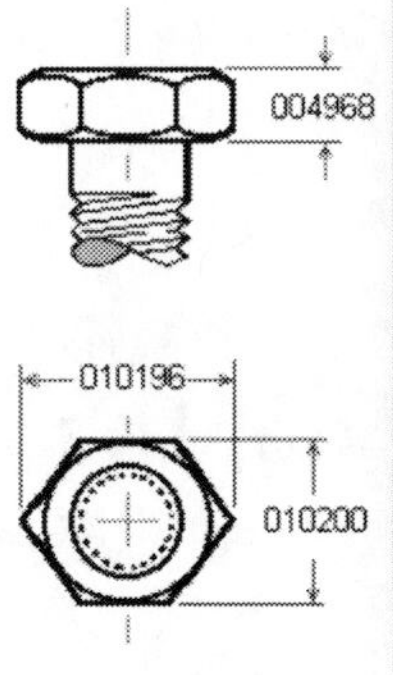

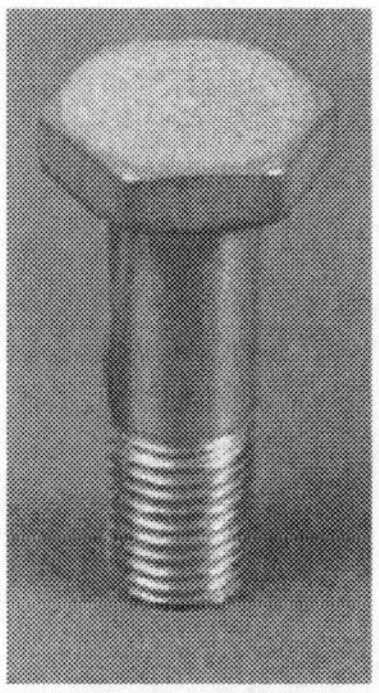

<Attribute EGAI="**027382**" Value="**014197**" />
<Attribute EGAI="**021636**" Value="**015326**" />
<Attribute EGAI="**027375**" Value="**3225020037**" />
<Attribute EGAI="**027376**" Value="**10**" />
<Attribute EGAI="**027378**" Value="**$0.80**" />
<Attribute EGAI="**023822**" Value=" **0.250 inches**" />
<Attribute EGAI="**010200**" Value="**0.425 inches**" />
<Attribute EGAI="**010196**" Value="**0.484 inches**" />
<Attribute EGAI="**004968**" Value="**0.150 inches**" />

Attribute coded

-<Attribute EGAI="**027382**" EGAI_Title="**ECCMA GLOBAL ITEM IDENTIFIER (EGII)**" Code_value="**014197**" Text_value="**BOLT:HEXAGONAL**" />
-<Attribute EGAI="**021636**" EGAI_Title="**ECCMA GLOBAL CLASS IDENTIFIER (EGCI)**" Code_value="**015326**" Text_value="**Hexagonal bolts**" />
-<Attribute EGAI="**027375**" EGAI_Title="**PRODUCT NUMBER**" Code_value="" Text_value="**3225020037**" />
-<Attribute EGAI="**027376**" EGAI_Title="**COUNT PER PACK**" Code_value="" Text_value="**10**" />
-<Attribute EGAI="**027378**" EGAI_Title="**PACK PRICE**" Code_value="" Text_value="**$0.80**" />
-<Attribute EGAI="**023822**" EGAI_Title="**NOMINAL THREAD DIAMETER**" Code_value="" Text_value="**0.250 inches**" />
-<Attribute EGAI="**010200**" EGAI_Title="**WIDTH ACROSS FLATS**" Code_value="" Text_value="**0.425 inches**" />
-<Attribute EGAI="**010196**" EGAI_Title="**WIDTH ACROSS CORNERS**" Code_value="" Text_value="**0.484 inches**" />
-<Attribute EGAI="**004968**" EGAI_Title="**HEAD HEIGHT**" Code_value="" Text_value="**0.150 inches**" />

Attribute Expanded

eOTD

Benefits of Standards

Standardized Names & Structured Attributes

- Avoidance of duplicate items entering inventory
- Items can be aggregated and compared programmatically
- Use of Coded Reply Tables accommodates Multilingual environment

eOTD

Inventory Visibility

Inventory visibility is a function of the ability to understand the terminology used by the individual that described the item

Characteristic data transcends brand names and allows buyers to find items that meet their needs

Characteristic data allows suppliers to differentiate their products

eOTD

Benefits of Standards

Common characterization can provide benefits to Customer and Supplier

- **Customer**
  - Provide easy way to limit search domain using characteristics
  - Provide validating information for functional equivalent items
- **Supplier**
  - Get items properly classified in customer's Logistics Information System
  - Allows product differentiation

eOTD

The DOD EMALL

DOD EMALL

Voice: (804)279-3646
Fax: (508) 302-5619

gabrielle.zimmerman@dla.mil

GABRIELLE ZIMMERMAN
Deputy Program Manager
DOD EMALL

Joint Electronic Commerce Program Office
8725 John J. Kingman Rd. DLA J671
Ft. Belvoir, VA 22060 http://www.emall.dla.mil

DOD EMALL
WWW.EMALL.DLA.MIL

EMALL Mission

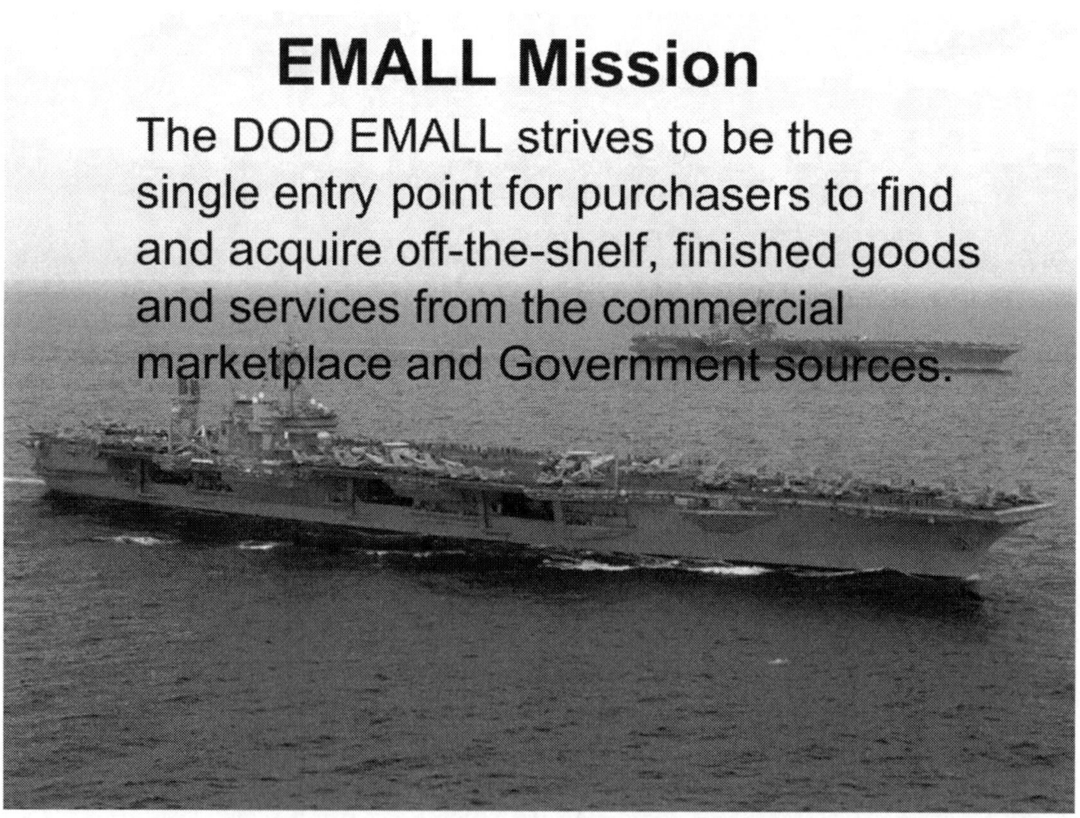

DOD EMALL Background

- The DOD EMALL was launched by the Defense Logistics Agency (DLA) in 1998 as the DLA EMALL.
- The FY99 DOD Authorization Act stated, "***... the Joint Electronic Commerce Program Office of the Department of Defense shall develop a single, defense-wide electronic mall system, which shall provide a single, defense-wide electronic point of entry and a single view, access, and ordering capability for all Department of Defense electronic catalogs."***
- DLA was named the executive agent for DOD EMALL which remains dedicated to its DOD-wide mission
- The DOD EMALL was created to leverage purchasing power across agencies to provide the warfighter and other Federal Government Agencies with volume discounts from Military and Commercial suppliers

DOD EMALL
WWW.EMALL.DLA.MIL

Virtual Inventory Electronic Window

◆**Joint Vision 2010** "...providing support in hours or days versus weeks."

◆**Empowers** customers to search, locate, compare, and order material armed with near real time visibility into public and private sector inventory levels and lead times.

◆ **Data source** for war planning and inventory management
- ◆Items in Commercial Distribution System
- ◆Items in DOD Distribution Systems
- ◆Items made On Demand

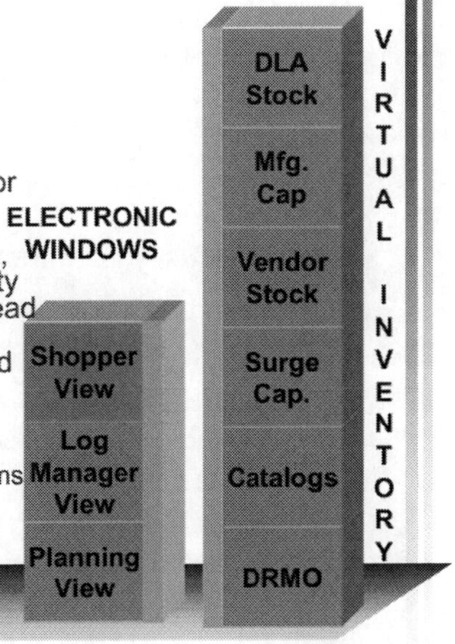

DOD EMALL
WWW.EMALL.DLA.MIL

Cost Avoidance Opportunity

- DOD EMALL reduces transaction costs
- DLA Specific Data
  - Cost Manual Purchase ($) (1) $146.00*
  - Cost EMALL Purchase ($) (2) $11.31
  - Cost Avoidance ($) (3) = [(1) – (2)] $134.69
- Credit Card Data
  - Baseline Credit Card Purchase $25.62
  - EMALL Purchase $11.31
  - Savings per Transaction $14.31

*Note: Morgan Stanley study of commercial industry shows manual purchases $125 – $175.

DOD EMALL
WWW.EMALL.DLA.MIL

Lower Inventory Costs

Newark Electronics Catalog (~200K SKUs)

Unique NSNs 11,499
With Stock 11,316 ➡ 98% Stock on Hand

DLA

For 11,499 NSNs 8,341 In DLA Stock ➡ 73% Stock on Hand

Annual Demand ordered from DLA (Baseline Cost) = $13,173,731

Apply rule:
Buy Annual Demand from the cheapest source *having stock:*
- Cost = $10,843,713

Customer Benefits

- $2.3M Cost Savings
- Stock Availability up 25% (73% to 98%)

DOD EMALL
WWW.EMALL.DLA.MIL

The Human Business Case

CUSTOMER DEMANDS
- High product availability
- Faster response time
- More goods and services from one place

FINANCIAL DEMANDS
- Reduce product cost
- Reduce process and other operations costs
- Reduce transaction cost

PROCESS DEMANDS
- Improve: Execution is manual & slow
- Improve: Timeliness & accuracy of information exchange
- Manage: Complex, multiple internal and external communications

GROWTH DEMANDS
- Amount of business done over the internet has to increase
- Keep customers loyal.

DOD EMALL
WWW.EMALL.DLA.MIL

How Does DOD EMALL Help?

- By providing the most robust Internet ordering solution offered to the Federal Government today.
- The EMALL solution set includes:
  - Broadest Possible Range of Supplies
  - Cross Catalog Shopping
  - Distributed Architecture
  - Advanced Searching Capabilities
  - Detailed Item Descriptions
  - Shipping Options
  - Payment Options
  - Order Management
  - Easy Re-ordering
  - Niche Market Customization

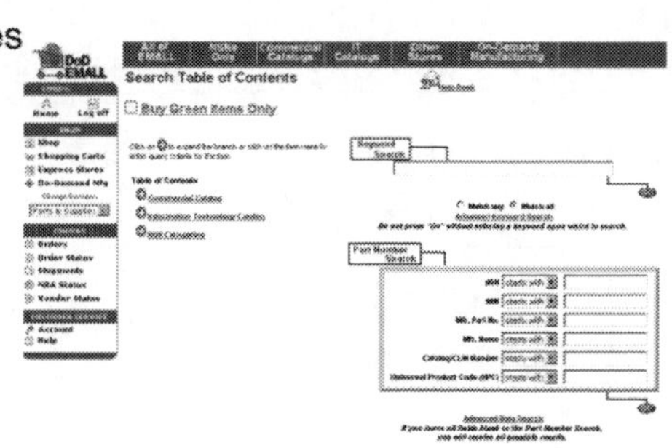

DOD EMALL
WWW.EMALL.DLA.MIL

Use of Standards

Problem: Commercial descriptions often limited and clear text

- **Makes search/find difficult**
- **Makes item and price comparison difficult**

Solution: Application of Standard Item Names

- Will facilitate searching
- Items can be aggregated and compared programmatically
- Will enhance data quality

DOD EMALL
WWW.EMALL.DLA.MIL

Parts and Supplies Vendors

NSN Catalogs

- **480 Vendors in Long-Term Contracts**
  - **Eastman Kodak**
  - **Allied Signal**
  - **Cummins Engine**
- **3.5 Million NSNs from the DLA managed catalogs**
- **2 Million GSA managed NSNs**

DSCP Clothing & Textiles

JWOD ITEMS

UNICOR ITEMS

DRMS CLASS A (Serviceable) ITEMS

COMMERCIAL VENDORS

- **3M**
- **AC Industrial**
- **Alexander Technologies**
- **DELL Computers**
- **Fastenal**
- **Fisher Scientific**
- **Innovative Sports**
- **Kennon Aircraft Covers**
- **Office Depot**
- **Maryland Nautical**
- **Morningstar Lighting**
- **Newark Electronics**
- **Rayovac**
- **W.W. Grainger**
- **....and many others**

DOD EMALL
WWW.EMALL.DLA.MIL

Our Business Model

- Contracts Are Good: See it…Order It
  - Address FAR and DFARS requirements up front:
    - Competition in Contracting Act
    - Price Reasonableness
    - Socio-Economic Considerations
    - Buy American Act/Trade Agreements Act/Berry Amendment
  - Clear Cut Responsibilities
    - Delivery
    - Warranty
    - Order formats and payment methods
    - Problem Resolution

DOD EMALL

DOD EMALL
WWW.EMALL.DLA.MIL

Third Party Logistics

- Contractors Ordering from DOD EMALL
  - Restricted to Scope of Contract Work
  - Monthly or Quarterly Contracting Officer Reviews
  - Fund Code, Government Purchase Card or Corporate Credit Card
  - DLA tracks demand and leverages pricing
- Boeing (KC-135), Lockheed Martin (T56 and TF39), E-RL (Army Vehicle Repairs): Target items are Weapons Systems Support Materiel managed by DLA

DOD EMALL
WWW.EMALL.DLA.MIL

e-Business and the Changing DOD Acquisition Environment
Supporting The Warfighter
Defense Acquisition University
Midwest Region
Richard "Brett" Andrews, CPL
Professor of Logistics
DAU Midwest Region
2950 Hobson Way
Bldg 641, Room 302
Wright-Patterson AFB, OH
45433-7765
Work: DSN 785-4915, x3374
Comm: (937) 255-4915, x3374
Fax: DSN 785-4987
Comm: (937) 255-4987
E-mail: richard.andrews@dau.mil

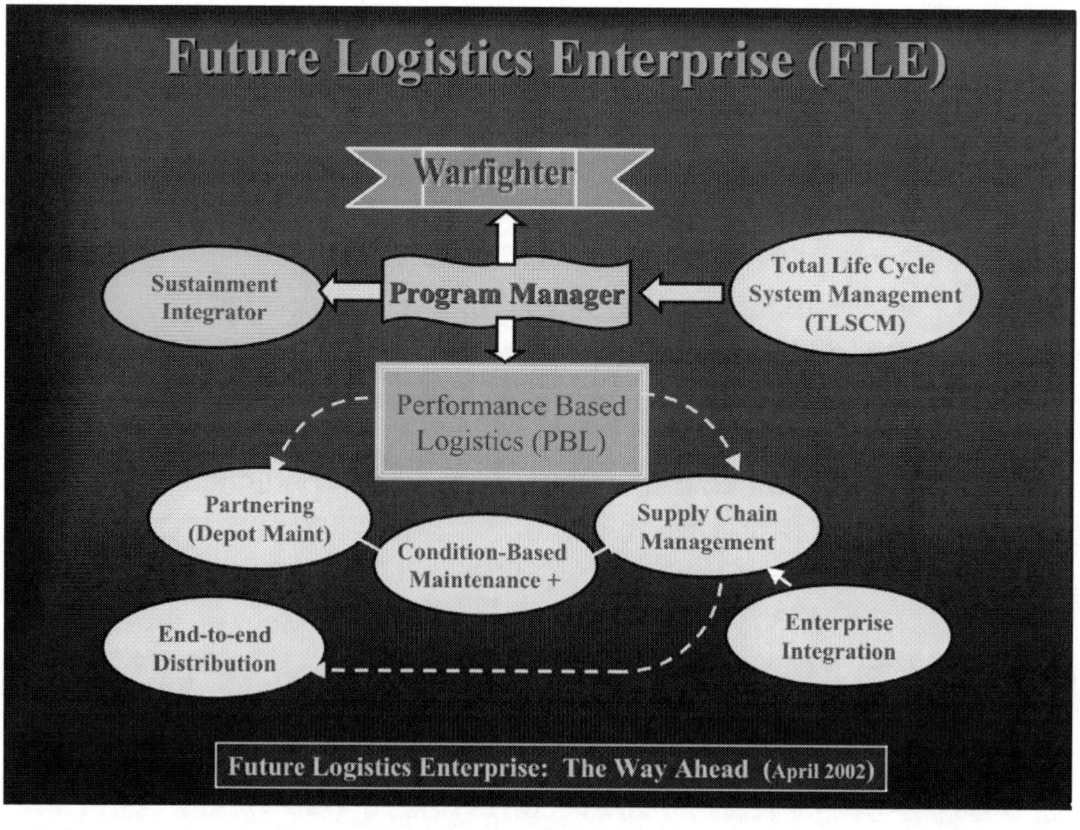

Future Logistics Enterprise (FLE)
Warfighter
Program Manager
Sustainment Integrator
Total Life Cycle System Management (TLSCM)
Performance Based Logistics (PBL)
Partnering (Depot Maint)
Condition-Based Maintenance +
Supply Chain Management
End-to-end Distribution
Enterprise Integration
Future Logistics Enterprise: The Way Ahead (April 2002)

The Need for Innovation

"Another priority element of the Department's corporate transformation strategy is the *reform of the acquisition process*. The Department is reducing cycle time and aligning acquisitions with a new capabilities-based resource allocation process built around joint operating concepts."

Secretary of Defense
Donald Rumsfeld

3

DODD 5000.1
"The Defense Acquisition System" (May 12, 2003)

- **Total Life Cycle Systems Management: "The PM shall be the *single point of accountability* for accomplishing program objectives for total life-cycle systems management, including *sustainment*."**
- **Evolutionary Acquisition: "…Evolutionary acquisition strategies are the *preferred approach* to satisfying operational needs."**
- **Performance Based Logistics: "PMs shall develop and implement performance-based logistics strategies that optimize total system availability while minimizing cost and logistics footprint. …*Sustainment strategies* shall include the best use of public and private sector capabilities through *government/industry partnering initiatives*, in accordance with statutory requirements."**

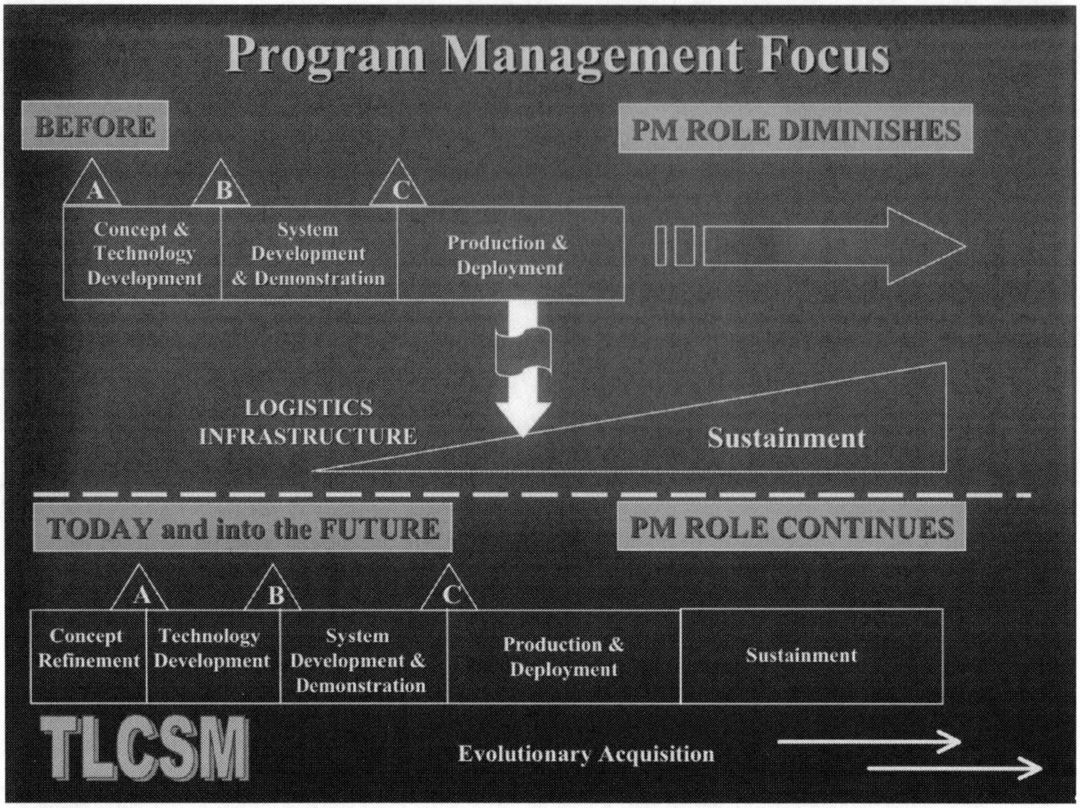
Program Management Focus
BEFORE
PM ROLE DIMINISHES
A
B
C
Concept & Technology Development
System Development & Demonstration
Production & Deployment
LOGISTICS INFRASTRUCTURE
Sustainment
TODAY and into the FUTURE
PM ROLE CONTINUES
A
B
C
Concept Refinement
Technology Development
System Development & Demonstration
Production & Deployment
Sustainment
TLCSM
Evolutionary Acquisition

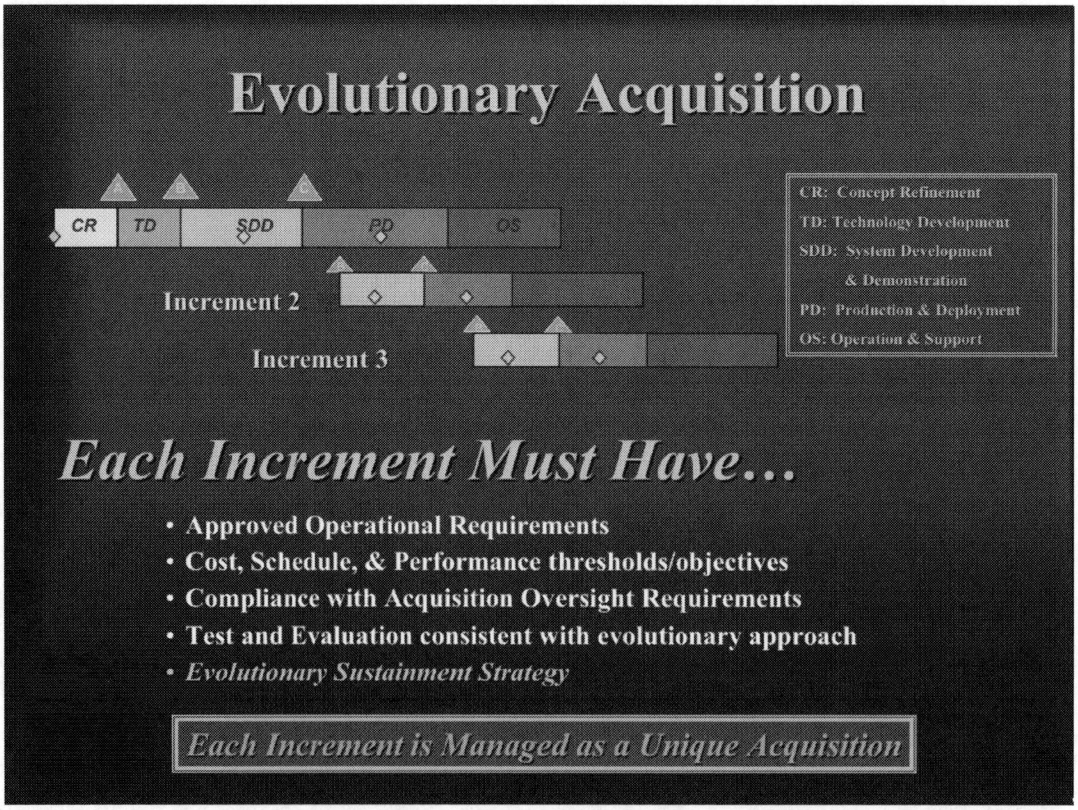
Evolutionary Acquisition
CR
TD
SDD
PD
OS
Increment 2
Increment 3
CR: Concept Refinement
TD: Technology Development
SDD: System Development & Demonstration
PD: Production & Deployment
OS: Operation & Support
Each Increment Must Have…
• Approved Operational Requirements
• Cost, Schedule, & Performance thresholds/objectives
• Compliance with Acquisition Oversight Requirements
• Test and Evaluation consistent with evolutionary approach
• Evolutionary Sustainment Strategy
Each Increment is Managed as a Unique Acquisition

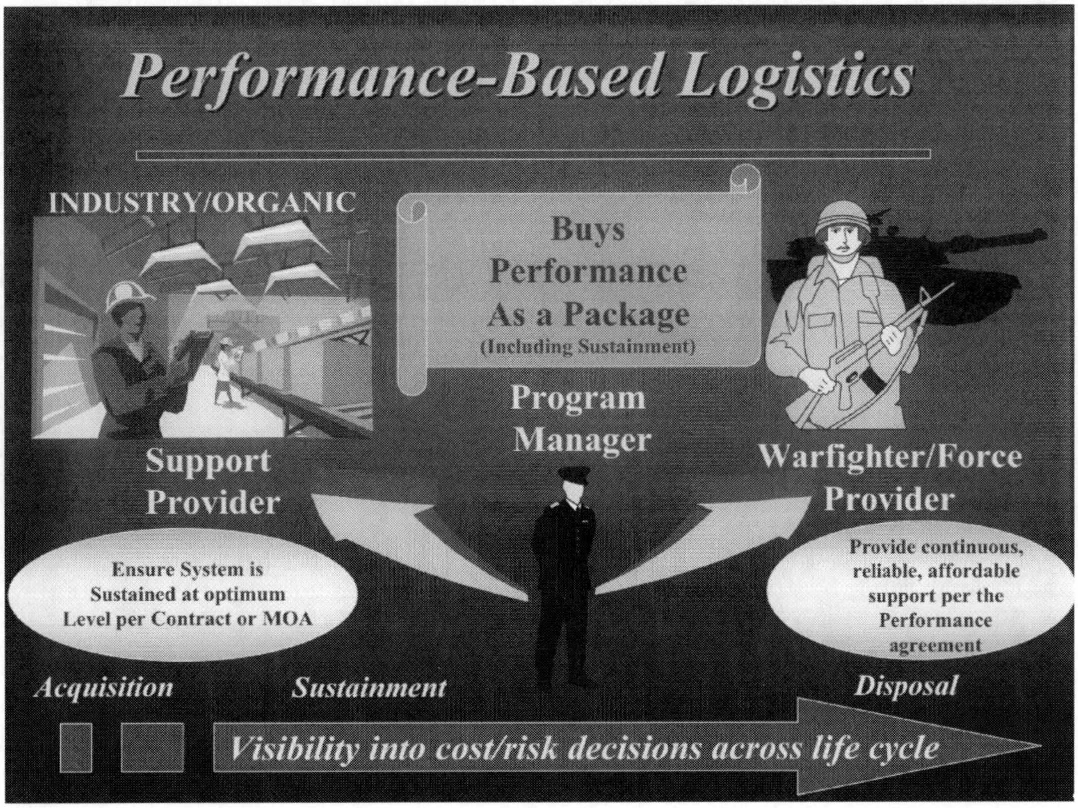
Performance-Based Logistics
INDUSTRY/ORGANIC
Buys
Performance
As a Package
(Including Sustainment)
Program
Manager
Support
Provider
Warfighter/Force
Provider
Ensure System is
Sustained at optimum
Level per Contract or MOA
Provide continuous,
reliable, affordable
support per the
Performance
agreement
Acquisition
Sustainment
Disposal
Visibility into cost/risk decisions across life cycle

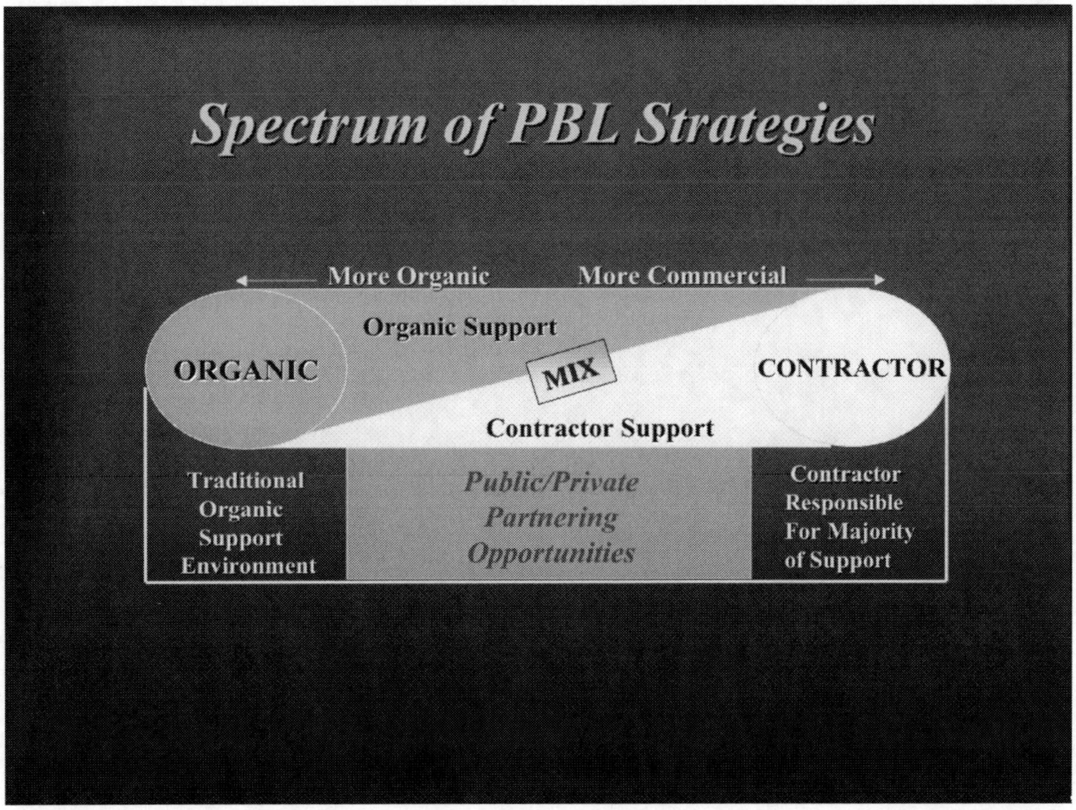
Spectrum of PBL Strategies
More Organic
More Commercial
Organic Support
ORGANIC
MIX
CONTRACTOR
Contractor Support
Traditional
Organic
Support
Environment
Public/Private
Partnering
Opportunities
Contractor
Responsible
For Majority
of Support

Innovation

"… MDAs [Milestone Decision Authorities] and PMs shall examine and, as appropriate, adopt innovative practices (including best commercial practices and electronic business solutions) that reduce cycle time and cost, and encourage teamwork."

Collaboration

"The DOD acquisition, capability needs, and financial communities, and operational users shall maintain continuous and effective communications with each other by using Integrated Product Teams (IPTs). Teaming among warfighters, users, developers, acquirers, technologists, testers, budgeters, and sustainers shall begin during capability needs definition.

DODD 5000.1
"The Defense Acquisition System"
May 12, 2003

DLIS Support to Acquisition Programs

- Participation in program formal provisioning efforts
- Data Base Systems:
  - Central Contractor Registration (CCR)
  - Hazardous Materials Information Resource System (HMIRS).
  - Military Engineering Data Asset Locator System (MEDALS)
  - Universal Directory of Commercial Items UPC
  - DOD EMALL
- Interchangeability and Substitutability determinations

DLIS and Mil-Prf-49506
(Logistics Management Information)

- LMI: Focuses on providing DOD a contractual method for acquiring support and support-related engineering and logistics data from contractors. *This data is used in materiel management processes such as initial provisioning, cataloging, and item management*.

- DLIS Assistance to Programs on LMI
  - Demilitarization Coding
  - Commercial & Government Entity (CAGE) Code
  - Assigning Item names and NSNs
  - Reviewing for preferred parts

For additional questions

E-mail: richard.andrews@dau.mil
Phone: DSN: 785-4915, x3374
Comm: (937) 255-4915, x3374

DATA AND CATALOGING SOLUTIONS THAT MELD DEFENSE AND COMMERCIAL LOGISTICS

DLIS—Information Brokers
Defense Logistics Information Service
"A Defense Logistics Agency (DLA) Activity"

E. GLENN HOLMWALL, CPL
Director

Cataloging Directorate (DLIS-K)
74 Washington Ave N Suite 7
Battle Creek MI 49017-3984
E-Mail: glenn.holmwall@dla.mil

Comm: (269) 961-5300
DSN: 932-5300
FAX: x5684
Cust Serv: 888-352-93334

1

CURRENT LOGISTICS ENVIRONMENT

Best Practices

Reduce Acquisition Costs

Total Life Cycle Management

2

FUTURE LOGISTICS ENVIRONMENT

"The overall goal ...is the creation of a force that is dominant across the full spectrum of military operations – persuasive in peace, decisive in war, preeminent in any form of conflict" Joint Vision 2020

3

WARFIGHTER NEEDS

"Interoperability is a mandate for the joint force of 2020 – especially in terms of communications, common logistics items, and information sharing." Joint Vision 2020

4

DLIS MISSION

To create, obtain, manage and integrate logistics data from a variety of sources and to disseminate it as user-friendly information to the warfighter

- Federal Logistics Information System (FLIS)
- Military Engineering Data Asset Locator System (MEDALS)
- Environmental Leadership
- Data Integration

DATA
- Interoperability
- Integration
- Integrity

- Logistics Information Products and Services
- International / NATO Support
- E-Solutions
- DOD Cataloging Provisioning Support

Customer Contact Center
E-Mail: DLIS-Support@dlis.dla.mil
Or Call: 1-877-352-2255

5

CATALOGING: THE GENETIC CODE OF LOGISTICS DATA

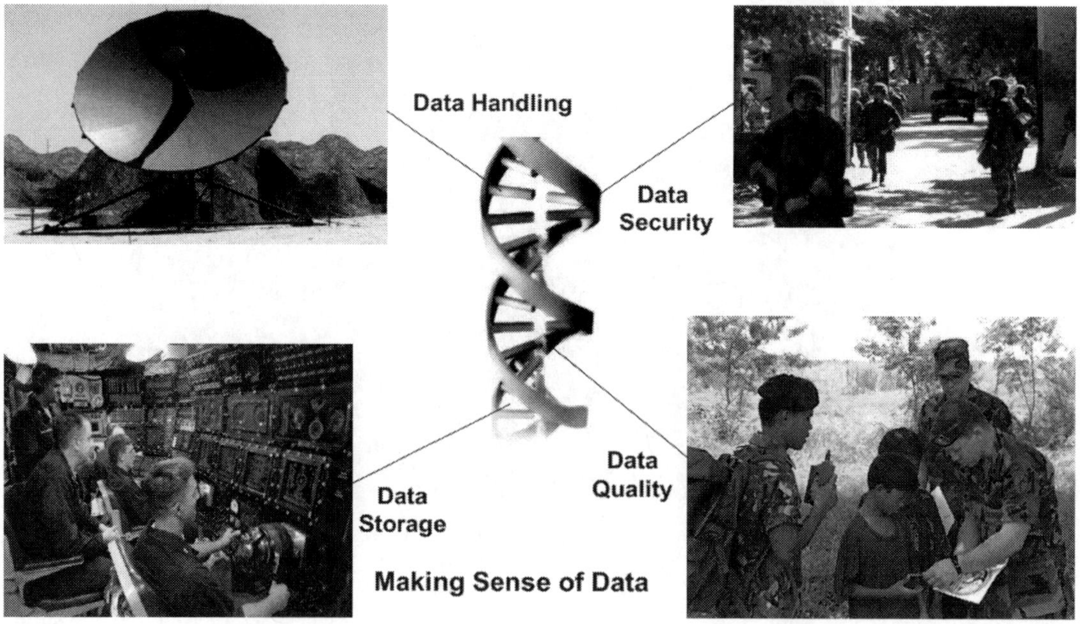

INTERNATIONAL CATALOGING

- NATO Codification System growing
  - 50 nations
  - 16M NSNs
- The DLIS to NATO interface
  - 47% of active NSNs
  - 30% of new NSNs
- DLIS services provided
  - Foreign Military Sales cases
  - NCB College (4th year)
  - In-theater cataloging seminars
  - Weblink International
  - Multilingual classification and naming publication

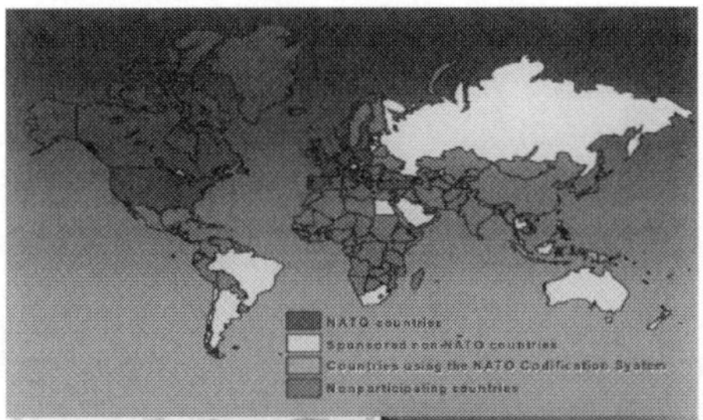

IMPROVED RIBBON BRIDGE

1070F HET

SCREW,MACHINE =Sroub, montázní =SCHROEF, MACHINE =SCHRAUBE, SCHLITZKOPF =VITE PER METALLO =WKRĘT DO CZĘSCI METALOWYCH (Z ROWKIEM) =TORNILLO, MECANICA

PROVISIONING IS THE BRIDGE FROM ACQUISITION TO SUSTAINMENT

8

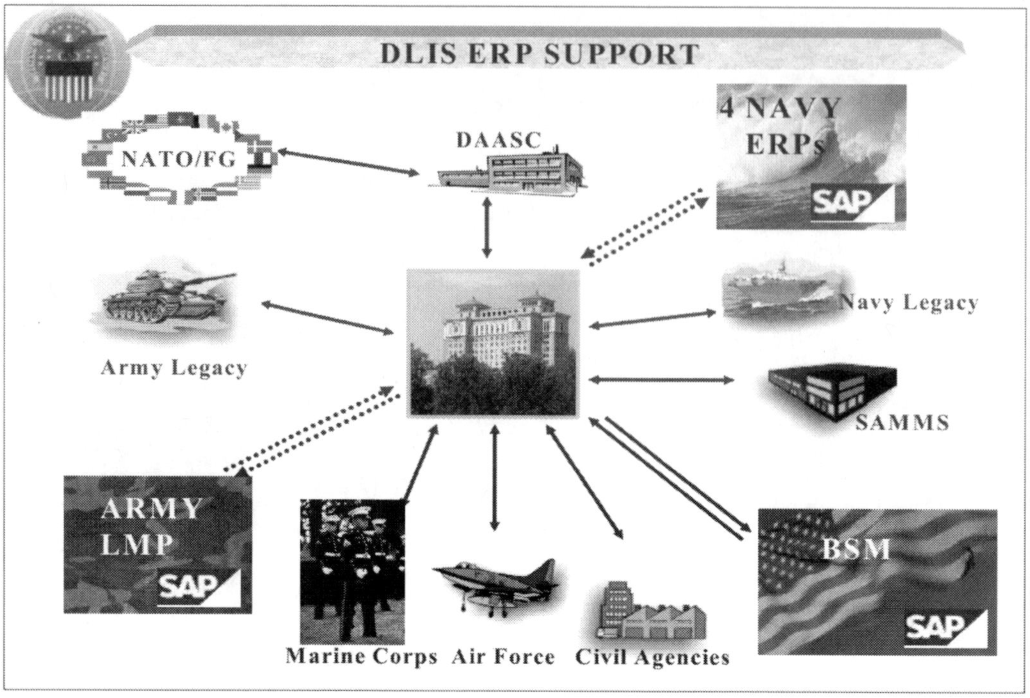

9

PRODUCTS AND SERVICES THAT SUPPORT THE WARFIGHTER

10

SUMMARY

"Changes in the information environment make information superiority a key enabler of the transformation of the operational capabilities of the joint force and the evolution of joint command and control " Joint Vision 2020

11

To Request DLIS Support

- DLIS Website...www.dlis.dla.mil
- DLIS Focal Points
  - Commercial: 269-961-xxxx or DSN: 932-xxxx
  - E-Mail (firstname.lastname@dla.mil)

- **Army ...Gerald Tilmann...x5708**
- **Air Force ....William Strough...x4675**
- **Navy...Rosemary Ludt...x4683 & Constance White...x4194**
- **Marine Corps...Rosemary Ludt..x4683 & Sheri Winget..x5725**
- **International/NATO...Christopher Yoder...x4286**
- **DLA...Jack Hunn...x4304**

12

INTEGRATION OF COMMERCIAL PRODUCTS INTO THE MILITARY SEARCH AND RESCUE PERSONEL RECOVERY (SARPR) SYSTEM

A BENEFIT TO BOTH SYSTEM PERFORMANCE AND COST

BY

MR. KENNETH H BROCKEL

MR. MICHAEL D. FREDERICKSON

MR. HARRY S. IVORY JR.

MR. DOUGLAS HOWE

This paper will review communications, navigational, and network-centric over-the-horizon SARPR systems required by the military aviation community. More specifically this paper will discuss the integration of existing commercial off the shelf technology (COTS) with existing and objective military search and rescue personnel recovery systems. Through this process, the military will achieve a highly accurate and efficient personnel recovery system for rescuing military aviators at an affordable acquisition and logistics cost. The ideas presented in the paper will look specifically at evolution of the network centric battle space and the evolution products and support structures that will be required to accomplish efficient effective personnel recovery missions. Further, the paper will provide an overview of commercial and military systems in use today and how all these products will be integrated into the evolving network centric battle space of the 21ST century.

Current DOD Combat SAR system architectures are in transition from a direct line- of-sight (LOS) non-Global Positioning System (GPS) to a more network-centric GPS based architecture that must be simple and highly reliable to achieve the end gold of timely, and failure free performance. It is most critical during the terminal phase of this mission to use redundant processes. Utilizing existing COTS technology will assure that the desired performance is achieved at and at affordable cost to own and operate the system. In order to achieve the embodiment of the ULTRA RELIABLE PERSONNEL POSITION LOCATING

SYSTEM (URPPLS), parts or complete commercial adapted survival radios in the current inventory will be used in the proposed system architecture. Key performance objectives for the system include:

- Assurance of at least dual redundant position information is transported from survivor radios to include but not limited to the AN/PRC-112 family of radios, and the objective Combat Survivor Evader Locator (CSEL) object radio to the rescue platform crew through use of an upgraded AN/ARS-6 position locator system.
- Employment of existing radio architecture already imbedded in the 112/CSEL radios integrated with a single board Pentium based computer to control and integrate three alternative position location processes identified as, GPS tagging (GPST), and Differential Position Integrated Network Global Positioning (DPING).
- Integration of current PLS software with other control, and computational logic necessary to communicate with the existing radio products and to transmit to and receive from these radios the position data necessary to assure efficient and timely rescue mission is archived.

Current inventory of survival radios known as the AN/PRC-112 family have two methods of position location for LOS communications of critical position data. The first is known as distance measurement processing (DMP). This is the primary method used by the AN/ARS-6 position locating system (PLS) that is embedded in the US DOD rescue aircrafts avionics system. The method includes a transponder capability to transmit a coded request to the 112. When the rescue platform gets within LOS radio range the 112 will respond to the transponder request with a coded message burst that includes critical information about the pilot. In addition, the AN/ARS-6 makes range calculation of distance to the survivor and through a multiple phased antenna system determines the direction that the pilot must navigate to reach the rescue. The range and steering information is displayed to the pilot. This method is efficient and accurate (few 100 feet) but requires a continuum of repetitive transponder responses to track the navigation path.

The Air Force and Navy currently use a variant of the 112 known as the Hook radio. This device has the DMP capability but also takes advantage of Global Positioning System (GPS). The process is defined in this invention disclosure as GPS tagging (GPST). In this process an imbedded GPS receiver in the survival radio determines the survivor's position and transmits the protected message to the rescue aircraft. Unfortunately this process requires a separate device on the rescue platform to receive the coded GPS message.

The Air Force is developing a network centric CSEL. This product also uses a variant of the 112 Hook GPST.

The URPPLS proposes a third position locating process that will be known as Differential Position Integrated Network Global Positioning (DPING) to improve mission reliability. This is similar to DMP in that it will use the transponder to request a coded response from the survivor's radio. In addition, URPPLS will use the on-board GPS capability in the AN/ARS-6 architecture or from imbedded on board aircraft GPS to determine a survivor position.

A single board computer in the AN/ARS-6 will then do the position location computations using navigation algorithms to determine the accurate (>100ft) survivor location in latitude, longitude or any other appropriate coordinate system. The intent is to integrate these three processes into the AN/ARS-6 platform PLS. The key critical system performance metric for terminal rescue mission reliability is assured by integrating these three processes. In addition, the integration of dual redundant communications and position location is obtained though the use of a single device that is usable by all DOD service users who have the legacy 112 radios or the future CSEL system radios.

Personnel Recovery Mission (PRM) – Joint Interim Technical Architecture Attributes

Need

- **Required to Support GO TO WAR Current/Near Term Operational Requirements.**
- **Assures Interoperability of all Joint PRM Assets**

Critical Issues

- **Interoperability - CSEL and all 112's variants**
- **Speed of Service**
- **Operational Visibility to National Command Authority**
- **Terminal Mission Communications/Protected Position Data**
- **Survivor Products Simplicity/Training Retention Key**
- **Logistics Plan is Supportable/Affordable.**

In conclusion the architecture diagram below depicts how the AN/ARS-6 as upgraded will allow all the survival products legacy and objective products to interoperate on the battlefield.

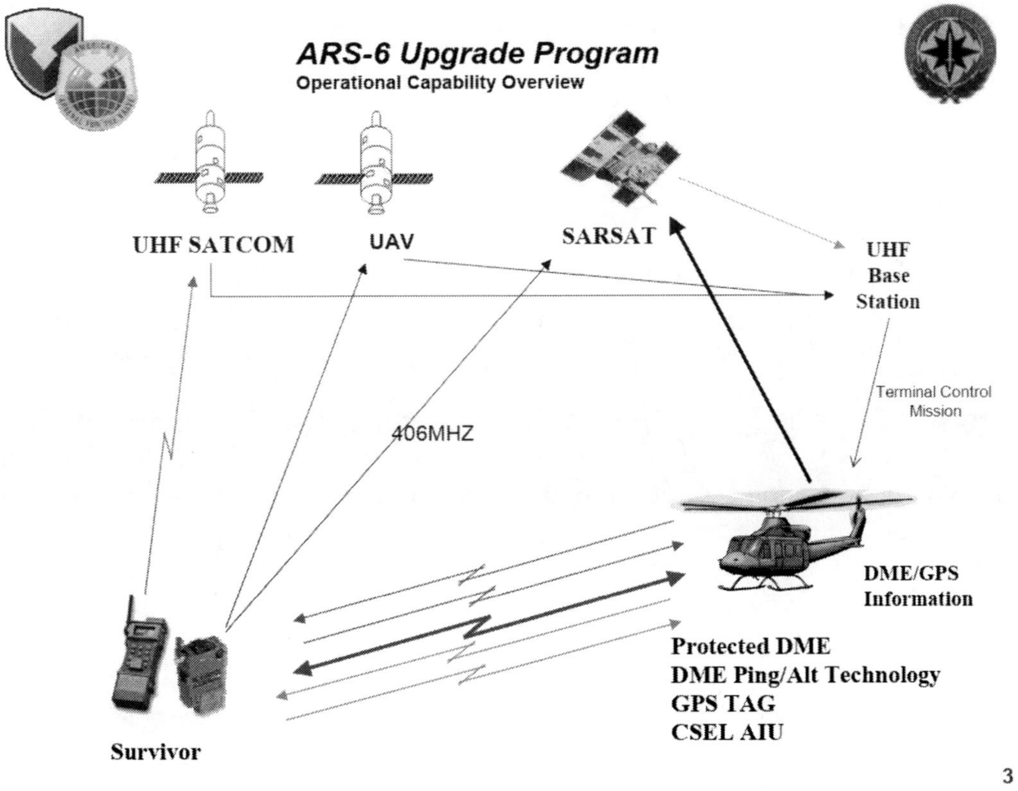
ARS-6 Upgrade Program
Operational Capability Overview
UHF SATCOM
UAV
SARSAT
UHF
Base
Station
Terminal Control
Mission
406MHZ
DME/GPS
Information
Protected DME
DME Ping/Alt Technology
GPS TAG
CSEL AIU
Survivor
3

A Case Study of a Dual Use Embedded Vehicle Computer

By Thomas White, SAIC and Mark Haslam, DriverTech, Inc.

Talk of dual use technology is pervasive throughout industry today. It is so attractive. Development risk is slashed. Sharing technology for both commercial and military applications promises to reduce not just acquisition cost, but life cycle costs through shared logistics. In practice commercial off the Shelf (COTS) products often require modification for DOD use. This paper traces the evolution of a transportation industry cab mounted computer for potential use in U. S. Army vehicles.

The DT 2000 is a small Windows CE computer used by over the road trucks, emergency services, and local delivery services. It is typically procured by mid to large organizations for fleet management. Typical on-board applications include navigation, driver communications, cargo tagging, diagnostics, and remote reporting.

The US military maintains vehicle fleets with many of these basic requirements. These requirements are augmented by a variety of extensions including interoperability with existing systems, harsher operating environment, and radically different buying habits. The DT 3000 is a design evolution of the DT 2000, designed for dual use and presently used in several Army Proof of Principle (POP) demonstrations.

This paper will present these products as a case study of technology, business practices and logistics of commercial technology in a military environment. It will show similarities and sharp contrasts of dual use technology and highlight some of the difficult trade-off decisions faced by hardware OEMs, material developers and military end users adapting commercial technology.

The Ground Vehicle Problem

The US Army has worked on vehicle diagnostic systems since the 1980's. A first generation system, the (Special Test Equipment-Internal Combustion Engine) STE-ICE, was a microprocessor based, custom box with simple buttons, a seven segment LED display and flip card instructions. A mechanic would connect the STE-ICE to a vehicle to perform tests. The STE-ICE supported multi-meter style measurements and transducer measurements. These transducers were defined in a Tank and Automotive Command (TACOM) developed Diagnostic Cable Assemble (DCA) design guide, which standardized transducers and gave guidance on implementation. Vehicle Original equipment Manufacturers (OEMs) would install some subset of the design guide transducers. These transducers consisted of current shunts, pressure sensors, etc. A number of derived parameters were also made from these simpler measurements.

This was replaced by a luggable PC designated the Contact Test Set (CTS) The CTS supported both the earlier ICE tests and added a Society of Automotive Engineers (SAE) J1708/J1587 capability to meet the then emerging trend of digitally controlled engines. It also added a graphical user interface, which integrated simple graphics to aid in troubleshooting.

This trend has continued to the present day with the Soldiers Portable On system Repair tool (SPORT) and Maintenance Service Device (MSD). Each of the programs retained the original ICE and J1708 functionality while upgrading the computer processing power and graphics. A limitation of this series was that a mechanic had to transport a device to a vehicle, connect, and manually interact with the system.

During the 1990's several programs attempted to embed data acquisition systems on the vehicle, and take diagnostic data without mechanic intervention. These lowered manpower usage, but posed problems in how to retrieve and interpret this data. Studies also investigated what data is required for diagnostics and if additional sensors are needed to supplement the J1708/J1587 or newer J1939 data. These additional sensors include cranking system instrumentation similar to the STE-ICE transducers, oil analysis, and vibration monitoring.

Acquisition reform during the past decade has placed increased emphasis on the use of Non Developmental Items (NDI). This offers both great benefits and challenges to material developers supporting diagnostic systems. Through the automotive industry in general and truck applications specifically there are a great number of similar applications, including maintenance, navigation, dispatch communication and cargo tracking. Challenges to using the technologies include the often-proprietary technology, and the relative benign environmental conditions, especially compared to combat vehicles, (e.g. tanks, armored personnel carriers). This is further complicated by the large number of stakeholders in the diagnostic systems. These include users, material developers, logistics and supply. This necessitates trade offs in the diagnostic system selection. Potential solutions include Commercial off the Shelf (COTS) laptops and Personal Digital Assistants (PDAs), industrial computers, and computers built to full military specifications.

The View from the Commercial Side

Industrial product lifecycles are typically much longer than similar consumer and commercial product lifecycles. How many iterations of the copy machine or the cell phone have there been in twenty years? Compare this to the relatively low number of iterations of the D9 Cat, or the Qualcomm OmniTRACs sat com system (also referred to as D-Tracs). Industrial product lifecycles are long because they are major capital expenses that have long useful lives and long depreciation schedules. Therefore they not only have to last a long time in use (durability), but they have to fit the customer's business model very well in order to provide ROI (return on investment) over a long period.

DriverTech Truck-PC History: Why is it important to describe life cycles? It is important to develop a perspective of the amount of time it takes to develop a new class of industrial products. This is a process that not only requires innovation on the part of the developer, but also a keen awareness of customer requirements, what we call market/product knowledge.

DriverTech's Truck-PC and Fleet Management System began development in 1996 when we teamed with the computer engineering department of Utah State University to assist us in developing the core of the system, the Truck-PC itself, and the basic software applications that run on it, email, mapping and diagnostics. DriverTech provided the team with a basic outline of what the Truck-PC needed to do for fleets, based on DriverTechs twelve months of market analysis and focus sessions. This list included the functions performed, as well as the feature set. We define *feature set* as the way we choose to perform the *functions*, for instance, color displays instead of monochrome; aviation style keypads, instead of PC style keyboards; touch screens instead of track balls; and so on.

In early 1997 DriverTech made a hard choice. We moved from our purely embedded computer development approach to Windows CE, a brand new operating system. Throughout 1997 we worked on software modules for mapping and e-mail, studied several hardware approaches compatible with this new operating system from Microsoft, made our choice of processors and began development of the Truck-PC. In late 1997, the National Automotive Center at TARDEC joined the development and provided additional cooperative funding, and suddenly we were able to increase the speed of development, and add a truck diagnostic interface. We were able to add this interface by taking one of our commercial products for the mass transit market, and integrating it with the Truck-PC.

In early 1999 we completed the initial Truck-PC and fleet management system and demonstrated it to the NAC. We joined with Northrop Grumman to compete on the Movement Tracking System RFP. Although the NG team did not win the contract, the Army's contract award team graded the Northrop Grumman in-vehicle portion of the system as the preferred choice.

From that point DriverTech concentrated on polishing our Truck-PC based system in preparation for commercial introduction, and debuted the system in April 2001 at the International Wireless Conference. We established several pilot accounts, and set about the job of proving the Truck-PC and software. As usual, some software tweaking was required, as well as the addition of new software modules for things like DOT logs (hours of service regulations), fuel tax recording, and event recording (speeding, hard braking, over revving, etc.). To our satellite wireless interface we added cellular IP packet data and Wireless LAN.

At about that time, the NAC and DriverTech decided it was time to improve the Truck-PC for tactical wheeled vehicle applications so that EMS software and predictive maintenance software could more easily be run by the system, and a true embedded diagnostic/prognostic capability could result. The concept of a Multi-Role driver computer was born, the DT-3000.

Markets: The fleet management market is large and varied. There are large pockets of homogenous users, but there are also a lot of unique applications. DriverTech has put a great deal of investment in making the Truck-PC and its software very configurable and widely applicable. However, you can't be everywhere at once, so we chose to concentrate on four widely divergent market sectors. First, we decided the food logistics market was a good choice because of the size of the market, and the fairly consistent requirements from user to user. We established our first pilot program with Sysco Foods in Salt Lake City. Second, we established a beachhead in the ambulance market with the largest ambulance operator in the country, American Medical Response. We then established a pilot program with a large well head remediation company, BJ Services, where our diagnostic capabilities and satellite communication were key ingredients. Finally, we agreed to keep the Army's requirements squarely in our sights, and to find ways to become the favored choice of the logisticians.

Other markets we are beginning to pursue as we go forward are the long haul market, also known as the full load contract carrier market. We bring some important improvements to the long haul carriers. We are also beginning to focus on service fleets, police/fire, construction and recreation. We can approach all of these fleets with the Truck-PC and our fleet management software, because of the openness of our architecture.

Functions: You can subdivide Truck-PC functions into over twenty. However, there are five central functional capabilities. These are e-mail, dispatch, map navigation, truck diagnostics and video.

1. Email: The Truck-PC provides for both free-form messaging and canned messages. The messages follow a path between the Truck-PC and a SQL server at the back office, where the message is routed to the intended recipient. The e-mail program is a closed loop program and not accessible from the Internet. However, with DriverTech's optional SMTP server, messages can be routed to/from standard e-mail addresses, similar to how Hotmail works.

2. Dispatch: Fleet Management is built on the principal of dispatching for pickup, delivery or performance of a service. A dispatch is a work order or job order. It includes where to go, who to contact, what to deliver/pickup, what job to perform, and includes other ancillary information and activities. In the case of DriverTech, our dispatch application is form based, where the dispatches are forms with fields of information to display to the driver, or fields to be filled out by the driver with information. The data is pushed through the DriverTech SQL server. When a form is created using DriverTech's form creator tool, a table is automatically created for that form in the SQL database. Data is moved back and forth through the SQL server using these tables. This is why it has been easy for DriverTech customers to integrate their enterprise management or logistics management databases with the DriverTech Fleet Management System. The most recent change is the modification of DriverTech's Fleet Management applications to be DotNet compliant and web enabled.

3. Map Navigation: Maps in vector format or raster format are displayed to the driver. On the map is an icon that represents the driver's vehicle, and indicates the direction of travel. Icons that represent stops along the route are sent down by the dispatch application. Controls include zoom and panning. Panning is done by touching the screen with your finger and dragging the map.

4. Diagnostics: The Truck-PC talks to both the SAE J1708 and J1939 networks simultaneously (J1850 and PLC4Trucks are coming soon). A Windows API on the Truck-PC allows a programmer to makes calls to our SAE hardware interface to get data or send messages. An RP-1210A dll provides a Windows compliant application, like the EMS2 (IETM), a standard interface. DriverTech's own software applications get events from the J1708 data bus for trip recording and accident recording, as well as putting the Truck-PC into Driving and Not-Driving mode, for safety considerations.

5. Video: New to the Truck-PC is the ability to take in standard NTSC output from a camera, thermal night vision cameras included, and display the output on the Truck-PC screen. Camera adjustments (gain, white hot/black hot) are made from the Truck-PC. Streaming MPEG2 video is played through a video decompressor chip for glitch free playback. This capability is included for future training videos.

The Commercial Acquisition Process: Buying (selling) capital equipment in the commercial sector is not exactly easy, although considerably simpler than selling to the military. This is especially true when looking at the entire process, instead of just the act of providing a quotation and receiving a purchase order.

In the commercial acquisition process we include the time from the point when the potential customer/user becomes aware of the product and its benefits, to the time for doing the due diligence dance, where the customer becomes comfortable that the product and seller will perform as advertised, and on through the process where the customer/user gets an acquisition approved through the financial vetting process.

These steps are very customer/user oriented, and provide a good filter for getting the right product. The process is user driven. All focus is on meeting the express purpose outlined in the customer requirements documents. GAP analysis has become central to the evaluation of competing products, and we see it more and more. Purchasers and contracting agents come into the process only after the customer's system acquisition team has decided which vendor and product offering most closely meets the objectives of the customer.

This process is optimized when the customer's system acquisition team forms a strategic partnership with the vendor after a single choice has been down selected to. The amount of time the acquisition team can focus on the preferred system before an actual purchase order is placed is very important. Fewer misunderstandings result, and more customizing can be started, prior to purchase commitments being made.

There are many variations on this process, but we have seen this basic series of events on most of our large accounts.

Purchase orders follow, and it is at this point that we require the customer place a non-refundable down payment on the system, mostly as a motivator for the customer to complete the project and not quit or cancel as the dynamics of their organization changes.

Current Army Demonstration and Procurement Programs with the DT-3000

The VID program (Voice Interactive Display), a NAC sponsored program, was in need of a computing platform that included a direct connection to the vehicle data bus, and a truck to demonstrate the voice interactive diagnostics on. DriverTech and Stewart and Stevenson were in a position to provide both of these. DriverTech had the basis for the computing platform, and had the diagnostics connection and fleet management software that would provide a context for a major system demonstration. Stewart and Stevenson had a truck, the FMTV A1, with the electronic data bus, intelligent components, and an agenda to explore embedded diagnostics capabilities for their ILS (Integrated Logistics Services) department.

The VID program prime contractor, MTS-Tech, subcontracted to DriverTech in late 2001 to make upgrades to the DT-2000. DriverTech decided to name the upgraded product the DT-3000. In addition to upgrading the electronics to run Windows NT, DriverTech developed a video capability for night vision and rear aimed cameras for the DT-3000. Embedded training video display capability was added in the form of an MPEG2 decompressor chip from Sygma. This chip enables the DT-3000 to process video using the same type of hardware used in set top box systems like Tivo.

MTS-Tech, with DriverTech's assistance, integrated an FMTV provided by Stewart and Stevenson with voice interactive diagnostics, RFID tag cargo scanning, map navigation, satellite communication and the FMTV IETM using the DT-3000 as the computing platform for the demonstration. The system was demonstrated to four key general officers and representatives of all TWV pm shops. Follow-on work underway adds the HEMTT, as well as adding integration of AIT capabilities on the trucks with DriverTech's dispatch software for tracking of cargo from a central location, as well as matching cargo with a manifest. This manifest matching will enable errors in pickups and deliveries to be signaled to the driver and to commanders immediately upon occurrence.

Mid way through the program the ADIP team at PM-TMDE decided to use the DT-3000 for demonstrations of embedded diagnostics and embedded prognostics. DriverTech was still in a position to make modifications to the DT-3000, and the ADIP specification under development helped guide us in making some changes for environmental ruggedness (temperature, vibration, humidity, moisture) and EMI (electro-magnetic interference).

Late in 2002, the DT-3000 was chosen as the embedded computer platform for the SBCT demonstration. The DT-3000 will be the on-board system for embedded diagnostics and satellite communication over the Movement Tracking System for the tactical wheeled vehicles. DriverTech's satellite communication software will be used on two of the vehicles, and will enable demonstration of these two SBCT vehicles over the internet through DriverTech's DotNet based web application.

One of the requirements of the SBCT demo is to demonstrate the capability of a mechanic at vehicle to utilize the embedded IETM. Rather than making the DT-3000 a portabe device that could be removed from the cab, creating lots of complications, DriverTech suggested a mechanic's walk around tablet terminal. DriverTech will be delivering five such devices in September. These five devices are based on our QTERM-G75 terminal, and use VNC as a method of remotely viewing the DT-3000 display, and remotely using the DT-3000 touch screen and keys over a wireless LAN.

Finally, the recent award of the FMTV rebuy cements for the Army the concept of embedded diagnostics for tactical wheeled vehicles. A requirement in the FMTV rebuy RFP for an embedded diagnostics capability caused Stewart and Stevenson to integrate the DT-3000 into their proposal. The Army noted in their award review process that Stewart and Stevenson had hit the nail on the head in understanding the requirement and had proposed a very good solution.

ESC
EMER
LOG ON
DEL
ADVANCED INTERACTIVE DIAGNOSTIC ENVIRONMENT - M1070A1
TECHNICAL MANUAL
UNIT
ARMY TM 9-2320-391-20
AIR FORCE TO 36A12-1B-1133-2
REVISION NO. 0
Introduction
Service Instructions
Troubleshooting
Maintenance
Preventive Maintenance Checks and Services
Appendices
Maintenance Allocation Chart
Repair Parts & Special Tools List Introduction
Repair Parts & Special Tools List
Subject Index
Department of the Army
2000-06-01
TAB
ENT

Application of Commercial Information Technology Tools to Support Defense Logistics Analysis and the Logistics of Fielded Defense Systems

Michael Davis, Jean Ann Davis, and Michael Gibbons

Sparta, Inc.
4901 Corporate Drive, Suite 102
Huntsville, AL 35805
256-837-5282, x1302
256-830-0287 (FAX)
davism@huntsville.sparta.com

ABSTRACT

Use of commercially available information technology tools to support the planning for and fielding of U.S. military systems provides a viable alternative to development of information systems to accompany each new or existing military system or unit. SPARTA, Inc. has developed information technology tools for commercial ventures that have been successfully adapted to the military logistics world.

SPARTA has developed the ShareIT™ system, an in-house tool for customers that have a need to share data in a Web-based environment over the Internet or an intranet. Originally designed for providing an Integrated Data Environment for medical records, ShareIT™ provides a collaborative virtual workspace for geographically separated groups using Internet protocols and your web browser. ShareIT™ supports up-front logistics design with its IPT/Workgroup module which provides a specially designed tool that permits IPTs/Workgroups to focus on tasks/projects. It allows creation of segmented working environments consisting of any ShareIT™ modules or any web-based legacy applications.

For a deployed commercial communications satellite system, SPARTA developed an asset tracking tool to assist in the operations and maintenance of satellite control facilities. SPARTA modified this tool, now called Logistics Multiple Asset Integrated Tracking (LogMAIT™) to accurately and comprehensively track assets through all phases of war. LogMAIT™ is a unique database system in that it tracks everything from supplies to maintenance actions. Today's fast paced military and industry needs require real-time information to prevent critical information lag during the build-up and battle phases of war. LogMAIT™ is designed to respond to today's needs by providing a single logistics Information System (IS) that utilizes the data in all categories through a relational database environment with automated linking functional applications. This approach directly reduces capacity, connectivity and processing requirements, making LogMAIT™ a one-stop tool that manages and tracks the total logistics requirements of an asset. This is achieved by utilizing a single data structure that is robustly linked, providing the decision maker with the ability to easily formulate the information required in making timely and optimal resource allocation decisions. This presentation will include a short demonstration of both LogMAIT™ and ShareIT™.

1.0 Introduction

SPARTA has developed information technology solutions and associated software development for government and commercial customers since its inception in 1979. For many of our customers, who work in Integrated Product Team environments to work complex Systems Engineering problems, we have developed a tool that enables them to share the information and data needed to work the necessary analysis. For other customers, especially those who work with logistics solutions for maintaining fielded systems efficiently, we have developed a tools to assist them in assessing system readiness and individual asset conditions. This paper summarizes those two tools, ShareIT™ and LogMAIT™.

2.0 ShareIT™

SPARTA has provided technology solutions and services to customers for over twenty years. Ten years ago, we were asked to develop a solution for the U.S. Army Battle Labs to exchange data between twelve distributed sites throughout the country. A simple interface was developed that allowed the Battle Labs to not only view their own data, but also the data from the other eleven Battle Labs. Since web-based solutions were not readily available at that time, we used data replication provided with Windows NT and custom programming to transmit data on a nightly basis.

With the arrival of the worldwide web, we began supporting customers with requirements for web-based solutions and services. After several years of developing specialized products for various customers, we realized that many of these products could be combined into a single product that would meet many of their business needs. The product that we created is called ShareIT™. This product was developed by SPARTA for customers that have a need to share data in a web-based environment over the Internet or an intranet. ShareIT™ provides a collaborative virtual workspace for geographically separated groups using Internet protocols and a web browser. Once ShareIT™ is installed on an Internet or intranet server, clients only require browser software to use ShareIT™. No other client software is required.

ShareIT™ is modular by design, so other web-based applications can easily be added to improve the capabilities. It is developed with HTML, ASP, VBScript, JavaScript, and Java. It uses Internet Information Server (IIS) as the web server and is database driven. Access, SQL Server, or Oracle may be used as the backend database. The desired database primarily depends on your legacy database applications or the expected growth of the system. ShareIT™ is continuously being enhanced for our current customer base. Every installed copy may have a unique look and feel because ShareIT™ was designed to allow administrators to customize it by changing text, buttons, and logos. Also different views may be seen based on the content that the user has permissions to access. All modules can be set for no-access, read-only access, or read/write access. The administrator sets these permissions with a robust administration utility that is delivered with the product. Figure 1 illustrates ShareIT™ screens and lists the six main functions provided by the tool.

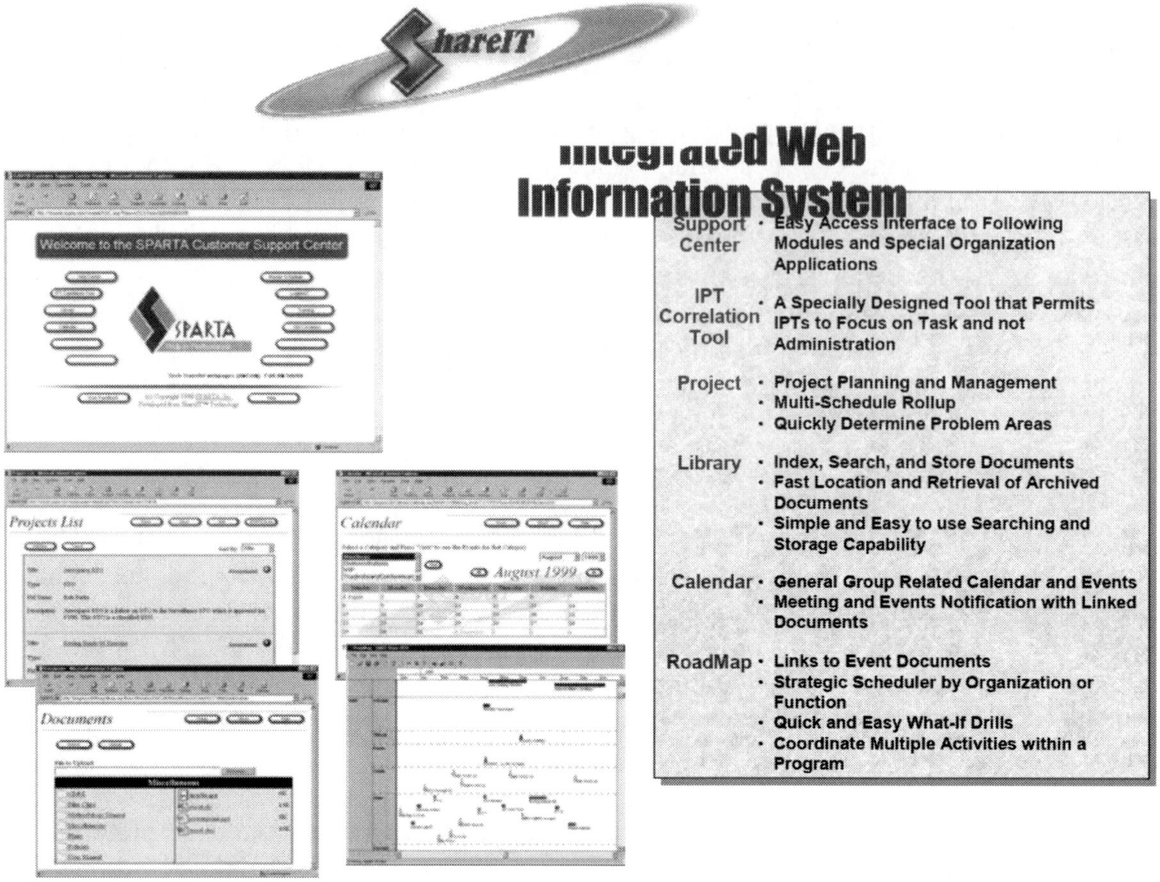

Figure 1. ShareIT™ System Sample Screens and Main Functions

Eight external customers are currently using ShareIT™ Raytheon is using it to support the Extended Air Defense Test Bed (EADTB) in virtually the identical way that the VA Financial Services Center plans to use its document library system. The U.S. Army Aviation and Missile Command (AMCOM) Research, Development and Engineering Center (RDEC) uses it as a repository for its digitized documents. The U.S. Army Space and Missile Defense Technology Center (SMDTC) uses ShareIT™ to manage its meetings and events and to organize its electronic documents. The Joint Center for Technology Integration (JCTI) uses it to catalog and organize its internal and contractor produced documents. The U.S. Air Force Space and Missile Command (SMC) uses it to support its Engineering, Analysis, Design & Development (EADD II) Integrated Product Team (IPT) process and related documentation. Spiral Technology uses it to receive and distribute all contract deliverables for NASA Dryden Flight Research Center. Advanced Logistics Solutions (ALS) uses ShareIT™ to organize and share documentation and task orders among its 23 subcontractors on its Omnibus 2000 Logistics contract with AMCOM. The Securities Assistant Management Directorate (SAMD) of AMCOM uses the system to coordinate activities among dispersed locations and to organize and share documentation.

In addition to these external uses, SPARTA currently uses four distinct installations of ShareIT™ for internal use. Our Human Resources department uses ShareIT™ to keep track of resumes and job applicant forms. When a job opportunity arises, managers are able to search the library for resumes that match the job criteria. Some Operations use ShareIT™ to store and track briefings and other documents for access by the group as well as to track meetings and conferences. Corporate working groups composed of key personnel from around the country use ShareIT™ to share documentation and to plan and manage projects and pursuit activities. SPARTA proposal development teams use ShareIT™ to organize proposal development material and to coordinate proposal activities among widely dispersed proposal team members.

3.0 Logistics Multiple Asset Integrated Tracking (LogMAIT™)

From SPARTA's four-year experience with IRIDIUM®, a global satellite and terrestrial telecommunication system requiring real-time global asset tracking and status, LogMAIT™ was created by SPARTA to provide a truly integrated logistics system that provides the keystone for maintaining and sustaining mid to large operating centers and systems. Leveraging the benefits of a relational database, coupled with point-and-click screen technology, LogMAIT™ provides the user with the capability to track a wide range of company assets -- hardware, software, test equipment, spares, consumables and other key logistics items, and the associated logistics metrics. It provides a host of logistics administrative functions such as vendor data, contract information, personnel information, purchases and shipping information. LogMAIT™ includes a "trouble ticket" maintenance system, a work order system, and a repair and calibration system in addition to facilitating read/write bar coding for quick asset tracking and inventory management. LogMAIT™ provides Battle Planners, resource managers and commanders on the Battlefield with instant visual readiness reporting for critical equipment and associated subsystems. A wide variety of logistics management reports, along with the capability to quickly customize these reports to meet immediate and changing operational requirements, is also available in LogMAIT™. Figure 2 illustrates LogMAIT™ interaction with the user community.

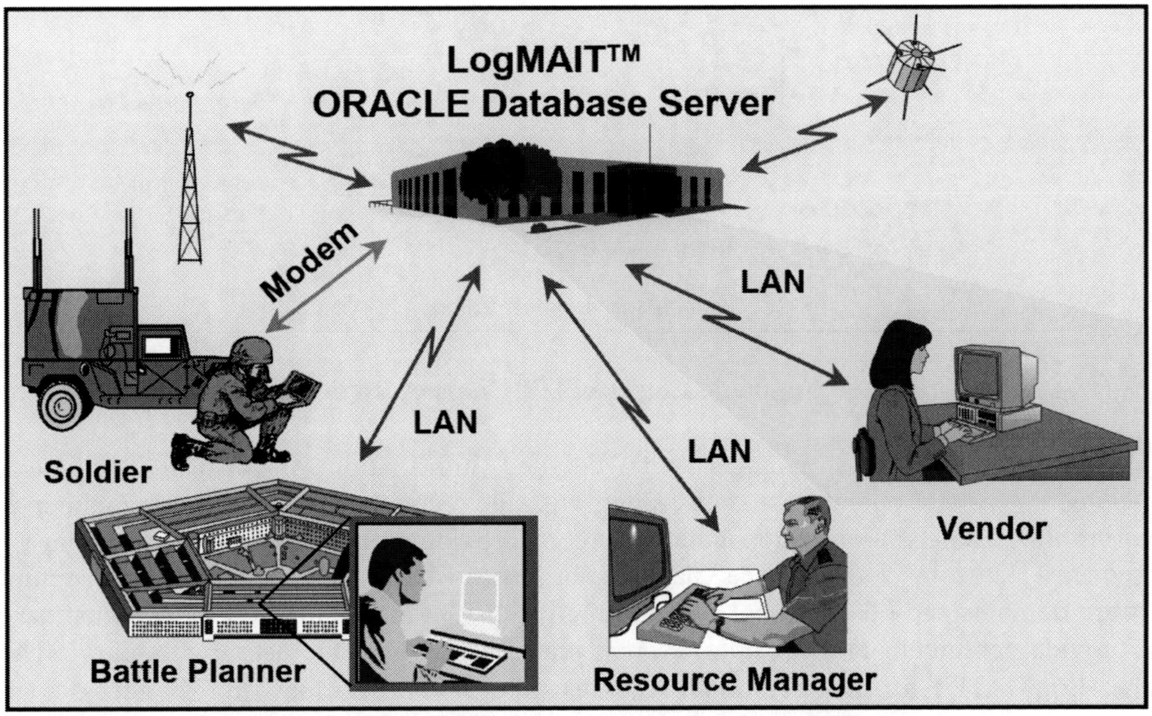

Figure 2. LogMAIT™ User Community Connectivity

LogMAIT™ serves as a "data warehouse" for all critical logistics information required to manage developing and/or deployed systems. Implemented as a client-server, object oriented database system, this tool utilizes Oracle data management back-end. LogMAIT™ accommodates both developmental and operational supportability requirements associated with system development; and includes the capability to capture data from test, prototype, operational, and logistical environments.

LogMAIT™ has over 20 pre-formatted and "linked" user screens that allow managers, maintenance, supply and contract personnel to quickly surf the logistics "data warehouse" to find information required to complete daily tasks. The tool has other uses including: configuration management of hardware, software, test equipment, and documentation; training requirements and accomplishments; employee certification management; maintenance scheduling; Reliability, Availability, and Maintainability (RAM) documentation; and Failure Reporting and Corrective Action System (FRACAS). Figure 3 displays LogMAIT™'s functional capabilities.

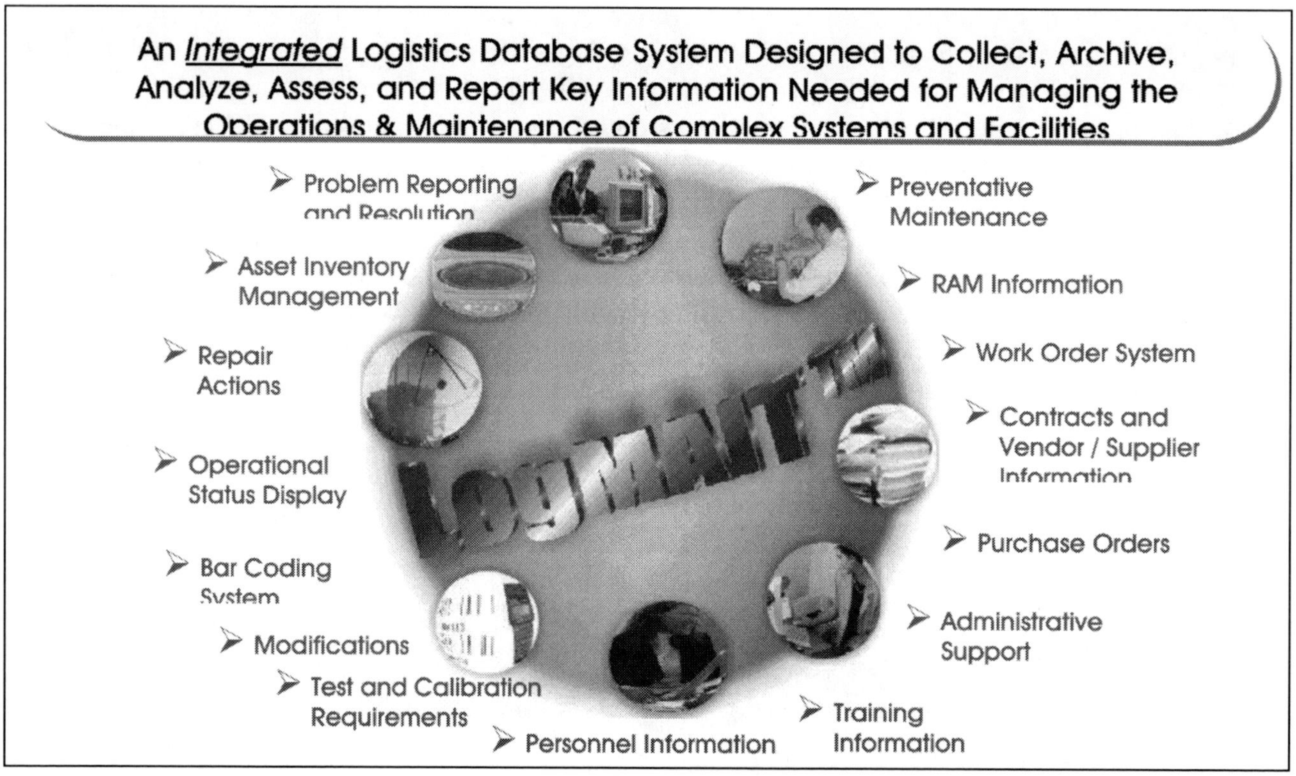

Figure 3. LogMAIT™ Characteristics

LogMAIT™ provides the manager with detailed information on critical equipment and associated subsystem operational status along with the Vendor name and phone number who is repairing the asset. The operational status screens provide a quick look at the program's major component status by reflecting red, amber, or green status for key operations, equipment, software domains and other critical system functions. Linking this feature with actual hardware will provide continuous and accurate weapon platform status to the user community. The user queries LogMAIT™ for the operational readiness of a system and may quickly access a specific problem report which identifies the time, date, and circumstances of the trouble. This process provides key data fields that capture information concerning the failure, as well as a disciplined means to resolving and closing out the incident.

LogMAIT™ is a truly integrated tool - all information types may be linked. When a property item is added to the system, management of that item begins immediately. Each item is associated with a vendor/supplier/contractor, point(s) of contact, documentation, etc. The user may quickly query the database for a property item's pertinent information and receive all associated information down to all repair actions associated with that item. Figure 4 is a typical scenario for LogMAIT™.

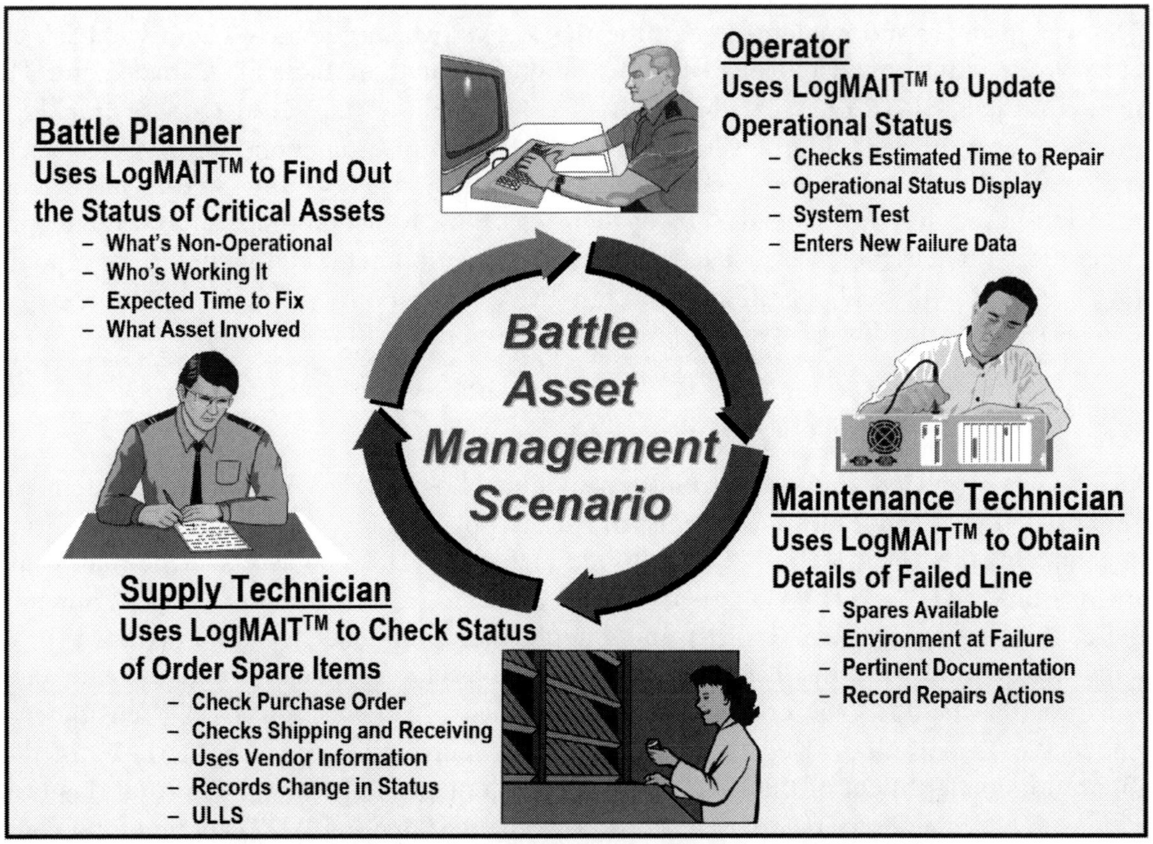

Figure 4. Typical Scenarios Serviced by LogMAIT™

3.1 Commercial Background for LogMAIT™

SPARTA is responsible for developing tools for analysis of manpower, supportability, reliability and systems availability for a number of Government and commercial customers. For the IRIDIUM® project, a worldwide satellite based telephone and paging system, SPARTA designed the **IRIDIUM® Logistics Support Database (ILSDB)** to identify and capture logistics requirements for satellite and ground control O&S needs. The ILSDB maintains a host of critical and vital logistics data for supply, transportation, maintainability, and reliability for real-time use.

The ILSDB, a forerunner to LogMAIT™, collects, archives, assesses and reports logistics information for asset tracking, trouble ticketing, maintenance and supply information, readiness display, bar code read/write, and other related administrative functions. The ILSDB is implemented as a client-server, object oriented database system using a Visual FoxPro front-end that provides the Graphical User Interface and a Sybase System Database back-end. The ILSDB was created to support First Launch operational logistics activities and subsequent build development efforts. LogMAIT™ is the central repository for the logistics information needed for developing, managing, operating, and improving the resources used to keep the IRIDIUM® system up and operating throughout its operational life to provide top quality service at minimum cost.

ILSDB was installed and implemented at the IRIDIUM® Master Control Facility (MCF) and the Telemetry, Tracking and Control (TTAC) Stations located in Iceland, Canada, and Hawaii. From this project, SPARTA created LogMAIT™ to provide a universal tool for tracking asset information, and for generating customized reports based on user input. LogMAIT™ provides general capabilities to support operation and maintenance of any mid-to-large complex information-based system. The ILSDB system was built to accommodate both developmental and operational requirements associated with system development; and includes the capability to capture test, prototype, and operational data. LogMAIT™ not only provides this same capability, but also currently provides greater functionality to assist in tracking key assets

3.2 Applications of LogMAIT™

SPARTA has provided and is currently providing LogMAIT™ to various systems in the community. Lockheed Martin in Huntsville used LogMAIT™ to manage the operation and maintenance of the Theatre High Area Altitude Defense (THAAD) assets. One major tailoring effort for LogMAIT™ is THAAD's requirement to provide a direct link to the government tools, Unit Level Logistics System (ULLS) and Supply and Maintenance System (SAMS). These systems are required for the Lockheed Martin Contractor to support and provide the asset information for the THAAD common army elements. Another LogMAIT™ customer is the Extended Air Defense Test Bed (EADTB), which is currently using LogMAIT™ to track the configuration management of the EADTB software elements. The major effort on this task is to provide web based modules of LogMAIT™ so that the worldwide EADTB community can easily and quickly submit a trouble report or software change request.

LogMAIT™ is now being used by the PEO-STRI to track the status of assets on training ranges in CONUS and OCONUS. This application of the tools provides status and locations of items such as targets that are required for soldier training. It also provides acquisition planners with input needed for update of assets and related cost estimates.

3.3 Reports and Data Output

Surprisingly, most logistics centers, operational commands, and test beds do not have real-time integrated logistics support databases such as LogMAIT™. Most rely on a mixture of databases, spreadsheets, and other tools that are "homegrown", frequently do not fulfill the requirements, and are costly to update and maintain. LogMAIT™ is a truly integrated data system, in which a user may navigate through all types of linked data through point-and-click screen access techniques. For example, the user may begin by viewing the readiness of key equipment. If the status is red or non-operable, the user may click to view the reason for the failure (trouble ticket), and then again click to view the repair screen to see detailed information on the repair. The user may then click to the assets to determine what hardware or software item is available or to obtain the vendor's phone number, and/or any additional information until he or she has a complete picture of the state and status of the system. Such an integrated system will substantially increase productivity for a variety of different organizations and result in increased system availability. LogMAIT™ also has a reliability, availability, and maintainability (RAM) capturing capability. It identifies key operational and support drivers that need to be addressed to improve the supported system. Figure 5 illustrates sample Navigation Screens from LogMAIT™.

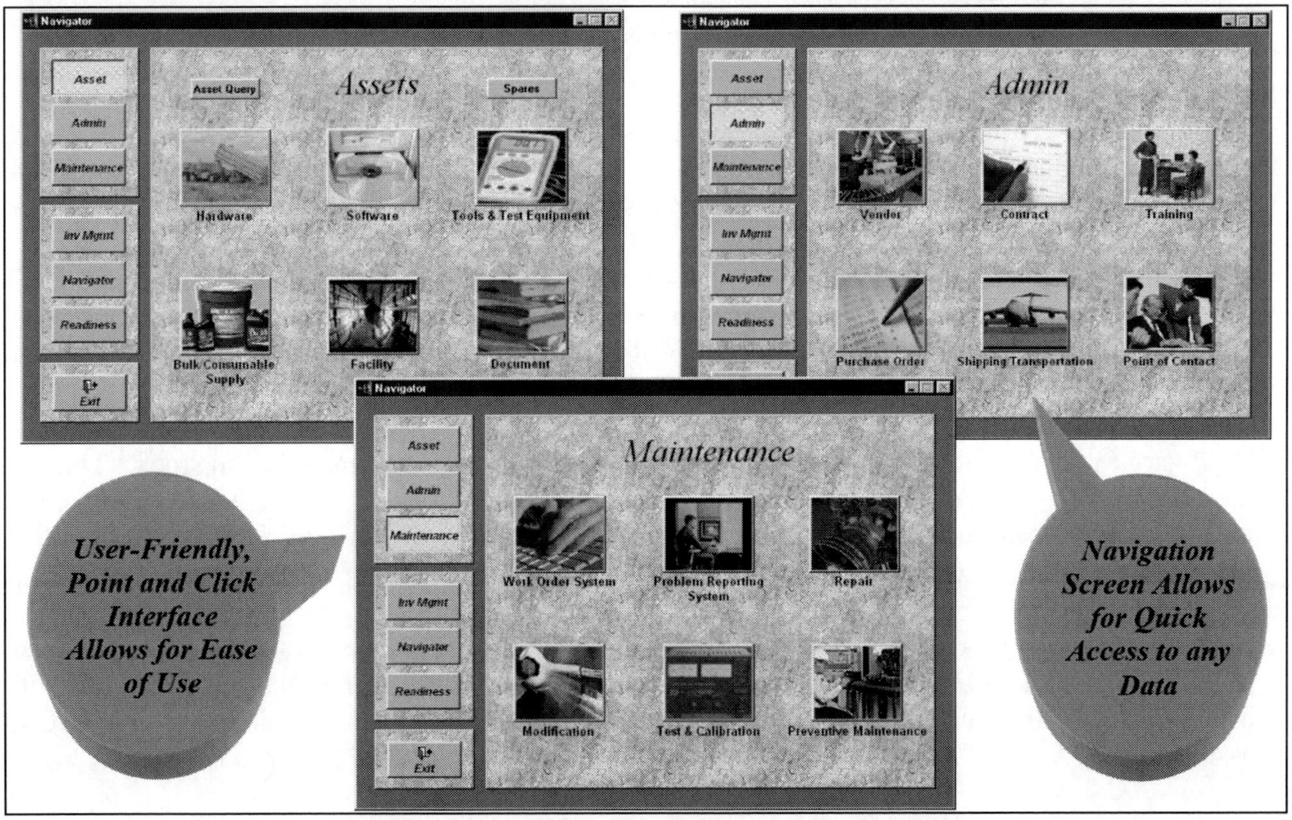

Figure 5. Top-Level Navigation Screens from LogMAIT™

The following data illustrates the type of customized reports available from LogMAIT™. However, any user may easily create a report using any field in the database. The user may select any number of fields in any order, sort this information, perform calculations, filter the data, and output the information in a variety of ways. The report may be displayed on the screen, printed, or saved for later use. Also, the report may be converted to HTML format, Excel spreadsheet, database format, word documents, text file, graphs, and the user may even send it email directly from LogMAIT™.

Software Master/Backup Inventory Summary Report - Provides a summary of on-hand software to report which version of software the site is using for operations. This information may be used for planning and installation of software updates, the quantity of a specific version of software required for the program, and where at a given site the software copies are stored.

Hardware Status Inventory Report - Provides a listing of all site assets, by part number, and current location. This report is used to assess a site's ability to sustain operations and determine the quantity, kind, and condition of assets on hand.

Hardware Washout Summary - Provides a listing of those assets washed out and disposed for each site. The report provides an audit trail to identify when the item was washed out, and source data to support new procurements.

Tools & Test Equipment Summary – Provides, by location, a summary of a given site's tools and test equipment.

Spares Status Report - Provides listing of all site spare assets, by part number, and current location. The report is used to access the site's ability to perform sustained operations, determine the quantity and condition of each asset on hand. These results may be used to update sparing numbers, expedite repair actions, or redistribute assets among sites.

Hardware Spares In-Repair - Provides a list of spare components designated as in repair. This list includes by site, the Name, Part Number, Serial Number, and criticality of the spare. This report is used to determine what portion of program assets are not serviceable and may be used to determine vendor effectiveness or the effectiveness of other support related activities.

Hardware Spares In-Stock - Provides a list of spare components designated as in stock. This list includes by site, the Name, Part Number, Serial Number, and criticality of the spare. This report will be used to determine a site's ability to sustain operations or support decisions concerning maintenance policies and additional procurements.

Hardware Spares In-Transit - Provides a list of spare components designated as in transit (between sites). This list includes by site, the Name, Part Number, Serial Number, and criticality of the spare. This report is used to determine the distribution of assets for other sites or in transit to a vendor.

Critical Hardware Spares Listing by Location - Provides a list of all critical spares by site. This report is used to determine the availability of critical spares especially during launch operations.

Logistics Control Number (LCN) Report - Provides an as-built indentured list of system hardware to the SRU level in LCN sequence. This report provides system configuration to support repairs, modifications, and asset management.

4.0 Summary

SPARTA, Inc. has successfully converted tools that were initially developed for commercial information technology applications to support the acquisition and fielding of U.S. military systems. This paper presented two such tools that are being used to support DoD programs. At this symposium, as part of our presentation, we are demonstrating these tools.

Authors:

Michael Davis
Mike Davis is currently the director of the Logistics and Supportability Directorate of the Technical and Acquisition Support Operation at SPARTA, Inc. Mike has provided Reliability, Availability, and Maintainability (RAM) and logistics analyses for both commercial and DoD efforts. He worked supported the IRIDIUM communications system in developing RAM requirements, and in development of the IRIDIUM Logistics Support Database, the forerunner of the LogMAIT™ tool. Mike has supported the modeling and simulation activities of the Army by maintaining and enhancing the Logistics Simulation (LOGSIM) and the Logistics Analysis Model (LOGAM). Mike graduated from Harding College (BS Mathematics) in 1977 and from the University of Arkansas in 1980 (MS Statistics). He is currently editor of *The Challenger*, the newsletter of the Tennessee Valley Chapter of SOLE. He received his Certified Professional Logistician (CPL) accreditation in July 1999. He received accreditation as a Certified Cost Estimator/Analyst in 2001.

Jean Ann. Davis
Jean Ann Davis is currently the Directorate Manager for the Software Products Directorate (SPD) at SPARTA, Inc. She manages the development of several software products including Logistics Multiple Asset Integrated Tracking (LogMAIT™), Multiple Launch Rocket System (MLRS) Automation Initiative International (MAII), Business Information Tracking System (BITS), Ground-Based Midcourse Defense (GMD) Technology Catalog, and the SMDC SBIR Database. She is responsible for tailoring LogMAIT™ for the Extended Air Defense Test Bed (EADTB) and the PEO-STRI's Training Range Support Services Contract. Ms. Davis graduated from the University of Alabama, Huntsville (BS, Mathematics) in 1993.

Michael Gibbons
Mike Gibbons is a Systems Analyst/Programmer within the Technology Program Integration Directorate at SPARTA, Inc. He designs, develops, and installs custom built client-server and web-based programs for various customers. He is the technical lead for ShareIT™, a web-based product that allows disbursed organizations to exchange data easily and is developed with a combination of HTML, ASP, VBScript, JavaScript, and Java code to provide a robust, yet easy to use product. He is the Website administrator for versions of ShareIT™ located at SMDC, AMRDEC, GMD JPO, and SAMD. Mr. Gibbons graduated from the University of Alabama, Huntsville (BSBA, Management Information Systems) in 1990. He is a Microsoft Certified Professional (MCP), implementing and supporting Windows NT Server and Microsoft Windows NT Workstation.

Information Technology:

Expediting Intermodal Military Logistics

Presented by:

Midshipmen Cornelio,

Perri & Chrosniak

Change is on its way

- Re-engineering
- Technology
- Visionary Concepts

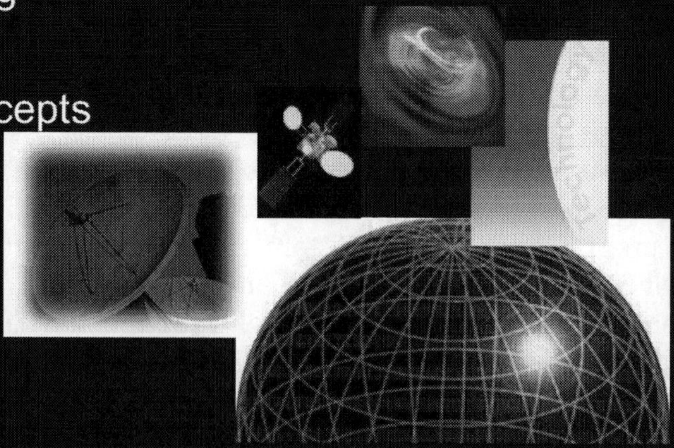

Learned Lessons

- Principal focus of military logistics has been
  - Large scale, and
  - Forward based forces, with
  - Logistics infrastructure

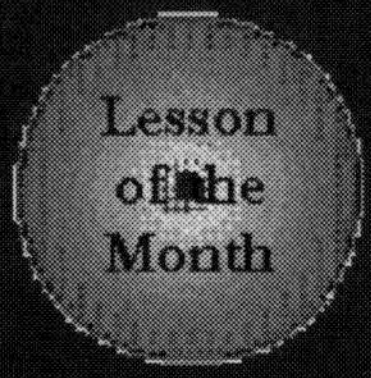

HOWEVER!

- Desert Storm,
- Desert Shield,
- Operation Iraqi Freedom showed us that US Forces cannot depend on a large logistics system

SO,

- Department of Defense (DOD) - allocating resources, and
- Exploring benefits of intermodalism

Process	DoD	Commercial Company A	B	C
Distribution (in stock items)	26 days*	1 day	3 days	2 days
Repair (cycle time)	4-144 days	3 days	14 days	14 days
Repair	8-35 days**	1 day	10 days	5 days

* DoD average

** Particular DoD item

How?

- Developing strategies,
- Prioritizing resources, and
- Directing joint programs

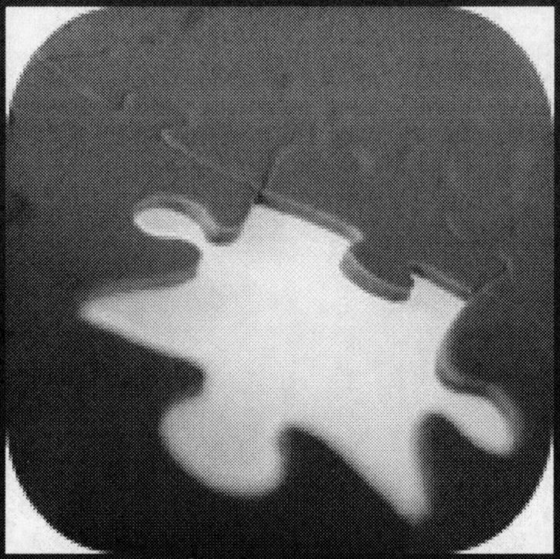

Strategies

- Customer-driven
- Pursue INTEGRATION
- To create a SEAMLESS structure
- Flexible technical architecture for change and the logistics systems environment

Air Lift Problems

- Wasted space
- Crippling - capability not fully utilized
- Moving air

What must be done

- Verify / Justify airlift capability
  - Check containers,
  - Open boxes, and
  - Look inside vehicles
- Not fully used = waste

Changes to Air Lift?

- Optimize space
  - New container shapes & sizes, instead of
  - Broken stowage and/or changing size of aircraft
    - Expensive
- Better tracking for aforementioned containers

Sealift

- Voluntary Intermodal Sealift Agreement (VISA), introduced in the mid-1990s
- Intermodalism allows the military and civilian transporters to work with one another

Sea Lift Problems

- Military intermodal technology… up to date?
- Majority of RRF ships are break bulk
- MSC - seeking to make commercial resources equal with military sealift needs

Possible Sealift Solutions

- New ships for the modern military
- Use more containers
- Ro-Ro and container vessels with minimal resources shore side needed

Army Traffic Management (ATM) Goals

- Cost analysis to determine economical feasibility
- Furnish containers in support of Operations Support Command (OSC) requirements and exercises
- Determine the routing of containers

Technological Solutions

- Site Based Container Handling Equipment (SB-CHE)
- Automated All-weather Cargo Transfer System (AACTS)
- Radio Frequency Identification
- Theater Support Vessel

Site Based Container Handling Equipment

- SB-CHE equipment will attach to a chassis to self-load from the ground
- The operator…
  - Perform operation from cab of the vehicle
    - Joystick, and
    - Video feedback

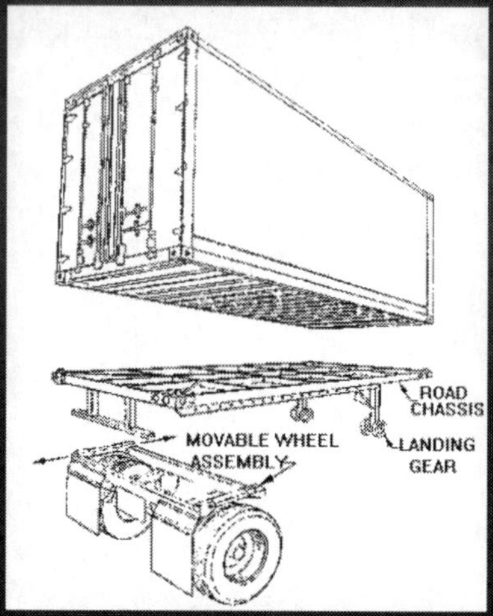

Automated All-weather Cargo Transfer System

- Under funds provided by the US Army Belvoir Center,
  - *Automated All-weather Cargo Transfer System* (AACTS)
- Use of robotic principles for the crane to handle the containers

AACTS

AACTS

AACTS avoids….

Radio Frequency Identification

- Combines radio waves and computer networks to track shipments

How RFID Works

- "Tags" containing microchips to cargo
- Tag emits radio waves with a unique ID code

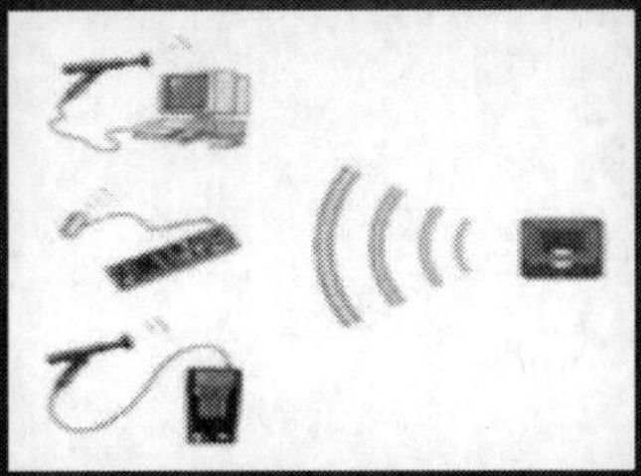

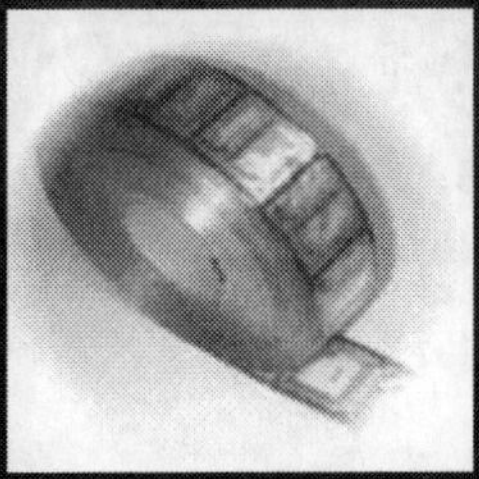

RFID System

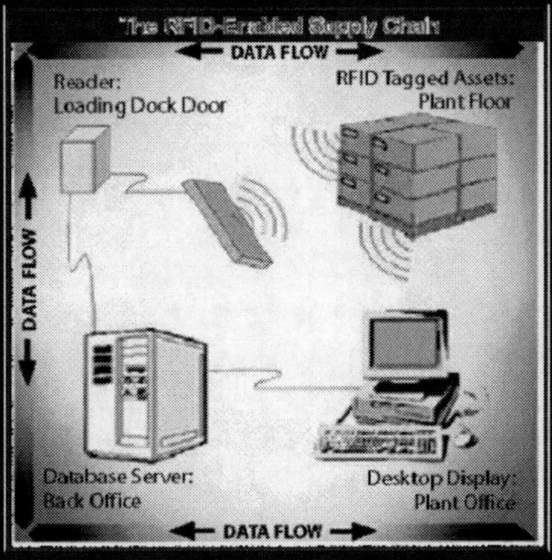

Theater Support Vessel (TSV)

Background: The Theater Support Vessel (TSV) will be the Army's Next Generation self-deploying Watercraft. Leveraging technologies developed within the commercial sector and DOD; the TSV will be optimized to support intra-theater operational & tactical movement and maneuver for the objective force while retaining the capability to provide intra-theater lift and sustainment support for the interim and legacy forces.

TSV

- - Speed: Threshold = 40 knots / Objective = 40+ Knots
- - Range: Threshold = 4726 NM @ 40 knots
- Objective = 8700 NM@ 24 knots & 4726 NM @40 knots
  - Cargo: Threshold = 1,250 ST/25,000+ Ft2 cargo area
  Objective = 1,500 ST/25,000+ Ft2 cargo area

TSV

- Status:
  - ORD approved Jan 00
  - TAA 09 Allocation Rule = 12 per MTW Theater
  - Mini-POM = UFR '05 / Fund 1 vessel per year FY06/07
- Basis of Issue:
  - 1 per TSV Detachment (AC & USAR)
  - TAA 7 AAO = 14-

TSV

C.1.2.1 LOAD PLAN, (ATTACHMENT 002)

So What?

Defense Acquisitions under the New DOD 5000 Series

By

Dr. Ralph L. Harper, Jr.

Defense Acquisitions under the New DOD 5000 Series

by

Dr. Ralph L. Harper, Jr.

ABSTRACT

The critical elements of the military acquisition systems infrastructure have been impacted by recent advances in Systems Sciences, Simulation Methods, and DOD 5000 series changes. This paper will look at the effect that each has on the other, as well as measure the comparative effectiveness that is essential in the defense acquisitions sector. It is possible to approach procurement by identifying the performance and other characteristics of equipment as they contribute synergistically on overall effectiveness in defense and military systems.

A major problem is how to specify acquisition requirements for a system many years in advance of delivery, such that it can be manufactured, supplied, supported in operation, and most important of all, that it will operate effectively when a need arises. The Infrastructure ensures that the best Engineering, Logistics, and Management practices are used throughout the DOD and industry to deal with emerging paradigm to develop and sustain systems

Defense Acquisitions under the New DOD 5000 Series

The end to the Cold War accelerates logistics improvements, enhances support to the warfighter, and aligns logistics processes with the operational demands of the 21st Century. This has brought about a change in logistics infrastructure which has as the primary objective to ensure consistent, reliable support that meets warfighter requirements.

Changes in the logistics infrastructure will have to meet the major challenges to maintain our technological superiority. Yesterday's technology may not be "good enough" on tomorrow's battlefield and U.S. industry may no longer have leadership in some areas of technology.

These changes have placed the Department of Defense (DOD) under three mandates:

1. To leverage the best technology available from both the commercial and defense sources.

2. The rapidly transitioning of technology into new material systems.

3. The refreshing of technology as needed to maintain the warfighter throughout the life cycle of a system.

Achieving success in the technology transition requires teamwork between four communities;

- **The requirements community** – the warfighter or their representatives who develop new warfighting concepts and outline the capabilities needed to support them.
- **The science and technology (S&T) community** – the government, industry, academic scientists, and S&T managers who develop knowledge in the key technologies, that will be needed for future equipment.
- **The acquisition community** – the program managers who insert the technologies into systems that are placed into the hands of the warfighters.
- **The logistics and sustainment community** – the program managers, item managers, and logisticians who maintain and improve the equipment through the decades of service that are expected for major systems.

The entire life cycle of an acquisition program from conception to removable from use requires identifying the technology, applying commercial and government science and technology, tradeoffs within the community, integrating the technology into development programs, and continuously upgrading of the technology.

To enable the technology challenges, the DOD 500 Series document for basic acquisition policy was rewritten. In particular, DOD Directive 5000.1 and DOD Instruction 5000.2

articulate evolutionary acquisition and technology insertion as a means of meeting technological challenges.

This guide assists in the implementation of the policies regarding technology insertion and evolutionary acquisition for DOD 5000 Series acquisitions as well as for smaller programs. As an evolving document, the guide's objectives are to help the program manager and the requirements:

(1) Plan for evolutionary technology integration.

(2) Achieve continuous technology enhancement by identifying the appropriate tools, business arrangements, programs, and incentives.

The acquisition technology and logistics memorandum from the Undersecretary of Defense on April 12, 2002, defines the evolutionary acquisition as:

> An acquisition strategy that define, develop, produce, or acquire and fields initial hardware or software increment (or block) of operational capability. It is based on technologies demonstrated in relevant environments, time-phased requirements, and demonstrated manufacturing or software deployment capabilities. These capabilities can be provided in a shorter period of time, followed by subsequent increments of capability over time that accommodate improved technology and allow for full and adaptable systems over time. Each increment will meet a useful capability specified by the user (i.e., at least the thresholds set by the user for that increment); however, the first increment may represent only 60 to 80 percent (or less) of the desired final capability.
>
> There are two basic approaches to evolutionary acquisition. In one approach, the ultimate functionality can be defined at the beginning of the program, with the content of each increment determined by the maturation of key technologies. In the second approach,

the ultimate functionality cannot be defined at the beginning of the program, and each increment of capability is defined by the maturation of the technologies matched with the evolving needs of the user.

The Evolutionary Acquisition use of the Acquisition Management System is defined by the DOD 5000 Series. These documents provide a flexible, yet disciplined, approach for meeting technology challenges. The approach incorporates three key objectives for acquiring new systems:

(1) Reduced cycle time

(2) Affordability

(3) Sustainability and Interoperability

The DOD 5000 Series documents emphasize evolutionary acquisition and spiral development. These concepts provide a framework for a complex system, focusing first on military utility – developing something useful and getting it to the warfighter faster – and then building on and improving that military utility. The requirements community is challenged to use a performance-based approach to define incremental blocks of combat capability that are not only useful to warfighters, but also executable in terms of manageability and risk. A time-phased approach allows technology to be transitioned from the lab into the field at multiple opportunity points.

The acquisition community includes acquisition executives, program executive officers, program managers, and their staffs. They provide new, improved, or continuing material, weapons systems, or information system capabilities or services in response to a validated operational and business need.

The acquisition community does not operate from a fixed template. They interface with requirements personnel and technology providers, and develop tailored acquisition strategies that fit the needs of particular programs, consistent with the time-sensitive needs of the user's requirement, applicable laws and regulations, sound business management practice, and common sense. The new acquisition policies allow and encourage program managers to enter the acquisition process at different decision points, depending on the maturity of the concept, requirements definition, and technology. Throughout the development of the system, program managers work with the requirements community to maintain a balance of cost, schedule, and performance. They can trade performance and schedule objectives to achieve the cost and affordability goals for the program. Sometimes, new or improved technologies that will reduce costs or improve performance become available during the development of the system. This gives the program managers flexibility to adopt these technologies.

The DOD must seek the state-of-the-art technologies being developed by industry, and leverage the advantages of industry's market-driven and cost-constrained products. Staying at the cutting edge of industry-driven technology requires different planning methods and tools from those the government has been accustomed to using.

Acquisition reform initiatives recognized this need and modified policies to provide for collaboration, cost sharing, and incentives when working with industry partners. Other changes including dropping the restrictive "military standard" specifications, a more flexible menu of contracting options, the option for integrated military and commercial development and production, and a program to support the development of dual-use technologies.

It is important to plan early for continuous technology insertion. DOD Directive

5000.1 discusses "Rapid and Effective Transition from Science and Technology to Products," an approach that requires the S&T community to understand and respond to the time-phased needs of the end users. Because the approach requires the acquisition community to plan for the initial system capability and incremental introduction of new technology, the acquisition community must have a thorough knowledge of the technology's readiness for transition.

The primary challenges faced in preparing for the transition of new technology are:

- **Contracting strategy** – motivating the contractor(s) to provide a best-value (from an overall life cycle cost-effectiveness perspective) solution and transitioning into procurement without loss of momentum.
- **Interoperability** – ensuring that the technology can interface with other systems on the battlefield.
- **Supportability** – ensuring that the fielded systems can be cost-effectively supported.
- **Test and evaluation** – early and continuous participation of the operational testing community and evaluators in the final stages of the technology development process, from the definition of data needs and associated military exercises to the completion of the operational assessment to support the production/transition decision.
- **Affordability** – assessing life-cycle affordability and application of a cost-as-an-independent-variable strategy to continuously look for ways to balance acquisition costs and life-cycle cost.
- **Funding** – choosing the proper strategy for obtaining the resources necessary for acquisition.

- **Requirements** – evolving from a mission need and associated performance goals, to a formal ORD and/or system performance specification, to an application.

The new DoD 5000 policy incorporates three key objectives. To meet the reduced cycle time for providing advanced technology faster, more efficient way of setting the cutting edge technology to the warfighter had to be created. The DOD 5000 documents introduce a new acquisition model that extends from S&T phases, through system acquisition, all the way to operation and support. The new model includes three distinct areas:

1. Pre-systems acquisition, which includes developing mission needs and technology opportunities, as well as concepts in technology development.
2. Systems acquisition, which includes systems development. demonstration, production, and deployment.
3. Production sustainment, which includes operation and disposal.

To make systems more affordable, the life cycle DOD 5000 policy emphasizes the need for a limited number of mission-oriented key performance parameters and for cost value to be addressed up front in the requirements documents, resulting in trade space and lower ownership cost.

To incorporate, one must understand how much is the warfighter willing to invest in a particular system for both acquisition and support; provide for competition throughout the life of the system at the system level if possible but clearly at the subsystem, component, and/or subcomponent level. They can accomplish this goal by moving from head-to-head competition for a specific requirement to competition for alternative solutions to meet mission need. In addition, they can require their prime contractors to continuously perform competitions at subsystem, component, and/or subcomponent levels. The result is capability and need combined at the lowest cost.

The third key objective is creating systems that interoperate and are supportable. We need focus on interoperability and supportability.

Interoperability means viewing each system in a family-of-systems context. In other words, how does each system interface with the other systems from which we seize information or support, and how does it feed information and support to other systems?

Supportability means building support into the design and emphasizes total system support and operational sustainment. To ensure supportability and interoperability, the documents emphasize the importance of including supportability as part of the performance envelope from the start of the development process.

The DOD 5000 gives a model that allowed entry into the acquisition process when a mission need requiring a material solution is matched with available technology. This can happen in any milestone.

- **Milestone A** – where the PM can explore alternative concepts or mature key technologies.
- **Milestone B** – if the PM knows the system's architecture, knows the technologies are mature, and has both the requirements and funding.
- **Milestone C** – if the PM already has developed the system and it works in a way that provides military utility.

The model (Figure 1) separates technology development from system integration, and production comes after capability demonstration. Ultimately, that allows PMs to reduce cycle time by concentrating on proven technology and produceable systems. All of these process features are captured in the entrance criteria, which must be met before entering each phase. Depending on the maturity of the technology and the user need, a program can begin at any point in this development continuum.

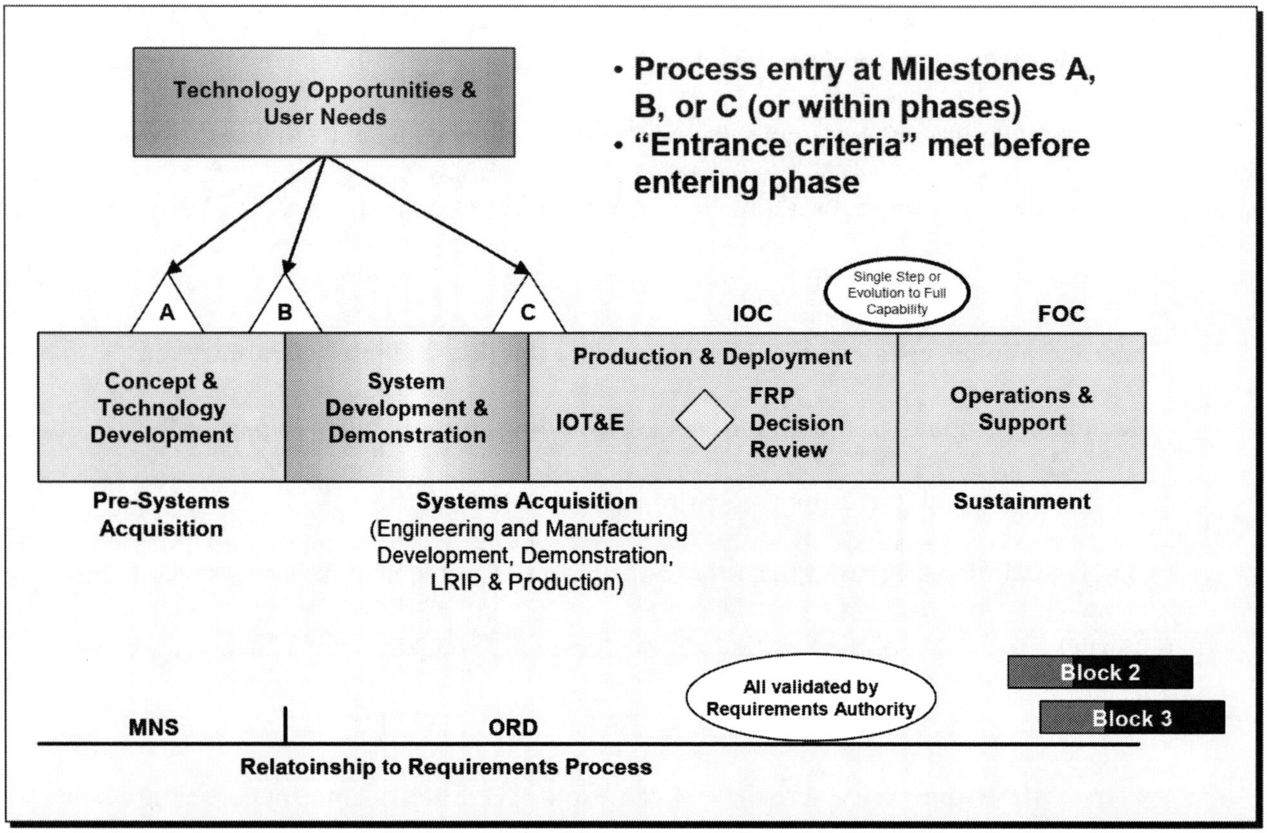

Figure 1. The 5000 Model

Summary

In summary, the new DOD 5000 process offers many benefits to the Government and its partnering prime contractor. The process takes away the arm's length approach and replaces it with a collaborative style of partnering that will not only provide the Government with best value but will also provide the prime contractor a sense of shared ownership and vision. It is through this process that all parties will be able to maintain open communication, improve relationships, and reduce time and costs associated with both the source selection process and program execution.

The new DOD 5000 process is structured in a manner that requires full participation by all support functions within the prime's organization, its subcontractors and the Government. The program must be organized in an IPT style that has dedicated resources and an energetic and skilled Program Manager. The program manager is the key integrator of this process and must be skilled in all areas of program management. Technical skills alone will not enable the program managers to be successful. The program managers must be capable of managing and have a well-founded knowledge of both business and financial requirements. Since this process involves joint participation with the Government, the program manager's decisions throughout this process will either have a positive or negative impact to the Government and company.

REFERENCES CITED

Department of Defense *"A Manager Guide to Technology Transition in an Evolutionary Acquisition Environment a Contact Sport"* Workshop Draft–AQ102; Washington, DC; February 17, 2003

Under Secretary of Defense (Acquisition, Technology, and Logistics); *"Evolutionary Acquisition and Spiral Development,"* memorandum; Washington, DC; April 12, 2002

Department of Defense; *"The Defense Acquisition System,"* DoD 5000.1 October 23, 2000, with Change 1, January 4, 2001

Department of Defense, *"Interim Defense Acquisition Guidebook;"* Washington, DC; October 30, 2002

Dr. Ralph Harper

8 Hampshire Drive, Derry, NH 03038
Phone: (H) 603-893-6682
Email: rth6274@aol.com

PROFESSIONAL QUALIFICATIONS

Over 40 years of experience in Acquisition and Logistics focused on product application and development. Thirty-seven years experience in the aerospace industry in the development and delivery of logistics products and services to government and commercial customers in the U.S. and overseas. Extensive experience in providing engineering. Training in logistics products and services through concurrent engineering and Integrated Product Team (IPT) applications. Experienced cost account manager from proposal development through final contract closure. Provides in-company and local level training for logisticians pursuing their Certified Professional Logistician status.

RELATED EXPERIENCES AND PERFORMANCE

Develop, manage and present logistics technical training for personnel seeking their Certified Professional Logistician recognition from SOLE – The International Society of Logistics – A 300+ hour train9ing program that covers all areas of logistics in the design, manufacturing, customer support and retirement segments of the product life cycle.

Develop in-house training for advanced technical education in Logistics Engineering and Management.

Member of Raytheon Six Sigma Team (Specialist) for implementation of Six Sigma for engineering change procedure.

EDUCATION

Nova Southeastern University – 2001; Doctor of Business Administration in Information Technology

New Hampshire College – 180; Master of Business

University of Maryland – 1978; Bachelor of Science/Business Administration

OTHER

The Sigma Beta Delta National Honor Society for Business, Management and Administration

Franklin Pierce College Graduate Advisory Council, 2001-2003

Adjunct Professor, Florida Institute of Technology, Master Program for Logistics, 2001-2003

Adjunct Professor, Franklin Pierce College, School of Graduate & Professional Studies, 2001-2003

Adjunct Professor, Southern New Hampshire University, School of Graduate & Professional Studies, 2002-2003

Director of Management and Strategy Division SOLE; 2002-2003

Logistics Education Foundation, Board of Governors; 2001-2003

Management and Strategy Application Director for SOLE; 2002-2003

Vice President, Professional and Technical Development, SOLE – The International Society of Logistics; 1999-2001

Vice President, Operations, Boston Chapter SOLE; 1998, 1999

Vice President, Administration, Boston Chapter SOLE; 1998

ROLE OF STANDARDS IN REALIZATION OF INTEGRATED LOGISTICS SUPPORT ON NATIONAL LEVEL

Rados Popadic, M.Sc.
Public Enterprise of PTT communication "Srbija", Serbia and Montenegro

Abstract

Leading along with modern tendency in development and appliance of computer and telecomunication technologies, in accordance with changed global social milieu and economy needs in Serbia, creating and installing activities of modern integral information system on national level are intensified. The most important standards of CALS strategy (Continuous Acquisition and Life-cycle Support) as basis for realisation of logistics support of national level in Serbia, that is for realization of participants' integration from civil and military sector. Paper presents characteristics of CALS strategies, standard's role and importance of installing CALS strategy, rezults of standard using in highly developed countries' economy, factors that would support reality of implementation and possible way of realization CALS strategy in Serbia building upon standards. With standardization and installing of unique language it would be possible heterogeneous system connect, and make effective and efficiant logistics support (maintainability, reliability, supportability, availability, testability, affordability…) possible and therefore providing more performance of bussines and military systems in and among those systems.

1. Introduction

If applied in an organised manner, IT ensures timely availability of support elements of military, business and technical systems, and their integrated action. Revolution in the field of communications and information provides for many abilities and presents a resource which changes manner of work and economic action. A concept that stands out by its achievements after it was widely applied first in military and then economic organisations, is known as the CALS integral logistics information system. That is a logistics concept that presents a logistics paradigm of modern military and economic action. It is dealing with rationalisation, integration and flexibility system increase in the most direct manner, thus raising effectiveness and efficiency of military and economic systems to the highest level. This strategy presents an acknowledged and standardised strategy of electronic documenting of processes within product lifetime and of systems on the whole. It enables timely performance of operation with minimal expenses. Assuming that the logistics today is dealing with integration issues of material, information and energetic flows by the integrated provision of qualitative (by sorts), quantitative (by quantity) and terminal (by time-limits) availability of system elements used for management at minimal costs, CALS strategy should stand as its information support.

At the beginning of 21st century, in the world of computer and communication technologies domination where an abundance of information is created, collected, exchanged and used in the shortest time and at the highest level of quality to meet the high demands of the market, employees and public opinion. In order to provide material, energetic and information resources, logistics requires application of the latest technologies. Thus, interconnection becomes important, for purposes of information exchange among a supplier, producer, distributor, shipper and seller, where the results of computer technology, such as Internet, Intranet, Extranet, Web, etc. have a decisive role.

2. Place of standards in CALS strategy implementation

Standardisation can be described as a process for solution choice, determination and application of technical and technological ideas and procedures, technology and practical experience, as well as prediction of both positive and negative effects, in order to reach solutions that have to comply with the development level, policy and goals of one country, region or with international requirements. In its essence, standardisation is directed towards reduction of product and procedure variants, towards easier communication, general efficiency and security. Standardisation helps people to satisfy various spheres of interest (of life, health, environment), then it helps to save energy and material, to protect customers, to defend a country, to eliminate technical obstacles in the international turnover, to provide a level of "socially justified quality and other goals".

What is often noted as a disadvantage of standardisation is a reduction of abilities for "freedom": for imagination and innovation, for example, in design, which is limited by standards or what they proscribe by some authors. It is most often the problem due to delay in updating and modernisation of standards.

The core of CALS concept is to change business processes. IT sets a framework for this change, while the standards provide support in creation and exchange of information. In strategy implementation, international standards are used (acknowledged by ISO and IEC, and related to ERP and telecommunication protocols, such as TCP/IP), but there are also standards which are now verified and used in the countries where the CALS strategy has been implemented. A motion to make them verified by the international standardisation institutions has been initiated and their adoption is expected. These standards have been created by the authors of CALS concept and have been for the first time developed in USA (series of military standards –MIL-ATD), and later also in other countries for their specific needs (e.g. Great Britain is known by *DEF STAN 00-60* standard).

The particular place of standard in CASL strategy implementation in USA is shown in the picture 1.

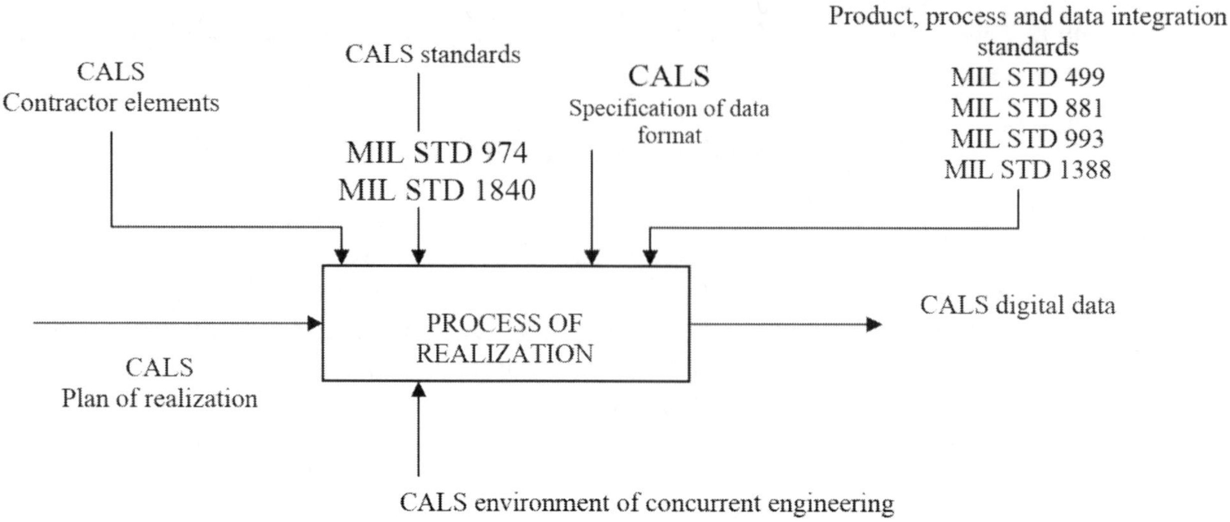

Picture1. Process of realization CALS strategy in u USA [5]

Needs and requirements of contracting party are specified in the following documents: Request for bid, Governmental operation concept and Contractor's approach to CALS strategy.

The CALS realisation plan describes ways in which the contractor will apply CALS strategy techniques during the contract validity, in order to meet the requirements related to services, infrastructure, data format and media to be specified in the contract. The CALS concept standards are used to strictly define procedures in connection with data format and source, manner of transfer and relations among users, so that there is no possibility for improvisation is left in their implementation.

Standard 974 defines framework for *on-line* approach and sharing of digital data of Government. Every contractor has ITISU *on-line* service. In this way, digital data are more easily updated, stored, controlled, reproduced and distributed.[8]

Standard 1840 – Automated technical information exchange. It defines format for exchange of digital technical data in CALS environment. This standard precisely defines interfaces of computer technology which automate creation, storing and dispatch of technical manuals, engineering drawings and other digital data. It also precisely defines standard formats and document productions, standards for document presentation, conventions for naming of documents and files for digital data transfer and shows how the data should be registered.[3]

CALS specifications of data formats. In this segment the data format specifications for data dispatch to Government are prescribed. These specifications are controlled by SGML Convention for textual documents processing, vector and graphic files, and engineering data on projecting and product. The following standards of series 28000 are used: *MIL-STD 28000, MIL -M-28001, MIL -R-28002, MIL -D-28003.*

Standards on integration of products, processes and data. Application of CALS strategy should enable competition and integrated work of all participants and teams: the ones dealing in projecting, development, production, support, etc, but first with assistance of high-quality shared data.

Standard *MIL-STD 499*: Engineering management. This standard is related to defining, execution, management and development of procedures used in order to decide upon business processes of procurement and technology development. The standard is applied as a technical foundation for competitive engineering, it supports integration of data related to the product, advances development while demanding simultaneous development of product and support for product, in order to meet user's requirements. All these is facilitated by use of multidisciplinary approach and methodology of system engineering.[4]

Standard *MIL-STD 881*: Standard on decomposition of material items. This standard determines the criteria of Government for preparation and establishment of approaches for consideration of data structure, and it is used during procurement of the necessary materials ordered by Government. Uniformity in procurement defining enables harmonisation of requirements defined in different manners. Therefore, the standard sets rules how to make a unique marking system for differently marked requirements.[2]

Standard *MIL-STD 973*: Configuration management. It describes a way for application of technical and administrative instructions through product lifetime and describes in technical documentation both functional and physical characteristics of present or future hardware and software solutions (which was necessary for better recognition of needs related to the product purpose).

Standard *MIL-STD 1388-1A*: Logistics support analysis. The standard lays out general requirements of Logistics Support Analysis (LSA) and describes support implemented during the product lifetime. It aims at a unique and uniformed access to the Logistics Support Analysis to perform necessary activities to accomplish the following:

a) To enable that support requirements be the integral part of design and development;
b) To define the requirements for support that optimally meets the needs in design and other system and equipment development processes;
c) To define the required support and, subsequently, the phases of exploitation;
d) To prepare data for product tracking – from the initial idea to the product withdrawal from use.[1]

Fundamental assumptions of the Analysis Logistics Support Analysis system are defined in a *MIL-STD* 1388-1A standard, as well as in the AMO Document No. 5000-39 under the name "Procurement and Management of the Integral Logistics Support of Systems and Equipment".

The management of the Analysis of the Logistics Support may be divided into three areas:

a) Resource definition and provision;
b) LSA process integration and handling;
c) Application of the LSA process results.[6]

According to the *MIL-STD 1388-1A* standard documents, the LSA system is divided into five general sections, and every section contains a certain number of activities (15 in total) and subactivites (77 in total). In addition to the section description, the respective activities and subactivities will be analysed, to demonstrate the application of the standards by their better understanding.

MIL-STD 1388-1A standard defines four elements for each and every one of the activities:

- goal;
- structure;
- input data;
- output data.

MIL-STD 1388-2A Standard. It is closely related to the *MIL-STD 1388-1A* standard, as it deals with the data sources requested for the logistics support analysis.[7]

The *MIL-STD 1388-2A* standard is a regulatory standard of the data registration domain, within the SRPI analysis of the logistics support. According to it, 15 groups are defined (from A to O) with total of 547 data. The standard sets rules for each of the data as follows:

- data type (belonging to the group);
- data meaning;
- data length;
- data codification (if there is one).

The data requested for the registration of the logistics support are grouped as follows:

A-Exploitation and maintenance requests;
B-Maintenance reliability and suitability properties;
B1- Analysis of failures and their effects;
B2-Analysis of failure danger and maintenance suitability;
C-Overview of exploitation and maintenance activities;
D- Analysis of exploitation and maintenance activities;
D1- Requests in human resources and support;
E and E1-Description of support equipment and educational instruments;
E2-Tested units and programs of automated testing;
F-Infrastructure description;
G-Assessment of staff qualification;
H-Identification of elements of support;
H1-Identification of support elements
J-Technical properties of the transportability.

The possible content of the realised database is shown at the Picture 2. As experiences are gained and the database grows, it comes possible to introduce knowledge-based system that records the past experiences and can be used to test new knowledges in relation to the troublemaking characteristics in the past. The experience of the advanced users has shown that the positive results of the simultaneous design engineering, as well as for holding of the working meetings, can be highlighted.

When the CALS strategy realisation is dealt with, one can conclude that it is composed of:

- re-engineering of some of or all the processes in the company, including design and engineering and procurement, as well as the product support management within the whole lifetime;

- practical application of advanced computing tools, techniques and successful operational results;
- use of shared integrated digital data in the system that is controllably open to the environment;
- harmonised use of specific information-related and other standards to enable successful information management, integration, and sharing with the environment.[12]

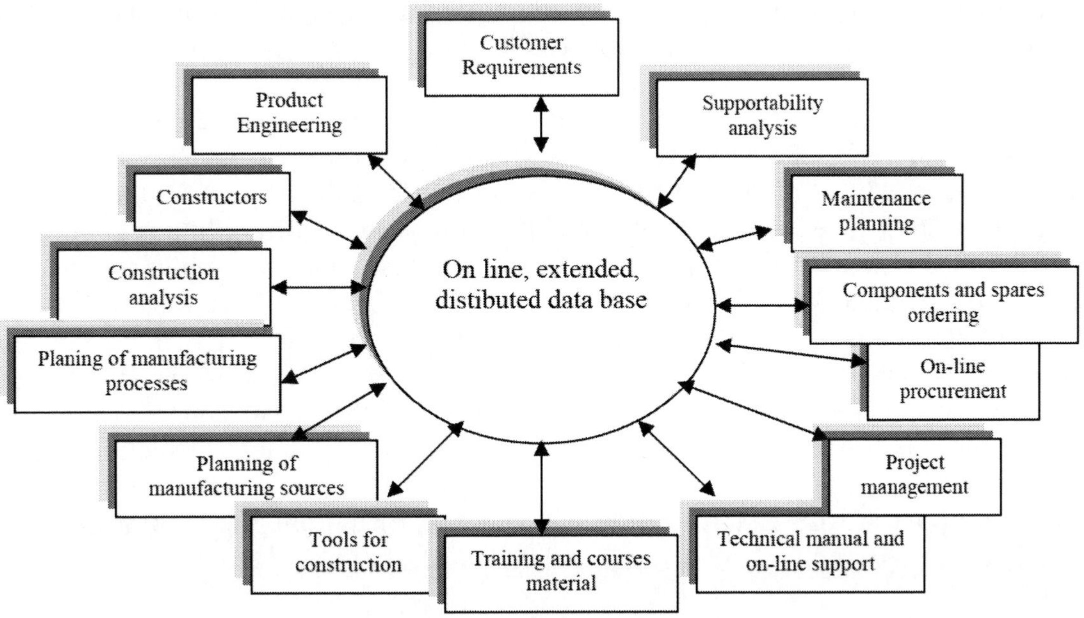

Picture 2. Shared data base in CALS environment [11]

Improvements at the business processes achieved by the CALS strategy include:

a) improved quality of information managing the system as a whole, and support to planning, procurement, and maintenance;
b) better system reliability;
c) modernisation of the generation of new products and services by linking databases and data requesting processes;
d) procurement and support cost reduction by elimination of manual, doubled and failure-generating operations;
e) reduction of footprint and weight of the stored matters;

f) creation of possibilities of operational modernisation: electronic ordering, contracting and payments, etc.
g) virtually immediate availability of the information requested from the environment.[4]

Thus is mentioned the example of the Boeing 777 aeroplane as the first constructed completely by computer programs, without physical prototype. Everybody wondered how it was made possible to carry out a very complicated project in such a manner. The answer lies in the application of the above-mentioned standards of the CALS strategy.

Good example is also the development of the "Viking" submarine, the project jointly realised by the governments of Finland, Sweden, Denmark and Norway. The CALS strategy's role in this business was to integrate all the participants from the very commencement. What was the most important to expect from the CALS concept was the reduction of the procurement and support expenses in the whole lifetime of this "product", the enhancement of the information flow among the participants and the provision of the adequate concept of relevant information management within the "Viking" project. The goals of the strategy of information management by CALS concept were the improvement of quality within the product lifetime, the data accuracy and the reduction of design, development and production costs by 10 per cent.

By implementation of the CALS concept for contracting the spare parts for B-1, F-15, F-16 and F-117 aircrafts, the U.S. Navy has decreased its expenses by 28.9%. Also, an information is presented that more than five billion US dollars will be spent for the ASP software support model by 2003. The percentage of companies doing businesses online is going strikingly upwards: 81% in the year 2000 (55% of companies with less than ten employees) and 63% in 1999 (only 15% of companies with less than ten employees).

The United States of America and Great Britain at the moment are the two leading countries in the world by use and reach of the CALS concept application. The best results of the CALS strategy application in the military and business systems of these two countries are presented above. The results are divided into four groups due to importance of each particular area.

Logistics support. CALS enables full implementation of the integrated information system (integrated database):

- data are created once and are used many times by many users;
- quality of the activity management is steady;
- tracking of completed jobs is easier;
- error number is decreased by 98% (errors due to manual labour, doubling and information transfer);
- data exchange is faster;
- multiple common levels of executive monitoring are enabled;
- education time "along the way" is decreased by 70-80%.

The access to the technical data is easier and they are more intelligible:

- 40% time is saved in the process of searching for the information;
- operability of the work is increased;

- the data are managed by a variety of media (audio, video, colour image, 3-D animation, virtual reality);
- value-recognition is easy, as well as authenticity check of the data sources;
- one and the same data group is interpreted in multiple ways;
- technical data are distributed more easily, as all employees are provided with the possibility of supplying technical information through various processes;
- feedback response is decreased by nine times.

Procurement. Assistance in process planning through:

- reduction in useless time (30%-70%),
- early detection of risks,
- eliminating of unnecessary expenses, by use of control points and continual check-up,
- recognition of risks and time reduction in delays, external control, supervision, tracking, reviews and prices,
- reduction in time for development and risk reduction by quick changes in engineering,
- ability for process automatisation for e-ordering, e-contracting and e-payment (10%-40% less activities for every process).[8]

Engineering. Integration of processes through Competitive Engineering:

- an approach which is oriented to entire lifetime of product (service) and business system (20% savings in support expenses),
- team work (multi-disciplinary groups or integrated production teams),
- introduction of right skills in right time,
- swifter response in processes of decision-making through entire lifetime of product, service, business system.

Production. Promotion of management processes in production through automation:

- 98% shorter time of system response,
- "right on time" production,
- reduction in currently unnecessary activities on quality tracking by 80%,
- reduction in number of production problems by 80%,
- reduced number of problems in work overlapping during production by 88%, by use of CAD/CAM/CAE.[9]

3. Feasibility of implementation CALS on the national level in Serbia

The CALS strategy is applied worldwide, so there are announcements for further prospects of this concept. Mr. Michio Naruto, Executive Vice-President in "Fujitsu Ltd" from Japan, claims that those who immediately take advantages that CALS strategy offers, would reach the top. Mr. Rod Leggeter, a GEC Marconi Manager from Great Britain, says that nature of their complex business systems facilitates presence of many participants in the projects; CALS strategy allows direct connection of suppliers and partners with their electronic data on product.

In favour of this concept application also speak successful use of it in the following countries: the USA, Canada, France, Great Britain, Germany, Spain, Portugal, Sweden, North Korea and Japan.

The European Community also advocates for full implementation of this concept, as another way for adequate business integration of European countries. So the CALS strategy implementation has begun in Czech Republic, and it is also planned to be introduced in Hungary. Since North Korea and Japan are not politically and economically close countries, they have chosen to implement this concept as their way to bring them closer together. An Economic Forum for PBS Strategy was founded in 1999 in Japan, which gathered together 130 companies from Japan by the end of the same year.

It should be noted that an adaptable organizational structure will be essential for the new generations of enterprises: training of highly-specialized and flexible teams, that can be quickly formed, completed and discharged after a performed task. Reduction of product life cycles implies reduction of development time. Mr. J.S. Mayo, President of "AT&T Bell Laboratories" anticipates that the cycles of designing for complex chips in 2010 will be only 3 days. According to him, flexible work force would be necessary for implementation of these projects, especially regarding skills, knowledge, location and availability.

In "UKCeB" organization Executive Guide for CALS strategy implementation stands an information that application of the strategy reduces the time for introduction of a new product by 50%. A basic advantage which is pointed out here is "Availability of the right information in the right moment".[10]

The announcement from 1992 of North Atlantic Treaty Organization study group (in charge of cooperation with economy), stating that "CALS strategy implementation in economy will bring about revolution in organization, management and performances of both big and small companies" is proved again and again: it is particularly obvious in relation to the increase of enterprise profitability, to the satisfaction of both employees and customers, and by raising military systems performances to a higher level.

Return of SaM (Serbia and Monte Negro) under the auspices of International Monetary Fund, open perspective for future cooperation with the World Bank, London and Paris Club, all these are facts that present conditions for economic stability of the country, and contribute to determination to "keep up the pace" with Europe. At a state level, the efforts are made to create preconditions for joining "Partnership For Peace". This would determine the Army of SaM for longer period, and the preparations for cooperation within South-Eastern Europe Stability Pact and OSCE. All the above facts present a very concrete steps towards full membership in European Community.

The mentioned tendencies make a good foundation for more serious approach to solving of issues related to information area in our country, so the following activities of competent bodies should be singled out:

- "Sinergija" Assembly, dealing with IT, at which the "Microsoft" company was promoted into an executive consultant for creation of future information strategy in Serbia,
- Draft Act on E-business and E-signature was submitted for consideration to the Government of the Republic of Serbia, which should be the first step in e-business implementation,

A two-day Seminar on assets codification was held in Belgrade at the close of April, 2001, supported by the Greek Defence Ministry. The lecturers at the Seminar were from "P.A.S.S defence" Greek agency, while the representatives of the SaM Army and military industry of our country were in the audience. At this Assembly which was first in a series of a few that took place until March 2003, the NATO Codification System was presented for the first time, and importance of its application for those who want to enter and act on the NATO Member Countries market was emphasized. It was also pointed out that the application of this way of nomenclature would signify the first step of a country for joining in "Partnership for Peace". Having in mind that our state policy is taking this course, one can conclude that the realisation of a unique nomenclature is a condition for always faster development of both logistics and national integrated information system.

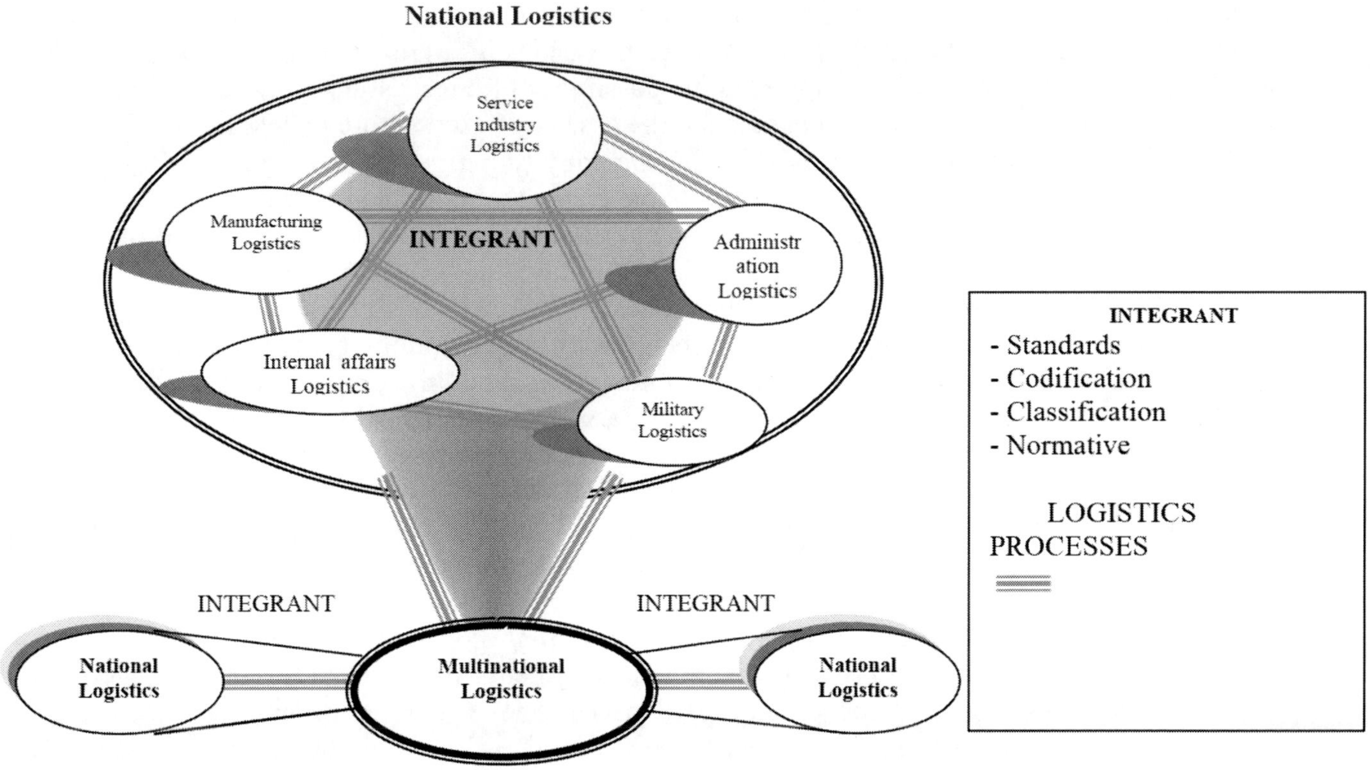

Picture 3. Integration concept on the national level

4. Effects of application of the CALS concept on the national level

The effects can be observed by analysis of the basic logistics processes.

Supply, storage and distribution. It is essential to carry out the system of timely supply – by using the JIT approach ('just in time'), while the timely supply is provided using the Material Requirements Planning – by types, quantities and periods of time. It is possible to realise the software support of the chains of supply, using modern approaches:

- WMS (Warehouse Management System)
- TMS (Transportation Management System)

- APS (Advance Planning and Scheduling)

In connection with the distribution logistics, there would be realised the concept of the distribution network, as well as the planning of the distribution processes.

Maintenance of technical systems. Functional ability of the system on the whole lifetime is secured at minimal expenses, by tracking and analysis of failures and modern models of maintenance of the technical systems. The On-Condition Maintenance (OCM) and Reliability Centred Maintenance (RCM), Model of Logistics Maintenance, Total Productive Maintenance, Model of Proactive Maintenance, as well as Model of Maintenance IT System would be realised.[13]

Money saving. Logistics managers should know where the stocks are and in what quantity. If the NATO codification system is used (as a part of the stocks control system), they have a tool to recognise the goods to be allocated to various locations within the system, whether it be the state or the world. Thus is avoided the possibility of unnecessary stock accumulation, as well as storage and stored assets expenses, and the assets are used before the expiration date. The recent paper of the *KPMG Peat Marwick LLP* company (a part of the US Agency of Logistics) has stated that the privately owned companies have created a 'more than fifty per cent' savings in the stocks, using standard methods of asset recognition and tracking. Also, the paper presented the example of two companies that used the NATO codification system and decreased their stock level by 75 and 97 million US dollars respectively.

Prevention of piling-up stocks. As new and old generations of equipment often have common parts, the Codification System eliminates the doubling of the funds at the supply system. The US experiences (as in the country of large production), show that 30 per cent of the newly-arrived parts have already been found at the existing catalogues. This percentage is often even larger in other countries using the Codification System (e.g., in Canada it is 60%), which means that 60% of the spare parts purchased to support the new equipment or weaponry system have already been in the old catalogues and are used with the total support of the NATO Codification System. Thus expire the needs in stock accumulation.[2]

Lower purchase price. Many branch offices across the country can buy the same assets. Within the NATO Codification System (its purchase system, more precisely), the managers can quickly recognise the same items and compare prices. They are given possibility to buy larger quantities of goods at a lower price. Just imagine the savings that would be made possible within the NATO pact on the whole. An independent study of the NATO Management and Supply Agency (NAMSA) has shown that the potential savings can be as much as 20 billion US dollars in the ten-year time. **Improvement of the logistics activities**. NATO Codification System assists the chains of supply among the military branches: Navy, Infantry, Air Forces, and between the private and the military industries.

The interoperability among the NATO member countries enables a shared supply support for several countries, as the NATO Codification System functions at an international level. For instance, Germany, Poland and Bulgaria, while cooperating within the 'Partnership for Peace' programme, can exchange the supply and maintenance much more readily. They use a *lingua franca* of understanding that enables the simplification of the technical dialogue between the countries and the customers.

Time savings in spare parts supply. If the managers at the military have a tool to quickly identify their spare part stocks, they have better position to supply the right spare part at the right place and at the right time.

Faster identification of goods to supply. Precise description of the goods to supply, followed by a simplier catalogue usage, enables the prompt procurement of needed goods.

Better tracking of suppliers. Codification System includes the system of recognition and tracking of the commercial suppliers. In combination with the supply systems, the managers can systematically trace any critical information as a contractor's performance, as well as the addresses and the phone numbers.

Commercial sources history. Logisticians can use the history of the data sources, in relation with the purchase. This can be useful if it is difficult to provide the goods.

Tracking of important information. System supports the availability of all important information in relation with the goods: type of material, environmental risks, special storage procedures, etc.

5. Conclusion

CALS presents an international initiative and is a result of the aspiration at achieving the systematic improvement of the business systems/projects effectiveness and efficiency. One can conclude that the CALS, as a concept established on the standard-based digital data transfer among diversed databases, enables the linking of the processes of research and development, design, supply, transport, production, maintenance, etc., all of which being the isolated 'isles of information' in the traditional sequential approach. In addition to the process linking, the process participants are integrated by using the ERP: contractors, shippers, suppliers, customers, consultants, providers. As the basis of integration at the level of international, national, civil and military logistics, CALS can serve as an opportunity to realise a comprehensive Serbian concept, instead of starting new and partial information system concept at a national level every once in a while.

One should bear in mind that the value generation from the information system needs organisational and procedural changes. Insofar as these changes are not accomplished, the chances of profitable implementation of the new information system are only too small. Most oftenly, the main reason behind the failure of many a similar project was the lack of paying attention to these issues. In our country, the technology was, most oftenly, not used to change the nature of the work, but to automate the old system of operation. As a result, the customers were frustrated by the information system acting not as a change catalyst, but as an obstacle to the changes. Traditional bureaucratic approaches, associated with the hierarchical structure, severely hinder the ability of an organisation to a prompt reaction, to it be flexible and modern.

To make the integration possible at a national level, it is inevitable to introduce a unique codification system. Thus, the resources are spared, the full visibility of any information related to the status of goods is possible, as well as the precise identification of troubles and standstills. The possibility of an immediate access to the requested logistics information and documents in order to provide logistics support regardless to the user location and distance, at minimal expenses, has become reality thanks to the appropriate codification system. It is true that the business systems in our country, provided that the state coordinates the activities, should implement a united codification system as one of the means of integration in the environment and of the more effective trade.

Changes in social conditions, the goals of the military authorities set to reorganise the Army of Serbia and Montenegro (ASaM) into a modern army of the 21st century with the high combat powers and readiness, accompanied by a reduction in size, are only a few of the reasons to consider the CALS concept as the possible solution. The US General Gordon Sullivan, while coining the term 'FORCE XXI' as the military concept for the 21st century, also defines further commitment of the information support in the military. "The 21st century army shall be digitised… FORCE XXI is directed toward a tactical units re-design, but must be more than that. Information technologies enable us a complete new overview of the entire organisation. Management and control depend on the present situation, the organisations make network that connect electronically and not geographically".

CALS has a perspective to completely solve the problem of logistics support at the military systems, the system built in peace to effectively function at the complex war activities, taking logistics support as a dynamic system continually developed and modernised. The author's assessment is that, provided that it is implemented correctly and with full functionality, the CALS strategy would have a positive impact to the development of the Serbian national logistics and would facilitate the involvement with the international community and the ASaM's collaboration within its framework.

As expected, it is not easy to realise such a comprehensive information system. The realisation must be well-considered, planned and supported by proper human resources (knowledge) and financial funds (money). It is an established practice to make assessments of possibilities and consequences of application of the CALS concept.

Bibliography

1. Vasiljević, D., Computer aided logistics*: models and trends*, FON, Belgrade, 2001.
2. "*A Metrics Model for NATO Use*", A report to the Conference of National Armament Directors, October 2000., www.dcnicn.com/ncmb
3. *"Managing in the 21st century"*, UKCEB, 1999.
4. Military Handbook, CALS - Implementation guide, www.acq.osd.mil
5. MIL-STD 1388-1A, www.nslc.fmso.navy.mil
6. Standard MIL-STD 1388-1A, www.kolacki.com
7. Standard MIL-STD 974, www.acq.osd.mil
8. Standard MIL-STD 1388-2A, www.kolacki.com
9. "*CALS-Integrating Business Process for Productivity and Quality*", Executuve Newsletter-CALS, August 2000.
10. "*CALS BENEFITS MATRIX* ", www.dao.defence.gov.au
11. *CALS-Implementation guide*, Military handbook 59B, www.acq.osd.mil/cals
12. *CALS-The Executive Guide*, UK CALS Industry Council, 1997.
13. "*What is CALS & How it help*", Executive Newsletter-CALS, September 1999.

SHORT BIOGRAPHY

30 years old from Yugoslavia. He finished the Faculty of Electrical Engineering in Belgrade 1997 and Master science program in logistics 2003. He has been participant of numerous congresses, conferences and symposiums in Yugoslavia and worldwide. He has published in Yugoslavia, scientific and expert papers on conferences, symposiums and journals. He works for Public Enterprise of Postal, Telegraph and Telephone traffic "Srbija", as a Head of Quality Department. He is SOLE member.

China's Logistics Industry and WTO: A Trend of Globalization

Daiheng Ni and Chunxia Feng

School of Civil and Environmental Engineering,
Georgia Institute of Technology, Atlanta, GA 30332

ABSTRACT

China's logistic industry catches eyes of those interested foreign firms and China's domestic enterprises. This research pieces together the general environment for logistics development in China, including economic situation, transportation infrastructure, and information technology systems. Based on this, logistics players are identified, the regulatory framework is outlined, and the challenges and opportunities are analyzed, especially those brought about by World Trade Organization (WTO). This paper highlights key issues in China's logistics industry and provides a comprehensive reference for Multinational Corporations that want to establish their footholds in China.

Key words: Logistics, WTO, Infrastructure, China, Globalization.

1. OVERVIEW

In the past two decades, East Asian and Pacific region has experienced dramatic economic growth. Following the success stories of Japan, Singapore, Hong Kong, South Korea, and Taiwan is the remarkable development of China. China has demonstrated, and will continue to show, its fast growth and vast potential. Even taking into consideration of Asian financial crisis that began in 1997, China achieved annual gross domestic product (GDP) growth rate of 7.79 percent in the past five years, contrasting the 2.77 percent of the world, 2.76 percent of European Union, and 3.70 percent of the United States *(1)*. Today, China's economy is measured at nearly 1.16 trillion U.S. dollars (US$) and trade volumes to and from Asian ports are growing at a healthy rate.

Modern logistics, known as the third profit source in China, is soaring following network fever. Fast developing transportation and information infrastructure and the great demand for mass production and fast circulation has prepared a huge stage for logistics in China. With the entry of China into WTO, enormous opportunities as well as challenges are faced by logistics players of both China's domestic and overseas. A basic understanding of the size of the logistics market, the infrastructure on which modern logistics runs, the regulatory systems that govern logistics activities, and the problems and future directions of the industry are, therefore, of great interest to those interested parties.

2. GENERAL ENVIRONMENT FOR CHINA'S LOGISTICS DEVELOPMENT

China is the third largest country in the world in terms of territory. One of the most fascinating parts of this country is, perhaps, the vast market brought about, at least in part, by its huge population - nearly 1.3 billion or 22 percent of the world population, with 30 percent of urban population and 70 percent of rural population. This population is growing at annual rate of 0.9 percent.

This section pulls together the sectors closely related to logistics development and gives a full picture of the general environment where logistics industry thrives. These sectors include economy situation, transportation infrastructure and information platform.

2.1 Economic Environment

Economic sector is too big a topic to fit in the limited space, so this section focuses on China's GDP growth and how it compares with the world, China's banking system, foreign trade and investment, and issues with China's economy.

General Economic Environment

The past decade has witnessed unprecedented improvement in China's economic development. According to The World Bank Group, China's GDP totaled US$1.16 trillion in 2001, nearly doubling that of 1990, and China's per capita GNI reached US$890 in 2001. These numbers compare with European Union's US$6.05 trillion and US$21,730, United State's US$10.17 trillion and US$37,870, and the world's US$31.28 trillion and US$5,140, respectively.

Banking System

There are four largest banks in China, namely, People's Bank of China (PBOC), Agricultural bank of China (ABC), China Construction Bank (CCB), and Industrial and Commercial Bank of China (ICBC). After more than a decade's reformation, PBOC is transformed to be a central financial institution and the sole source of currency issue. The nation's international accounts and foreign currency arrangements are the primary concern of PBOC, which has nearly 50 foreign branches, including offices in New York, Hong Kong, Singapore, and London.

Foreign Trade and Investment

Despite difficult international circumstances, China's foreign trade volume in 2001 reached US$509.8 billion, a year-on-year growth of 7.5 percent according to China's customs statistics. Of the total, exports grew 6.8 percent to US$266.2 billion and imports rose 8.2 percent to US$243.6 billion. The contracted volume of foreign investment totaled US$69.2 billion, 10.4 percent increase, with the amount of foreign investment in place jumping 14.9 percent to US$46.9 billion. China's primary trading partners include the United States, Japan, Taiwan, South Korea, Hong Kong, Germany, Singapore, and Russia.

In the past few decades, China has been seeking ways to integrate into the world's trading system. In 1991, China jointed the Asia Pacific Economic Cooperation group (APEC), which promotes free trade and cooperation in economic, trade, investment, and technology issues. The long road to the entry of WTO was yet another endeavor. In November 1999, the United States and China reached a bilateral market-access agreement, paving the way for China to WTO. As part of the agreement, China agreed to lower its tariffs and abolish market impediments after its entry of the world trading body. The agreements with EU and other trading partners are reached in summer 2000, and China became a member of WTO in 2001.

Key Issues in Economic Development

China runs a unique system: Socialism and Market Economy. Very often, this system suffers the downsides of the combination: bureaucracy, lassitude, and corruption of socialism, and windfall gains and stepped-up inflation of capitalism. The transition from "rule by personnel" to "rule by law" has a long way to go, which partly contributes to the unsatisfactory economic environment.

The national banking system is heavily exposed with tremendous bad loan burdens. Most of them are related to State-Owned Enterprises. The state sector is the core of the challenge faced by China's economy. The problem of long run declining efficiency in the use of resources, a major stimulus for undertaking reform, is most acute in the state sector. Reform taken by the government has yet to achieve the expected result.

The absence of reliable data on markets is another big problem. Business people are very skeptical to the pronouncements from the National Bureau of Statistics and the rosy government brochures. This has implications for both the government and the potential investors.

2.2 Transportation Infrastructure

China's transportation has undergone profound changes in recent years. According to National Bureau of Statistics (NBS) of China, Chinese government poured US$ 761 billion into 1,553 infrastructure projects in the past decade. China now boasts over 70 thousand km of railway with an annual increase rate of 2.87%, 1.7 million km of highways with an annual increase rate of 3.47%, 121.5 thousand km of inland navigable waterways with an annual increase rate of 0.88%, 1.55 million km aviation routes with an annual increase rate of 16.88% , and 27.6 thousand km of oil and gas pipeline with an annual increase rate of 5.25%). In addition, China has launched a total of 1,143 airlines for domestic and overseas travel. On the other hand, many serious problems still exist in China's transportation sector, which, if not addressed properly, will hamper the country's economic development. First, undeveloped infrastructures significantly raise the costs of inventory and transportation. According to World Bank statistics, goods lost due to poor or obsolete transportation infrastructure amounted to one percent of China's GDP in mid 1990's. Even though this has been constantly improving, the avoidable goods lost is still considerable. Second, service quality and efficiency are often poor because the maintenance groups are small and not well equipped. Employee training has yet to be improved, and quality assurance has yet to be strengthened. Third, coastal ports are themselves competing for container transportation. There are thirteen major shipping ports with a capacity of over 5 million tons per year. Most of the hinterlands for these ports are overlapped. This unfortunately undermines the utilization rate of fix assets of major ports, such as Shanghai and Shenzhen, which are ranked as the top two container ports in China.

2.3 Information Platform

Information platform is a critical to modern logistics industry. This section gives a general overview of China's national information infrastructure, with an emphasis on e-commerce.

National Information Infrastructure

Since the 9th Five-Year Plan period (1996-2000), China's postal and telecommunication industries have been developed at a quick pace and equal in proportion to the country's GDP growth. This trend is speeded up during China's 10th Five-Year Plan (2001-2005) that gives IT industry the top priority for development. China has now become the third largest information industry in the world. The Ministry of Information Industry estimated that China's electronic and IT industry is expected to grow by 30 percent to US$ 253 billion in 2003. The scale of communication networks of both fixed (135 million main lines in use) and mobile (65 million mobile cellular) are next only to the United States (194 and 69 million, respectively). In this period China's whole value for communication business reached $48.2 billion to show a yearly increase of 33 percent. The market for basic telecom business, previously dominated by China Telecom, has been opened to various telecom developers.

Internet in China has developed rapidly since the start of Internet in the early 1990's. Backbone networks (ISP's) in China have grown from the first 4, namely China Telecom Network (ChinaNet, 163), China Golden Bridge Network (ChinaGBN, 167), China Science & Technology Network (CSTNet), and China Education & Research Network (CERNet), to 10 with China Unicom Network (UniNet, 165), China Netcom Network (CNCNet, 171), China Great Wall Network (CGWNet), China International Ecomomy & Trade Network (CIETNet), China Mobile Network (CMNet), and China Statellite Network (CSNet) added to the pool. The number of Chinese Internet subscribers is nearly 35 million, and is growing at an annual rate of 100 percent. However, 80% of China's data traffic is still carried by the largest backbone, ChinaNet, which is owned by China Telecom. ChinaNet has 2.5Gbps backbone bandwidth and 4,580Mbps international bandwidth, but the others are relatively weak in network coverage and bandwidth capability. International connectivity has reached a total of 2,799Mbps including 213Mbps for Voice over IP (VOIP). Figure 1 partially shows the connectivity of China's backbone networks.

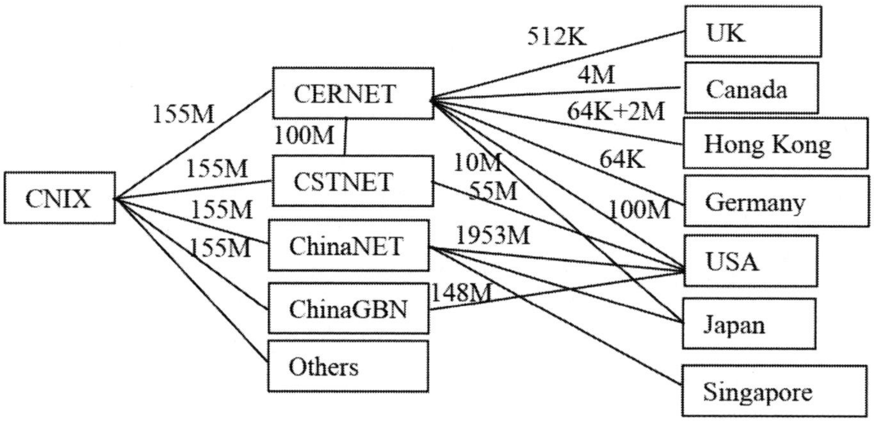

Where: CNIX (China Network Interchange)
Source: Jianping Wu, China Education & Research Network (CERNET).

Figure 1 China's National Information Technology Platform

E-Commerce

E-commerce relies heavily on the Internet and its users. To give a flavor of the size of Internet in China and how it compares with that of the United States, let's take a look at the estimates of . , China has 33.7 million Internet users and 25 million personal computers in 2001, according to International Telecommunication Union (ITU). These numbers compare with the United States' 143 million and 178 million, respectively. Translating to measures of per 100 population, China has 2.6 Internet users and 1.93 personal computers, while the United States has 49.95 and 62.25, respectively.

E-commerce in China is really at its incipient stage. The concept of E-commerce was introduced to China in 1993, but the first online sale didn't appear until 1998. China Electronic Commerce Association estimated that China has more than 1500 E-commerce websites at the end of April 2001, among which 44.5% are for Business-to-Consumer (B2C), and 24.7% are for Business-to-Business (B2B). B2C transaction is small in absolute terms, making up 0.018% of total retail trade in this country, comparing 1.4% in the Untied States. In 2000, the E-commerce business amounted US$9.3 billion, with B2B market predominates 96.7 percent, and B2C taking the remainder.

E-commerce is going to be profitable in the long run, but companies may not be able to benefit from it in short terms. There are many issues to resolve before E-market becomes mature. First of all, it needs time to shape people's view and habit of purchasing and nurture a culture for e-commerce. In China, especially urban area, traditional retail network is so ubiquitous that getting to stores is rarely the concern of buyers. On the other hand, with relatively low workload for the employed or the elders sitting at home, time is rarely a major concern. Ironically, the most likely e-shoppers, the young middle-class, shop online primarily for novelty. Second, China is in much need of a national credit system to foster buying on credit and protect against fraud. Meanwhile, an effective nation-wide e-banking system is called for to support online transaction. Third, barriers have to be lowered in setting up payment authentication system as well as maintaining and promoting web sites.

3. ANALYSIS OF CHINA'S LOGISTICS INDUSTRY

Frankly speaking, there were no real logistics enterprises in China in the past. Only in recent years did professional logistics companies emerge, but the number is few and the scale is small. They are far from meeting the market demand. An investigation conducted by the China Warehouse Storage Association showed that, in the next one or two years, some 45 percent of the enterprises will select new providers, of which 75 percent will choose new-type logistics enterprises instead of the old storage and transportation enterprises; and 60 percent will contract all their materials distribution business to logistics enterprises *(2)*. This implies lots of business opportunities for China's logistics market.

3.1 Logistics Market

How big is China's logistics market in a general sense? National Bureau of Statistics of China shows that China's GDP totaled US$1.16 trillion in 2001, of which logistics production accounted for 5.4 percent. A reasonable estimate of the logistics market should be somewhat around US$62.6 billion. Sharply in contrast to this was the logistics cost, which amounted to

US$215.4 billion or 18.6 percent of GDP. There was a wide margin and possible source of profit to reduce the cost to 10 percent, which is often seen in advanced countries.

A rough-cut estimate of market segmentation results in the following 7 broad categories of logistics services related to material flow:

- Material flow generated by industrial enterprises amounted to US $598.40 billion in 2001, of which 87% was generated by manufacturing industry and 13% by construction industry. Annual increase rate was 9.8% in the latest five years.
- Material flow generated by commodity circulation industry translated to US $452.95 billion in 2001, an increase rate of 10.6% in the latest five years.
- Material flow generated by agricultural produce was 777.41 million tons in 2001, increasing at a rate of 3.5% in the latest five years.
- Material flow generated in bonded areas amounted to US $18.7 billion in 2000.
- Material flow generated by import and export reached US $509.8 billion in 2001, in which 9.1% was exported to Hong Kong. The average annual increase rate was 11% in the latest five years.
- Material flow generated by recycling was approximately 150 million ton in 2000.
- Material flow handled by transportation industry in 2001 was 4630.4 billion ton-km, an annual increase rate of 4.5% in the latest five years.

Third party logistics (3PL) demand analysis *(3)* shows that urban goods distribution leads the market (taking 24.4% of the market), with storage and warehousing being the next (17.6% for each), followed by logistics forwarding (16.8%), and customs clearance, logistics information service, barcode scanning, and supply chain system design at the bottom (5.9% for each). As far as the willingness to employ 3PL service, 66.7% of electronic enterprises and 66.7% of daily chemical enterprises say yes, followed by food industry (53.7%), telecommunication (50%), medical industry (50%), and household electronics (33%).

3.2 Logistics Enterprises

Generally, there are three types of logistics enterprises. The first type includes those self-contained in large and medium sized state-owned enterprises that, traditionally, are responsible for all their logistics activities from inbound to outbound. The second type includes those private companies featuring warehousing and distribution services as their major businesses. The third type is mainly logistics joint ventures who provide 3PL services. The first two are typically domestic enterprises and the third usually involves foreign players.

China's Domestic Logistics Players

As far as services provided, there are basically two types of logistics companies. One is material flow-oriented enterprises, and the other information-oriented dotcoms. Material-oriented logistics enterprises provide value-added services such as freight transportation, warehousing, consolidation, packaging, etc. for other enterprises. Movement of goods and value-added processing are the products of this type of enterprises. Accompanying material flow is information flow, and collecting and disseminating such information is the main business of the second type of logistics firms. Internet is the environment where they thrive and logistics websites are their major products. Some Multinational Corporations (MNCs) have adopted Chinese localization strategy and are seeking cooperative partners in China or seek to renovate Chinese logistics enterprises, such as P&G, IBM and Nokia. According to International Business

Database of China, there are over 700,000 domestic logistics companies, in which 3000 offer international logistics services. Unfortunately, the number of the professional logistics companies is little, and the scale is small. They are far from meeting the market demand. China Ocean Shipping Company (COSCO) is striving to be a transnational comprehensive logistics provider featuring shipping service, marine bunker supply, road transport, air freight forwarding and Internet business. P.G. Logistics Group, the main third-party logistics enterprise in China, has built up an extensive network comprising 6 branches and 43 offices covering more than 40 mainland cities.

The pace of development of logistics in developed coastal areas in China is faster than in other places, due primarily to their advanced logistics infrastructure and equipment, such as transportation and storage facilities, information communication, goods packing and shipping. Up to now, a number of professional logistics enterprises have emerged in China's coastal areas, and some local governments have begun to study and promulgate development plans for logistics. Shenzhen, Guangzhou, Tianjin, Shanghai and Beijing are expected to become regional logistics centers in future.

Problems and opportunities facing material flow-oriented enterprises will be further discussed later. Here, let's take a look at the information-oriented enterprises. The ultimate goal of any business is profit. Logistics dotcoms are no exception. Where do their profits come from? Advertisements and premium services are the possible options. How to get people pay for these services? It depends on many things. One of the key issues is the firm's ability to access the market, which is not something that a pure dotcom can manage. On the other hand, the market for on-line B2B transaction is not bright. For example, small enterprises are either short of the finance or lack of the need, while big companies with enough resources to process logistics information tend to establish their own logistics information networks. The latter has been confirmed by industry giants such as IBM, HP, Legend, and GM. After the excitement of dotcom bubble, it is now generally believed that horizontal integration with logistics enterprises is a feasible outlet, which benefits both parties by mutually-promoting and mutually-complementing. In June 2002, Legend Group Holdings Co., one of China's leading corporations, and APL Logistics (APLL), the logistics arm of the NOL Group, a global transportation and logistics company engaged in shipping, signed a shareholding agreement in Beijing for a joint venture to provide supply chain service for China's IT businesses. Joint ventures will be a major source of third party logistics services in China. The scope of their businesses includes domestic and international ocean, land, inland waterways and air transportation, freight forwarding, warehousing and customs house brokerage. It also extends to after-sale services such as "reverse logistics" which deals with returns. Their partnership will not only provide logistics professional support to China’s IT sector in China, but also helps to sharpen its competitive edge.

Foreign Logistics Players

With its entry to WTO, China is committed to gradually relax its restrictions on logistics sector. Given the huge market size and enormous business opportunities, foreign companies are competing with each other to establish their footholds in China so as to secure their market shares within the shortest possible time. Logistic businesses open to the outside include freight transportation, freight forwarding, storage and warehousing, courier service, road and water transportation infrastructure, port facilities, etc. The majority of the businesses are classified as encouraged, with a small portion being restricted or prohibited. The way a business operates can be minority-owned, majority-owned, and wholly-owned, with each requires successively longer time to obtain permission. For example, minority-owned are generally allowed upon entry, majority-owned requires generally one year after entry, and wholly-owned generally five years. Finding business partners and establishing joint ventures are the major means by which a foreign logistics company enters Chinese market. Many of the world's leading logistics companies have setup their offices in China mainly in the form of joint venture. Businesses they operate are largely 3rd and 4th party logistics as well as self-support logistics. For example, logistics giants such as FedEx, UPS, Maersk Logistics, Exel Logistics, DHL, TNT, Nippon Express, APL Logistics, NYK Lines, Mitsui OKK Lines (MOL), and OOCL cooperated with their Chinese partners offering 3rd and 4th party logistics services. Some others have established their own logistics system in China, such as Metro, Mitsubishi, McDonald's, KFC, and Ito Yokado. Recently, the Beijing International Technology Co-operation Center reached an agreement with Essen-Based Multinational Schenker to establish a logistics joint venture in Beijing operating with a Class A license for international forwarding. Expected to begin operations in 2003, the new company will be among the first to apply for foreign majority share holding in the industry. The new joint venture will have a registered capital of US$5.7 million, of which 70% will come from Schenker and 30% from the co-operation center. The company plans to build a state-of-the-art multi-functional logistics center one kilometer from the Beijing International Airport, with a storage area of 6,000 square meters.

3.3 Regulatory Framework

Logistics in China is a new concept and is experiencing its learning process. Much has yet to be done to put it in order before the system functions smoothly and efficiently. Currently logistics is regulated or associated with multiple agencies such as governmental departments or non-governmental associations, the relationship of which is depicted in the following figure.

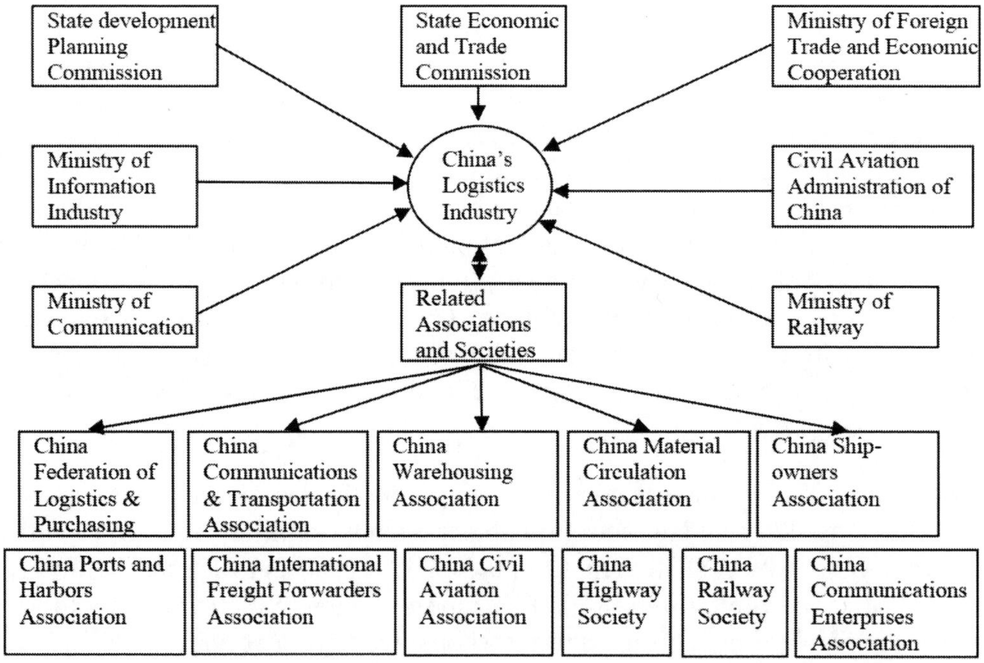

Figure 2 China logistics industry and its related agencies

The problem is that logistics sector hasn't yet formed a well-defined industry in China. Different components of logistics services are in the jurisdictions of different government ministries. For foreign companies, a single license which covers the entire scope of logistics activities does not exist. The following table lists, in part, the relationship between logistics sub-sectors and government agencies.

Table 1 Regulatory Framework for Foreign Participation in Sub-sectors

Sub-sector	Foreign Participation Encouraged/Regulated	Related Authority for License Approval
International freight forwarder	Regulated	MOFTEC
Air freight forwarder	Regulated	CAAC, MOFTEC
Logistics center	Encouraged	MoC, MOFTEC
Domestic trucking	Regulated	MoC, MOFTEC
Consolidation	Regulated	MoC, MOFTEC
Warehousing	Encouraged (sole-owned enterprise possible)	MoC, MOFTEC
Customs brokerages	Heavily regulated	CGA, MOFTEC
Shipping line	Regulated	MoC, MOFTEC
Airline	Heavily regulated	CAAC, MOFTEC

Where: MOFTEC - Ministry of Foreign Trade and Economic Co-operation, PRC
CAAC - Civil Aviation Administration of China
MoC - Ministry of Communications of the People's Republic of China
CGA - Customs General Administration People's Republic of China
Source: Hong Kong Trade Development Council

3.4 Key Issues

There are many key issues in China's logistics industry, but on the top of the list, perhaps, are the following 6:

Inefficient regulation system

As indicated in the regulatory framework, China's logistics industry is under control of multiple governmental agencies, each of which takes away a piece of cake and there is a lack of coordination. The separate and divided regulation system is manifested in long-term logistics planning. For example, government departments and many municipalities compete with each other planning for their own logistic networks. Shanghai announces its resolution of incorporating logistics as one of its 4 pillar industries, with 6 logistic centers already planned, each of which about 5000 acres in size. Shenzheng is going to invest $19.3 billion in its logistics infrastructure. Ministry of Railway plans to add another 50 big freight yards to its pool. Ministry of Communications also shows interest in building 50 hubs in the next few years. Enough lessons have learned from the past, and the nightmare of repeated construction is still around. Strategic planning in a coordinated and cooperated manner is critical to avoid the pitfall.

On the other hand, the efficiency of logistic system is hurt due primarily to separation of modes of transportation, i.e., railroads is the business of Ministry of Railway, highway and waterway belong to Ministry of Communication, aviation is run by Civil Aviation Administration. This separate regulation inevitably sets up barriers to multimodal through transportation. This is also the reason of loose connection between backbone transportation systems and municipal logistic systems.

Inter-region or inter-industry logistics operations usually face unexpected difficulties because of industry protection or regional protection. Permission of this kind of business has to go through a very complicated procedure before granted. Fine and detention are often encountered by those who ship from one region to another. As a result, charge of using roadway amounts to 20% of transportation cost, and this will inevitably bring a negative impact on logistics cost and service level.

Unfledged 3rd party logistics market

Conventionally business and enterprises in China operate in a self-contained or all-in-one mode, meaning the logistic activities from raw material purchasing in the upstream to product selling in the downstream are carried out by the companies themselves, and consequently these companies have to maintain enough logistic facilities by their own. This partly explains the lack of demand in 3rd party logistics. On the other hand, enterprises in China have yet to establish a modern view of business. They need to be updated with how a modern enterprise operates and how 3rd party logistics can help them reduce costs.

Ironically, resistance to 3PL may also come from those enterprises who are aware of the benefit and importance of modern logistics. The problem lies in information-sharing, a necessary step to operate 3PL. These companies are reluctant to employ 3PL because commercial secret might be revealed, or something that, in the past, can be played under the table has now to be exposed to more eyes.

In addition, 3PL logistics relies on a nation-wide integrated market. This means industries and regions have to give up part of their power and benefit to achieve this market integration. On the other hand, traditional enterprises have to tradeoff between incorporating and separating their cumbersome logistics sectors. Separation is certainly in favor of those enterprises with advanced technologies who can now focus more on their key products. However, objection to separation can be heard from some other enterprises to which supply chain itself is part of their profitable business and the leverage to negotiate with downstream companies.

To-be-improved logistic infrastructure

Though China has achieved great progress in its transportation infrastructure construction, the coverage is relatively light considering China's huge population and vast territory. For example, roadway coverage averages to 0.13 km/km^2 or 1.0 km/1000 population, far less than that in advanced countries.

The connection between different modes of transportation shows large improvement potential because these jurisdictions are competing with each other rather than forming a partnership. For example, railroad authority puts its finger on short distance freight transport and highway administration keeps an eye on long-distance hauling. The absence of coordination and cooperation deteriorates the efficiency of already-sluggish transportation network.

Unbalanced development

China, due to its particular geography, has an unbalanced regional economy, with the most advanced areas clustered along the southeast coast. Government policies which give priority to these areas even sharpen the contrast. For instance, logistics production in south area translates to about $48.2 billion in 1999, 1.38 multiples of that of north area, and the trend is expected to amplify if policies continue to be in favor of south area.
The second type of unbalanced development can be found between urban and rural areas. This is due largely to the unbalanced distribution of resources, technologies, and investments. Urban areas, which are characterized by modern industries and economies, generate far more material flows than rural areas which deal mainly with elementary farming.

Under-equipped logistics facilities

This includes the shortage of logistics equipments, the lack of uniform standards of material handling between modes of transportation (eg., loading, packaging, measuring, etc.), and the need for advanced logistics management systems. On the other hand, freight hauling in China is operated in a lighter weight (typically by 3, 5, or 10 ton trucks) than in the United States, not only because rigs are not widely available but also the road surface is generally not good enough to support 18 wheelers.

Shortage of logistics talents

It is estimated that the need for logisticians by 2010 will have reached 250,000.The imminent problem, above all, is probably the preparation of educated talents who really know what modern logistics is and how it works. A prevailing view of logistics is simply warehousing plus transportation, which services as the main strategy of many logistics companies. Logistics activities, however, cover a broader category. For example, demand forecast, distribution management, and customer service. To compete effectively in the information age, logistics talents must become an infomediary for their companies, their suppliers and their ultimate customers.

4. WTO AND CHINA'S LOGISTICS INDUSTRY

Perhaps the greatest impact on China's logistics industry comes from WTO. This section presents the commitments that China made to WTO upon its entry regarding logistics and analyzes the challenges and opportunities face both China and foreign players.

4.1 China's Commitments to WTO

According to the Compilation of the Legal Instruments on China's Accession to the World Trade Organization *(4)*, China has made the following commitments to the WTO with regard to logistics: China will gradually eliminate the restrictions regarding the presence of foreign service providers in China. Related services include, but not limited to, distribution services, communication services, transport services, and packaging services. Restrictions in these areas will be lifted in 3-4 years, during which, foreign service providers may go through joint ventures to wholly-owned subsidiaries or operational organizations. More specifically, the phased elimination of restrictions related to logistics is listed in the following table.

Table 2 Limitations on market access related to logistics services

Sector or sub-sector	Limitations on market access w.r.t. Commercial presence
Communication Services	
Courier Services	• Upon accession, foreign service suppliers will be permitted to establish joint ventures with foreign investment not exceeding 49 per cent. • Within one year after China's accession, foreign majority ownership will be permitted. • Within four years after China's accession, foreign service suppliers will be permitted to establish wholly foreign-owned subsidiaries.
Telecommunication Services, including: Electronic data interchange, On-line information and database retrieval, On-line information and/or data processing	• Foreign service suppliers will be permitted to establish joint venture value-added telecommunication enterprises, without quantitative restrictions, and provide services in the cities of Shanghai, Guangzhou and Beijing. Foreign investment in joint venture shall be no more than 30 per cent. • Within one year after China's accession, the areas will be expanded to include Chengdu, Chongqing, Dalian, Fuzhou, Hangzhou, Nanjing, Ningbo, Qingdao, Shenyang, Shenzhen, Xiamen, Xi'an, Taiyuan and Wuhan and foreign investment shall be no more than 49 per cent. • Within two years after China's accession, there will be no geographic restriction and foreign investment shall be no more than 50 per cent.
Transport Services	
Maritime Transport Services	(a) Establishment of registered companies for the purpose of operating a fleet under the national flag of the People's Republic of China: - Foreign service suppliers are permitted to establish joint venture shipping companies. - Foreign investment shall not exceed 49 per cent of the total registered capital of the joint venture. - The chairman of board of directors and the general manager of the joint venture shall be appointed by the Chinese side. (b) Other forms of commercial presence for the supply of international maritime transport services: Unbound
Auxiliary Services, including Maritime cargo-handling services, Customs clearance services for maritime transport	Only in the form of joint ventures, with foreign majority ownership permitted.
Container station and depot services	Only in forms of joint ventures, with foreign majority ownership permitted.
Maritime agency services	Only in forms of joint ventures, with foreign equity share no

	more than 49 per cent.
Internal Waterways Transport	Unbound
Air Transport Services	Foreign service suppliers are permitted to establish joint venture aircraft repair and maintenance enterprises in China. The Chinese side shall hold controlling shares or be in a dominant position in the joint ventures. Licenses for the establishments of joint ventures are subject to economic needs test.
Rail Transport Services Road Transport Services	• Only in the form of joint ventures, with foreign investment not to exceed 49 per cent. • For rail transport, within three years after China's accession, foreign majority ownership will be permitted and within six years after China's accession, wholly foreign-owned subsidiaries will be permitted. • For road transport, within one year after China's accession, foreign majority ownership will be permitted, within three years after China's accession, wholly foreign-owned subsidiaries will be permitted
Services Auxiliary to all Modes of Transport	
Storage and warehousing services	Upon accession, only in the form of joint ventures, with foreign investment not to exceed 49 per cent. Within one year after China's accession, foreign majority ownership will be permitted. Within three years of China's accession, wholly foreign-owned subsidiaries will be permitted.
Freight forwarding agency services	• Upon accession, foreign freight forwarding agencies which have at least three consecutive years experience are permitted to set up freight forwarding agency joint ventures in China, with foreign investment not to exceed 50 per cent; within one year after China's accession, foreign majority ownership will be permitted. Within four years after China's accession, wholly foreign-owned subsidiaries will be permitted. • The minimum registered capital of the joint venture shall be no less than US$ 1 million. Within four years after accession, national treatment will be accorded in this respect. Operation term of the joint ventures shall not exceed 20 years. • After one year operating in China, the joint venture can set up branches when the registered capital of both sides has been provided. Another US$ 120,000 shall be added to the original registered capital of the joint venture for the set-up of each branch. Within two years after China's accession to the WTO, this additional registered capital requirement will be implemented on the national treatment basis. • A foreign freight forwarding agency may set up a second joint venture after its first joint venture has been in

	operation for five years. Within two years after China's accession to WTO, this requirement will be reduced to two years.
Other Business Services	
Packaging services	• Foreign service suppliers will be permitted to establish joint venture in China. • Within one year after China's accession, foreign majority ownership will be permitted. • Within three years after China's accession, foreign service suppliers will be permitted to establish wholly foreign-owned subsidiaries.

4.2 Challenges and Opportunities Brought about by WTO

Perhaps the greatest impact on China's logistics industry comes from its entry of WTO. With China's entry of WTO, future challenges will come not only from foreign companies but also from domestic buyer's market. It is, therefore, critical for Chinese enterprises to lower their logistics cost and improve their competitiveness. Opportunities, however, are the huge inflow of capital and technology and examples of modern enterprises, which are bound to help shaping China's modern logistics network and establishing China's role of world-class logistics centers. Chances of success of both sides heavily rely on the following issues:

Improving regulation system

The deep involvement of government in business is a big issue. Though the scenes where opening a business has to go through tons of departments are not common today, the efficiency of government is still one of the top issues that foreign companies should consider when moving their businesses to China. The fact that Gerling Insurance Group, a German-based company, recently decided to quit their businesses in China is an example of such a difficulty. As an emerging industry in China, logistics not only represents a future trend but also shows a good profitability. It is not surprise that everyone wants to get a piece of the cake, and this partially contributes to the multiple and overlapped regulation. Therefore, in the next few years, it is critical for government to focus on its key functions - standardizing processing procedure and increasing policy transparency – so as to create a healthy environment for players of both domestic and overseas.

Encouraging coordination between industries

Traditionally, the operation of logistics was undertaken by a number of closely related but separate industries, such as transportation, telecommunication, postal services, and port authorities. Even in transportation, services are traditionally segmented by modes. On the other hand, state-level backbone transportation networks and urban transportation networks are typically separated. These pose hardship in organizing multimodal transportation and door-to-door delivery.

To overcome these barriers, industrial associations can play an important role in bringing together the related parties and helping communicating with each other. For example, logistics-related state-level associations, such as China Communications and Transportation Association,

China Warehousing Association, and China Material Circulation Association, are such examples that can provide coordination, consultation, and communication services between government agencies and industries and between industries themselves.

Nurturing logistics market

Traditional mode of self-contained logistics service should be reformed to nurture an integrated nation-wide logistics market. This is not only the general trend, but also for the good of enterprises themselves to reduce cost and concentrate on core businesses. In addition, attention should also be paid to training and preparing logistics talents as well as to the establishment of a training mechanism for logistics operation, managerial and working personnel.

Dealing with cultural shock

China's WTO accession provides a best chance for players of domestic and overseas to compete with and learn from each other. Accompanying business competition is the conflict of enterprise cultures. Chances of their success depend not only on the efficiency of the culture, but also the fitness of the culture to the general environment. There is much that deserves Chinese enterprises learning from foreign companies, but it is equally pains-taking for foreign enterprises to adapt to Chinese market. The great success of American fast food in China is a wonderful example of the combination of Eastern and Western cultures.

CONCLUSION

Globalization is a general trend, and China is no exception. China's logistics industry is experiencing, and will continue to be driven by, such trend, especially with China's entry of WTO. General environment, including economy, transportation, and information, is undergoing continuous improvement, and is expected to be in a better shape in the future. The huge market is gradually opening to the outside, and constraints on logistics are expected to be removed in the near future. Logistics players in the world are competing to establish their footholds in this market, and competition will be increasingly intensive in the future. Opportunities and challenges, inevitably, co-exist for players of both domestic and overseas. Success of the industry as well as logistics players depends heavily on how the above-mentioned key issues are resolved.

ACKNOWLEDGEMENT

The authors would like to acknowledge and thank Dr. John Vande Vate, Professor at Georgia Institute of Technology, for prompting the idea of this paper and providing many valuable suggestions.

BIBLIOGRAPHY:

1. Data source: World Development Indicators (WDI) 2002, The World Bank Group.
2. Z. Tian. *Present situation and prospective development of logistics in China*. Economic Information & Agency. August 26, 2002

3. *Research Report on China's Logistics Industry*. Allchinadata.com. 2002.
4. MOFTEC, PR China.
http://preview.www.moftec.gov.cn/article/200207/20020700032358_1.xml.

Linking Equipment Supportability Databases and Support Publications for the Full Service Life of Complex Assets

Patrick Read, Nik Barron and Frank Hallam
Pennant Information Services, Inc

Abstract

Defense forces and industry are partnering to ensure effective and optimal support of fleets of complex assets throughout their full and lengthy service life. Continuous improvements – both of equipment fleets and of their associated support systems – inject ongoing change to the foundation information used to resource, plan and execute the support activities necessary to sustain the readiness of these fleets. Many defense forces are relying on effective performance monitoring of support to trigger structured maintenance reviews to re-optimize support based on actual support transaction histories captured in Enterprise Resource Planning (ERP) information systems. For the Canadian Forces (CF), this has led to the creation, configuration management and on-going use of in-service Equipment Supportability Databases (ESDs) centered on Logistics Support Analysis (LSA) data and related analytical tools. These ESDs provide approved current data to be used in ERP transactions, and provide expected performance values to set triggers and to form the basis for analysis of variances or of proposed changes.

Key to effective delivery of in-service is the dynamic linkage of ESD approved data and the various maintenance and support publications that are used by maintainers and logisticians to sustain their fleets. This paper explores evolving concepts to manage ESD baseline data, and to create and operate a two-way dynamic link for content management between ESDs and electronic publications, at the data element level. It cites recent experience in creating an ESD for all CF Navy ships from legacy data, and in linking this equipment fleet data to SAP R/3 transaction systems (as part of the Canadian Department of National Defence Materiel Acquisition and Support Information System – **MASIS** – Project), and describes potential for more effective content management of electronic technical publications critical to supporting complex equipment fleets.

Background

Effective through-life maintenance and logistics support of complex equipment systems (such as major weapons systems of defense forces) throughout their often extended service lives relies on the right information being readily available to those operating and sustaining each equipment. Operators need correct operating and user maintenance information, relevant to the specific equipment upon which they rely. Maintainers need to execute correct maintenance procedures; they need to identify and obtain the correct repair parts; and their supporting supply chain need to hold and deliver the right items to sustain each equipment within these systems at optimal readiness. Primary sources of data for all these operating and support actions are the various logistics support documents held for the equipment system. For many organizations with extensive and complex equipment systems, this document set is massive. By example, the US Army has over 21,500 Technical Manuals, of about 3.5 Million pages that are required to be kept up-to-date and accessible in order to support its diverse equipment/weapon system inventory[1]. Lags in updating publications contribute to maintenance errors and inefficiencies[2].

But logistics support documents only ***present*** significant amounts of data that is ***sourced*** and copied/transcribed from other datasets. During the acquisition phases of the life cycle of many

---

[1] Source USALIA website, see bibliography

[2] Caldwell, V. Research of USMC AH-1W helicopter maintenance practices confirmed more than 30% of maintenance costs were due to improper maintenance being performed.

complex systems, logistics support analysis record (LSAR) databases have been used to hold key baseline logistics support data elements which form much of the foundation dataset for various logistics support documents produced to enable effective in-service support of the equipment/weapon system. However, in many instances the follow-on update of publication ***presentation*** of the correct logistics support data ***content*** has lagged well behind changes to equipment system design and its support. In the past, related publications using the same LSAR data were often authored and then updated independently, creating document production inefficiencies and data inconsistencies. While the introduction of electronic file and content management systems for publications can reduce both data errors and these publication update process inefficiencies, logistics support publications still need a common source of equipment-system specific data that is maintained as a continuously revised baseline aligned with changes to design and support throughout the system's in-service life, a time period often measured in many decades.

The introduction of Enterprise Resource Planning (ERP) solutions that also rely on single-source reliable datasets for equipment system master data[3] has reinforced the value of expanding LSAR datasets traditionally used in acquisition to meet the needs of ***Equipment Supportability Database (ESD)***[4] baseline datasets to hold up-to-date equipment/weapon systems data throughout the extended in-service life cycle within large commercial and government enterprises. In fact, this requirement to have solid through-life ESD datasets to support "*optimizing weapon system performance throughout the life cycle*"[5] led the Canadian Department of National Defence (DND) to adopt a solution that integrated LSAR-centred ESDs and supportability analysis tools with the SAP R/3 ERP software for department- and Canadian Forces-wide engineering and maintenance transactions[6], commencing with the Navy in 2003.

Recently, the evolution of product/equipment system publication data standards – both towards web-enabled formats and towards managing content at the SGML/XML fragment level[7] [8] - will enable better sharing and management of publication data ***content*** at a data element level. By maintaining an LSAR-centred ESD as a core through-life equipment system baseline dataset to meet ERP and other data uses, and by taking full advantage of these growing electronic data interchange (EDI) capabilities, the ongoing synchronization of baseline equipment system data elements and the various publications that present them is made easier and more effective,

---

[3] The term ***master data*** is used here in an ERP context (based on SAP R/3 concepts), to reflect re-usable equipment system data (e.g. system name or part numbers) that are used across many ERP transactions, and that change less frequently that data that is created with each transaction (e.g. a specific maintenance work order number).

[4] The term Equipment Supportability Database (ESD) has been used to indicate this dataset – although usually centred on LSAR data – may be broader that just traditional LSAR data produced to various standards. For example, it may include client-defined identification codes (e.g. VIN numbers) and data necessary to link LSAR data to other datasets, such as SAP R/3 Functional Location structures used to pass LSAR functional breakdown hierarchies into SAP R/3.

[5] the mission statement of the DND Material Acquisition and Support Information System (MASIS) Project that is to deliver an integrated engineering and maintenance solution to all services within DND. This statement is taken from the Materiel Acquisition and Support Information System (MASIS) Business Case, January 2000, see bibliography.

[6] See MacDonald, B. et al for description of through-life LSAR-based ESDs linked to ERP solutions.

[7] The NATO Integrated Technical Data (ITD) Interoperability Task Force Roadmap provides a useful overview of this thrust and summarizes key relevant standards. See bibliography.

[8] For an overview of the shift of the ISO 10303 Standard Exchange for Product Data (STEP) towards SGML/XML and resulting EDI impacts, see Harvey, B. in bibliography.

provided that linkages are made between ESDs and support publications, and between the efforts of the logistics engineers/equipment managers and authors who work with these related aspects of equipment systems support.

This paper will present concepts for managing data content between LSAR-centred Equipment Supportability Databases (ESDs) and electronic support publications, based on Pennant Information Services, Inc experiences in developing solutions for defense and automotive clients.

Equipment Supportability Databases (ESDs) as Integrating "Middleware"

LSAR-centred equipment supportability databases (ESDs) are the initial coordinating dataset developed during design and delivery of an equipment/weapon system for use by both the producer and a client to capture key support data elements related to the specific project/acquisition/support package. In particular, these data elements:

- Define the ***structure, logistic breakdown and piece parts*** that make up an equipment system, each of its variants, and any supporting equipment.
- Describe the ***reliability, availability and maintainability characteristics*** related to how the system will fail.
- Define the ***maintenance actions*** necessary to maintain equipment system readiness.

This ESD baseline data is then used to produce a number initial logistics support deliverables, including the data baseline for authoring of logistics support publications.

As explored in two previous papers presented at SOLE 2001[9] and SOLE 2002[10], ESDs maintained as such a coordinating baseline dataset can become core elements of effective full-life logistics support of many complex systems, adapting to changes in use, design, and support of the equipment/weapon system that affect both producer and owner/operator. In effect, the ESDs can act as "middleware" datasets that either draw from or provide to multiple users the correct data for support to an equipment/weapon system. The figure below shows some of these key through-life data integration linkages, and they are discussed in the following paragraphs.

An ESD can exchange data with producers' ***Product Data Management (PDM)*** datasets, particularly to identify hierarchical breakdowns and the relevant technical drawings and specifications for the system and its component items. Key to sustaining this synchronization is effective configuration management discipline applied to both the PDM and ESD environments.

An ESD used for in-service management will also need to synchronize data with ***Client Asset Databases*** that provide additional asset identification information applied by the user to a product (e.g., an airline aircraft registration information associated with a specific aircraft; equipment identification codes used within a military force; vehicle registration plates, etc).

An ESD may also provide data to ***Simulation and Training*** products, such as failure trees and troubleshooting data used within maintenance simulators to train technicians.

As being implemented within the Canadian Department of National Defence (DND), an ESD can be a crucial source of key master data used to manage and execute transactions within ***Enterprise***

---

[9] MacDonald B et al, see bibliography
[10] Read, P.O. and Hallam, F, see bibliography

Resource Planning (ERP) and Support Management applications. In DND, an ESD centred on the Pennant OmegaPS software is used to define functional locations, equipments, materials, equipment bills of materials, and maintenance task information used within the SAP R/3 transaction system for executing maintenance and engineering activities. Our SOLE 2001[11] paper presented key aspects of this use of ESD data to *"optimize weapon system performance throughout the life cycle"*[12].

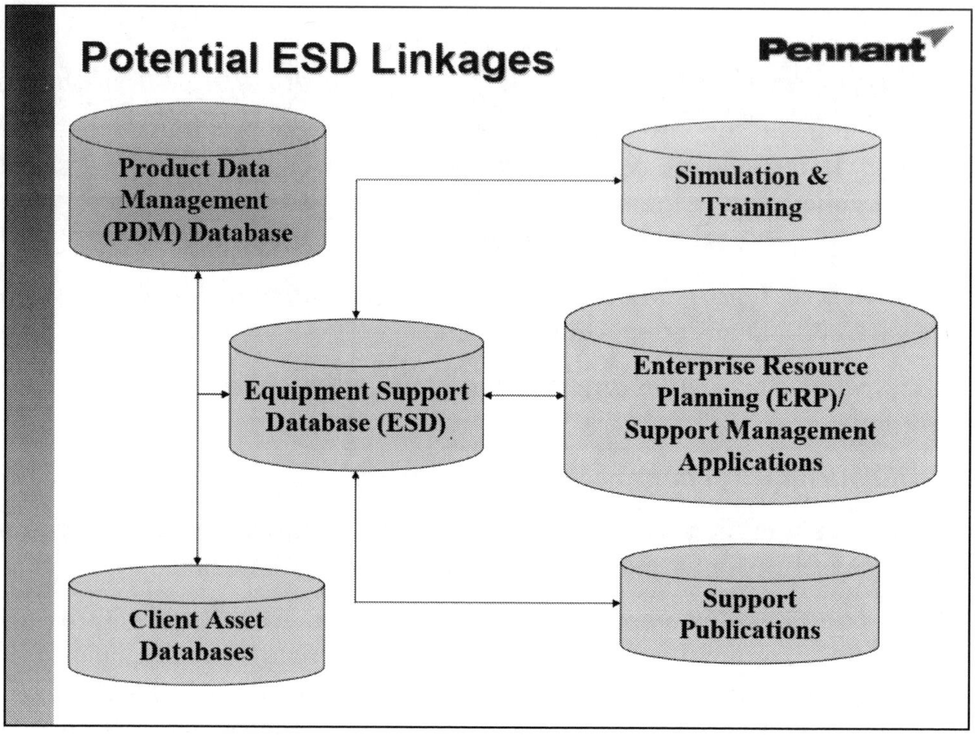

Figure 1 - Potential Equipment Supportability Database (ESD) Linkages

A key and direct linkage of ESD-sourced information and equipment/weapon system ***Support Publications*** was formed for many systems during acquisition, where data sourced from LSAR-centred ESDs was used to develop initial delivered versions of maintenance and support publications.

ESDs can thus be seen as a "***middleware***" data integrator of multi-source data relevant to the support of a specific equipment/weapon system for a specific user/owner. By retaining ESDs past initial delivery, the follow-on integration of data throughout the lengthy in-service phase is enhanced, and synchronization between diverse data sources can be enabled.

---

[11] MacDonald, B. et al, see bibliography

[12] the mission statement of the DND MASIS Project. This statement is taken from the Materiel Acquisition and Support Information System (MASIS) Business Case, January 2000, see bibliography.

Why Link ESDs and Support Publications During the In-service Phase?

For many complex systems, the ESD and associated support publications are synchronized through the integrated logistics support processes applied before initial delivery of the system. If an ESD is not maintained after delivery, however, the update of publications may become detached from frequent changes to source data that would normally flow from and ESD. As support publications remain a primary tool used in the actual execution of support by maintainers, it is imperative they reflect the accurate and most current data on the specific equipment being supported. As design and support changes are introduced, the data describing them may originate from or cause updates to existing ESDs, reinforcing the role of ESDs as a primary data source for support publications.

In the past, ESDs provided extract reports or data files that were used to produce support publications. As a result time lags existed between changes being defined in an ESD and these changes being reflected in publications. By example, changes to Naval Preventive Maintenance Schedules used by the Canadian Navy can take up to 18 months to be promulgated into the formal publication due to author, translation and publication delays[13]. As a result, though the ESD related to the equipment has been updated, the technicians may still be using outdated maintenance procedures for years pending publication of the update.

By establishing effective content management between publication author/managers and equipment logistics support/ESD managers, these delays in presentation of support data within publications can be significantly reduced. As well, by recognizing ESDs as a continuing source of accurate logistics data for in-service equipment systems, the use of incorrect or inconsistent data in key support publications should be eliminated. An additional value of content management linkage between authors and logistics engineers can be the enabled feedback of ESD errors from authors[14].

Further, the use of web-based presentation of technical information can initiate significant increases in feedback from maintainers and operators on errors in publications that may also reflect underlying ESD errors. Major Vern Caldwell indicated that once the UMSC UH-1W maintenance mentoring program presented technical manual-sourced maintenance information in a simple web-based format with one-click feedback, the level of technician-generated publication error reports increased 10-fold.[15]

Key Characteristics of a Linked ESD/Publication Content Management System

In order for the benefits of a linked content management system for publications and ESDs, certain key characteristics need to form part of any solution. These include:

- The linkage needs to ***sustain two working environments***, in that publication authors need to continue working in a familiar publication revision process, while logistics engineers and other work in and ESD revision process. Each group needs to work in common software

---

[13] Data from DND sources provided to the author.

[14] Nik Barron personal experience as an author of support publications for electronic systems confirms authors are a useful source of feedback on technical data anomalies to logistics engineers.

[15] As discussed with author. This program that was recognized as the 2002 best "Great Idea" by 1,000 maintainers attending the 2002 USDoD Maintenance Symposium in Reno, Nevada in October, 2002. It provides simple Internet presentation of maintenance information for the UH-1W attack helicopter fleet, built by a joint DoD/GM team using the GM commercial "Mr Goodwrench" program as a model.

tools for their environment (e.g., author using publishing tool such as Interleaf while logistics engineers work in OmegaPS LSAR databases).

- The linkage needs to work below the traditional full publication level, by focussing on the specific support data ***fragments*** within it. It is at this level that specific ESD data elements impact on the related support publications, and that one-to-many mapping is possible to enable concurrent update of multiple publications impacted by an ESD data element change (e.g. a change in part number in an ESD linked to its use in both parts and maintenance manuals).
- The linkage needs to ***dynamic***, in that changes to shared data elements are detected and passed to the affected stakeholders to be considered.
- The linkage needs a ***content management*** engine to control data changes between these two work areas, and this content management system should have imbedded ***workflow*** capabilities to enable effective passage of changes to stakeholders for consideration, approval, and/or necessary action.
- For maximum utility in the future environment, the linkage system should make good use of Internet ***web enabled data formats*** to facilitate open sharing of data files. The use of SGML or XML fragments seems to offer the best potential for open sharing of data element fragments.
- The linkage relies on ***data mapping*** rules linking ESD data elements with document fragments and on ***document data models*** to facilitate assembly of data fragments into suitable publication presentation formats.

Support Publications from an ESD Perspective

Support publications can generally be grouped into two categories when viewed from their use of ESD-sourced data elements.

ESD Data Presentation Documents (e.g. Parts Manual). A parts manual is an example of a publication that largely ***presents*** data directly from an ESD. It may include breakdown hierarchical information, parts identification data and linkages to related drawings or illustrations. Generally, these data elements can exist or be hyperlinked direct from data elements within the ESD, and the publication process is limited to adding a presentation layer on the data elements sourced from the ESD. As such, these documents may be produced from ESD data with little or no human intervention required by authors. Equally, changes entered in these documents can be passed back to update the ESD with only limited approval/review necessary.

ESD Data Enrichment Documents (e.g. Maintenance Manual). Unlike parts manuals, many maintenance manuals contain significant author-added content that builds upon basic maintenance task data drawn from the ESD. Here, much valuable information is added within the authoring process before publication of the document. As such, significant human intervention is required to take either an initial or updated ESD data load and create the mew or revised document.

Electronic and Integrated Electronic Technical Manuals (ETMs & IETMs) can be considered another form of electronic ***presentation*** document, in that they present an assembly of SGML/XML source data fragments, an assembly that may be stable or be adjusted to meet each need.

From Concept to Reality – Linking ESD and Support Publications

To move from concept to reality in linking ESDs and support publications requires the development of interfacing software products that embody the key aspects listed above and that are used to link together ESD datasets and support publications. An example product is the Pennant Information Services Inc OmegaPS Publisher™ product when used in conjunction with the OmegaPS™ LSAR software and with publication authoring toolsets. It integrates an SGML/XML authoring environment with the OmegaPS LSAR database via a content management system with workflow control of actions. An overview is shown in the figure below.

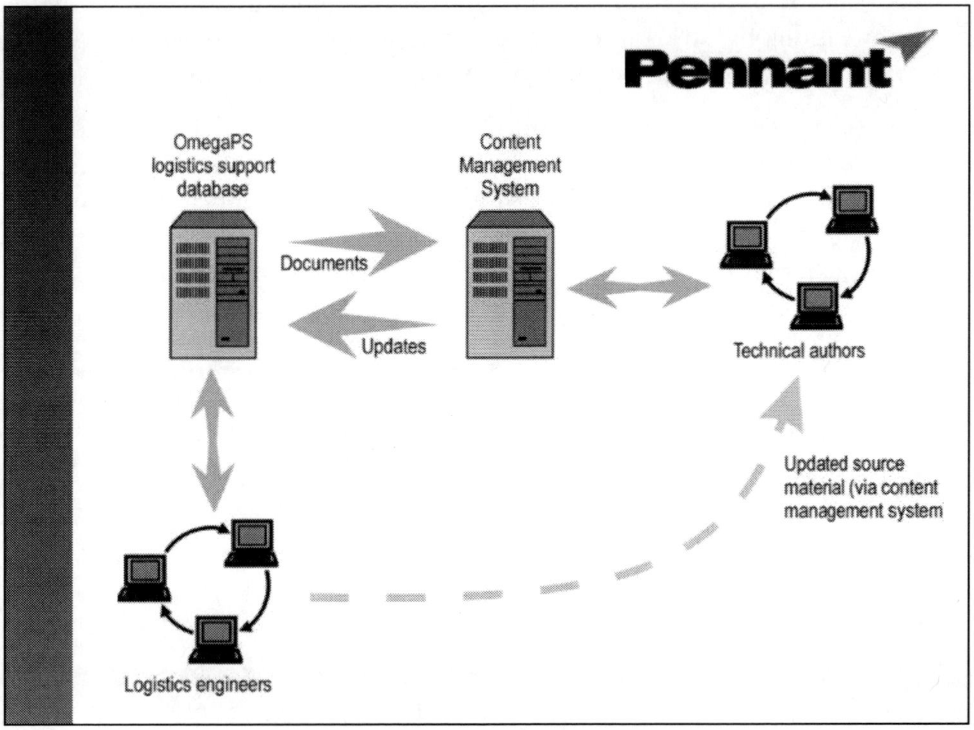

Figure 2 - OmegaPS Publisher Overview

The OmegaPS Publisher™ solution allows authors to continue working in a familiar SGML/XML document publication system, and allows logistics engineers to work in their familiar LSAR/ESD environment. A document content management system is added between the two working environments, and data mapping between ESD data elements and the associated document XML fragments within agreed document type definitions is completed. It enables two-way flow of data elements, their updates and changes between the two working environments, controlled by the workflow rules established within the content management system. OmegaPS Publisher™ uses the Content@ ™ product to enable this linkage and workflow control[16]. In general:

---

[16] Content@ is a product of XyEnterprise, a leading producer of publishing systems since 1983.

- Draft SGML/XML document files can be ***assembled*** from LSAR/ESD data and passed through the content management system to be then edited into published format within the author environment.
- Equally, ESD-relevant data can be ***extracted*** from support publications and processed through the content management system to build LSAR/ESD datasets, with controlled review/acceptance of document-sourced changes to the baseline ESD.
- Lastly, these two environments can then ***update*** each other on a regular basis with the changes entered in either environment. These updates are passed through the content management workflow control system to be approved and accepted in each environment.

The use of effective content management to complement electronic publications has proven to offer significant benefit, in one automotive technical publication example by increasing shared data between publications by 90%, and also by reducing time to translate (into 20 languages) and distribute a new publication from 6 months to 3 weeks[17].

The content management system and its workflow element serve to also provide a discipline and visibility to the document production control process. The following figure is a screen capture from Content@™ that illustrates the editing tool to develop a workflow map that then will be applied to the review cycle for a document revision, and to the specific authors/reviewers associated with each step.

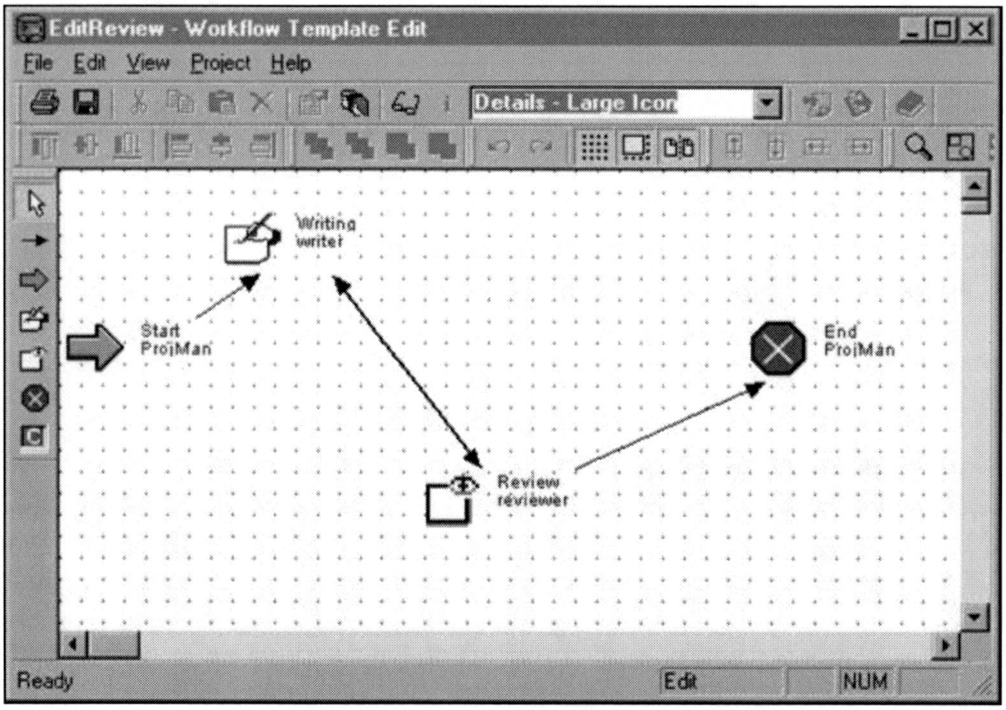

Figure 3 - Workflow within a Content Management System

[17] Data provided by XyEnterprise regarding use of Content@XML by Tweedle Litho for Ford/Chrysler technical manuals

In organizations using ESD datasets to keep in-service equipment support data aligned across multiple data users – including with publications – linking ESD datasets with publications can significantly reduce the coordination needed to ensure accurate and most recent data from an updated ESD is reflected in all associated publications in an expedient fashion, avoiding wasted effort performing incorrect maintenance tasks, and perhaps the dire consequences of wrong data within publications. Support costs can be significantly lowered and equipment readiness enhanced by this improved accuracy and currency of support publications linked with well-maintaned in-service ESD datasets. And, as these ESD datasets are maintained for other purposes – for example to manage master data used on ERP electronic maintenance work orders -, linkage to publications would be an incremental investment towards better data integration and resultant equipment support efficiency across the enterprise.

Concluding Remarks

This paper has discussed the concepts and perceived value in providing effective linkage of LSAR/ESD datasets with the support publications related to these equipment systems, with changes managed within a content management system. The introduction of producer and client ERP solutions that use ESDs as "middleware" to synchronize equipment/weapon system support data across all users further underscores the value of such linkage of ESD datasets to the primary tools used by maintainers to keep equipment ready, the support publications relied on to provide correct and accurate data. The adoption of in-service ESD → publication data management links helps ensure the publications used for maintenance describe the right maintenance and parts as defined in the most recent ESD, and can provide enhanced feedback to the ESD logistics engineers. The key characteristics of such data linkage were discussed and the example OmegaPS Publisher™ toolkit provides a model of how these characteristics can be embodied in an integrated solution.

Both equipment/weapon system producers and the users of fleets of such complex assets are moving towards a much more integrated data structure. Adopting linkages between LSAR/ESD datasets and the related support publications is an important enabler to help ensure optimum readiness and support efficiency through-out the lengthy in-service lives of these costly fleets.

Biographical Notes

Pat Read, BSc (Mechanical Engineering), PEng is a former senior Canadian Forces (CF) officer with 30 years experience leading Army maintenance and equipment management organizations in Canada, in Germany and in both United Nations and Multinational Forces in Egypt. He is a graduate of the Canadian Land Forces & Canadian Forces Staff Colleges, as well as the Royal Military College of Science (UK) Army Staff Course – Division One. For the last decade he has been a key member and lead proponent of Canadian Forces and Department of National Defence (DND) efforts to re-engineer equipment fleet management processes. Retiring from the CF in 2000 as a Lieutenant-Colonel, he became a senior supportability consultant within Pennant Information Services, Inc. Most recently, his team of logistics consultants commenced the transfer of existing CF Navy data into the MASIS solution, as well as the definition of associated supportability business process models. He is also the PLCS lead for Pennant Information Services, Inc.

E-mail: pat.read@pennantcanada.ca

Nik Barron has over 10 years of practical experience in the use of technology to enhance the provision and presentation of technical support information for both commercial and military requirements. Currently specializing in SGML, XML and their integration with existing production environments, he is the Pennant Software Services Limited (UK) lead for development of the OmegaPS Publisher software that enables content management between logistics support databases and electronic technical documents. He also writes a regular column for Secure Computing, one of the largest circulation information security publications in Europe and the USA.

E-mail: Nik.Barron@pennantplc.co.uk

Frank Hallam, MEng(Software Engineering), PEng served in the Canadian Navy for over 14 years, as an engineering officer and software engineer. He is an SAP-certified Plant Maintenance consultant and the Pennant Product Manager for the certified Complex Asset Support System (CASS) interface with SAP R/3. Since August 2000, he has been the Team IBM supportability team lead for the Canadian Department of National Defense tri-service MASIS solution for enterprise equipment engineering and maintenance.

E-mail: frank.hallam@pennantcanada.ca

Bibliography

1. Caldwell, V., Major USMC, Electronic Performance Support : Maintenance Mentoring, Presentation to the USDoD Maintenance Symposium, October 2002, *Society of Automotive Engineers,* presentation online @ http://www.sae.org/calendar/dod/presentations.htm

2. Courtney, J., Lieutenant-Colonel USAF, AF Logistics Integration : In Plain English, *Logistics Spectrum,* July-September 2001, pp. 28-32.

3. *Defense Collaboration Network / International Collaboration Network (DCN/ICN)*, NATO Integrated Technical Data (ITD) Interoperability Task Force Roadmap, revised July 31, 2002, website http://www.dcnicn.com/IETMCentral/Roadmap_2002/default.asp

4. *Department of National Defence (DND), Canada*, Materiel Acquisition and Support Information System (MASIS) Business Case, January 2000.

5. Harvey, B., How STEP/SGML and XML/EDI Initiatives Will Impact Future Development of IETMs , *Electronic Commerce Connection, Inc,* http://www.eccnet.com/papers/ietm.html

6. *Institute of Configuration Management*, University of Arizona website http://www.icmhq.com/

7. Kratz, L., Achieving Logistics Excellence through Performance-Based Logistics, *Logistics Spectrum,* July-September 2001, pp. 12-15.

8. MacDonald, B., P.O. Read and G.R. Ellis, Integrating Through-Life Supportability Analysis within Enterprise Resource Planning (ERP)-Enabled Solutions for Organizations with Complex Equipment *Proceedings of the 36th Annual International Logistics Symposium: (SOLE 2001),* May 2001.

9. Meyer, M.M., Why IBM is Linking Information and Logistics , *Logistics Spectrum,* October-December 2001, pp. 17-20 (reprinted from *Supply Chain Management Review*, 2001).

10. *PLCS, Inc,* website www.plcs.org

11. Read, P.O., DGLEPM Logistics Support Analysis Record (LSAR) Data Elements For Through-Life Supportability Analysis, *Pennant Information Service, Inc* Report, March 29, 2001.

12. Read, P.O. and Frank Hallam, From Product to Asset Information : Bridging the Two-Way Information Gap in Effective Enterprise-wide Support of Multi-Source Asset Fleets, *Proceedings of the 37th Annual International Logistics Symposium: (SOLE 2002),* May 2002.

13. *United States Army Logistics Integration Agency* (USALIA) website https://lia13-www.army.mil/. Information on IETM initiative is found under Future Logistics.

Product support logistics based on product design characteristics and operating environment

Behzad Ghodrati [*], Uday Kumar [†]
Division of Operation and Maintenance Engineering
Luleå University of Technology
SE 971 85 Luleå - SWEDEN
Tel.: +46 (920) 491456 [*], +46 (920) 491826 [†] - Fax: +46 (920) 491935
E-mail: Behzad.Ghodrati@ce.luth.se [*], Uday.Kumar@ce.luth.se [†]
Dhananjay Kumar [‡]
Nokia Research Center, Nokia House, Summit Avenue
Farnborough, Hampshire, GU14 ONG, UK
Dhananjay.Kumar@nokia.com [‡]

Abstract

To improve the reliability, maintainability, and supportability (RMS) of a product, it is necessary to understand the factors influencing the product performance. This factors can be user environment, human (operator) aspects like training, and technical characteristics of the product. The environmental conditions in which the equipment is to be operated, such as temperature, humidity, dust, road conditions, maintenance facilities, maintenance crew training, operator training, etc, often have considerable influence directly on the product reliability and indirectly on the product supportability characteristics. Thus operating environment should be considered seriously while dimensioning product support and service delivery performance strategies since it will have an impact on operational and maintenance cost and service quality to provide product support plan in an optimal condition.
Spare parts are classified, as a product support items whose availability is important when planned or unplanned maintenance is to be carried out. Forecasting the required support/spare parts based on technical characteristics and operating environmental conditions of a system, is the one of the best ways for optimizing unplanned stoppages.
This paper discusses about product support (required spare part) logistics based on product design characteristics and operating environment both for conventional and functional products

1. Introduction

A product is an object that is made by manufacturer/producer for consumption or for production of other products. Generally, it can be classified according to product characteristics into two groups: Consumer products and Industrial products. Consumer products are made for consumption such as personal computer, TV, car, etc. Industrial products are those, which are being used for production goods or for producing other products either for consumer or industry. Industrial product's customer may be a more professional customer and may set up special product criteria, specification, requirements, etc (Kumar and Kumar, 2003). Mining equipment, car assembling machine, crusher, and etc are the examples of this type of product.

On the other hand, product can be classified based on ownership as well. According to this, a product can be classified into two groups: Functional products and Conventional products. In functional products category, the user does not buys a machine/system but the function it delivers (Markeset and Kumar, 2002a). To avoid the complexities of maintenance management, many customers/users prefer to purchase only the required function and not the machines or systems so that the responsibility of maintenance and product support lies with organization delivering the required function.

The conventional product is that; the customer buys and uses the product and accepts the responsibility of maintenance, and the service provider delivers product support and services according to the requirements and agreement.

Every product, and especially the industrial product need support in their working during the lifetime. Typical forms of support include installation, maintenance, repair services, availability of spare parts, warranty schemes, and documentation to user guiding and training. In fact product (or customer) support entails all activities "to ensure that a product is available for trouble-free use to consumers over its useful life span" (Loomba, 1998).

Product support can briefly be defined as any form of assistance that manufacturers/suppliers offer to users/customers to help them gain maximum value (profit) from the manufactured products, and it is important in the recent industrial world scenario. Meanwhile, the management considers and pays more attention to product support, because it:

- Plays a key role for many products in achieving customer satisfaction.
- Can be a considerable source of revenue and profit.

- Can provide a competitive advantage in marketing.

On the other hand, it is undeniable that the environmental conditions in which the equipment is to be operated, such as temperature, humidity, dust, etc. often have considerable influence on the product reliability characteristics (Kumar and Kumar, 1992; Kumar et al., 1992). Thus operating environment should be considered seriously while dimensioning product support and service delivery performance strategies since it will have an impact on operational and maintenance cost and service quality. In general, since new products are often employed under conditions that are also new and many items are intended for uses different from typical applications, it is common in many applications to modify predicted values by application of environmental and other factors. The intent is to account for different conditions, such as temperature, humidity, dust, voltage stress, etc.

2. Product support

Product support which sometimes known as customer support and/or after-sale support, is the name given to the different forms of assistance and aid that manufacturers offer customers to help them gain maximum value (profit) from the product. This assistance can be provided in different forms and stages of product life cycle. With this concept, product support falls into two board categories, namely support to customer and support to product (Figure 1)(Markeset and Kumar, 2002a, Mathieu, 2001). Support to customer is based on client characteristics such as culture, their educational level, geographical location, social/political environment, organization's vision, goal and strategy. This type of support addresses the general quality of interactions between a seller and a customer (Parasuraman, 1998), and includes, extra documentation, consultancy, training, and etc. Support to product, which is based on product characteristics, includes support from the initial phase of product generation to phase of product in use. These are in the form of installation, maintenance, up gradation, and improvement in the reliability and maintainability with respect to product operating environmental characteristics such as dust, humidity, temperature, employees/human, level of competence, and etc. In other word, we can compare the support to product as hardware side, and support to customer as software side of product support.

Maintenance and spare parts support are two basic and critical issues of support to product, because often due to lack of technology and other compelling factors (like economy, environmental situations, etc), in the design phase it is impossible to design a product that will fulfill its function. So the need for support is becoming vital to enhance system effectiveness and prevent unexpected failure (Figure 2).

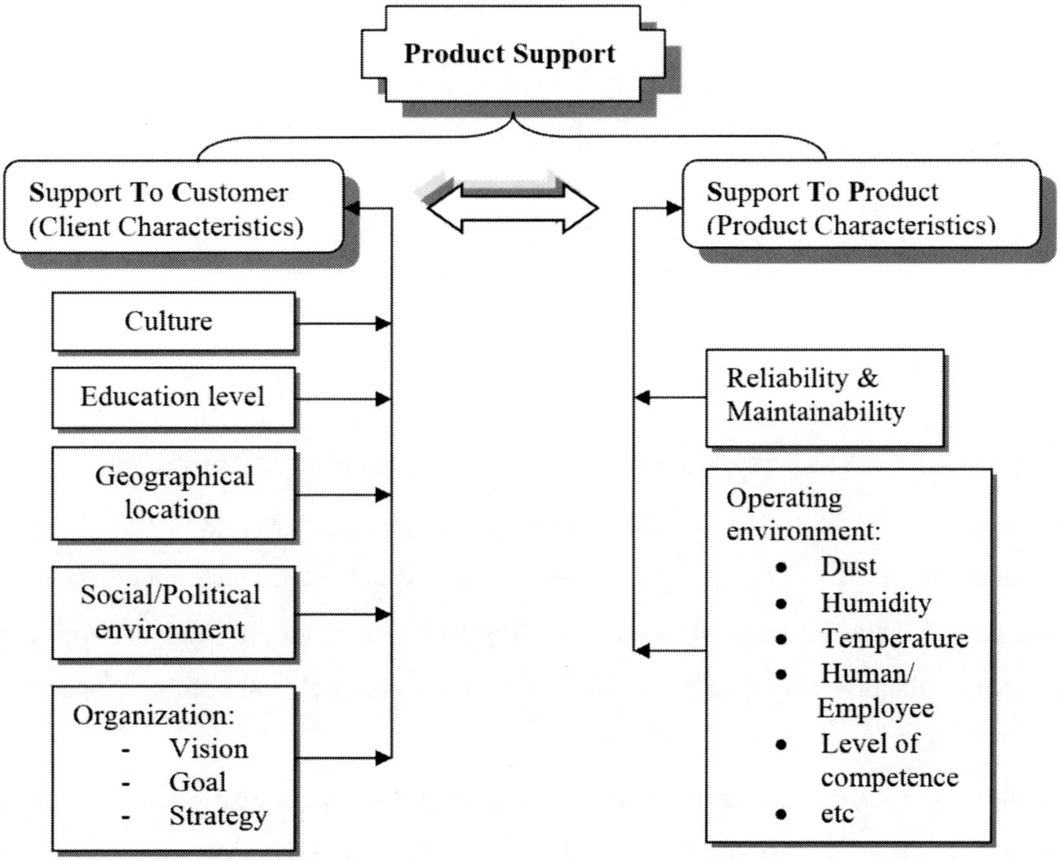

Figure 1. *Classification of product support*

Product technical characteristics such as product reliability and maintainability are more useful factors in defining and obtaining the required maintenance and especially spare parts needs. Meanwhile, it can be used in decision making between design for and design out maintenance, in design phase.

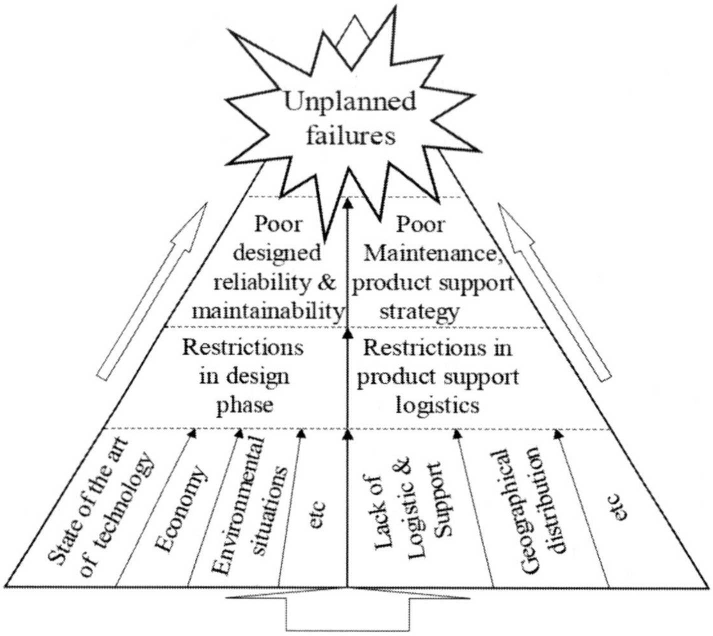

Figure 2. *Typical restrictions that cause unexpected failure*

In other words, while considering maintenance in design, either we can try to design out maintenance or try to optimize the design with respect to maintenance issues, and decision can be made for each alternative relating to different factors such as: application type, geographical distribution, cultural, socio-political situation, operational environment, and etc of the product/system.

Furthermore, the state of the art of technology is important in decision-making. Lack of available technology might not allow the desired elimination of maintenance, or it might be too costly.

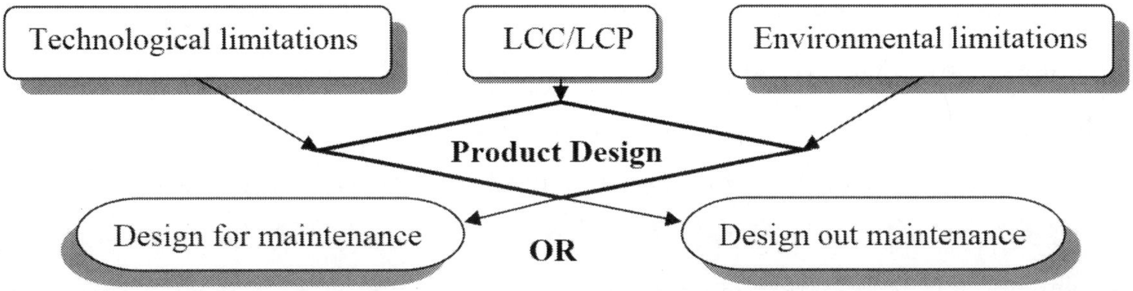

Figure 3. *Integration of different parameter in product design to make decision for design out/for maintenance*

3. Product support strategy

The manufacturers due to some factors and restrictions, mentioned earlier, attempt to optimize maintenance needs during product development & manufacturing phases, and the spare parts are becoming an important issue in this scenario. How many spare parts are required? When and how much should be ordered? And so on, are some questions that should be answered in product support management phase and discussion.

Spare parts forecasting differs for repairable and non-reparable systems, and in this paper we are discussing just about non-repairable parts. Non-repairable spare parts need can be studied in two categories as:

a. For new product
b. For existing product

And each of the above categories can be further subdivided into two sub-categories as:

i. Conventional product
ii. Functional product

In the class **ai** (new and conventional product), the customer is owner of system, and owner normally performs operation and maintenance processes. The manufacturer attempt to optimize the reliability of system and its components based on product LCC, competitive market, customer competence and needs. In this case, support generates revenue for manufacturer, but cost for customer. So, manufacturer profits from selling the system/machine and deliver support services to product. Meanwhile the manufacturer wants maximum profit at lowest cost, then focus on optimum reliability, since by improving reliability, not only the cost of product is increased, but also revenue from product support will be decreased. Then the manufacturer should focus on trade-offs between product price (market competitive), performance (customer needs) and costs.

In the category **aii** (new and functional products), the manufacturer is responsible for delivering *total functional performance* instead of just delivering and supporting a physical product performing a function. The physical function needs to be designed for maximum performance effectiveness and efficiency at minimum LCC (Markeset and Kumar, 2003). This means that the operational and maintenance costs needs to be as low as possible.

Product weaknesses causing the need for services to support product, must be designed out, if possible. If not, the product needs are to be designed for cost effective reliability, and thereafter for easy maintenance and support at lowest cost.

Services and maintenance, which are directed at enhancing product exploitation, need to be minimized by incorporating them into the training of operation and maintenance personnel, or designed out through improved product reliability, improved documentation, etc. The manufacturer will not make any profit in maintenance and support. In this scenario, the manufacturer would like to optimize product reliability based on geographical location of operating of system (distance between manufacturer and operation place), customer competence, political and geopolitical situation of customer, and infrastructure facility and utilization in operation place. Then the required spare parts can be obtained and managed to procure.

Customer is responsible for anything (operation, maintenance, upgrade, etc), as mentioned earlier for **bi** (existing and conventional products). Then he/she can calculate and procures required spare parts based on product condition and its technical parameters.

In **bii** (existing and functional products), the manufacturer is delivering performance with an existing product, and has less possibility to influence performance through product design. Since the manufacturer owns the product/machine, and hence has to live with the weaknesses, there will be no profit from conventional services to support the product or customer. In other words, improved profit is coming from improved operational, maintenance and product support strategies. Reliability is influenced by how the product is used, by the operation environment, load, etc. Improving the preventive maintenance strategy and product support strategy (availability of spare parts in situ when required) also can influence system/machine availability. Consequentially, training of operation, maintenance, and support personnel will be important to ensure effective and efficient function performance (Markeset and Kumar, 2003).

4. Product reliability characteristics

Reliability of a system is a function of time and the environment, under which the system is operating. Reliability of a system is the probability that it will perform or operate the required functions without failure under a given condition for an intended operating period. Lower reliability means increased unscheduled repairs and decrease availability. More stand-by units may increase the system availability but do not decrease the incidence of system failures (Kumar and Granholm, 1988).

Life Cycle Cost (LCC) analysis can be used to compare and making decision between design alternatives. If the life cycle cost of one alternative is higher compared to the other one, then the lowest life cycle cost alternative is naturally preferred (figure 4).

If the reliability of a system is too low, maintainability issues such as accessibility to spare parts that need to be maintained, serviceability and interchangeability of parts and systems, use of modular design have to be considered (Blanchard et al., 1995, Kumar, 2001).

4.1 Operating environment based reliability analysis

Our literature survey shows that most of the researches and articles on reliability considers the failure time as the only variable for estimating reliability of a system. The reliability models, which also uses only time as an influencing factor, may not be suitable for the reliability analysis, because there are other factors that may influence the reliability characteristics of a system during its working lifetime (Kumar, 1993). For example if a system is used in different geographical or climatic conditions, then its reliability characteristics will not be equal in different condition. These variables may, for instance, include working environment (e.g. temperature, pressure, humidity, dust, or voltage stress), operating history of a machine (e.g. overhauls, effects of repair or type of maintenance) or the type of design or material, which are referred to as risk factor or covariates.

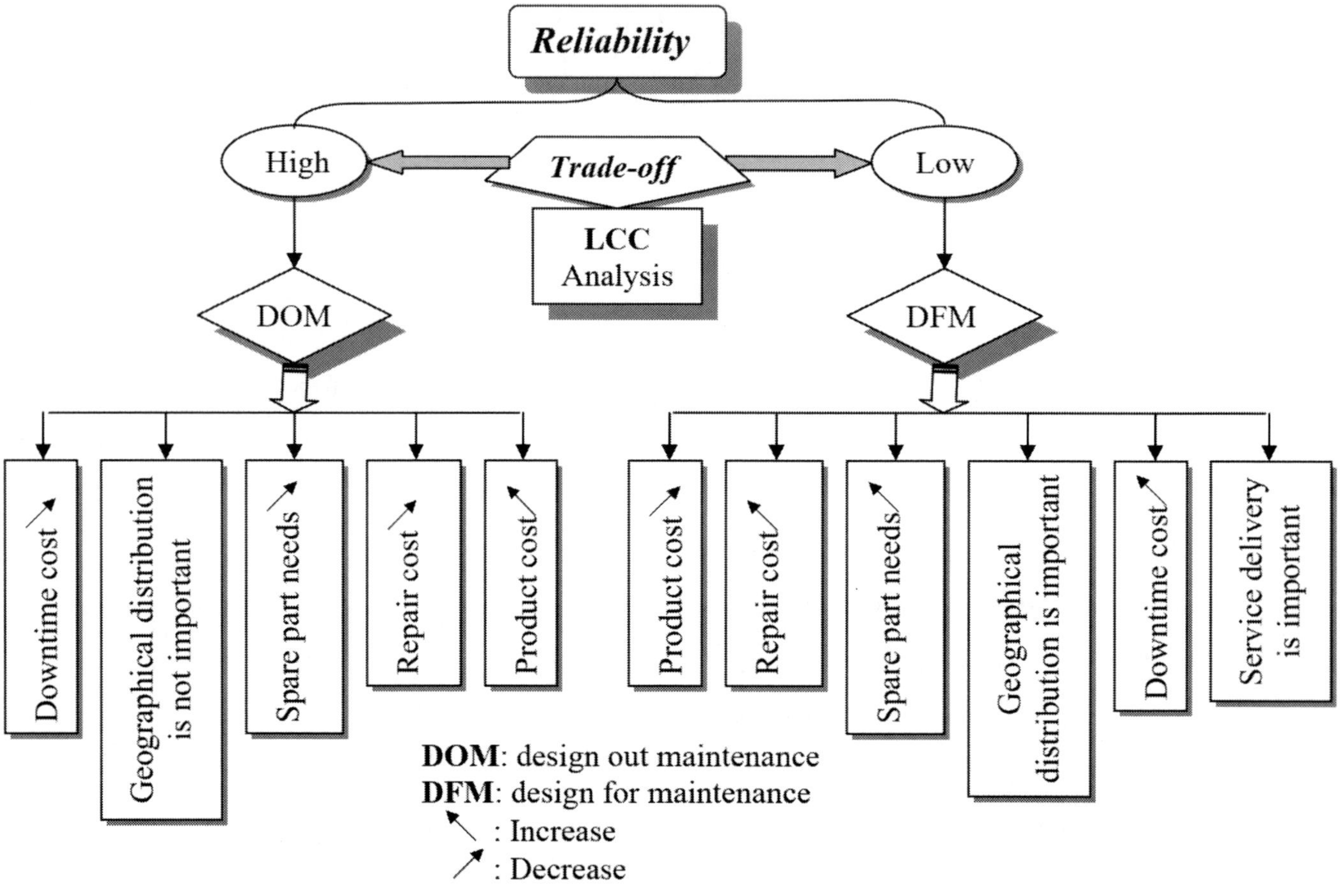

Figure 4. *Comparison between high and low reliable products*

For an item under consideration, with failure density function *f(t)* and reliability function *R(t),* the failure nature can be modeled by the hazard rate $\lambda(t)$ given by the relation: $\lambda(t) = \frac{f(t)}{R(t)}$, where $\lambda(t)dt$ is approximately the conditional probability of failure in the time interval *(t, t+ dt)* given survive to time *"t"*. As mentioned earlier, the hazard rate of a system, in general, is influenced not only by the time, but also by the covariates under which it operates. The hazard rate of a system is the product of baseline hazard rate $\lambda_0(t)$, dependent on time only, and one another positive functional term, basically independent of time, which incorporates the effects of a number of covariates. The baseline hazard rate is assumed to be identical and equal to the total hazard rate when the covariates have no influence on the failure pattern. The covariates may influence the hazard rate so that the observed hazard rate is either greater (e.g. in the case of poor maintenance or incorrect spare parts) or smaller (e.g. a new improved component of a system or reliable components) compared to the baseline hazard rate. The basic concept of this model is shown in figure 5 (Kumar and Klefsjö, 1994).

So, the actual hazard rate (failure rate) with respect to exponential form of time independent function, which incorporating the effects of covariates can be defined as (Kumar and Klefsjö, 1994):

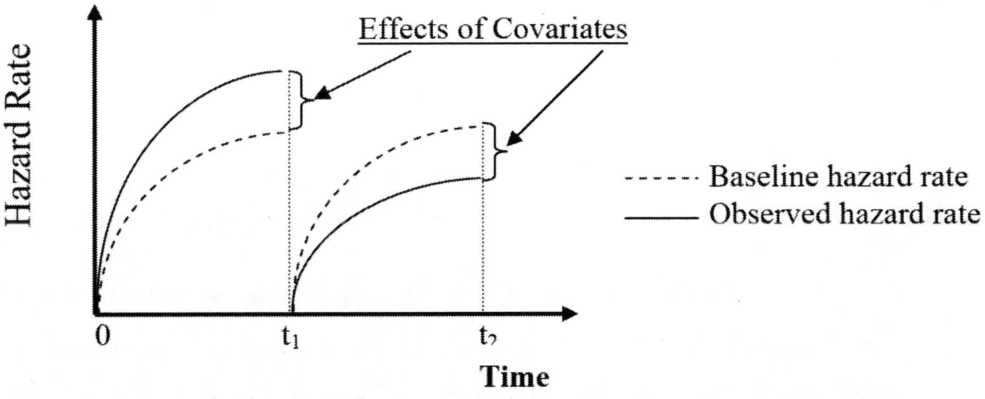

Figure 5. *Effects of risk factors (covariates) on hazard rate of system (Kumar and Klefsjö, 1994)*

$$\lambda(t^{\cdot}, z) = \lambda_0(t)\exp(z\alpha) = \lambda_0(t)\exp(\sum_{j=1}^{n}\alpha_j z_j) \qquad (1)$$

where z_j, $j = 1, 2, ..., n$, are the covariates associated with the system and α_j,

$j = 1, 2, \ldots, n,$ are the unknown parameters of the model, defining the effects of each one of the n covariates. The above model is commonly known as proportional hazards model (PHM) (see for details Kumar and Klefsjö, 1994)

5. Required spare parts calculation

For several types of spare parts, subassemblies and modules, replacing them, upon failure is more economical than repairing them. Bearings, gears, electronic modules, computer parts, gaskets, seals, filters, light bulbs, hoses, and valves are some of such parts, which are mostly replaced rather than repaired. In real life situation as mentioned earlier, there are several factors except time that has influence on reliability characteristics of parts/system. To account for these covariates into calculation we can assume the term $\exp(\alpha z)$ in the hazard rate function [$\lambda(t, z)$] proportionate to actual working condition, as a constant coefficient. Then:

$$R(t) = \exp(\sum_{j=1}^{n} \alpha_j z_j) \times \exp\left[-\int_0^t \lambda_0(x)dx\right] = \exp(\sum_{j=1}^{n} \alpha_j z_j) \times \exp[-\Lambda_0(t)] \quad (2)$$

where $\Lambda_0(t)$ is the cumulative baseline hazard rate.

The above exponential reliability model is generally a simple, applicable, and probably the best model while the effects of covariates are coming into calculation, If specially, the under study items are non-repairable (as mentioned before). In case of non-repairable items, the number of required spare parts can be calculated by (adapted from Billinton and Allan, 1983):

$$P(t) = \exp(-\lambda t) \times \sum_{X=0}^{N} \frac{(\lambda t)^X}{X!} \quad (3)$$

where:

P = Confidence level of spare parts' availability [1- p (shortage)]

$\lambda =$ Failure rate of objective part (with regarding to effect of covariates)

$t =$ operation time of system

$N =$ Total number of required spare parts in period "t"

If there is q number of same part that are in use at the moment; then q is entering in equation in form of multiplying by λtq. So the calculated $\boldsymbol{N}$ will represent the total required number of spare parts for whole system.

6. Case study

Life today would be difficult without such basics as water and electricity. In industry the same could be said with regard to hydraulic power. The hydraulic loaders are used commonly in the open pit mines for loading, hauling, and pilling up of ore and gangue. The hydraulic bucket lifting system of these loaders, which includes different repairable and non-repairable parts, plays a key role in the operation of machine. The hydraulic seal, which is used in hydraulic jacks, is one of non-repairable parts that were studied for analyzing of the effect of operating environment on mean time to failure and consequently forecasting of spare part needs. The figure 6 shows a number of seals that was mounted on hydraulic lifting jack.

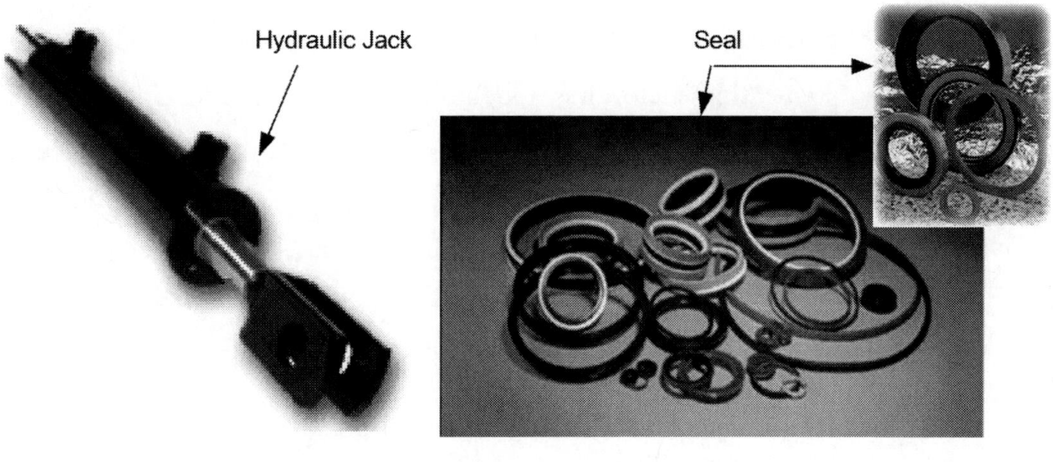

Figure 6. Hydraulic jack and seals

For studying of operating environment influence on failure rate of these seals, we analyzed the failure time data, which has been obtained from an Iron ore mine in Iran. We identified the important environmental factors influencing the performance of the seals, and codified them by numeric value. With respect to importance of selection and formulating of covariates in statistical inference, the covariates are formulated as follows in this case study:

1. *Roughness of jack rod:* The indicator "RNR" is used to denote the hydraulic jack rod condition regarding to rod surface finishing and smoothness, which is assigned the value ***–1*** for rough, and ***1*** for smooth surface.
2. *Type of hydraulic oil:* the indicator "**OILTYPE**" is used to denote the type of hydraulic oil is assigned ***1*** for the standard/manufacturer recommended type and –***1*** for other types.
3. *Dust:* this factor is denoted by the indicator "**DUST**", and is assigned ***1*** for insignificant (less and soft material such as clay…) and ***–1*** for significant (excessive and hard material like sand, quartz…) dust.
4. *Pollution (oil, gasoline, chemical water…):* this parameter appears as a corrosion that accelerated the failure, and denoted with indicator "**POLUTION**", which is assigned value ***–1*** for pollution existence and ***1*** for non existence.
5. *Temperature:* the temperature of parts and operation environment influences the abrasion and failure rate of the seals. The indicator "**TEMP**" is used to denote this covariate, and is assigned the value ***–1*** for temperature above +35 °C or below –15 °C , and ***1*** for temperature between –15 to +35 °C.
6. *Operator's skill:* this factor has much influence on failure rate of seals, and appears in the form of the hydraulic jack's interior oil pressure (excessive oil pressure at the time of lifting more than allowed load). The indicator "**OPSKILL**" is used to denote this factor and assigned the value ***1*** for skilled and ***–1*** for inexpert operator.

For checking the IID (independent identical distribution) assumption for data (inherent assumption of the exponential reliability model, eqn no. 2), cumulative time to failures

(TTFs) Vs cumulative failure number is plotted in Figure 7. The plotted points form a straight line. It implies that there is no trend in the failure data. Then the assumption of identical distribution for the TTFs under consideration is not contradicted. On the other hand, regarding to non-reparability of part we allow concluding data as independent.

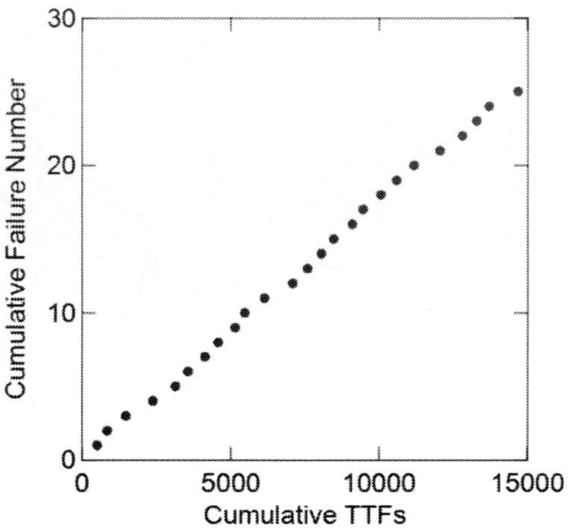

Figure 7. *Showing no trend in the TTFs of hydraulic seals*

Same baseline hazard rate $[\lambda_0(t)]$ for seals after failure and replacement have been assumed.

The SYSTAT software was used for estimating the correspond value of α, and were tested for their significance on the basis of *p-value*. In the other word, *1-p* for a covariate indicates the importance of its considerations in the model. The following table shows the estimates of α for the six covariates (*t-ratio* in table 1 indicates the t-test statistic for each covariate, uses for determining *p-value*).

The results show that the effects of three covariates (**DUST, OPSKILL, OILTYPE**) are significant at 10% *p-value*.

The best model for hazard rate of seal according to the result of the PHM analysis is:

$$\lambda(t,z) = \lambda_0(t) \times exp(-0.783\ DUST - 0.777\ OPSKILL + 0.397\ OILTYPE) \quad (4)$$

To satisfy the proportionality assumption of the hazard rates, the plots of the logarithm of the estimated cumulative hazard rates against time should be simply shifted by an

Table 1. *Estimation of covariates*

Step number 0

	t-ratio	"p"
Variables included:		
DUST	-2.678	0.007
TEMP	0.056	0.955
RNR	-1.240	0.215
OILTYPE	1.104	0.270
POLUTION	1.432	0.152
OPSKILL	-2.586	0.010

Step number 1

	t-ratio	"p"
Variables included:		
DUST	-2.698	0.007
RNR	-1.240	0.215
OILTYPE	1.205	0.228
POLUTION	1.531	0.126
OPSKILL	-2.728	0.006
Variables excluded:		
TEMP	0.056	0.955

Step number 2

	t-ratio	"p"
Variables included:		
DUST	-2.760	0.006
RNR	-2.025	0.043
POLUTION	1.438	0.150
OPSKILL	-2.803	0.005
Variables excluded:		
TEMP	-0.480	0.631
OILTYPE	1.212	0.226

Step number 3

	t-ratio	"p"
Variables included:		
DUST	-2.820	0.005
RNR	-1.376	0.169
OPSKILL	-2.872	0.004
Variables excluded:		
TEMP	0.227	0.820
OILTYPE	1.088	0.277
POLUTION	1.474	0.140

Step number 4

	t-ratio	"p"
Variables included:		
DUST	-2.630	0.009
OPSKILL	-2.672	0.008
Variables excluded:		
TEMP	-0.732	0.464
OILTYPE	1.705	0.088
POLUTION	0.195	0.845
RNR	-1.394	0.163

Step number 5

	t-ratio	"p"
Variables included:		
DUST	-2.831	0.005
OPSKILL	-2.802	0.005
OILTYPE	1.670	0.095
Variables excluded:		
TEMP	0.316	0.752
POLUTION	1.013	0.311
RNR	-0.500	0.617

Final Model Summary

Parameter	Estimate	S.E.	t-ratio	p-value
DUST	-0.783	0.277	-2.831	0.005
OPSKILL	-0.777	0.277	-2.802	0.005
OILTYPE	0.397	0.238	1.670	0.095

95.0 % Confidence Intervals

Parameter	Estimate	Lower	Upper
DUST	-0.783	-1.325	-0.241
OPSKILL	-0.777	-1.320	-0.233
OILTYPE	0.397	-0.069	0.862

additive constant α, the estimate of the regression parameter α of the covariate which is taken as strata (Kalbfleisch and Prentice, 1980). Therefore; the plots should be approximately parallel and separated appropriately corresponding to the different values of the regression parameter α, if the proportionality assumption is correct as is seen for example in figure 8 (Kumar and Klefsjö, 1994).

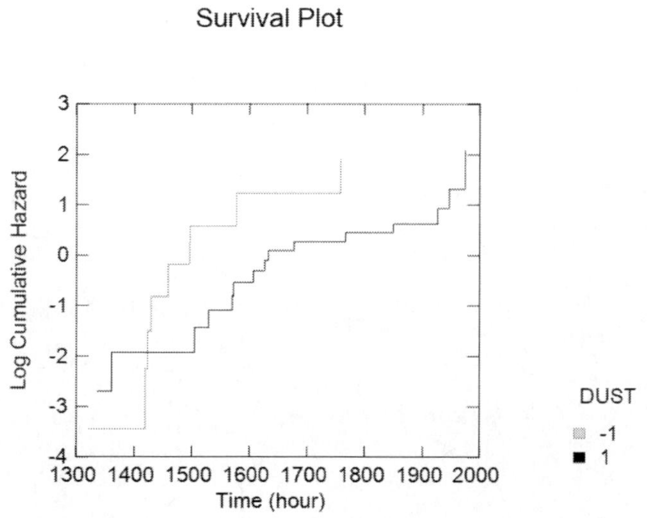

Figure 8. *An example (DUST covariate) of graphical test for proportionality assumption of the hazard rates*

With assuming 3000 hour as a mean time to failure for this part (seal), and applying the exponential reliability model as a common model in analyzing of system characteristics,: the constant baseline hazard rate is given by

$$\lambda_0(t) = \frac{1}{MTTF} = \frac{1}{3000} \approx 3.33e-4 \qquad (5)$$

In this case study, the loader operators are almost expert, and hydraulic oil is standard and adapted to manufacturer recommendations. Dust in this mine due to the nature of rocks, is excessive. So according to this condition:

$$\lambda(t,z) = 3.33e\text{-}4 \times \exp(-0.783 \times (-1) - 0.777 \times 1 + 0.397 \times 1) = 4.98e\text{-}4 \qquad (6)$$

The predictable number of required seal in one working year (two working shift per day) with respect to 2007 hours as a mean time to failure of seals with 90% confidence of accessibility when it is required, is equal to:

$$0.90 = \exp(-4.98e-4\times 5450\times 2)\times \sum_{X=0}^{N}\frac{(4.98e-4\times 5450\times 2)^{X}}{X!} \qquad (7)$$

$N \approx$ ***8*** *(units/Y/loader)*

In the ideal circumstance, where no covariate existing, the required number of seals is equal to:

$$0.90 = \exp(-3.33e-4\times 5450\times 2)\times \sum_{X=0}^{N}\frac{(3.33e-4\times 5450\times 2)^{X}}{X!} \qquad (8)$$

$N \approx$ ***6*** *(units/Y/loader)*

In comparison the number of required seals in both conditions, with or without considering the operating environmental factors' affect, the significance of these factors and their role in actual life of parts is appeared. We can also conclude for optimizing of system organization with respect to real life factors, operating environmental parameters should be taken into account in process management of system/machine.

7. Inventory management requirements

Lead-time is one of important factors in the inventory management. This factor has influence on when and how many/much should order to minimize inventory cost and maximize the availability of parts when is required. On the other hand the criticality of parts is also another important factor in decision making about its quantity in warehouse. Then we can evaluate and classify the spare parts in term of lead-time (which represents indirectly geographical location of system) and criticality (Table 2).

The number of stars for each item indicates the importance of the item to consider and pay more attention for its availability when required. Since the studied loader's model in our case study is Volvo, many dealers in different parts of world are offering this part to sale. With considering a dealer in Sweden, due to the distance between operating location (Iran) and dealer, and also the criticality of part, it can be classified in the S_{LM}^{***} category.

Table 2. Classification of spare parts (adapted from Sheikh et al., 2000)

Lead-time \ Criticality	Low	Moderate	High
Short	S_{SL}^{*}	S_{SM}^{*}	S_{SH}^{*}
Moderate	S_{ML}^{**}	S_{MM}^{**}	S_{MH}^{***}
Long	S_{LL}^{**}	S_{LM}^{***}	S_{LH}^{***}

Another option is that the user decide to purchase from local dealers, then it can be classified in the S_{HM}^{*} category.

With assumption the cost of one seal equal 500 SEK, the cost of ordering one lot equal 300 SEK, and the annual holding cost equal 15% of the part cost, the economic order quantity with respect to annual demand rate (8) is (Krajewski and Ritzman, 1999):

$$EOQ = \sqrt{\frac{2DS}{H}} = \sqrt{\frac{2\times 8\times 300}{75}} \approx 8 \text{ (Units/loader)} \qquad (9)$$

This is the quantity which with that the total inventory cost will be minimum. For the "continuous review (Q) system" as inventory position controlling and management, we need to calculate the "reorder point". The "reorder point" is equal to the sum of average demand during lead-time and safety stock. The safety stock is calculated based on the confidence level of cycle service and the number of standard deviations from mean. If average lead-time in this case is 45 days, and assume 90% confidence level of cycle service, then:

$$\sigma_{D(1year)} = \sqrt{\frac{t}{\overline{T}}} = \sqrt{\frac{5450}{2007}} \approx 1.65 \text{ (Units/loader)} \qquad (10)$$

$$\textit{Reorder point} = d\times L + \sigma_D \times \sqrt{L}\Phi_{(p/2)} = 0.667\times 1.5 + 0.1375\times 1.5^{1/2}\times 1.645 \approx \mathbf{2} \text{ (U. /L.)} \qquad (11)$$

It means whenever the inventory position reaches 2 units/loader (1 unit/loader, is safety stock), we should order 8 units/loader.

8. Conclusion

In the beginning, one attempts to make a product as reliable as possible, with less maintenance needs and cheap, But this approach is not feasible mainly due to technological limitations. Then the design for maintenance alternative becomes mooted, and this option demand that the reliability and maintainability characteristics with supportability issues like required spare parts of the product should be taken in account. Using the reliability techniques can optimize the forecasting and calculating for required spare parts during the product life.

The reliability analysis of the hydraulic seal failure time data shows that the environment in which the machine/system is used, plays a critical role in reliability and consequently availability characteristics of machine, and some times cause more spare parts requirements. These covariates cause the hazard rate increase. Then the formulation and selection of a covariate is very important in the sense that the statistical inferences are based on the covariates considered. However, we can optimize it with modifying some effective parameters, such as user/operator training, and use of high performance material such as low friction composite or abrasion resistant polyurethane which enhance the performance characteristics of the seal and leading to a longer seal life.

References

1. Billinton, R. and Ahllen, R.N., (1983), "*Reliability Evaluation of Engineering Systems: Concepts and Techniques*", Boston, Pitman Books Limited

2. Blanchard, B.S., Verma, D. and Peterson, E.L. (1995), "*Maintainability: A Key to Effective Serviceability and Maintenance Management*", New York, John Willey and Sons Inc.

3. Kalbfleisch, J.D. and Prentice, R.L. (1980), "*The Statistical Analysis of Failure Time Data*", New York, John Willey and Sons Inc.

4. Krajewski, L.J. and Ritzman, L.R. (1999), "*Operations Management-Strategy and Analysis*", 5th ed., New York, Addison-Wesley Publishing Co. Inc.

5. Kumar, D. (1993), "*Reliability Analysis Considering Operating Conditions in a Mine*", Licentiate thesis, Luleå University of Technology, Luleå, Sweden

6. Kumar, D., Klefsjö, B. And Kumar, U., (1992), "Reliability Analysis of Power Transmission Cables of Electric Mine Loaders Using the Proportional Hazard Model", *Reliability Engineering and System Safety*, Vol. 37, pp 217-222

7. Kumar, R. and Kumar, U. (2003), "A General Framework for Development of Service Delivery Strategy for Industrial System in a Multinational Environment", Submitted for publication in *Journal of Business and Industrial Marketing*

8. Kumar, U. & Granholm, S. (1988), "Reliability Technique – a Powerful Tool for Mine Operators", *Mineral Resource Engineering*, Vol. 1 No. 1

9. Kumar, U. (2001), "Design and Development of Service and Maintenance Concepts for Mechanized and Automatic Mining system", *in Proceedings of the 4th Regional Symposium on Computer Applications in the Mineral Industries*, 3rd to 5th September, Tampere. Finland

10. Loomba, A. P.S. (1998), "Product distribution and service support strategy linkages (An empirical validation)", *International Journal of Physical Distribution & Logistics Management*, Vol. 28, No. 2

11. Markeset, T. and Kumar, U. (2002a), "Integration of RAMS and risk analysis in product design & development work processes – A case study", *in Proceeding of Maintenance Management and Modeling Conference of International Foundation for Research in Maintenance*, 6-8 May, Växjö, Sweden

12. Markeset, T. and Kumar, U. (2003), " Study of Product Support Strategy: Conventional versus Functional Products", Submitted for publication in *Journal of Quality in Maintenance Engineering*

13. Mathieu V. (2001), "Product services: from a service supporting the product to a service supporting the client", Journal of Business & Industrial Marketing, Vol. 16 No. 1

14. Parasuraman, A. (1998), "Customer Service in Business-to-Business Markets: An Agenda for Research", *Journal of Business and Industrial Marketing*, Vol. 13 No. 4/5, pp. 309-321

15. Sheikh, A.K., Younas, M. and Raouf, A. (2000), "Reliability based spare parts forecasting and procurement strategies", *Maintenance, Modeling and Optimization*, pp. 81.108, Kluwer Academic Publishers, Boston

About the authors

BEHZAD GHODRATI

Behzad Ghodrati obtained his B.Sc. and M.Sc. in Mining Engineering from Technical Faculty – Tehran University, Iran in 1989 and 1993 respectively. Then he jointed to Sahand University of Technology, Tabriz, Iran in 1994 as a lecturer and was actively involved in teaching and research in the field of Mining Machinery, Mining Economy and Management. He joined the postgraduate program of Luleå University of Technology, Sweden in September 2000. At the present, he is doing his Ph.D. in the field of product support management, and the temporary title of his research is:
INTEGRATION OF PRODUCT DESIGN CHARACTERISTICS IN DIMENTIONING OF PRODUCT SUPPORT FOE EFFECTIVE SUPPLY CHAIN MANAGEMENT.

E-mail: Behzad.Ghodrati@ce.luth.se

Uday Kumar, PhD
Professor of Mechanical Engineering (Operation and maintenance Eng.)

Dr. Kumar obtained his B. Tech from BHU, India during the year 1979. After working for 6 years in Indian mining industries, he joined the postgraduate program of Luleå University of Technology, Sweden in 1986 and obtained a PhD degree in field of Reliability and Maintenance during 1990. He worked as a Senior Lecturer and Associate Professor and was actively involved in teaching, research and consultancy in the field of reliability and maintenance at Luleå University. In 1997, he was appointed as a Professor of Mechanical Engineering (Maintenance) at Stavanger University College, Stavanger, Norway. Since July 2000, he has taken up a position as a Professor of Mechanical Engineering at Luleå University of Technology, Luleå.
He is also member of the editorial boards and reviewer for many international journals. He has published more than 80 Papers in International Journals and Conference proceedings mainly in the field of reliability and maintenance.
His research interests are Product support, Equipment management, Equipment maintenance, Reliability and maintainability analysis, Life Cycle Costing, Risk analysis, System analysis, etc.

e-mail: uday.kumar@ce.luth.se

Dhanajay Kumar, PhD

Dhananjay Kumar graduated in Mechanical Engineering in 1987 from India. He worked for a utility company from 1987-1990 in India. In 1996, he obtained a PhD in Reliability Engineering from Lulea University of Technology, Sweden. He worked for a utility company from 1996-1999. Presently, he is working as a senior research engineer for Nokia since 1999 in the area of Reliability Engineering.

E-mail: dhanajay.kumar@nokia.com

Impact of RCM on Performance and Customer Perception

By Melkote Ramaswamy, Ph. D.
(3910 Pebble Creek Drive, Indianapolis, IN 46268)

ABSTRACT

Traditionally, based on product testing and Failure Mode and Effects Analysis, manufacturers develop a service maintenance schedule to ensure optimum performance during the product life. The maintenance may entail such tasks as cleaning, adjustment or replacement, However, of late, the focus of maintenance has shifted from routine preventative maintenance to reliability-centered maintenance (RCM). The crux of RCM is maintenance as and when required and not on a preset schedule. The judgment is based on careful inspection. The British Royal Navy has recently applied RCM to its fleet of submarines and appears to have achieved impressive reduction in maintenance costs without compromising performance.

Here we apply the RCM concept to the following scenarios:
Pharmaceuticals (drug administration—dosage and frequency), healthcare (type and frequency of various tests, for example: mammograms and other screenings), the auto industry (oil change, tire rotation, balance and replacement, battery replacement), home appliances (furnace filters, water heating elements, carpets, etc.) and the workplace (certification frequency, number and duration of tests, etc.).

INTRODUCTION

Maintenance Concept

Unless designed as a throwaway, a product's usefulness is determined principally by maintainability and availability. While maintenance and maintainability are customer-centered, availability is a function of design elements, some of which dictate certain maintenance constraints.

A product can be an individual component or a system of components. Maintenance schedule is largely a result of conservative estimates based on studies of mean time between failures (MTBF) and Failure Mode and Effect Analysis (FMEA).

The product warranty in turn reflects the manufacturer's confidence in product performance. Warranty is always conditional, subject to the customer doing certain things at certain times as spelled out in a maintenance schedule. While such a schedule may be described as suggested, it has an implicit mandatory overtone.

Reliability Centered Maintenance (RCM)

This scheme is a departure from the traditional schedule-based maintenance and consists of doing things and tasks only as and when necessary. At the heart of the concept is careful inspection. Maintenance is based not on a static preventive philosophy but on a dynamic performance-based scenario. In some sense, the approach parallels the Just-in-time (JIT) method of inventory control.

SCOPE

We examine here the relevance, application, and impact of RCM in various product scenarios—from DOD to Automobiles to Pharmaceutical. Validity in domestics, academics and healthcare is also explored.

APPLICATIONS

Department of Defense (DoD)

According to a report in the October 2002 issue of IndyLog (the newsletter of SOLE's Indianapolis chapter), the British Royal Navy recently implemented RCM on a small fleet of submarines, (a sophisticated system) and achieved significant cost savings with no impact on performance. However, the small size of the study sample (less than 12) raises questions on the statistical validity of the results. The results, however, signal the emergence of a new trend in maintenance and point to a potential alternative to the traditional schedule-based maintenance.

The United States DoD has an enormous number of assets in various branches of the armed forces and is a natural candidate for proving the RCM in a more convincing way. What is needed is a re-examination of current maintenance schedule and a revamped inspection schedule and a reliable diagnostics application on which to base the RCM. A risk evaluation game plan is a necessary corollary to the inspection regime. Yearly cost savings can be in millions of dollars.

Similar considerations apply to the commercial aviation sector.

Auto Industry

RCM finds an attractive proving ground in the automobile industry. American automobiles are built to last around 100,000 miles with scheduled maintenance. Because owners do not keep their car for more than 5 years on an average (they either sell or trade or give to charity), it is difficult to trace the history after it leaves the original owner. Foreign cars built abroad or in the US appear to last at least 150,000 miles sometimes with no trace of rust even and owners appear to stick to their automobiles lot longer than an American car. Of late, some imports are offering 7 year/70,000 miles and some 10 year/100,000 mile warranty. To keep up with this challenge, US car manufacturers are beginning to offer similar warranties. Also, so-called certified used cars are becoming popular because of the nearly new-car-like warranties and the transferability feature.

Of course, these warranties have certain exclusions.. Warranties are contingent on the customer strictly adhering to a rigid maintenance schedule and offering proof of such compliance. The impact of RCM on the validity of warranty is an open issue.

The following table (typical of the auto industry) lists the maintenance task, the interval in miles for scheduled maintenance and likely RCM intervals based on inspection

Maintenance Task	*Interval (Miles)*	*RCM (Example)*
Oil and Filter Change	3,000	4,500
Air Filter	30,000	40,000
Fuel Filter	60,000	70,000
Tire Rotation	6,000	8,000
Wheel Balance	12,000	15,000
Alignment	12,000	15,000
Wiper Blades	6,000	12,000
Cooling System Flush	30,000	45,000
Brake Fluid Flush	30,000	45,000
Transmission Fluid Flush	30,000	40,000
Power Steering Fluid Flush	30,000	35,000
Belts and Hoses	60,000	75,000
Fuel Injection Cleaning	30,000	40,000
Maintenance Tune-up	30,000	40,000
PCV Valve	30,000	38,000
Battery Replacement	40,000	45,000
Tire Replacement	30,000	42,000

The above tasks differ in their degree of criticality. This raises the question: what if we deviate from the above intervals. Instead of blindly and rigidly sticking to the schedule, suppose we inspect and then decide if we need that service. We are then gravitating to RCM. The third column lists what we describe as RCM services which are the result of careful inspection and a reliable diagnostics system. Notice that the customer comes out ahead since the intervals are longer than manufacturer-scheduled. Also note that because of care in inspection and use of quality components, performance has not been compromised. The customer may not mind if the dealer charges a little more for the same services.

Auto leasing companies have a lot to gain by switching to an RCM regimen.

Pharmaceutical Industry

The rising cost of healthcare stems partly from prescription and other drugs. Drugs dictate a regimen (strength and frequency) of dosage administration to deliver maximum benefit to the patient.

It is tempting to speculate what would happen if the regimen is slightly modified.
Will it matter if the dosage is reduced by 25% or the interval increased by 25%?
Manufacturers definitely build a cushion and employ a play-it-safe philosophy.
While life and death situations allow for very little deviation from the cushion, less critical situations might lend themselves to lower dosages or longer intervals with no loss

in efficacy. Only research can tell which drugs lend themselves to such deviations. The benefits to the customer in terms of cost reduction are obvious.

Healthcare

Time was women were kept in the hospital for at least 7 days after normal delivery before being sent home. Notice that this has come down to more like 2-3 days. Only abnormal and caesarian cases are sent home after a relatively longer stay. Patients are happy to go home earlier and the insurance industry is pleased with the cost benefit.

Mammograms were recommended to be taken every year. Depending on age, once in two years is the current practice. Research is the key to the exact interval. For instance, why not once in 30 months?

Routine physicals are another example of RCM-like maintenance. Education is the key. The Internet, if used with caution, could be a valuable learning tool.

Since some of the physician services require a co-payment, switching to RCM will save money for both the patient and the insurance company.

Domestics

Refrigerators, microwave ovens; washer-dryers, dish washers and garbage disposers require very little scheduled maintenance and are ideal candidates for RCM concept. Bathroom and attic fans seem to last for ever and are simply replaced when they stop working. Inspection, not a hard and fast schedule should dictate changing furnace filters, electric bulbs, water heating element and lawn mower parts.

A maintenance schedule for a PC and accessories appears non-existent. PC's are either upgraded or discarded for a newer version.

Academics

Many professional certifications require continuous updating of training and licensing requirements. This may mean taking courses and attending workshops or conferences. One obvious way to cut costs is to tailor the frequency of updates to developments and advances in the field. For example, if nothing has changed in the way a certain surgical procedure is done, there is not need for new training. On the other hand, if changes occur rapidly (for instance laser applications), one needs to update more frequently.

Driver license renewal for senior citizens should be response-based instead of on a fixed 4-year interval to ensure that the driver is reliable and does not a pose safety hazard.

With the increased popularity of online and distance learning, face-to-face instruction, workshops and conferences can perhaps be made less frequent and shorter, thus reducing travel costs.

Along the same lines, removing a foreign language requirement from graduation may have little impact on the quality of the graduate. On the other hand, changing numerical grade system to Pass/Fail will have significant impact since it is impossible to tell how well a student had done in a given course.

CONCLUSIONS

RCM is a viable option for product maintenance and is likely to become more popular as careful inspection procedures are developed and implemented. It promises to bring significant cost savings to a variety of stakeholders.

Author's Bio
Melkote Ramaswamy received his BS and MS from India and Ph. D in physics from Johns Hopkins University. After pursuing a career in physics, Mel switched to Technical Writing. His writing career has spanned commercial and DoD sectors. His most recent job has been as a Validation Lead/Senior Technical Writer as a Crew Technical Services contractor at Eli Lilly. Prior to that he worked for Hurco Companies, Wavetek Wandel Goltermann and Systems Maintenance & Technology.

Mel has taught physics in India and US and also Business Writing as an adjunct faculty at the University of Indianapolis. He has published over 100 research and technical articles. He has given presentations at SOLE's Annual Symposia in Las Vegas (2001), in Orlando (2001), and in Phoenix (2002). He is a Fellow of the Indian Academy of Sciences. He has published two books and has just finished a book *An Immigrant Celebrates America*.

Mel joined SOLE in 1996 and has been active in its publications. He has received the *Excellence in Logistics Literature* award from SOLE's Indianapolis Chapter in 1996, 1999, 2000 and 2001and 2002. He served on the Board of Contributors of *Logistics Spectrum*.

UNCLASSIFIED

OPERABILITY IN SPACE: Commonality, Interchangeability, and Robotics – An Approach to Cost Reduction

Presentation to

SOLE 2003
Von Braun Center
Huntsville, AL

12- 14 August 2003

Dr. Mike Baran
SAIC, Huntsville, AL

With Contributions from Drs. Jim Odom and Doug Baker,
SAIC Huntsville, AL

And Dr. Mike Battaglia,
HQ NASA

UNCLASSIFIED

PURPOSE:

This paper is intended to stimulate thought and discussion concerning the concept of operability applied to space systems and operations with the intent of reducing costs to achieve and sustain orbital operations.

APPROACH:

Postulate a simple view of what may drive recurring costs and operations risks

Define Five Categories of "Things" to Get to Orbit and to Provide Sustained Operability in Space

- **Minimize Recurring Costs to Orbit**

BASELINE PARAMETERS

1. Bulk of on-orbit weight is in fuel for satellite operation
2. Next item for weight is satellite supporting structure
   - Power and power management
   - Cooling and thermal control
   - Station keeping
   - Command and control
3. Last items in terms of weight are generally specialized components related to satellite primary mission or function
   - Boxes, boards, and cabling / intra-satellite comms

COST DRIVERS

1. Overcoming gravity –
   - Can not do too much about that directly
   - Get fuel & booster costs as low as possible
2. Pre-launch labor costs – the more sophisticated and complex the carrier vehicle,
   - The greater the skill and manpower levels required to prepare for launch
3. Vehicle requirements – the more complex the requirements, the more expensive to design, build, and maintain.
   - Boost phase and re-entry loads vs. in-space ops only

A SIMPLE VIEW OF COST DRIVERS

CONCEPT FOR DISCUSSION:

Define Five Categories of "Things" to Get to Orbit and to Provide Sustained Operability in Space

- Minimize Recurring Costs to Orbit

1. Nineteen Inch Rack Satellite Concept
2. On-orbit, In-plane Service Stations
3. Robotic Service Vehicles
4. Two Types of "Trucks" and One "Bus" to Haul to Orbit
5. Rescue Vehicles

1. NINETEEN INCH RACK SATELLITE CONCEPT

Concept based on form-fit-function / plug-and-play approach –

Standardization of key structural and support elements:

 # 2 Weight Driver

- **Satellite structural approach for long on-orbit life – Design to reduce space debris – recycle used components to earth**
- **Interfaces for power, cooling, intra-satellite communications**
- **Refueling interface (as done on military aircraft – UARSI – Universal Air Refueling System Interface)**
- **Design for robotic servicing: remove / replace / repair**
    - **Apply industrial robot assembly technology**
    - **Indexing and fiducial marks built-in for robot docking, refueling, servicing, and component replacement**

2. ON-ORBIT, IN-PLANE SERVICE STATIONS, 1/2

Purpose of Stations: On-orbit trans-shipment points

1. **Interface between heavy "trucks" & busses, and orbital service vehicles that stay in space – "The Freight Terminal"**
2. **For starters, consider them to be unmanned**
    - **Fuel Storage – Fuel "trucks" offload, on-orbit service vehicles "tank up" to service satellites**
    - **Parts storage for satellites to be serviced**
    - **Consider capability for limited manned operation on as-needed basis**
3. **Number and locations in orbital planes TBD by operational and supporting cost studies**
4. **Could reduce space debris – place to deliver "used parts" for return to earth**

2. ON-ORBIT, IN-PLANE SERVICE STATIONS, 2/2

Requires definition of orbital planes and altitudes of most interest and use. Nothing new really:

Wanted: Traffic Cops for Space
New York Times
By Andrew C. Revkin
February 18, 2003

But three regions in space that are growing very popular with companies lofting commercial satellites **are particularly vulnerable to a continuing buildup of space junk, according to analyses by NASA and other researchers: the band from** 480 to 600 miles up, **another** 840 to 900 miles up, **and finally the** special zone 22,300 **miles from the Equator, called geosynchronous orbit, where satellites can remain nearly stationary over a spot on the surface.**

That region already has some 320 satellites parked in coveted spots, with dozens more planned as space-based enterprises continue to expand.

> This is probably more of an international political issue as opposed to a technical issue.

3. ROBOTIC SERVICE VEHICLES

Optimize design for long space life

- **Aerodynamics and associated loads not a factor**
- **Minimize weight**
- **Deliver fuel and new parts to satellites on-orbit**
  - **One design vs. Two – fuel vs. parts – TBD by studies**
- **Return old parts from satellites for return to earth –**
- **Help address space junk issue**

> Another international political issue as opposed to a technical issue.

4. TWO TYPES OF "TRUCKS" AND ONE "BUS" TO HAUL TO ORBIT

Not really a new idea. Military and commercial practices have done this for years –design (size & use) of vehicles to optimize performance in a broad sustained operational sense that supports the enterprise

- **Type 1: Bulk cargoes that are not time-urgent – fuel for satellites**
  - **Use simple, rugged, "heavy lifters" to take fuel, etc., to on-orbit transfer points.**
- **Type 2: Just-in-time deliveries: Smaller, less expensive unmanned system to deliver to orbital transfer stations**
  - **Replacement and / or upgrade parts – send on pre-planned basis or when needed**
- **Type 3: The "Bus" – Man-rated system to deliver personnel and limited supplies to orbit and return when needed**
  - **Robust Safety Margins & designed to simplify refurbishment**

5. RESCUE VEHICLES

Again, a concept long used by both military and commercial enterprises

- **USAF / USN / USCG Rescue Teams – Combatant and Non-Combatant**
  - **Coal and other hard-rock mines**
    - **Petro-Chemical Plants**
      - **HEMSI ...**

Three types of vehicles – Rich field for Operations / Cost Analyses

1. **On-orbit "life-boats" – at on-orbit stations.**
2. **Stand-by vehicles on ground – Simple, robust, reliable**
3. **"Lifeboat Module" on Bus?**

REGARDING CONCEPTS DISCUSSED HERE

Wanted: Traffic Cops for Space
New York Times, By Andrew C. Revkin February 18, 2003

The United States, starting in the 1990's, became the first country to adopt strict national standards for cutting risks that space activities would add to debris-collision risks. The regulations apply both to NASA and military launchings and to any company seeking the federal licenses required to launch or operate a satellite.
...result could mirror a problem with ship registration: owners can register their vessels under "flags of convenience" to avoid strict laws elsewhere.

The motivation to skirt rules lies in money. **One of the biggest expected costs to commercial satellite owners from the proposed standards will be holding in reserve some of the fuel that is used to keep certain satellites precisely positioned.**

The standards will require those satellites, toward the end of their useful lives, to be boosted into "graveyard orbits," said Dr. Phillip D. Anz-Meador, a physicist and NASA consultant in Houston

This could cost some companies hundreds of millions of dollars in lost revenue from the abbreviated missions of their equipment.

SOME CLOSING THOUGHTS

Concept offers possible range of services that NASA could sell to commercial ventures:

1. Refueling
2. Address space junk issue on incremental basis, sustainable in the long run
3. Satellite Servicing

Alternative approach might be for NASA to develop and license technologies

WOULD APPEAR TO BE A RICH AREA FOR OPERATIONS AND COST ANALYSES

Keep Human Role in Space Focused on What Humans Can Do Uniquely – EXPLORE, ANALYZE, & CREATE

Data Modeling Change Detection of Inventory Flow and Instrument Calibration

Holger M. Jaenisch, James W. Handley, and Louis A. Bonham
Sparta Inc., 4901 Corporate Drive, Suite 102, Huntsville, AL 35805

ABSTRACT

Data Modeling is a new mathematical tool for logistics research. It enables reference points to be established for complex dynamic processes such as inventory control and instrument calibration. This paper presents an overview of Data Modeling and how it can be used to achieve mathematical models that are a basis of comparison for detecting significant changes either in inventory flow or instrument calibration.

1. INTRODUCTION

1.1 Inventory Flow

Data Modeling for inventory flow and control involves the creation of a mathematical equation such as

$$y' = f(V, \Delta V, PO, PD) \tag{1}$$

that describes the relationship between inventory levels and their usage as measured by **volume** (V), **change in volume** (ΔV), **point of origin** (PO), or **point of departure** (PD). Simple metrics that are part of traditional logistics analysis of inventory levels can be monitored autonomously to give a new level of self-awareness to business as usual for complex operations. For example, keeping munitions and supplies at the proper levels between storage points and required field or transition points requires careful orchestration of delivery schedules, volumes, and queuing time arrival events.

If the intricacies contained in the complex inventory flow system or process can be adequately modeled, the model can be used as a diagnostic and predictor for assessing when inventory flow has changed in an off-nominal fashion. Such change detection (novelty detection) would enable monitoring and detection of inappropriate allocations of resources and potentially generates derivative indicators of impending critical events and disasters.

1.2 Inventory Abnormality

The time directly preceding possible escalations of hostilities frequently results in an increase in the requisition of certain materials or the unusual storage of quantities of certain items. This change in the flow of business as usual is very difficult to detect while it is happening, because this form of anomalous behavior is usually spread out over time and across many nodes in the inventory flow structure. If an accurate mathematical model of the nominal flow characteristics of the inventory site were available for comparison, then changes in the underlying dynamics would be easily seen and would draw the logistic analyst's attention.

1.3 Instrument Response Modeling

Aircraft use sophisticated instruments in the form of Improved Data Modems (IDM), flight recorders, transponders, radar, communication links, leveling instrumentation, and flight and attitude controllers. Whenever one of these instruments is suspected of being out of calibration, it is removed from the aircraft and returned to the manufacturer for recalibration and testing. This process is both costly and lengthy, and is done many times unnecessarily. Data Modeling can be used to eliminate the unnecessary removal and recalibration of an instrument. Using Data Modeling, the response of a newly calibrated instrument to a known stimulus for different instrument settings can be monitored and recorded during the early history of its useful life or whenever the instrument is known to be functioning adequately. These stimuli need not be the same as those prescribed by the manufacturer for use during test bench calibration. Instead, the stimulus can be something that is readily available for use in the field.

These settings and responses are used to generate a tuned equation Data Model that associates these instrument readings and nominal variations to a nominal output. This Data Model captures the performance curve of the instrument, and is sensitive to any changes or variations. Once generated, the Data Model can then be used to determine at any point and time in the future if the current instrument is within nominal bounds, or if the instrument is now out of calibration and must be removed from the device and returned to the manufacturer.

2. DATA MODELING

2.1 Introduction

Data Modeling is the process of finding a mathematical expression that provides a good fit between given finite sample values of the independent variables and the associated values of the dependent variables of the process. The mathematical expression that fits the given sample of data is called a Data Model. This process involves finding both the functional form of the Data Model and the numeric coefficients for the Data Model. Data Modeling differs from conventional methods such as linear, quadratic, and polynomial regression techniques that only solve for the numerical coefficients for a function whose form is specified ahead of time. Data Modeling also differs from genetic algorithms and symbolic regression because it incorporates fractal interpolation functions for achieving mathematical modeling of complex multivariable processes. The Data Modeling process of discovering automatic functions is an evolutionary and genetic directed approach where the set elements consist entirely of simple polynomial building blocks.

The final form of the Data Modeling equations and the polynomial order shown in (2) are solutions to the Kolmogorov-Gabor polynomial with n representing the number of layers in the final Data Model and $x(b_i(t))$ the inputs mapped from the previous layer.

$$\begin{aligned} x(t) &= f(t, x(b_1(x(b_2(t(\ldots(x(b_n(t))))))))) \\ O[x(t)] &= 3^n \end{aligned} \tag{2}$$

Data Model polynomials on the order of $\sim$ O[3^{10}] have been generated within minutes which adequately capture high degrees of nonlinearity but still execute in real-time.

2.2 Change Detection

The power of statistical quality control charts is the ability to flag when a dynamic process such as inventory flow or instrument response is not in statistical control. One commonly used type of control chart is the X-Bar Chart defined by the upper control limit (UCL) and the lower control limit (LCL)

$$\begin{aligned} UCL_{\overline{X}} &= \overline{X} + A_2 \overline{R} \\ LCL_{\overline{X}} &= \overline{X} - A_2 \overline{R}. \end{aligned} \tag{3}$$

The X-Bar chart plots how far away from the average value of a process the current measurement falls. According to Shewhart, values that repeatedly fall outside of three standard deviations of the average have assignable causes and are labeled as being out of statistical control (off-nominal).

2.3 Calibration on Demand (COD)

A Data Model of a complex process in statistical control can be used to generate a lookup table (LUT), which is analogous to the X-Bar chart. Such a Data Model is built using only nominal cases. Tuning makes the model sensitive to feature values that fall outside the training boundaries. Whenever these new features fall outside of nominal boundaries, tip-off is flagged. Combinations of incoming feature values that are not anticipated or that are within valid ranges but in combinations not seen before can be instantly detected with this approach. This enables calibration to be specified and monitored dynamically or on demand (COD). The lookup table trial limits are set using the polynomial output from the training data. The upper and lower boundaries are assigned to be one-half (½) of a standard deviation (ε) above and below the mean value of the polynomial output from the training data.

Fig. 1 illustrates how either inventory flow sensor measurements or instrument responses are converted into features and analyzed to detect if a change has occurred in system status from nominal to yield tip-off conditions from the model.

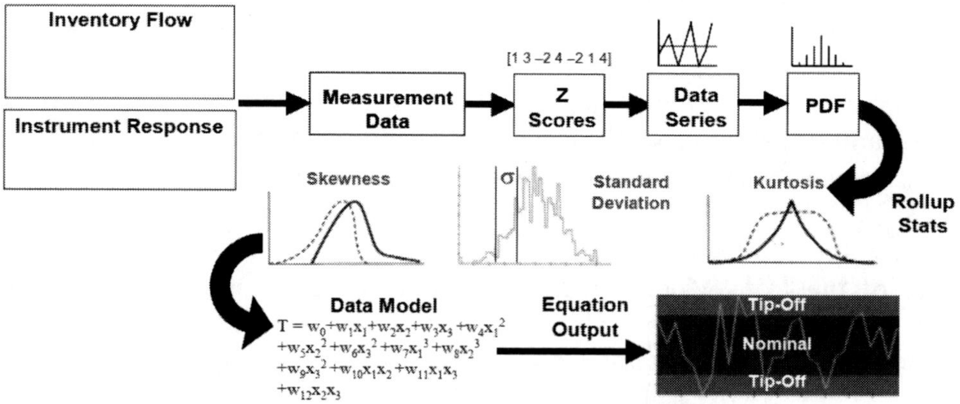

Fig. 1. Calibration on Demand using Data Modeling.

COD can monitor individual sensor measurements, feature vector elements, and overall system snapshots for change detection. Individual sensor measurements provide a characterization of system level calibration states.

3. APPLICATIONS

3.1 Inventory Flow and Monitoring

An inventory flow scenario was created using the Dynamic Inventory Model (DIM) and associated inputs given in the Appendix that simulates an inventory problem on a period-by-period basis. This inventory model was run using two different products stored at a single location (e.g., warehouse). Two different customers that were the end users of these two products were also modeled ordering inventory from this storage location. These orders were placed and filled along with inventory reordering and backordering by the storage location for a total of 256 time periods. During each of the 256 time periods, the number of orders received, inventory, quantity of sales lost, and quantity of units sold was recorded. These quantities were recorded on a customer by product basis, and summed in order to determine the overall inventory flow, number of orders, number of sales lost, and number of units sold for the storage location. The goal was to construct a LUT picture of nominal inventory flow conditions and to predict what off-nominal conditions might be.

Our approach does not directly use the inventory feature values as inputs into the Data Model. Instead, each of the 256 nominal feature examples was rolled up, thereby characterizing the feature distribution independently. This was done for each nominal example using the following parametric and non-parametric statistics where N=4, x_1 is inventory flow, x_2 is the number of orders, x_3 is the sales lost, and x_4 the quantity of units sold, and the Range is the difference between the highest and lowest x_j.

$$\bar{x} = \tfrac{1}{N}\sum_{j=1}^{N} x_j \qquad (4)$$

$$\sigma^2 = \tfrac{1}{N-1}\sum_{j=1}^{N} (x_j - \bar{x})^2 \qquad (8)$$

$$Skew = \tfrac{1}{N}\sum_{j=1}^{N}\left[\frac{x_j - \bar{x}}{\sigma}\right]^3 \qquad (5)$$

$$Kurt = \left\{\tfrac{1}{N}\sum_{j=1}^{N}\left[\frac{x_j - \bar{x}}{\sigma}\right]^4\right\} - 3 \qquad (9)$$

$$M_6 = \left\{\tfrac{1}{N}\sum_{j=1}^{N}\left[\frac{x_j - \bar{x}}{\sigma}\right]^6\right\} - 15 \qquad (6)$$

$$M_8 = \left\{\tfrac{1}{N}\sum_{j=1}^{N}\left[\frac{x_j - \bar{x}}{\sigma}\right]^8\right\} - 105 \qquad (10)$$

$$\mathrm{Re}(J_{i+1}) = \min\left(\lim_{\Delta J \to 0}\left[\frac{\log\left(\frac{Range}{\sigma N J_i}\right)}{\log\left(\frac{1}{N}\right)}\right]\right) \qquad (7)$$

$$D_f = 1 + \log\left(\tfrac{1}{N}\sum_{j=1}^{N-1}\sqrt{1 + \left(\tfrac{x_{j+1} - x_j}{Range}\right)^2}\right) \qquad (11)$$

Once the rollup features in Eq. (4) through Eq. (11) were calculated, a Data Model was tuned to

$$f(\bar{x}, \sigma^2, Skew, Kurt, M_6, M_8, J, D_f) = \tfrac{1}{2} \pm \varepsilon \qquad (12)$$

where ½ is the target regression value and ε is the variation of the regression fit about ½. Once the equation is trained and tuned, boundaries are placed on either side of the target regression value that characterizes the fluctuation ε of the polynomial about ½. The Data Model generated is shown in Fig. 2, and the boundaries that characterize the polynomial fluctuation were set at 0.4992 and 0.5010.

```
DEFCUR A-Z
ON ERROR RESUME NEXT
OPEN "input" FOR INPUT AS #1
INPUT #1, nvlmean
INPUT #1, vlstdev
INPUT #1, nvlskew
INPUT #1, nvlkurt
INPUT #1, invlm6
INPUT #1, invlm8
INPUT #1, nvlJaen
INPUT #1, nvlHand
CLOSE #1
nvlmean = (nvlmean - 13.8184) / 2.6513
vlstdev = (vlstdev - 18.8322) / 5.025
nvlskew = (nvlskew - .5742) / .1255
nvlkurt = (nvlkurt - -1.8193) / .0994
invlm6 = (invlm6 - -12.7127) / .39
invlm8 = (invlm8 - -100.2993) / 1.1112
nvlJaen = (nvlJaen - .3742) / .0162
nvlHand = (nvlHand - 1.4469) / .0139
llol = .188
llol = llol -.0738 * nvlHand
llol = llol +.1997 * vlstdev
llol = llol -.1798 * invlm6
llol = llol -.102 * nvlHand * nvlHand
llol = llol -.1341 * vlstdev * vlstdev
llol = llol -.1567 * invlm6 * invlm6
llol = llol + .0974 * nvlHand * vlstdev
llol = llol -.2089 * nvlHand * invlm6
llol = llol + .18 * vlstdev * invlm6
llol = llol -.1183 * nvlHand * vlstdev * invlm6
llol = llol + .05 * nvlHand * nvlHand * nvlHand
llol = llol -.0898 * vlstdev * vlstdev * vlstdev
llol = llol -.0411 * invlm6 * invlm6 * invlm6
llol = llol -.1631 * vlstdev * nvlHand * nvlHand
llol = llol + .0964 * nvlHand * vlstdev * vlstdev
llol = llol -.107 * nvlHand * invlm6 * invlm6
llol = llol + .0324 * invlm6 * nvlHand * nvlHand
llol = llol + .3845 * invlm6 * vlstdev * vlstdev
llol = llol -.2312 * vlstdev * invlm6 * invlm6
llo2 = .0955
llo2 = llo2 -.2848 * SIN(6.2832 * nvlHand) -.0622 * COS(6.2832 * nvlHand)
llo2 = llo2 -.0136 * SIN(6.2832 * nvlmean) +.0643 * COS(6.2832 * nvlmean)
llo2 = llo2 +.0822 * SIN(6.2832 * nvlkurt) +.3904 * COS(6.2832 * nvlkurt)
llo2 = llo2 -.0682 * SIN(6.2832 * nvlJaen) -.1297 * COS(6.2832 * nvlJaen)
llo2 = llo2 -.069 * SIN(6.2832 * vlstdev) -.053 * COS(6.2832 * vlstdev)
llo2 = llo2 -.002 * SIN(6.2832 * nvlskew) +.2364 * COS(6.2832 * nvlskew)
llo2 = llo2 +.2457 * SIN(6.2832 * invlm6) -.3747 * COS(6.2832 * invlm6)
llo2 = llo2 -.1293 * SIN(6.2832 * invlm8) -.1807 * COS(6.2832 * invlm8)
l2ol = -.0165
l2ol = l2ol + 1.3121 * (llo2)
l2ol = l2ol + .1672 * (nvlskew)
l2ol = l2ol + .6759 * (llol)
l2ol = l2ol + .1137 * (llo2 * llo2)
l2ol = l2ol -.0826 * (nvlskew * nvlskew)
l2ol = l2ol -1.0685 * (llol * llol)
l2ol = l2ol -.8677 * (llo2 * nvlskew)
l2ol = l2ol + .771 * (llo2 * llol)
l2ol = l2ol + .0947 * (nvlskew * llol)
l2ol = l2ol + .215 * (llo2 * nvlskew * llol)
l2ol = l2ol -.9928 * (llo2 * llo2 * llo2)
l2ol = l2ol -.0375 * (nvlskew * nvlskew * nvlskew)
l2ol = l2ol -.6721 * (llol * llol * llol)
l2ol = l2ol -.5831 * (nvlskew * llo2 * llo2)
l2ol = l2ol -.463 * (llo2 * nvlskew * nvlskew)
l2ol = l2ol + 4.73 * (llo2 * llol * llol)
l2ol = l2ol + .7141 * (llol * llo2 * llo2)
l2ol = l2ol + .1766 * (llol * nvlskew * nvlskew)
l2ol = l2ol + .4821 * (nvlskew * llol * llol)
l2ol = l2ol * (.0005) + (.5)
iflg = 0
IF l2ol < .4992 THEN iflg = 1
IF l2ol > .501 THEN iflg = 1
OPEN "output" FOR OUTPUT AS #1
PRINT #1, l2ol, iflg
CLOSE #1
END
```

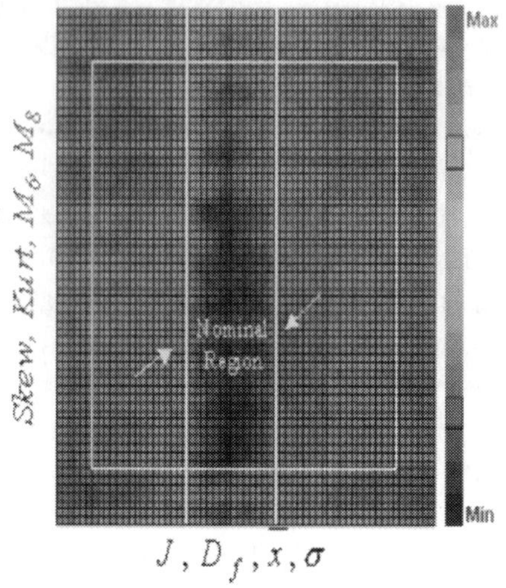

Fig. 2. Data Model of the Dynamic Inventory Model (DIM).

Fig. 2 also contains a Decision Map (LUT) generated using the Data Model. The white box represents the training range of the nominal cases. From the Decision Map, only the features shown on the x-axis need to be monitored in order to determine if the inputs will produce nominal or off-nominal inventory flow, since the nominal region is bounded to a narrow band along the x-axis but extends along the full range of values for the y-axis. This boundary is marked on the Decision Map and represents the values $0.33 < J < 0.37$, $1.43 < D_f < 1.45$, $12.3 < \bar{x} < 16.3$, and $16.1 < \sigma < 22.7$. This model now predicts what inventory statistics would fall outside of the boundary, indicating unusual inventory dynamics that demand scrutiny by the analyst.

3.2 Instrument Calibration

To demonstrate instrument calibration, the MiniOx oxygen analyzer with an accuracy of plus or minus 1% was used. Since this type of oxygen sensor is based on measuring oxygen partial pressures (PPO_2), the manufacturer specifies that concentrations of 100% oxygen (EAN100) and 20.9% oxygen (air or EAN21) be used for calibrating these instruments at a constant flow rate. The instrument is first connected to the EAN100 source, and once the sensor response has come to equilibrium, the instrument is then adjusted until the reading is 100%. If the instrument cannot be adjusted so that the reading is 100%, then the sensor should be replaced. Once the reading is adjusted, the instrument is disconnected from the EAN100 source, exposed to EAN21, and the reading noted. If the sensor reading does not return to indicating between 20-22%, then the sensor should be replaced. As the sensor nears the end of its useful life, it is possible to calibrate the sensor to 20.9% in air, but it may read only as much as 85% in 100% oxygen. This makes it necessary to check the sensor periodically at both EAN100 and EAN21. However, in field applications EAN100 is not always available for calibration of oxygen sensors and analyzers. For this reason, it is not always possible to explicitly follow the manufacturer's procedures to check instrument calibration in the field. However, EAN21 is generally readily available at varying pressures or flow rates in the form of SCUBA cylinders or tire fill stations.

3.2.1 Performance Curve Modeling

Using Data Modeling, the performance curve of a new or in-calibration oxygen analyzer instrument can be modeled using varying flow rates of air as a stimulus. Using a flow meter, known flow rates of air can be applied to the calibrated sensor and the oxygen percentage or voltage output from the sensor recorded. From this, a tuned equation based Data Model is constructed that can be used in the field using the same flow rates. All that is then required in the field to determine if the instrument or sensor is still calibrated is a flowing air source to yield the constant flow rates. Alternatively, a flow meter to regulate the flow of air across the sensor in a quantified manner may be used.

The sensor exhibits a small hysteresis effect that slightly elevates the reading of oxygen and then rebounds to a low value. We propose to characterize this hysteresis curve for a calibrated sensor and then compare to this model in the field to determine instrument calibration based solely on airflow induced perturbations to shift the hysteresis curve.

To do this, an oxygen analyzer sensor that was in calibration was characterized. Ten different measurement realizations were recorded as shown in Fig. 3, consisting of 1) Flow rate in liters per minute (L/min), 2) the power on equilibrium oxygen sensor percentage readings, 3) instrument oxygen percentage reading with air flowing across the sensor, and 4) final oxygen sensor percentage reading (including any hysteresis effects) once the airflow was removed from the sensor. Using the power on instrument readings as a baseline, the amount of change in the instrument readings while air was flowing across the sensor from the initial power on value and the change in the final readings from the power on values (thereby capturing the sensor hysteresis) were calculated.

Calibrated

Flow Rate (L/min)	% O_2 (Power ON) (P)	% O_2 (AirFlow) (A)	**% O_2 (Final) (R)**	A-P	**R-P (Dr)**
6.0	20.4	20.2	19.9	-0.2	-0.5
6.0	20.9	21.0	20.6	0.1	-0.3
5.9	20.5	19.3	19.6	-1.2	-0.9
5.75	20.0	20.2	20.3	0.2	0.3
5.75	20.1	20.2	20.0	0.1	-0.1
4.6	20.5	20.55	20.3	0.05	-0.2
4.5	20.4	20.5	20.3	0.1	-0.1
4.5	20.5	20.6	20.4	0.1	-0.1
4.5	20.5	20.6	20.5	0.1	0.0
4.5	20.5	20.6	20.4	0.1	-0.1

Rollup of All Calibrated % O_2 Measurements
Mean = 20.3
Standard Deviation = 0.34

+6% Out of Calibration

Flow Rate (L/min)	% O_2 (Power ON) (P)	% O_2 (AirFlow) (A)	**% O_2 (Final) (R)**	A-P	**R-P (Dr)**
6.0	22.2	22.3	22.15	0.1	-0.05
6.0	22.3	22.5	22.1	0.2	-0.2
5.75	22.0	21.65	21.5	-0.35	-0.5
5.75	21.6	21.4	21.2	-0.2	-0.4
5.75	22.3	22.4	22.3	0.1	0.0
4.8	22.0	21.9	21.2	-0.1	-0.8
4.8	21.4	21.6	21.3	0.2	-0.1
4.75	21.75	21.95	21.9	0.2	0.15
4.7	22.3	22.4	22.2	0.1	-0.1
4.5	22.4	21.85	21.6	-0.55	-0.8

Rollup of All Out of Calibration % O_2 Measurements
Mean = 21.9
Standard Deviation = 0.40

Fig. 3. Tabulated sensor measurements.

An additional ten measurements (also shown in Fig. 3) from a +6% calibration biased sensor were also measured using the same conditions and flow rates as the nominal cases. Both the calibrated and biased measurements were within the manufacturer's accuracy specifications for acceptability for EAN21 (between ~ 20-22% as stated above), making it impossible to conclude that the sensor was out of calibration based on the measurements alone.

The Data Modeling process ranks these inputs and builds a tuned equation, which characterizes the performance curve using only knowledge derived from the nominal sensor measurements. The tuned Data Model only required the final instrument reading (R) and the sensor hysteresis (Dr) to model the performance curve. This yielded 100% correct classification. The equation for this Data Model is shown at the top of Fig. 4, labeled as *nom1*. If *nom1* gives a value between 0.499 and 0.501, the sensor is calibrated. Any other values indicate the sensor is out of calibration. The lookup table graphic can be used directly in the field by simply taking the power on and final oxygen analyzer percentage readings to determine the values for R and Dr and the calibration status. Alternatively, the equation for *nom1* itself can be evaluated if a calculator is at hand. Additionally, the known off-nominal cases were run against the tuned Data Model and all ten (100%) were flagged as off-nominal, indicating that the sensor needed to be either recalibrated or replaced.

$$nom1 := 111.632 \cdot Dr + 383.752 \cdot R + 10.818 \cdot Dr^{2.} - 18.9819 \cdot R^{2.} - 10.86 \cdot Dr \cdot R + 7.736 \cdot 10^{-2} \cdot Dr^{3.} + .312949 \cdot R^{3.} - .5324 \cdot R \cdot Dr^{2.} + .2641 \cdot Dr \cdot R^{2.} - 2585.369$$

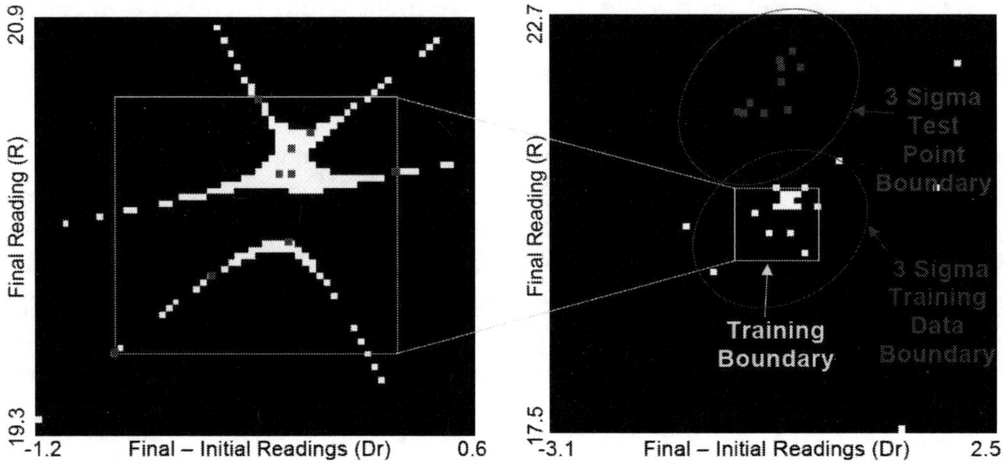

Fig. 4. Lookup table generated using Data Model for oxygen sensor monitoring and calibration.

The LUT shown in Fig. 4 can be used to see if the oxygen sensor is out of calibration. The current values for R and Dr are determined and the intersection for the two values can be read directly from the chart. If the value falls in a white region, the sensor is calibrated. If the value falls into black, the instrument is out of calibration. The tuned equation Data Model is able to predict that regions of calibration and out of calibration exist outside of the training box region.

On the left side of Fig. 4, the training region and boundary for the tuned equation based Data Model is enlarged and shown in detail. The box on the interior represents the training boundary and encompasses the region where the training examples (shown as points on the graph) reside. Shown on the right side of Fig. 4 is a larger interrogation region derived from the tuned equation based Data Model, the same training boundary box, and the off-nominal points used for testing the model.

4. CONCLUSIONS

Data Modeling has been successfully applied to inventory flow and instrument calibration monitoring. A Data Model was created that defined the boundary for nominal inventory dynamics. Additionally, Data Modeling was used to demonstrate in field Miniox calibration monitoring. This was accomplished by modeling the response hysteresis of the sensor to various flow conditions. This created an equation and lookup table that can be used in the field to determine if the Miniox is still in calibration without the use of a pure O_2 source.

ACKNOWLEDGMENTS

The authors would like to thank Marvin Carroll, Tec-Masters, Level-13, Licht Strahl Engineering INC, and Kristi Jaenisch and Technical Dive College for the use of the MAJQANDA algorithm suite during the course of this work, and Greg Ogle of Southeastern Divers Inc. for his assistance in the oxygen sensor data collection process.

BIBLIOGRAPHY

1. Blanchard, B. *Logistics Engineering and Management.* Englewood Cliffs, NJ: Prentice-Hall, 1981.
2. Buzacott, J.A. and J.G. Shanthikumar. *Stochastic Models of Manufacturing Systems.* Englewood Cliffs, NJ: Prentice-Hall, 1993.
3. Fraden, J. *Handbook of Modern Sensors.* New York: AIP Press, 1996.
4. Grant, E. *Statistical Quality Control.* New York: McGraw-Hill, 1952.
5. Jaenisch, H.M. and J.W. Handley, "Data Modeling for Radar Applications," *Proceedings of the IEEE Radar Conference 2003*, May 5-8, 2003. Huntsville, AL.
6. Jaenisch, H.M., J.W. Handley, L. Bonham, "Enabling Calibration on Demand for Situational Awareness", Army Aviation Association of America (AAAA), Tennessee Valley Chapter, Huntsville, AL, February 12, 2003.
7. Jaenisch, H.M., J.W. Handley, J.C. Pooley III, S.R. Murray. "Data Modeling For Fault Detection," 58th MFPT, Virginia Beach, VA, 2003.
8. Jaenisch, H.M., J.W. Handley, K.H. White, J.W. Watson Jr., C.T. Case, C.G. Songy, "Virtual Prototyping With Data Modeling", Proc. SPIE. Seattle, WA July 7-11 2002.
9. Lamb, J.S. *The Practice of Oxygen Measurement for Divers.* Flagstaff, AZ: Best, 1999.
10. Lotfi, V. and C. Pegels. *Decision Support Systems for Operations Management & Science.* Chicago, IL: Irwin, 1996.
11. McNitt, L.L. *BASIC Computer Simulation.* Blue Ridge Summit, PA: TAB Books, 1983.
12. *MiniOx I Oxygen Analyzer Instruction Manual.* Pittsburg, PA: MSA Company, 1995.
13. Webster, J.G. *Medical Instrumentation: Application and Design.* Boston, MA: Houghton Mifflin, 1978.

BIOGRAPHY

Dr. Holger Jaenisch has over 20 years experience working in the field of applied mathematics and algorithm creation. Dr. Jaenisch's experience has included the application of Data Modeling to advanced discrimination algorithms and concepts, data, message, and image compression techniques and simulation modeling. His expertise covers the areas of signal and data processing, image processing, and the modeling of processes, simulations, and systems with neural and equation based architectures. His concepts have been successfully applied in the development of two commercially sold software packages for non-linear data analysis.

APPENDIX

Dynamic Inventory Model Inputs

```
Number of customers 2
Number of products 2
#######################################
Customer 1 Product 1
# Demand levels 2
Level 1 # Items 1 Prob of Demand Level .8
Level 2 # Items 10 Prob of Demand Level .2
# Lead times 2
Lead Time 1 # Periods 5 Prob of lead time level .8
Lead Time 2 # Periods 15 Prob of lead time level .2
Cost per order placed ($) 100
Annual per unit-holding cost ($) 10
Stockout cost per unit ($) 100
Number of periods per year 52
Order quantity 2
Reorder point 2
Beginning inventory 10
Number of periods to simulate 256
#######################################
Customer 1 Product 2
# Demand levels 1
Level 1 # Items 3 Prob of Demand Level .5
# Lead times 2
Lead Time 1 # Periods 2 Prob of lead time level .5
Lead Time 2 # Periods 4 Prob of lead time level .5
Cost per order placed ($) 10
Annual per unit-holding cost ($) 1
Stockout cost per unit ($) 5
Number of periods per year 52
Order quantity 20
Reorder point 10
Beginning inventory 20
Number of periods to simulate 256
#######################################
```

```
Customer 2 Product 1
# Demand levels 2
Level 1 # Items 3 Prob of Demand Level .7
Level 2 # Items 4 Prob of Demand Level .3
# Lead times 1
Lead Time 1 # Periods 3 Prob of lead time leve
Cost per order placed ($) 100
Annual per unit-holding cost ($) 20
Stockout cost per unit ($) 30
Number of periods per year 52
Order quantity 10
Reorder point 25
Beginning inventory 5
Number of periods to simulate 256
#######################################
Customer 2 Product 2
# Demand levels 3
Level 1 # Items 1 Prob of Demand Level .5
Level 2 # Items 5 Prob of Demand Level .25
Level 3 # Items 10 Prob of Demand Level .25
# Lead times 3
Lead Time 1 # Periods 1 Prob of lead time leve
Lead Time 2 # Periods 5 Prob of lead time leve
Lead Time 3 # Periods 10 Prob of lead time lev
Cost per order placed ($) 125
Annual per unit-holding cost ($) 25
Stockout cost per unit ($) 10
Number of periods per year 52
Order quantity 15
Reorder point 20
Beginning inventory 20
Number of periods to simulate 256
#######################################
```

Dynamic Inventory Model Source Listing

```
'Dynamic Inventory Model (DIM)
'Holger M. Jaenisch, Ph.D. and Jamie Handley
CLS
DIM l(50, 2), d(50, 2), y(50)
OPEN "input.log" FOR OUTPUT AS #1
INPUT "Number of customers"; ncust
PRINT #1, "Number of customers"; ncust
INPUT "Number of products"; nprod
PRINT #1, "Number of products"; nprod
PRINT #1, "#######################################"
REDIM max1(ncust)
mx1 = 0
FOR nc = 1 TO ncust
  REDIM nrow(nprod)
  maxval = 0
```

```
  FOR np = 1 TO nprod
    PRINT
    PRINT "Currently on Customer"; nc; "and Product"; np
    PRINT #1, "Customer"; nc; "Product"; np
916 GOSUB 1106
920 GOSUB 1206
924 GOSUB 1306
928 GOSUB 1406
932 GOSUB 1506
    nrow(np) = n2
    IF n2 > maxval THEN maxval = n2
    IF U$ = "1" THEN 924
    IF U$ = "2" THEN 920
    IF U$ = "3" THEN 916
  NEXT np
'rollup by customer
  REDIM w(maxval, 8)
  FOR np = 1 TO nprod
    zz$ = "c" + FORMAT$(nc, "0") + "p" + FORMAT$(np, "0") + ".dat"
    OPEN zz$ FOR INPUT AS #2
    FOR i2 = 1 TO nrow(np)
      FOR kz = 1 TO 8
        INPUT #2, h
        w(i2, kz) = w(i2, kz) + h
      NEXT kz
    NEXT i2
    CLOSE #2
  NEXT np
  zz1$ = "c" + FORMAT$(nc, "0") + ".dat"
  OPEN zz1$ FOR OUTPUT AS #2
  FOR i2 = 1 TO maxval
    FOR kz = 1 TO 8
      PRINT #2, w(i2, kz);
    NEXT kz
    PRINT #2,
  NEXT i2
  max1(nc) = maxval
  IF maxval > mx1 THEN mx1 = maxval
  CLOSE #2
NEXT nc
'final rollup
REDIM w(mx1, 8)
FOR nc = 1 TO ncust
  zz1$ = "c" + FORMAT$(nc, "0") + ".dat"
  OPEN zz1$ FOR INPUT AS #2
  FOR i2 = 1 TO max1(nc)
    FOR kz = 1 TO 8
      INPUT #2, h
      w(i2, kz) = w(i2, kz) + h
    NEXT kz
  NEXT i2
  CLOSE #2
NEXT nc
zz1$ = "rollup.dat"
OPEN zz1$ FOR OUTPUT AS #2
FOR i2 = 1 TO mx1
```

```
  FOR kz = 1 TO 8
    PRINT #2, w(i2, kz);
  NEXT kz
  PRINT #2,
NEXT i2
CLOSE #2
PRINT
CLOSE
END
1106 PRINT
  PRINT "Probability distribution for demand period"
  PRINT
  PRINT "3 Demand levels = Low, Med, High"
  PRINT "Input Demand levels and probabilities in ascending order"
  PRINT "to build histogram"
  PRINT
  INPUT "Number of levels of demand"; k1
  PRINT #1, "# Demand levels"; k1
  PRINT "demand, probability"
  p = 0
  e1 = 0
  FOR i = 1 TO k1
    PRINT "Level"; i
    INPUT "# Items"; d(i, 1)
    INPUT "Prob of Demand Level"; d(i, 2)
    PRINT #1, "Level"; i; "# Items"; d(i, 1);
    PRINT #1, "Prob of Demand Level"; d(i, 2)
    e1 = e1 + d(i, 1) * d(i, 2)
    p = p + d(i, 2)
    d(i, 2) = p
  NEXT i
  PRINT
  PRINT "Expected demand for period"; e1
  PRINT
  PRINT "Probability distribution for lead time"
  PRINT
  PRINT "Number of different lead times";
  INPUT k2
  PRINT #1, "# Lead times"; k2
  PRINT
  PRINT "3 Lead time levels = Low, Med, High"
  PRINT "Input Lead time levels and probabilities in"
  PRINT "ascending order to build histogram"
  PRINT
  PRINT "If period is defined as month"
  PRINT "# Periods/yr=52 below), 3 weeks"
  PRINT "would be 0.75"
  PRINT
  PRINT "lead time (# time periods), probability"
  p = 0
  e2 = 0
  FOR i = 1 TO k2
    PRINT "Lead Time"; i;
    INPUT "# Periods"; l(i, 1)
    INPUT "Prob of lead time level"; l(i, 2)
    PRINT #1, "Lead Time"; i; "# Periods"; l(i, 1);
```

```
   PRINT #1, "Prob of lead time level"; l(i, 2)
   e2 = e2 + l(i, 1) * l(i, 2)
   p = p + l(i, 2)
   l(i, 2) = p
  NEXT i
  PRINT
  PRINT "Expected lead time", e2
RETURN
1206 PRINT
  PRINT "Cost per order placed ($)";
  INPUT c1
  PRINT #1, "Cost per order placed ($)"; c1
  PRINT "Annual per unit-holding cost ($)";
  INPUT c2
  PRINT #1, "Annual per unit-holding cost ($)"; c2
  PRINT "Stockout cost per unit ($)";
  INPUT c3
  PRINT #1, "Stockout cost per unit ($)"; c3
  PRINT
  PRINT "52 periods/year = week, 12 periods/year = month"
  PRINT "Number of periods per year";
  INPUT n1
  PRINT #1, "Number of periods per year"; n1
1299 RETURN
1306 PRINT
  PRINT "Order quantity";
  INPUT q
  PRINT #1, "Order quantity"; q
  PRINT "Reorder point (Quantity threshold for reorder)";
  INPUT r
  PRINT #1, "Reorder point"; r
  PRINT "Beginning inventory";
  INPUT b
  PRINT #1, "Beginning inventory"; b
  PRINT "Number of periods to simulate";
  INPUT n2
  PRINT #1, "Number of periods to simulate"; n2
  PRINT #1, "###########################################"
  FOR i = 1 TO k3
   y(i) = 0
  NEXT i
RETURN
1406 t1 = 0
  t2 = 0
  t3 = 0
  t4 = 0
  k3 = l(k2, 1)
  zz$ = "c" + FORMAT$(nc, "0") + "p" + FORMAT$(np, "0") + ".dat"
  OPEN zz$ FOR OUTPUT AS #2
  FOR i2 = 1 TO n2
   'UPDATE PIPELINE
   GOSUB 2006
   'GENERATE DEMAND
   GOSUB 2106
   'PLACE ORDER
   GOSUB 2206
```

```
    PRINT #2, t1; t2; t3; t4; jwh; b; s2; s1
    t2 = t2 + b
    t3 = t3 + s2
    t4 = t4 + s1
  NEXT i2
  CLOSE #2
  'DISPLAY RESULT
  GOSUB 2306
RETURN
1506 PRINT
  PRINT "MENU OF OPTIONS"
  PRINT "1 TRY ANOTHER SET OF DECISIONS"
  PRINT "2 TRY ANOTHER SET OF COSTS "
  PRINT "3 TRY ANOTHER SET OF PROBABILITIES"
  PRINT "4 NEXT/TERMINATE "
  PRINT
  PRINT "ENTER OPTION";
  INPUT U$
  IF U$ = "1" THEN 1599
  IF U$ = "2" THEN 1599
  IF U$ = "3" THEN 1599
  IF U$ = "4" THEN 1599
  PRINT "INVALID RESPONSE"
  GOTO 1506
1599 RETURN
'UPDATE PIPELINE
2006 b = b + y(1)
  FOR i = 1 TO k3 - 1
    y(i) = y(i + 1)
  NEXT i
  y(k3) = 0
RETURN
'GENERATE DEMAND
2106 p = RND
     FOR i = 1 TO k1
       IF p > d(i, 2) THEN 2116
       z = d(i, 1)
       i = k1
2116 NEXT i
IF z > b THEN 2126
s1 = z
s2 = 0
GOTO 2130
2126 s1 = b
s2 = z - b
2130 b = b - s1
RETURN
'PLACE ORDER
2206 v = b
  FOR i = 1 TO k3
    v = v + y(i)
  NEXT i
  jwh = 0
  IF v > r THEN 2299
  p = RND
     FOR i = 1 TO k2
```

```
    IF p > l(i, 2) THEN 2226
    l1 = l(i, 1)
    i = k2
2226 NEXT i
 t1 = t1 + 1
 jwh = jwh + 1
 IF l1 > 0 THEN 2236
 b = b + q
 GOTO 1299
2236 y(l1) = y(l1) + q
2299 RETURN
'DISPLAY RESULT
2306 PRINT
 PRINT "RESULT OF SIMULATION"
 PRINT "DEMAND", t3 + t4
 PRINT "UNITS SOLD", t4
 PRINT "SALES LOST", t3
 PRINT "ORDERS", t1
 PRINT "AVERAGE INVENTORY LEVEL ", t2 / n2
 t5 = (n1 / n2) * c1 * t1
 t6 = c2 * t2 / n2
 t7 = (n1 / n2) * c3 * t3
 t = t5 + t6 + t7
 PRINT
 PRINT "COSTS ADJUSTED TO ANNUAL BASIS"
 PRINT
 PRINT "ORDERING", t5
 PRINT "HOLDING", t6
 PRINT "STOCKOUT", t7
 PRINT "TOTAL", t
 PRINT
 PRINT "TYPE THE VALUE 1 TO CONTINUE";
 INPUT U$
RETURN
```

SECONDARY ITEM MANAGEMENT

AUTHOR: John LaFalce, U.S. Army Aviation and Missile Command (AMCOM)

ABSTRACT:

Fielded weapons systems require a constant in-flow of spare and repair parts to remain in operational condition. The U.S. Army depends on its Army Materiel Command (AMC) to provide this in-flow of secondary items to maintain its war fighting capabilities. The AMC relies on its Commodity Command Standard System (CCSS) and four primary Major Subordinate Commands to manage its $12 billion secondary item inventory. Within the CCSS, the Requirements Determination and Execution System (RD&ES) is the primary tool for accomplishing the secondary item management mission of the MSCs. Like the balance of CCSS, the RD&ES is comprised of a suite of COBOL programs run via batch processing on mainframe computers. Many functional and technical upgrades have been bolted on over the years, but the core of the requirements system is still based on 1970s era 80-column card format processing technology. Irregardless, the RD&ES still provides the MSC item manager with very accurate procurement, repair, retention, and disposal forecasts on an individual item basis. The AMC has entered into a multi-year program with Computer Sciences Corporation to privatize and upgrade its automated logistics systems.

The steps for conceiving, designing and developing weapon systems within the Department of Defense (DOD) are well known. They are also fairly standardized among the services thanks to DOD 4140 series instructions. Once weapon systems are fielded and operational, the means by which the services and the Defense Logistics Agency provide spare parts support diverges. The flow of parts from the manufacturer, to the depot, and then to the user is standardized throughout DOD. However, the computation systems and business process procedures used by each DOD element to buy and repair those parts are unique. To those working inside the secondary item management community, the myriad processes and Byzantine systems provide a daily challenge to navigate and master. To those outside of the item management functional area, the procedures and systems used to control the inventory are not well known, or understood.

The focus of this paper is how the U.S. Army Materiel Command (AMC) computes secondary item requirements and translates them into repair, procurement, redistribution and disposal actions that are the ebb and flow of the inventory. At this stage, the reader may be wondering, "What the heck is a secondary item?" These are the spare (reparable) and repair (non-reparable) parts, components, kits and subassemblies that make up the "primary" end item, or weapon system. In Army lingo, Tanks, Helicopters, Missiles, Radars, etc. are "major" items. Armor plates, rotor blades, ignition igniters and trailer tires are secondary items. DOD categorizes secondary items as the "Class IX" inventory and major items as the "Class VII" inventory.

Day-to-day management of AMC's $12 billion, 119 thousand secondary item inventory is the responsibility of these Major Subordinate Commands (MSCs):

- Aviation and Missile Command (AMCOM), Huntsville, AL
- Communications and Electronics Command (CECOM), Ft. Monmouth, NJ
- Tank, Automotive and Armaments Command (TACOM), Warren, MI, and Rock Island, IL
- Solider, Biological and Chemical Command (SBCCOM), Natick, MA

The MSCs utilize the Commodity Command Standard System (CCSS) to accomplish their varied functional tasks. The CCSS was internally designed and developed by Army functional and technical experts beginning in the early 1970s, and has been significantly modified and upgraded over the years. There are 21 million lines of COBOL programming in hundreds of functional programs (called "applications") that comprise CCSS. These programs are still batch processed on mainframe computers, but the AMC has a modernization program underway (see below). The CCSS Requirements Determination and Execution System (RD&ES) is used to individually compute the requirements levels and inventory management actions for each of AMC's secondary items on a monthly basis.

Fig. 1: SECONDARY ITEM SUPPORT CONCEPT

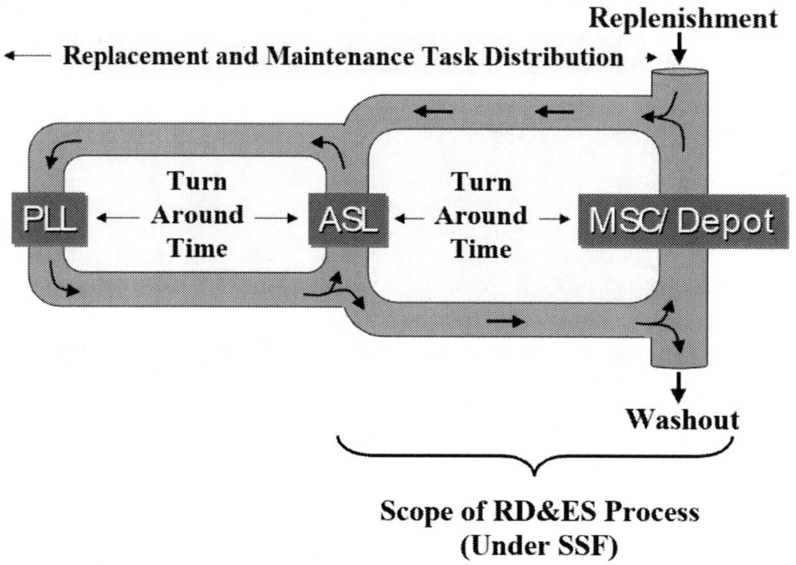

The basic secondary item support concept employed by AMC and the CCSS RE&ES is summarized in the figure 1 "pipeline" diagram. There are three echelons of spare parts support, the commodity oriented MSCs and their repair depots, the Authorized Stockage List (ASL) inventories maintained in field Supply Support Activities, and the Prescribed Load Lists (PLLs) maintained by Army units. The depth and breadth of the inventory decreases from each successive echelon (from the MSCs, thru the SSAs to the unit levels). The MSCs stock most items required to support customers world-wide. The

SSAs stock to support units in their footprint, and PLLs are lean and mobile inventories of items essential to combat operations.

The MSC initially "fills" the pipeline with the required quantity of an item based on provisioning model recommendations and budget constraints. These items flow thru the pipeline, eventually being consumed by the customer. If the item is non-reparable, the unserviceable item is "washed out", i.e., disposed of and a replacement item is ordered. If the item is reparable, the echelon authorized to repair the item (the maintenance task distribution) and the percent of time it cannot be repaired (the replacement task distribution) are assigned. The lead-times required to retrograde and repair the item are factored into the RD&ES stockage computation. To keep the reparable item pipeline full, the MSC initiates repair programs to fix unserviceables, and procurement actions to replace the unserviceable items that "wash out" of the inventory.

Similar to an end item, or weapon system, secondary items have a predictable lifecycle. First they are provisioned, then they have an active operational life, and then they are replaced or phased out and enter a period of inventory retention and disposal. The RD&ES accommodates each of these lifecycle stages, and accounts for different configurations of the same item via interchangeability and substitutability relationships. The phases of a secondary item's lifecycle are summarized in figure 2:

Fig. 2: SECONDARY ITEM LIFECYCLE STAGES

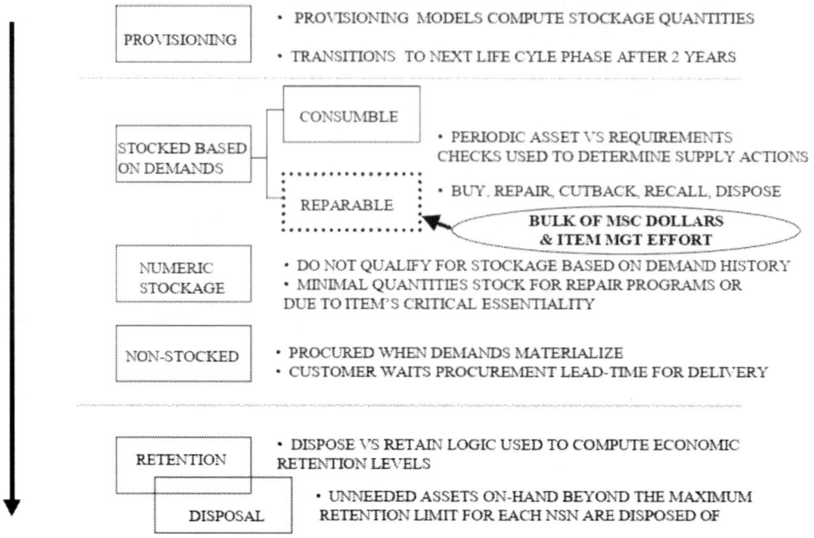

In the provisioning stage, failure estimates from the weapon system developer are processed through custom math models that compute how many of the new items to initially stock. As replenishment requisitions from the field are received, they are recorded in the CCSS Demand, Return and Disposal (DRD) File. Over the first two years of the provisioning secondary item's life, a weighted monthly demand rate is used by the RD&ES to compute overall requirements for the item. Initially, the demand rate is based solely on the engineering failure estimates. Over the two-year demand development period, the field demands from the DRD File are weighted in and eventually replace the provisioning estimates.

After the secondary item exits the provisioning stage of the lifecycle, RD&ES will categorize it either as a stocked, a numerically stocked, or a non-stocked item. The determination is based upon customer usage, essentiality and demand volume in the DRD File. For most army commodities (e.g., automotive, munitions and communications), a secondary item requires 12 separate demands within a 12-month time frame to warrant a depot-based inventory to support forecasted demands. Lower-volume commodities, such as missiles, require just 3 demands every 12 months to qualify for depot stockage. These items with dependable and recurring demand history are routinely procured, stocked and issued by Army Item Managers at the MSCs. RD&ES performs various levels of requirements computations on these items dependent upon dollar value of past demands and the item's reparability.

A subset of the routinely stocked items are those that fall into the "numeric stockage objective" (NSO) category. NSO items do not qualify for stockage based on demand history, but may be essential to the operation of the next higher assembly, or end item. For these "insurance" items, the RD&ES computes a minimal depot stockage "just in case" they are needed. A second type of NSO item are those required only to support depot repair programs. The CCSS forecasts these requirements based on consumption data from past repair programs.

Non-stocked items are the third general stockage category. These very low demand, non-essential items are only procured when validated demands are received from DOD and International Logistics customers. The downside of non-stocked items is that the customer has to wait the administrative and production lead-times before receiving the part. This could be as short as a few months, or in worst-case situations, several years.

Fig. 3: RD&ES REQUIREMENTS LEVELS

Figure 3 lists the requirements levels that RD&ES compares to asset levels when computing how many units to procure, repair and, or dispose of. The Administrative Lead-Time (ALT) is the average number of months it takes the MSCs to award procurement contracts and purchase orders. The trend in AMC is to minimize ALTs via the use of flexible and long-term procurement contracts (that qualify for a one-month ALT, or less). The Production Lead-Time (PLT) is the number of months it takes to manufacture the item and deliver it to the storage depot. Both the ALT and the PLT are calculated for each item based on representative procurement history.

War reserve requirements are computed by various CCSS applications for each item, and are intended for use in future contingency operations. A procurement safety level is individually computed for each item by the RD&ES. It is protects against unexpected demand surges and delays in procurement actions. For reparable items, the RD&ES

computes a repair safety level and a repair cycle quantity. This safety level protects against repair program delays and the repair cycle is a small pipeline of recoverable unserviceable assets required to maintain a smooth flow of assets into repair programs.

The sum of the ALT, PLT, war reserves, safety level(s) and repair cycle levels is called the reorder point (ROP). To this is added a reorder cycle level that is computed by an economic order quantity model embedded within the RD&ES. The sum of the ROP and reorder cycle levels is called the requirements objective (RO). When inventory asset balances (both on-hand and due-in) fall below the ROP level, a procurement is initiated for a quantity equal to the delta between the RO and the asset balance. For reparable items, a similar computation is made between a "repair action point" and inventory asset balances to determine how many unserviceable items to repair. The RD&ES computation is an intensive process; each requirement and asset level is computed for a 72 month forecast for each item on either a monthly, quarterly or annual basis.

All secondary items eventually migrate from the active stage of their lifecycle to a retention, and then to a disposal stage. Often, the item configuration is upgraded, leaving behind an inventory of items built to old specifications. The replaced items may, or may not be issued in place of the new item. The RD&ES takes this interchangeability and substitutability information into account when determining requirements levels. When weapon systems are phased out of the Army arsenal, the secondary item support inventory for that weapon system must also be drawn down. The RD&ES accounts for these inactive inventories using the three levels of retention stockage shown in figure 4:

Fig. 4: RD&ES RETENTION LEVELS

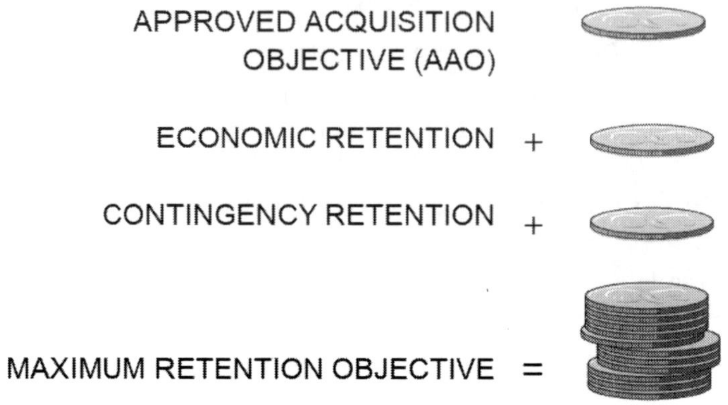

The Approved Acquisitions Objective (AAO) is a compilation of all anticipated requirements for an item through the budget horizon. Economic retention is computed by a math model embedded in the RD&ES and determines the amount of stock, in addition to the AAO stock, that is economical to retain. This is factor by comparing the benefits of disposing the item (and not paying inventory holding costs) vice the probability and cost of potentially having to reprocure it down the road. Following AMC policy, the item manager is authorized to add an additional level of contingency stockage, justified by events and factors unique to the item or weapon system. The sum of these three retention levels is called the maximum retention level (MRL). The RD&ES will recommend that the item manager dispose of inventory that exceeds this maximum stockage limit. The MRL is computed for all items in every secondary item category: provisioning, active stocked, NSO and obsolete items. Due to the myriad of variables involved, excess stock can potentially accrue at any stage of the item's lifecycle. However, most disposal actions are initiated on obsolete items with diminished, or no known requirements.

The RD&ES generates a hardcopy printout called a "supply control study" for item managers to analyze, and if necessary to modify using information and data not programmed into the CCSS data files. The item manager will then initiate supply actions as required (e.g., initiate, revise, expedite, reduce, or cancel procurement and repair programs). Several years ago, AMC introduced an on-line version of the supply control study that automatically recalculates the 72 month requirement forecast based on data element changes input by the item manager. The on-line study also submits data file update transactions, and routes the digital study through the required levels of management review and approval. This, and many, many other enhancements and upgrades have been made to the RD&ES and CCSS during the past three decades.

In December, 1999, the AMC leadership initiated the Logistics Modernization Program (LMP), which will replace CCSS and the Standard Depot System. The LMP is being developed, and will be sustained by CSC Corporation under a 10-year, $680M contract with the Army. The goal of the LMP is to upgrade both the data systems and the business processes used within AMC. The commercial off-the-shelf system selected to be the core of the LMP is the German-developed Systems, Applications and Processing (SAP) enterprise resource planning tool. Replacing a system as integrated and complex as CCSS is proving to be a challenge. Introducing commercial business practices and inventory management processes to the AMC workforce will also be a challenge. The initial pilot implementation of LMP is scheduled for the 4Q FY03 at CECOM.

The CCSS and RD&ES were conceived in the waning years of the Vietnam Conflict. These systems, and the AMC staff that created and maintained them, helped the Army to win the Cold War, and two Gulf Wars. However, the era of COBOL programming, 80-column cards, and organic systems development has come and gone. Its time to say, "farewell old friend" to CCSS.

John LaFalce is the Requirements Team Chief in the UH-60 Black Hawk Airframe Division, Integrated Materiel Management Center, U.S. Army Aviation and Missile Command. He has also worked as an inventory management specialist on the HAWK Missile System (at AMCOM) and on the M113 Armored Personnel Carrier at the U.S. Army Tank, Automotive and Chemical Command, Detroit MI. He served as a logistics management specialist in the Troop Support Branch of the U.S. Army Europe ODSCSLOG, Heidelberg, Germany. He was a requirements systems analyst in the AMCOM IMMC, and in the Lead AMC Integration Support Office, where he represented the Army on the Joint Logistics Systems Center project. He is a graduate of the University of Kentucky, Texas A&M University (Texarkana) and attended the University of London (Burbeck College).

SOLE 2003

Melding Defense and Commercial Logistics to Optimize Key Performance Indicators Using Porters Value Chain Secondary Activities

By Paul Wilcox

August 2003

SOLE 2003

- Porter's Value Chain-Secondary Activities
- Key performance indicators
- Compare to intercompany, intracompany, industry, S & P 500
- Customer Satisfaction

Generic Value Chain

(After Porter, 1985, 1998)

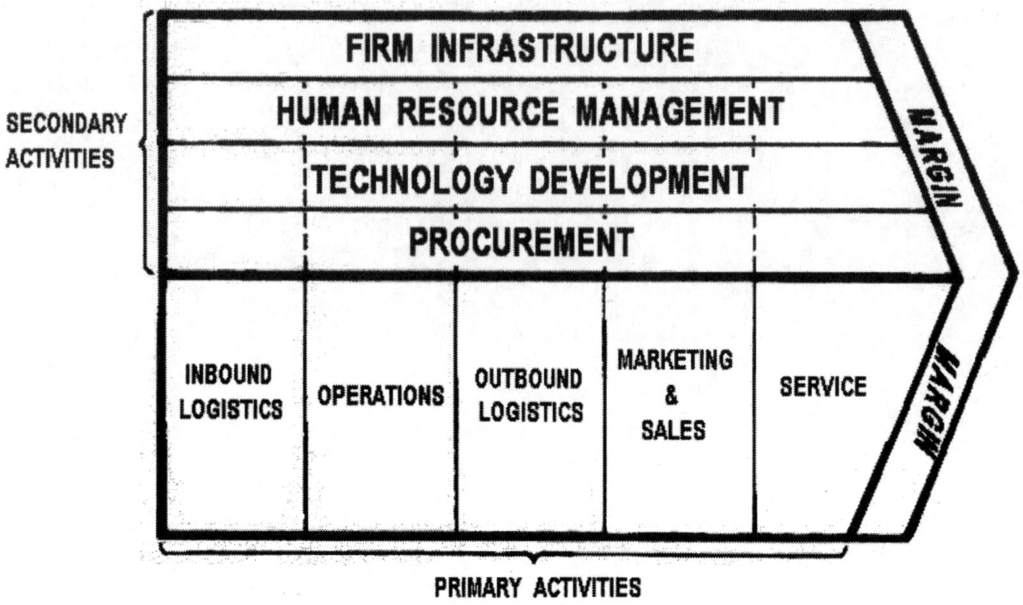

Value Chain: Example Cost Drivers

(After Porter, 1985, 1998)

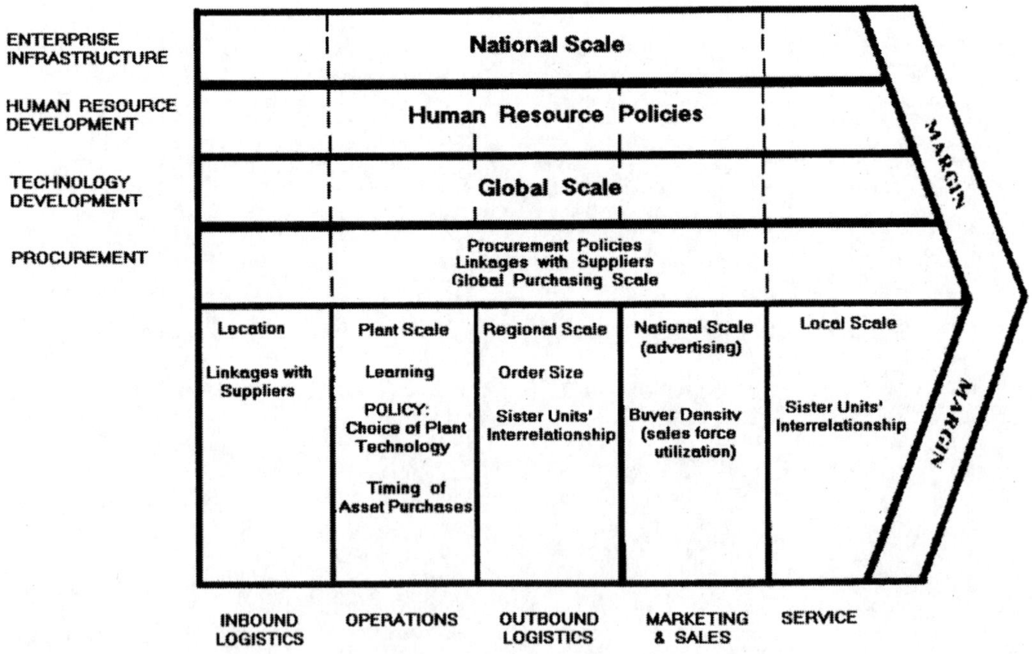

Procurement

- Price effectiveness
- Cost savings
- Workload
- Administration and control
- Efficiency
- Vender quality and delivery

Procurement-cont

- Material flow control
- Regulatory, societal and environmental measures
- Procurement planning and research
- Competition
- Inventory
- Transportation

FIGURE 12–3

How procurement contributes to return on net worth

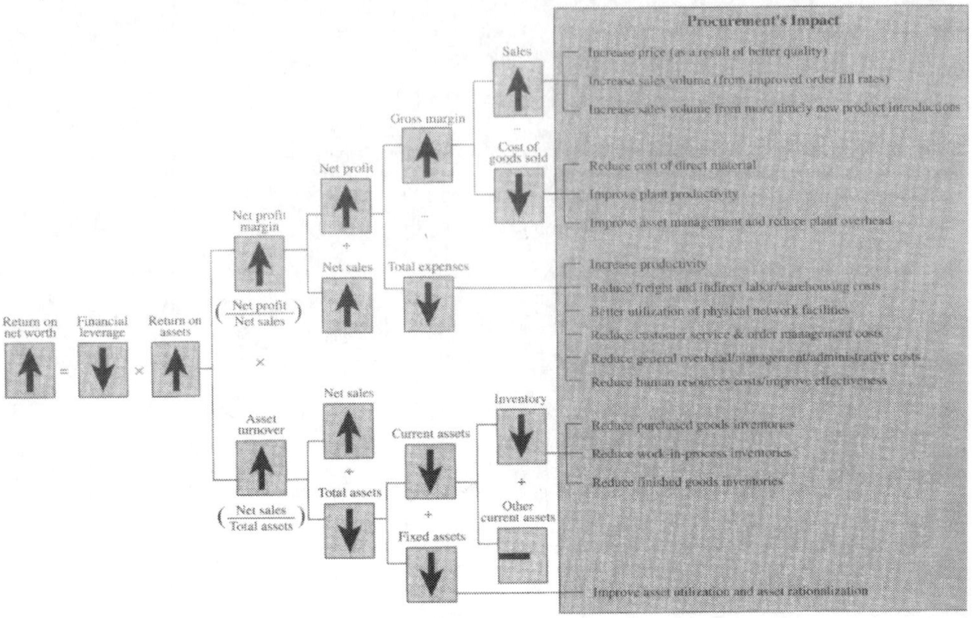

Technology Development

- Inventory levels and measures
- Transportation costs and customer locations (GPS)
- Use of e-commerce
- System down time

Human Resource Mgmt

- Number of people working
- Number of new hires
- Number of minorities
- Turnover ratio
- Total dollar labor cost
- Number of promotions
- Amount of training
- Number of certifications

Firm Infrastructure

- Total dollar of facilities
- New construction and improvements
- New property, plant and equipment
- Property plant and equipment sold

Conclusion

- Porter's Value Chain
- Key performance indicators
- Compare to intercompany, intracompany, industry, S & P 500

Questions?

APPLYING TREND ANALYSIS TECHNIQUES TO LOGISTICS NEEDS

J R MILLER
SCIENCE APPLICATIONS INTERNATIONAL CORPORATION
HUNTSVILLE ALABAMA

ABSTRACT

One of the persistent needs of all logistical systems, military or commercial, is demand forecasting. There are many methods to make forecasts however an often overlooked question is this: What is the accuracy of the forecast? In this paper we describe methods to obtain forecasts together with error limits on them. With considerable experience using trend analysis we illustrate the techniques used with several examples. Although used in other venue adaptation to logistics problems is relatively straightforward. Ways to make forecasts with the attendant error limits is given. The relation to anticipatory logistics is discussed. The effect of volatile data and changing user history is explored. Another facet of the use of trend analysis to establish demand forecasts is the question of how often to take data. This is explored.

Introduction

We often wish to know the future. Man has in the past relied on astrologers, wizards. prophets and psychics to foretell events. The Romans studied the entrails of fowl for signs before going into battle.

In modern organizations looking into the future is necessary so that intelligent planning can be accomplished. One needs forecasts of the future.

The forecasting we will be describing relies on past history, it is quantitative forecasting. There is a fundamental limitation to all forecasts …if the future is not reflected by past data then forecasts may be untrue. So we must be continuously on guard for changes in these patterns.

There is always error in our forecasts and one of the challenges is to specify what the error limits are for a particular forecast, this point is often ignored.

In the logistics world we run across (ref 1) a new phrase "anticipatory logistics" which means predicting needs of users before they actually develop. To do this one needs to predict component failures using historical data. This is one of the main functions of the project we support, the Army Common Embedded Diagnostics managed by the PM-TMDE office at Redstone Arsenal Alabama. It is apparent how interrelated these goals and functions are.

Clearly it is important to be able to use historical data to make predictions and do it quantitatively. Predictions are best if quantitative; the prediction and its accuracy should be known and stated.

So we see our methodology is applicable to logistics problems and should be of interest to persons working in that field. Logistics people want to forecast demand for repair parts, replacement parts, military munitions, etc.

The methods and mathematics used are quite general in nature and can be applied to a universe of needs. We have been using this math/science for well over twenty years (2). We are currently using it to predict time to exceedance (failure) for various Army vehicle systems (engines, transmissions, alternators, batteries, etc). We have also used it to predict the time for spacecraft amplifier electronics to drift out of tolerance. The original use was to calculate the time before recertification of calibration standards was required.

This paper will describe the adaptation of this methodology to logistics needs.

Demand Forecasting

A supply system needs to know what the demand for the product they stock is, so they will not run out. Given a set of historical data one can use the average of that data, not a good idea! Why? The average has an inherent problem best exemplified by this example, see figure 1.

BANG!
BANG!

Figure 1 Duck and Hunter Illustration

A duck hunter went hunting, first time he shot in front of the duck, second time he shot behind the duck, on the average he had duck for dinner!

The average ignores wide variations in the data, so sometimes it is a very misleading number. The standard deviation or standard error, is used to give a measure of the variability of the data, and should always be used with it to indicate this variability.

A better scheme is to do the following: One can do a best fit to the data using any number of off-the -shelf software routines….best , most common being EXCEL linear regression, a straight line fit. This is a form of averaging, except it tries to minimize the deviations by squaring and summing them. It gives correlation between variables but does not give the accuracy of the curve fit.

The demand forecast based on this curve fit can be used and often is…. the accuracy of the forecast should be known and used.

Two ways to obtain it: one can calculate the standard deviation using the data, multiply it by a certain factor (Student T number and then one has plus and minus tolerances, a few textbooks recommend this approach.

There is a potential problem …the accuracy bounds are independent of time i.e., future use of this demand forecast does not depend how far in the future one uses it, not intuitively satisfying. See Figure 2

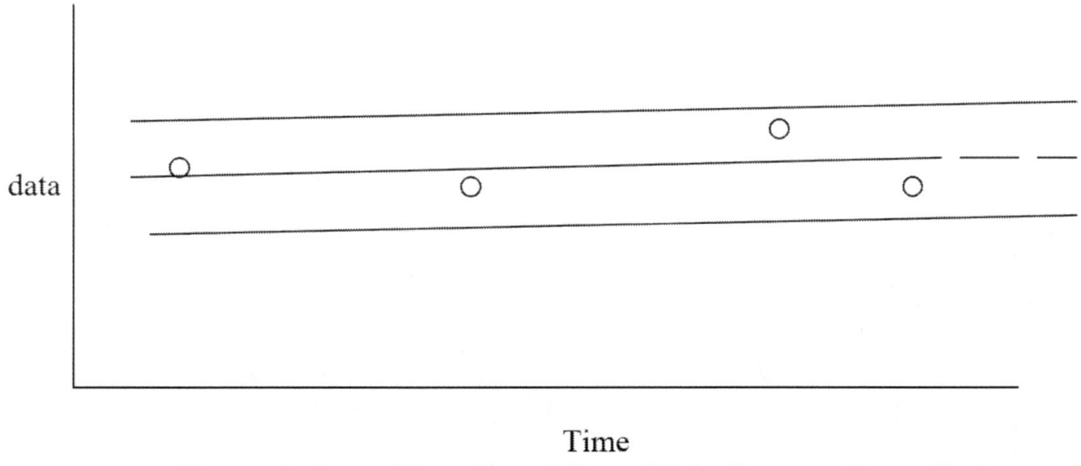

Figure 2 Some Time Trend Data With *Constant* Error limits

A better solution is to have demand error limits that do depend on time, illustrated by fig 6. As shown the error limits get bigger as we extend into the future. Their size depends on the variability of the data, the confidence level we use and how far we extrapolate into the future. Let's show the differences just discussed with an example table 1, [3].

Table 1 Forecast Demand Example

Month	Demand	
1	497	
2	454	
3	624	
4	764	
5	631	
6	624	
7	821	
8	1017	
9	709	
10	715	
11	1794	
12	1242	Confidence Level = 90%

A plot of this data is shown in fig 3

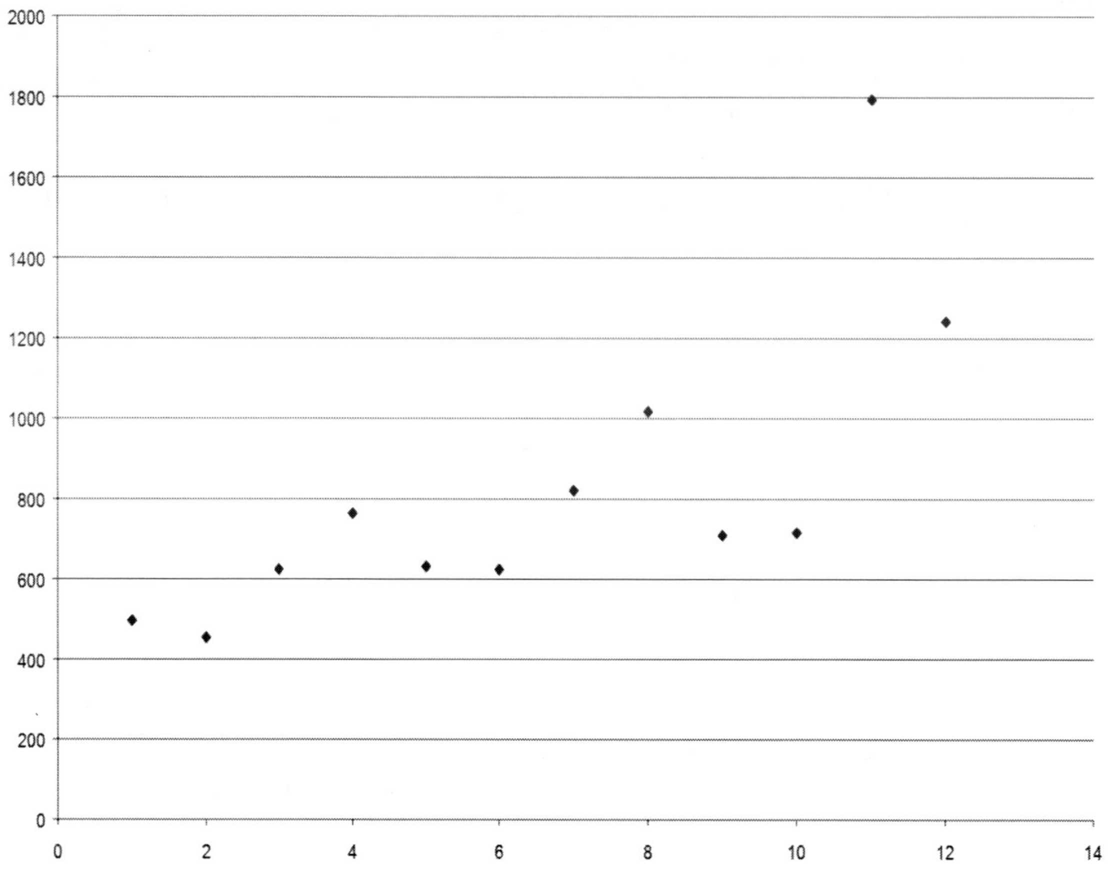

Figure 3 Demand Data (example)

Figure 4 Demand Data Fitted With Offset, Periodic and Linear Trend Terms

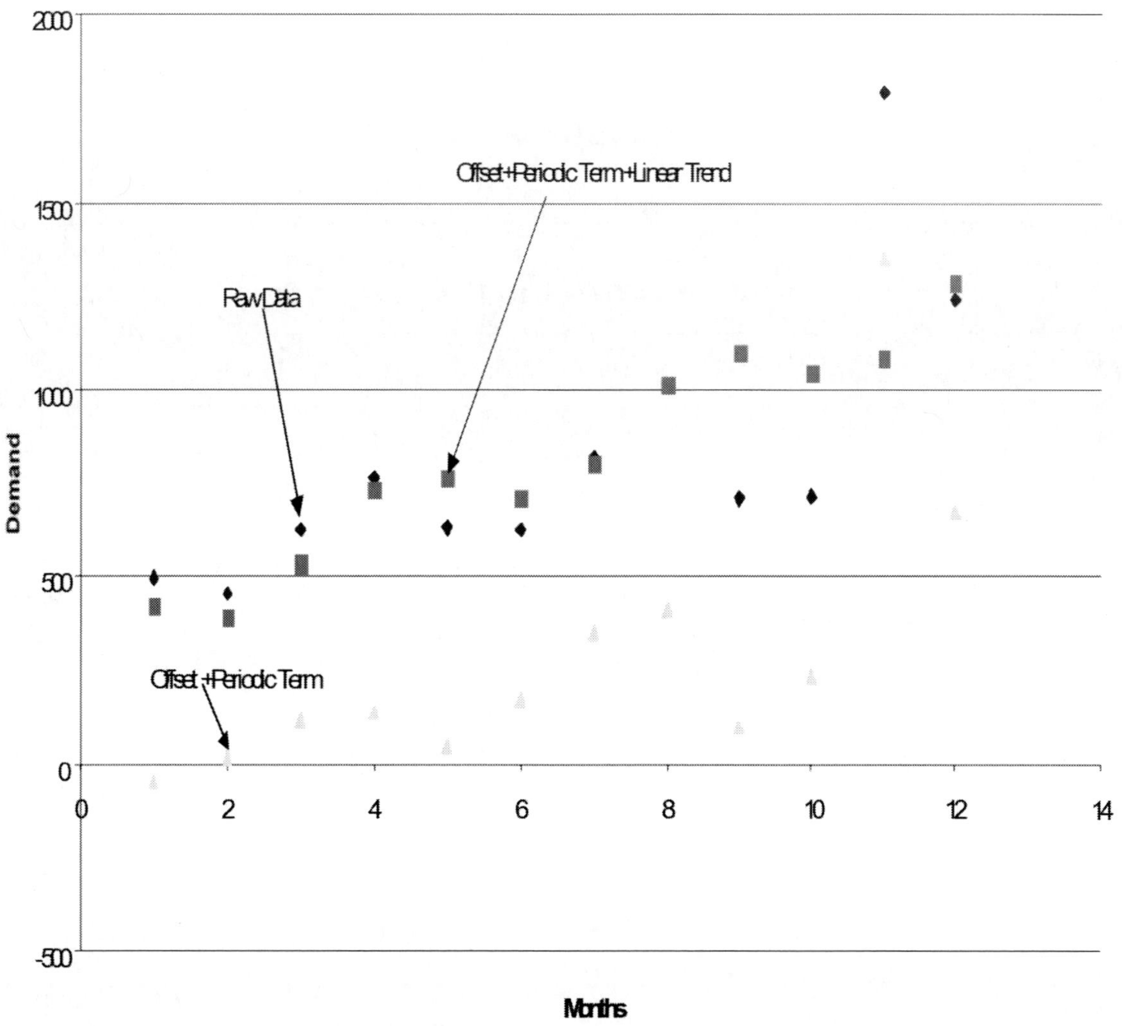

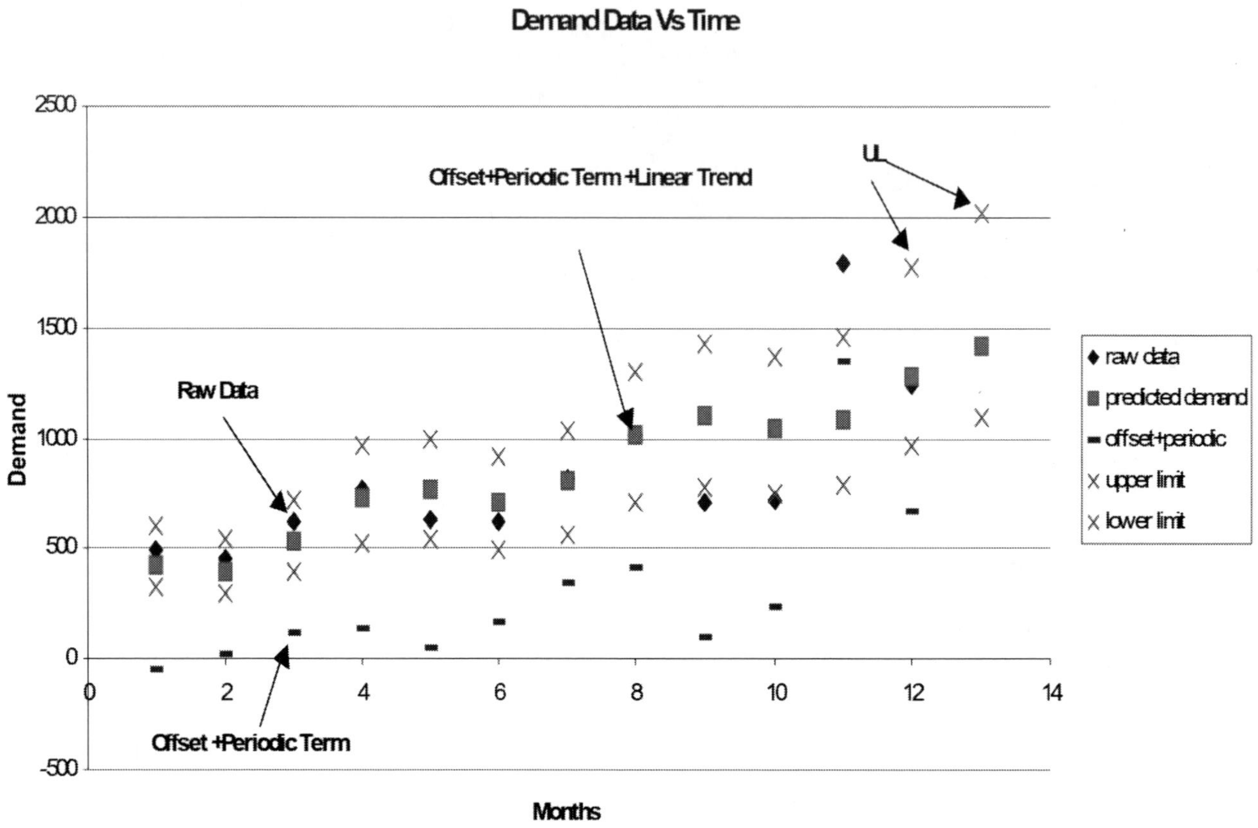

Figure 5 Demand Data With Prediction at 13th quarter and Error Limits

Figure 6 General Time Trend data

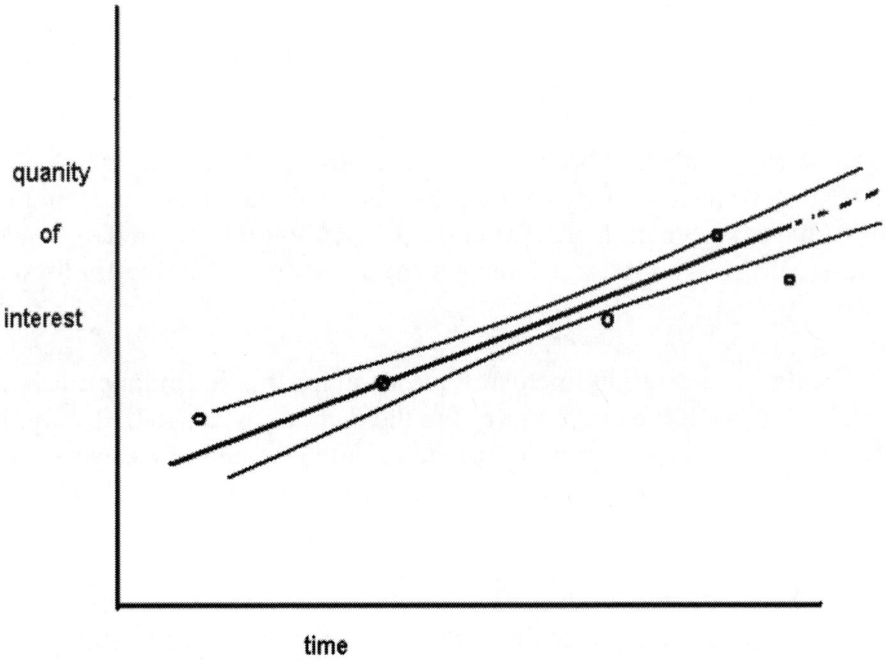

Now using them we will predict the demand for the 13th month and it is **1421 (+595,-323)**. Then error limits around this prediction,figure 5 , are found from how well the curve fits the data and how far into the future we want to extraploate. The next section expands on this.

Some Linear Trend Details

If one has a set of data that only exhibits a steady change, with time, a straight line may be the best curve to fit it. This is often the case with data from wear and tear situations. One must have historical data .,real data, not artifically generated, to analyze. For illustration purposes suppose we have a set of data as plotted in figure 6.

We fit the data to a straight line using least squares math, finding the slope and intercept. Now we test to see if the curve really fits the data, do whats called a significance test. This test compares the slope to the spread of data of data ; makes sure the slope is stronger than the data dispersion. If that is the case we proceed ,if not we stop. Cannot use the curve if not significant.

Now we estimate the error limits of this curve. They are found from the confidence level, number of points and spread of the data around the line and how far into the future we want to go. Note this error limit is found from the math used, it is a general error estimate not based on specific experimental results. This is the preffered method if a single method must be had. Doing this we have the upper and lower error bounds.To see how this is done consult reference 2,3,4,5..

Note the error bounds get larger the more into the future we venture. This can be used to solve various problems such as finding how long to wait to recalibrate some calibration standard (our original use,3), how long it takes for some drifting item to exeed specification limits(amplifier in a space craft ,an engine where oil pressure is too low). The methods used are quite general and can be adapted to many problems.

There are however limits on the useage; the past must reflect the future i.e., the item being studied must remain the same, one cannot change out the engine and use data from the previous engine. There are a certain number of data points required. A preliminary idea of a possible trend can be sought with a minimum of 3 points but we really need 6 or 7. When one gets about 9 to 10 points then a good answer can be had. One can have too many points so that old numbers will tend to obscure a new effect. To prevent this one should use last in first out to throw out old data and detect change faster. So much for some of those details

Logistical Applications

Some applications/data are not particurarly stable, for example military supply requirements can be expected to change rapidly as force requirements ramp up and down.

In the previous example what happens if we use just the last 6 data points? This question is best answered by refering to prior ,2,3,4,5.

How many data points to use? Recent work 3, on this question suggests that 7 is about the minimum, to keep about that number;to put in new numbers and throw out the old.

What if a linear curve does not fit good enough? At least two other choices exist; Brownian or Drunkards walk models
for purely random data and for "stronger" data quadratic curve fits may suffuce.. Both have error limits ,can be found and used.

So now how to do demand forecasting for an organization when the situation becomes volatile and the demand data is volatile.? Go back to past history when things were volatile, that is the only data that is appropiate, then input fresh data
as it becomes available. If one can shorten the time interval between data samples this may be useful to track the trend earlier.

Error Limits of Different Forecasting Methods

Table 2 summarizes the error limits found by theoretical methods (math) for most forecasting methods.In some cases it is not clear such exists, that is what the question mark means.An experimentally found error is often given as a general error limit, this is a confused understanding of the subject. Experimentally based error limits are special case situations
and fit the particulars of that experiment. One should be able to derive error limits from the theory used to make the prediction. The best of all worlds is to have both methods and for both to agree. It is quite difficult to have a significant number of experiments to establish and justify error limits.

There are many off the shelf software programs available to do demand forecasting, they should be clear what the accuracy of the forecast is, and how found. Furthermore it is often the case that the error limits are used rather than the actual prediction, this is true for our technique.

TABLE 2 ERROR LIMITS OF FORECASTS

FORECAST TYPE	**ERROR LIMITS**	**REMARKS**
average	dispersion around average, Standard Error, a general result	independent of time, not realistic
best fit straight line	dispersion around line+ time dependence, general result	error limits depend on time
random, Brownian or drunkards walk	dispersion around line+ time dependence, general result	same as above, very wide limits
2nd Order, Quadratic	dispersion around prediction line,unclear time dependence ,general result	require more data than above
exponential	same as above ,general results	
artificial intelligence methods, Neural net	?,special case, limited	Difficult to generalize ?

SUMMARY and CONCLUSIONS

In conclusion demand forecasts can be found in many different ways. To be quanatitive is desired.
We have described one method, the use of a linear regression. All forecasts should include an estimate of
their error limits and how found. General demand data can exhibit several components; offsets, periodic and
time trends, An example with these components was worked through and a prediction made. The results are
applicable to military and civilian users.

One should be alert to the question of accuracy of forecasts and their method of determining such. Additionally one must consider the use of such error limits when employing predictions.

REFERENCES

1.Anticipatory Logistics: The Army's Answer To Supply Chain Management, Major J.M.Lenzini, *Army Logistician*, Sept-Oct 2002.
2.Mofification Of Calibration Intervals Using Measurement Data, J R Miller III, NCSL Symposium, 1983, Boulder Colorado.
3. What Are The Important Factors Affecting Prognostics? J R Miller and J Grimes, AutoTestCon 2002,HuntsvilleAl
4. Results Using Trend Analysis For Predicting Automotive Maintenance Needs, J R Miller, AutoTestCon 2002, Huntsville Al.
5. Performance History For Multifunction Calibrator, J R Miller III and Patrick Curry, NCSL, 1995
6. *Principles of Inventory and Materials Management,* 3rd Edition, Tersine,R J,North-Holland,1988, pg 82.

A Review of Logistics Management Information

Author: Joe Ketron, USAMC Logistics Support Activity, Redstone Arsenal, AL
256-955-9926 donald.ketron@us.army.mil

Abstract:

It has been 7 years since the MIL-STD-1388-2B, Logistics Support Analysis Record (LSAR) was eliminated. Since then the performance specification MIL-PRF-49506, Logistics Management Information (LMI) and MIL-HDBK 502 have served to help DOD acquire the data the government needs to ensure logistics support is properly managed throughout the life cycle.

The question now is, how is the LMI performance specification working out? Are programs really using it? How will future and legacy LMI data feed the Logistics Modernization Program (LMP)? It is difficult to provide definitive answers to these questions, but in our presentation we'll give our observations, the problems uncovered, and possible solutions.

Paper:

On May 17, 1995, the Defense Standards Improvement Council ruled that MIL-STD-1388-2B, DOD Requirements for a Logistic Support Analysis Record (LSAR), be replaced with a performance specification. Similar to the LSAR, the subsequent performance specification, MIL-PRF-49506, Logistics Management Information (LMI), describes information required by the government to perform logistics management functions. However, the LMI looks radically different from MIL-STD-1388-2B.

One of the main differences is the number of data elements in the two documents. The LSAR, Notice 1, contained 518 data elements while the LMI was drastically reduced to only 159. The LMI data elements are mainly in the areas of provisioning, cataloging, and support equipment, whereas the LSAR data elements covered those areas plus, reliability, maintenance tasks, facilities, skills, and transportation. While this seems to be a limiting factor on the breadth and depth of logistics data that the government can get on contract through the LMI document, the positive, and often overlooked, aspect of the LMI performance specification is that requirements can be tailored out or tailored in (e.g., data elements can be removed or added for a specific contract if necessary) according to guidance from MIL-STD-961D, Defense

Specifications Standard Practice. It is this tailoring flexibility that many programs have utilized and continue to utilize.

There are numerous DOD system programs that have utilized MIL-PRF-49506, LMI, as a contractual method for acquiring logistics and support-related engineering data. For instance, the Air Force's C-5A program tailored the LMI to fit their specific needs. However, there is a perception that there are many programs that still utilize either MIL-STD-1388-2A or –2B, Logistic Support Analysis Record (LSAR), to get their logistics data. To validate this perception and to find out how many programs were utilizing the LMI, a survey was conducted of the Army's ACAT I and II programs listed in the Acquisition Information Management (AIM) database. Results of the survey are depicted in the following table.

	NUMBER OF RESPONSES	NUMBER WITH LOGISTICS DATA DELIVERY RQMTS	NUMBER USING LMI SPEC	NUMBER USING LSAR STANDARD	NUMBER USING LSAR SYSTEM FOR DATA DELIVERY
ACAT I	23	19	13	5	19
ACAT II	14	10	4	4	6
TOTAL	37	29	17	9	25

Based on the gathered information above, it infers that the LMI is being utilized by government organizations on contracts issued since its release. Furthermore, some of the program offices are tailoring the basic set of LMI data elements, as they should be, quite often including additional data requirements. There are still some programs that are utilizing the LSAR standards. Most of those are older programs and are "grand-fathered in" under the LSAR standards. From the OEMs perspective on satisfying the government's logistics data requirement needs, they are taking to heart one of the first statements in the LMI, "The contractor may, and is encouraged to, suggest alternative means of satisfying requirements of this specification to make information more readily available and to utilize more efficient business practices." This statement gives the contractor the freedom to choose from many different systems and methods to deliver the LMI data, but they typically have utilized LSAR software programs. The final column of data reveals this trend. One of the main reasons for this goes back to the LMI statement above, they can efficiently deliver the data since the government legacy systems can accept and load data from the LSAR software. In addition, the contractor already has an investment in the LSAR system and their personnel are trained on it.

There are some contractors that do not utilize LSAR software and, quite often in these cases, the data interchange formats are not clearly spelled out in the contract. This is problematic since each LMI contract can be tailored with a different set of data elements that have unique formats and data relationships. This presents a problem anytime the data is fed to a central government data repository such as the Commodity Command Data System (CCSS) or, in the future, the Logistics Modernization Program (LMP). Since the data is not in a standard format, quite often a time consuming and expensive effort is required to convert that data before it can be loaded into the government repository.

So, is anything being done to alleviate future data interchange problems concerning logistics data feeds between industry and government, especially for the future LMP system? Recognizing this potential issue, the Department of the Army (Deputy for ILS, ASA Acquisition, Logistics, and Technology) requested support from LOGSA in addressing it. Following are excerpts from the memo. "We request your support in developing interim and long-term solutions for data interchange of logistics information between industry and government organizations. This specifically includes, but is not limited to, interchange of logistics data with the Logistics Modernization Program (LMP). The acquisition community needs a way to ensure that logistics data is being developed properly and that it has a standard format for passing data back and forth between government and industry. Additionally, this data must be able to flow, without conversion, to the many data systems currently being developed in the Army such as the LMP initiative. Currently, there is no contractual mechanism to ensure this will happen." "…an interim solution must be developed to provide specific Department of the Army contractual guidance for data interchange with LMP to include the necessary formats and data elements." "Ultimately, a long-term solution must be developed. Other Army organizations and other services have voiced concerns on contracting for the LMI data. Since LOGSA is the preparing activity for MIL-PRF-49506, we feel it will be necessary for your organization to either develop a Logistics Support Interface standard and associated XML schema, or update the existing LMI document and convert it to an Interface Standard or Standard Practice."

Currently, we are working with personnel from the LMP office to develop an interim solution for data delivery utilizing MIL-PRF-49506, Logistics Management Information. The LMP personnel are providing us necessary data elements, formats, and definitions in the areas of Provisioning, Packaging, and Environment, Health, and Safety so that we can develop contractual guidance via a tailored MIL-PRF-49506, specifically for delivery to that system. This will include policy guidance with examples of how to use data worksheets to select the appropriate data elements based on program needs. It is our belief that this guidance should emanate from the LMP office.

Since the LMP system is Army unique, the long-term solution will most likely be to develop a limited coordination (Army) Interface Standard, or Standard Practice, specifically for interchange of data with it. For this to be accomplished, system requirements containing data elements, their attributes and definitions, data schema and associated rules must be identified and solidified by the LMP office. In addition, the mode of data transfer must be established and it is likely that the Extensible Markup Language (XML) protocol will be used. The effort to identify the necessary system requirements is not ready to be undertaken since the LMP is currently in a state of flux. When the time comes, it will require coordination with ongoing efforts such as Enterprise Product Data Management, as well as input from Major Subordinate Commands, Program Executive Offices, Project Managers, and other services if necessary.

In summary, the LMI is being utilized by government organizations to contract for logistics data and the ability to tailor it allows for program unique data requirements to be addressed. On the other hand, this flexibility also causes concern anytime the data must be fed to a government data repository and this issue is currently being addressed with the future LMP system.

Author's Biography: Mr. Ketron is a graduate of the University of Kentucky, with a Bachelor's degree in Chemical Engineering and a Master's in Business Administration. He has worked for the government in the Logistics Field for over 17 yrs at MRSA and LOGSA. He has taken part in the development and authoring of MIL-STD-1388-2B, Logistic Support Analysis Record, MIL-PRF-49506, Logistic Management Information (LMI), and MIL-HDBK-502, Acquisition Logistics Handbook. Also, he performed the Functional Economic Analysis and served as lead functional person for the Post Fielding Support Analysis project. Currently, Mr. Ketron serves as the lead functional person in the effort to provide logistics data to the Logistics Modernization Program (LMP) via LMI tailoring and associated guidance.

IBM

Business Consulting Services

On Demand in the US Department of Defense

Flexible, Light and Agile
August 11, 2003

DRAFT

Video Presentation in Original e-media

How is the DoD of the future able to respond so quickly to eminent threats, hostile events, and make such quick decisions?

Scenario Attributes

- Smooth cooperation with coalition partners, foreign governments, and industry
- Executive level dashboard of readiness with views into operational deployment times, supply chains, personnel preparedness, and budgets
- Rapid deployment of forces
- New review process: Who, doing what, using what assets, at what cost
- Fused coalition capabilities
- Integrated set of Financial, HR, and Logistic data, starting at field level and rolling up to service level.

How was this possible?

Enabling Capabilities

- **Dynamic Human Capital:** Identify and deploy the right people at the right time
- **Fully Integrated Fact Based Decision Making:** Comprehensive understanding of decision implications for all decision alternatives
- **Seamless Integrated Logistics:** Logistical intelligence responsive to strategic direction changes
- **Utility IT Services:** Variable IT capacity, dedicated surge IT partner resources

Scenario stakeholders: value and benefits

Stakeholder Segment	Value	Benefits
Tactical Commander	Outside mission real-time analysis and assistance	• Increased mission effectiveness and safety • Lethality of all in theater combined arms available
Joint Force Commander	Common Operating Picture of mission operations and capabilities	• Superior battle field intelligence • Real-time analytical support • Operational scenario development • Interoperability
National Command Authority	Overall assessment of mission effectiveness, cost estimates, and personnel impacts, leading to realistic national budget planning	• Integrated knowledge set per mission: - Warfighter capabilities/readiness - Financial estimates - Personnel
On demand Partners	Collaboration and directed activity	• Increased scope of response possibilities • Defines specific contribution of coalition and other partners

Agenda

- Defense operations of the future
- On demand attributes
- Capabilities to get to the future
- On demand roadmap
- Next steps – Transformation approach

This scenario highlights the impact of a world of increasing uncertainty and dynamic changes for the Department of Defense

Drivers

Asymmetric Threats

- Threats are increasingly asymmetric and sophisticated in nature
- Projection of power is increasingly dependent upon intelligence and information superiority
- Development of warfighting capabilities and weapons on the outer edges of state-of-the-art
- Conflicts are increasingly occurring in urban areas

Political Pressures

- Increased congressional oversight
- Meeting political leadership's management agenda
- Internal, self imposed goals for efficiency and effectiveness
- Increased need for cleaner, smarter weapons
- Increased interdependence on world trading partners

Geographically Dispersed Conflict

- Conflicts are increasingly decentralized
- Numerous and dispersed nature of conflicts/ missions
- Need for increased resource flexibility and interchange among service branches and nations
- Increasing littoral operations

Security / Privacy

- Global concern for protecting citizens and their information
- Threats from increased information 'viruses'
- Privacy and Information security needs
- Information sharing requirements expanding rapidly
- Multi level security complications and host nation agreements

Role Evolution

- Broadening of role to pre/post conflict stabilization – e.g. peacekeeping
- Rebuilding and governance development
- Nation building activities are increasing
- Creation of professional warfighters: non-core military activities moving to civilian sector
- Redefining historic use of National Guard Forces

The DoD is able to respond to these pressures by becoming an *'on demand'* organization

An on demand organization is…

…an enterprise whose **business processes – integrated end-to-end** across the company and with key partners, suppliers and customers – can respond with **flexibility** and **speed** to any **customer demand, market opportunity** or **external threat**

Sam Palmisano, CEO, IBM, October 30, 2002

…a military enterprise whose **support processes – integrated end-to-end** across the uniformed services, mission partners, and suppliers– can respond with **agility** and **flexibility** to any **mission, direction** or **external threat**

Bill Phillips, Managing Partner, DoD, IBM

An on demand DoD fulfills its transformation vision by becoming focused, responsive, variable and resilient

Department of Defense vision…

Flexible *Light* *Agile*

"We learned on September 11, 2001,that our nation is vulnerable to enemies who hide in caves and shadows and strike in unexpected ways. That is why we must transform our armed forces. Our forces need to be flexible, light, and agile, so they can respond quickly and deal with surprise. The same is true of the man and women who support the Department of Defense. They also need flexibility so that they can move money, shift people, design and deploy new weapons more rapidly and respond to the continuing changes in our security environment." – *Secretary of Defense, Donald Rumsfeld*

… on demand Attributes

Focused
Committed to **concentrating on core mission** capabilities, using tightly integrated strategic partners to manage selected non-mission critical activities

Responsive
Seeming almost intuitive in its ability to **sense and respond rapidly** to unpredictable changes in the market environment and the needs of all its constituents

Variable
Able to adapt cost structures and business processes **flexibly**, in order to reduce risk and to do business at higher levels of productivity, cost control, capital efficiency and financial predictability

Resilient
Prepared for changes and threats – be they technological, economic, or political – enabling the business to continue operating with consistent availability, security and privacy

On demand enables the new opportunities for DoD

Transformation philosophy captured in the Defense Guidance directs the services to provide these attributes

New Rules for DoD	On Demand Attributes			
Fight first for *information superiority*	✓			✓
Speed of command		✓		
Access to information: *shared awareness*		✓		✓
Dispersed forces: noncontiguous operations			✓	✓
Demassification	✓		✓	
Elimination of *process lines*	✓		✓	
Elimination of *structural lines*			✓	
Self-synchronization	✓		✓	✓
Alter initial conditions at *higher rates of change*		✓	✓	✓
Compression of levels of war	✓			

A focused DoD can concentrate its resources on mission critical activities

Focused DoD

What it means for the DoD to Be "Focused"

- Has precise understanding of what is core and non-core activities
- Is committed to building its core competencies
- Outsources *non-core* elements to partners or shared services centers
  - Logistics, medical, personnel, finance, communications, etc
- Enables result oriented outcomes
- Compresses the battle space by focusing more resources on mission critical areas

Why it matters

- **Enables DoD to focus on areas which it does better than any other military in the world**
- **Reduce operational costs through efficient resource allocation**
- **Accesses best-in-class capabilities and leverages scale efficiencies through partners**
- **Concentrates effort on functions that increase core warfighting capabilities**
- **Frees overhead savings for use in warfighting capabilities**

A responsive DoD can better react to continuous change in national threats and political priorities

Responsive DoD

What it means for the DoD to Be "Responsive"

- Capable of anticipating, sensing, and dynamically responding to operational shocks and threats
  - Unpredictable and elusive enemies
  - Emerging partner, supplier and warfighter needs
  - Unexpected operational needs and rules of engagement
  - Conducting new concepts of operations
- Has the organizational capacity to act quickly based on collective intelligence
  - Real-time data gathering and analysis pulled as needed by the warfighter
  - Continuous generation of feedback and actionable insights
  - Total awareness based decision making

Why it Matters

- **Rapidly develops new mission capabilities and response packages**
- **Customizes operations to fit target profiles and maximize force multiplier**
- **Minimizes risk against premature military action**
- **Enables its people to rapidly make well-informed, timely decisions**
- **Optimizes readiness and mission capabilities**

A defense enterprise that can move from fixed to variable levels of resources to meet surge requirements while optimizing warfighting capabilities

Variable DoD

What It Means for the DoD to Be "Variable"

- Lowering overall costs by replacing fixed costs with needs based variable costs
- Reduces excess capacity and associated sustainment while increasing ability to meet surge level requirements
- Drives mission performance to higher levels of readiness, capital efficiency and financial predictability
- Partners with industry to provide fast and flexible resources
- Strengthen the ability to deploy the appropriate enterprise capabilities for each mission or situation

Why it matters

- **Allows use of military's total force to perform core mission capabilities while industry performs non-core tasks**
- **Aligns the size and type of response to the operational need**
- **Maintains resource capacity for average day-to-day demand versus peak demand**
- **Augments internal capabilities to achieve peak capacity**
- **Alleviates current funding gaps and capital requirements by paying for resources used**

A resilient DoD anticipates and prepares for the unexpected and learns from past experience while reducing current total cost of ownership and maintaining operational assuredness

Resilient Defense

What It Means for the DoD to Be "Resilient"

- Rapidly adapts based on current and expected experience
- Leverages industry and coalition resources to reduce total cost of ownership for operational continuity
- The warfighter can depend on consistent, reliable, secure service, 7X24 across the entire organization, all around the globe
- Prepares for unforeseen shocks to the DoD and protects the assets, safeguards service personnel, and reduces operational risks

Why it matters

- **Effectively manage risk among DoD, its coalition partners and industry**
- **Reduces capital requirements**
- **Minimize costs of reacting to external shocks**
- **Can recover quickly from disruptions to operations**
- **Shocks to IT infrastructure are mostly transparent to the warfighter**

Maturing capabilities move the DoD towards the overarching goal of Total Operational Effectiveness

Agenda

- Defense operations of the future
- On demand attributes
- ⇨ **Capabilities to get to the future**
- On demand roadmap
- Next steps – Transformation approach

The on demand journey helps the DoD to drive towards joint operations and total operational effectiveness

The evolution from single service operational models to the creation of adaptive partnerships among the DoD, its coalition partners and industry that possess specific discrete roles in delivering value to the warfighter

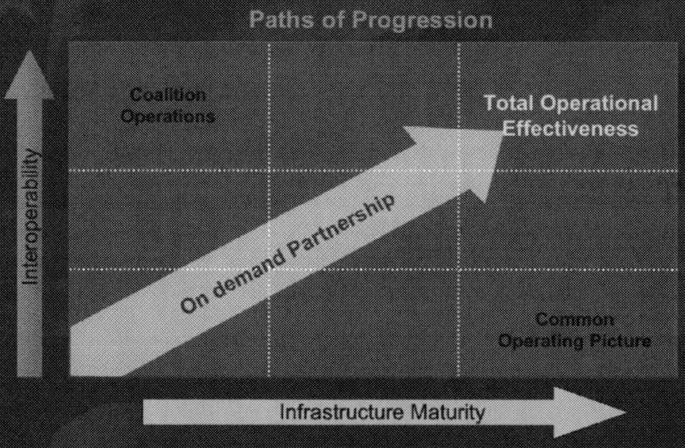

A flexible, integrated, open technology architecture that relies on sophisticated operational processes and promotes organizational flexibility

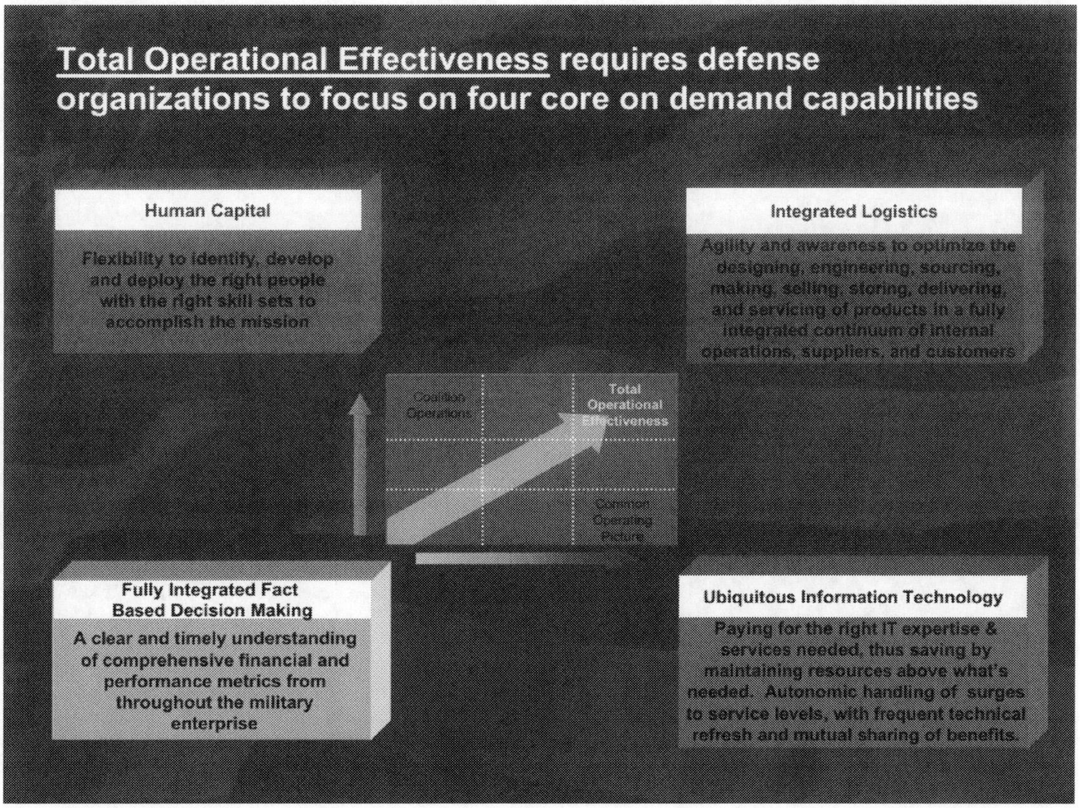
Total Operational Effectiveness requires defense organizations to focus on four core on demand capabilities
Human Capital
Flexibility to identify, develop and deploy the right people with the right skill sets to accomplish the mission
Integrated Logistics
Agility and awareness to optimize the designing, engineering, sourcing, making, selling, storing, delivering, and servicing of products in a fully integrated continuum of internal operations, suppliers, and customers
Coalition Operations
Total Operational Effectiveness
Common Operating Picture
Fully Integrated Fact Based Decision Making
A clear and timely understanding of comprehensive financial and performance metrics from throughout the military enterprise
Ubiquitous Information Technology
Paying for the right IT expertise & services needed, thus saving by maintaining resources above what's needed. Autonomic handling of surges to service levels, with frequent technical refresh and mutual sharing of benefits.

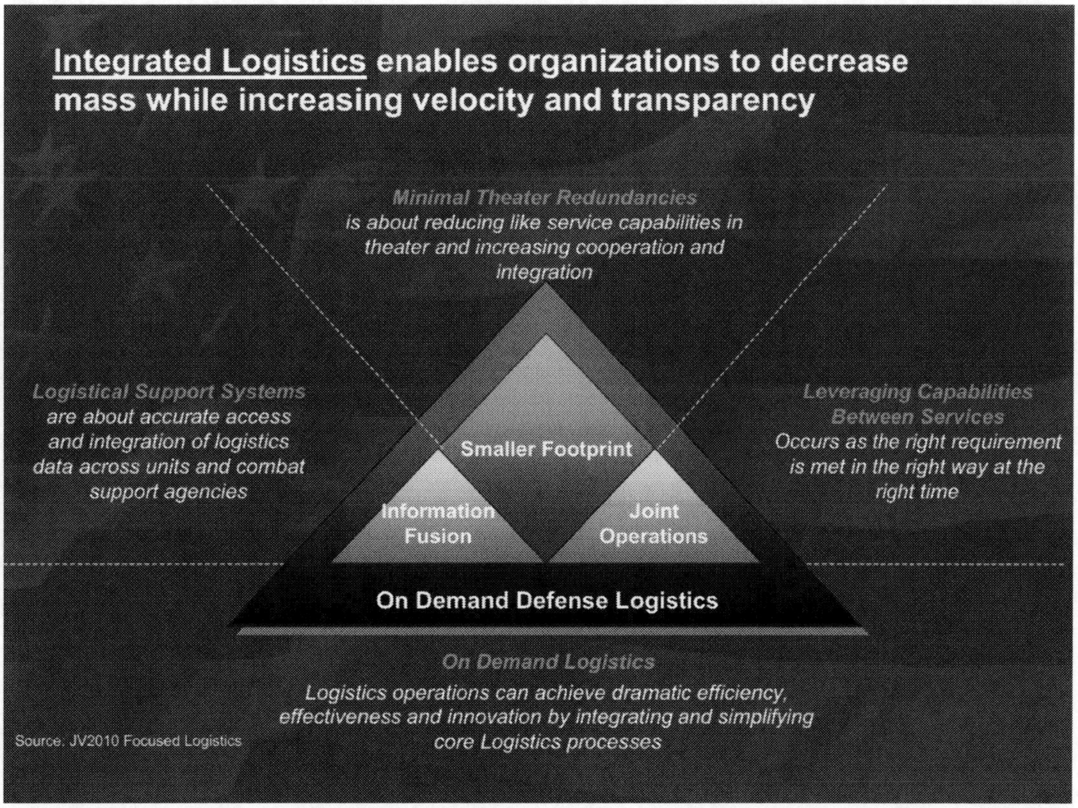
Integrated Logistics enables organizations to decrease mass while increasing velocity and transparency
Minimal Theater Redundancies
is about reducing like service capabilities in theater and increasing cooperation and integration
Logistical Support Systems
are about accurate access and integration of logistics data across units and combat support agencies
Leveraging Capabilities Between Services
Occurs as the right requirement is met in the right way at the right time
Smaller Footprint
Information Fusion
Joint Operations
On Demand Defense Logistics
On Demand Logistics
Logistics operations can achieve dramatic efficiency, effectiveness and innovation by integrating and simplifying core Logistics processes
Source: JV2010 Focused Logistics

How did on demand Integrated Logistics contribute to success in the scenario?

Characteristics

- Consolidation of logistics data across services
- Demand prediction – built in on going analytics that predict mission supply needs based on multiple mission scenarios
- Intelligence feeds linked to logistics systems coordinate
- Detects possible need before occurrence, taking into account on-hand supplies and times to re-supply with necessary codes and dependencies
- Built in links to supplier systems, automatically ordering replacement equipment

Value to DoD

- Reduce cost of logistical systems due to consolidation and associated efficiencies of procurement
- Increased warfighter preparedness; despite changing mission criteria to last minute
- Right equipment arrives at the right place from the closest source
- Minimizes forward logistics footprint

To achieve Seamless Integrated Logistics, on demand partnerships focus on this core set of building blocks

People

- Overall DoD logistics management staff
- Corporate level auditors and inspectors
- Standard DoD logistics skills and training
- Liaisons to external entities

Process

- Unified planning
- Accurate & timely expenditure reporting
- Holistic decision support
- Documented lessons learned & program effectiveness

Seamless Integrated Logistics

Technology

- Integrated financial & performance management systems
- Logistics systems integrated through entire DoD, coalition partners and suppliers
- Accurate accountability for legacy systems

Knowledge

- Real time access to current logistics information
- Ability to accurately project logistical and performance health
- Model cause and effect relationships
- Full & marginal cost analysis

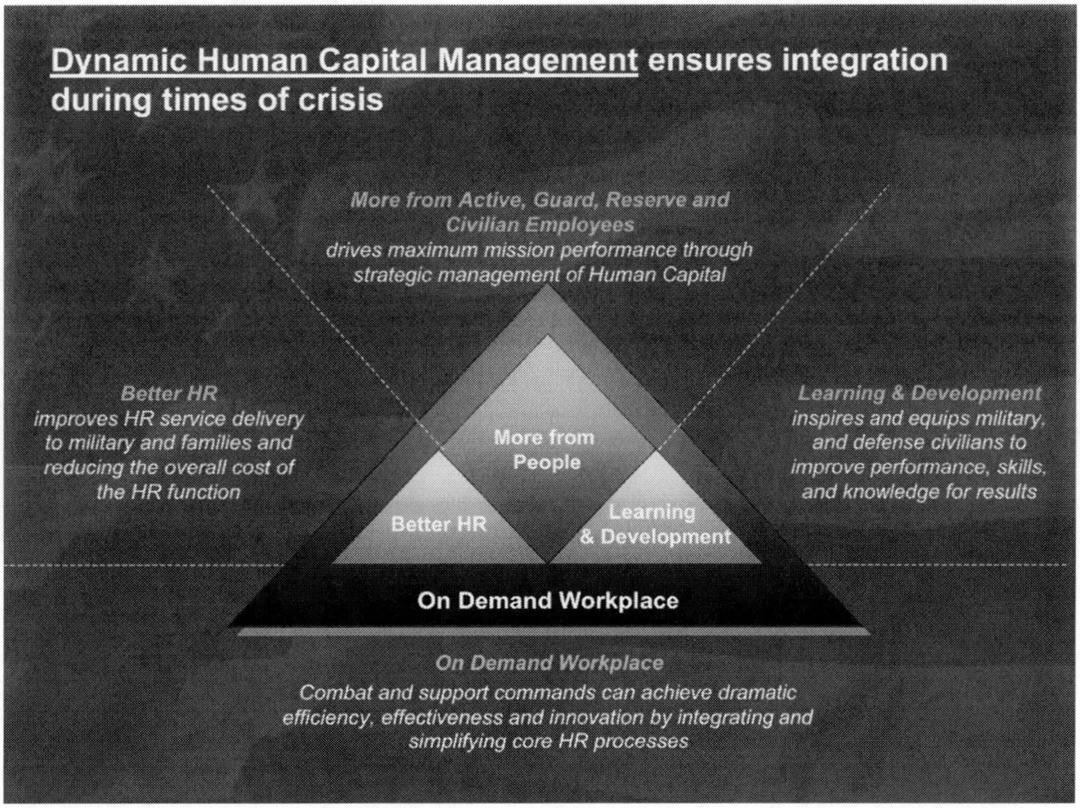
Dynamic Human Capital Management ensures integration during times of crisis
More from Active, Guard, Reserve and Civilian Employees
drives maximum mission performance through strategic management of Human Capital
Better HR
improves HR service delivery to military and families and reducing the overall cost of the HR function
Learning & Development
inspires and equips military, and defense civilians to improve performance, skills, and knowledge for results
More from People
Better HR
Learning & Development
On Demand Workplace
On Demand Workplace
Combat and support commands can achieve dramatic efficiency, effectiveness and innovation by integrating and simplifying core HR processes

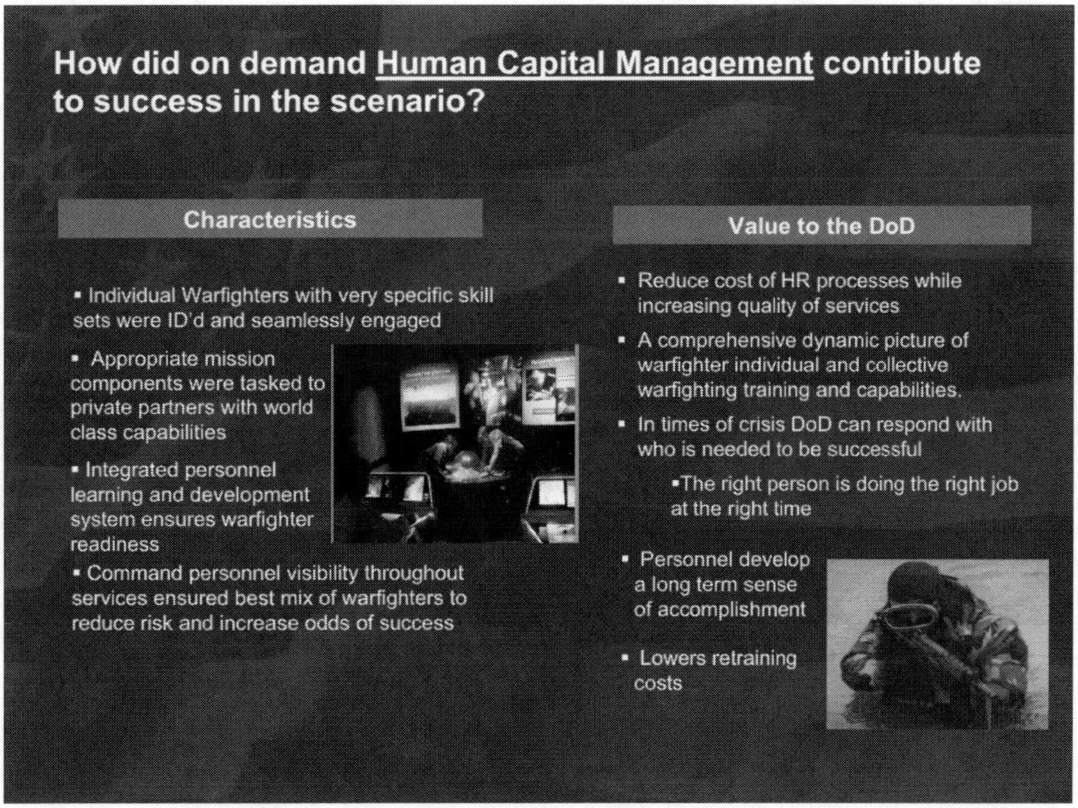
How did on demand Human Capital Management contribute to success in the scenario?
Characteristics
▪ Individual Warfighters with very specific skill sets were ID'd and seamlessly engaged
▪ Appropriate mission components were tasked to private partners with world class capabilities
▪ Integrated personnel learning and development system ensures warfighter readiness
▪ Command personnel visibility throughout services ensured best mix of warfighters to reduce risk and increase odds of success
Value to the DoD
▪ Reduce cost of HR processes while increasing quality of services
▪ A comprehensive dynamic picture of warfighter individual and collective warfighting training and capabilities.
▪ In times of crisis DoD can respond with who is needed to be successful
▪The right person is doing the right job at the right time
▪ Personnel develop a long term sense of accomplishment
▪ Lowers retraining costs

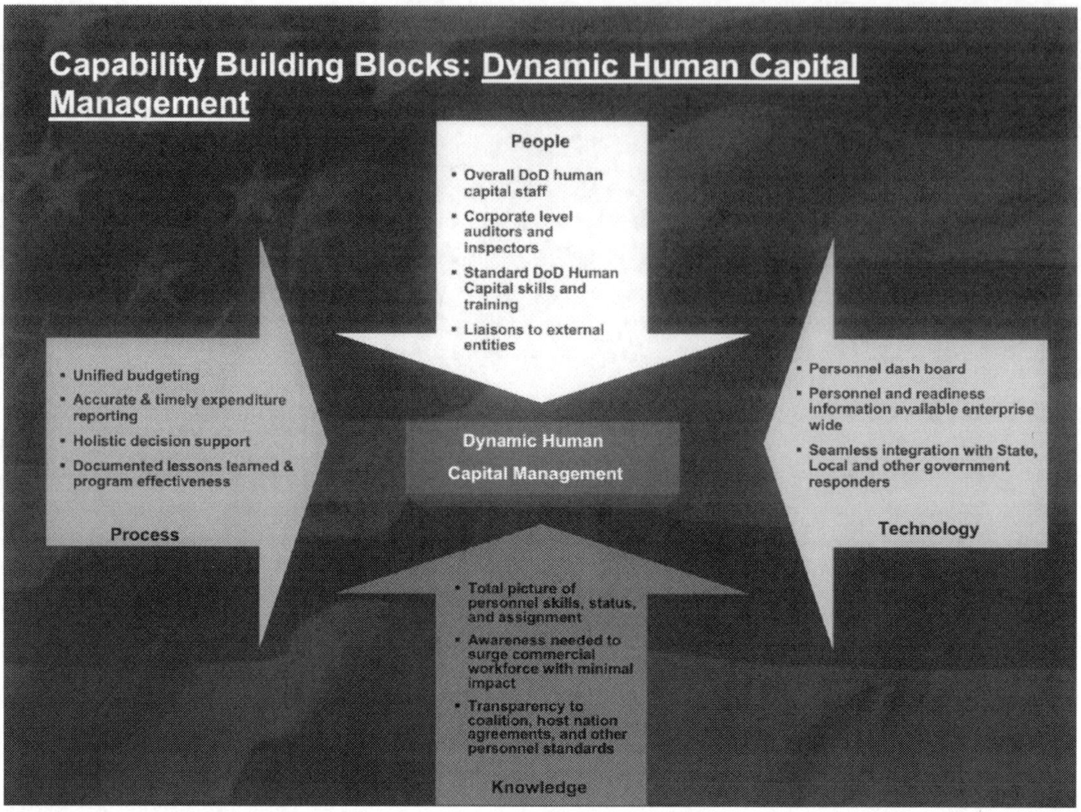
Capability Building Blocks: Dynamic Human Capital Management
People
• Overall DoD human capital staff
• Corporate level auditors and inspectors
• Standard DoD Human Capital skills and training
• Liaisons to external entities
• Unified budgeting
• Accurate & timely expenditure reporting
• Holistic decision support
• Documented lessons learned & program effectiveness
Process
Dynamic Human Capital Management
• Personnel dash board
• Personnel and readiness information available enterprise wide
• Seamless integration with State, Local and other government responders
Technology
• Total picture of personnel skills, status, and assignment
• Awareness needed to surge commercial workforce with minimal impact
• Transparency to coalition, host nation agreements, and other personnel standards
Knowledge

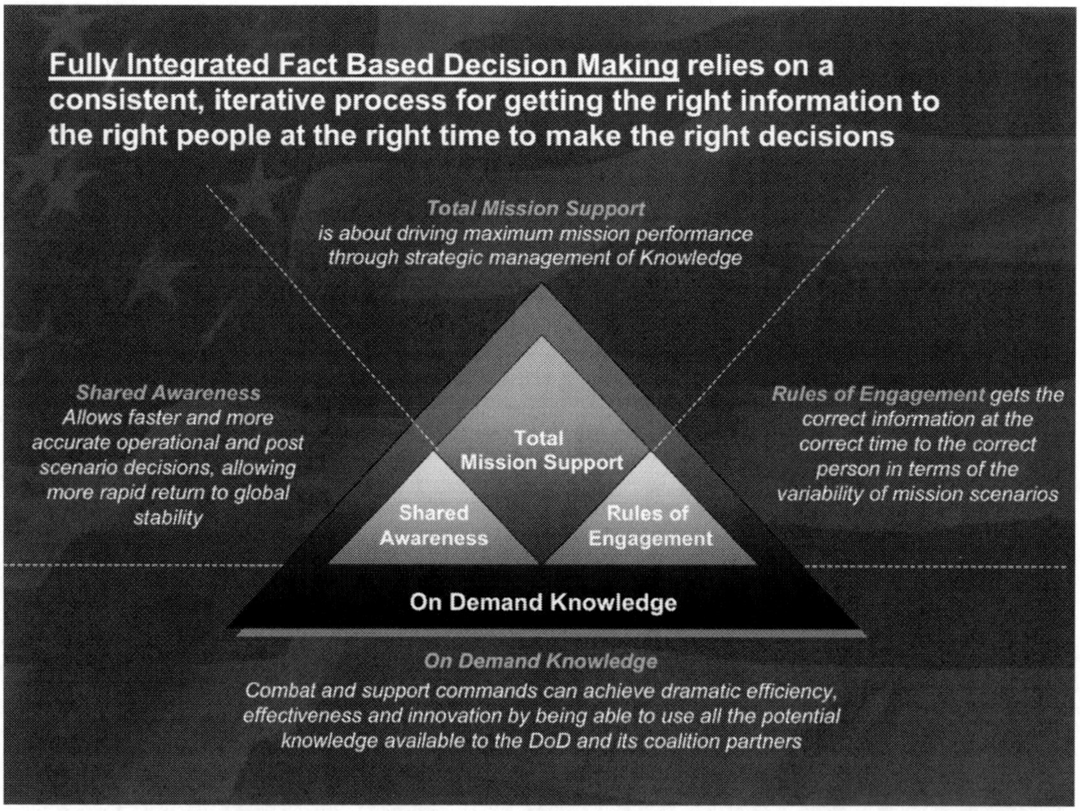
Fully Integrated Fact Based Decision Making relies on a consistent, iterative process for getting the right information to the right people at the right time to make the right decisions
Total Mission Support
is about driving maximum mission performance through strategic management of Knowledge
Shared Awareness
Allows faster and more accurate operational and post scenario decisions, allowing more rapid return to global stability
Rules of Engagement gets the correct information at the correct time to the correct person in terms of the variability of mission scenarios
Total Mission Support
Shared Awareness
Rules of Engagement
On Demand Knowledge
On Demand Knowledge
Combat and support commands can achieve dramatic efficiency, effectiveness and innovation by being able to use all the potential knowledge available to the DoD and its coalition partners

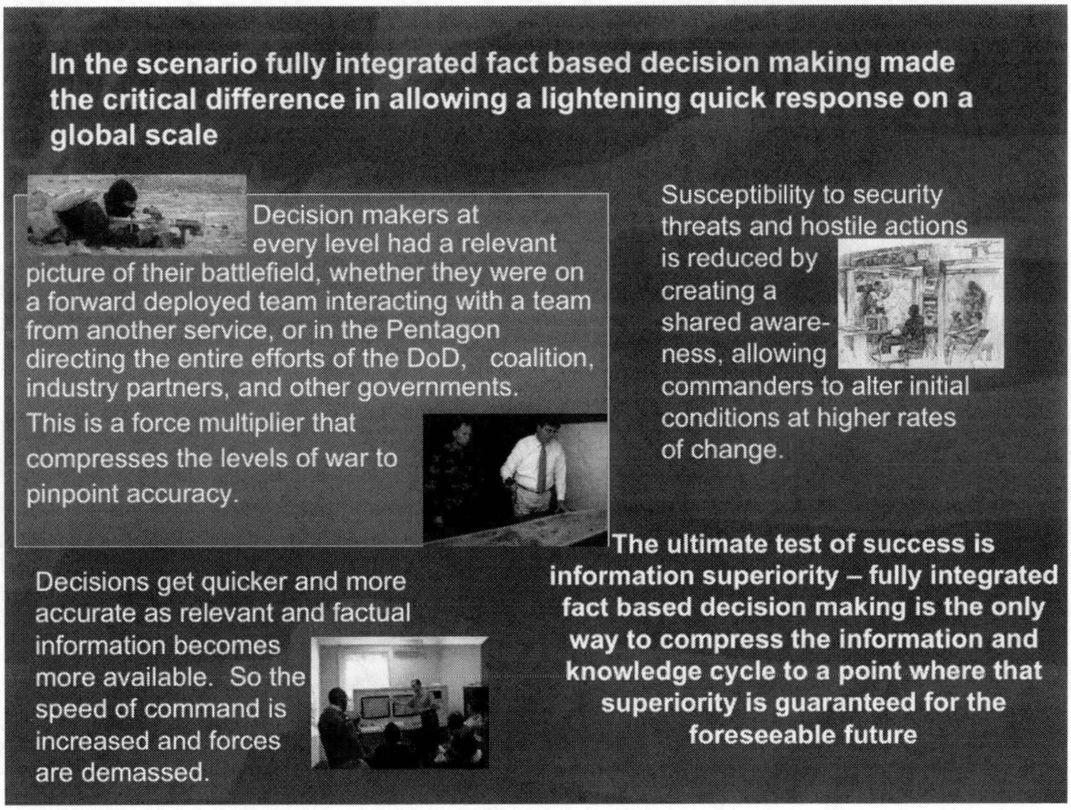
In the scenario fully integrated fact based decision making made the critical difference in allowing a lightening quick response on a global scale
Decision makers at every level had a relevant picture of their battlefield, whether they were on a forward deployed team interacting with a team from another service, or in the Pentagon directing the entire efforts of the DoD, coalition, industry partners, and other governments.
This is a force multiplier that compresses the levels of war to pinpoint accuracy.
Susceptibility to security threats and hostile actions is reduced by creating a shared awareness, allowing commanders to alter initial conditions at higher rates of change.
Decisions get quicker and more accurate as relevant and factual information becomes more available. So the speed of command is increased and forces are demassed.
The ultimate test of success is information superiority – fully integrated fact based decision making is the only way to compress the information and knowledge cycle to a point where that superiority is guaranteed for the foreseeable future

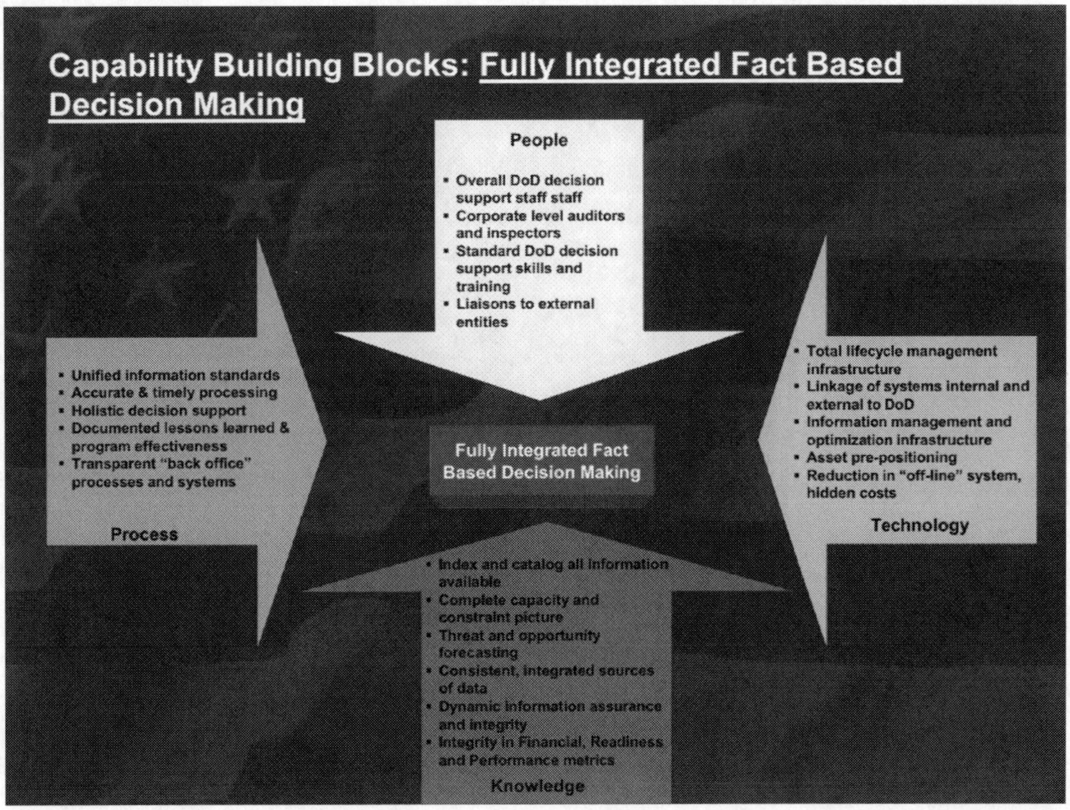
Capability Building Blocks: Fully Integrated Fact Based Decision Making
People
▪ Overall DoD decision support staff staff
▪ Corporate level auditors and inspectors
▪ Standard DoD decision support skills and training
▪ Liaisons to external entities
▪ Unified information standards
▪ Accurate & timely processing
▪ Holistic decision support
▪ Documented lessons learned & program effectiveness
▪ Transparent "back office" processes and systems
Process
Fully Integrated Fact Based Decision Making
▪ Total lifecycle management infrastructure
▪ Linkage of systems internal and external to DoD
▪ Information management and optimization infrastructure
▪ Asset pre-positioning
▪ Reduction in "off-line" system, hidden costs
Technology
▪ Index and catalog all information available
▪ Complete capacity and constraint picture
▪ Threat and opportunity forecasting
▪ Consistent, integrated sources of data
▪ Dynamic information assurance and integrity
▪ Integrity in Financial, Readiness and Performance metrics
Knowledge

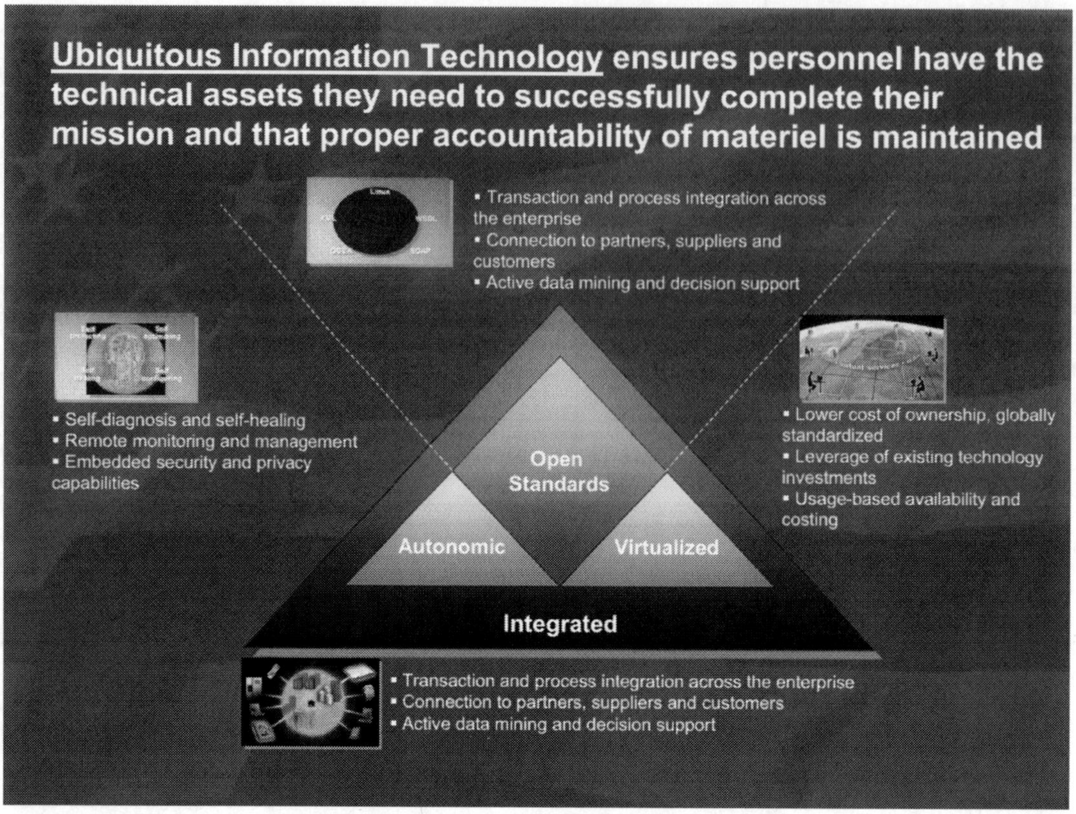
Ubiquitous Information Technology ensures personnel have the technical assets they need to successfully complete their mission and that proper accountability of materiel is maintained
▪ Transaction and process integration across the enterprise
▪ Connection to partners, suppliers and customers
▪ Active data mining and decision support
▪ Self-diagnosis and self-healing
▪ Remote monitoring and management
▪ Embedded security and privacy capabilities
▪ Lower cost of ownership, globally standardized
▪ Leverage of existing technology investments
▪ Usage-based availability and costing
Open Standards
Autonomic
Virtualized
Integrated
▪ Transaction and process integration across the enterprise
▪ Connection to partners, suppliers and customers
▪ Active data mining and decision support

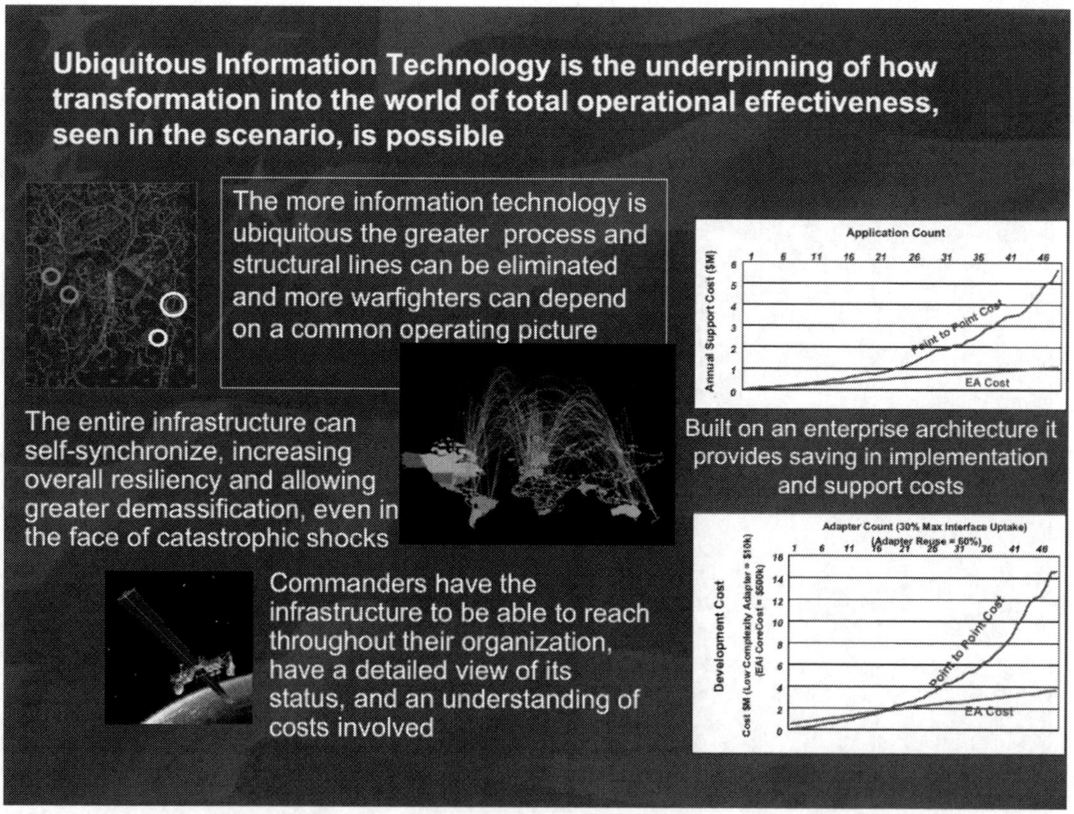
Ubiquitous Information Technology is the underpinning of how transformation into the world of total operational effectiveness, seen in the scenario, is possible
The more information technology is ubiquitous the greater process and structural lines can be eliminated and more warfighters can depend on a common operating picture
The entire infrastructure can self-synchronize, increasing overall resiliency and allowing greater demassification, even in the face of catastrophic shocks
Commanders have the infrastructure to be able to reach throughout their organization, have a detailed view of its status, and an understanding of costs involved
Application Count
Annual Support Cost ($M)
Point to Point Cost
EA Cost
Built on an enterprise architecture it provides saving in implementation and support costs
Adapter Count (30% Max Interface Uptake)
(Adapter Reuse = 60%)
Development Cost
Cost $M (Low Complexity Adapter = $10k) (EAI CoreCost = $500k)
Point to Point Cost
EA Cost

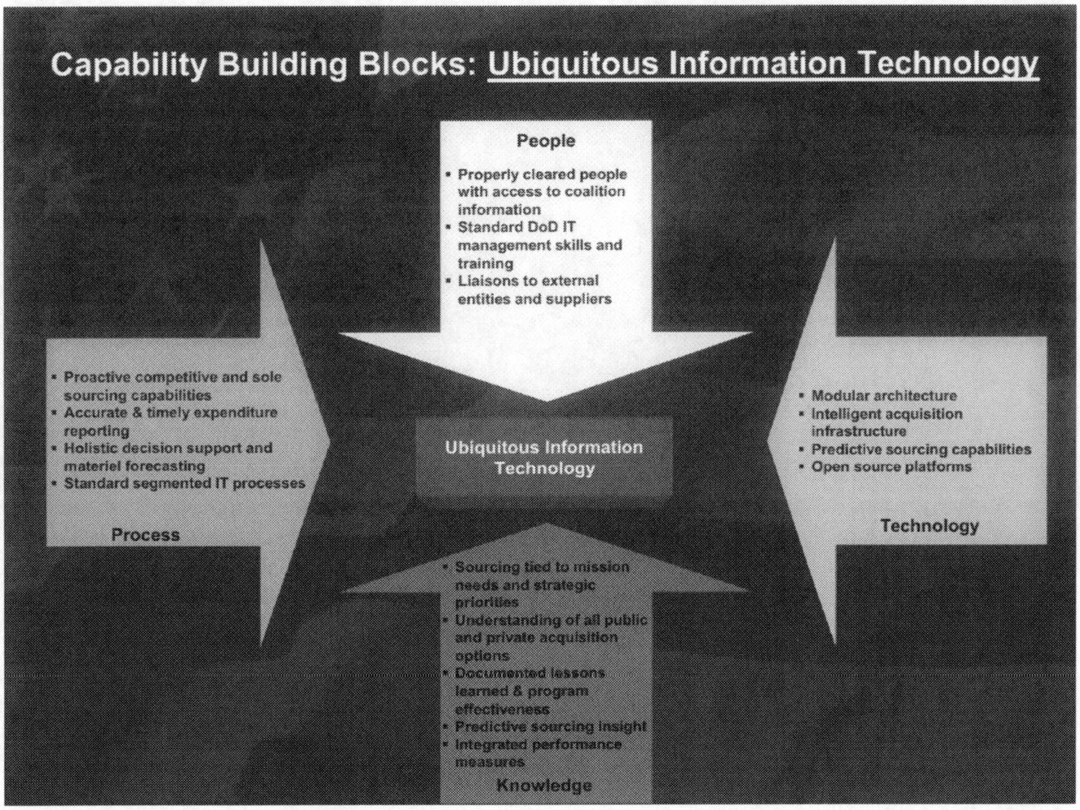
Capability Building Blocks: Ubiquitous Information Technology
People
▪ Properly cleared people with access to coalition information
▪ Standard DoD IT management skills and training
▪ Liaisons to external entities and suppliers
▪ Proactive competitive and sole sourcing capabilities
▪ Accurate & timely expenditure reporting
▪ Holistic decision support and materiel forecasting
▪ Standard segmented IT processes
Process
Ubiquitous Information Technology
▪ Modular architecture
▪ Intelligent acquisition infrastructure
▪ Predictive sourcing capabilities
▪ Open source platforms
Technology
▪ Sourcing tied to mission needs and strategic priorities
▪ Understanding of all public and private acquisition options
▪ Documented lessons learned & program effectiveness
▪ Predictive sourcing insight
▪ Integrated performance measures
Knowledge

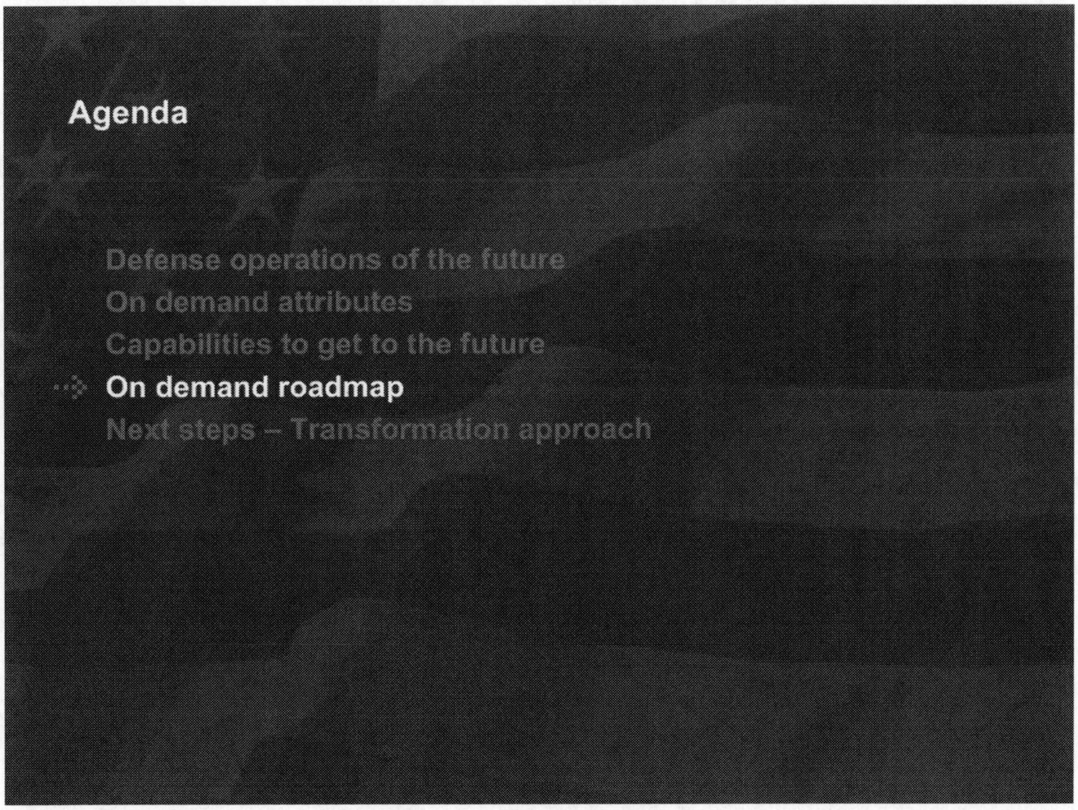
Agenda
Defense operations of the future
On demand attributes
Capabilities to get to the future
On demand roadmap
Next steps – Transformation approach

The on demand journey helps the DoD to drive towards joint operations and total operational effectiveness

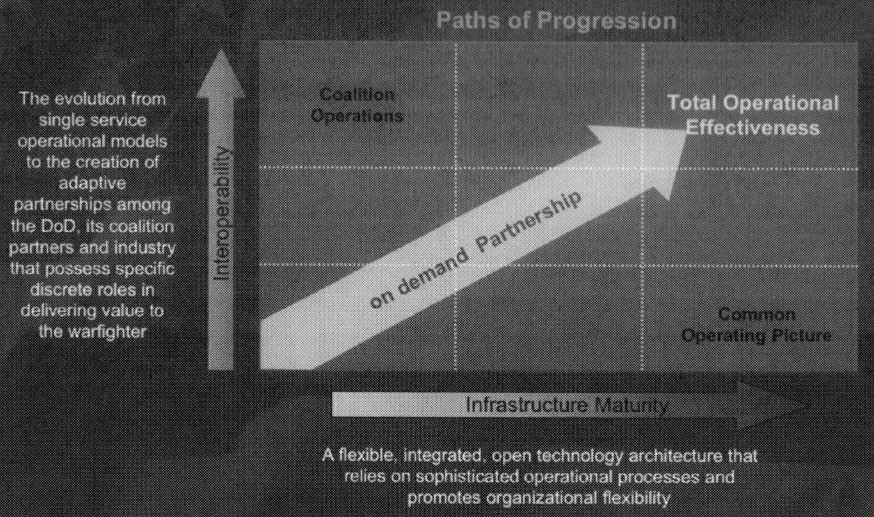

Evolution to Total Operational Effectiveness

Current State of the Art → **Capability Maturation** → **Total Operational Effectiveness**

Current State of the Art

- Current readiness is mostly manually gathered and display via spreadsheet or operational situation boards
- Separate pieces of the total situation may be available via many different systems with different timings and orientations
- Drill down details are difficult to obtain
- Mission options and current readiness to perform each option is mostly manually driven
- Operations and mission planning is a real art today in the DoD -- mostly performed by the most experienced and capable.
- Lengthy time and processes are needed to derive non-optimized plan

Capability Maturation

- Readiness of selected assets are available and integrated
- Selected portions of the total situation are integrated onto one system
- Critical drill down areas are identified
- Mission options and current readiness virtualized
- Mission planning support is virtualized, and knowledge collected

Total Operational Effectiveness

- Real time readiness of personnel, units, weapon systems, etc with drill down details to unique items and their status are available
- The COP is achieved by adhering to standards and up-to-the-minute update of information presented in the right context with detail actions-to-be taken and status drill downs
- Mission capabilities and their readiness are given real time status is provided. Drill downs with details are available
- Optimized time phased deployments that take minutes are available.
- Optimized mission planning with many ready-to-go scenarios will support faster multi-operations

Evolution to Seamless Integrated Logistics

Current State of the Art → Capability Maturation → Total Operational Effectiveness

Current State of the Art

- Multiple requisitions of an item made in the hopes of an on time arrival
- Excessively heavy logistical footprint
- Significant in theater service capability redundancies
- Separate service supply chains

Capability Maturation

- Reduction in theater service redundancies
- Specific asset tracking per request
- Coordination between coalition components and civilian/commercial resources

Total Operational Effectiveness

- In between "just in case" and "just in time," with focus on "just enough."
- Global automatic asset tracking interfaced with industry suppliers
- Proactive decision support systems
- Minimal theater redundancies between services. Leveraging of capabilities between services
- Replace mass with velocity

Evolution to Dynamic Human Capital Management

Current State of the Art → Capability Maturation → Total Operational Awareness

Current State of the Art

- Separate HR processes and systems by Service Department
- Manpower resources isolated by component-command and industry specialization
- Non-browser based technology

Capability Maturation

- Shift to "virtual" command assets
- Consolidation of manpower systems and overall view of readiness on each warfighter
- Sunset and migrate legacy systems
- Complete picture of deployable assets across services at any point of time
- Ability to tap into non-DoD resources for non-warfighter roles

Total Operational Awareness

- Integration across all services and NATO
- Skills-based manpower profiling
- Mission-based warfighting unit profiling
- Reach into manpower assets of mission partners and key suppliers
- Migration to outsourced mode – maintained by supplier

Evolution to Fully Integrated Fact-Based Decision Management

Current State of the Art	Capability Maturation	Total Operational Effectiveness
▪ Inaccurate, untimely and standard financial information ▪ Stovepipe financial systems, by Service Department and Component Command ▪ Sporadic and non-integrated performance data (readiness, service levels, operating capacity, quality and cycle time data, etc) ▪ Non-browser based	▪ Convergence of ERP systems ▪ 100% Compliant ▪ Sunset and migrate legacy systems ▪ Performance-based management ▪ "Virtual" financial management and modeling	▪ Integration across all services – standardized ▪ Cause-and-effect visibility over financial/resource decisions and performance outcomes ▪ Predictive modeling for scenario decision support ▪ Migration to outsourced mode – maintained by supplier

Evolution to Ubiquitous Information Technology

Current State of the Art	Capability Maturation	Total Operational Effectiveness
▪ Autonomous corporate and division systems with limited LOB process integration and shared services	▪ Business process outsourcing, shared business process infrastructure / applications across the organization	▪ BTO and shared services models applied throughout organization
▪ Low utilization, heterogeneous systems with limited integration	▪ Moving non-differentiated and some differentiated systems to capacity on demand	▪ Highly utilized, interconnected and autonomic infrastructure
▪ Localized management of some applications and infrastructure	▪ Partial automation and limited portal-based app and infrastructure mgmt	▪ Consolidated, virtual and local application and infrastructure mgmt
▪ Internal hosting and ASP delivery models	▪ Infrastructure and horizontal applications delivered in utility manner	▪ Infrastructure, applications and business processes delivered in a utility manner over the network
▪ Redundant infrastructure	▪ Partial automated BCRS and self-diagnosing infrastructure components	▪ Resilient Infrastructure that is self-diagnosing and self-healing
▪ Linux, Unit, Windows competing; heterogeneous environments	▪ Migration to open standards, adoption of web services	▪ Open standards-based integration up and down the stack
▪ Disparate, non-connected computing resources	▪ Experimentation with Grid and industry utilities	▪ Virtualized data centers with grids of capabilities across partners

Source: IBM Institute for Business Value

Agenda

- Defense operations of the future
- On demand attributes
- Capabilities to get to the future
- On demand roadmap
- Next steps – Transformation approach

Transformation occurs along three simultaneous paths to reach total operational effectiveness

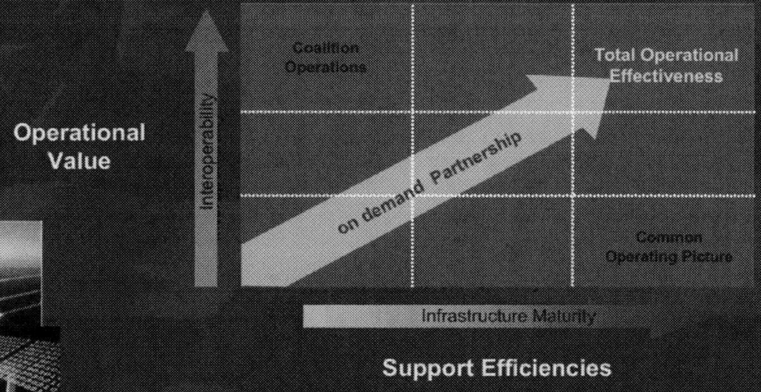

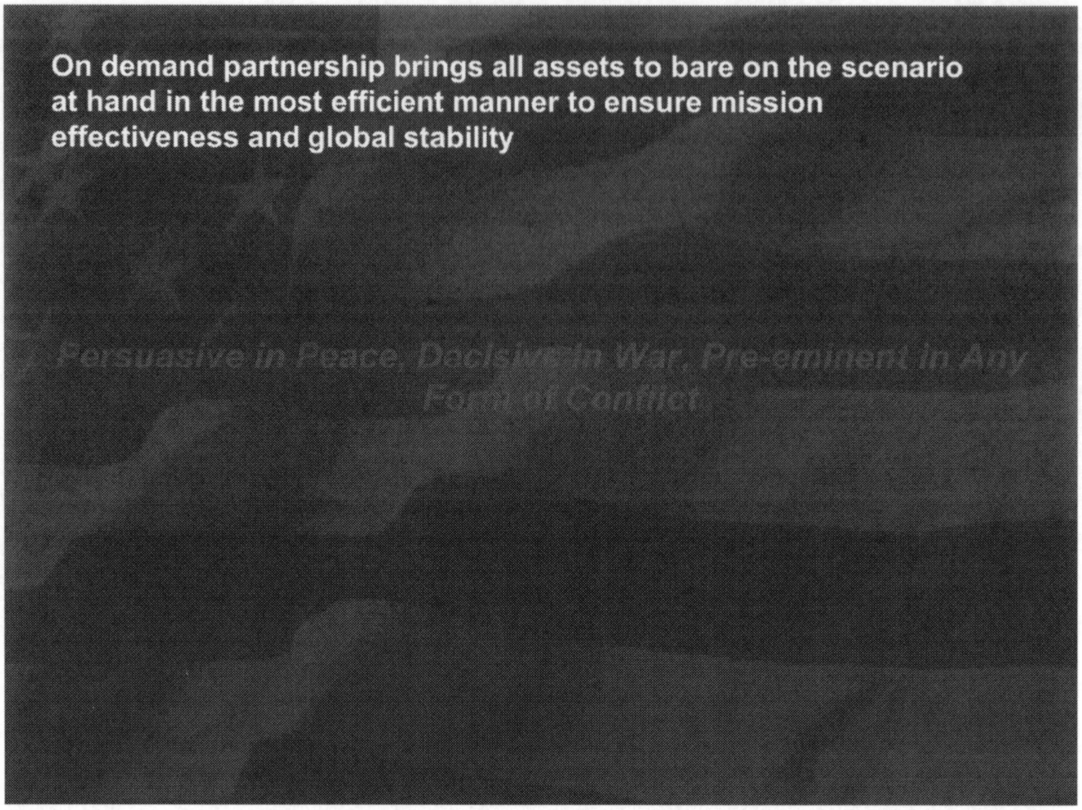
On demand partnership brings all assets to bare on the scenario at hand in the most efficient manner to ensure mission effectiveness and global stability
Persuasive in Peace, Decisive in War, Pre-eminent in Any Form of Conflict

Backup Slides

Key Steps to Joint Operations

Joint Operations

Step 1 Create Governance System

- Establish leader reporting to senior commanders
- Mission leaders as champions
- Clear ownership and accountability for results

Step 2 Identify core and non-core processes

- Deconstruct the business architecture
- Identify natural processes for integration – e.g. administrative processes – HR, Finance, Procurement)
- Determine critical functions

Step 3 Establish Partnership Models

- Assess partnership benefits, costs and risks
- Set performance standards and establish monitoring framework
- Establish secure, compatible technology environments
- Evaluate different funding models

Key Steps to Common Platforms

Common Platforms

Step 1 Optimize the Infrastructure

- Consolidate to reduce cost & complexity
- Build security into the system – it is not an 'add-on'

Step 2 Establish architecture & standards

- Use real industry standards – not product defaults
- Define overall enterprise architecture
- Define enterprise portal strategic – look/feel, linkages, updates

Step 3 Extend infrastructure to suppliers & other defense agencies

- Identity, security, privacy
- Interfaces based on industry standards
- Force electronic interchange whenever possible

Step 4 Consider utility I/T capabilities

- Grid computing – dynamic/variable compute power
- Autonomic features – manageability, availability
- Sourcing alternatives

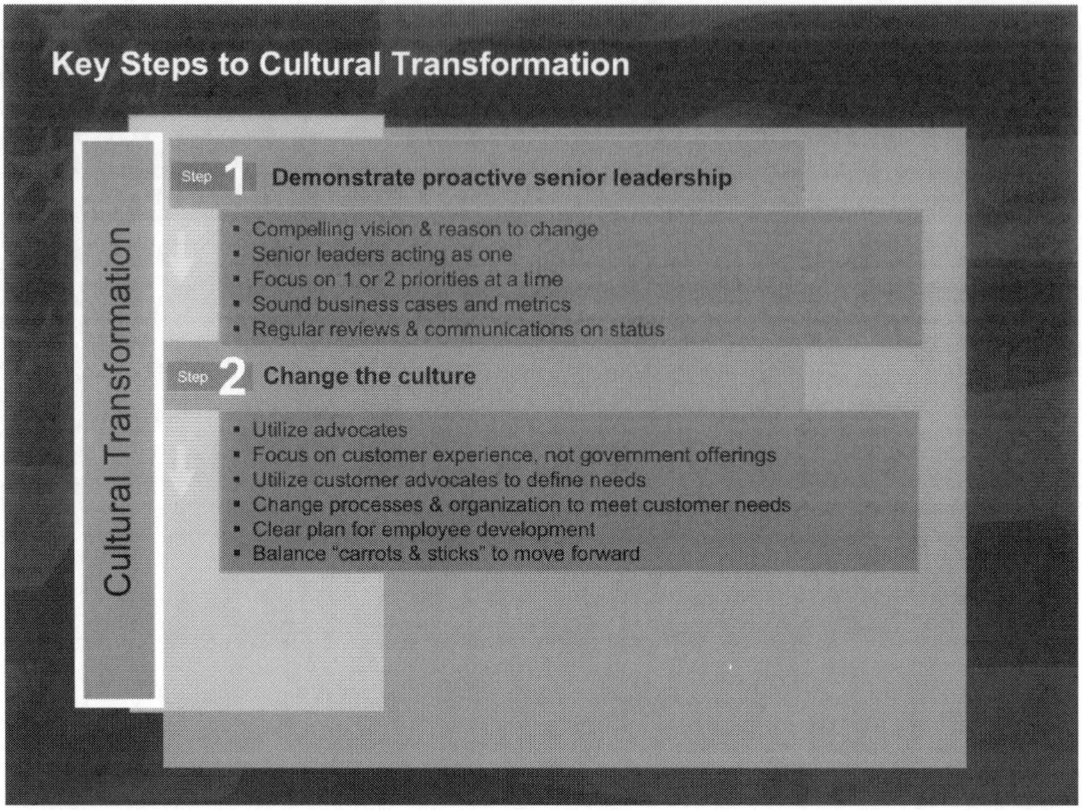
Key Steps to Cultural Transformation
Cultural Transformation
Step 1 Demonstrate proactive senior leadership
▪ Compelling vision & reason to change
▪ Senior leaders acting as one
▪ Focus on 1 or 2 priorities at a time
▪ Sound business cases and metrics
▪ Regular reviews & communications on status
Step 2 Change the culture
▪ Utilize advocates
▪ Focus on customer experience, not government offerings
▪ Utilize customer advocates to define needs
▪ Change processes & organization to meet customer needs
▪ Clear plan for employee development
▪ Balance "carrots & sticks" to move forward

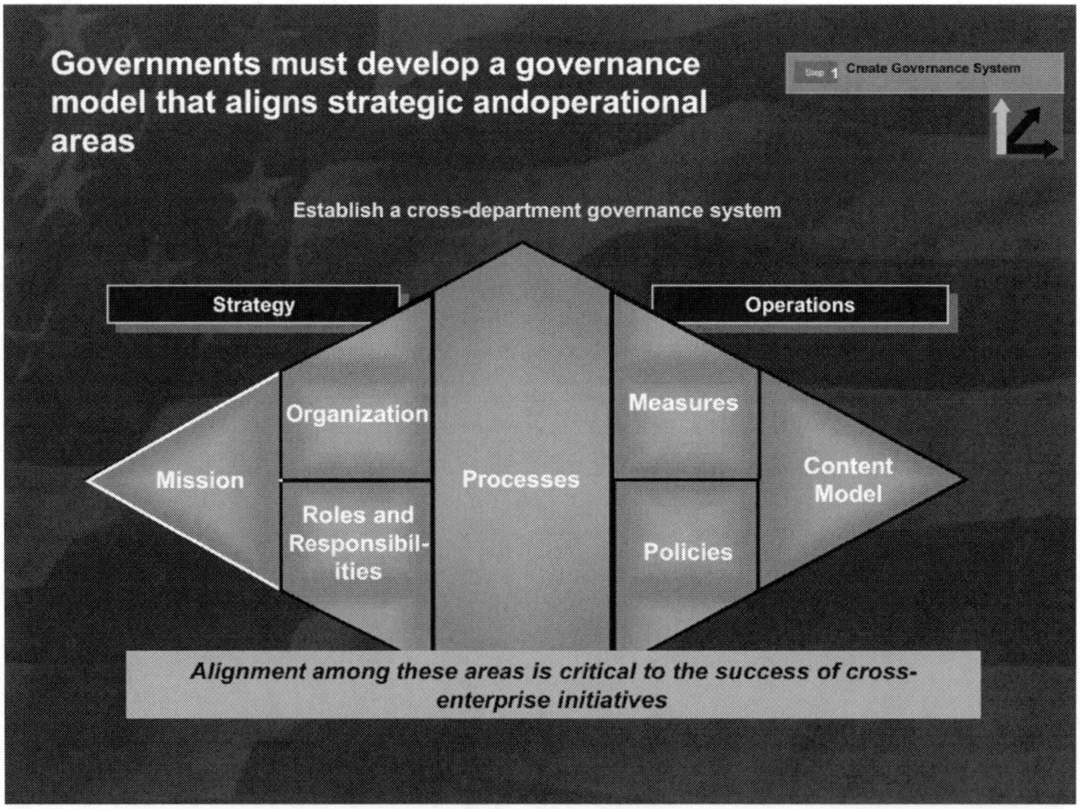
Governments must develop a governance model that aligns strategic andoperational areas
Step 1 Create Governance System
Establish a cross-department governance system
Strategy
Operations
Mission
Organization
Roles and Responsibil-ities
Processes
Measures
Policies
Content Model
Alignment among these areas is critical to the success of cross-enterprise initiatives

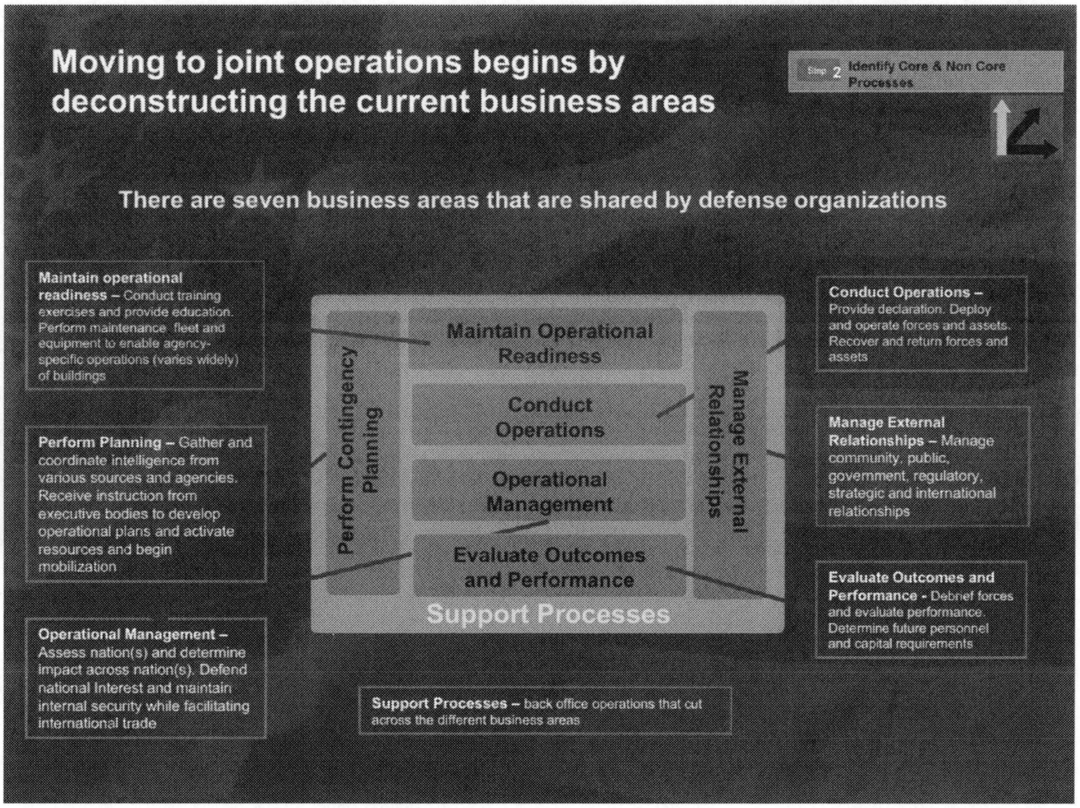
Moving to joint operations begins by deconstructing the current business areas
Step 2 Identify Core & Non Core Processes
There are seven business areas that are shared by defense organizations
Maintain operational readiness – Conduct training exercises and provide education. Perform maintenance fleet and equipment to enable agency-specific operations (varies widely) of buildings
Perform Planning – Gather and coordinate intelligence from various sources and agencies. Receive instruction from executive bodies to develop operational plans and activate resources and begin mobilization
Operational Management – Assess nation(s) and determine impact across nation(s). Defend national Interest and maintain internal security while facilitating international trade
Perform Contingency Planning
Maintain Operational Readiness
Conduct Operations
Operational Management
Evaluate Outcomes and Performance
Manage External Relationships
Support Processes
Conduct Operations – Provide declaration. Deploy and operate forces and assets. Recover and return forces and assets
Manage External Relationships – Manage community, public, government, regulatory, strategic and international relationships
Evaluate Outcomes and Performance - Debrief forces and evaluate performance. Determine future personnel and capital requirements
Support Processes – back office operations that cut across the different business areas

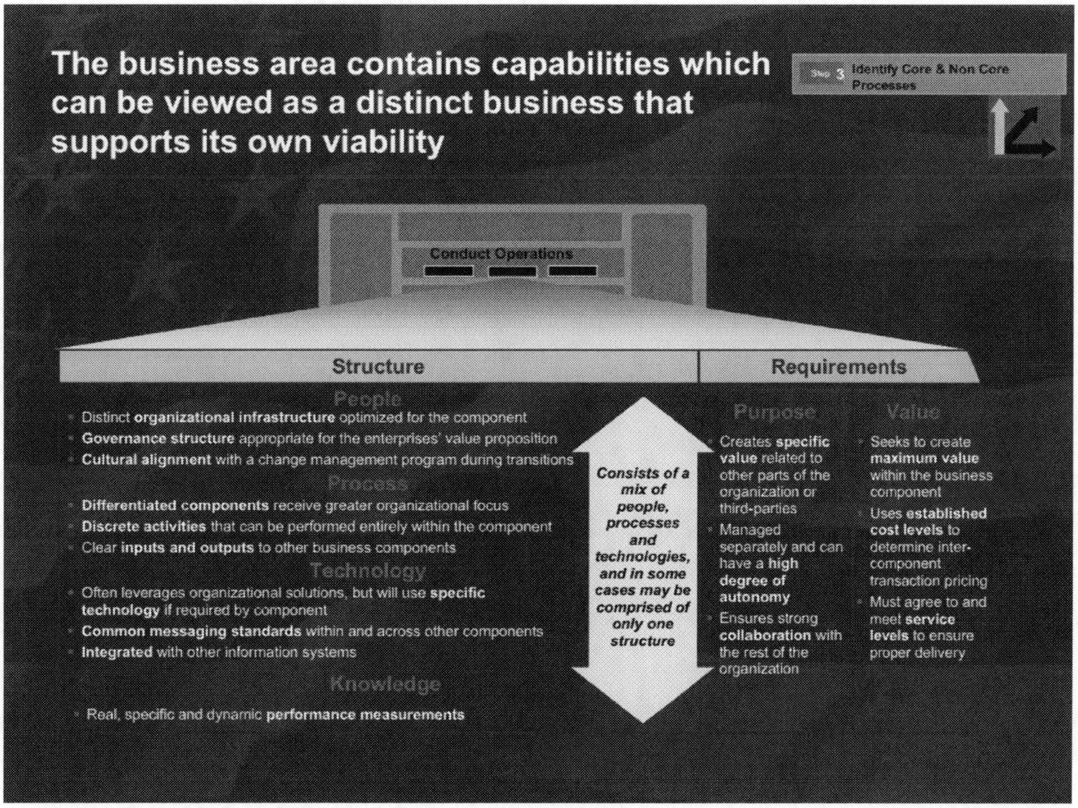
The business area contains capabilities which can be viewed as a distinct business that supports its own viability
Step 3 Identify Core & Non Core Processes
Conduct Operations
Structure
Requirements
People
Distinct organizational infrastructure optimized for the component
Governance structure appropriate for the enterprises' value proposition
Cultural alignment with a change management program during transitions
Process
Differentiated components receive greater organizational focus
Discrete activities that can be performed entirely within the component
Clear inputs and outputs to other business components
Technology
Often leverages organizational solutions, but will use specific technology if required by component
Common messaging standards within and across other components
Integrated with other information systems
Knowledge
Real, specific and dynamic performance measurements
Consists of a mix of people, processes and technologies, and in some cases may be comprised of only one structure
Purpose
Creates specific value related to other parts of the organization or third-parties
Managed separately and can have a high degree of autonomy
Ensures strong collaboration with the rest of the organization
Value
Seeks to create maximum value within the business component
Uses established cost levels to determine inter-component transaction pricing
Must agree to and meet service levels to ensure proper delivery

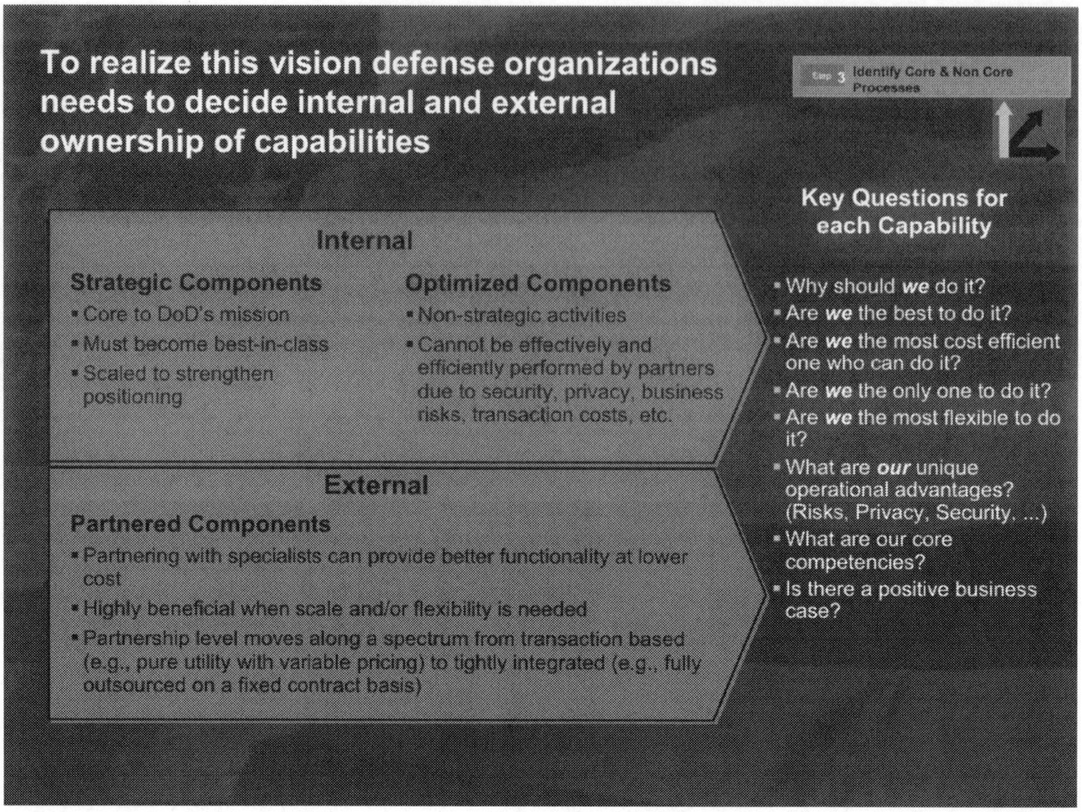
To realize this vision defense organizations needs to decide internal and external ownership of capabilities
Step 3 Identify Core & Non Core Processes
Internal
Strategic Components
Core to DoD's mission
Must become best-in-class
Scaled to strengthen positioning
Optimized Components
Non-strategic activities
Cannot be effectively and efficiently performed by partners due to security, privacy, business risks, transaction costs, etc.
External
Partnered Components
Partnering with specialists can provide better functionality at lower cost
Highly beneficial when scale and/or flexibility is needed
Partnership level moves along a spectrum from transaction based (e.g., pure utility with variable pricing) to tightly integrated (e.g., fully outsourced on a fixed contract basis)
Key Questions for each Capability
Why should we do it?
Are we the best to do it?
Are we the most cost efficient one who can do it?
Are we the only one to do it?
Are we the most flexible to do it?
What are our unique operational advantages? (Risks, Privacy, Security, ...)
What are our core competencies?
Is there a positive business case?

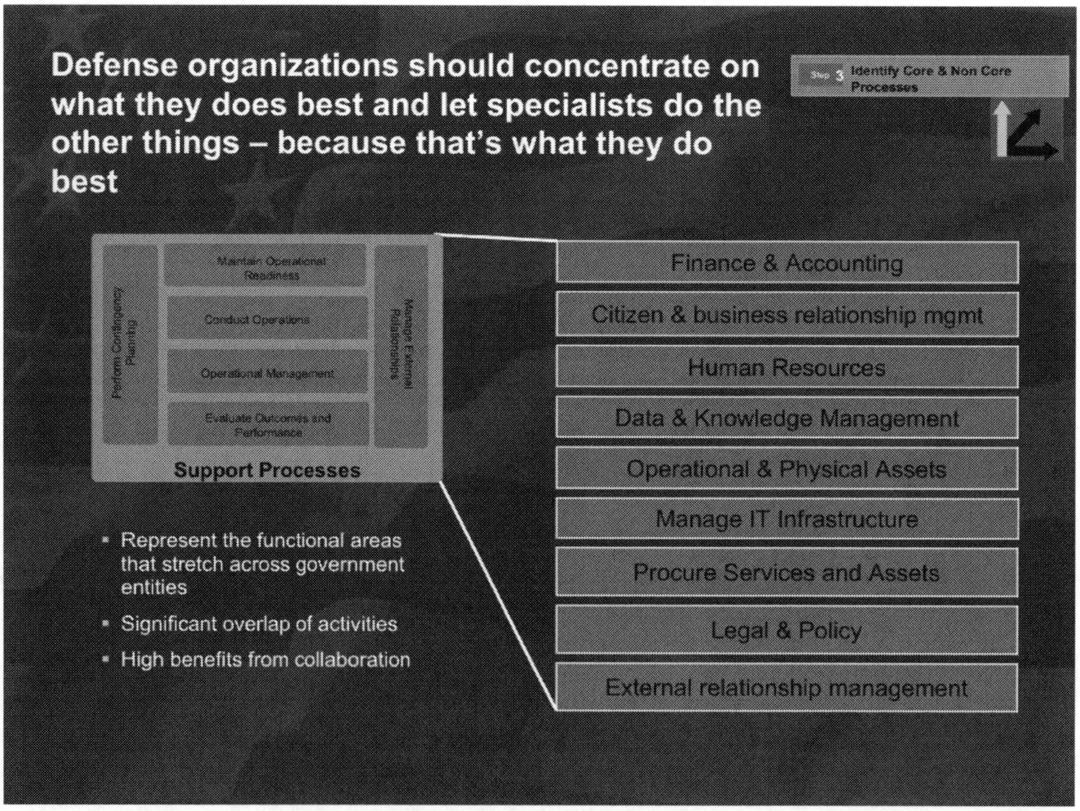
Defense organizations should concentrate on what they does best and let specialists do the other things – because that's what they do best
Step 3 Identify Core & Non Core Processes
Perform Contingency Planning
Maintain Operational Readiness
Conduct Operations
Operational Management
Evaluate Outcomes and Performance
Manage External Relationships
Support Processes
Represent the functional areas that stretch across government entities
Significant overlap of activities
High benefits from collaboration
Finance & Accounting
Citizen & business relationship mgmt
Human Resources
Data & Knowledge Management
Operational & Physical Assets
Manage IT Infrastructure
Procure Services and Assets
Legal & Policy
External relationship management

A full range of internal and external partnership models are available for maximizing efficiencies

Step 4 Determine Partnership Models

	Government Integration	Outsourcing	Public – Private Partnerships	Privitization
Description	Governments link processes across departments, levels or jurisdictions	Organizational are contracted to third party, private sector companies	Government and private sector share costs, risks and benefits	Transfer public assets or enterprise to private ownership – with or without competition
Strengths	▪ Maintain control ▪ Dedicated resources	▪ Enables specialized firms to manage function ▪ Enhances internal mgmt ▪ Increases efficiency	▪ Potential for use of performance based contracts ▪ Fund services that previously could not	▪ Better performance from private sector ▪ Receive revenue from sale of government assets
Weaknesses	▪ Lack of marketplace competition ▪ Limited performance incentives	▪ Limit flexibility ▪ Complex, fixed contracts ▪ Personnel disruptions	▪ Roles and responsibilities might not be clear	▪ Potential for private sector monopolies ▪ Potential regulations limit market competition
Government Risks	▪ Government finances and maintains obligation to deliver service	▪ Government finances and maintains risk to delivery	▪ Risk shared between government and private sector –government risk is higher then privatization	▪ Private sector maintains risk to source and deliver services – governments have ceded control

Gansler, Jacques. The Changing Role of Government as the Provider. IBM Endowment for the Business of Government Report

Government integration provides a valuable method to enhance process an IT sophistication

Step 4 Determine Partnership Models

Government Integration

Create Value

Tax Administration on demand will cut across Agency and Government processes and systems to provide a focused end-to-end client approach

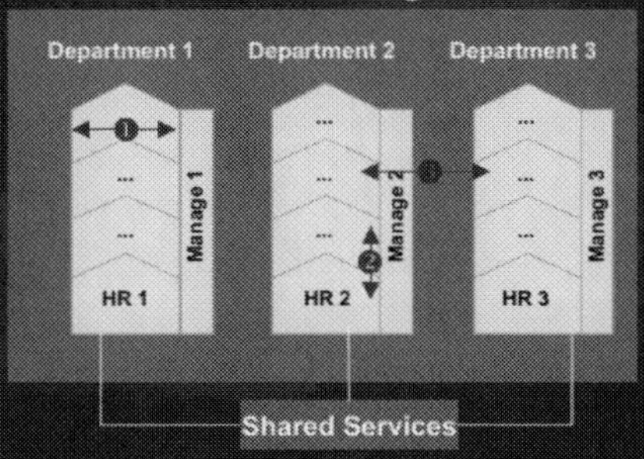

Optimize Costs

Functions that perform similar actions in the same manner are identified across the Government → A shared services area is created that serves the silo organizations, providing standardized service at a lower price

Within Function

- The business and technology architecture at a functional level needs to optimized
- Best practices can be adopted – or created – to position the department for future centralization

Across Functions

- The speed and accuracy of coordination and communication between functions needs improvement
- Building connectivity should reflect the on demand model that is likely to be adopted in the future

Across Agency Silos / Across Jurisdictions

- New connectivity must be created that allows for sharing across silos
- The platform temporarily will be leveraged for within and across component connectivity in the future

Enterprise Architectures incorporate specific components of IT systems: application, information, infrastructure and management architectures

Step 2 Establish Architecture and Standards

Strategic Enterprise Architecture Components

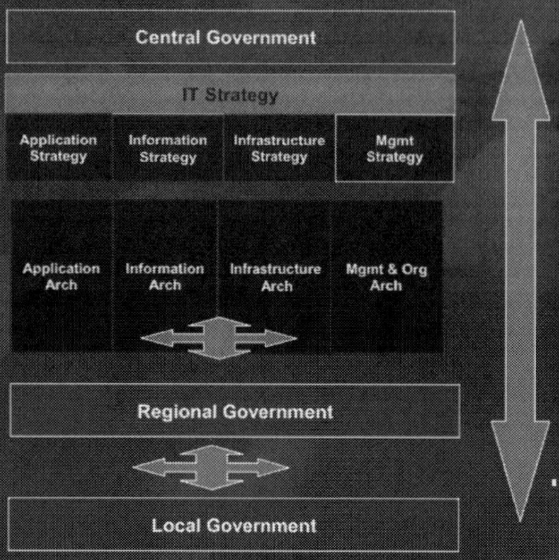

- Application
  - Application design must reduce the need for widespread customization, but must leverage best of breed applications
- Information
  - Delivery of Information must be coordinated, secured, and incorporate privacy protocol
- Infrastructure
  - Creative intermingling of infrastructure across jurisdictions will be driven by a need to achieve greater economies of scale.
- Management
  - Multi-jurisdictional Management Committee must be formed with strong authoritative presence and mandate

"We have to balance the benefits of [information sharing] with privacy protection, civil liberties and intellectual property rights," *Mark Forman, Associate Director of Information Technology and E-Government, OMB*

Following creation of the enterprise architecture, common languages or protocols must be employed

Step 2 Establish Architecture and Standards

Common languages and standards build interoperable systems and databases

- Use common languages and protocols to facilitate information and communication flow
  - Internet Standards such as Transmission Control Protocol/Internet Protocol (TCP/IP)
  - Secure Socket Layers (SSL) for communications
  - HTML/Java-enabled thin clients
  - eXtensible Markup Language (XML)
- Common language
  - HTML enables the presentation of content
  - Java enables cross system applications, Java = portable code
  - XML brings data to the web, completing the necessary component for 90% of e-government applications it is a standard way to share structured data, XML = portable data

In addition, common standards are critical for the development interoperable systems and databases

Step 2 Establish Architecture and Standards

Standards provide a common framework

- Employ business and integration patterns to assist with structuring the technology infrastructure, reducing development cost and selecting the best IT model to follow
  - Business and Integration Pattern offer the basic components upon which to develop architecture. Business and integration pattern provide the basic structure from which to begin the discussion about how to structure the IT architecture
  - Integration Patterns include: (1) Access and (2) Application and are focused around processes of access and application connectivity with the IT system
  - Business Patterns include: (1) Self-Service, (2) Information aggregation, (3) Collaboration and (4) Extended Enterprise
- Develop systems which are flexible, reliable, and scalable, in order to aid successful integration projects
  - Flexible with the acceptance of software and hardware components into the IT structure without generating expensive development and maintenance expense
  - Reliable systems to handle performance demands should be planned and constructed
  - Scalable systems should be constructed to handle addition process demands while maintaining high levels of service availability and fast response times

Inter-operable Technology Characteristics

Open software development	Common, open standards/data definitions
Common language (e.g. XML) and templates	Open source, scalable infrastructure
Self-correcting, self-healing common security	Open protocols, interfaces and file formats

Value of enterprise architecture

Step 2 Establish Architecture and Standards

Enterprise Architecture

- Enterprise Architecture (EA) should be driven by Business Mission and Requirements, Technology Pragmatics
- EA Governance must be integrated into IT Investment Planning
- To gain the most benefit out of EA, it is important that the EA be prescriptive
- Real benefit of the EA can be reaped incrementally
- EA includes: Active Enterprise Portfolio Management (EAM), Enterprise Architecture Standards, and Technology Change Management

COTS Integration

- Multiple applications using the same COTS do not "automatically" integrate
- Integration to legacy systems and ERP/COTS requires robust scalable middleware
- Data Cleansing & Migration is a critical path
- COOP & Disaster Recovery should be planned at outset
- Never modify COTS in ways which prevent upgrade (e.g., business rule and workflow)

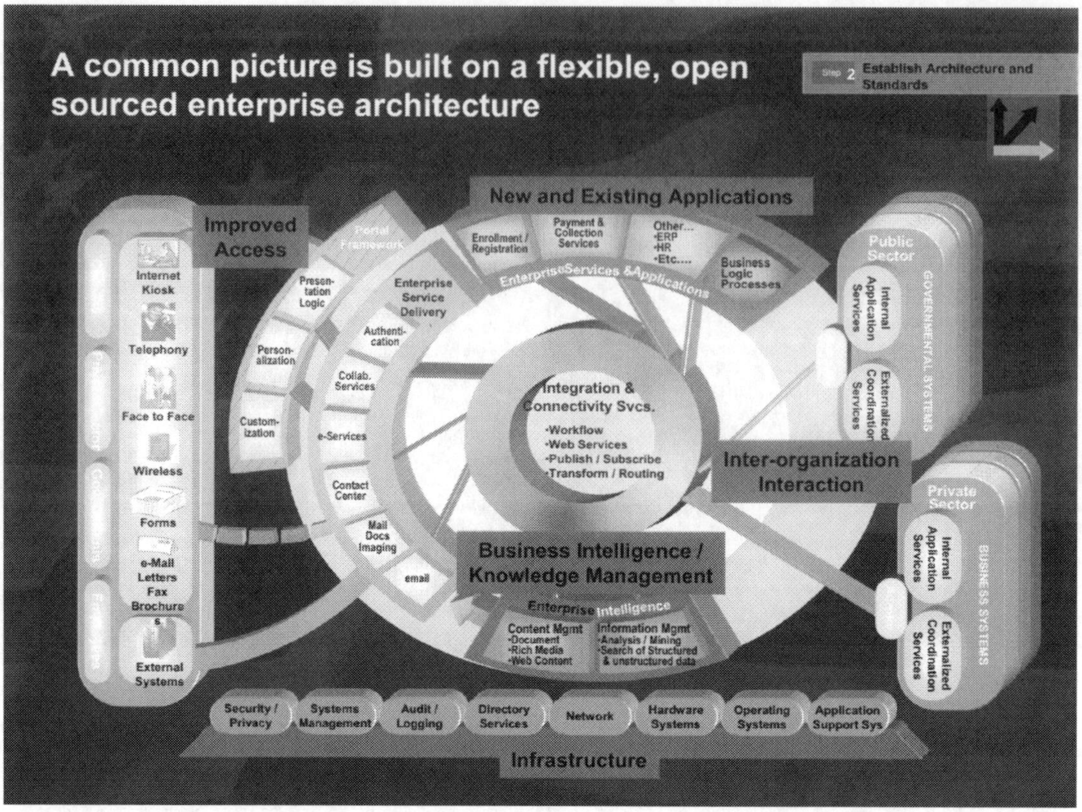
A common picture is built on a flexible, open sourced enterprise architecture
Step 2 Establish Architecture and Standards
New and Existing Applications
Improved Access
Internet Kiosk
Telephony
Face to Face
Wireless
Forms
e-Mail Letters Fax Brochures
External Systems
Portal Framework
Presentation Logic
Personalization
Customization
Enterprise Service Delivery
Authentication
Collab. Services
e-Services
Contact Center
Mail Docs Imaging
email
Enrollment / Registration
Payment & Collection Services
Other... •ERP •HR •Etc....
Business Logic Processes
Enterprise Services & Applications
Integration & Connectivity Svcs.
•Workflow
•Web Services
•Publish / Subscribe
•Transform / Routing
Inter-organization Interaction
Business Intelligence / Knowledge Management
Enterprise Intelligence
Content Mgmt •Document •Rich Media •Web Content
Information Mgmt •Analysis / Mining •Search of Structured & unstructured data
Public Sector
Internal Application Services
Externalized Coordination Services
GOVERNMENTAL SYSTEMS
Private Sector
Internal Application Services
Externalized Coordination Services
BUSINESS SYSTEMS
Security / Privacy
Systems Management
Audit / Logging
Directory Services
Network
Hardware Systems
Operating Systems
Application Support Sys
Infrastructure

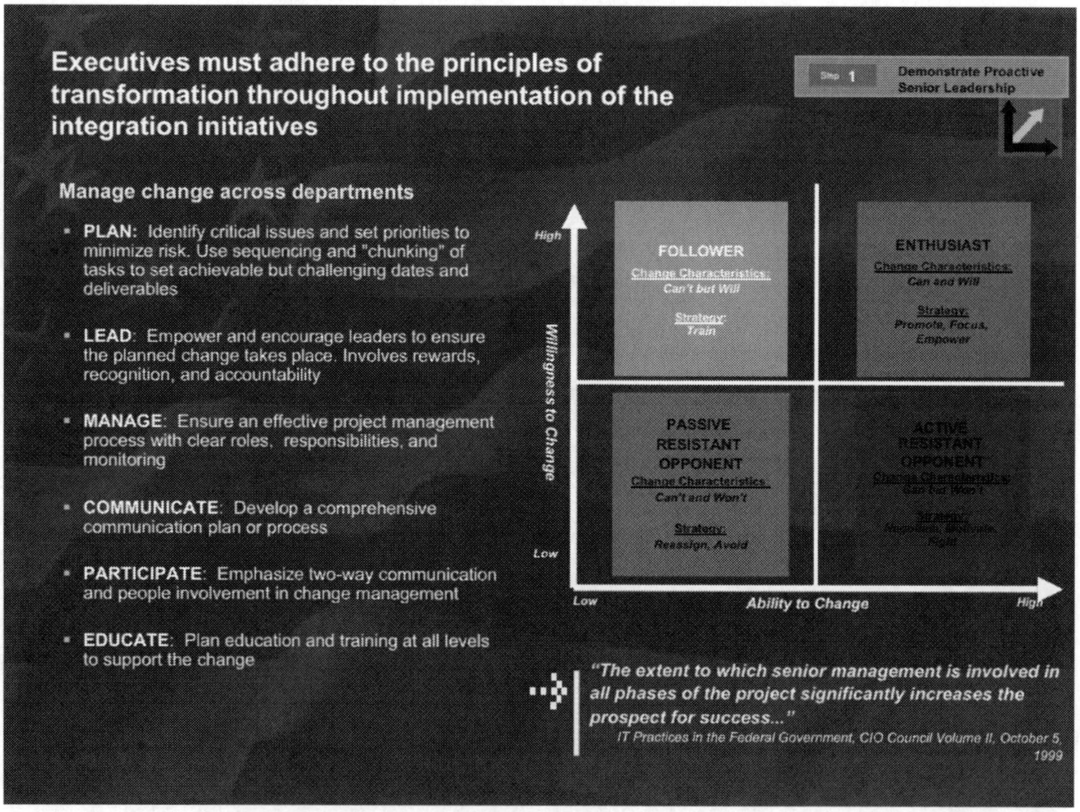
Executives must adhere to the principles of transformation throughout implementation of the integration initiatives
Step 1 Demonstrate Proactive Senior Leadership
Manage change across departments
PLAN: Identify critical issues and set priorities to minimize risk. Use sequencing and "chunking" of tasks to set achievable but challenging dates and deliverables
LEAD: Empower and encourage leaders to ensure the planned change takes place. Involves rewards, recognition, and accountability
MANAGE: Ensure an effective project management process with clear roles, responsibilities, and monitoring
COMMUNICATE: Develop a comprehensive communication plan or process
PARTICIPATE: Emphasize two-way communication and people involvement in change management
EDUCATE: Plan education and training at all levels to support the change
High
Willingness to Change
Low
FOLLOWER
Change Characteristics:
Can't but Will
Strategy:
Train
ENTHUSIAST
Change Characteristics:
Can and Will
Strategy:
Promote, Focus, Empower
PASSIVE RESISTANT OPPONENT
Change Characteristics:
Can't and Won't
Strategy:
Reassign, Avoid
ACTIVE RESISTANT OPPONENT
Low
Ability to Change
High
"The extent to which senior management is involved in all phases of the project significantly increases the prospect for success..."
IT Practices in the Federal Government, CIO Council Volume II, October 5, 1999

On demand initiatives represent dramatic change. Executives must actively lead these efforts

Step 1 Demonstrate Proactive Senior Leadership

Actively lead the implementation

- **Quick Decision Making** — Utilize a strategic planning approach that acts fast; strategic planning does not have to be 100% complete to begin to implement solutions
- **Know the Costs & Benefits** — Decide what capability is worth the cost; i.e., the value proposition for doing more than publishing: use a solid business case approach
- **Decentralize Decision Making** — Overcome resistance to change, especially in integrating a business design, by increasing authority for managers to make decisions
- **Manage Risk** — Manage the risk of early e-government implementations to gain momentum - this includes effective privacy frameworks
- **Provide Strong/ Visible Support** — Provide **unified and committed executive presence** that clearly communicates and supports the need for change
- **Use Partners/Other Organizations** — Integrate other players, such as service delivery/strategic partners, project champions and change agents, etc.

On demand Defense enables process and technology sophistication by shattering traditional cultural barriers

Step 2 Change the Culture

Traditional Cultural Barriers to Change

- Silo mentality with a history of ineffective implementations and missed ROI opportunities
- Slow decision making processes and a lack of partnering capabilities
- Inability to simultaneously nurture and control innovative ventures
- Inflexible organizational structures and rigid measures of success

Characteristics of an On Demand Organization

- ✓ Maintains a formal and informal network, within and beyond organizational boundaries
- ✓ Anticipates and responds rapidly to needs of customers, partners, and value network
- ✓ Embraces individuality, diversity, creativity and change
- ✓ Self-organizes and re-shapes itself constantly as organizational needs dictate

"In all of my business career, I would have always said that culture is one of the five or six things you worry about if you're a leader… a corporation is nothing more than the collective ability of its people to do two things: create value and execute the strategies of the company."

-- Lou Gerstner, Who Says Elephants Can't Dance? Inside IBM's Historic Turnaround

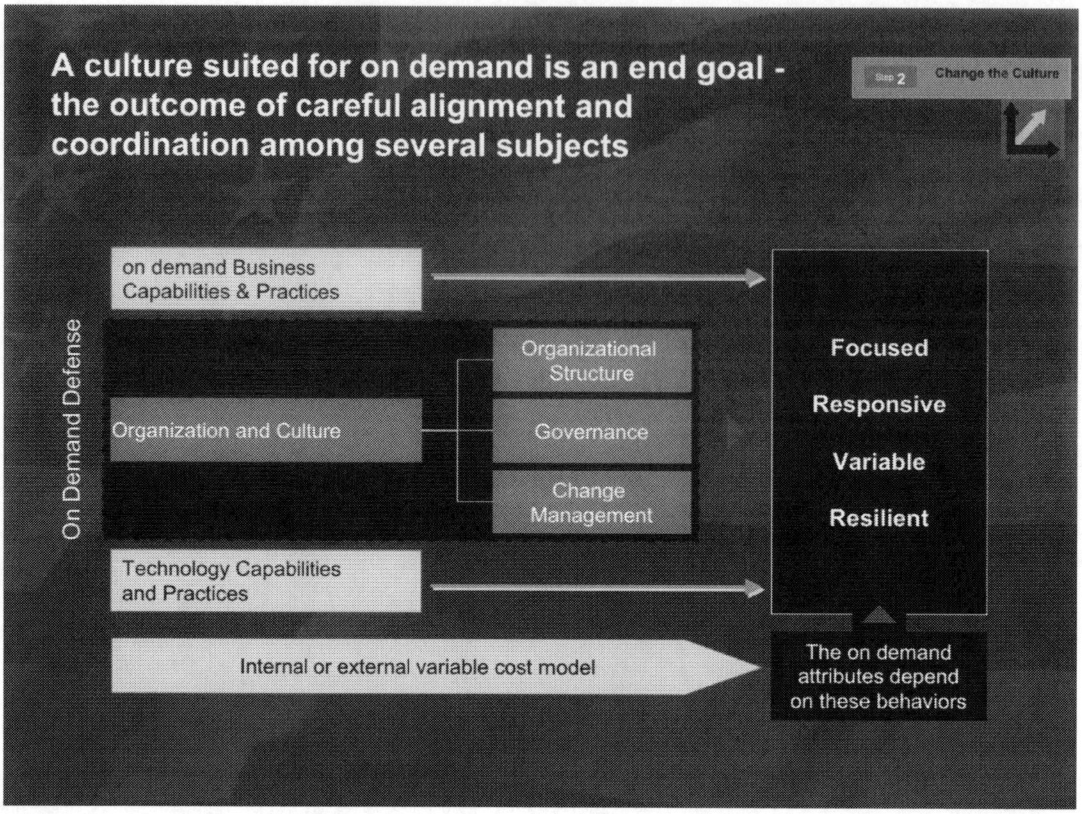
A culture suited for on demand is an end goal - the outcome of careful alignment and coordination among several subjects
Step 2
Change the Culture
on demand Business Capabilities & Practices
On Demand Defense
Organization and Culture
Organizational Structure
Governance
Change Management
Technology Capabilities and Practices
Internal or external variable cost model
Focused
Responsive
Variable
Resilient
The on demand attributes depend on these behaviors

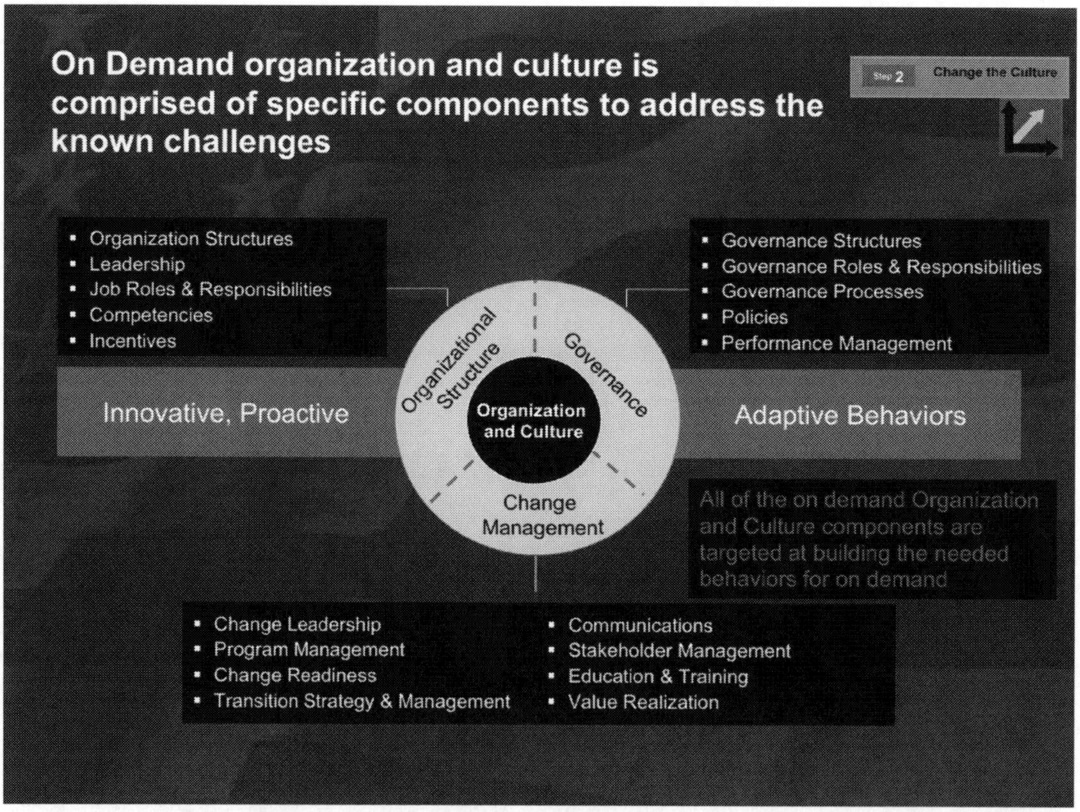
On Demand organization and culture is comprised of specific components to address the known challenges
Step 2
Change the Culture
▪ Organization Structures
▪ Leadership
▪ Job Roles & Responsibilities
▪ Competencies
▪ Incentives
▪ Governance Structures
▪ Governance Roles & Responsibilities
▪ Governance Processes
▪ Policies
▪ Performance Management
Innovative, Proactive
Organizational Structure
Governance
Organization and Culture
Change Management
Adaptive Behaviors
All of the on demand Organization and Culture components are targeted at building the needed behaviors for on demand
▪ Change Leadership
▪ Program Management
▪ Change Readiness
▪ Transition Strategy & Management
▪ Communications
▪ Stakeholder Management
▪ Education & Training
▪ Value Realization

Sustaining the 21st Century Battlespace

Mr Tom Edwards
Deputy to the Commander
Combined Arms Support Command

Outline

- Logistics System Architecture
- Logistics Common Operating Picture
- Future Combat System
- Performance Based Logistics
- Contractor Support

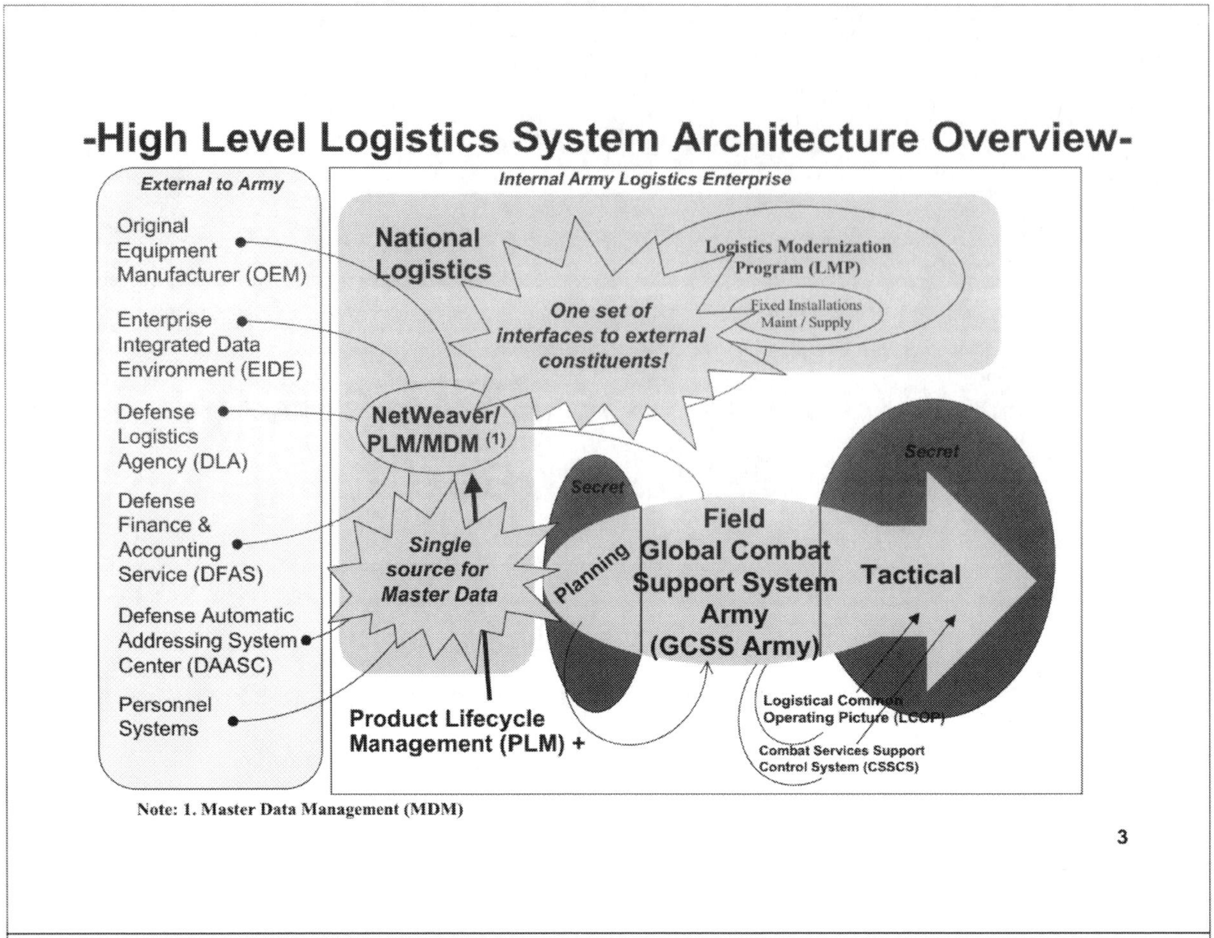

-High Level Logistics System Architecture Overview-
External to Army
Original Equipment Manufacturer (OEM)
Enterprise Integrated Data Environment (EIDE)
Defense Logistics Agency (DLA)
Defense Finance & Accounting Service (DFAS)
Defense Automatic Addressing System Center (DAASC)
Personnel Systems
Internal Army Logistics Enterprise
National Logistics
Logistics Modernization Program (LMP)
Fixed Installations Maint / Supply
One set of interfaces to external constituents!
NetWeaver/ PLM/MDM (1)
Single source for Master Data
Secret
Planning
Field Global Combat Support System Army (GCSS Army)
Tactical
Product Lifecycle Management (PLM) +
Logistical Common Operating Picture (LCOP)
Combat Services Support Control System (CSSCS)
Note: 1. Master Data Management (MDM)
3

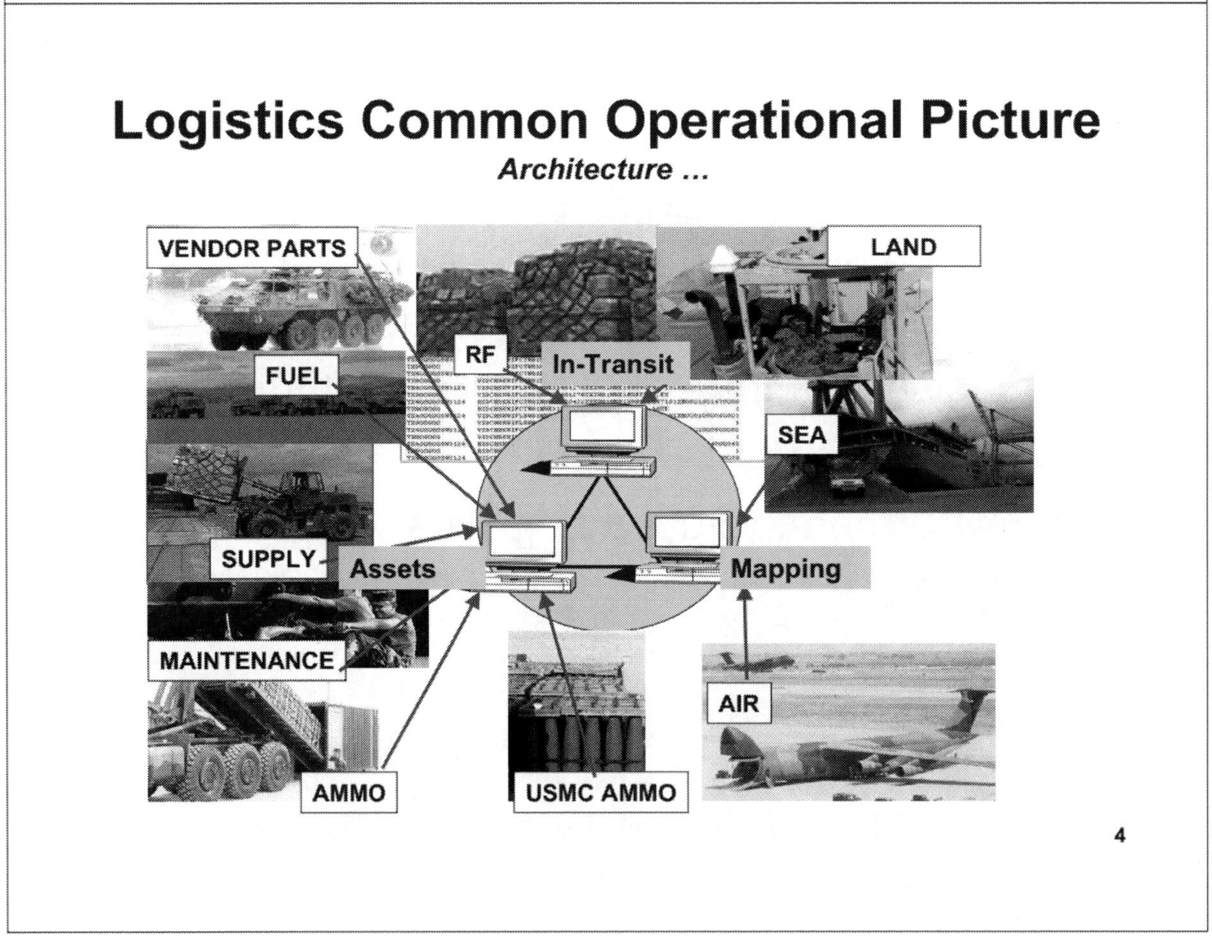

Logistics Common Operational Picture
Architecture ...
VENDOR PARTS
LAND
RF
In-Transit
FUEL
SEA
SUPPLY
Assets
Mapping
MAINTENANCE
AIR
AMMO
USMC AMMO
4

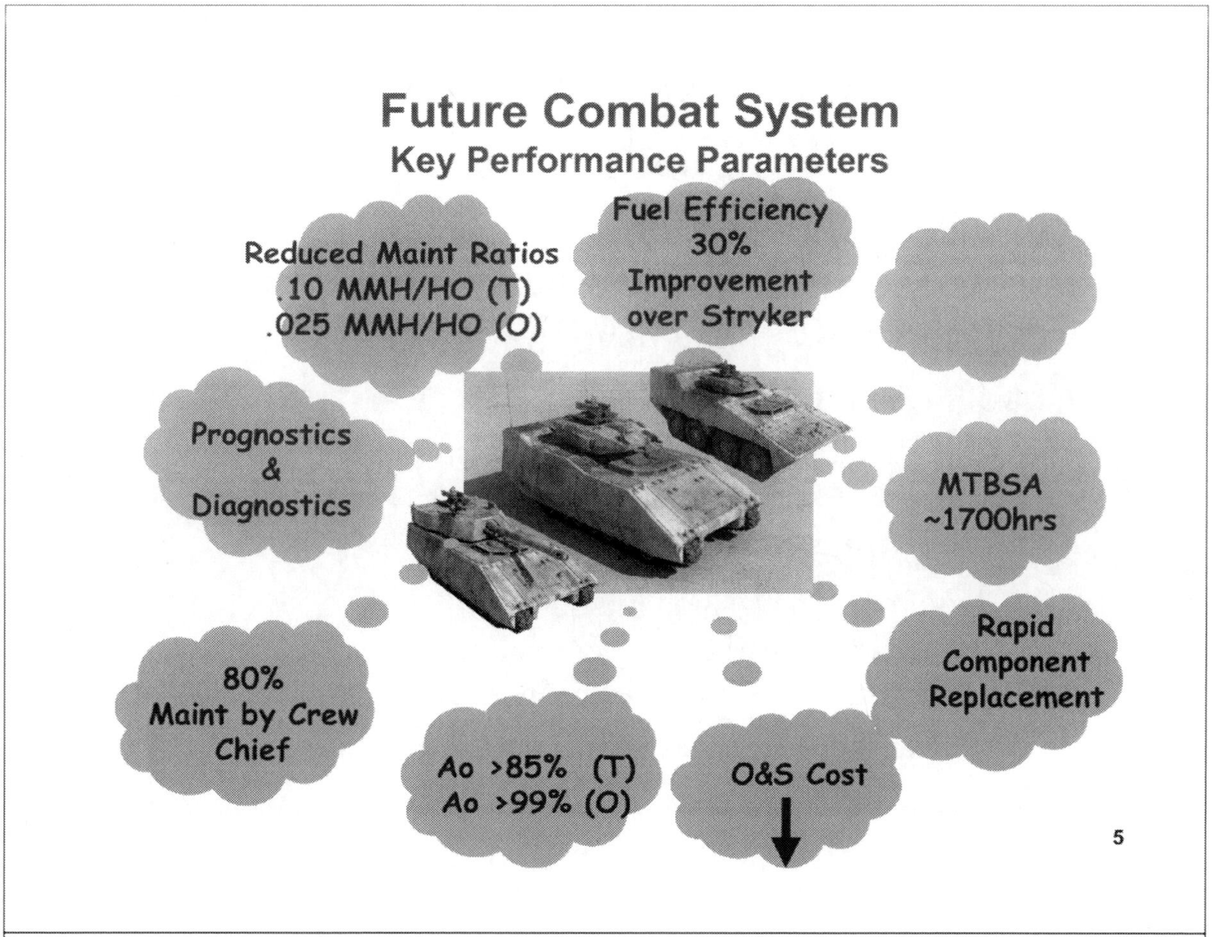
Future Combat System
Key Performance Parameters
Reduced Maint Ratios
.10 MMH/HO (T)
.025 MMH/HO (O)
Fuel Efficiency
30%
Improvement
over Stryker
Prognostics
&
Diagnostics
MTBSA
~1700hrs
Rapid
Component
Replacement
80%
Maint by Crew
Chief
Ao >85% (T)
Ao >99% (O)
O&S Cost
5

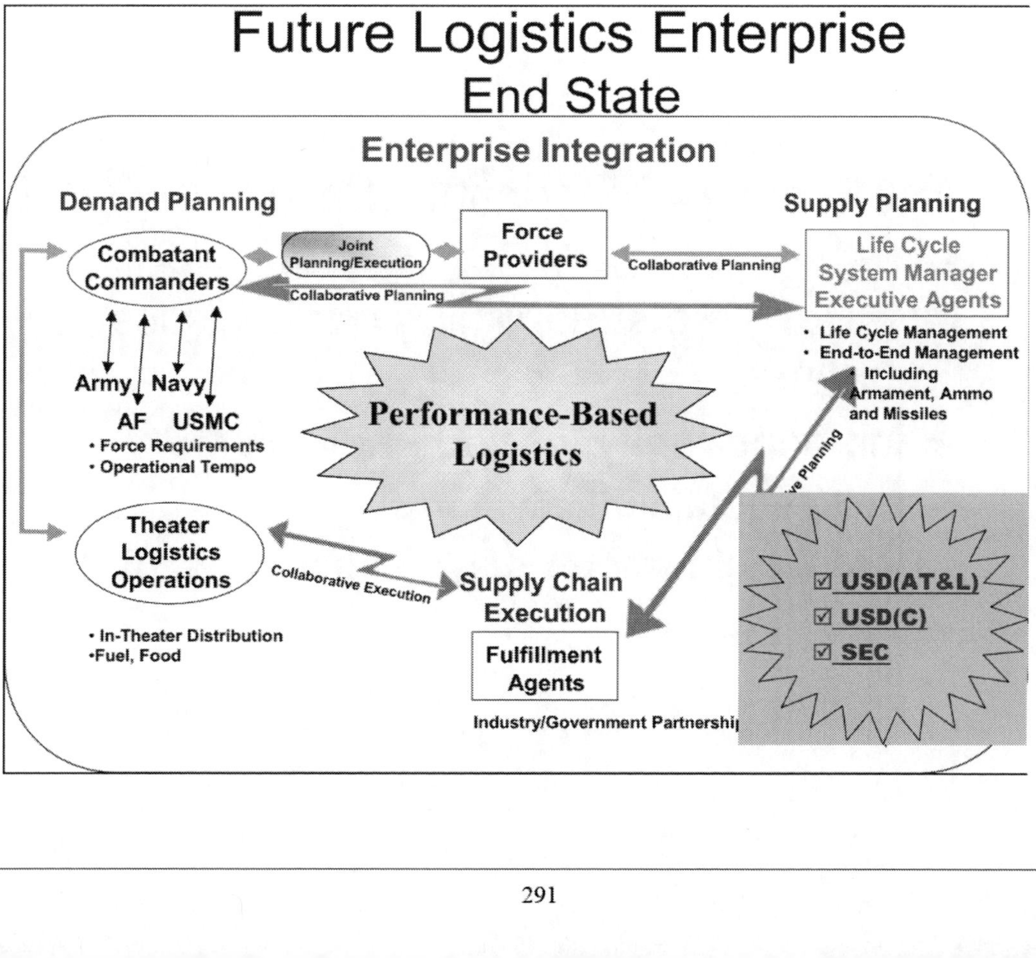
Future Logistics Enterprise
End State
Enterprise Integration
Demand Planning
Supply Planning
Combatant
Commanders
Joint
Planning/Execution
Force
Providers
Collaborative Planning
Life Cycle
System Manager
Executive Agents
Collaborative Planning
• Life Cycle Management
• End-to-End Management
Including
Armament, Ammo
and Missiles
Army
Navy
AF
USMC
• Force Requirements
• Operational Tempo
Performance-Based
Logistics
Theater
Logistics
Operations
Collaborative Execution
Supply Chain
Execution
Fulfillment
Agents
• In-Theater Distribution
•Fuel, Food
Industry/Government Partnershi
☑ USD(AT&L)
☑ USD(C)
☑ SEC
6

Systems Contractors On The Battlefield

- If it breaks—you fix it:
  wherever and whenever required.
- Consider this an incentive for quality…
- Iraqi Freedom
  - 4th ID deployed with 246 civilians supporting systems
    - ✓ Nearly 75% are Systems Contractor personnel
- Stryker Brigade Combat Team
  - Requires 115 civilians in support
    - ✓ 86% are Systems Contractor personnel
    - ✓ 59 Systems Contractor personnel embedded in the Brigade AO

What can Industry do to reduce the Contractor Footprint?

7

Wrap Up

- The Future is Performance Based Logistics
- We (DoD) are streamlining our Logistics Enterprise
- Huge opportunity for you (Industry) to
  - **Build sustainable systems**
  - **Reduce contractor dependence forward**

Technology Focus For The Future

manugistics

SOLE Conference
Huntsville

August 2003

Focus on Benefits

- > **Grow Revenues**
  - 95% - 99+% customer service
- > **Lower Operating Costs**
  - 5% - 12% reduction in transportation costs
  - 10% - 25% reduction in logistics costs
- > **Maximize Asset Return**
  - 5% - 20% improvement in yields
  - 15% - 65% reduction in schedule changes
  - Reduction of cycle times (order and manufacturing)
- > **Reduce Working Capital**
  - 40% - 60% obsolete and stale inventories
  - 20% - 60% finished goods inventory
  - 10% - 35% raw materials inventories

manugistics

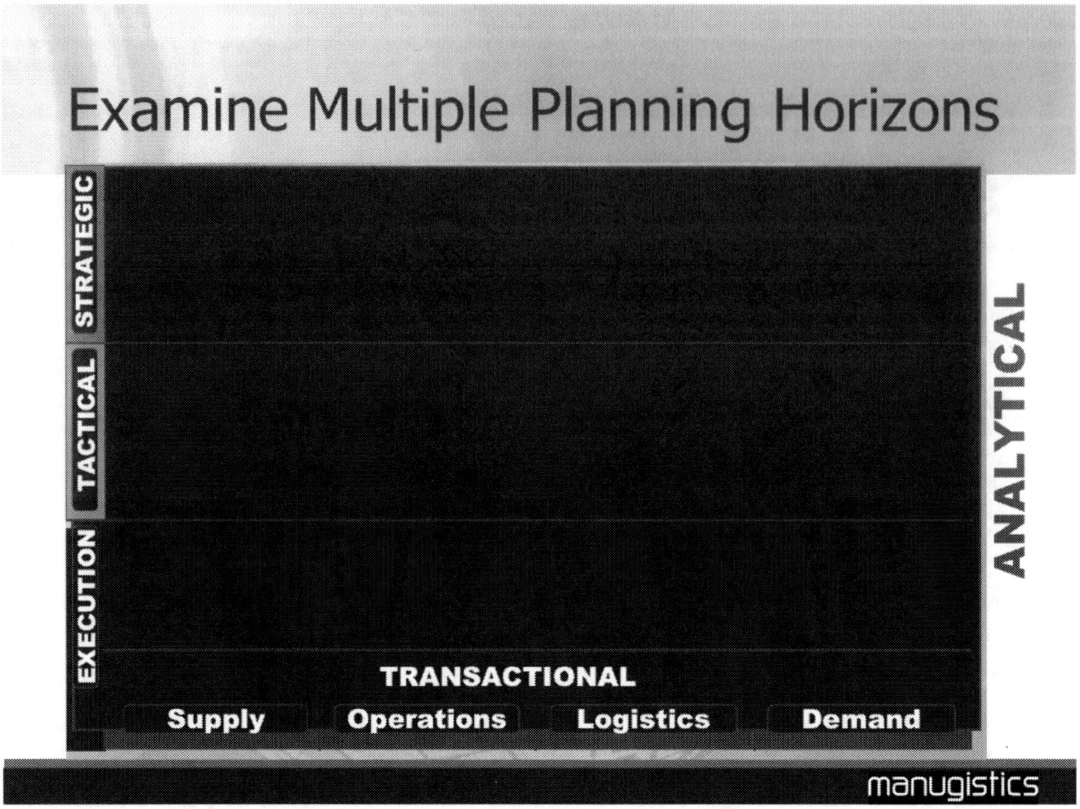
Examine Multiple Planning Horizons
STRATEGIC
TACTICAL
EXECUTION
ANALYTICAL
TRANSACTIONAL
Supply
Operations
Logistics
Demand
manugistics

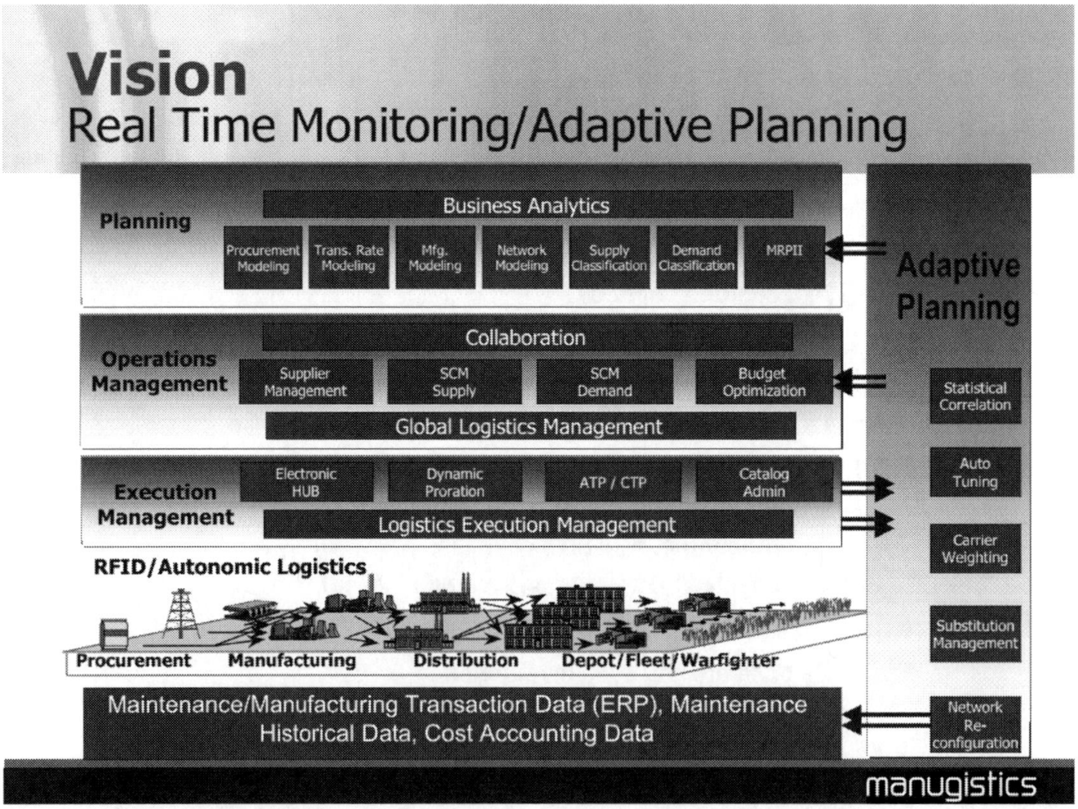
Vision
Real Time Monitoring/Adaptive Planning
Planning
Business Analytics
Procurement Modeling
Trans. Rate Modeling
Mfg. Modeling
Network Modeling
Supply Classification
Demand Classification
MRPII
Operations Management
Collaboration
Supplier Management
SCM Supply
SCM Demand
Budget Optimization
Global Logistics Management
Execution Management
Electronic HUB
Dynamic Proration
ATP / CTP
Catalog Admin
Logistics Execution Management
RFID/Autonomic Logistics
Procurement
Manufacturing
Distribution
Depot/Fleet/Warfighter
Maintenance/Manufacturing Transaction Data (ERP), Maintenance Historical Data, Cost Accounting Data
Adaptive Planning
Statistical Correlation
Auto Tuning
Carrier Weighting
Substitution Management
Network Re-configuration
manugistics

Current Operating Environment

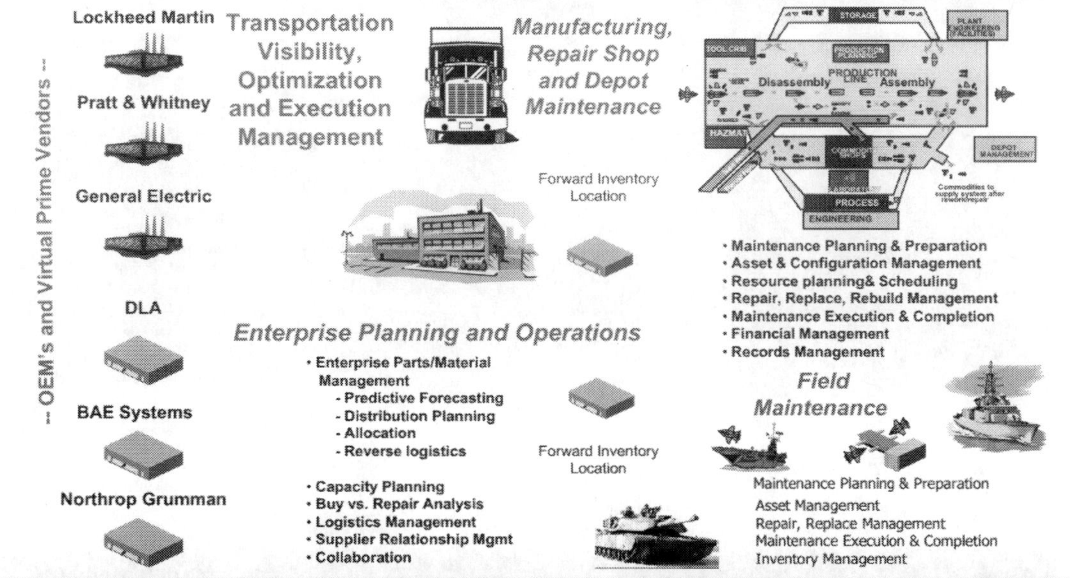

manugistics

Operating Challenges

> Replacing inventory, capital and costs with information and speed

> Converting from mass material acquisition and management to targeted material acquisition and management

> Optimizing complex manufacturing and repair supply chains that extend across customers, suppliers and other partners globally

> Reducing overall cycle times and improving reliability by providing real-time visibility across the supply chain

> Integrating SCM, ERP, MRO and legacy environments and systems

manugistics

Vision
Enabling the End-to-End Supply Chain

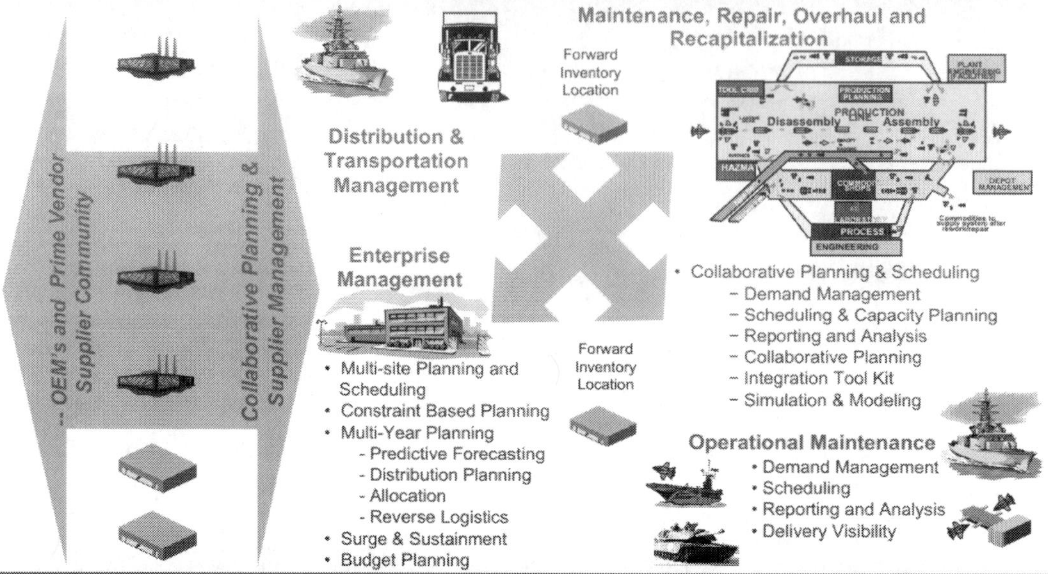

manugistics

Technology Solution Overview

End-to-End Supply Chain planning and execution
- From materials sourcing through to mission fulfillment

Transformation of data into information for logistics operations
- Direct linkage to detailed historical utilization data
- Significant improvement in predictive forecasting
- Collaborative planning ... internal and external
- Service level based management

Simultaneous constraint-based operations management
- Constraint-based planning and scheduling
- Multi-location / function scheduling and sequencing

Delivery and transportation management
- Visibility to the inbound and outbound flow of materials

Speed of information
- Capable of real-time simultaneous distribution of information

Supply Chain Execution
- Reporting and analysis ...real-time

manugistics

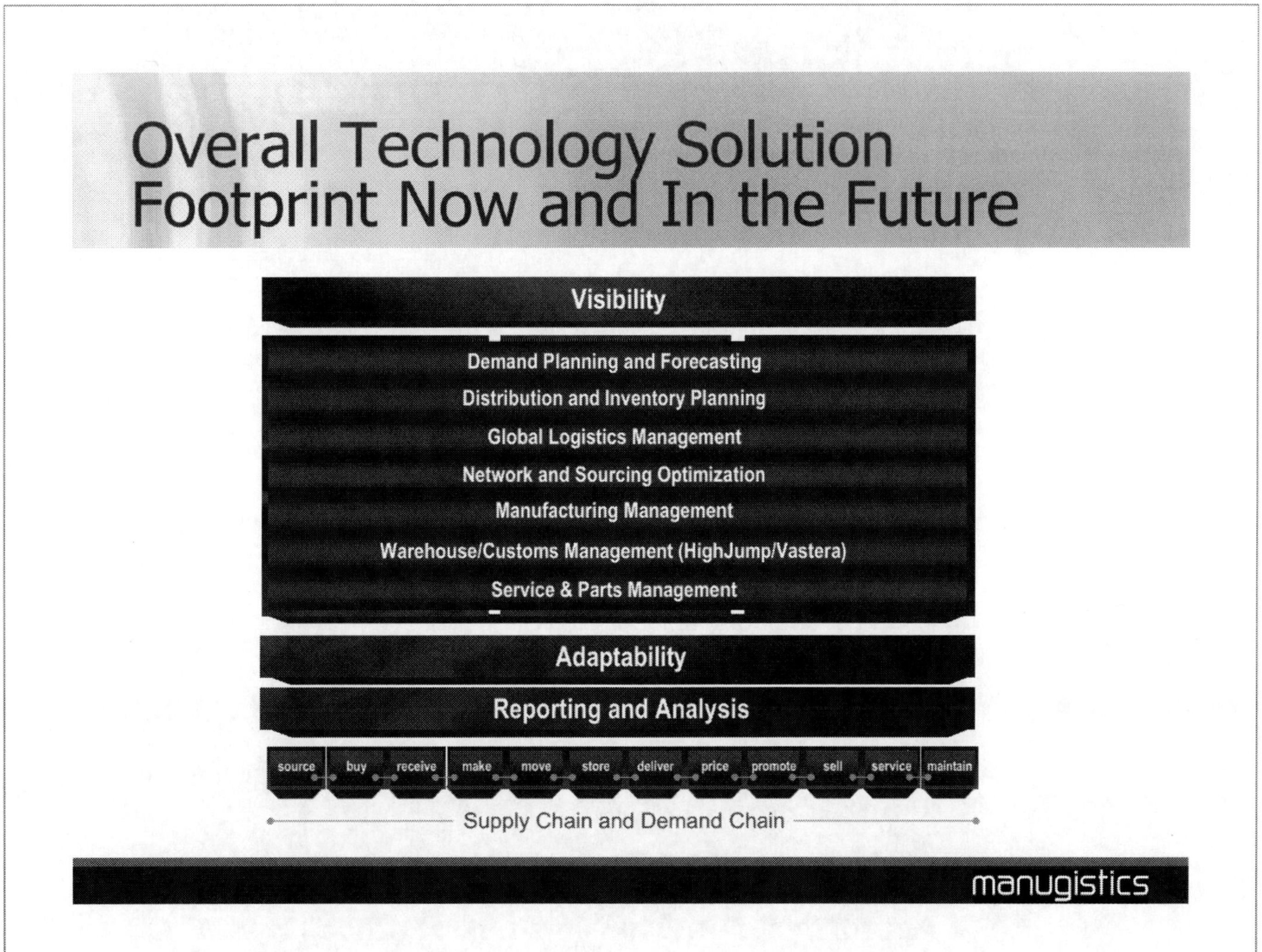

Overall Technology Solution Footprint Now and In the Future
Visibility
Demand Planning and Forecasting
Distribution and Inventory Planning
Global Logistics Management
Network and Sourcing Optimization
Manufacturing Management
Warehouse/Customs Management (HighJump/Vastera)
Service & Parts Management
Adaptability
Reporting and Analysis
source
buy
receive
make
move
store
deliver
price
promote
sell
service
maintain
Supply Chain and Demand Chain
manugistics

CTC

Concurrent
Technologies
Corporation

1 CTC Concurrent Technologies Corporation

About *CTC*

- Independent nonprofit
- Applied research and development professional services organization
- Staff of over 1,200 professionals
- Approximately 1,000,000 sq. ft. of office, laboratory, and demonstration factory space
- More than 25 *CTC* sites throughout the U.S.
- ISO 9001 & 14001 certified

2 CTC Concurrent Technologies Corporation

New Sustainment Paradigms

- Sea Based Logistics
  - Logistics base will maneuver with sea base operational forces
  - Eliminates shore based facilities with inherent security requirements
- National Inventory Management Strategy

3

CTC Concurrent Technologies Corporation

Improved Technologies for Weapons Systems

- New weapons systems will be:
  - Lighter
  - Use less fuel
  - On-board diagnostics
- Technology Improvements:
  - New Materials
  - New Technologies for manufacturing

4

CTC Concurrent Technologies Corporation

Optimum use of IT

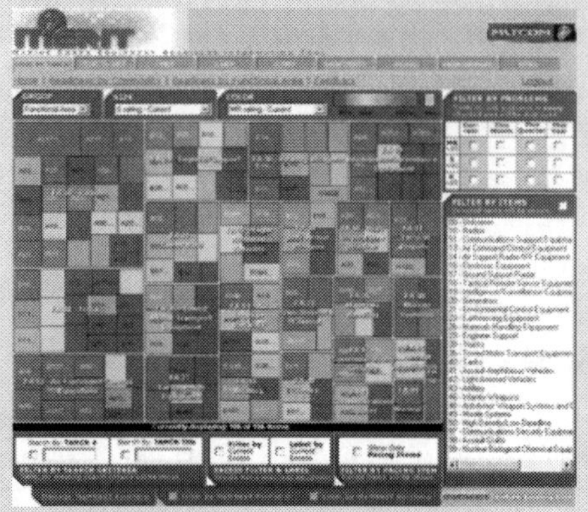

- Web-enabled, collaborative environments
- Integrated Data Environment (IDE) to provide total asset visibility
- Improved Decision Support Systems
- Use of Intelligent Agents for diagnostics

Need for Innovative Ideas

- Advances in the area of Logistics Chain Management are accelerating
- Leading organizations are viewing and improving their competitiveness by taking a supply chain perspective vice an organizational perspective
- Organizations demand that improvements result in financial benefit

CTC Concurrent Technologies Corporation

CTC

Concurrent Technologies Corporation

7

CTC Concurrent Technologies Corporation

Senior Executive Partnership Round Table
Innovative Logistics Partnering
with the Department Of Defense
Honeywell, Inc.
John Phillips
Vice President of Logistics Services and Senior DoD Advisor,
Former Deputy Under Secretary of Defense and Major General
(ret.)
December 5, 2002
UOM 102802 Page 1

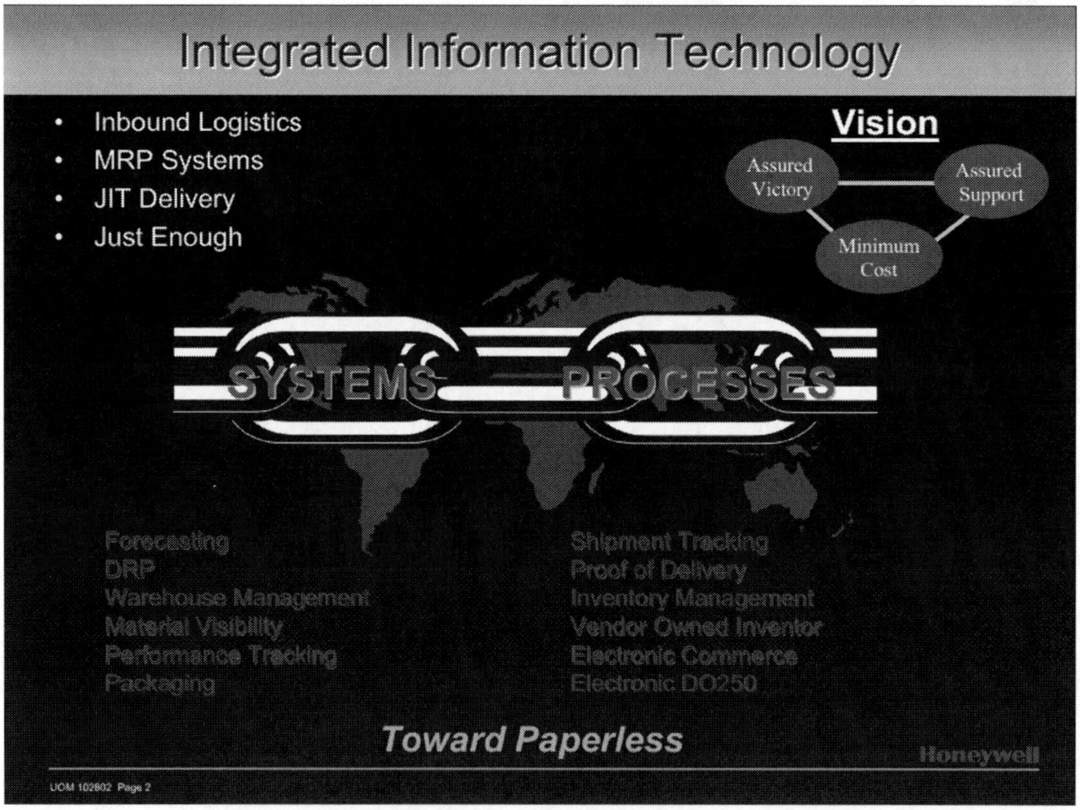
Integrated Information Technology
• Inbound Logistics
• MRP Systems
• JIT Delivery
• Just Enough
Vision
Assured Victory
Assured Support
Minimum Cost
SYSTEMS
PROCESSES
Forecasting
DRP
Warehouse Management
Material Visibility
Performance Tracking
Packaging
Shipment Tracking
Proof of Delivery
Inventory Management
Vendor Owned Inventor
Electronic Commerce
Electronic DO250
Toward Paperless
Honeywell
UOM 102802 Page 2

Supply Chain Management Program Goals

Supply Chain Support

- Demand forecasting
- Repair requirement forecasting
- Material requirement forecasting
- Material ordering/procurement (acquisition and delivery)
- Material expanding
- Inventory management for supply system
- "G" Condition Code (awaiting parts)
- "F" Condition Code (carcass movement and tracking)

General Expectations

- Improve material availability
- Improve logistics response time
- Improve product quality
- Improve price/total cost
- Improve supply services
- Improve technical support
- Exploit technology
- Manage industrial readiness
- Socioeconomic compliance

Honeywell

UOM 102802 Page 3

Digitization: Cradle-to-Grave Life Cycle

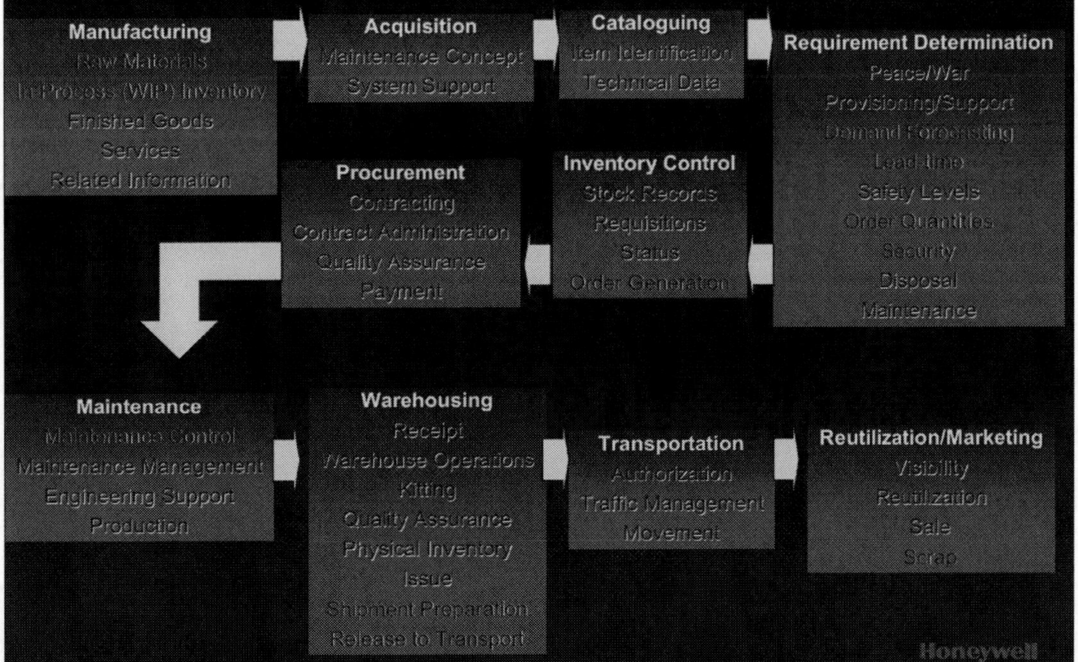

Honeywell

UOM 102802 Page 4

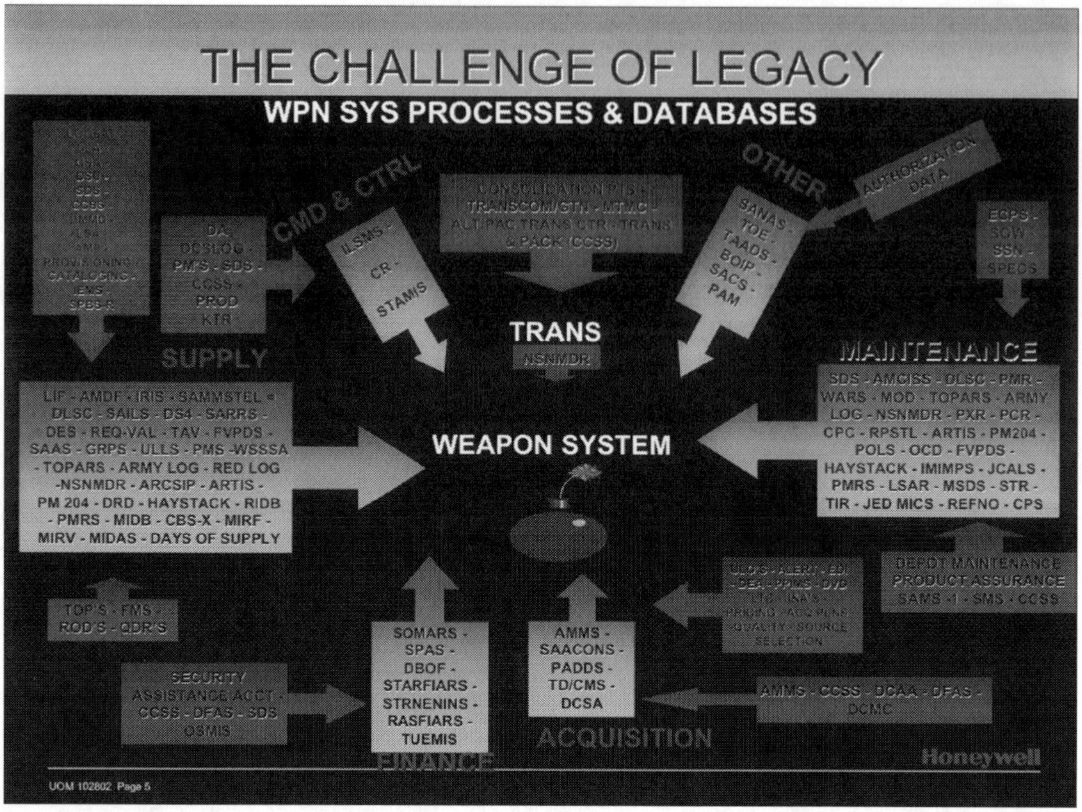
THE CHALLENGE OF LEGACY
WPN SYS PROCESSES & DATABASES
DSU - SDS - CCSS -
PROVISIONING - CATALOGING - IEMS - SPBS-R
DA DCSLOG - PM'S - SDS - CCSS - PROD KTR
CMD & CTRL
ILSMS - CR - STAMIS
TRANSCOM/GTN - MTMC - ALT PAC TRANS CTR - TRANS & PACK (CCSS)
OTHER
AUTHORIZATION DATA
SANAS - TOE - TAADS - BOIP - SACS - PAM
ECPS - SOW - SSN - SPECS
TRANS
NSNMDR
SUPPLY
LIF - AMDF - IRIS - SAMMSTEL - DLSC - SAILS - DS4 - SARRS - DES - REQ-VAL - TAV - FVPDS - SAAS - GRPS - ULLS - PMS -WSSSA - TOPARS - ARMY LOG - RED LOG -NSNMDR - ARCSIP - ARTIS - PM 204 - DRD - HAYSTACK - RIDB - PMRS - MIDB - CBS-X - MIRF - MIRV - MIDAS - DAYS OF SUPPLY
WEAPON SYSTEM
MAINTENANCE
SDS - AMCISS - DLSC - PMR - WARS - MOD - TOPARS - ARMY LOG - NSNMDR - PXR - PCR - CPC - RPSTL - ARTIS - PM204 - POLS - OCD - FVPDS - HAYSTACK - IMIMPS - JCALS - PMRS - LSAR - MSDS - STR - TIR - JED MICS - REFNO - CPS
DEPOT MAINTENANCE PRODUCT ASSURANCE SAMS -1 - SMS - CCSS
TOP'S - FMS - ROD'S - QDR'S
SECURITY ASSISTANCE ACCT - CCSS - DFAS - SDS OSMIS
SOMARS - SPAS - DBOF - STARFIARS - STRNENINS - RASFIARS - TUEMIS
FINANCE
AMMS - SAACONS - PADDS - TD/CMS - DCSA
ACQUISITION
AMMS - CCSS - DCAA - DFAS - DCMC
Honeywell
UOM 102802 Page 5

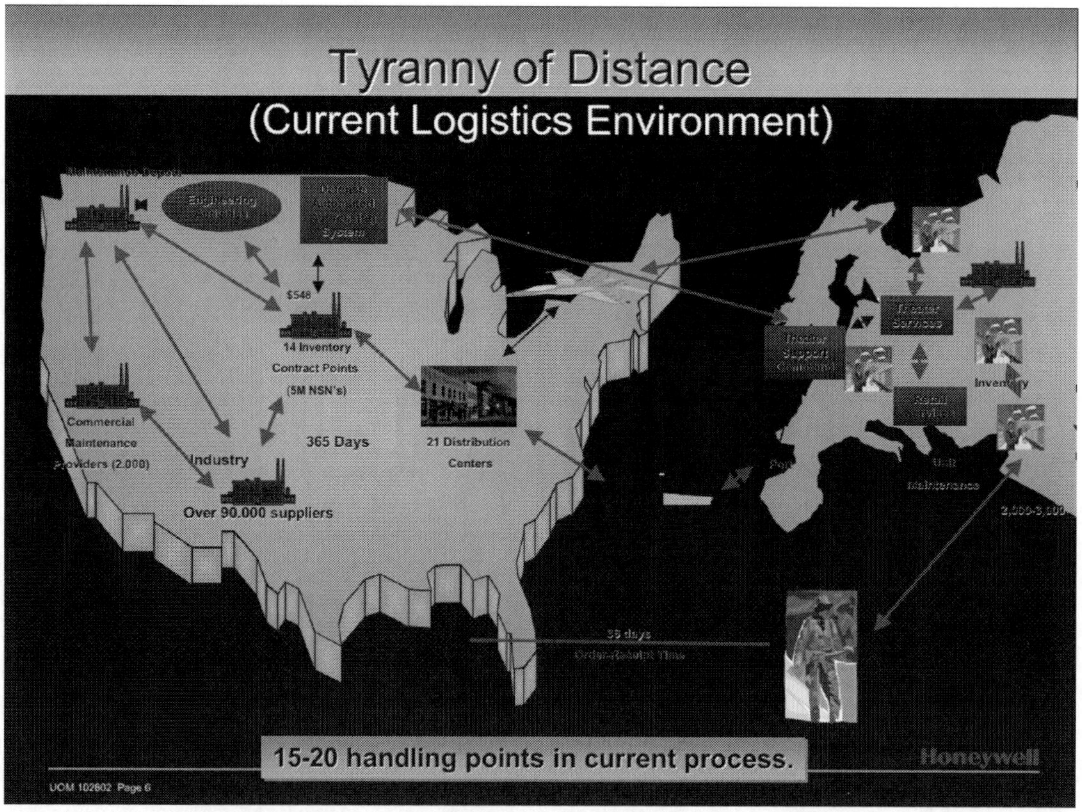
Tyranny of Distance
(Current Logistics Environment)
$548
14 Inventory Contract Points
(5M NSN's)
365 Days
21 Distribution Centers
Commercial Maintenance Providers (2,000)
Industry
Over 90,000 suppliers
Inventory
15-20 handling points in current process.
Honeywell
UOM 102802 Page 6

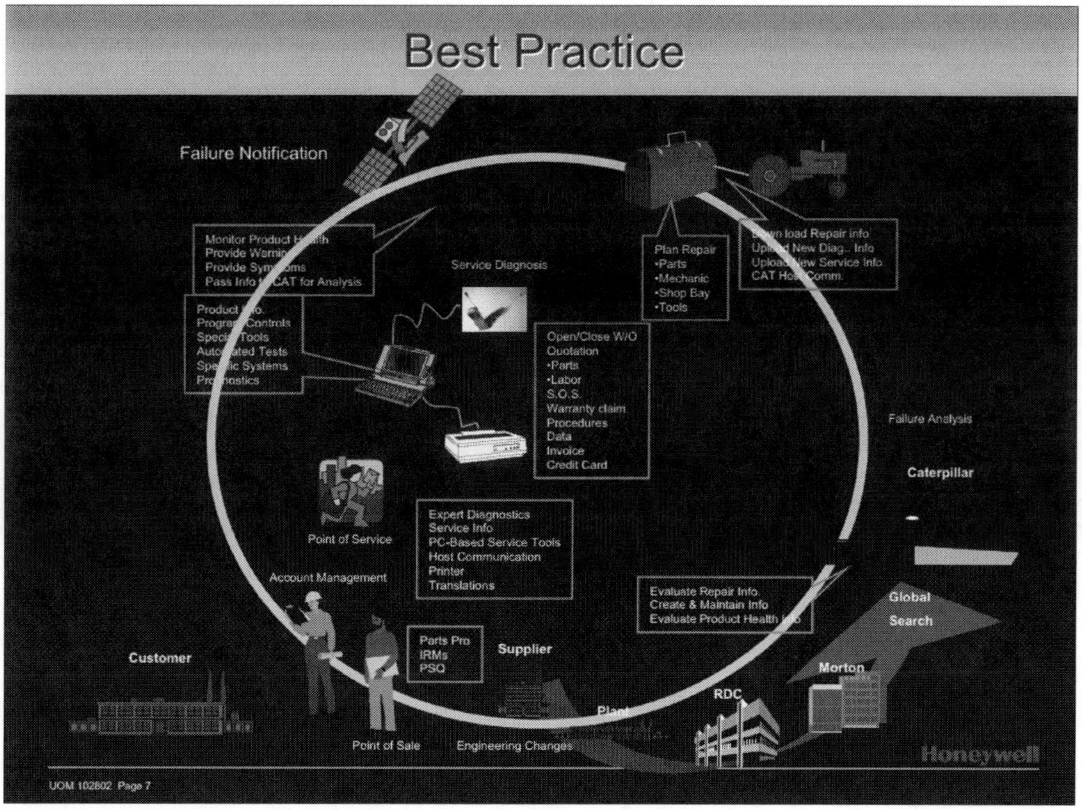
Best Practice
Failure Notification
Monitor Product Health
Provide Warnings
Provide Symptoms
Pass Info to CAT for Analysis
Product Info.
Program Controls
Specific Tools
Automated Tests
Specific Systems
Prognostics
Service Diagnosis
Plan Repair
•Parts
•Mechanic
•Shop Bay
•Tools
Down load Repair info
Upload New Diag.. Info
Upload New Service Info
CAT Host Comm.
Open/Close W/O
Quotation
•Parts
•Labor
S.O.S.
Warranty claim
Procedures
Data
Invoice
Credit Card
Failure Analysis
Caterpillar
Point of Service
Expert Diagnostics
Service Info
PC-Based Service Tools
Host Communication
Printer
Translations
Account Management
Evaluate Repair Info.
Create & Maintain Info
Evaluate Product Health Info
Global
Search
Customer
Parts Pro
IRMs
PSQ
Supplier
Morton
RDC
Plant
Point of Sale
Engineering Changes
Honeywell
UOM 102802 Page 7

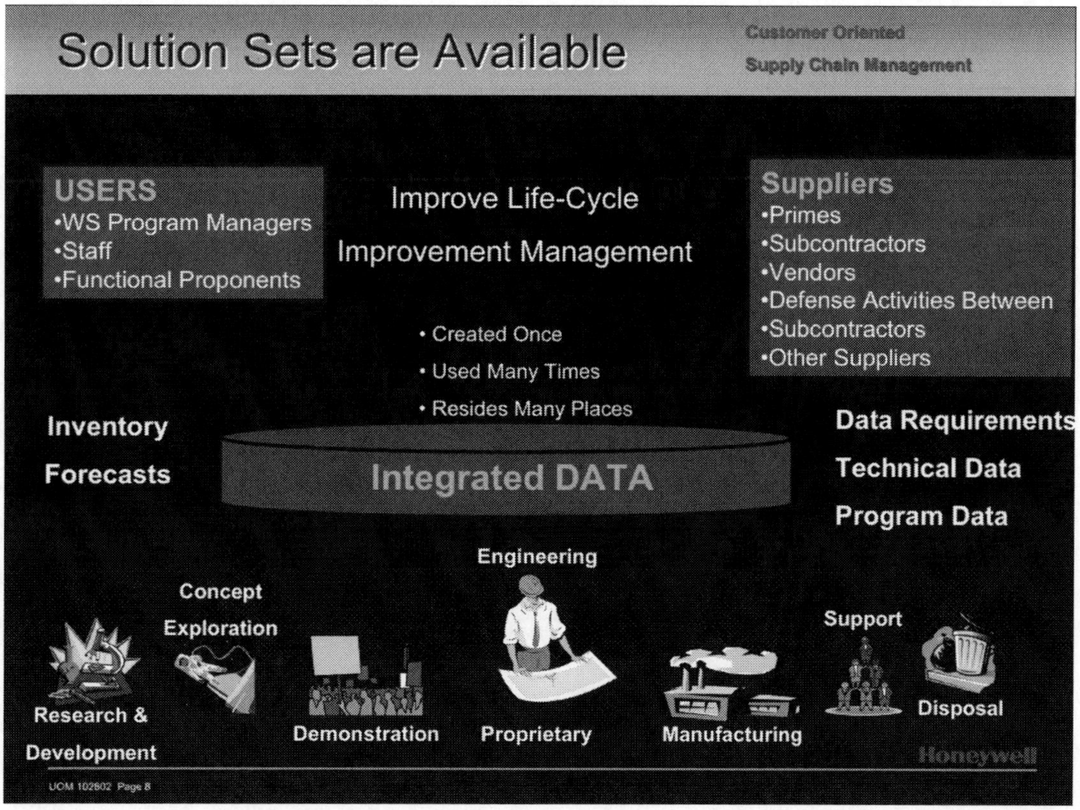
Solution Sets are Available
Customer Oriented
Supply Chain Management
USERS
•WS Program Managers
•Staff
•Functional Proponents
Improve Life-Cycle
Improvement Management
Suppliers
•Primes
•Subcontractors
•Vendors
•Defense Activities Between
•Subcontractors
•Other Suppliers
• Created Once
• Used Many Times
• Resides Many Places
Inventory
Forecasts
Integrated DATA
Data Requirements
Technical Data
Program Data
Engineering
Concept
Exploration
Support
Research &
Development
Demonstration
Proprietary
Manufacturing
Disposal
Honeywell
UOM 102802 Page 8

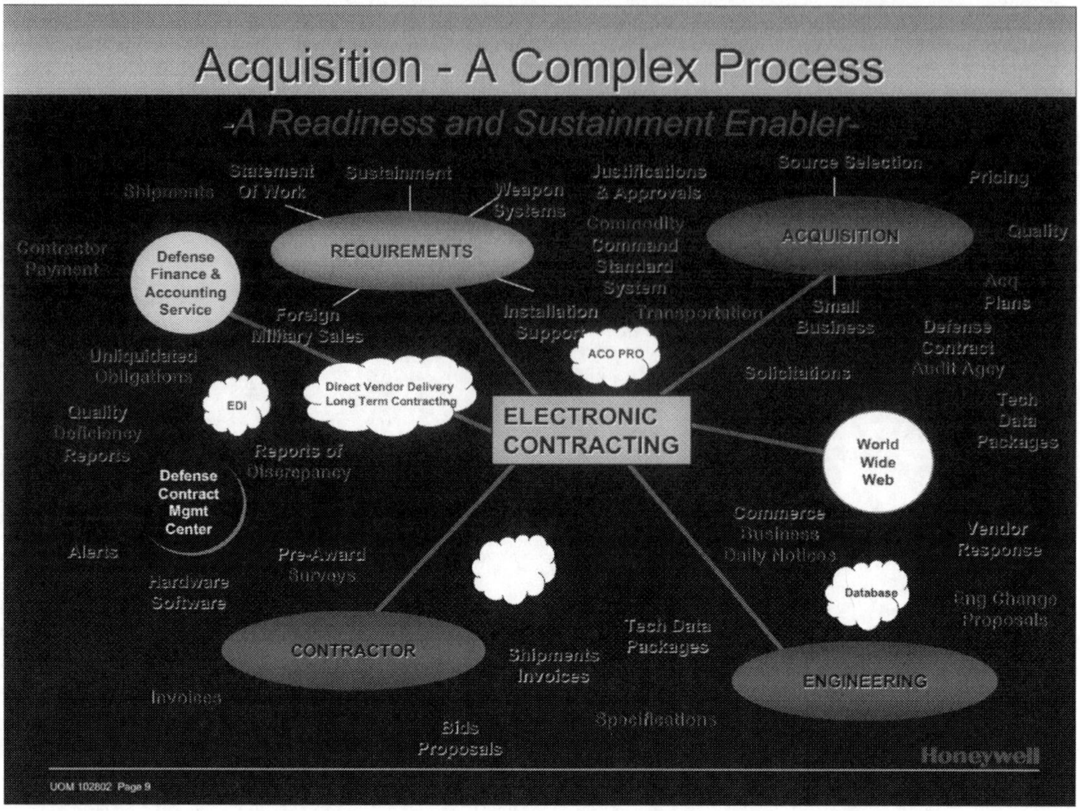
Acquisition - A Complex Process
-A Readiness and Sustainment Enabler-
Shipments
Statement Of Work
Sustainment
Weapon Systems
Justifications & Approvals
Source Selection
Pricing
Contractor Payment
Defense Finance & Accounting Service
REQUIREMENTS
Commodity Command Standard System
ACQUISITION
Quality
Acq Plans
Foreign Military Sales
Installation Support
Transportation
Small Business
Defense Contract Audit Agcy
Unliquidated Obligations
ACO PRO
Solicitations
EDI
Direct Vendor Delivery
Long Term Contracting
ELECTRONIC CONTRACTING
Tech Data Packages
Quality Deficiency Reports
Reports of Discrepancy
World Wide Web
Defense Contract Mgmt Center
Commerce Business Daily Notices
Vendor Response
Alerts
Pre-Award Surveys
Hardware Software
Database
Eng Change Proposals
Tech Data Packages
CONTRACTOR
Shipments Invoices
ENGINEERING
Invoices
Specifications
Bids Proposals
Honeywell
UOM 102802 Page 9

Industry Re-Structuring - Strategic Issues
Changing Relationships with the Mega Primes
✞ Spin Offs
✞ Financial Problems
✞ Few New Starts
✞ Price Pressuring Subs
✞ Seeking Investments
Changing Relationships with Europe/Asia
✞ EU Successes
✞ Defense & Space Industry Consolidation
✞ Japanese Recession
✞ War on Terror
More Subsystem Integration Roles ?
Honeywell
UOM 102802 Page 10

Integrated Solutions Covers Many Aspects of Homeland Defense

Integrated Solutions Capturing Cross Honeywell Capabilities & Technologies

- **Homeland Defense and Govt. Facility Security**
- **Anti Terrorist Operations**
- **Protecting our Military Forces**

Physical and Cyber Security
- Fire and Security
- Asset Tracking -RF Tags
- Digital Video for Sensing Stress and Anxiety
- Intruder Detection Ground Sensor Network
- Damage Resilient Communications Networks

Building Controls
- Enterprise Security
- Crisis Management
- Biological and Chemical Warfare Immune Buildings
  - -Chemical/Biological Detectors
  - -Air Filtration and Purification
  - -Heating Ventilation Air Conditioning Controls

Secure and Enhanced Comm
- Secure Airborne Messaging (ACARS)
- Secure Aviation Communications
- Voice and Video Transmission
- Advanced Friend or Foe Identification
- Data Links
- Message Encryption

Advanced Materials
- Bullet and Explosion Proof Armor and Containment Materials (Spectra TM)
- Air Filtration and Purification Materials and Catalysts

Avionics
- Chemical and Biological Sensor Systems
- Safety of Flight
- Miniaturized and Integrated Electronics, Sensors and Systems

Propulsion Power Environmental Controls
- Chemical and Biological Filters
- Air and Water Filtration and Purification
- Main, Auxiliary and Emergency Power on Military Vehicles and Aircraft

Growth Initiatives: Working with our Government Customers on Post 911 Solutions

Honeywell

UOM 102802 Page 11

Industry Restructuring Summary

- **Wall Street Opinions Continue to Exert Significant Pressure on Industry Management.**
- **Procurement Budget Increases Benefits Some, Not All.**
- **DoD Decisions on Domestic Industrial Base Restructuring Aimed at Maintaining Some Level of Competition.**
- **Some Concern Over the Robustness of the Industrial Base Remains.**
- **Size of Upper-Tier "Mega Players" and "Mid-Tier Players" Moving Into Balance.**
- **Trans-Atlantic Deals and/or Globalization Are Wildcards.**
- **We Stand on Threshold of Industrial Realignment.**

Honeywell

UOM 102802 Page 12

23L

Future Growth Through Technology

- Information Systems
  - Battlespace Management, Situational Awareness, Combat ID
- C41
  - Secure Comm., Electronic Mods and Upgrades, Intel Systems, Targeting, Small Unit Operations (SUO)
- Platform Automation
  - UCAVs/UAVs
  - SC-21
  - Warfighter
  - Health Monitoring
  - VMS
- Space Asset Control and Exploitation
  - Space Based Radar
  - Directed Energy Weapons
- Missile Defense
- Deep Precision Strike and Navigation
- Simulation and Training
- JSF
- Fuel Cells
- Electric Power Generation
- Ceramics

Honeywell

UOM 102802 Page 13

JV2010 Provides The Vision....

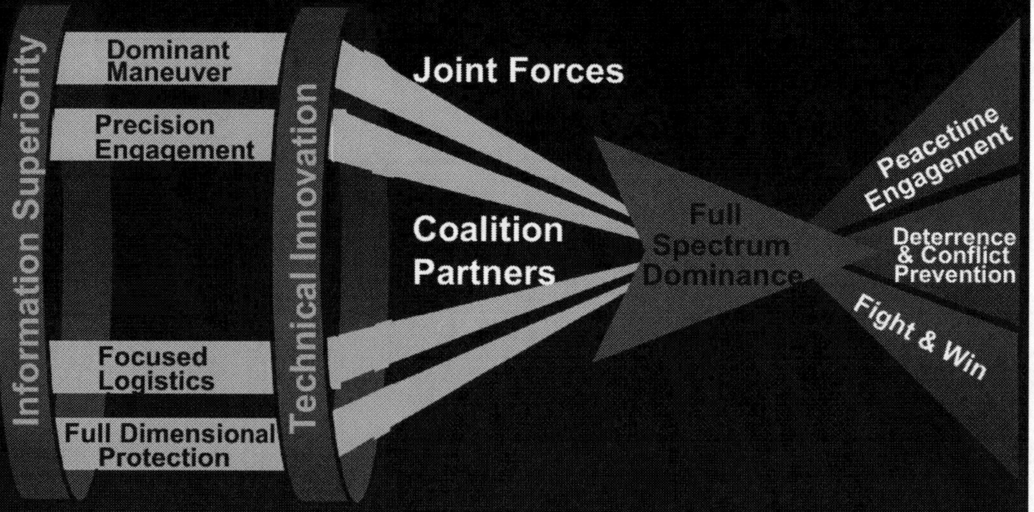

Honeywell

UOM 102802 Page 14

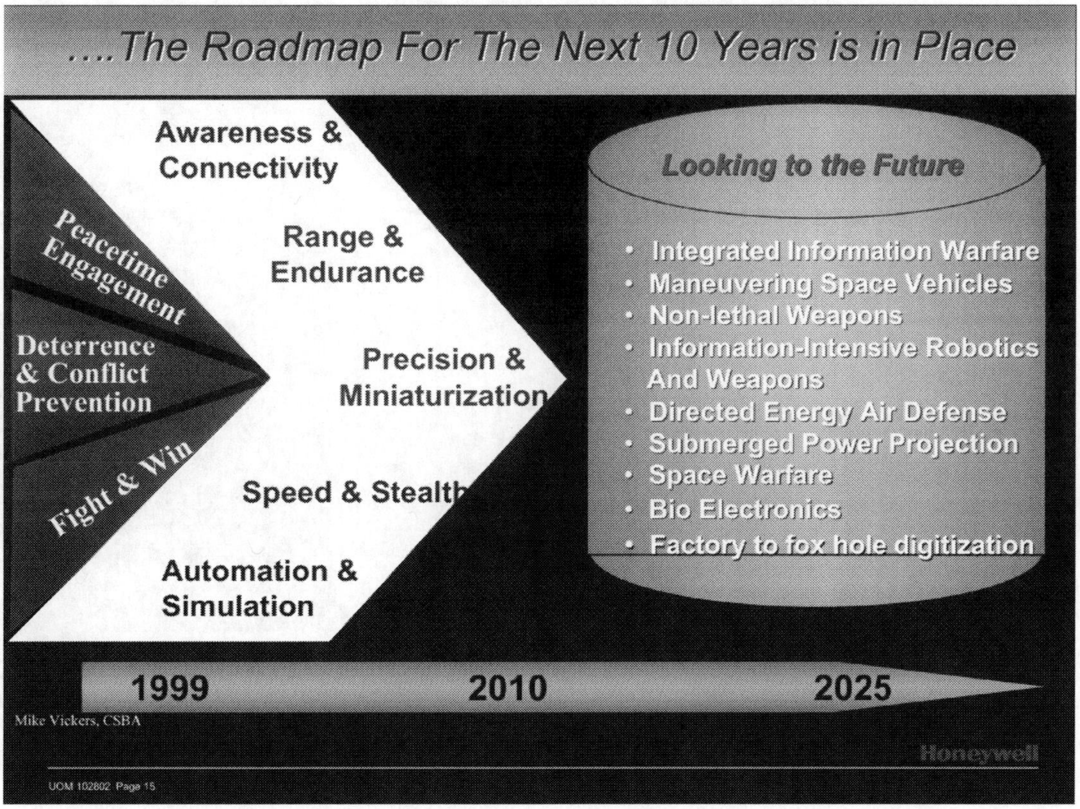
....The Roadmap For The Next 10 Years is in Place
Awareness & Connectivity
Range & Endurance
Precision & Miniaturization
Speed & Stealth
Automation & Simulation
Peacetime Engagement
Deterrence & Conflict Prevention
Fight & Win
Looking to the Future
• Integrated Information Warfare
• Maneuvering Space Vehicles
• Non-lethal Weapons
• Information-Intensive Robotics And Weapons
• Directed Energy Air Defense
• Submerged Power Projection
• Space Warfare
• Bio Electronics
• Factory to fox hole digitization
1999
2010
2025
Mike Vickers, CSBA
Honeywell
UOM 102802 Page 15

Hi-Priority Customer Concerns
Deterrence & Mission Success
Superiority (Information Dominance)
Safety
Reliability
Affordability
Digitization
Surveillance & Communication
Standoff / Precision Strike
Un-inhabited Combat Air Vehicle
National Missile Defense
Asset Tracking
Vehicle Health Mgt.
CNS-ATM GATM
Commercial Buying
Outsourcing
Upgrades
Aftermarket
Honeywell
UOM 102802 Page 16

Aging Aircraft Dilemma

Military Aircraft Projected to Remain Active Longer Than Expected:

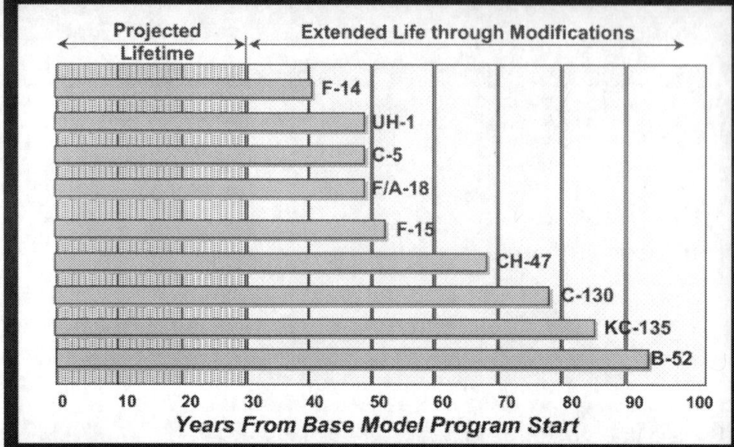

The Cost of Aging

- Last Year the Air Force Spent $2B More to Fly the Same Number of Aircraft the Same Number of Hours As in the Previous Year.
- The USMC Average Cost Per Flying Hour Has Risen From $2,341 in FY96 to $3,481 in FY98.
- Overall DoD Flying Hour Costs Have Risen Almost 70% Over the Past Four Years.

Aging Aircraft Will Fuel Mod/Retrofit and Logistics Support Opportunities

Honeywell

UOM 102802 Page 17

Conclusions - Aircraft

- Aging Aircraft Demand Modernization
  - New Fighter Development & Production Programs Will Dominate Budgets
  - Non-fighter Aircraft Will Be Modernized Through Avionics and Propulsion Modifications
- Lower Cost of Ownership is Required
  - Must Be Designed Into Modernization Programs
  - Prerequisite for Service & Congressional Funding Support in U.S.
- Shortfalls Will Exist and May Result In:
  - Additional JSF Development Schedule Slippage
  - Stretching Out And/or Trimming Size of Other Major Programs

Honeywell

UOM 102802 Page 18

Industry View: Digitization Strategies for the Supply Chain

Strategy	Business Functions	Metrics
eProcurement/ eCommerce	Cross-enterprise system-to-system integration	Productivity Reduced cost/cycle time contract compliance customer reach
eCollaboration	Cross-enterprise technology/ design interaction	Design cycle time design synergy, reuse revenue
Integrated planning/ manufacturing	Cross-enterprise planning/ execution system-to-system integration/ outsourced manufacturing visibility	Lead time, margin accuracy/flexibility inventory levels on-time delivery
Integrated delivery	Cross-enterprise logistics management/consignment visibility	Logistics cycle time reduced cost lead time
On-line marketing	Product boundary extension new products/services creation new markets/channel creation	Market segment share

(Source: INTEL)

Honeywell

UOM 102802 Page 19

DoD Supplement Critical Processes

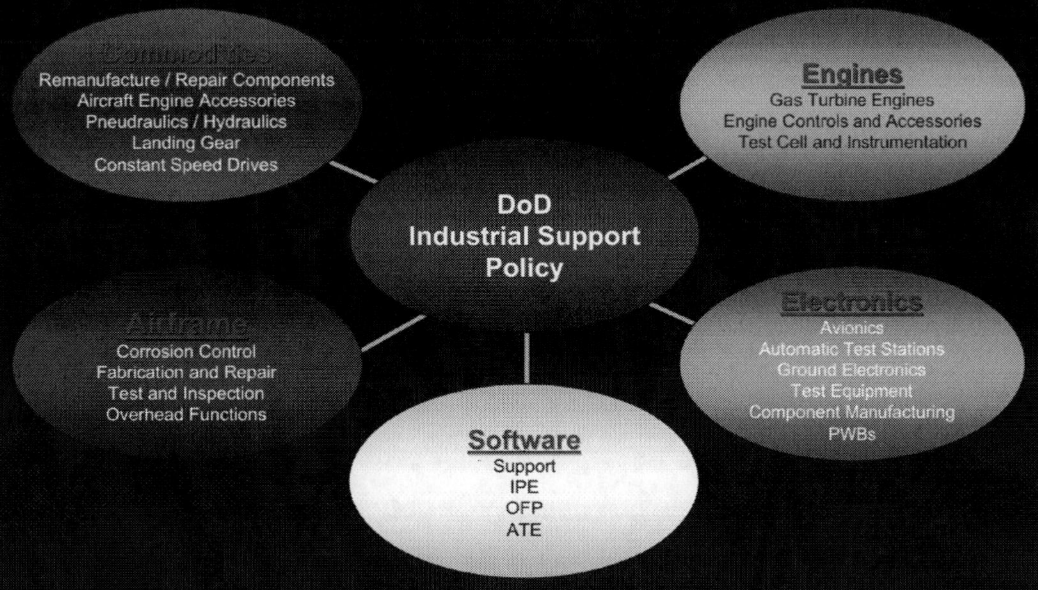

Honeywell

UOM 102802 Page 20

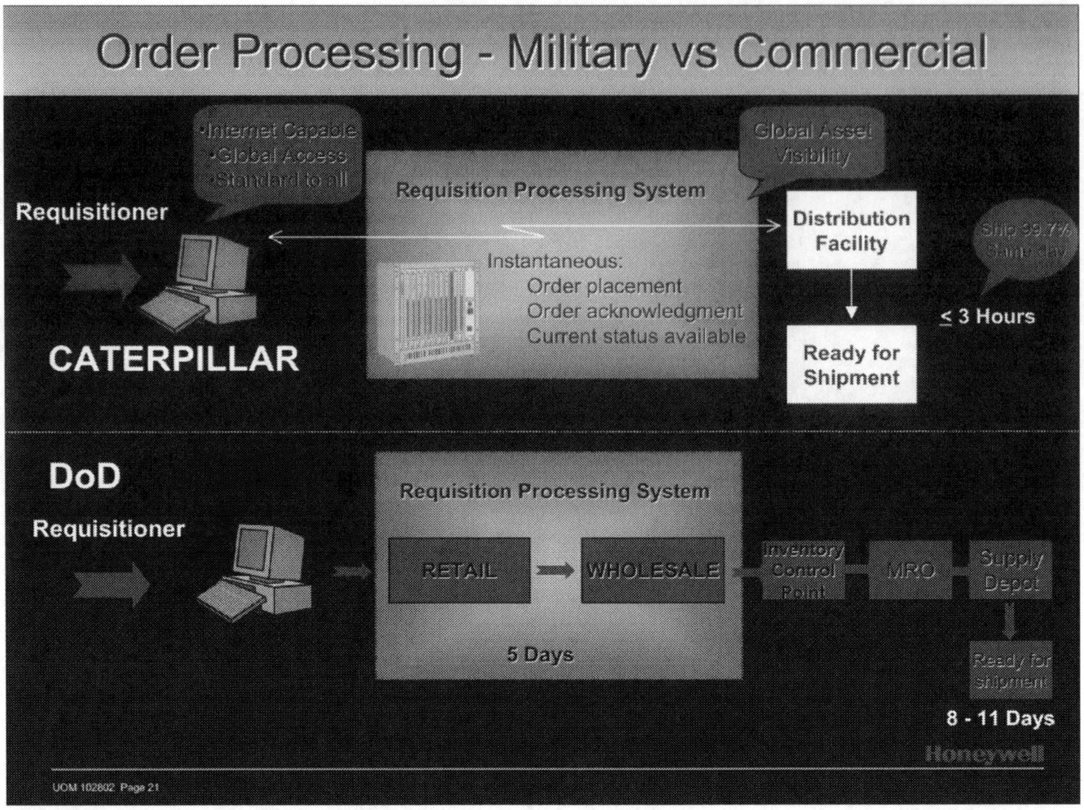

Order Processing - Military vs Commercial
•Internet Capable
•Global Access
•Standard to all
Global Asset Visibility
Requisitioner
Requisition Processing System
Distribution Facility
Ship 99.7% Same day
Instantaneous:
Order placement
Order acknowledgment
Current status available
≤ 3 Hours
CATERPILLAR
Ready for Shipment
DoD
Requisitioner
Requisition Processing System
RETAIL
WHOLESALE
Inventory Control Point
MRO
Supply Depot
5 Days
Ready for shipment
8 - 11 Days
Honeywell
UOM 102802 Page 21

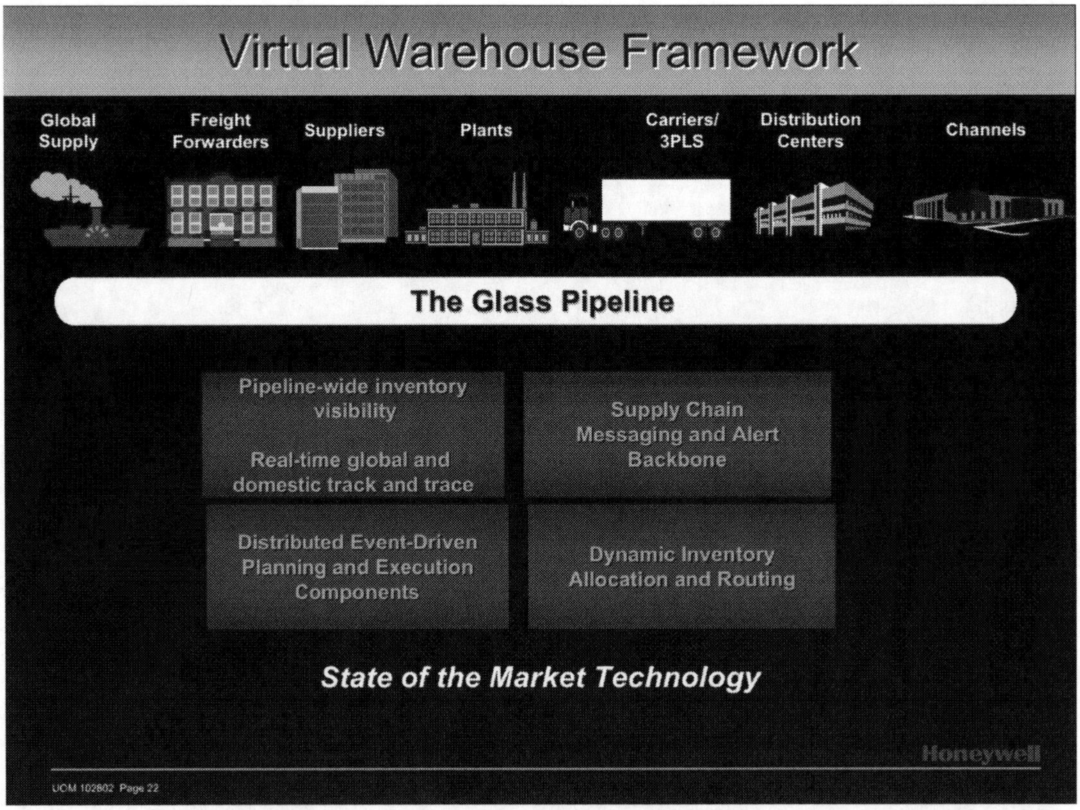

Virtual Warehouse Framework
Global Supply
Freight Forwarders
Suppliers
Plants
Carriers/ 3PLS
Distribution Centers
Channels
The Glass Pipeline
Pipeline-wide inventory visibility
Real-time global and domestic track and trace
Supply Chain Messaging and Alert Backbone
Distributed Event-Driven Planning and Execution Components
Dynamic Inventory Allocation and Routing
State of the Market Technology
Honeywell
UOM 102802 Page 22

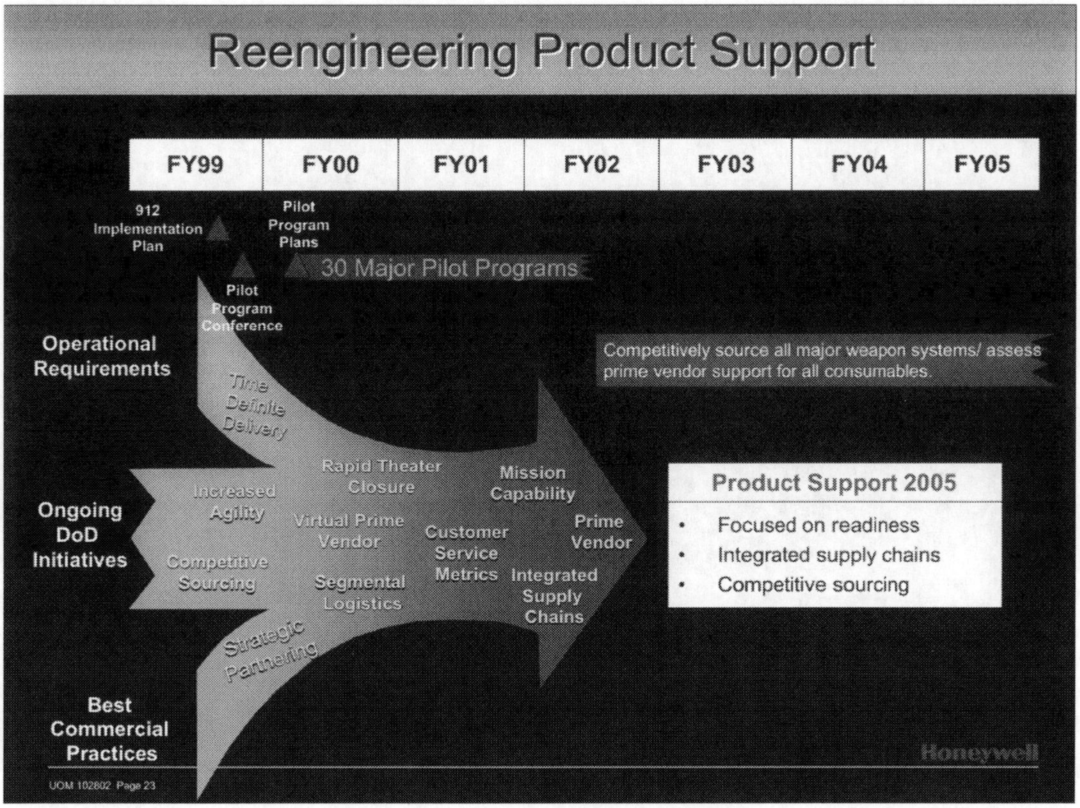

Reengineering Product Support
FY99
FY00
FY01
FY02
FY03
FY04
FY05
912 Implementation Plan
Pilot Program Plans
30 Major Pilot Programs
Pilot Program Conference
Operational Requirements
Competitively source all major weapon systems/ assess prime vendor support for all consumables.
Time Definite Delivery
Rapid Theater Closure
Mission Capability
Increased Agility
Virtual Prime Vendor
Customer Service Metrics
Prime Vendor
Ongoing DoD Initiatives
Competitive Sourcing
Segmental Logistics
Integrated Supply Chains
Strategic Partnering
Product Support 2005
• Focused on readiness
• Integrated supply chains
• Competitive sourcing
Best Commercial Practices
Honeywell
UOM 102802 Page 23

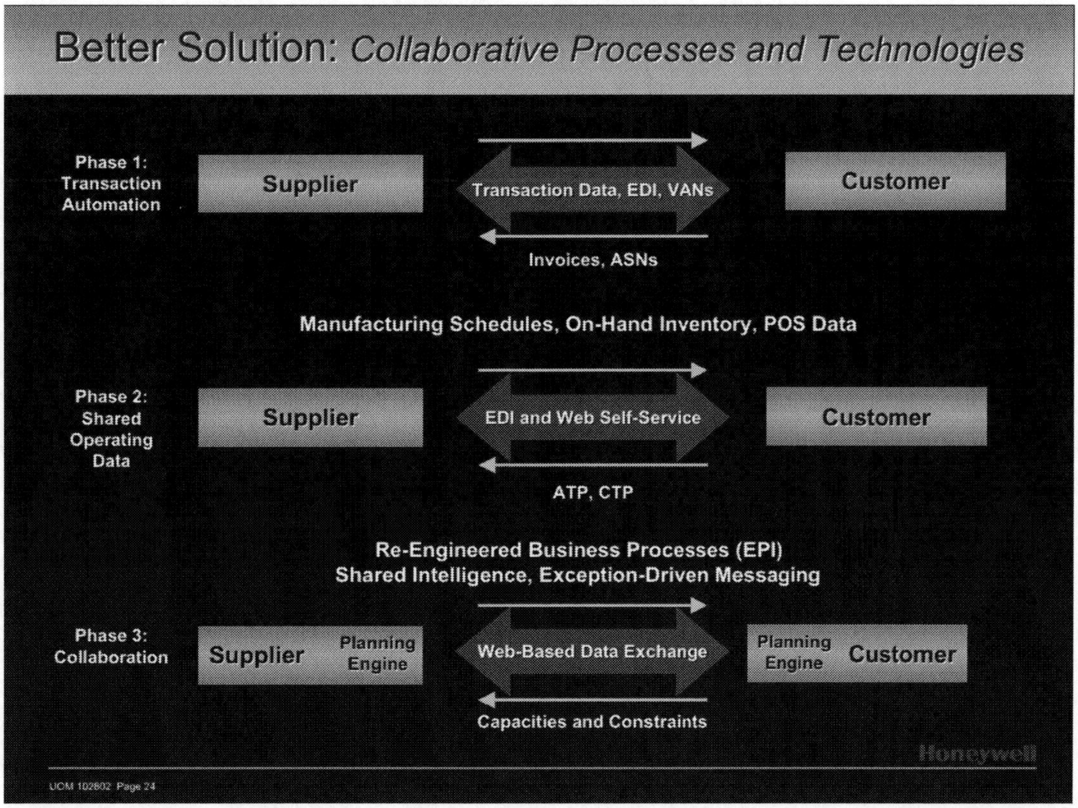

Better Solution: Collaborative Processes and Technologies
Phase 1: Transaction Automation
Supplier
Transaction Data, EDI, VANs
Customer
Invoices, ASNs
Manufacturing Schedules, On-Hand Inventory, POS Data
Phase 2: Shared Operating Data
Supplier
EDI and Web Self-Service
Customer
ATP, CTP
Re-Engineered Business Processes (EPI)
Shared Intelligence, Exception-Driven Messaging
Phase 3: Collaboration
Supplier
Planning Engine
Web-Based Data Exchange
Planning Engine
Customer
Capacities and Constraints
Honeywell
UOM 102802 Page 24

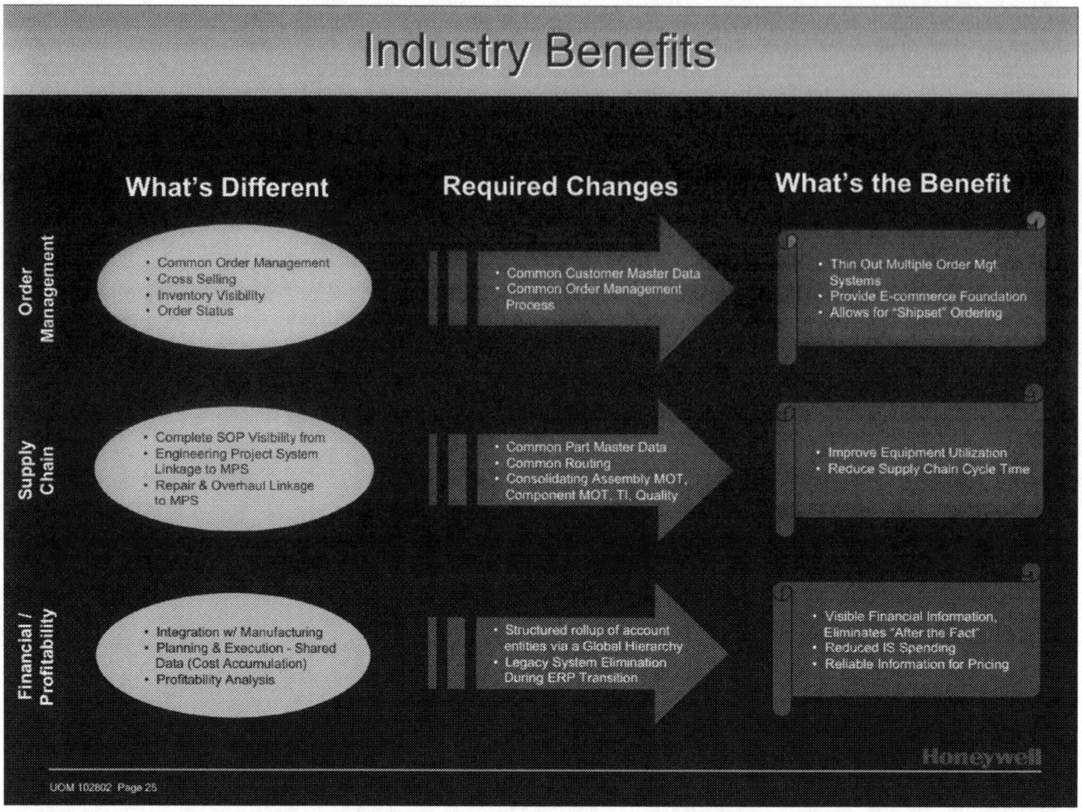
Industry Benefits
What's Different
Required Changes
What's the Benefit
Order Management
• Common Order Management
• Cross Selling
• Inventory Visibility
• Order Status
• Common Customer Master Data
• Common Order Management Process
• Thin Out Multiple Order Mgt Systems
• Provide E-commerce Foundation
• Allows for "Shipset" Ordering
Supply Chain
• Complete SOP Visibility from
• Engineering Project System Linkage to MPS
• Repair & Overhaul Linkage to MPS
• Common Part Master Data
• Common Routing
• Consolidating Assembly MOT, Component MOT, TI, Quality
• Improve Equipment Utilization
• Reduce Supply Chain Cycle Time
Financial / Profitability
• Integration w/ Manufacturing
• Planning & Execution - Shared Data (Cost Accumulation)
• Profitability Analysis
• Structured rollup of account entities via a Global Hierarchy
• Legacy System Elimination During ERP Transition
• Visible Financial Information, Eliminates "After the Fact"
• Reduced IS Spending
• Reliable Information for Pricing
Honeywell
UOM 102802 Page 25

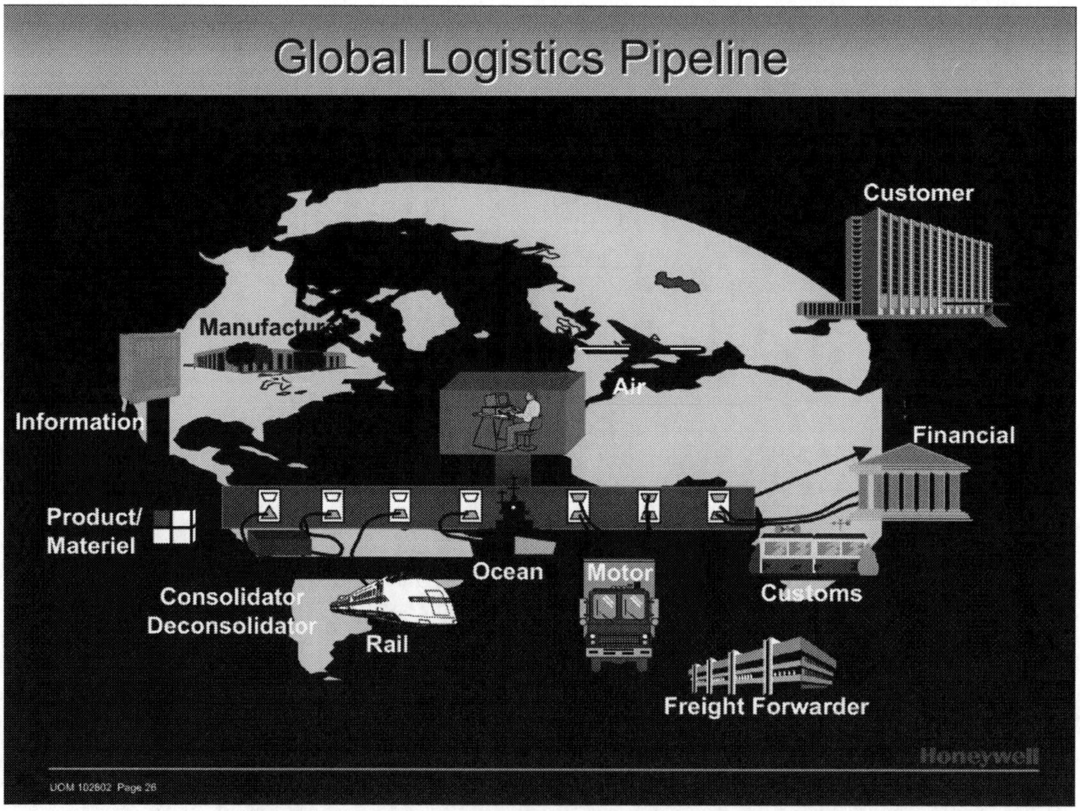
Global Logistics Pipeline
Customer
Manufacture
Air
Information
Financial
Product/ Materiel
Ocean
Motor
Customs
Consolidator Deconsolidator
Rail
Freight Forwarder
Honeywell
UOM 102802 Page 26

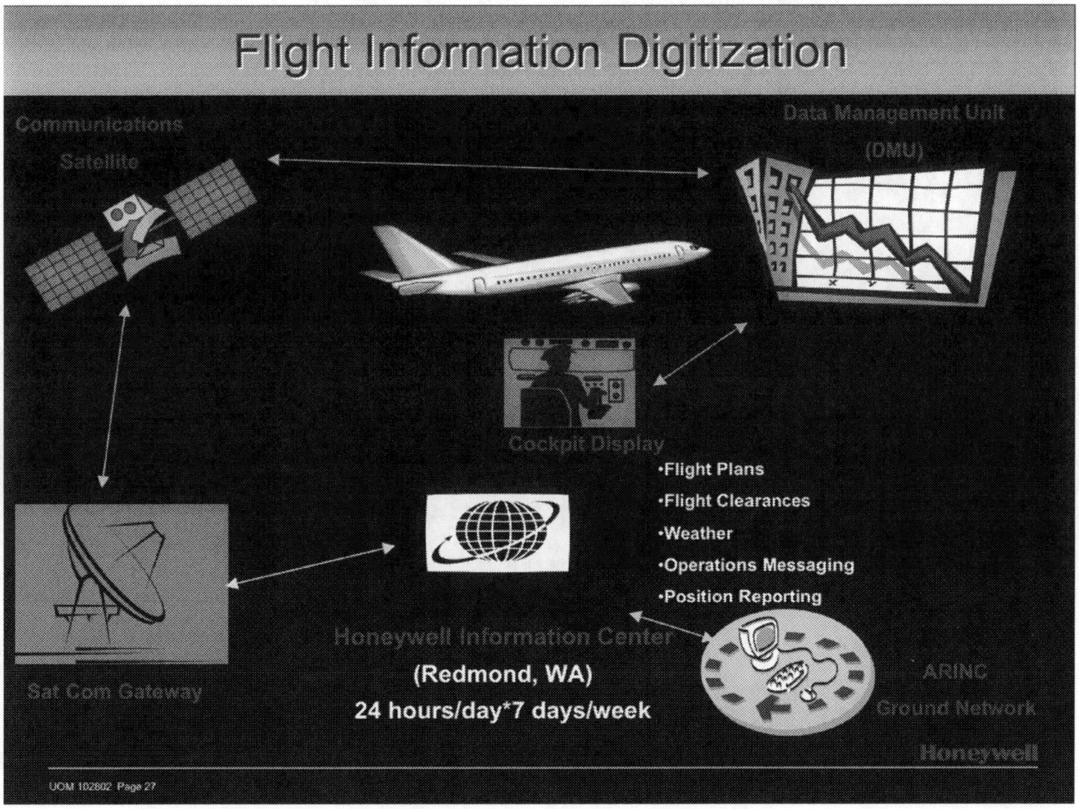
Flight Information Digitization
Communications
Satellite
Data Management Unit
(DMU)
Cockpit Display
•Flight Plans
•Flight Clearances
•Weather
•Operations Messaging
•Position Reporting
Honeywell Information Center
(Redmond, WA)
24 hours/day*7 days/week
Sat Com Gateway
ARINC
Ground Network
Honeywell
UOM 102802 Page 27

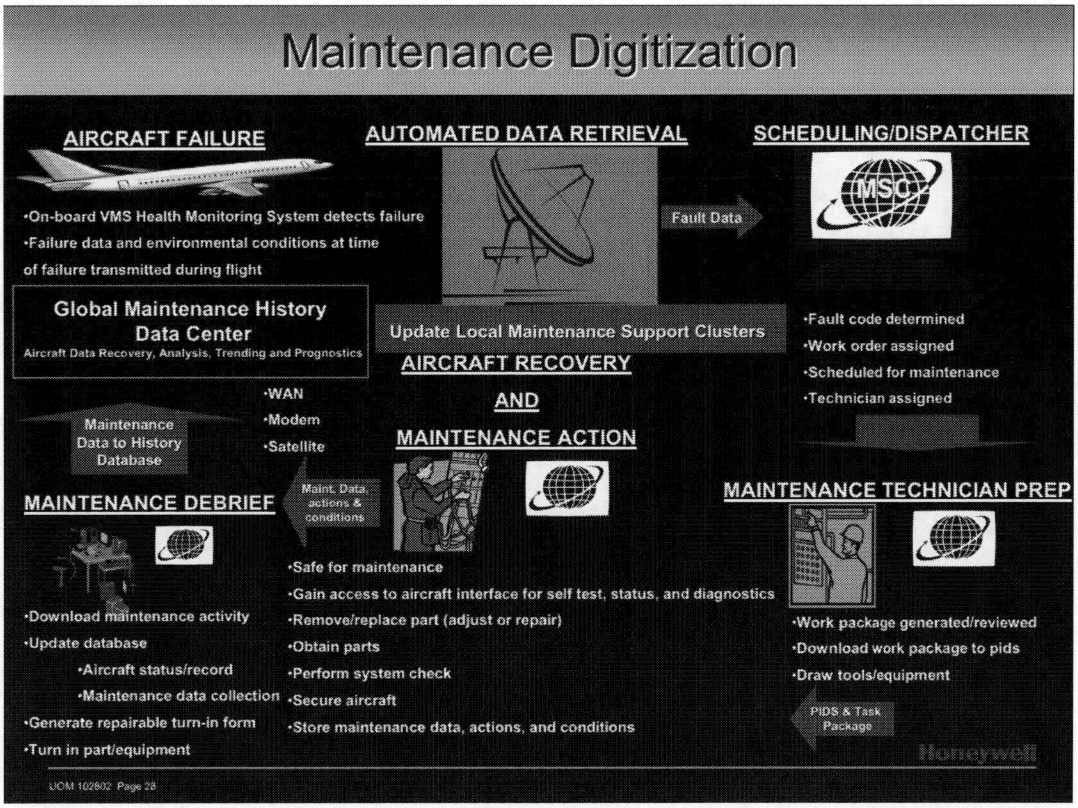
Maintenance Digitization
AIRCRAFT FAILURE
•On-board VMS Health Monitoring System detects failure
•Failure data and environmental conditions at time
of failure transmitted during flight
AUTOMATED DATA RETRIEVAL
Fault Data
SCHEDULING/DISPATCHER
MSC
Global Maintenance History
Data Center
Aircraft Data Recovery, Analysis, Trending and Prognostics
Update Local Maintenance Support Clusters
•Fault code determined
•Work order assigned
•Scheduled for maintenance
•Technician assigned
AIRCRAFT RECOVERY
AND
MAINTENANCE ACTION
Maintenance
Data to History
Database
•WAN
•Modem
•Satellite
MAINTENANCE DEBRIEF
Maint. Data, actions & conditions
MAINTENANCE TECHNICIAN PREP
•Safe for maintenance
•Gain access to aircraft interface for self test, status, and diagnostics
•Remove/replace part (adjust or repair)
•Obtain parts
•Perform system check
•Secure aircraft
•Store maintenance data, actions, and conditions
•Download maintenance activity
•Update database
•Aircraft status/record
•Maintenance data collection
•Generate repairable turn-in form
•Turn in part/equipment
•Work package generated/reviewed
•Download work package to pids
•Draw tools/equipment
PIDS & Task Package
Honeywell
UOM 102802 Page 28

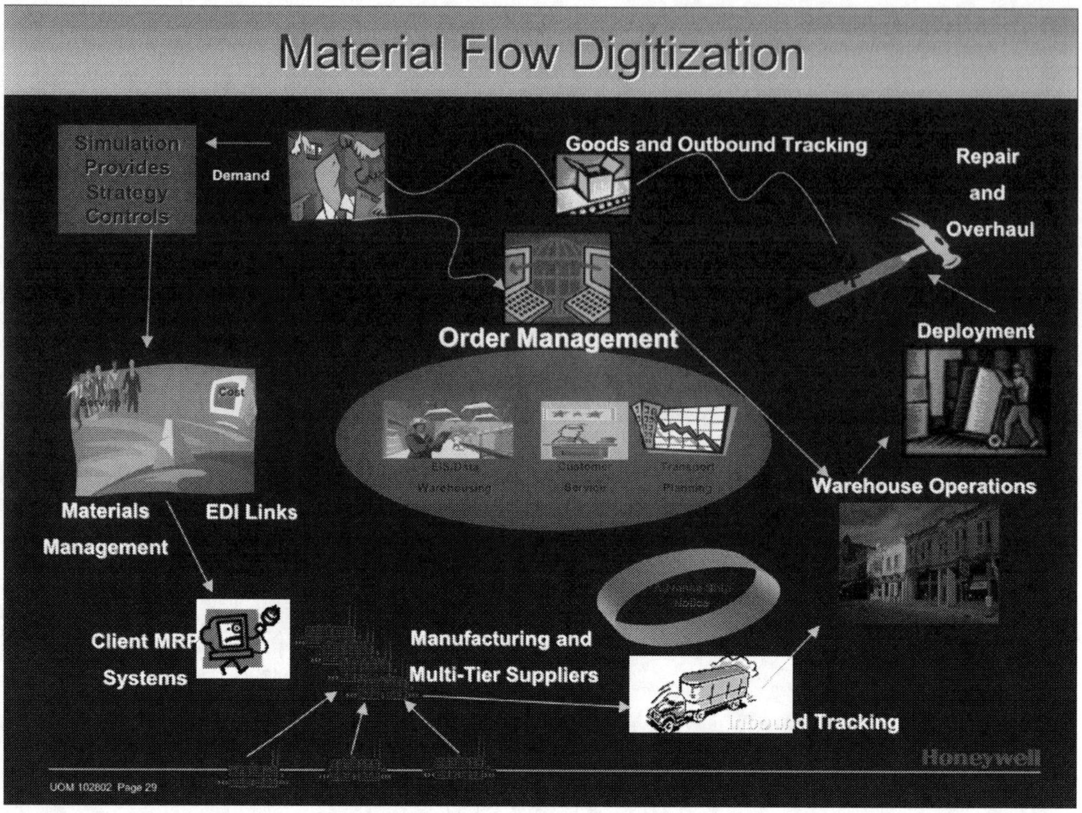

Material Flow Digitization
Simulation Provides Strategy Controls
Demand
Goods and Outbound Tracking
Repair and Overhaul
Order Management
Deployment
Warehouse Operations
Materials Management
EDI Links
Client MRP Systems
Manufacturing and Multi-Tier Suppliers
Inbound Tracking
Honeywell
UOM 102802 Page 29

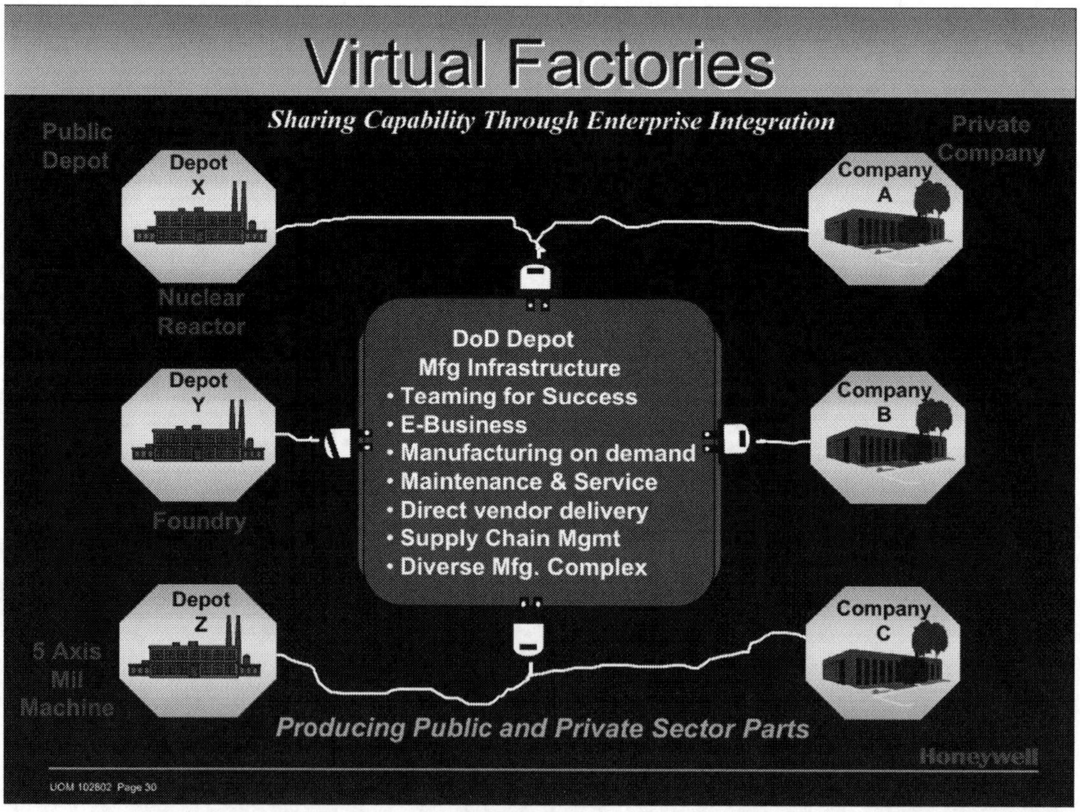

Virtual Factories
Sharing Capability Through Enterprise Integration
Public Depot
Private Company
Depot X
Company A
Nuclear Reactor
DoD Depot
Mfg Infrastructure
• Teaming for Success
• E-Business
• Manufacturing on demand
• Maintenance & Service
• Direct vendor delivery
• Supply Chain Mgmt
• Diverse Mfg. Complex
Depot Y
Company B
Foundry
Depot Z
Company C
5 Axis Mil Machine
Producing Public and Private Sector Parts
Honeywell
UOM 102802 Page 30

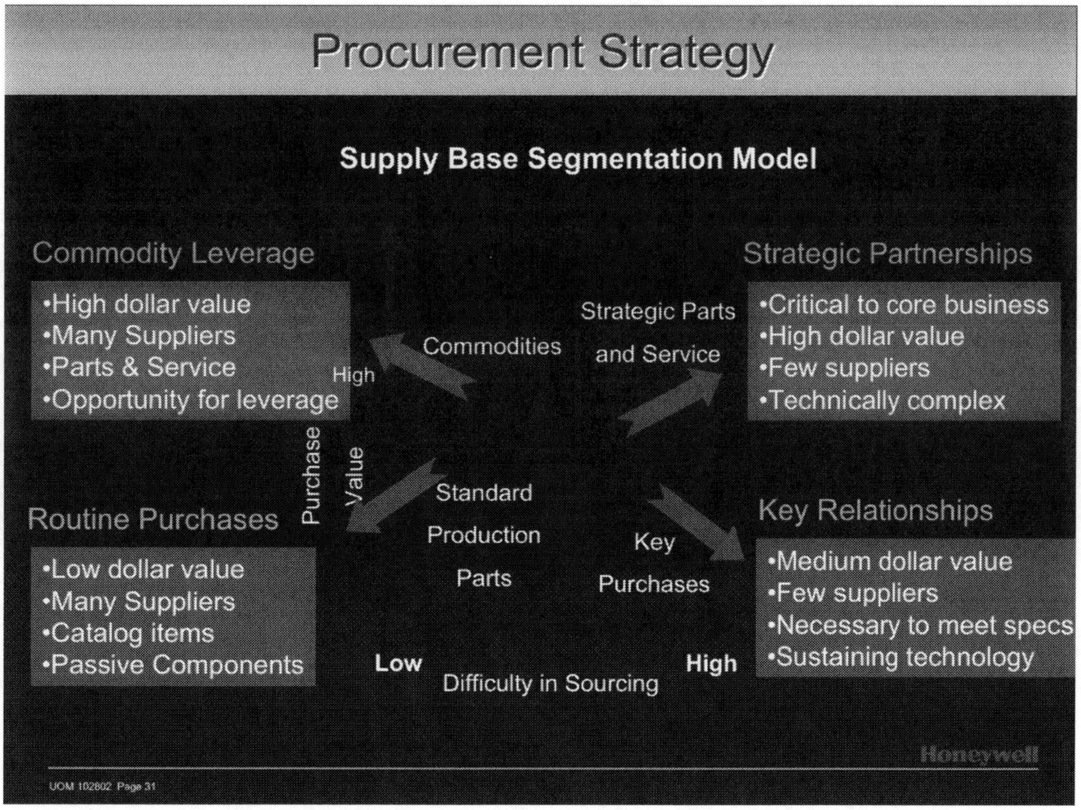

Performance-Based Contracting

- **Establish jointly-determined levels of performance**
- **Reward superior performance and risk taking**
- **Value increases as mutual goals are attained**

Metric	Goal, %	Actual, %
Receipts (Same day)	100	99.75
Shipments (Same day)	90	100
Emergence Shipments	100	100
On Time delivery	98.00	98.27
Inventory accuracy	99.99	99.99
Delivery accuracy	99.99	100

Goals and results of sample Cat Logistics client

Honeywell

UOM 102802 Page 32

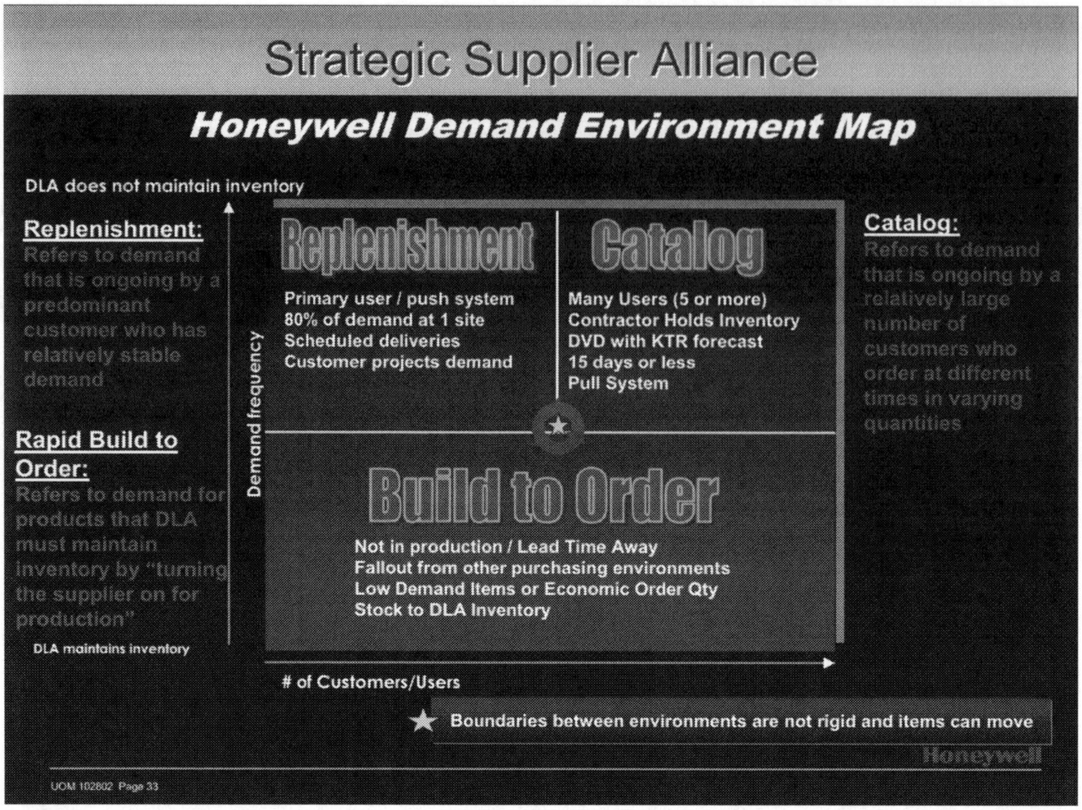

SSA - EXPAND/GROW THE PROGRAM

- Add Parts (2300/yr current pace)
  - Sole Source (150K population)
  - Competitive (300K population)
  - 3rd Party (TBD)
- Add Sites (currently only 5 cages under contract: 99193, 59364, 70210, 9X173 & 64547)
  - Aircraft Landing Systems, South Bend, IN (CAGE 55284)
  - Hardware Products Group, Tempe, AZ (CAGE 1RDZ1)
  - Urbana, OH (CAGE 72919)
  - Albuquerque, NM (CAGE 55972)
  - Boyne City, MI (CAGE 96774)
- Add Services (Honeywell can provide additional value)
  - List Management
  - Surge
  - Accelerated Virtual One Pass Pricing Events
- Add Non-Aerospace Products (Honeywell is not just an aerospace company)
  - Automotive
  - Home Controls
- Add Customers
  - Navy, Army, Air Force, Coast Guard, National Guard
  - FMS
  - DOE
  - NASA

Value Proposition Can Be Expanded

Honeywell

UOM 102802 Page 34

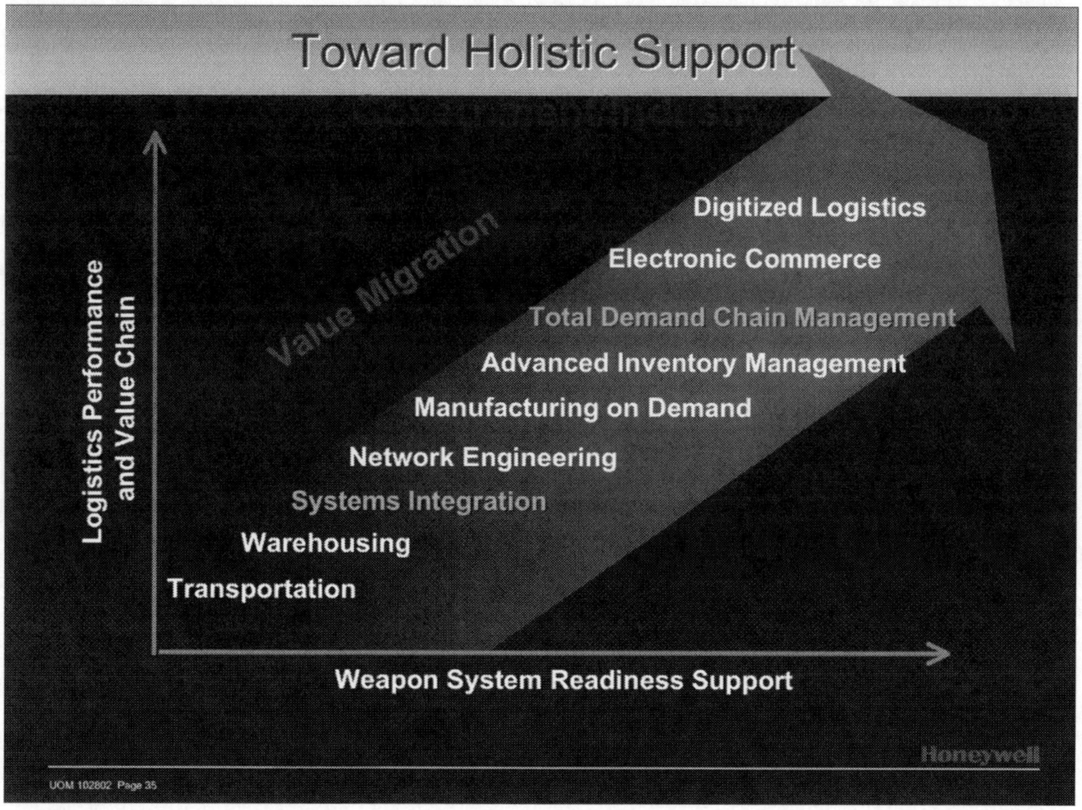
Toward Holistic Support
Logistics Performance and Value Chain
Value Migration
Digitized Logistics
Electronic Commerce
Total Demand Chain Management
Advanced Inventory Management
Manufacturing on Demand
Network Engineering
Systems Integration
Warehousing
Transportation
Weapon System Readiness Support
Honeywell
UOM 102802 Page 35

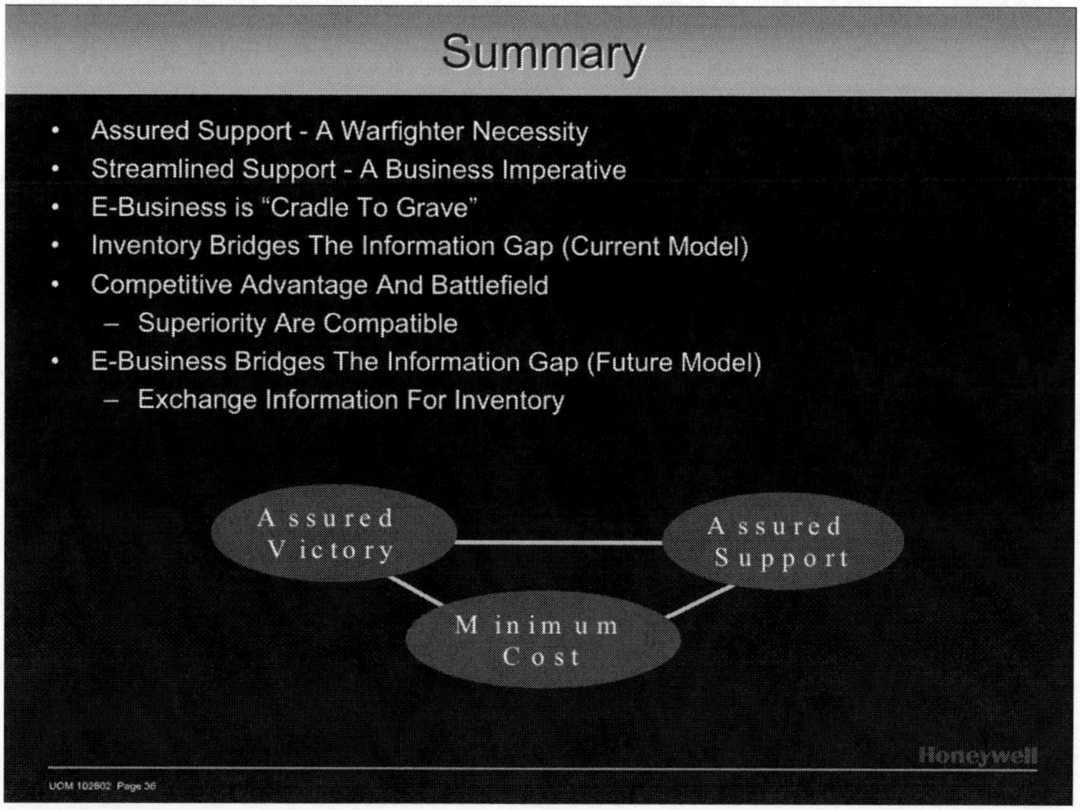
Summary
• Assured Support - A Warfighter Necessity
• Streamlined Support - A Business Imperative
• E-Business is "Cradle To Grave"
• Inventory Bridges The Information Gap (Current Model)
• Competitive Advantage And Battlefield
– Superiority Are Compatible
• E-Business Bridges The Information Gap (Future Model)
– Exchange Information For Inventory
Assured Victory
Assured Support
Minimum Cost
Honeywell
UOM 102802 Page 36

From Silos to Satisfaction: The Next Level of Logistics Performance

SOLE 2003 Conference

Eric Stange
13 August 2003

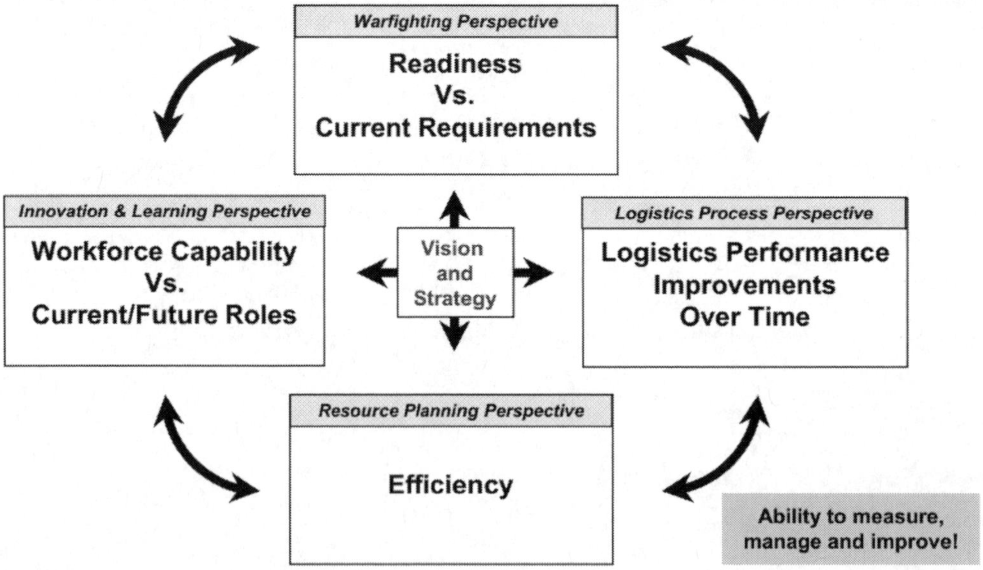

accenture

Management Principles

Enterprise Integration is the overarching enabler – governance/corporate decision making is the key!

- **Use BSC Key Drivers to align/converge selected programs**
- **Make definitive plans to shut off laggards/resource drains**
- **Enterprise approach for 6 key solution components (next)**
- **Take advantage of SLA's and performance based contracts to minimize "business risk" and maximize potential return on investment**

A handful of key decisions can make the difference between success and failure…

accenture

Key Enterprise Solution Components

- ***ERP*** **– delivers standard and flexible business processes, consistent transaction engine, dependable management information, integrated financial data**
- ***APS/SCM*** **– enables sophisticated demand planning and forecasting, supply planning and synchronization, collaboration across enterprise and with external stakeholders**
- ***IDE*** **– supports extended transformed business processes across enterprise, best of breed event management solutions**
- ***Corporate Data Strategy/Active Data Warehouse*** **- delivers critical support to BSC, TAV, and DRRS objectives from a single data source – "one version of the truth"**
- ***Customer Relationship Management*** **– defines enterprise customer, simplifies customer contact points, provides integrated customer view, cost savings from faster problem resolution and staff optimization**
- ***Integrated Performance Management*** **– provides basis for learning and institutionalizing transformed business model across workforce**

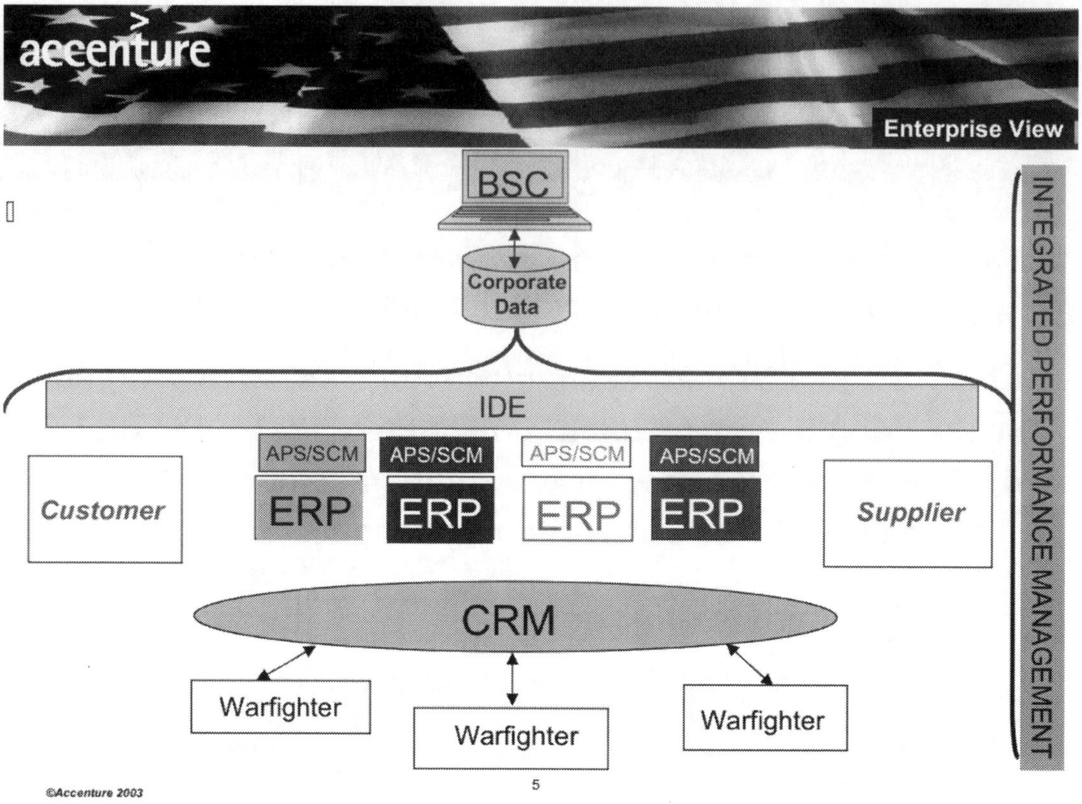
accenture
Enterprise View
BSC
Corporate Data
IDE
APS/SCM
APS/SCM
APS/SCM
APS/SCM
Customer
ERP
ERP
ERP
ERP
Supplier
CRM
Warfighter
Warfighter
Warfighter
INTEGRATED PERFORMANCE MANAGEMENT
©Accenture 2003
5

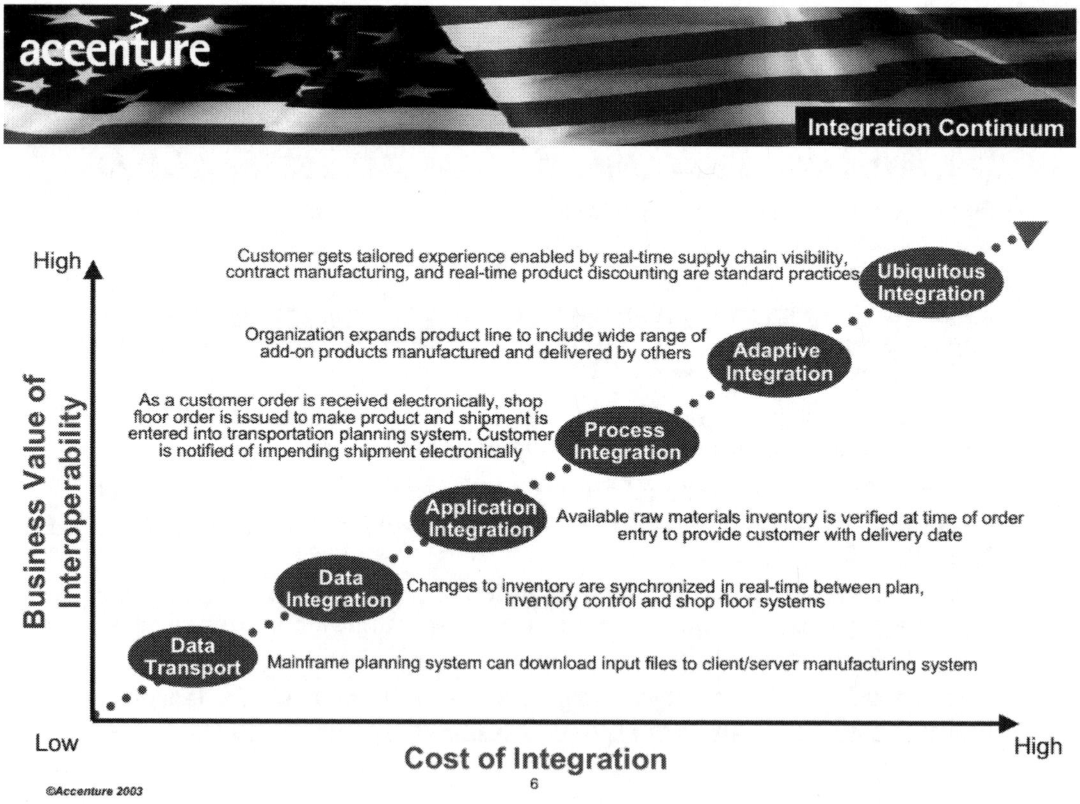
accenture
Integration Continuum
High
Business Value of Interoperability
Low
Cost of Integration
High
Data Transport
Mainframe planning system can download input files to client/server manufacturing system
Data Integration
Changes to inventory are synchronized in real-time between plan, inventory control and shop floor systems
Application Integration
Available raw materials inventory is verified at time of order entry to provide customer with delivery date
Process Integration
As a customer order is received electronically, shop floor order is issued to make product and shipment is entered into transportation planning system. Customer is notified of impending shipment electronically
Adaptive Integration
Organization expands product line to include wide range of add-on products manufactured and delivered by others
Ubiquitous Integration
Customer gets tailored experience enabled by real-time supply chain visibility, contract manufacturing, and real-time product discounting are standard practices
©Accenture 2003
6

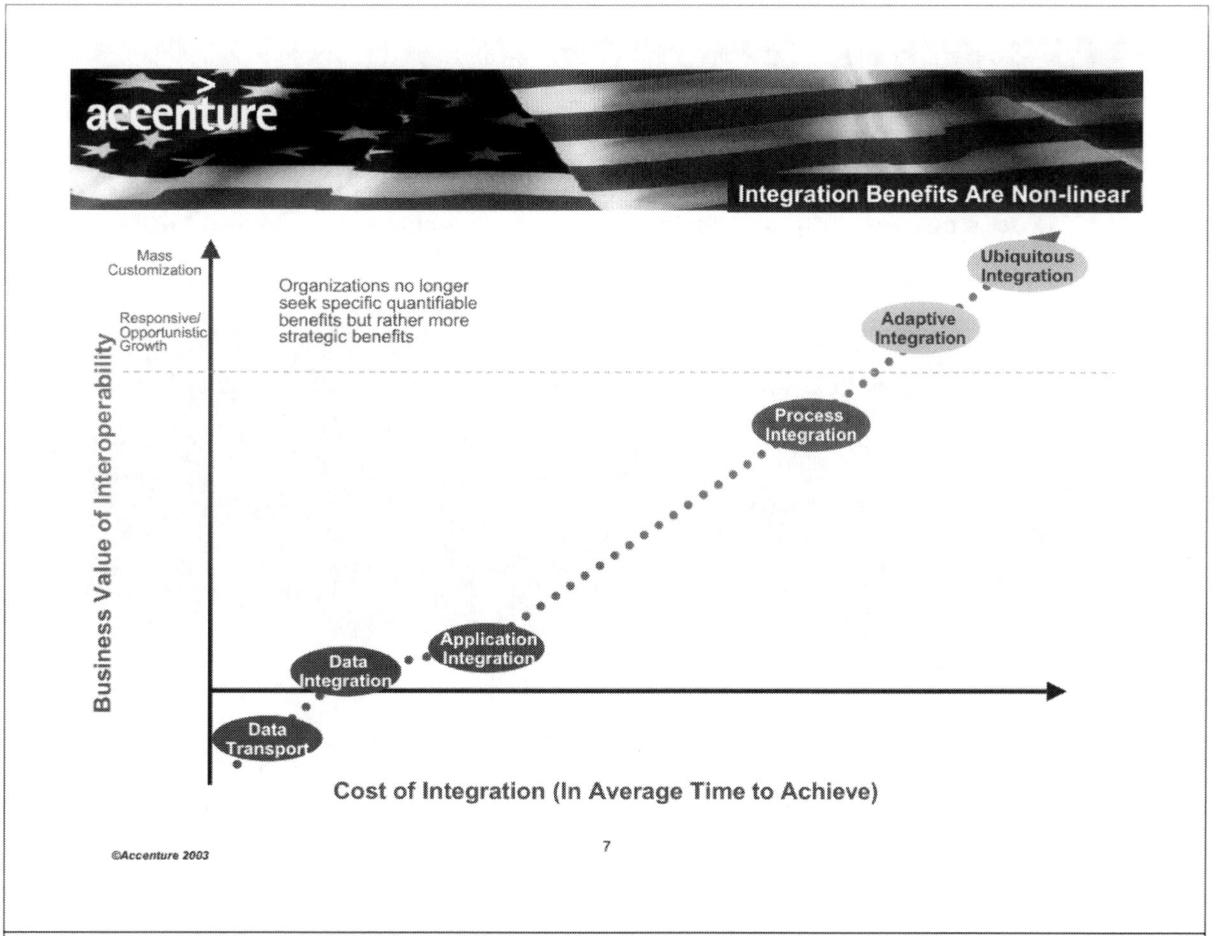
accenture
Integration Benefits Are Non-linear
Mass Customization
Responsive/ Opportunistic Growth
Organizations no longer seek specific quantifiable benefits but rather more strategic benefits
Ubiquitous Integration
Adaptive Integration
Process Integration
Application Integration
Data Integration
Data Transport
Business Value of Interoperability
Cost of Integration (In Average Time to Achieve)
©Accenture 2003
7

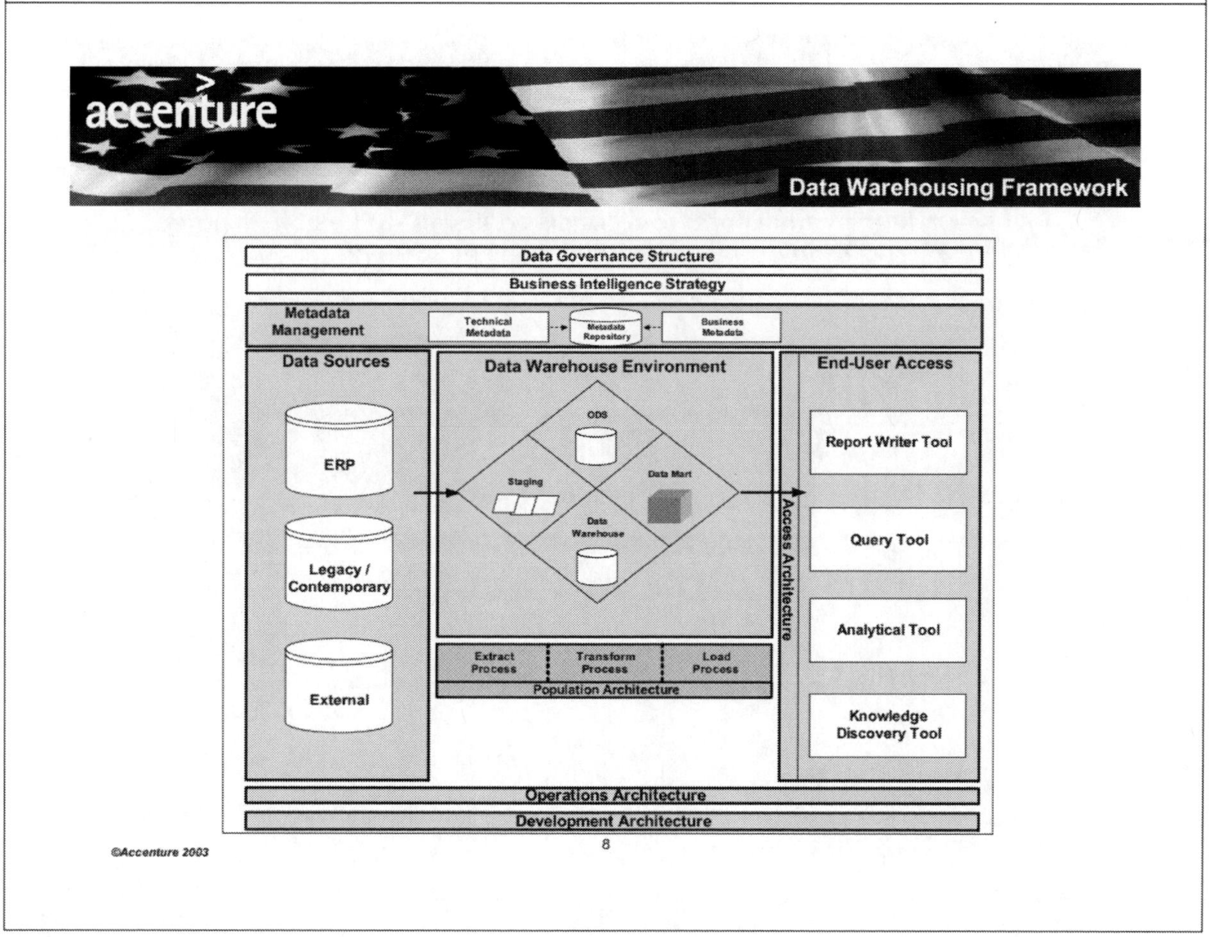
accenture
Data Warehousing Framework
Data Governance Structure
Business Intelligence Strategy
Metadata Management
Technical Metadata
Metadata Repository
Business Metadata
Data Sources
ERP
Legacy / Contemporary
External
Data Warehouse Environment
ODS
Staging
Data Mart
Data Warehouse
Extract Process
Transform Process
Load Process
Population Architecture
Access Architecture
End-User Access
Report Writer Tool
Query Tool
Analytical Tool
Knowledge Discovery Tool
Operations Architecture
Development Architecture
©Accenture 2003
8

accenture

Customer Relationship Management

Focus on providing the capabilities needed to achieve the desired future state

Today's Challenge	Service Effectiveness	Tomorrow's Outcomes
• Internal Optimization Focus		• Warfighter Outcome Focus
• Reactive to Customer Complaints		• Collaborative Planning
• Limited, Ad-hoc Dialogue		• Structured Customer Relationships
• One Size Fits All		• Customized Services @ Enterprise Scale
• Redundant, Siloed Customer Touchpoints		• Integrated Service Channels
• Internal and Warfighter Confusion		• Common Expectations and Understanding
• No Consolidated Customer View		• Enterprise Customer Portal
• Services defined by Provider		• Flexible Services Negotiated w/ Customer
• Limited Enterprise Integration		• Customer-Centric Enterprise Integration
• Missing Data Limits Fact-based analysis		• Fact-based Hypothesis Testing
• Limited Customer Analytic tools and training		• Robust, Flexible Customer Analytic Capability
• Cannot measure Customer Cost to Serve		•Customer Cost to Serve managed

9

accenture

CRM for the Warfighter...

... involves a fundamental shift from "one size fits all" to flexible, tailored warfighter services which can evolve and scale as needed.

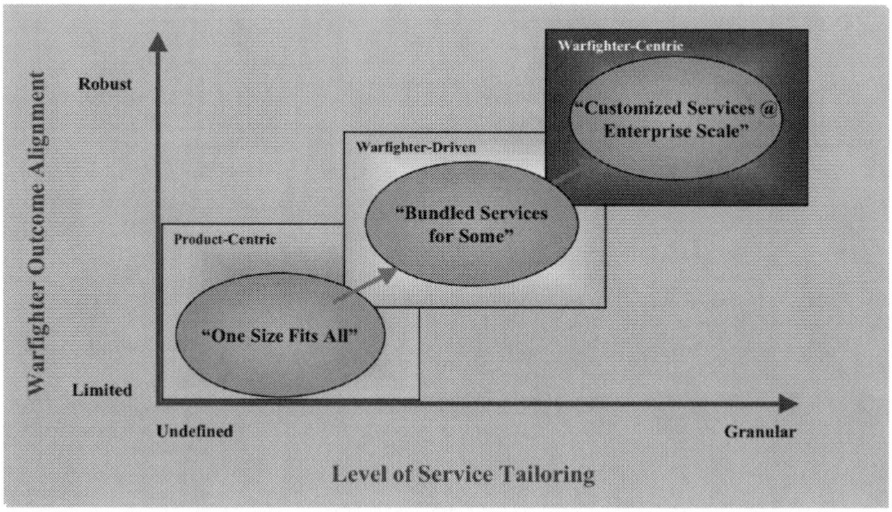

10

accenture

True Transformation is Hard, and Relying on IT Alone is Risky

Transformation Program Facts

- **ERP** implementations fail at a very high rate. Some have suggested that 70 percent of implementations fail to meet stated objectives[1]
- Upwards of 70, 80, even 90% of **CRM** implementations don't deliver on their original promise.[2]
- 61% of **acquisitions** in the past three years destroyed shareholder value[3]

Contributing Factors

- Leadership/Sponsorship
- Organizational Awareness and Alignment
- Interdepartmental Communication & Integration
- Workforce Performance
  - Competence
  - Capability
  - Confidence
- Motivation
- Commitment and Incentives

[1] "APICS – The Performance Advantage," Volume 10 No. 13, January 2001
[2] "Why CRM Implementations Fail ...and What to Do About It", LGH Consulting
[3] "Mergers: Who Most Big Deals Don't Pay Off," *BusinessWeek*, 10/14/2002

11

accenture

A Different Approach May Be Necessary

Focus on performance improvement...not just training

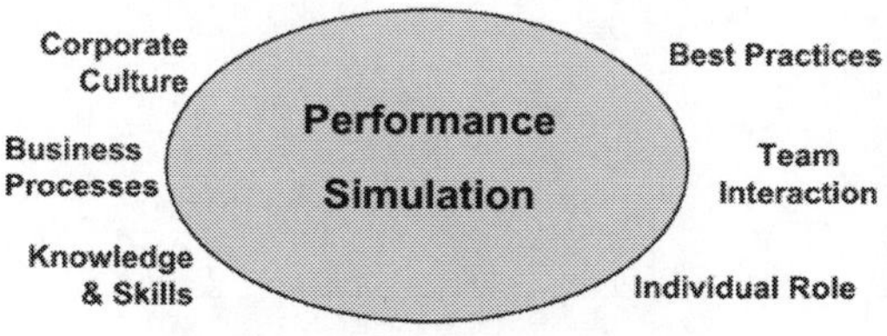

Multi-dimensional behavior change

Increase Retention

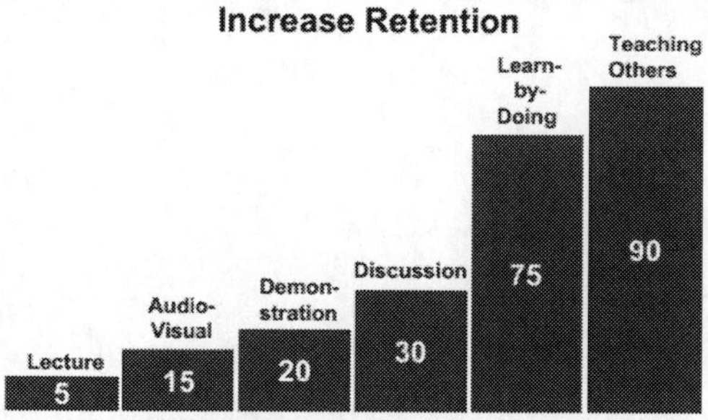

Improve decision-making skills

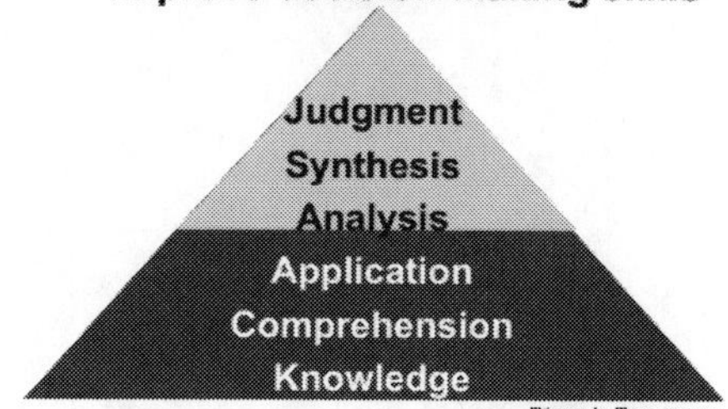

Bloom's Taxonomy

Reduce time to competency and decrease time away from the job

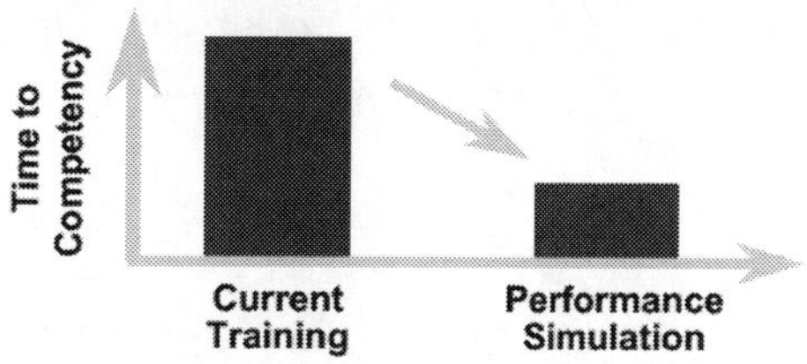

2

accenture

Summary

- IT Solution Components Available, Proven and Getting Even Better Every Day
- Enterprise Integration Necessary to Achieve Next Level of Performance
- Complete Success Requires Greater Attention and New Approaches to Institutionalize New Ways of Doing Business

LOGCOM

INTERNATIONAL SOCIETY OF LOGISTICS (SOLE)

13 AUG 2003

MR. R. KEN TRAMMELL
DEPUTY COMMANDER
MARINE CORPS LOGISTICS COMMAND

Operational Relevance

LOGCOM

LOGCOM — Our Mission

- Provide worldwide, integrated logistics/supply chain and distribution management; depot level maintenance management; and strategic prepositioning capability in support of the operating forces and other supported units to maximize their readiness and sustainability and to support enterprise and program level Total Life Cycle Management (TLCM).

Operational Relevance

LOGCOM — Who We Are – Department Level

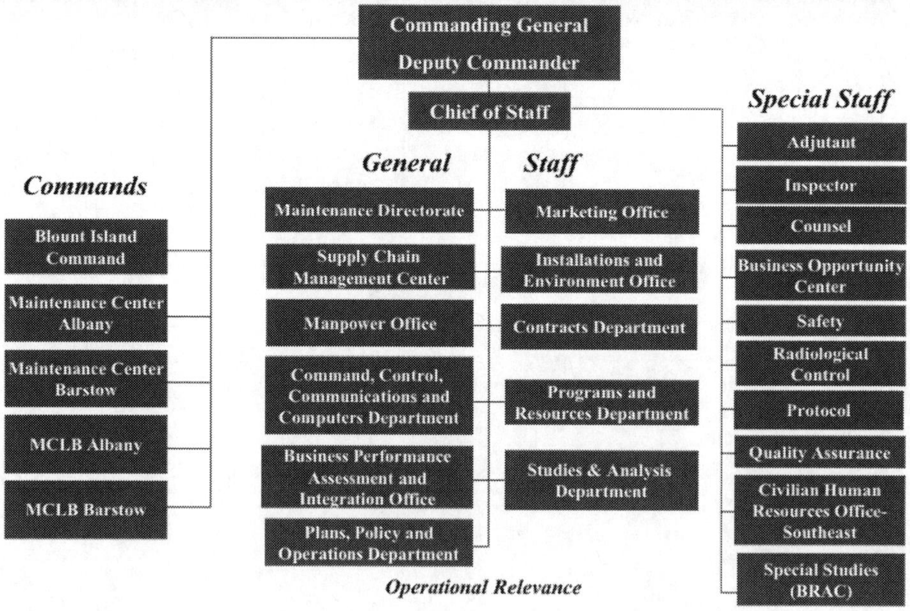

Operational Relevance

LOGCOM

Where We Are

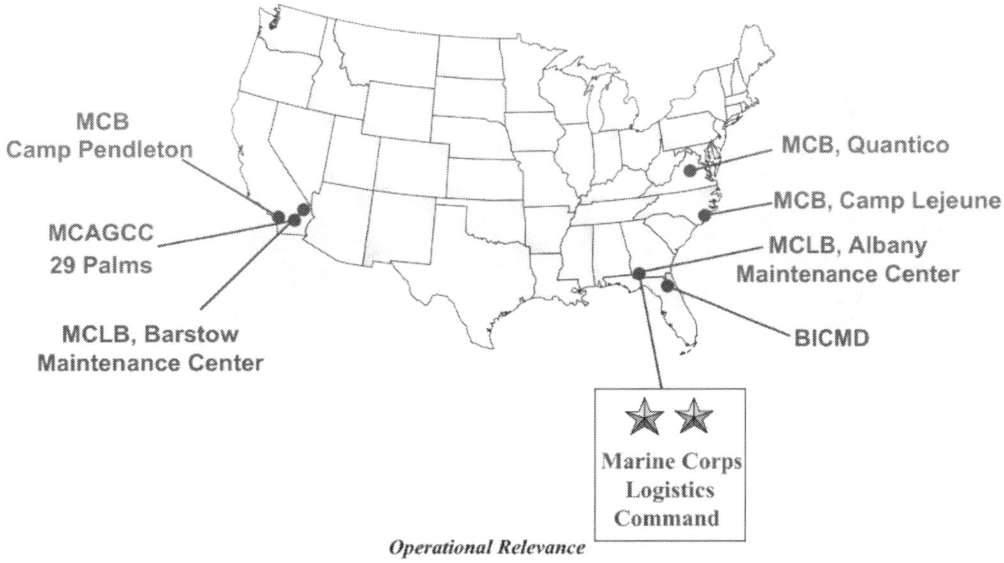

Operational Relevance

LOGCOM

Blount Island Command
Jacksonville, FL

Maintenance Center
Barstow, CA

Maintenance Center
Albany, GA

LOGCOM What We Do

- Maintenance Management
- Supply Chain Management
- Strategic Prepositioning

Operational Relevance

LOGCOM Maintenance Center

Operational Relevance

LOGCOM

Supply Chain Management Center

- Materiel Management Across the Supply Chain
- Inventory Strategies and Policies
- Maintenance Planning
- Distribution Planning
- Supplier Relationship Management
- Customer Relationship Management
- Logistics Information Management
- Initial Issue Provisioning Support

Operational Relevance

LOGCOM

Maritime Prepositioning

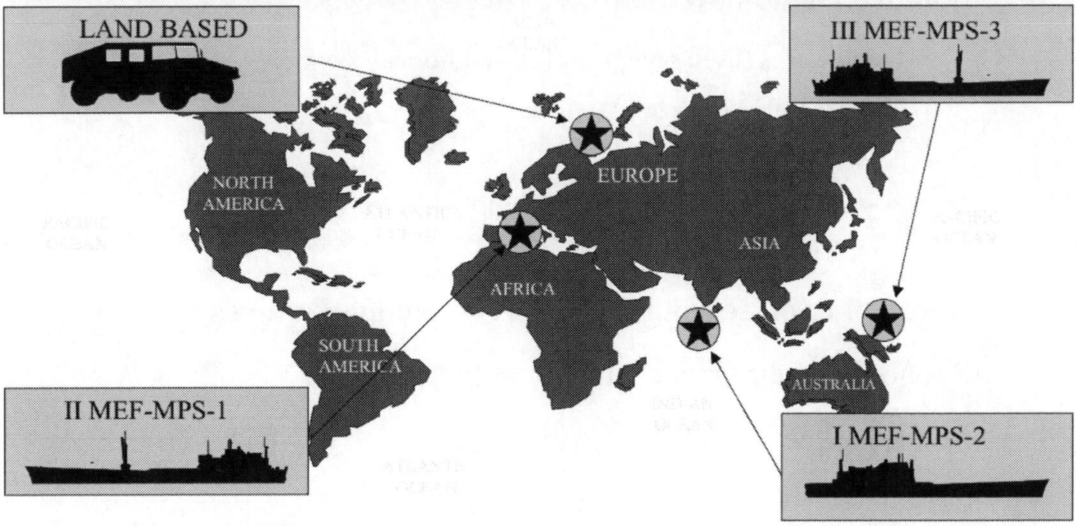

Operational Relevance

LOGCOM

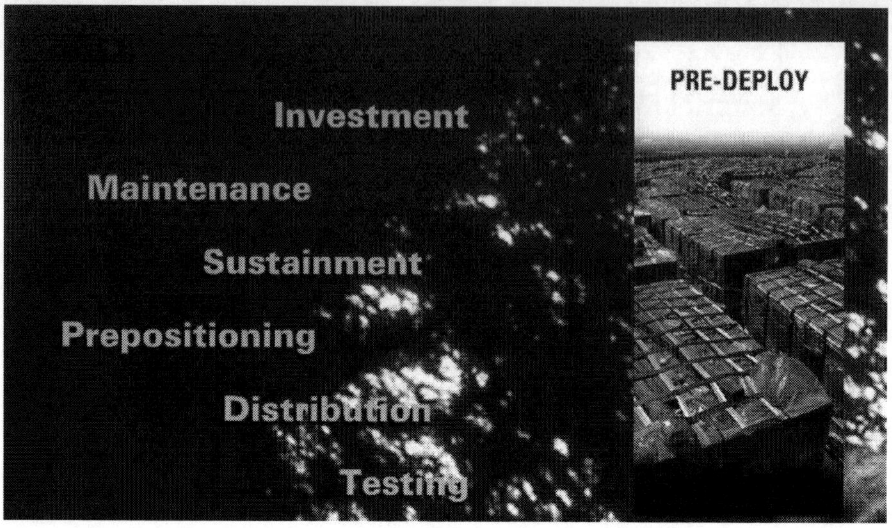

Operational Relevance

LOGCOM

THEORY OF CONSTRAINTS

- Improved Readiness
  - Marine Corps (used savings to fund additional workload)
    - Added 30 MK48's to FY-02 line
    - Added 10 MK15 Trailers
    - Added 4 LAV-25's and 2 POP (SLEP) vehicles
    - Added 4 MK17 Trailers
- Ahead of or on schedule for all TOC production lines
- Reduced Repair Cycle Time by at least 50%
- Reduced Quantity of Assets in Maintenance (WIP) by up to 50%

Operational Relevance

LOGCOM

THEORY OF CONSTRAINTS

MK-48
Repair Cycle Time (Days)

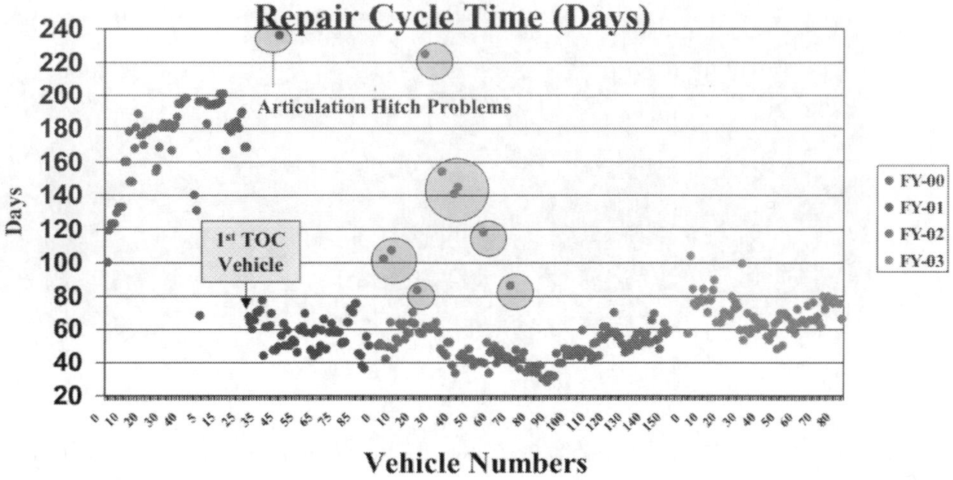

Data Source: Concerto Activity By Project Records

Operational Relevance

LOGCOM

GROUND COMBAT EQUIPMENT READINESS

MERIT

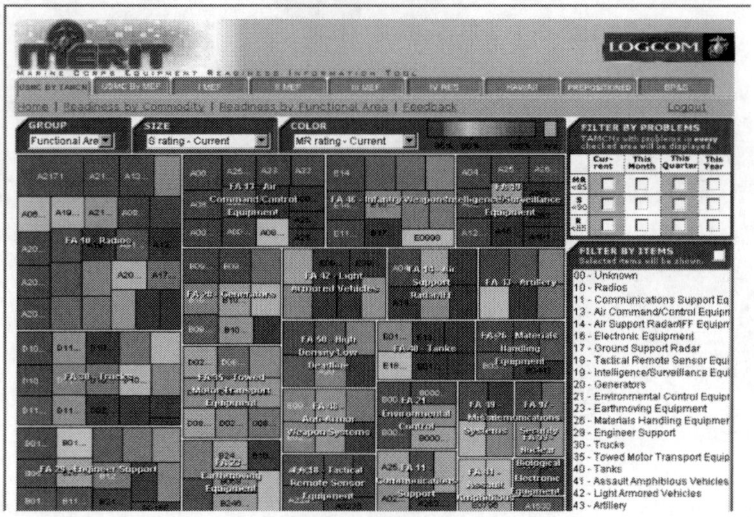

Operational Relevance

LOGCOM

Operational Relevance

LOGCOM

Successes

Loading / Unloading Teams

Operational Relevance

Operational Relevance

Operational Relevance

LOGCOM

Supply Challenges

Operational Relevance

LOGCOM

Operational Relevance

LOGCOM BA 5590 SUBSTITUTE

Operational Relevance

LOGCOM

Operational Relevance

LOGCOM

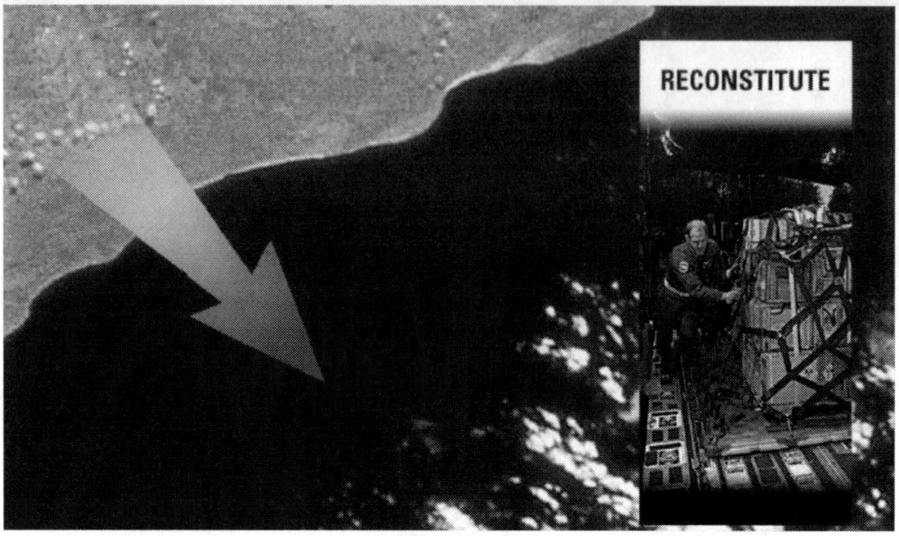

Operational Relevance

LOGCOM Contact / Liaison Teams

Operational Relevance

LOGCOM

Operational Relevance

LOGCOM

Operational Relevance

LOGCOM

Operational Relevance

LOGCOM

Operational Relevance

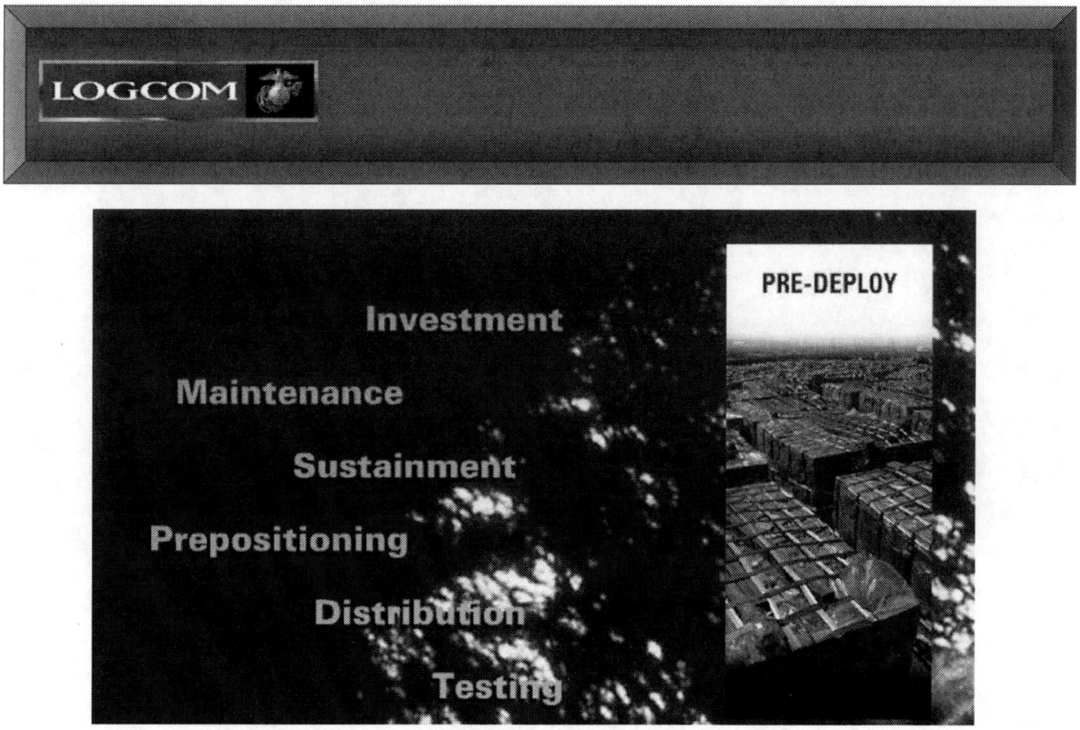

Operational Relevance

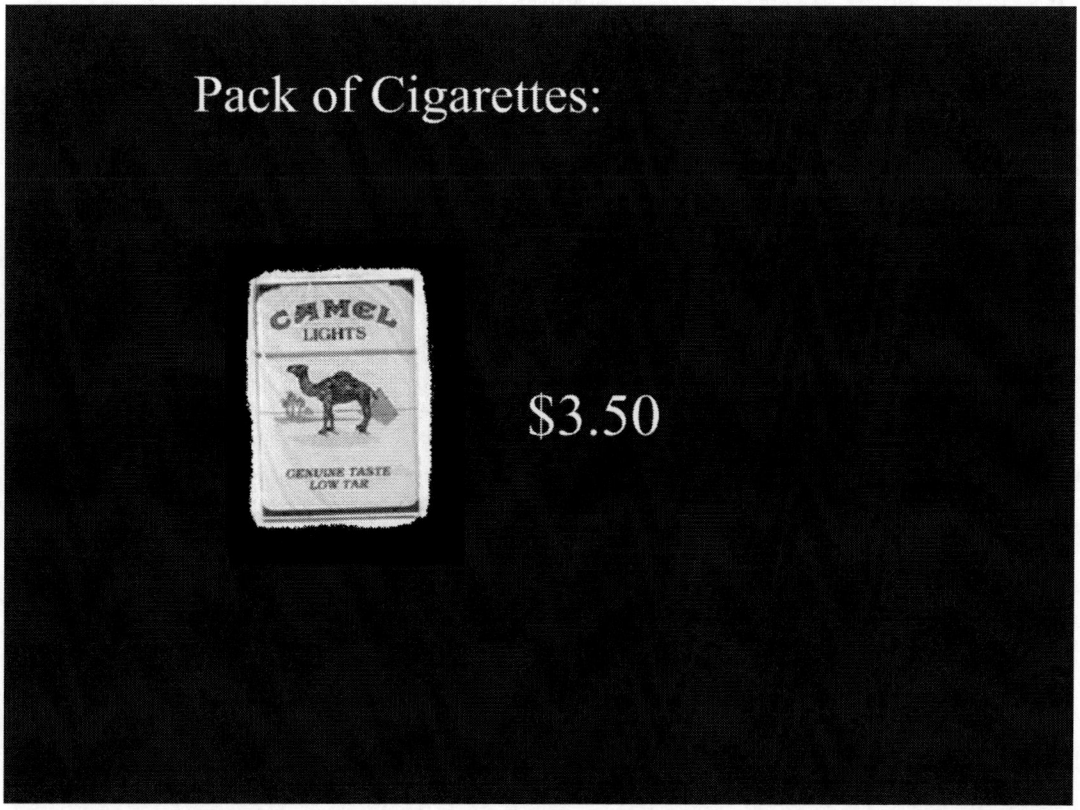

French Provincial Chair:

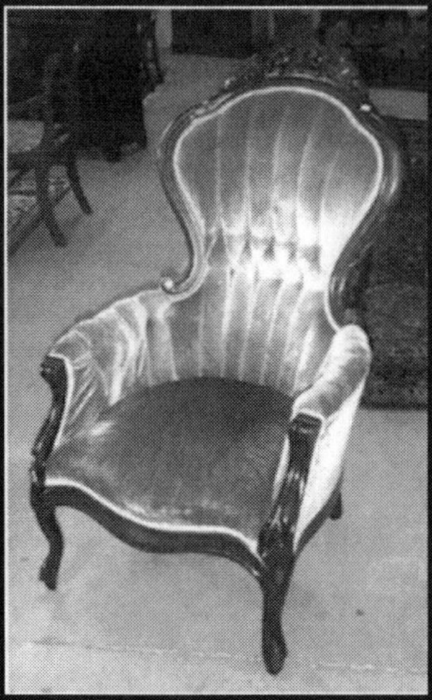

$500.00

Lighting up in Saddam's living room and dropping your ashes wherever the Hell you want:

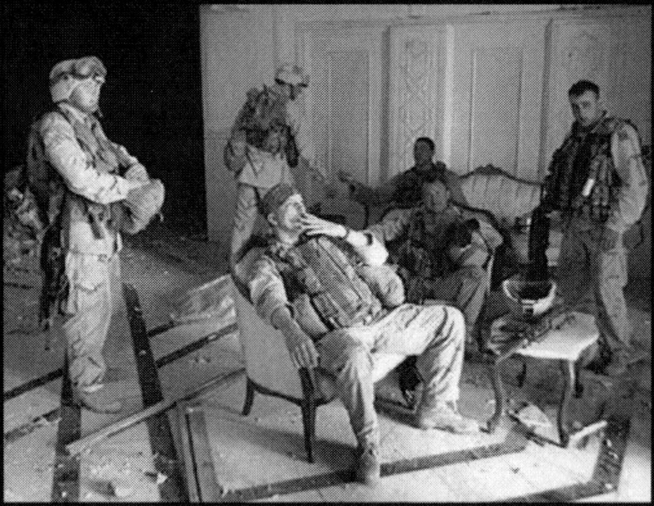

PRICELESS!

There are some things diplomacy can achieve.

For everything else, there's the

United States Marine Corps

Marines

UNITED STATES MARINE CORPS

Anywhere They Want To Be!

SOLE 2003

The Future Logistics Workforce for SOLE-The International Society of Logistics
Huntsville, Alabama
13 August 2003

Frank J. Anderson, Jr.
President, Defense Acquisition University
BOA Member: SOLE The International Society of Logistics

CUBIC

0157-0

0181-0

DAU: A Focus on Practitioner Training

Mission: Provide practitioner training and services to enable the Acquisition, Technology, and Logistics community to make smart business decisions and deliver timely and affordable capabilities to the warfighter

The Evolving AT&L Workforce

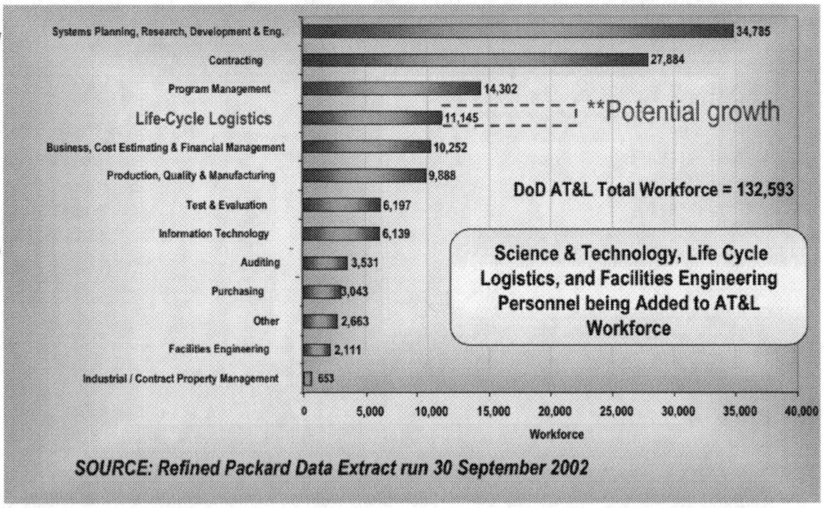

Shifting Logistics Workforce Skill-set

OLD Integrated Logistics Support (ILS) Manager

NEW Life Cycle Logistics Manager

Overwhelming **L**ogistics **D**ogma
- "ilities" zealots
- Support element cults
- Forgot the "integrated"
- Transactional Logistics
- Drove PM's crazy

Networked **E**2E for **W**arfighters
- Systems engineering driven
- Commercial practices enablers
- Product support integrators
- Outcome (readiness) oriented
- Service to the PM's

At the Heart of the Transformation

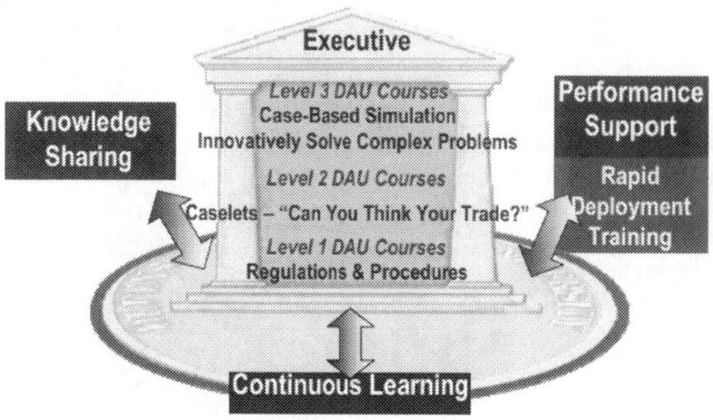

AT&L Performance Learning Model

- **Curriculum modernization**
- **Continuous learning**
- **Performance support**
- **Evolving practices**
- **Knowledge sharing / Communities of Practice**

DAU Alignment with FLE Implementation

Certification Curriculum and Executive Education

- Executive Program coverage (emphasis on TLCSM) – Nov 01
- PM Curriculum increased coverage – Jan 02
- PBL Course Deployment – October 2003
- Sustainment Fundamentals Course Deployment – Jan 04
- EIS/COTS PM Track Development – Sep 04
- **Life Cycle Logistics Portfolio – Oct 04**

Logistics Community Of Practice (LOG CoP)

- LOG.DAU.MIL – Oct 01
- FLE Info Source – Jan 02
- TLCSM/PBL References and Tools – Jun 02
- Performance Agreement Workshop – Oct 02
- Business Case Analysis Workshop – Feb 03
- Logistics Training and Education Information Repository – May 03
- **LOG CoP Deployed – Jul 03**

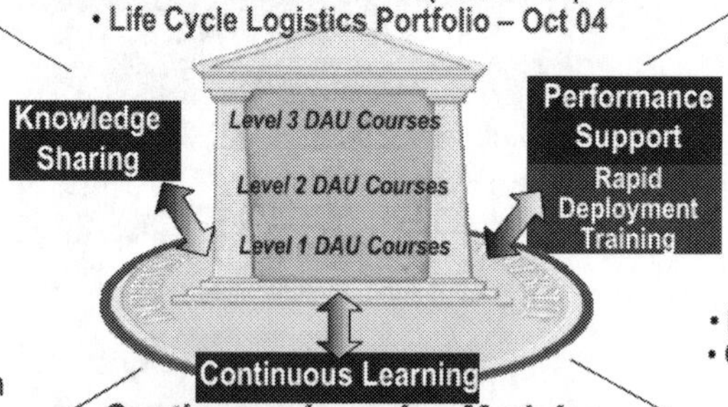

PS/RDT

- PBL Consulting – Jan 02
- Sustainment Training at Regions – Dec 02
- DoD 5000 Awareness Training – May 2003
- CJCSI 3170 Requirements/Capabilities Training – June 03
- **PBL Roadshows – Aug 03**
- Contracting for PBL – FY 04

Continuous Learning Modules

- PBL Course – Jun 2002
- Reducing Total Ownership Costs – Jan 2003
- Depot Maintenance Partnering – Jul 2003
- DLA Best Value Services – Sept 2003
- **Future Logistics Enterprise – Oct 2003**
- Supportability Emphasis in Requirements/Capabilities Development – Dec 2003
- Designing and Assessing Supportability to Reduce Logistics Footprint – FY 04
- Business Case Analysis Toolkit – FY 04

DAU Strategic Partnerships

Enhancing learner opportunities by establishing partnerships with institutions of higher learning, industry, professional associations, and other agencies

- Credit for DAU courses toward degrees (SDOE/Stevens Institute)
- Joint DAU-Industry curriculum development (Boeing and Raytheon)
- Logistics alternative certification (SOLE)
- Training MOUs with Australia and Taiwan
- GAO training

DAU…AT&L's Corporate University is helping to reshape the Logistics Workforce to meet the warfighter needs in the 21st Century.

Your Challenge:

Help Us Better Serve the Logistics Community

0157-7

0181-7

The Future Logistics Workforce

August 2003

Logistics Challenges

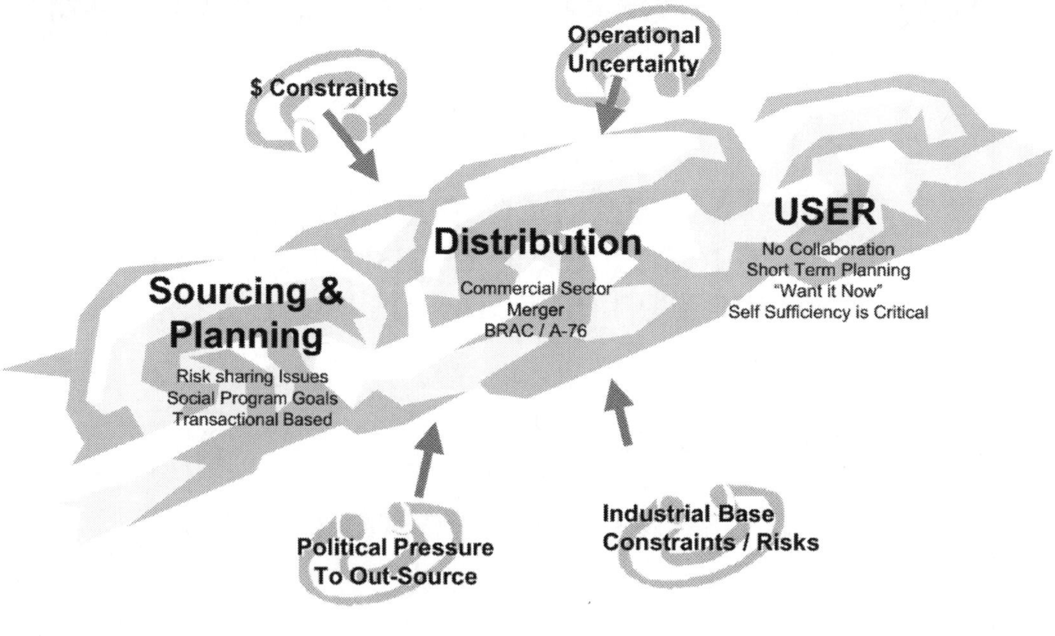

Operational Strategies

- Develop end to end policy framework
- Change the sustainment model - from breakout – not just contract out
- Foster a long term depot maintenance strategy
- Make effective use of technology and maintenance resources
- Work future demand reduction solutions with acquisition and technology

Change Strategies

- Language in QDR, DPG, and ADR
- Reports & studies
- Speeches and conferences
- Policy & doctrine
- Education and training
- Information systems
- Significant events – usually negative
- Forcing functions or personalities

My Experience

- Item and financial management
- Operational logistics
- Programming and budgeting
- Acquisition – limited
- Joint issues
- Office of the SECDEF
- The "Hill"

Observations – 30 Years

- Three distinct groups of logisticians
- Long term view is often missing
- Training and career development are by accident
- People are variable costs
- Commercial concepts are often lost in the translation
- Worked with the best people in the world

Ideas to Consider

- Enable new civilians to experience all three areas early in their careers
- Modify OPM's rules for hiring and classification
- Adopt the good parts from the military model
- Make mentoring part of senior managers' jobs
- Communicate changes and be honest
- Enable civilians to transition out to industry and back

THE FUTURE LOGISTICS WORKFORCE

Roy Beauchamp
August 2003

TRADITIONAL VIEW OF LOGISTICS

- ***Supply***

- ***Maintenance***

- ***Transportation***

4/17/2017 2

ISSUES AFFECTING THE EVOLUTION OF LOGISTICS

- Technology
- Organizational Structure
- Velocity of Operations
- Competition
- Education
- Understanding
- Globalization

4/17/2017 3

EVOLUTION OF A LOGISTICIAN

FROM A SINGLE FUNCTION		TO MULTI FUNCTIONAL
Supply Clerk/ Manager	→	Supply/Maintenance Mgr
Maintenance Technician/ Manager		Supply/Transportation Mgr
Transportation/ Traffic Manager		Maintenance/Transportation Mgr
		Supply/Maintenance/ Transportation Mgr

LOGISTICS MANAGER

SUPPLY CHAIN MANAGER

DISTRIBUTION MANAGER

4/17/2017 4

EVOLUTION OF LOGISTICS PROCESS

- Supply "Chain" Management
- E-Commerce
- Prognostics/Diagnostics
- Cargo Tracking
- In Transit Visibility
- Distribution Management
- Lifecycle Management

4/17/2017 5

IMPLICATIONS FOR THE FUTURE LOGISTICS WORKFORCE

- Know More
- Know More… Sooner
- Educated
- Trained
- Must Understand the Power of Integrated Management

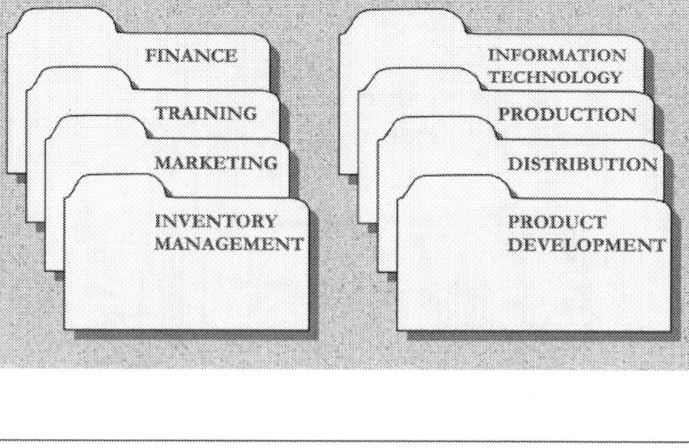

4/17/2017 6

A REDEFINITION OF LOGISTICS MANAGEMENT

The Management of All the Processes Which Affect the <u>Life Cycle Cost</u> and the <u>Life Cycle Capability</u> of a System.

4/17/2017 7

PROFILE OF THE 21ST CENTURY LOGISTICIAN

- **Realize That Logistics Is a <u>Lot</u> More Than Supply, Maintenance and Transportation**
- **Realize That It Requires "Integrated Understanding"**
- **Realize That It Requires "Integrated Management"**
- **Realize That Logistics Is a "Profession"**
- **Realize That It Is a Life-long Learning Experience**

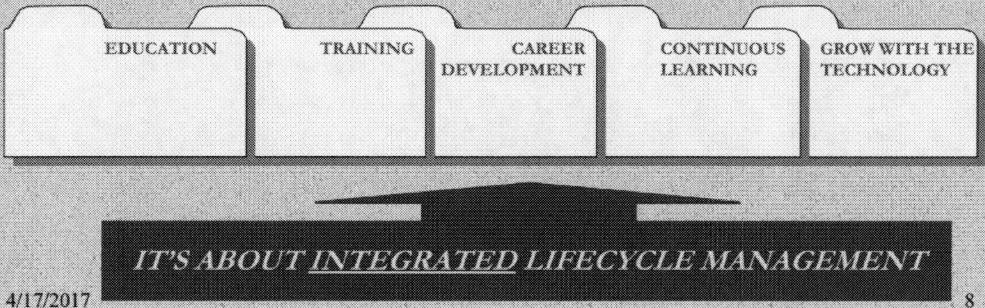

4/17/2017 8

WHAT IS REQUIRED TO ADVANCE THE PROFESSION?

- Recognition That Logistics Is a Profession!
- University Programs That Educate and Train Logisticians
- Programs That Produce "Integrated Thinkers" Because They Have an "Integrated Understanding"
- Strong, Vibrant Professional Associations
- Demanding and Comprehensive Programs That Lead to Certification
- A Commitment to Continuous Education

4/17/2017 9

WHAT SHOULD THE FUTURE LOGISTICS WORKFORCE LOOK LIKE?

- Must Be Multi-Functional -- Know
- Must Be Multi-Capable -- Do
- Must Be Leaders and Managers -- Integrate
- Must Know a Lot, But…
- Must "Know About" a Lot More

The World Has Changed From "Supply Chain Management" To…

4/17/2017 10

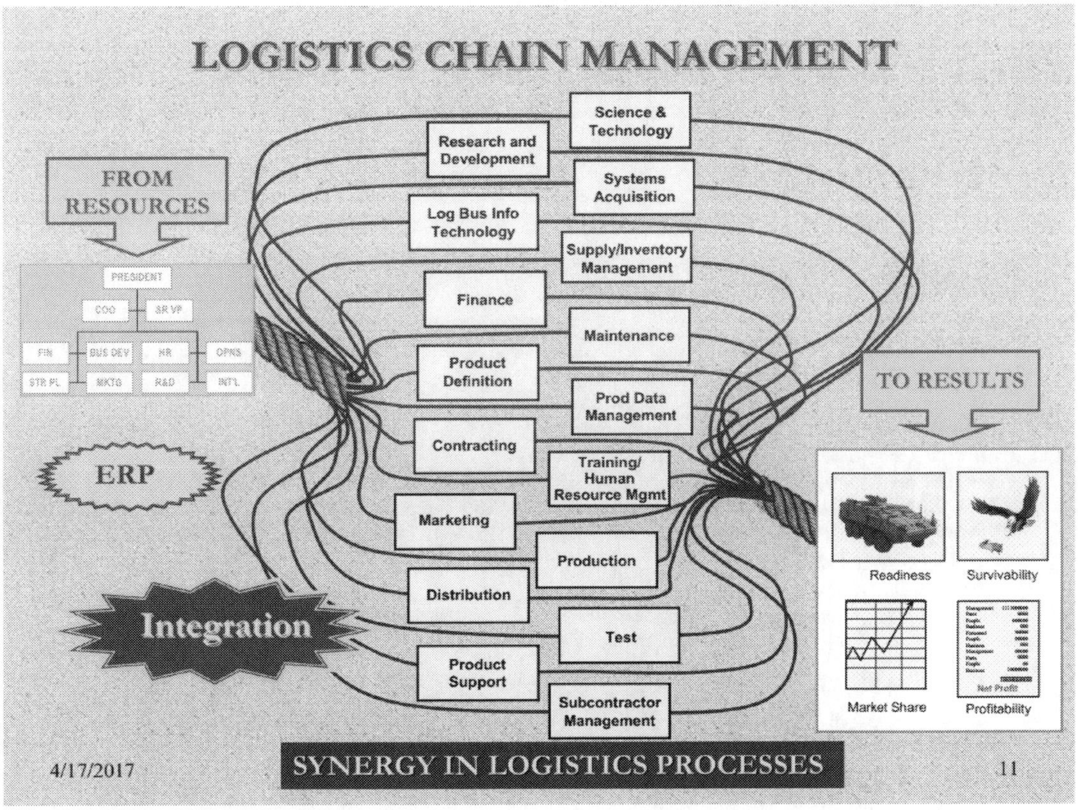

CONCLUSIONS

- These Principals Apply Universally – Military, Civilian
- This Is Not a Profession for the Faint Hearted
- Our Profession Must Grow:
  - In Stature
  - Through the Professionals Who Populate It
- Write About It – Talk About It – Practice It

BE PASSIONATE ABOUT IT!

4/17/2017 12

INTERNATIONAL SOCIETY OF LOGISTICS
4/17/2017
13

The Future Logistics Workforce

SOLE-The International Society of Logistics
38th Annual International Conference

William T. Powell, Jr.
President, Institute for Defense & Business
Executive Director, LOGTECH
University of North Carolina

"Computers in the future will weigh no more than 1.5 tons."

- *Popular Mechanics*, 1950

INSTITUTE FOR DEFENSE & BUSINESS

LOGTECH
CENTER OF EXCELLENCE IN LOGISTICS & TECHNOLOGY

"This telephone has too many short-comings to be seriously considered as a means of communications."

- Western Union analysis, 1876

★★★★★★★★
INSTITUTE
FOR DEFENSE
& BUSINESS

LOGTECH
CENTER OF EXCELLENCE IN
LOGISTICS & TECHNOLOGY

"Professor Goddard does not know the relation between action and reaction … He seems to lack the basic knowledge ladled out daily in high schools."

- *New York Times*, 1921

★★★★★★★★
INSTITUTE
FOR DEFENSE
& BUSINESS

LOGTECH
CENTER OF EXCELLENCE IN
LOGISTICS & TECHNOLOGY

"I think there is a world market for maybe five computers."

- Thomas Watson, then IBM chair, 1943

"$100 million is way too much to pay for Microsoft."

- IBM senior leadership, 1982

INSTITUTE FOR DEFENSE & BUSINESS

LOGTECH
CENTER OF EXCELLENCE IN LOGISTICS & TECHNOLOGY

Generally, what has changed?

- Communications, the Internet, Standardized Platforms
- Private Sector Logistics Trends and Practices

INSTITUTE FOR DEFENSE & BUSINESS

LOGTECH
CENTER OF EXCELLENCE IN LOGISTICS & TECHNOLOGY

What does this mean?

- Professor La Londe surveyed managers, directors and vice presidents, CLM members.
- In last 5 years, the number of logistics executives at:
  - Vice President level increased fourfold
  - Directors doubled

INSTITUTE FOR DEFENSE & BUSINESS

LOGTECH CENTER OF EXCELLENCE IN LOGISTICS & TECHNOLOGY

Where has this taken the Logistician?

"Logistics is now becoming a boardroom function as opposed to a loading dock function"

- M. Anthony Burns, Chairman of Ryder Systems, Inc.

INSTITUTE FOR DEFENSE & BUSINESS

LOGTECH CENTER OF EXCELLENCE IN LOGISTICS & TECHNOLOGY

What are the impacts to DoD?

CHANGE

INSTITUTE FOR DEFENSE & BUSINESS

LOGTECH CENTER OF EXCELLENCE IN LOGISTICS & TECHNOLOGY

"I think we've got to reach out and go to industry and get their best practices…[and use] commercial solutions to meet many military challenges."

- General Hugh M. Shelton, (Ret.) while Chairman, JCS

INSTITUTE FOR DEFENSE & BUSINESS

LOGTECH CENTER OF EXCELLENCE IN LOGISTICS & TECHNOLOGY

"[DoD's transformation efforts will require] transforming our people, processes and military forces."

- Honorable Donald H. Rumsfeld, Secretary of Defense

INSTITUTE FOR DEFENSE & BUSINESS

LOGTECH
CENTER OF EXCELLENCE IN LOGISTICS & TECHNOLOGY

What will impact the future logistics workforce?

1. The pace of organizational and cultural change, as well as the discovery and development of new technologies, will continue to accelerate. The truly successful logistician of the future will be an independent and critical thinker readily adaptable to diverse organizational environments.

INSTITUTE FOR DEFENSE & BUSINESS

LOGTECH
CENTER OF EXCELLENCE IN LOGISTICS & TECHNOLOGY

2. The U.S. military forces of the future will be much more nimble and flexible, and that agility must be reflected in the supporting business processes, practices and professionals.

INSTITUTE FOR DEFENSE & BUSINESS

LOGTECH
CENTER OF EXCELLENCE IN LOGISTICS & TECHNOLOGY

3. Logisticians will continue to grow more collaborative within the DoD and the military, and with the private sector as well.

INSTITUTE FOR DEFENSE & BUSINESS

LOGTECH
CENTER OF EXCELLENCE IN LOGISTICS & TECHNOLOGY

4. The importance of, and demand for, logistics professionals will continue to grow, with resulting increases in responsibility, status and (one hopes) compensation.

INSTITUTE FOR DEFENSE & BUSINESS

LOGTECH CENTER OF EXCELLENCE IN LOGISTICS & TECHNOLOGY

5. Advanced education as well as training, with a solid grounding in evolving technologies, finance, risk assessment and other business fundamentals, will be a key enabler for upwardly mobile logistics professionals.

INSTITUTE FOR DEFENSE & BUSINESS

LOGTECH CENTER OF EXCELLENCE IN LOGISTICS & TECHNOLOGY

LOGTECH

- MBA
- Research
- Executive Education
- Forums and Seminars
- SME Board
- Other Programs
  - Depot and Arsenal Commanders
  - U.S. Navy Leadership Program
  - USMC ILC Programs

INSTITUTE FOR DEFENSE & BUSINESS

LOGTECH CENTER OF EXCELLENCE IN LOGISTICS & TECHNOLOGY

"It was the best of times, it was the most challenging of times"

- with apologies to Charles Dickens

INSTITUTE FOR DEFENSE & BUSINESS

LOGTECH CENTER OF EXCELLENCE IN LOGISTICS & TECHNOLOGY

BAE SYSTEMS

Lean Thinking Applications to the Military

Managing the Flow

Larry DesSureault
Director of Supportability
BAE SYSTEMS IEWS

BAE SYSTEMS Information & Electronic Systems Integration Sector

---

BAE SYSTEMS

BAE SYSTEMS, Information & Electronic Warfare Systems (IEWS) Business Unit, Defense Electronics

IEWS "Big Blue Arrows"

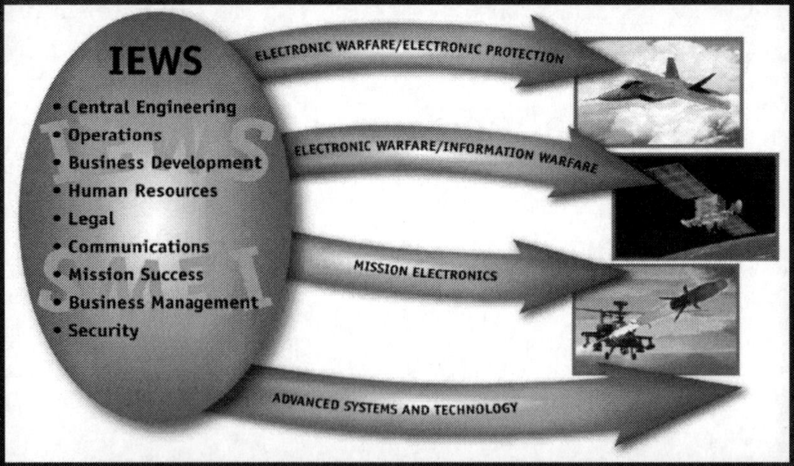

BAE SYSTEMS

BAE SYSTEMS Information & Electronic Systems Integration Sector

BAE SYSTEMS

Lean Manufacturing

BAE SYSTEMS

BAE SYSTEMS

Lean Manufacturing-Through Life Cycle Process

- DSSM (Design for Six Sigma Manufacturing) program
  - Provides product cost control from concept development through repeat production (NRE)
- Perform advanced process development activities needed to transition products from design to production (Recurring)
- Provide the Process and Test Engineering in the factories
  - Support the on-time delivery of a cost-competitive, quality product (Recurring)

BAE SYSTEMS

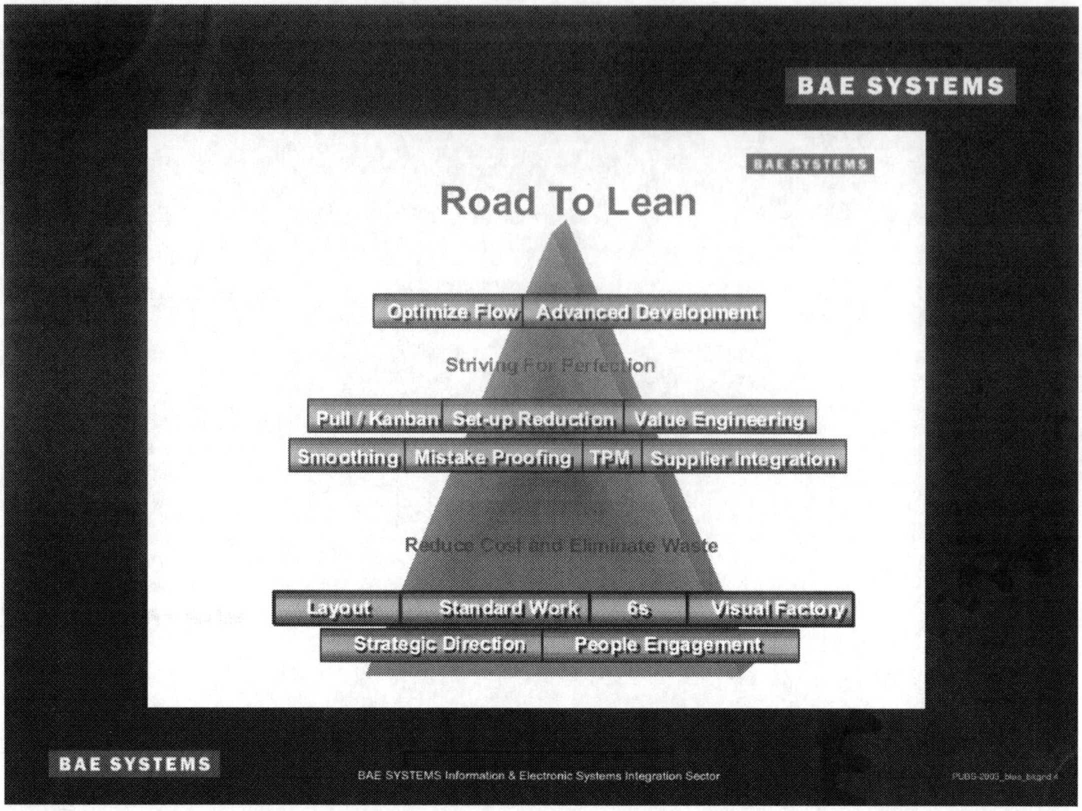
BAE SYSTEMS
BAE SYSTEMS
Road To Lean
Optimize Flow
Advanced Development
Striving For Perfection
Pull / Kanban
Set-up Reduction
Value Engineering
Smoothing
Mistake Proofing
TPM
Supplier Integration
Reduce Cost and Eliminate Waste
Layout
Standard Work
6s
Visual Factory
Strategic Direction
People Engagement
BAE SYSTEMS
BAE SYSTEMS Information & Electronic Systems Integration Sector

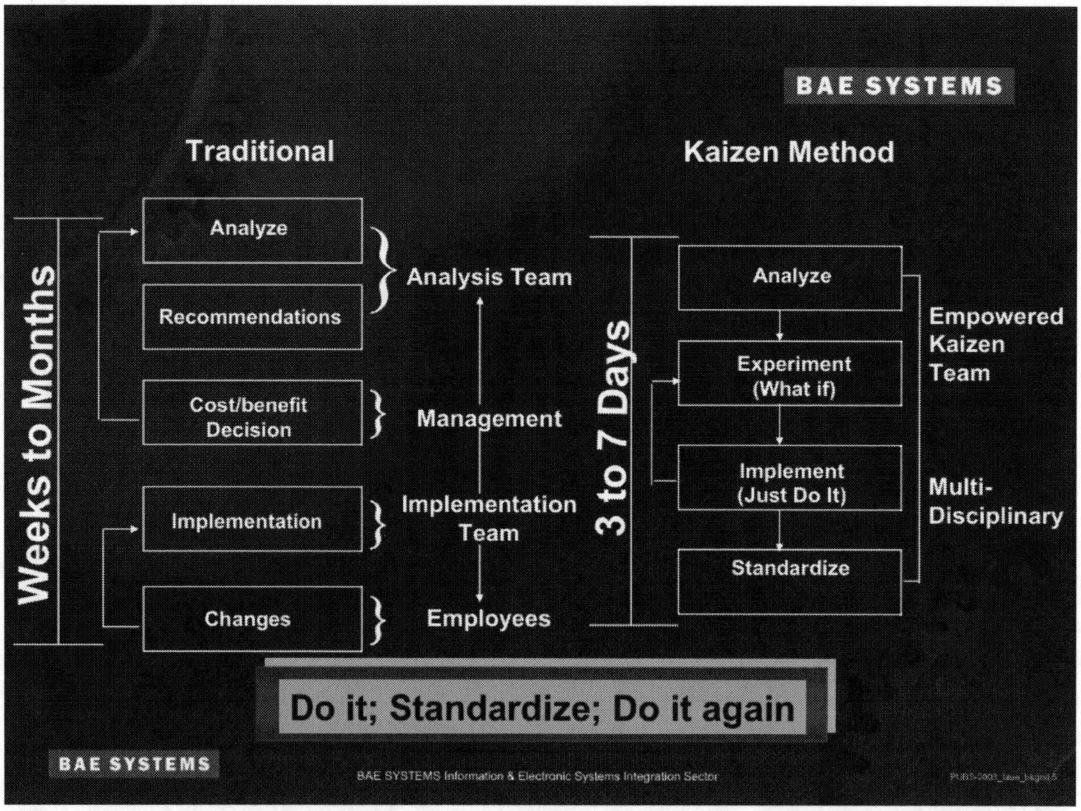
BAE SYSTEMS
Traditional
Kaizen Method
Weeks to Months
Analyze
Recommendations
Analysis Team
Cost/benefit Decision
Management
Implementation
Implementation Team
Changes
Employees
3 to 7 Days
Analyze
Experiment (What if)
Implement (Just Do It)
Standardize
Empowered Kaizen Team
Multi-Disciplinary
Do it; Standardize; Do it again
BAE SYSTEMS
BAE SYSTEMS Information & Electronic Systems Integration Sector

BAE SYSTEMS

Lean Manufacturing

- F-22 expanding Lean Initiatives in partnership with customer and Operations
  - 40 Kaizen events 1999-2000
  - Lean tools and techniques as standard practice
  - Extending application to Engineering and Business Systems
  - Cost benefits captured in "actuals"
- Implementation across multiple IEWS Programs
  - Longbow (Recurring production)
  - ALQ-144A (Recurring production)
  - JSF (Development)
  - Navy Support Equipment PBL (Repair)

BAE SYSTEMS

BAE SYSTEMS Information & Electronic Systems Integration Sector

BAE SYSTEMS

F-22 Example

Process	Improvement
Set-up	92%
Kitting	50%
Tools	87%
WIP	67%
Cycle Time	63%
Process Steps	67%
6S eval	75%

BAE SYSTEMS

BAE SYSTEMS Information & Electronic Systems Integration Sector

BAE SYSTEMS

Other Examples

Longbow Housing
Reduced hours/unit by 51%
Reduced lead time by 60%

Longbow RF/IF
Reduced hours/unit by 54%
Reduced lead time by 60%

ALQ-144 Final Assembly
Reduced lead time by 81%
Reduced travel distance by 85%
Reduced area support by 50%

JSF
Reduced estinmated production cost by 13% this year

BAE SYSTEMS BAE SYSTEMS Information & Electronic Systems Integration Sector PUBS-2003_blue_bkgnd 8

BAE SYSTEMS

Performance Based Logistics

(Applied Lean Principles)

BAE SYSTEMS BAE SYSTEMS Information & Electronic Systems Integration Sector PUBS-2003_blue_bkgnd 9

BAE SYSTEMS

Performance Based Logistics

Background

	Philosophy	Critical Path	ICP Role	Results
Historically	Inventory Based	Lowest Price Per Repair	Manage Supplies 	• Focus on supply availability • Solve problems by buying more inventory
Today	Performance Based	Best Value	Manage Suppliers 	• Focus on customer service and readiness • Solve problems by buying response time, quality and reliability

Change Driven by: Infrastructure Reduction, Acquisition Reform, & Technology Advances

BAE SYSTEMS

BAE SYSTEMS Information & Electronic Systems Integration Sector

BAE SYSTEMS

EW Support Equipment PBL

- Structure to provide Navy customer with "AVAILABILITY" of spare parts
- Navy spares turned over to BAE SYSTEMS
- BAE services to meet availability include:
  - Inspection
  - Rework
  - Modification
  - Repair
  - Test and calibration
  - Logistic and asset management
  - Obsolescence support
  - Shipment of assets

BAE SYSTEMS

BAE SYSTEMS Information & Electronic Systems Integration Sector

BAE SYSTEMS

EW Support Equipment PBL

- **24 hour turn around on "A" assets priority 1-3**
  - Actual to-date, meeting same-day shipping
- **30 day turn around on "A" assets priority 4 and above**
  - Actual to-date, average 4 days
- **97% availability required**
  - Actual to-date, 100% availability has been achieved

BAE SYSTEMS

EW Support Equipment PBL
Manage the Flow

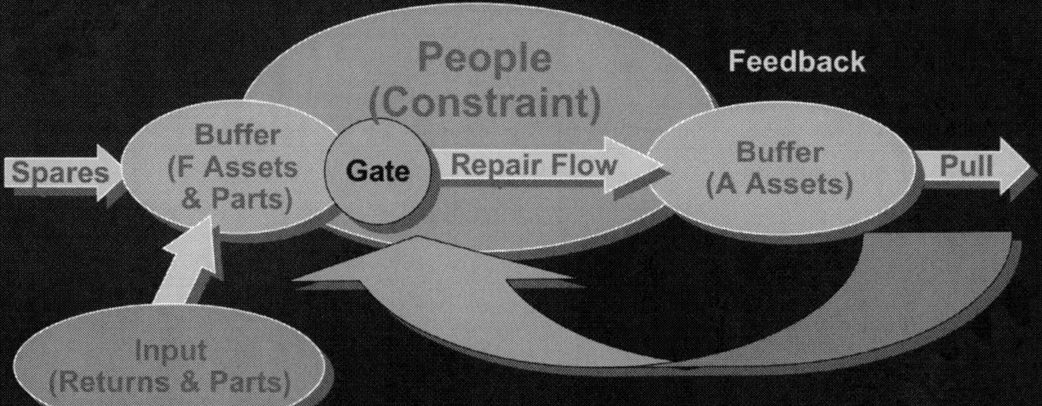

The rate of pull gates the repair flow

"We will not tire,
we will not falter,
we will not fail."
... as we work to
Protect Those Who Protect Us
BAE SYSTEMS

Leading Lean:
The Application of Lean Principles in Administrative Areas

By: Prof. Robert A. Miller, CPIM, CPL

Abstract: The application of Lean principles at Warner Robins Air Logistics Center (WR-ALC), Robins AFB, GA began to take shape in 2000 as the ALC's production-oriented business areas sought to becomemore efficient and competitive. In early 2002, the Space and Special Systems Directorate (WR-ALC/LK) became the first administrative area to adopt Lean techniques for process improvement. Following a brief description of Lean techniques and principles, this paper describes the successes, failures, and lessons learned from the first year of Lean in LK.

Introduction: Lean from the Airpower Perspective

"Fly, find your enemy, shoot him down—all the rest is rubbish." Manfred von Richtoven's (otherwise known as the Red Baron) response to a reporter's question about his methods for becoming the highest scoring ace of World War I serves as an excellent description of Lean thinking. Let's consider Richtoven's career in terms of the five principles of Lean philosophy:

I. Define the value of your product/service to your customer.

Von Richtoven's ultimate customer—Germany—demanded one service from the fighter ace: the efficient destruction of Allied aircraft.

II. Define the value stream as it flows from initial customer demand to the delivery of the product/service

His response was equally simple—he would define the "value stream" as doing only what was required to accomplish his mission continually over time--an act that required pilots and many specialized support personnel to work together as an integrated team.

III. Create flow within your value stream

Although Richtoven's 70 kills gained by far the greatest notoriety, his tireless efforts as a champion of Lean principles extended into all elements of his value stream. When not actively engaged in shooting down Allied aircraft, the Red Baron worked with support personnel to enhance mission readiness of his aircraft, designers to optimize fighter designs for future use, and other exceptional fighter pilots to document effective tactics. Richtoven was instrumental in creating a training system that served as the backbone of Luftwaffe pilot development for the next quarter-century. Richtoven's efforts resulted in a steady flow of optimally-trained pilots and effective, efficiently supported aircraft—and ultimately, lots of downed Allied aircraft.

IV. Allow your product/service to be pulled downstream by the customer

Although war is inherently push-oriented (the nation who out-produces the opponent in terms of war materials is virtually always the victor), Richtoven's philosophy centered around "pulling" personnel and equipment into the fight: neither pilots nor new aircraft models were sent to the front until proper training was conducted and a support structure available for them. Aircraft themselves were not to be introduced into combat until they were available in adequate numbers to be able to influence the air battle.

V. Strive for Perfection

Striving for perfection was self-evident not only in the Red Baron's own outstanding performance during the First World War, but also in the performance of his unit--the "Flying Circus"--which attained the War's highest kill ratio for a unit of its size, the Luftwaffe pilot training and aircraft development program, and the many Richtoven disciples who survived the First World War to attained leadership positions in Hitler's

Luftwaffe. Adherence to the philosophy of their mentor allowed this new generation of leadership to re-build the Luftwaffe from a virtually non-existent organization to the world's most formidable air force within the decade of the 1930s.

The Adoption of Lean Principles at Warner Robins ALC

Lean Production: The journey begins

The adoption of Lean principles at Warner Robins was driven by two ultimately synergistic factors: first was the core desire of the Warner Robins community to serve the warfighter in an ever more effective manner; second was the ever-present specter of a future round of Base Realignment and Closure (BRAC). It was reasoned that if measures from key metrics that indicate direct service to the warfighter were improved [e.g. Mission InCapable Awaiting Parts (MICAP) hours, Programmed Depot Maintenance (PDM) flow days, BackOrders (BO)s] through more efficient, effective processes, employee morale would rise, and other critical metrics (e.g. labor grievances) would likewise move in a positive direction.

Although a number of false starts did occur, the results garnered once properly supported Lean activities began were both significant and immediate. One example of such success was the C-5 inbound inspection activity. The inspection was determined to be a time-consuming, inefficient event which not only directly slowed PDM, but also indirectly caused delays downstream in the PDM line when crucial parts or needed repairs not ordered during inbound inspection were necessitated. The aircraft's critical path to PDM completion was often affected by the re-work required from such tardy discoveries.

To address this problem, a team made up of randomly selected workers executed this initial Lean event—mapping the value stream and re-designing the inspection process to better align with that stream, then testing the new process—and were able to cut the process from 37 to 22 days, noting further mid- to long-term changes potentially reducing the flow to 17 days, while virtually eliminating down-stream re-work. Not only did a once-loathed process become a crown jewel of Lean innovation, but initially skeptical "average" workers became dynamos and champions of Lean in the workforce.

The Lean Vocabulary

Value Stream Mapping(VSM): An activity that defines the value stream of any process in terms of present, future (desired), and ideal states. At a macro level, it is the process of defining the value stream for the most critical processes within the organization. Rapid Improvement Events, Projects, and Do-Its are defined and scheduled during this activity.

Rapid Improvement Event (RIE): An activity aimed at seeking out and implementing improvements to a defined process.

Projects: The activity of a small team designated to execute tasks defined by a VSM activity (e.g. If VSM defines a requirement to automate a process, a defined project may be the development of an automation tool).

Do-Its: Immediate activities that can be taken to improve processes (e.g. Operational Instructions from senior management).

Initially, Lean activity at Robins was focused by upon manufacturing processes, which most immediately and visibly impacted the warfighter. For the ALC to ever operate at peak effectiveness, the geriatric processes associated with ALC administrative areas would also need to be reinvigorated. By late 2001, the time was ripe for the Center to begin applying Lean principles in administrative areas.

Lean Administration: A little dab will do you…?

By the winter of 2001 some form of Continuous Process Improvement (CPI) was taking place in virtually every administrative directorate at Robins. From Just-In-Time to Activity Based Management to Theory of Constraints, each directorate worked with little overall coordination toward optimization of shared processes. Although the Depot Reengineering Directorate worked with established Lean representatives in each production directorate to ensure coordination, no such attention was given to administrative areas.

Following a Lean seminar attended by ALC leadership at Directorate-level and above, WR-ALC/LK's Director chose to embark on the journey of applying Lean to the directorate's administrative processes. Following an educational briefing to division chiefs, the Director requested nominations for an individual to coordinate Lean efforts within the directorate and represent LK for Center-level activities. Due to the immaturity of administrative Lean development, and resistance on the part of middle management to take personnel "out of hide," it was decided that a part-time Directorate Lean Change Agent—along with an alternate, to represent the directorate in the event of the primary agent's absence—would adequately support the defined role. Likewise, one part-time Lean Change Agent was assigned to each division to support Division-level activities and represent the divisions at Directorate-level events.

The mandate to this embryonic team was to observe, report, and recommend places for change to be implemented. The power to actually execute change was left in the hands of directorate and division leadership. LK's first Lean Change Agent was selected in January 2002: The agent was, at age 27, both relatively young and new to the

6S's to Success

6S is a key (and in many cases the initial) phase of Lean Implementation, and may be both physical and process-oriented. For example, a Lean team may need to remove all unnecessary equipment and materials on the shop floor in order to view a given process in action, and thereby consider possible alternatives and their implications. From a process standpoint, new Lean processes are much more difficult to implement in a cluttered, unsafe, or unsanitary working environment—or a workplace where processes are largely undefined.

1) Sort: Get rid of what isn't needed.
2) Straighten: Organize what belongs.
3) Scrub: Clean up.
4) Safety: See and fix unsafe conditions.
5) Standardize: Define how things are done.
6) Sustain: Constant practice of the first five S's.

Civil Service, having less than five years of experience. His youthful energy, exceptional performance to date, experience in leading CPI activity at his previous assignment, and newness to LK (less than 6 months) were all seen as advantages. In February 2002, the agent was educated through a one-week Lean training seminar and began working to institute Lean within LK.

Initial LK Lean activity focused on parallel efforts to give training to LK Division Change Agents (some general training along with additional training to be provided on a Just-In-Time basis), along with attempting to execute elementary Lean activities. The initial implementation plan for LK was focused on familiarization of personnel with Lean terminology and process activity (learning Lean by doing), while building confidence with small, quick victories (picking the low-hanging fruit). Meanwhile at the Center-level, activity to integrate all Directorate-level activities into one center-wide CPI program was underway. This activity focused on ensuring CPI priorities were driven by overall Center needs, redundant efforts were eliminated, and corporate knowledge was effectively shared.

By late February 2002 LK was on the verge of executing its first Lean event. As this event was being planned, the LK Lean Change Agent was forced to depart for the better part of two months due to family emergency. Although the initial Value Stream Mapping (VSM) activity went ahead as scheduled, and the remainder of the LK Lean Team received overview training and executed a directorate-wide 6S sweep in late April, most Lean activity came to a halt until early summer.

May and June 2002 saw two major milestones in the implementation of Lean throughout LK: the first was the comprehensive briefing of findings from the directorate-wide 6S sweep to directorate and division leadership. Although it was determined that flaws in scoring prevented the sweep from providing a true "baseline," many actionable findings—including some safety concerns—were noted to leadership. A schedule for future 6S sweeps was agreed upon, allowing for two of LK's six divisions to be "swept" each month.

By the end of June, a second major milestone was reached as each member of the 200+ strong directorate received at least one hour of Lean training. Despite early actionable success, leadership determined that any work to garner "low-hanging fruit" might be diverting Lean energy in directions that might not prove cost-beneficial. Further events were postponed until a Directorate-level VSM activity could take place in order to determine priorities & receive requisite buy-in from all stakeholders. Due to the necessity of coordinating the schedules of so many high-ranking personnel, Directorate-level VSM could not be executed until early August.

By the time of the August VSM, the second round of 6S sweeps were underway. A wide variation in results were noted not so much from the variation in inspection worksheets or from the training of the inspectors; rather, it was noted that middle management applied the first sweep's recommendations based upon their own perceptions of Lean's importance. One division, with a Lean/6S program already underway for some months was predictably far ahead of its sister divisions, while one other division made tremendous gains. The other four divisions made minor to no progress since initial inspections were conducted.

The August 2002 LK Directorate-wide VSM effort proved tremendously successful, as each division participated in defining the directorate's primary value streams to the warfighter. Although many processes were left undefined, the "80% solution" enlightened all participants to the waste currently inherent in their administrative processes—a plethora of ideas for follow-on lower-level VSM and RIE activities, Projects, and Do-Its followed. Prioritization for future activity was agreed to by all parties in light of an envisioned Future State and Ideal State. Last, a pace was set for activities—a rate of one event per month (the pacing item being the mandate that all activity be coordinated with the ALC's consulting activity) plus one 6S sweep for two of the divisions.

Momentum for Lean improvement built once again following the August VSM. In September, a second VSM was executed outlining the Purchase Request process—designated by LK and later the Center as a whole as the process most in need of improvement. Though the pace of one event per month was considered attainable by the entire directorate's leadership, managers unwilling to sacrifice an ever-expanding amount of scarce resources for Lean improvement successfully appealed to indefinitely push back planned events in order to execute Projects, Do-Its, and other residual tasks from previous events. By the winter of 2002, with Lean implementation undergoing cyclical spurts of effectiveness, the LK management team completely changed: a full time Lean Change Agent was appointed for LK, while both the organization's Director and Deputy Director were assigned to new positions. Lean implementation in LK was at a crossroads.

Lean Administration: Turning the Tide

Following a transitory period of education for the newly assigned personnel, Lean implementation for the organization finally began a slow, steady state of improvement. Other administrative directorates came on board, pooling resources and ideas. Many areas addressed for improvement in the LK VSM of August 2002 were tackled and exploited by Center-level teams representing many directorates. Seeing that Lean was here to stay, middle management began taking activities such as 6S events more seriously, while becoming more supportive of freeing up limited resources. Resources themselves were being demanded far less frequently as the full-time Directorate Lean Change Agent was able to more effectively coordinate with his counterparts in drawing from a vast talent pool. Very slowly, but with an ever building pace through the spring of 2003, Lean implementation in the administrative areas of Robins was becoming a reality.

Conclusion/Lessons Learned

Many lessons on the strategic and tactical level can be drawn from the first year of leading Lean in administration at Robins. Many difficult days and a multitude of headaches have led to marked improvement in some ALC processes, and a template for what to do—and in many more cases what not to do—when attempting to implementing Lean in their administrative areas.

1) **You get out what you put in**: Not dedicating people to Lean means that people won't be dedicated to Lean. At least one full-time person, supported by several personnel officially designated to support Lean implementation is a must for any office. Managers must also remember that as Lean implementation gains momentum, more resources will be needed to make change happen. The positive side is that many more times that number of resources should be freed up as a result of Lean process improvement. Although young talent with a fresh view is helpful on the team, experienced personnel who already have established credibility within the organization must lead the team.

2) **Power to the people**: Those responsible for determining what should be changed must be given the power to make change happen. If upper or middle management does not delegate authority, Change Agents become quickly discouraged, change is unevenly applied, and implementation as a whole loses momentum. Properly empowered, those responsible for making change happen must also work with an approved implementation strategy in mind. You can't get where you want to be unless you know where you want to be, and have a plan to get there.

Knowledge is another form of power that must be distributed as widely as possible. Overall education should be provided to a level of understanding for the entire workforce and to as great a depth as available to each member of the Lean implementation team. Single point failures should never happen—the absence of one team member can't be allowed to shut down activity for the whole organization.

Knowledge must also take the form of keeping the workforce aware of ongoing and projected Lean activity—especially those driven by the suggestions of the workforce.

The greater the education, the easier the implementation, and the more quickly an office can transition from being in need of consultants to providing consultant support to other organizations.

3) **Set the pace, then stick to it**: It is imperative that any organization pick a steady (initially slow) pace of change, then allow Lean implementation to accelerate by itself, dedicating additional resources as required. Not dedicating the amount of resources at the right time causes implementation—and the results gained from implementation—to slow down just as it should naturally be speeding up.

4) **Kamikaze or common sense**: Leadership must recognize the difference between "Kamikaze Kaizen"—a term used to refer to a desperately energetic shotgun effort at process improvement not dedicated to hit anything specifically, and common sense efforts to make widely-recognized process problems more bearable. Some initial efforts to implement Lean prior to the formalization of an overall plan can be effective in scoring quick successes, teaching people the mechanics of Lean, and familiarizing the organization with Lean thinking. Organizations should not necessarily strive to measure return on investment for such activity, as it is many times qualitative and therefore subjective in nature. A vision and macro-level VSM effort must be affected quickly to guide overall activity; however, the organization need not wait for months coordinating schedules and pooling resources required for such an undertaking in order to begin their Lean journey.

5) **Pool your resources**: Administrative Lean implementation accelerated dramatically in the spring of 2003 as more directorates became involved in Lean efforts. Allowing processes to be defined at the highest common level allows organizations to

draw less frequently from a deeper pool of talented personnel, get results faster, develop process uniformity over the broadest business area, and prevent redundancy. Lead organizations for such activities should be those most significantly impacted by the potential process change.

The implementation of Lean in administrative areas, just like in production facilities, will be come with difficulty and pain, as all change does. It is most of all important to keep in mind that those who first endeavor to make positive change happen will inevitably be the first to taste its fruit.

Bibliography

Although not directly quoted, themes and information for this paper were derived from the following texts:

Lean Thinking, James P. Womack & Daniel T. Jones, Simon & Schuster, 1996

The Red Baron Combat Wing, Peter Kilduff, Arms & Armour Press, 1998

The Red Baron: Beyond the Legend, Peter Kilduff, Sterling Press, 2000

Author's Biography

Prof. Rob Miller, CPIM, CPL is currently assigned as an Adjunct Professor of Logistics Management, Georgia College & State University/Robins Logistics Center. Prof. Miller instructs upper-level undergraduate and graduate students in Supply Chain Management, Warehousing, and Distribution Management. Prof. Miller received a BA in History from Oglethorpe University in 1997 while completing Air Force ROTC at the Georgia Institute of Technology. Prof. Miller received Certification in Production & Inventory Management (CPIM) from the American Production & Inventory Control Society (APICS) in 1998, an MS in Logistics Systems from Georgia College & State University in 2000, and Certified Professional Logistician (CPL) designation from SOLE in 2002.

Prof. Miller is a six-year Civil Service veteran with the US Air Force. Assigned to Warner-Robins Air Logistics Center in 1997 through the Palace Acquire logistics management internship program, Prof. Miller has served as Program Manager in the Special Operations and Support Equipment Directorates prior to his current assignment as a Program Manager in the Space and Special Systems Directorate.

The Asymmetric Threat and Defense Transportation Planning

Roy G. Bowman
Vice President, Government Affairs
APL Limited

Presented to the Transportation & Distribution Panel, SOLE
38th Annual International Logistics Conference & Exhibition, August13, 2003

As the 21st century dawns, we find ourselves coping with a global economy. This hackneyed phrase is often heard in economic discussions, but let's first start by establishing what it means. To me, the hallmarks of a global economy are a world in which manufacturing can be sourced anywhere, in which ideas move around the world at the click of a computer keyboard, a world in which politicians have lost control of tax policy and exchange control provisions are history because every business in the world can move to a more friendly jurisdiction and still remain in touch with its markets and its suppliers. This is a world in which your telephone query can be answered by your neighbor in Virginia or by a Indian sitting in Bombay speaking perfect English.

What makes this world possible are two technological marvels. One, of course, is the computer and the worldwide web, but second only to the computer and the web is the ocean transportation system. This ancient service is at the center of the global economy. It's only through the speed and efficiency of ocean transportation and its associated inland distribution that manufacturing can be located a world away from both its market and its suppliers. Sneakers manufactured in China can be in Chicago in what amounts to the blink of an eye in this modern world.

In order to make this global economy work, the transportation system has been integrated into a just-in-time inventory management manufacturing regime. Successful ocean transportation companies can coordinate supplies from any point on the globe, organize a delivery to a manufacturing facility in time to be incorporated in the production line and then take the output of that factory and distribute the products to the most profitable markets or most in need of product. The system depends on agility and adaptability.

With that background, then, let's turn our attention to defense logistics to see how these characteristics can be matched with developments in international military affairs. I'm fond of saying that in the last two years, that is, since 9/11, military tactics and concepts have changed more than in the last 50 years, since World War II. The Afghanistan and Iraqi freedom actions are the proof of this statement. But of course, you in the audience know far better than I how these changes affect the defense planner.

Let us examine for a moment some of the changes that the international political scene has imposed. The fall of the Soviet Union and the transformation of Russia into a sometime ally rather than an implacable enemy means that we must now shift our planning attention from a potential conflict in a specific geographic location, the European theater, where we had immense depots and concentrations of troops and equipment, to a far different contingency. In those days, transportation was pretty straightforward, in the sense that the destination for huge inventory and supply depots was limited to certain strategic areas in the world -- Western Europe, Japan, Korea -- and the transportation planner could concentrate on linking the supply sources in the continental United States with defined locations in these areas. Moreover, he had the luxury of maintaining significant inventory depots in these areas.

The new world order, however, dictates that the day of the iron mountain of logistics supplies ready for distribution to a defined geographical area is over. Now, instead of facing a well-defined threat of a large, monolithic enemy state, we face the asymmetric threat -- an enemy with no defined state, that is everywhere and nowhere. Al Queda and the 9/11 attacks are typical. An attack on the homeland of the United States from an enemy that vanished in the hazy deserts of Afghanistan. This threat means we may need to deploy forces in short order to a geographic part of the world where we have scant infrastructure. Instead of supply dumps in the theater, we will have to supply forces either from the continental United States or from other locations around the world. Because of the speed with which both the policy planner and the military strategist will be required to react, there will be little time to create transportation links to the theater in question.

Let's examine now a few things that these elements have in common with our commercial markets. The commercial markets emphasize speed-to-market for their product, the just-in-time inventory systems for their manufacturing facilities and always, the desire to minimize the cost of inventory or supplies in the pipeline. Moreover, this system has to be flexible. It has to be able to divert product to that market which is most in need of inventory and which is most profitable. It also must be able to re-source raw material and sub-assemblies as prices change or supplies are curtailed.

Add to this the latest requirement generated by the changed world situation -- security. As the United States Customs takes forward-looking action to protect homeland security, the supply chain and ocean transportation are now subjected to procedures designed to heighten the security of the supply chain. For instance, ocean carriers now must submit their complete manifests 24 hours in advance of inbound sailings to the United States. These manifests must be submitted electronically and speed and accuracy are the watchwords. Very shortly, we will enter into a similar procedure for exports from the United States, where the focus is a little bit different. On the export side, the U.S. is intent on limiting the export of materials that could be used to create weapons of mass destruction. Interestingly, we have found that the military is not exempt from these 24-hour advance notification requirements and is often ill-equipped to provide the electronic interface with Customs in the form that Customs requires.

I suggest to you that transportation requirements for defense planning in the future will require just these attributes. The ability to react quickly, to change sources of supply, to direct equipment to unexpected spots on the globe and to do so with a secure supply chain that is integrated with existing security measures. I suggest to you that this puts a premium on dealing with ocean transportation companies that have the following attributes:

- A widespread network of terminals and intermodal connections that will permit the defense planner to respond to the requirement to deliver equipment to the most unexpected and often God-forsaken spots on the globe -- for instance, Afghanistan.

- The ability to adapt and re-source its equipment to accommodate the military planner.

- The ability to utilize the electronic interfaces to achieve in-transit visibility and total-asset visibility to efficiently support the effort.

- The knowledge of the U.S. military, the procedures and limitations of procurement practices and other arcane elements that the customer, the U.S. military, requires and which are not replicated in commercial operations.

Now, having said all this, I just wanted to give you an example of how a company like APL fits into this pattern. To do this, I want to talk about Karachi, Pakistan. APL has been serving Karachi since World War II. Pakistan is an important market because of the textile imports that come into the United States and has long been a part of the APL service. In 1995 or 1996, APL decided that the Karachi terminal was not adequate for efficient container movement. In fact, there was no container crane in downtown Karachi, and the ports of Karachi were serviced with the same technology that existed after World War II.

The ocean transport companies that had containerized their ships for many years were trying to unload containers in the Karachi port with antiquated machinery and facilities. The result was mind-boggling inefficiencies. APL decided to go forward to modernize this terminal. The obstacles were formidable. Although the Karachi government and the government of Pakistan endorsed the modernization, ferocious opposition was encountered from the operators of the break-bulk ports that were not scheduled for modernization. One of the owners and investors in the competing port happened also to be a newspaper columnist, so that constant attacks appeared in the Karachi newspapers.

If that were not difficult enough, let me just give you some idea of the financing necessary to accomplish this. The package of financing included supplier credits granted through a Japanese trading house, German development bank funds extended in Deutsch marks and a syndicate of local Pakistani banks lending in Pakistani rupees. All this had to be done against the backdrop of Islamic law, which doesn't permit charging interest. Over a period of two to three years, this project was developed and financed, notwithstanding excruciating obstacles which would take far too long to recount here. Nevertheless, at the end of the day, APL controlled a modern container port in downtown Karachi.

This story was, I should guess, of supreme indifference to the defense planner at the time it was unfolding.

After 9/11, however, the indifference to Pakistan and Karachi changed. Almost overnight, Pakistan went from a troubled, backward country best left to its own devices, to a valued ally of the United States in the war against terrorism, then principally headquartered in Afghanistan under the supervision of Osama Bin Laden and the Taliban.

As the focus began to concentrate on military action in Afghanistan to oust the Taliban, the supply routes became critical. Looking at the map, we can see that the objective is a landlocked state bordered on the west by Iran (hardly an appropriate staging area for U.S.

military activities), on the south by Pakistan and on the north by the Stans – Turkmenistan, Uzbekistan and Tajikistan. Again, hardly inviting places.

Separated from Pakistan by towering mountains, accessed only through the historic Khyber Pass between Pakistan and Afghanistan, lay the objective of military action. It was at this stage, that having a transportation provider like APL begins to pay off. The investment in the Karachi container terminal and APL's familiarity with the trucking infrastructure in Pakistan permitted us to put together a chain of supplies that took containers entering the port of Karachi, trucked them by trusted suppliers used to dealing with APL and its commercial activities, up the length of Pakistan and over the Khyber Pass, into Afghanistan and Kabul. APL was able to put this chain together because it had the commercial infrastructure in place: the truckers, the port, the ships, and secondly, because it had the nimbleness and innovation acquired from years of reacting to commercial supply and demand changes to react with dispatch. Not least, it also had the knowledge of the local political customs in Pakistan and the ability to work with the all-important Pakistan army. One amusing story is told by our agent in Karachi, who went up to the Khyber Pass to a town called Peshawar to investigate the availability of truckers to go over the pass. He reported back that in a local café in this little town, the scene was reminiscent of the bar scene in "Star Wars", where every manner of life form congregated to sip tea and do business.

Another recent APL experience illustrates the use of commercial flexibility to serve changing requirements. The Army recently deployed a whole division from the U.S. to the Middle East. Before the ships could reach the initial destination, the requirement had changed and the division was redirected to Afghanistan. The ships carrying the division also had other cargo not scheduled to be deployed with the division. The solution was to find a safe locale in the Middle East with adequate force protection at which to discharge and direct the cargo. Air transport from this locale to the Afghani destination was not available on a timely basis. Working with APL, the Army directed the vessels to a transshipment location in the Middle East and APL is now redeploying the entire division's cargo through its Karachi entry point to Afghanistan.

The point of all of this is simply that the transportation providers that are likely to be of real value in the 21st century are the transportation providers who can integrate resources all over the world and respond on short notice to unanticipated and unpredictable demands. The nature of conflict in this new world order is such that there will seldom be the time to build iron mountains of supplies or even to predict the location in which combat will occur. The moral, it seems to me, is that the transportation provider in the logistics chain has got to be one that 1) has resources throughout the world, 2) that can react nimbly and innovatively to new demands and 3) that understands the customer and is familiar with the interface with his U.S. military customer.

Obviously, I believe that APL fits this description. We are not the only one, of course, but as the decline of U.S.-flag shipping accelerates, the number of providers who can meet this bill will grow smaller and, in my view, it will be important to have a good working relationship long before the President gives the order to send U.S. forces to another unusual and remote spot in the world.

I would like to close with a quote from General Doornink, Commander of MTMC printed in the July, 2003 issue of American Shipper magazine commenting on the civilian partnership. She said,

> "We capitalized on . . . [the commercial] infrastructure, which meant that the Department of Defense didn't have to put additional soldiers, airmen, sailors or Marines on the ground, because our commercial partners took care not only of picking up the cargo in the U.S. and taking it by ship to a port in Pakistan, let's say, en route to Afghanistan."

Operation Iraqi Freedom

Logistics First Impressions

Logistics Environment

- Lines of Communication extended over **600 miles**
- Marine Logistics Command culminating point was **430 miles**
- Modes of **distribution** included contracted line haul, US Army line haul, USMC tactical lift, C130s, air delivery, internal and external helo lifts
- "Push" concept of logistics support combined with pull
- Critical to success was providing **fuel** to rapidly advancing forces

Fast Facts

- Contracted over 400 trucks and drivers from 14 different countries
- I Marine Expeditionary Force consumed 450,000 gallons of fuel daily
  - Fuel hose reel system extended 84 miles
    - Supported USMC and US Army
- Helo lifted 1,590 warehouse pallets
- By 22 April 03 had moved over 1million pounds of mail to forward forces

Good

- USMC contingency contracting
- Maritime Prepositioning Force (MPF) concept
  - 11 ships in 16 days
- Operational Distribution
- Process Re-engineering (Integrated Logistics Capability (ILC)) concept for maintenance
  - High readiness rates
  - Repaired over 4,000 end items
    - Put two years of usage on tanks in 1 month

Good

- "Log Light" Division Concept: light, lean and lethal
  - **No black sleeping bags**
  - **No Cots**
  - **Prepared to go to 1 MRE per day**
  - **Water funnel for every four Marines**
  - **Staff reach back – reduced manning**
  - **Fuel test kits to use with seized Iraqi fuel**
  - **Gypsyrack for HMMWV's (2,000) – doubled fuel capacity**
  - ***Flexcells* on M1A1 tanks and *FAST* fuel storage devices on AAVs**

Bad

- Lack of communication assets for logistics units
- In-transit visibility
- Logistics C2 system
- Minimal bandwidth to support Logistics
- Tactical distribution / Line haul
- Class VIII (Medical)
  - Need to treat medical supplies like other supply items, not as a separate commodity

Ugly

- RFF process vs. TPFDD process – CSS Forces arrival
- Lack of drivers and Assistant-drivers
- Force protection
- Materiel Handling Equipment/Container Handling Equipment allocation
  - Extended Boom Forklift not popular with troops
  - Rough Terrain Container Handler tough to move
- Heavy Engineer equipment hauling
  - Need to replace 870 trailer with on/off road trailer
- Contractor Logistics Support

Key Take-Away's

- Distribution
  - Strategic / Operational / Tactical
- Logistics IT
  - TAV / ITV / LOG C2 / Data Storage & transmition
- Logistics Processes & Organizations
  - Supply / Maintenance / Transportation / Distribution

"Systems Logistics Integrated Management -- a Unified Multidimensional Logistics Vision"

LOGISTICS VISIONS

Dr. Ralph Harper, Jr.
RLH6274@aol.com

 Sole 2003

CONTEXT of the OPPORTUNITY

LOGISTICS offers a VISION for success in operationalizing "the Big Picture"!

SPECIFICALLY an ALL ENCOMPASSING Logistics Vision--a Systems Logistics Integrated Management approach to the Transformation of Business

 Sole 2003

THE OPPORTUNITY

Recent New Vision Need Indicatos:

- *"Reinventing Initiatives Corporation & Governments [Global scale]*
- *Calls for Transformations in both Business and Government*
- *Emphasis on determining and sustaining Core Competencies*
- *Emphasis on quantifying systems performance capabilities*
- *Requirements for "Rapid Response" and lifecycle considerations in decision*

R Harper © 2003 *Sole 2003*

THE OPPORTUNITY

INFORMATION does

provide competitive advantage,

BUT FLEXIBILITY in USING

[deploying] that INFORMATION

is the true

STRATEGIC WEAPON!

Rivers-Harper © 2002 U-SLIM

Our Environment is Forever Changed!

- **ESCALATING COMPETITION**
- **RAPID CHANGE on MANY FRONTS**
- **GLOBAL & CONNECTED MARKETS**

Doing the *"right thing"* is not enough--

Doing the *"right thing, better, more consistently, faster, and more efficiently"*
AND KNOWING WHEN TO CHANGE.

a.k.a. **SYSTEMS AGILITY !**

Rivers-Harper © 2002 U-SLIM

Evolving Environment

- Continually evolving and changing state within the Government and Commercial area.
- In today's environment, procedures are shifting from Military Specifications and Standards to Commercial Standards
- 6-SIGMA, Evolutionary Acquisition, and Spiral Development

R Harper © 2003 Sole 2003

Evolving Environment

Changes and New Direction in DOD for the following:

DOD 5000.1, *The Defense Acquisition System.*
DOD 5000.2, *Operation of the Defense Acquisition System.*
DOD 5000.2-R, *Mandatory Procedures for Major Defense Acquisition Programs (MDAPs) and Major Automated Information System (MAIS) Acquisition Program*

 Sole 2003

CONTEXT of the OPPORTUNITY

To address the critical organizational realities of implementing INNOVATIVE PRACTICES

New Wave Strategies in management and manufacturing *advocate integrating*

- Operational
- Organizational
- Human Considerations

 U-SLIM

Research Support

OPTIMIZATION

process of orchestrating efforts of all components toward achieving the stated aim. Optimization is management's job.
Deming (1993)

Rivers-Harper © 2002 U-SLIM

Research Support

Scenarios for 21st Century Organizations:

1. Shifting Networks of Small Firms

2. All-Encompassing "Virtual Countries"

   Laubacher, Malone, and MIT Scenario Working Group **(1993)**

Rivers-Harper © 2002 U-SLIM

Development

- For the 21st century we must recognize International Markets and include them in professional and personal development
- Promotes innovative Strategic Management practice with an integrated, cross-functional, technology and life cycle focused perspective

 U-SLIM

Logistics Theory

- A multidimensional approach to business is needed in Logistics
- The multi-dimensional model used by logisticians provides the initial planning, funding, and controlling activities
- A total systems integrated management system approach and life cycle management

 U-SLIM

Logistics Theory

- Logistics practice offers a blended management and leadership approach based on an integrated synthesis of all methodologies, theories, tools, and techniques of management

 U-SLIM

Transformation Goals

Achieve credibility and effectiveness in the acquisition and logistics support process

Revitalize the quality and morale of the DOD Acquisition, Technology, and Logistics workforce

Improve the health of the defense industrial base

Rationalize the weapons systems and infrastructure against our national security needs

Initiate high leverage technologies to create the warfighting capabilities, systems, and strategies of the future

 Sole 2003

RECOMMENDATION

Develop a Unified Theory for
Professional Logistics Practice

Today's Invitation:

THINK OUTSIDE THE BOX

Contribute to the* Transformation of *the dimensions.

Sole 2003

SYSTEMS LOGISTICS INTEGRATED MANAGEMENT:
Multi-Dimensional and Cross-Function

Geography Arenas

CORE PROCESSES ?

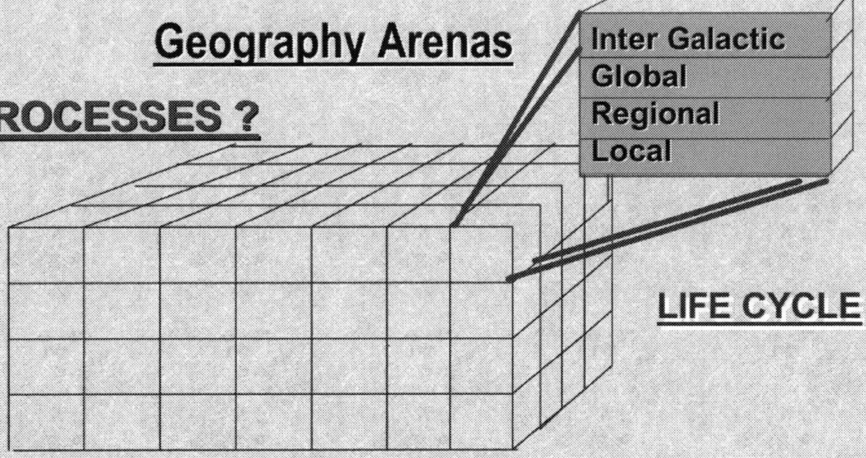

LIFE CYCLE

LOGISTICS SPECIALTY FOCUSES?
APPLICATION AREAS?

U-SLIM

Rivers-Harper © 2002 U-SLIM

Low Demand Design:

Sustainability as a Key Performance Parameter

Mr. Tom Edwards
Deputy to the Commanding General
Combined Arms Support Command
Fort Lee, Virginia

Objective Force Concept

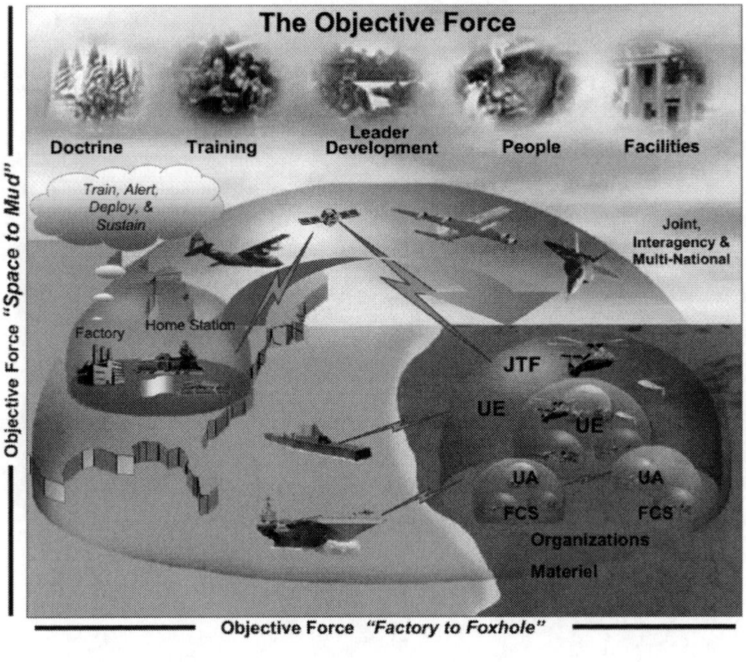

- Joint, Interagency & Multi-National Capabilities
- Increased Strategic Responsiveness
- Dominant across Full Spectrum Operations
- Campaign Quality Force
- Enabled by Knowledge
- Adaptive Modular Organizations
- 3-7 Days Self-Sustainment
- FCS: Family of Systems / System of Systems
- Soldiers and Leaders enabled by technology

Achieving the Objective Force Mandates
• Deployable in 96 hrs
• Reduce log footprint
• Reduce O&S costs
S&T
TRADOC, CASCOM, AMSAA, and other Requirements
Fuel Efficiency
Water Generation
Multi Purpose Ammo
Embedded Diag/Prog
CROP
Pit Stop Maint
Increased Reliability/ Availability
• Quantitative Analysis (Science)
• Qualitative Analysis (Art)
Log Corporate Enterprise
Distro-Based Logistics
Demand Reduction
Business Processes
Sense and Respond
More Capable Formations
+ Logistics Footprint Reduction
+ More Deployable Formations
+ Reduced O&S Cost

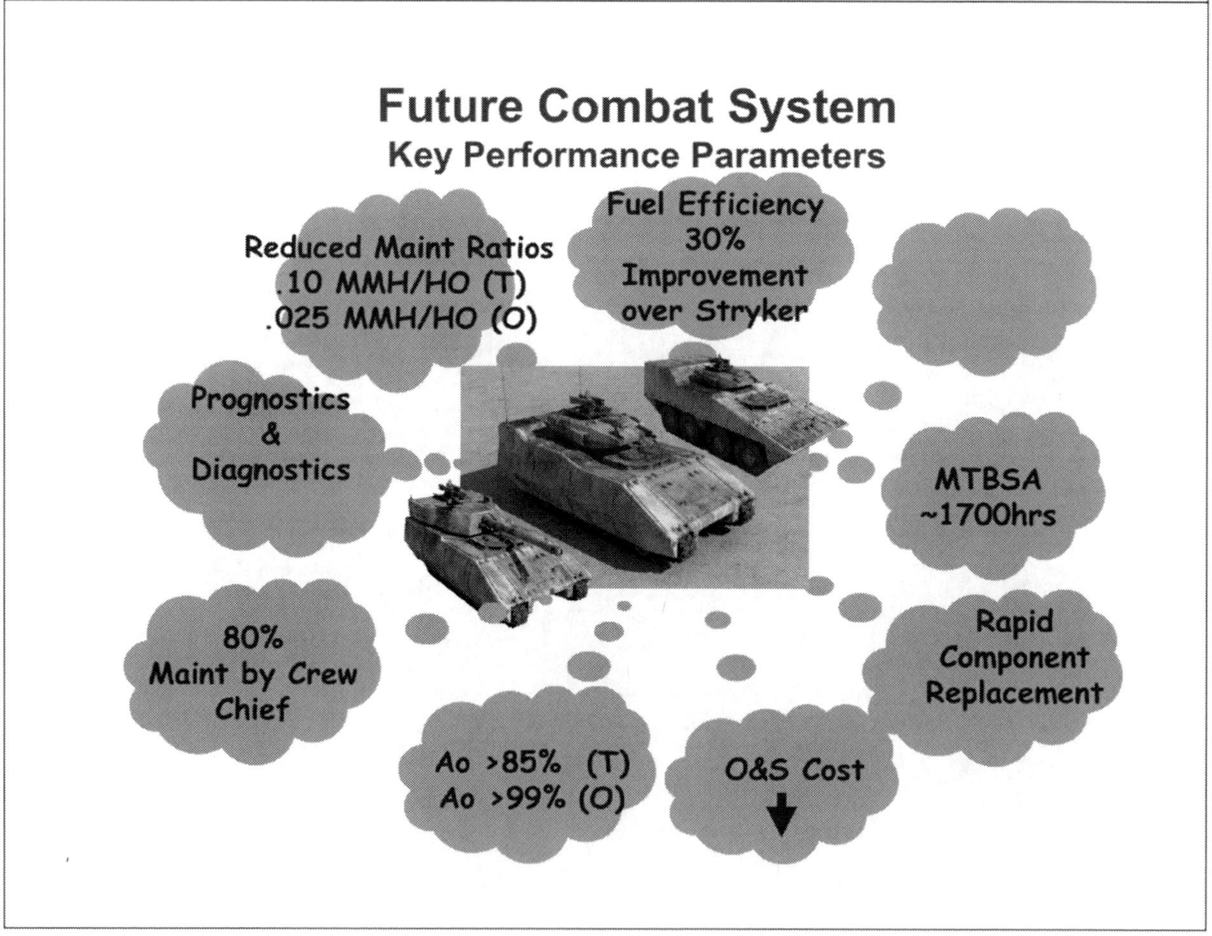
Future Combat System
Key Performance Parameters
Reduced Maint Ratios
.10 MMH/HO (T)
.025 MMH/HO (O)
Fuel Efficiency
30%
Improvement over Stryker
Prognostics & Diagnostics
MTBSA ~1700hrs
80% Maint by Crew Chief
Rapid Component Replacement
Ao >85% (T)
Ao >99% (O)
O&S Cost

Design Practices

- Which do you prefer?

A **B**

Design Practices

- Which do you prefer?

A **B**

Design Practices

- **Which do you prefer?**

A

B

Design Practices

- **Which do you prefer ?**

A

B

Design Practices

- Which do you prefer ?

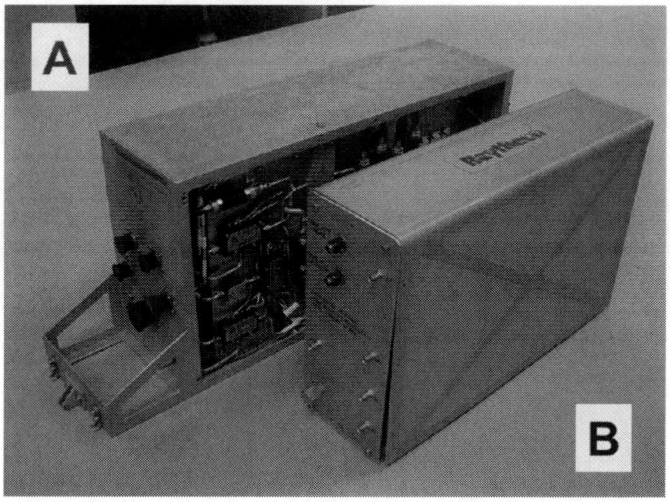

Wrap Up

- Objective Force capabilities require new design thinking

How are you changing the way you think about product design?

Backup Slides

Comanche
Key Performance Parameters

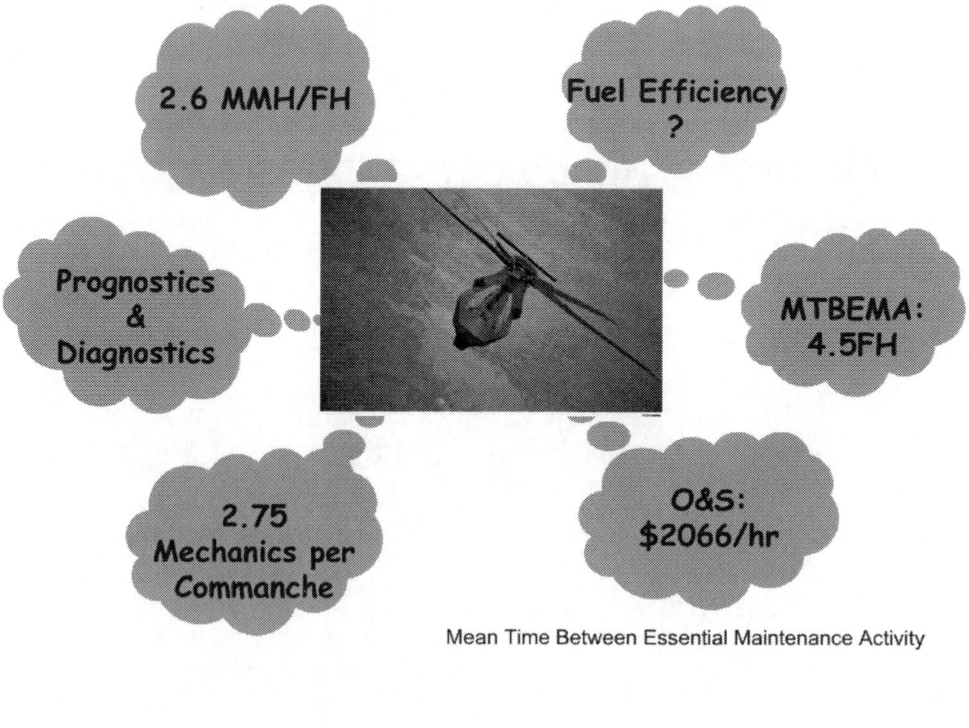

Mean Time Between Essential Maintenance Activity

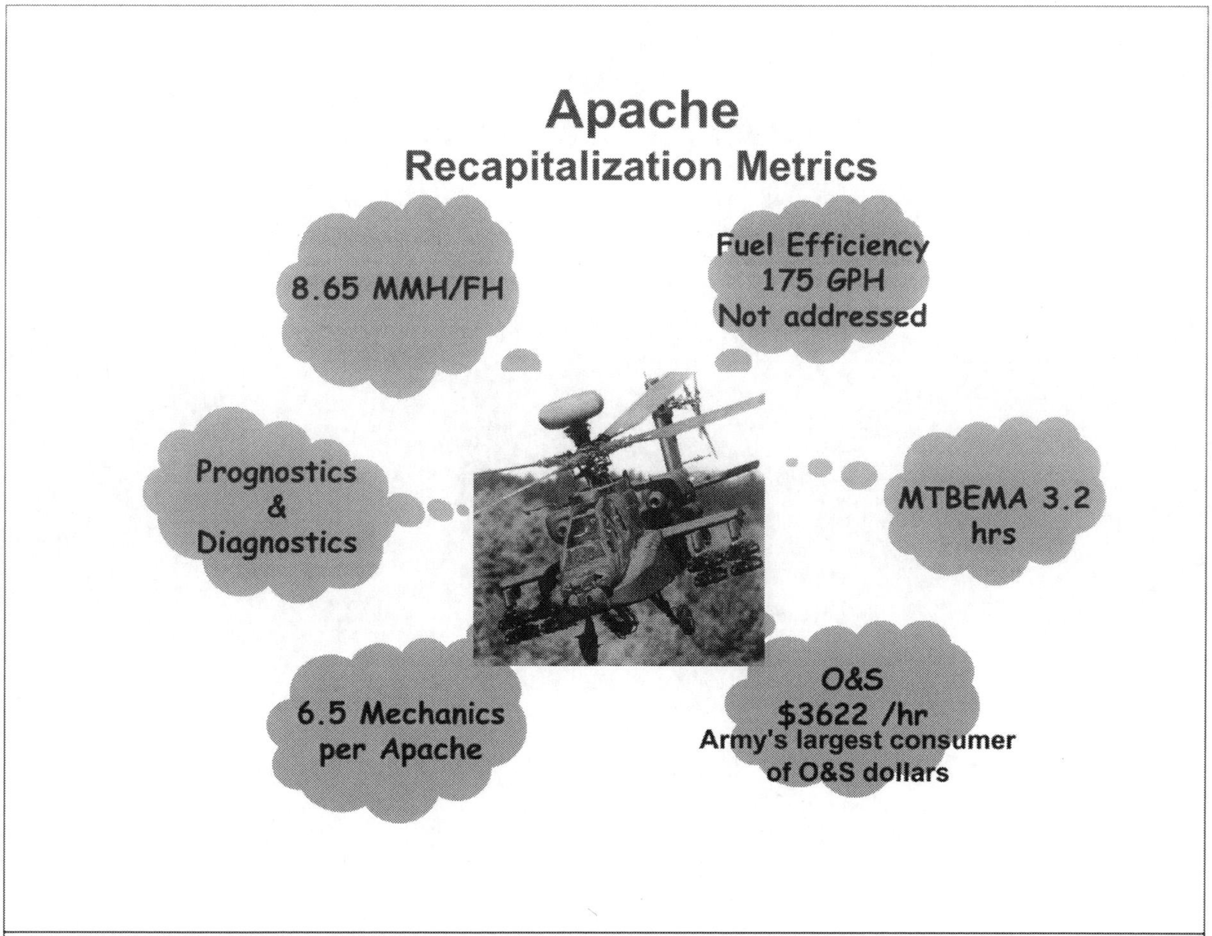
Apache
Recapitalization Metrics
8.65 MMH/FH
Fuel Efficiency
175 GPH
Not addressed
Prognostics
&
Diagnostics
MTBEMA 3.2
hrs
6.5 Mechanics
per Apache
O&S
$3622 /hr
Army's largest consumer
of O&S dollars

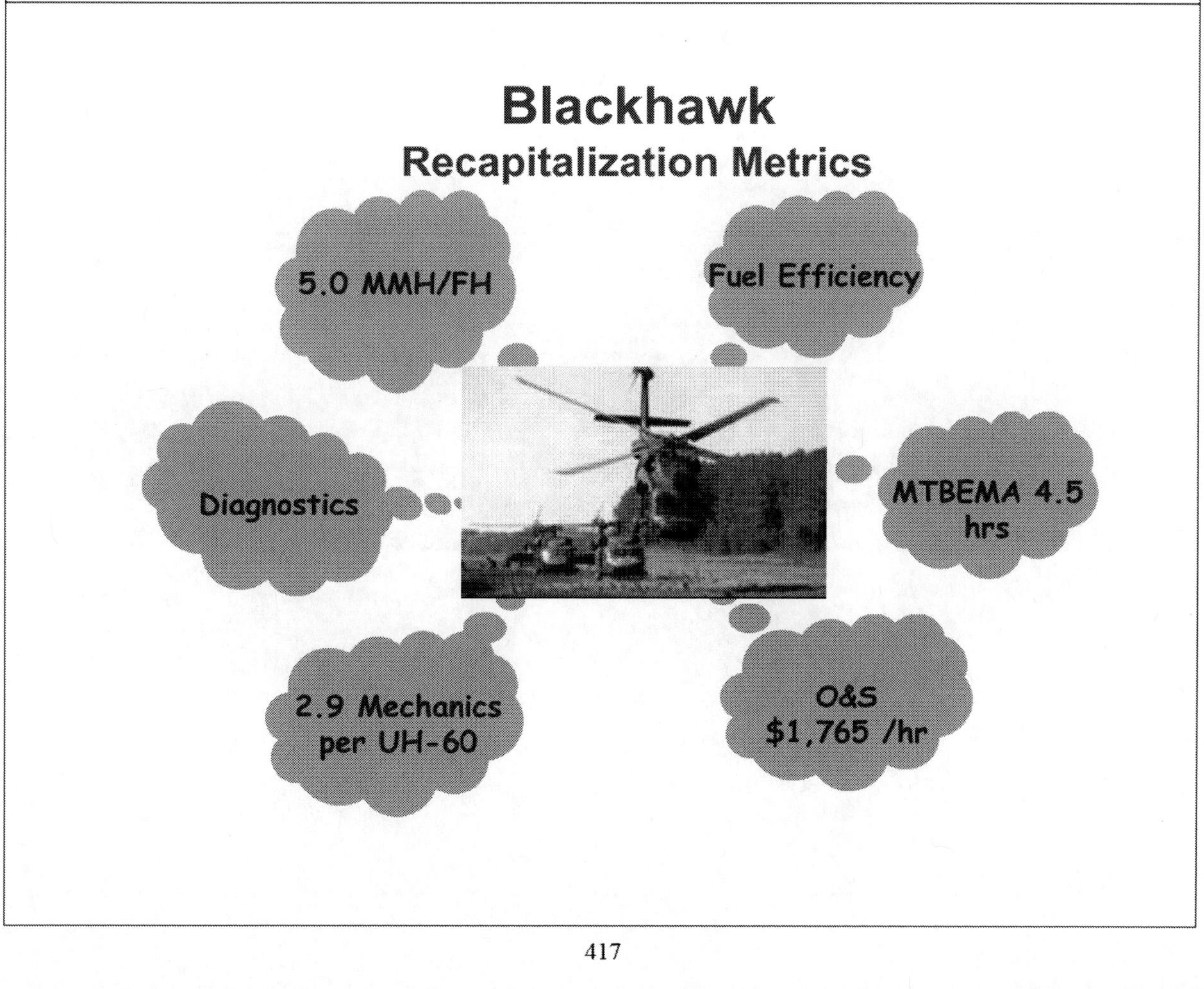
Blackhawk
Recapitalization Metrics
5.0 MMH/FH
Fuel Efficiency
Diagnostics
MTBEMA 4.5
hrs
2.9 Mechanics
per UH-60
O&S
$1,765 /hr

Chinook
Recapitalization Metrics

9.8 MMH/FH
300% Increase
in last 10 Years

Fuel Efficiency
Not Addressed

Diagnostics

MTBEMA 3.3
hrs

8.2 Mechanics
per Chinook

O&S
$1,900- $2,800
/hr

UAV

? MMH/FH

Fuel Efficiency
Addressed, but
Type?

Prognostics
&
Diagnostics

MTBEMA ?

? Mechanics
per UAV

O&S
$?

AMD Battlespace

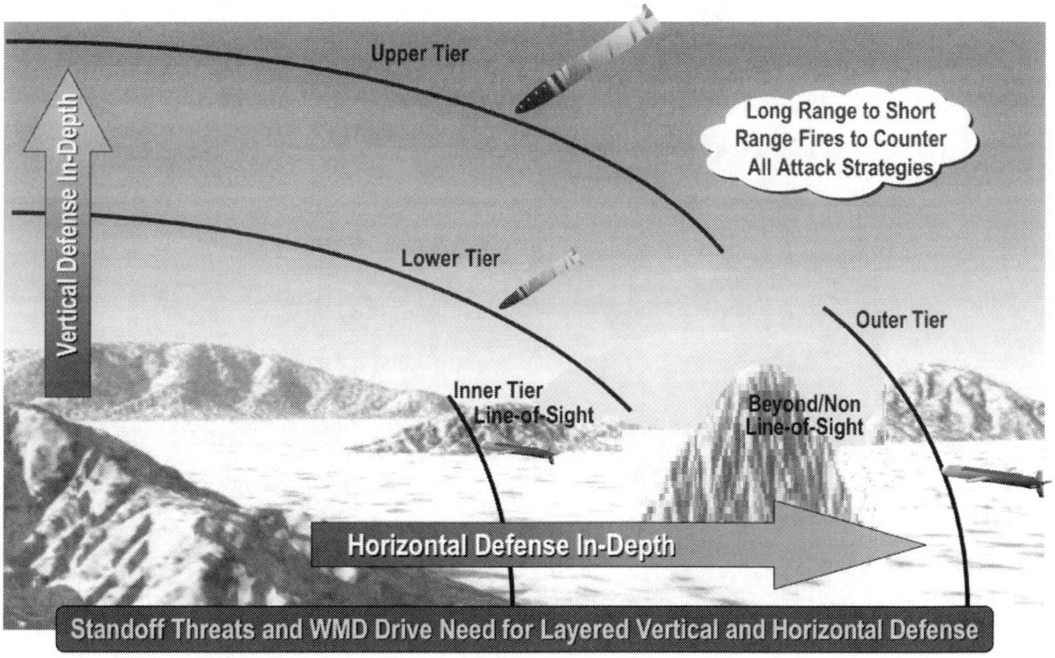

MEADS
Key Performance Parameters

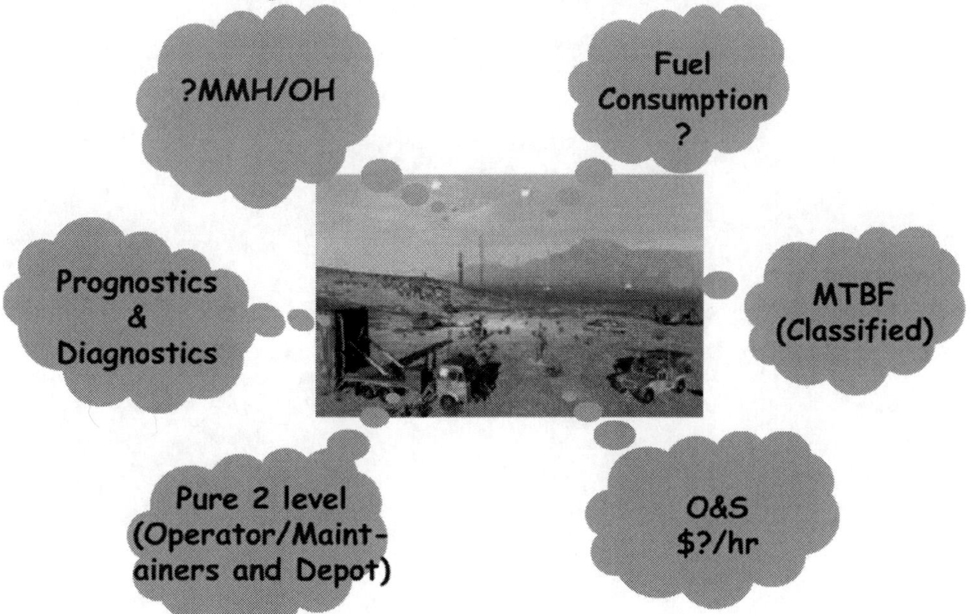

SLAMRAAM
Key Performance Parameters

MMH/OH

Fuel Efficiency

Prognostics & Diagnostics

MTBF
150hrs (T)
220hrs (O)

Pure 2 level (Operator/Maintainers and Depot)

$/hr

PAC-3 Patriot
Recapitalization Metrics

3.5 MMH/OH

Fuel Consumption

Diagnostics

MTBCMF
19.8 hrs

~114 Mechanics per Battalion

?$/hr

Stinger/Avenger
Not Due for Recapitalization

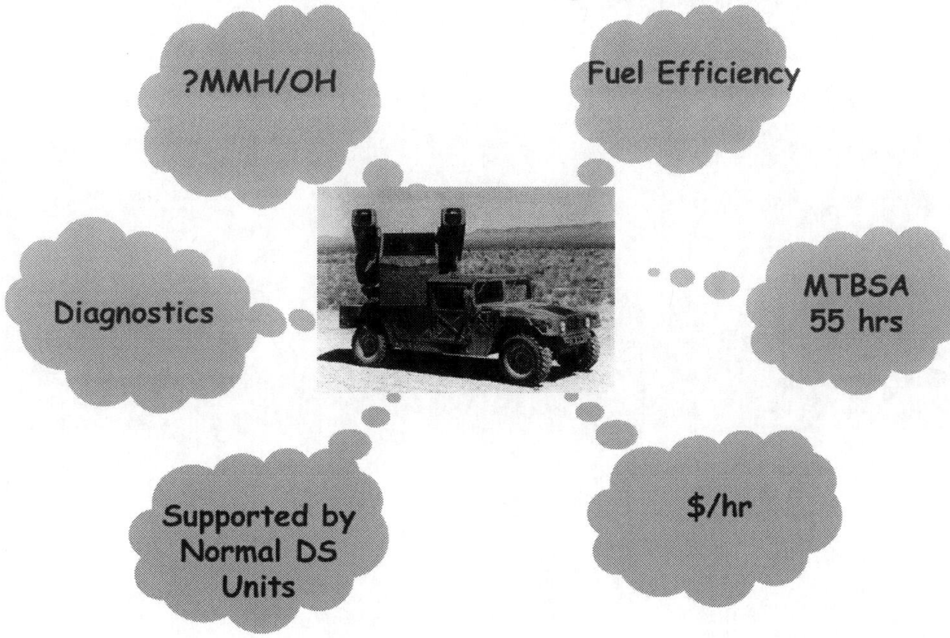

It's <u>not</u> about showing what is wrong….

…it <u>is</u> about finding better ways to do business!

- Lee Iacocca

Business Strategy

Dick O'Neill
Concurrent Technologies Corporation
August 13, 2003

We don't need a strategy!

- Market is too volatile!
- Technology is changing too rapidly!
- We have to be lean, mean – ready to adjust to market changes.

J. Edwards Deming

Everyone giving their best efforts without a strategic direction results in a random walk!

Why do we need a business strategy?

“

If you don't know where you're going,
you'll end up someplace else.

Yogi (Lawrence Peter) Berra (b.1925)

”

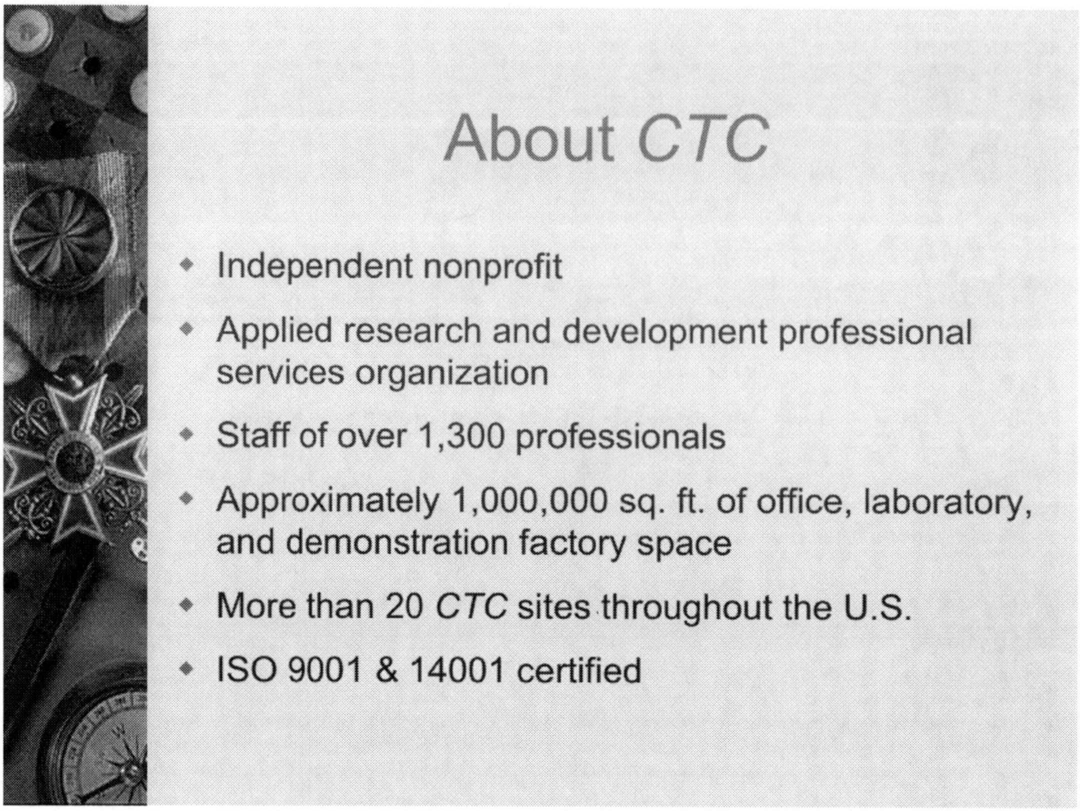
About *CTC*
Independent nonprofit
Applied research and development professional services organization
Staff of over 1,300 professionals
Approximately 1,000,000 sq. ft. of office, laboratory, and demonstration factory space
More than 20 *CTC* sites throughout the U.S.
ISO 9001 & 14001 certified

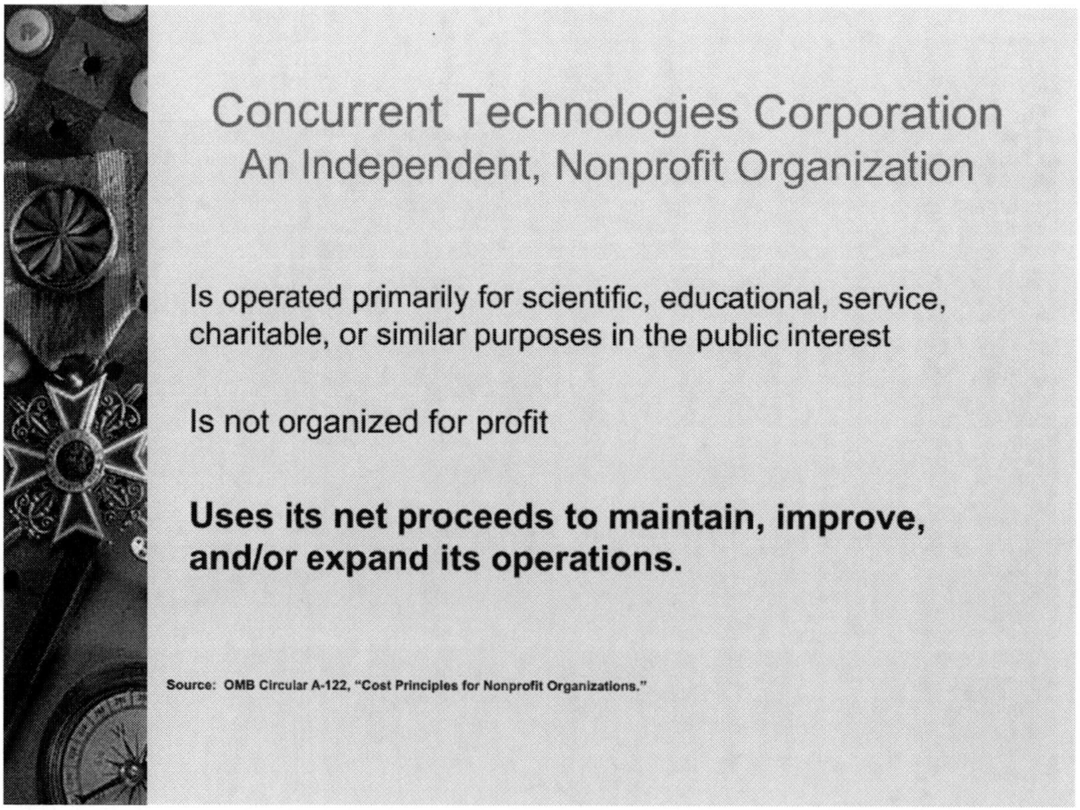
Concurrent Technologies Corporation
An Independent, Nonprofit Organization
Is operated primarily for scientific, educational, service, charitable, or similar purposes in the public interest
Is not organized for profit
Uses its net proceeds to maintain, improve, and/or expand its operations.
Source: OMB Circular A-122, "Cost Principles for Nonprofit Organizations."

Performance Based Marketing

- Critical to success
- Must exceed customer expectations
- Must ensure customer succeeds
- Key for obtaining client support for follow-on efforts

Strategic Partnering

- None of us possess all the skills/expertise required in today's environment
- Strategic partners are known quantities
- High degree of integrity and trust
- Easy to align for next opportunity

Final Thoughts

- **Must understand needs of client and help them succeed**
- **Value must be viewed from the Client's Perspective**
- **Value must be Measurable**
- **Strive for Perfection through rapid feedback & mistake proofing**
- **Today's state-of-the-art "system" is tomorrow's museum piece**

UNCLASSIFIED
GMD JPO Logistics Directorate
Melding Defense and Commercial Logistics
SOLE Symposium 2003
MISSILE DEFENSE AGENCY
DEPARTMENT OF DEFENSE
GROUND-BASED MIDCOURSE DEFENSE
Team GMD
JOINT PROGRAM OFFICE
14 August 2003
Mr. Gordon Porter
Deputy Director, Logistics Directorate,
Ground-Based Midcourse Defense
UNCLASSIFIED

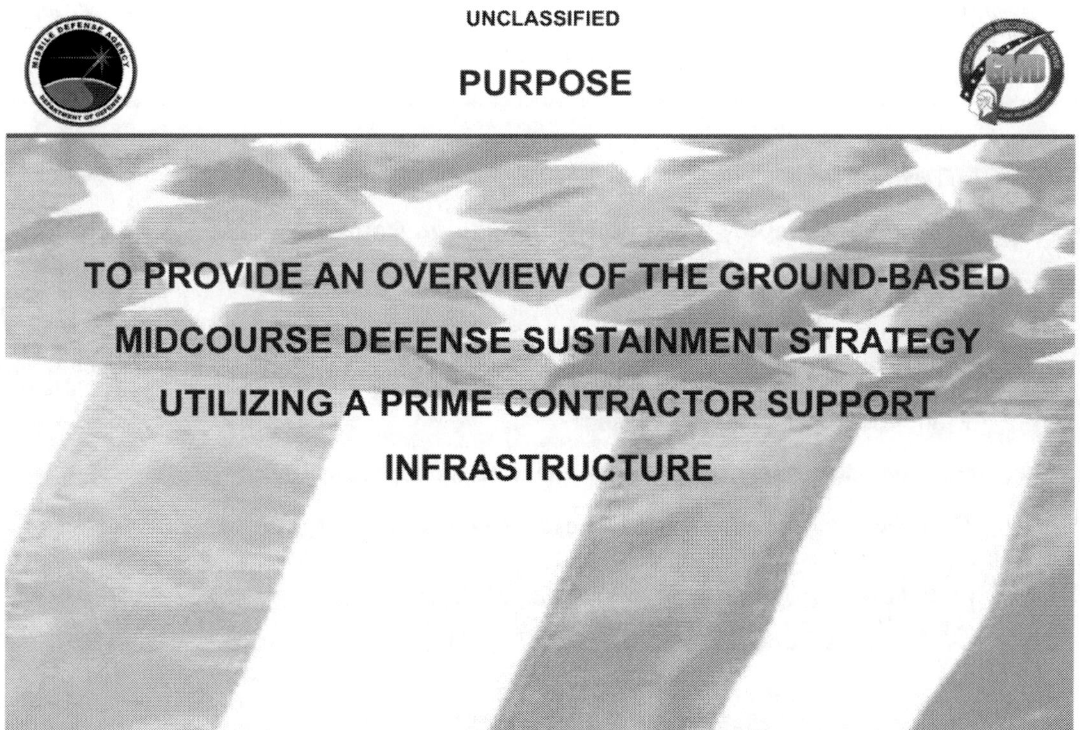
UNCLASSIFIED
PURPOSE
TO PROVIDE AN OVERVIEW OF THE GROUND-BASED MIDCOURSE DEFENSE SUSTAINMENT STRATEGY UTILIZING A PRIME CONTRACTOR SUPPORT INFRASTRUCTURE
Approved for Public Release Case No. 03-MDA-0177
GMK-03-07-0011-SOLE-U
UNCLASSIFIED
Team GMD Forging America's Shield

UNCLASSIFIED

OUTLINE

- GMD Program Synopsis
  - Mission and Tasks
  - Operational Concept
  - Organizational Structure
  - GMK Logistics Integration Role
- GMD Total System Performance Responsibility Strategy
  - GMD Support Strategy
  - Contractor Life Cycle Support
  - Prime Contractor Support System Overview
- Lessons Learned

GMK-03-07-0011-SOLE-U UNCLASSIFIED

Approved for Public Release Case No. 03-MDA-0177

TEAM GMD *Forging America's Shield*

UNCLASSIFIED

MISSION AND TASKS

•GMD Mission

–Develop and Deploy a Credible Capability to Defend Against ***Intermediate*** and ***Long-Range Ballistic*** Missile Attacks in the ***Midcourse Phase*** of Flight

•Tasks

–Build, Test, and Verify an Initial Defensive Operations Capability

–Place the GMD System on Alert

–Execute Concurrent Testing and Defensive Operations

–Continue Development to Incrementally Improve Capability

Bottom Line: Field Initial Missile Defense Capability

GMK-03-07-0011-SOLE-U UNCLASSIFIED

Approved for Public Release Case No. 03-MDA-0177

TEAM GMD *Forging America's Shield*

Approved for public release by MDA/EA on 20 May 03

UNCLASSIFIED

GROUND-BASED MIDCOURSE DEFENSE COMPONENTS

Sensors

Defense Support Program/ Space Tracking & Surveillance System (DSP/STSS)

Space-Based Infrared System (SBIRS High)

Early Warning Radars

Sea-Based Test X-Band Radar

Interceptor

Boost Vehicle

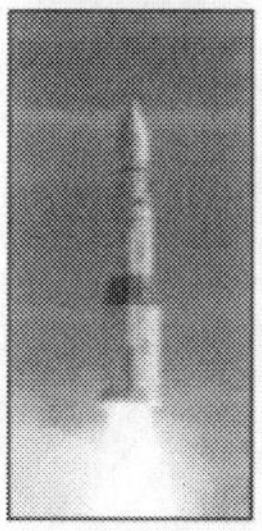

Kill Vehicle

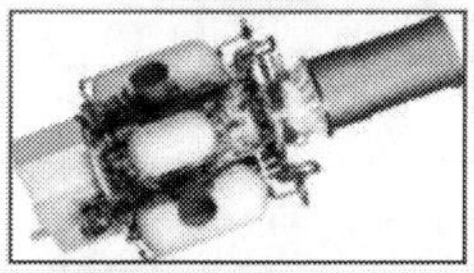

Leverages Existing Technology

Command & Control

GMD Fire Control & Communications

GMD Communications Net

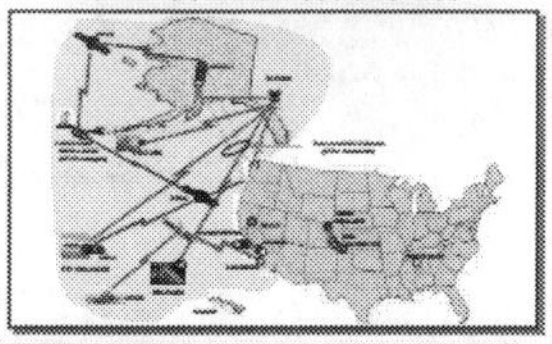

Key Functions	Acquire	Track	Classify	Discriminate	Control	Intercept	Assess
	✓	✓	✓	✓	✓	✓	✓

Assumes Completion of Appropriate Environmental Study(s)

Approved for Public Release Case No. 03-MDA-0177

TEAM GMD *Forging America's Shield*

Approved for public release by MDA/EA on 20 May 03

GMK-03-07-0011-SOLE-U

UNCLASSIFIED

UNCLASSIFIED

GMD ENGAGEMENT CONCEPT

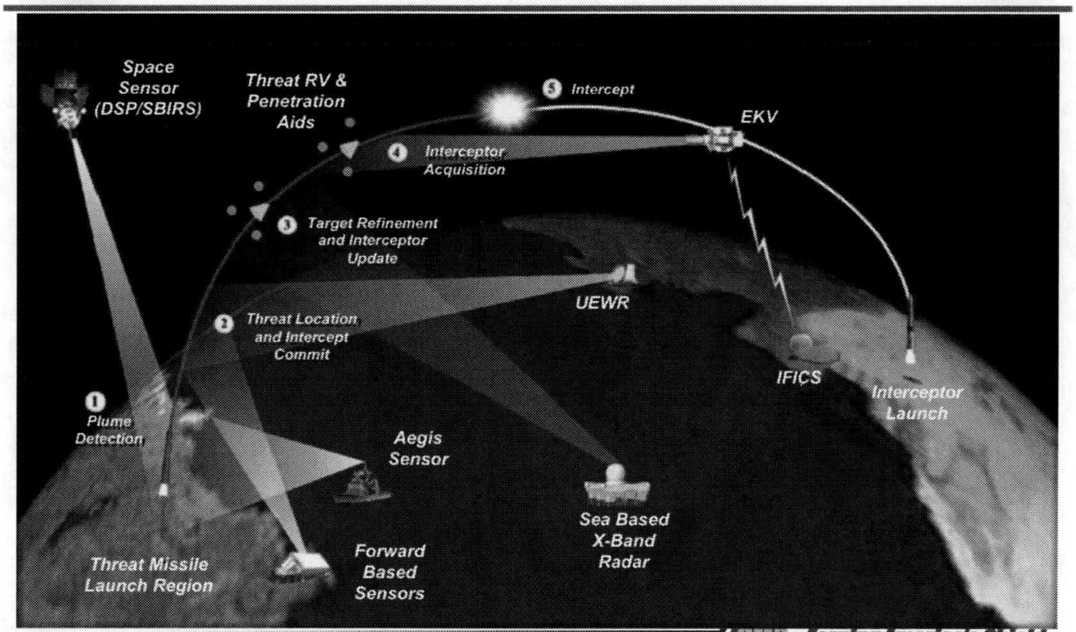

GMK-03-07-0011-SOLE-U

UNCLASSIFIED

GMD *Forging America's Shield*

Approved for public release by MDA/EA on 20 May 03

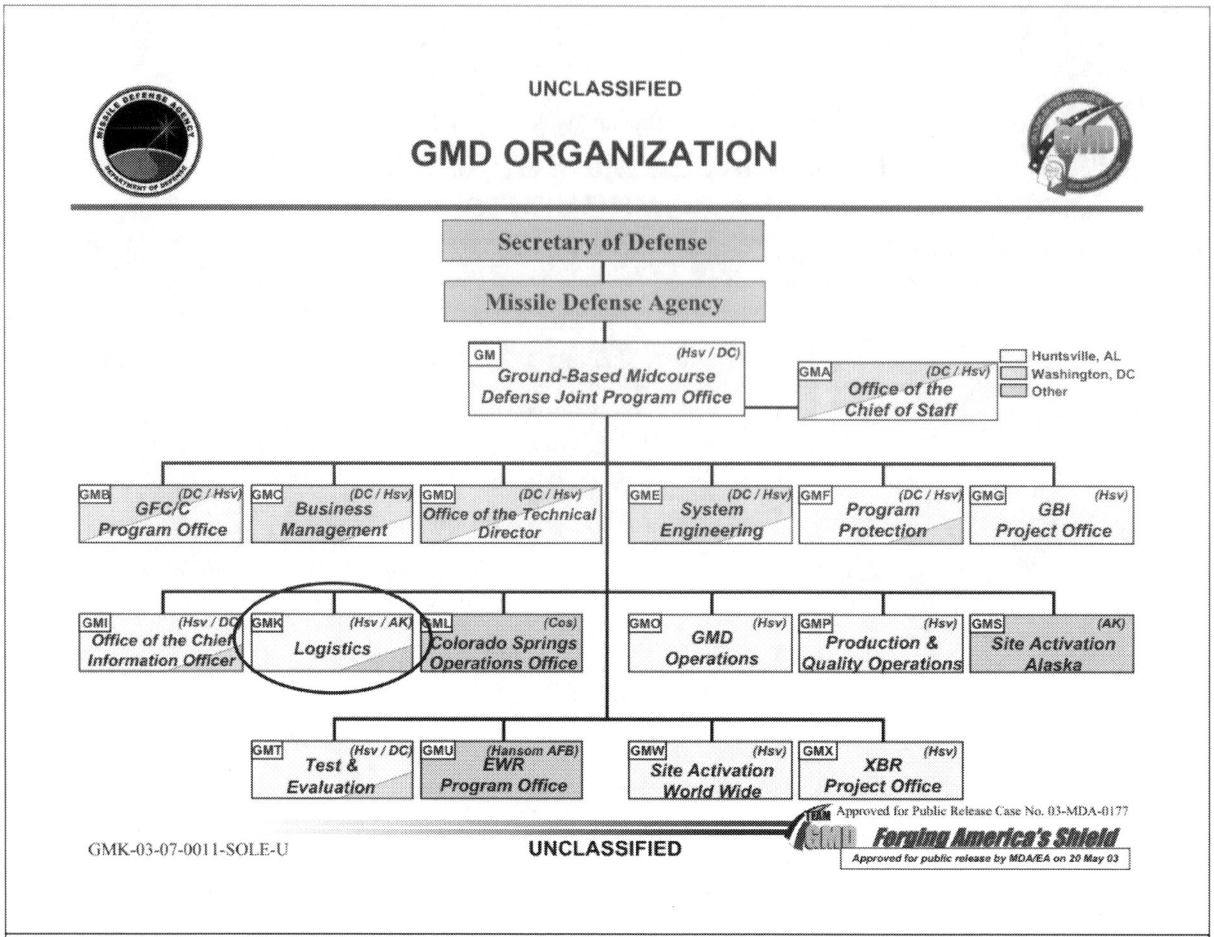
UNCLASSIFIED
GMD ORGANIZATION
Secretary of Defense
Missile Defense Agency
GM (Hsv / DC) Ground-Based Midcourse Defense Joint Program Office
GMA (DC / Hsv) Office of the Chief of Staff
Huntsville, AL
Washington, DC
Other
GMB (DC / Hsv) GFC/C Program Office
GMC (DC / Hsv) Business Management
GMD (DC / Hsv) Office of the Technical Director
GME (DC / Hsv) System Engineering
GMF (DC / Hsv) Program Protection
GMG (Hsv) GBI Project Office
GMI (Hsv / DC) Office of the Chief Information Officer
GMK (Hsv / AK) Logistics
GML (Cos) Colorado Springs Operations Office
GMO (Hsv) GMD Operations
GMP (Hsv) Production & Quality Operations
GMS (AK) Site Activation Alaska
GMT (Hsv / DC) Test & Evaluation
GMU (Hansom AFB) EWR Program Office
GMW (Hsv) Site Activation World Wide
GMX (Hsv) XBR Project Office
Approved for Public Release Case No. 03-MDA-0177
GMK-03-07-0011-SOLE-U
UNCLASSIFIED
Forging America's Shield
Approved for public release by MDA/EA on 20 May 03

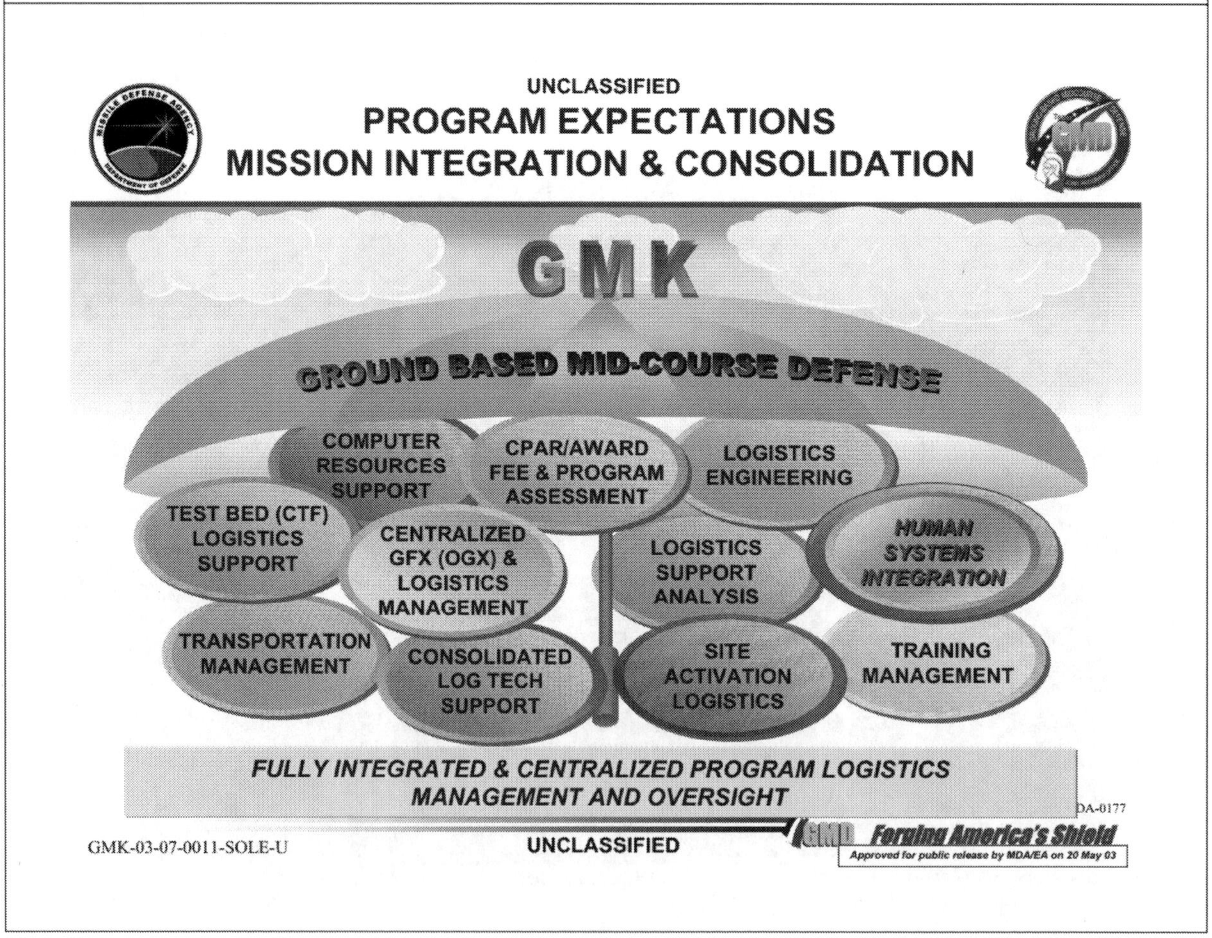
UNCLASSIFIED
PROGRAM EXPECTATIONS
MISSION INTEGRATION & CONSOLIDATION
GMK
GROUND BASED MID-COURSE DEFENSE
COMPUTER RESOURCES SUPPORT
CPAR/AWARD FEE & PROGRAM ASSESSMENT
LOGISTICS ENGINEERING
TEST BED (CTF) LOGISTICS SUPPORT
CENTRALIZED GFX (OGX) & LOGISTICS MANAGEMENT
LOGISTICS SUPPORT ANALYSIS
HUMAN SYSTEMS INTEGRATION
TRANSPORTATION MANAGEMENT
CONSOLIDATED LOG TECH SUPPORT
SITE ACTIVATION LOGISTICS
TRAINING MANAGEMENT
FULLY INTEGRATED & CENTRALIZED PROGRAM LOGISTICS MANAGEMENT AND OVERSIGHT
DA-0177
GMK-03-07-0011-SOLE-U
UNCLASSIFIED
Forging America's Shield
Approved for public release by MDA/EA on 20 May 03

UNCLASSIFIED

GMD PRIME CONTRACTOR RESPONSIBILITIES

- Total System Performance Responsibility Support Strategy:
  - Performance Based Incentive Fee
  - Provides for a Level of Service
- Prime Contractor Will Provide:
  - System Hardware & Software and Integration Capabilities
  - Maintenance on Mission Equipment
  - Repair Parts and Supply Support Management
  - Modernization Through Spares
  - Engineering Support
  - Base Operations Support--If Required
  - Training
  - Test, Training and Exercise Capability

User Provide Operators
JPO Provides Contract Management
Prime Contractor Provides Everything Else

Approved for Public Release Case No. 03-MDA-0177

GMK-03-07-0011-SOLE-U UNCLASSIFIED TEAM GMD *Forging America's Shield*

UNCLASSIFIED

CONTRACTOR LIFE CYCLE SUPPORT

- Boeing Provides a CLS Infrastructure to Maintain the Primary Equipment, ASOIE, TMDE and STTE.
- CLS Is Accomplished Through Integrated Prime Contractor Support System (PCSS).
- PCSS Supports Deployment, Activation and Sustainment of the GMD Architecture.

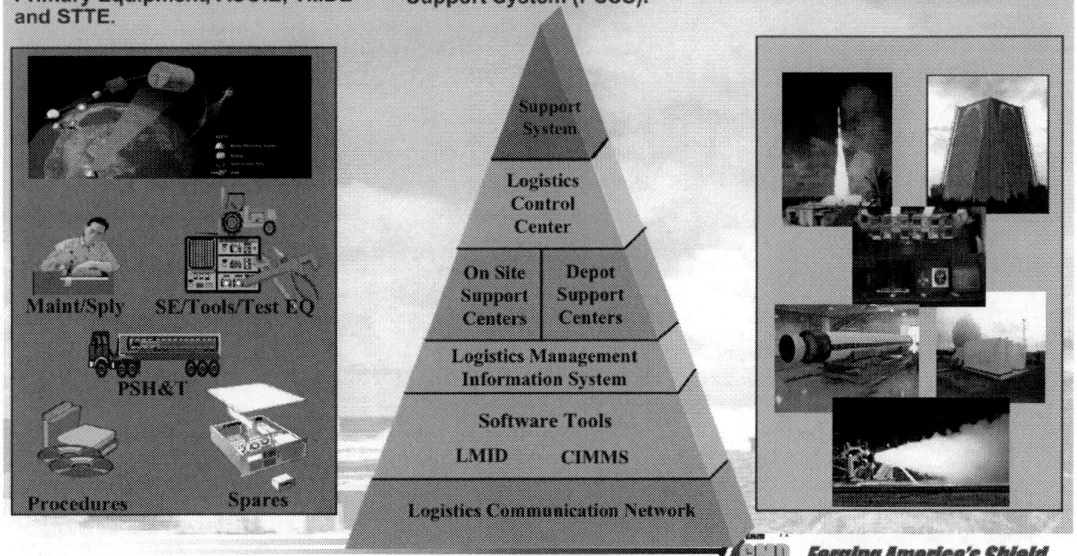

GMK-03-07-0011-SOLE-U UNCLASSIFIED TEAM GMD *Forging America's Shield*

CONTRACTOR LIFE CYCLE SUPPORT
Continued

- Prime Contractor (PC) to Provide a Lifecycle Sustainment Capability That Will Support Initial Defensive Operations (IDO) and Test Activities
- The Prime Contractor Support System (PCSS) Major Components Are The:
  - Logistics Control Center (LogCC)
  - On-Site Support Center (OSSC)
  - Off-Site Support Center(s) (OFSC)
  - Logistics Management Information System (LMIS)

- PC Provides All of the Necessary Resources to Sustain the GMD Element's Performance
- PC Retains Responsibility for Total GMD Element Performance and Conducts All GMD Maintenance Activities

CONTRACTOR LIFE CYCLE SUPPORT
Continued

- LogCC Provides the Centralized Logistics Functional Support and Overall Control of the PCSS System
- On-Site Maintenance Consist of Removal and Replacement of Defective Line Repairable Units (LRUs)
- Off-Site Maintenance, Consisting of Repair of Defective LRUs, Will Be Performed at Contractor/Vendor Facilities
- Legacy Component Interface (UEWR, Cobra Dane, Etc.), Sustainment Strategy:
  - Prime to Perform Depot Level Maintenance for GMD Developed Equipment, Software, and Material Support
  - The Prime Will Retain Responsibility for All Off-Site GMD Hardware/Software
  - CLCS Maintenance Will Be Implemented Through Associate Contractor Agreements and Memorandum of Agreements With Services

CONTRACTOR LIFE CYCLE SUPPORT
Continued

- **LMIS Uses Two Relational Databases to Support the PCSS**
  - **Logistics Management Information Database (LMID)**
    - **Element-level Logistics Support Analysis Record (LSAR)**
    - **Commercial Off-the-shelf Product Called SLIC Wave^{tm}**
  - **Computerized Maintenance Management System (CIMMS)**
    - **Monitors the Quantity, Location and Status of GMD Assets**
    - **Commercial Off-the-shelf (COTS) Product Called Datastream 7i ^{TM}**
  - **The Boeing Intranet Provides the Primary Communications Connectivity for the LMIS**

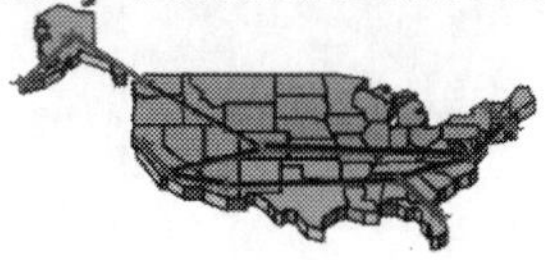

- **GMD Logistics Directorate Is the Provider of All Government Requested Logistics Information and Reports**

LESSONS LEARNED

- **Fix Responsibility to a Single Prime Contractor to Provide for Total System Performance**
- **Utilize the Alpha Contracting Process to Achieve Efficiencies in Contract Development**
- **Establish a Performance Based Incentive Contracting Strategy**
- **Develop Assessment Plan Based on Objective Evaluation Criteria**

Back Up

UNCLASSIFIED

"Maximizing Your SCOR with Lean Six Sigma"

A Balanced Approach

CMM/SEI

SCOR Model

Lean Six Sigma

Charlie Murphy
USA Logistics Process Owner

August 14, 2003

Who is United Space Alliance?

- NASA prime contractor responsible for Space Shuttle maintenance and operations
- Workforce of approximately 10,000
- Limited Liability Company formed in 1996 equally owned by The Boeing Company and Lockheed Martin Corporation
- Supports multiple NASA Centers:
  - NASA HQ
  - KSC
  - JSC
  - MSFC

SCOR Supply Chain Definition

SCOR Supply-Chain Council

SCOR defines supply chain as the integrated processes of Plan, Source, Make, Deliver and Return, spanning suppliers' supplier to customers' customer, aligned with **Operational Strategy**, **Material**, **Work** & **Information** Flows.

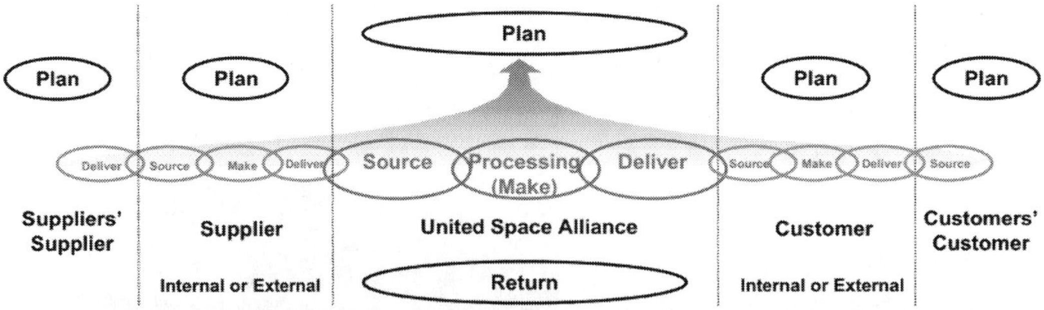

← Supply Chain Operations Reference Model →

USA SCOR Level I Supply Chain

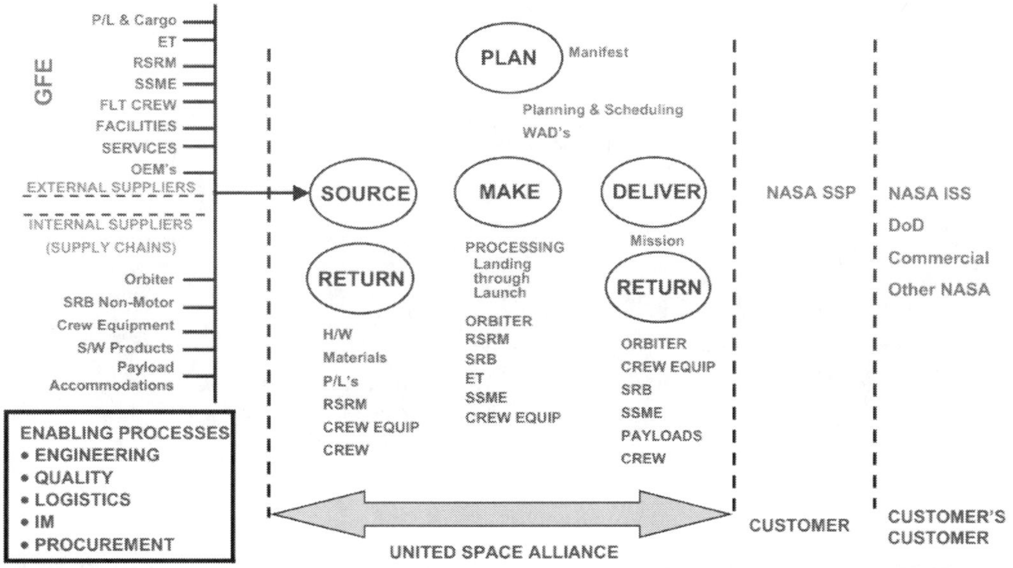

Supply Chain Processes & Products

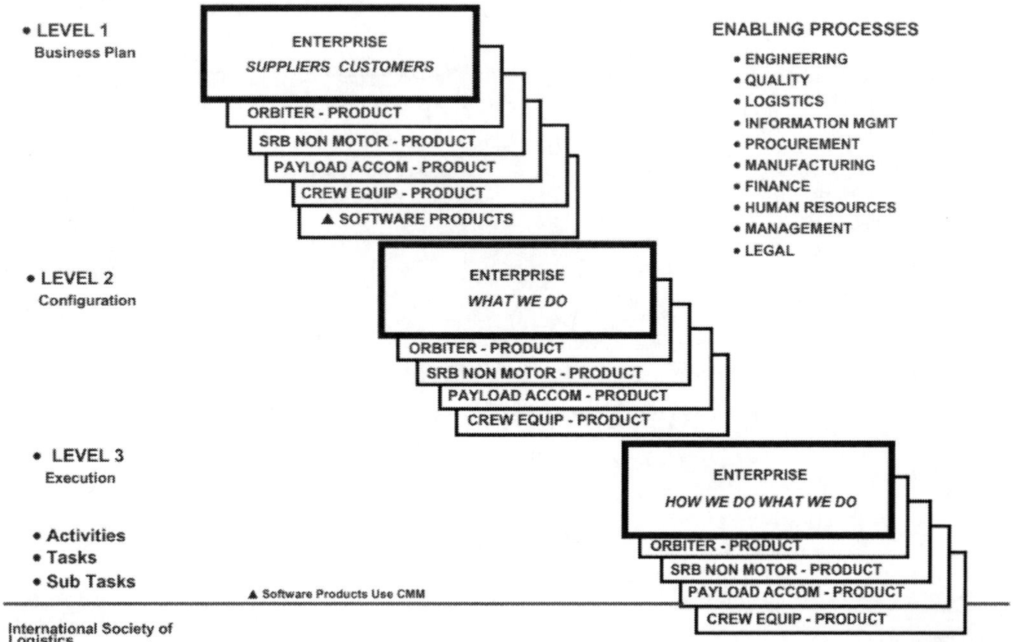

USA Processes & Products

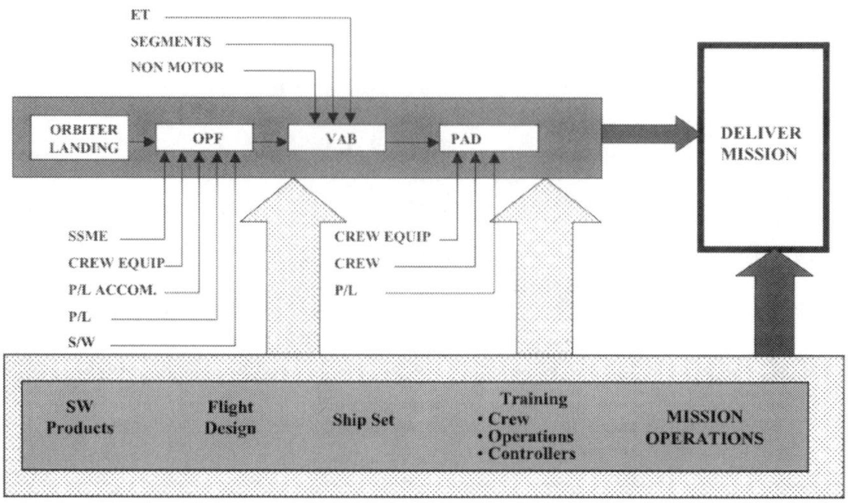

Toolset Effectiveness & Strengths

Lean

- *Work Flow Control*
  - Work Place Organization
  - Flow Analysis
  - Waste Elimination

Six Sigma

- *Variation Control*
  - Diagnosis for Variability
  - DMAIC

SEI/CMM

- *Product Development*
  - Integration of Different Practices to Create Products

SCOR

- *Supply Chain Performance*
  - Structured
  - Process Definition
  - Metrics Hierarchy

- *All Valid Tools with some Commonality*
- *All Have Strengths*
- *Integration Maximizes Strengths*

Toolset Integration

CMM/SEI – Tools to develop products.

SCOR – Tool to model processes, integrate products, define & measure performance.

L6S – Tool to analyze, improve & control process improvements.

Enterprise SCORCard

	Level 1 Metric	Level 1 USA to NASA	Level 1 Actuals FY '02	Level 1 Actuals SFOC	Benchmark	FY'02 Gap	FY'02$	SFOC LOC Gap	SFOC LOC $
Exte	Supply Chain Delivery Reliability	Delivery Performance	100.0%	90%	100%	0		16.1%	
		Perfect Order Fulfillment	100.0%	95%	100%	0		4.3%	
	Supply Chain Responsiveness	Order Fulfillment Lead Time (Calendar Days)	235	200	121	114		80	
	Supply Chain Flexibility	# of Problem Reports per flow	2577		100%	7.88%			
		# of Customer Change Requests per flow	150						
Shareholder	Supply Chain Cost	Cost of Goods	84.2%		73%	11.20%	$200,000,000		
		G&A+ Svc. Centers	8.7%		6%	2.70%	$50,000,000		
		Warranty / Returns Processing Costs	0.09%	0.13%	0%	0.09%	$2,000,000	0.13%	$10,000,000
		Cash-to-Cash Cycle Time	183.0		93	90			
		Inventory Days of Supply	206.0		53	153	$80,000,000		
	Profitability	Gross Margin	15.8%		22%	5.8%	$100,000,000		
		Operating Income	6.6%		12%	5.1%	$40,000,000		

USA's SCOR Top-Down Project Approach

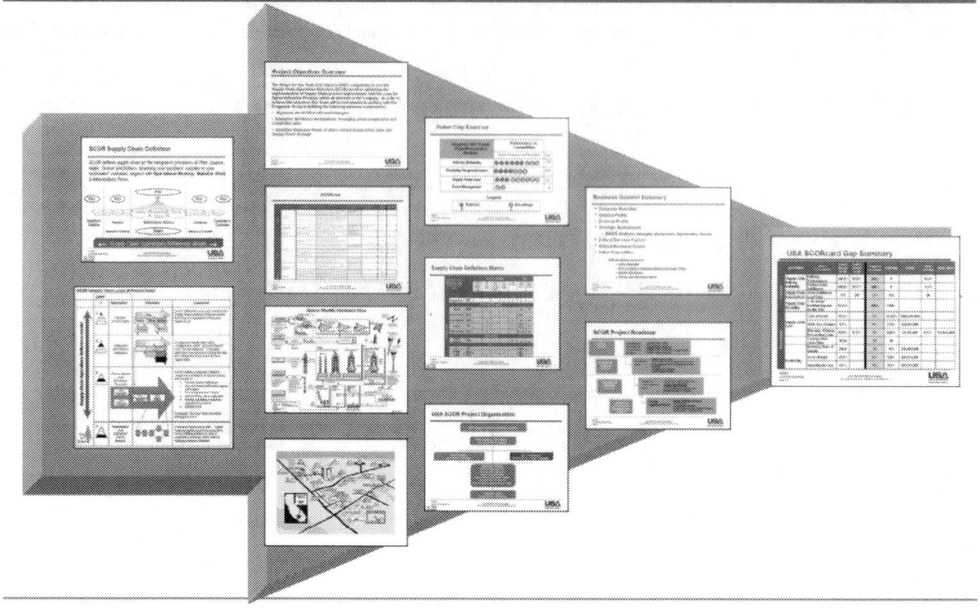

USA's SCOR Project Approach – Phase II

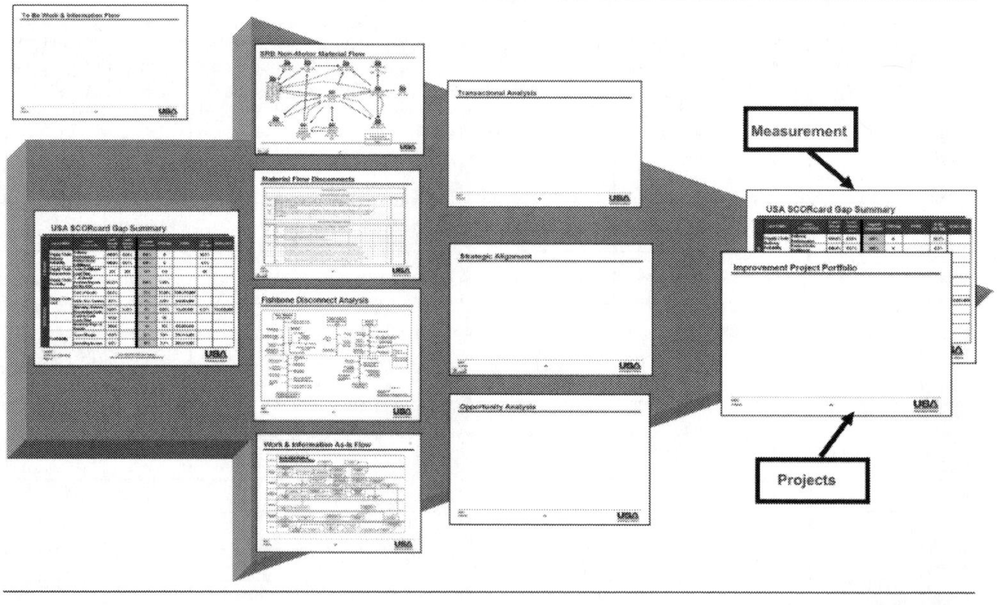

NASA Strategy Defined and Supported

- Integrated Space Transportation Plan
  - Shuttle
  - Orbital Space Plane
  - Next Generation Launch Technology
- Service Life Extension Program (SLEP)
- Clear Long Term Roadmap
- USA Actions Fully Support the Strategy
- Improved Productivity & Cost Reductions to Be Applied to SLEP Initiatives

Summary

- L6S Provides Effective Process for Improvements
- SCOR Provides Effective Process to Identify Enterprise Level Improvement Projects and Measure the Results
- Supply Chain Definition using SCOR Model can be Effective for Services as well as Durable Goods

HOMELAND SECURITY

SOLE – THE INTERNATIONAL SOCIETY OF LOGISTICS

38TH Annual INTERNATIONAL Conference & Exhibition

Huntsville, Alabama

August 14, 2003

Dr. Russell A. Vacante

Director of Sector Leadership

Defense Acquisition University &

SOLE BOA Member

Homeland Security -- A Challenge to Balance Competing Societal Forces

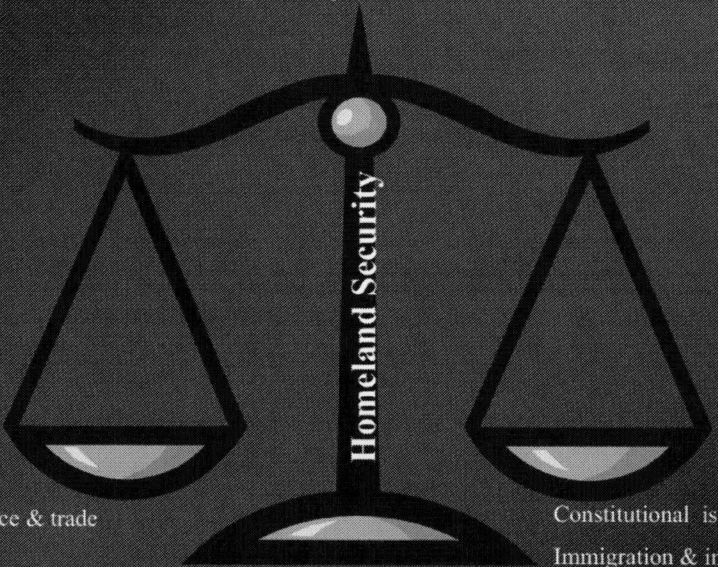

- Commerce & trade
- Security
- Economics
- Socio-political considerations

- Constitutional issues
- Immigration & intellectual capital
- Travel & import considerations
- Democracy & global leadership

HOMELAND SECURITY
Conclusion

- A Challenge to Logisticians and SOLE Members:

  - Make homeland security part of your daily thinking & activity—do the analysis
  - Understand and use the technology & safe guards associate with your job
  - Assist others in acquiring a homeland security consciousness
  - Challenge the requirements and procedures
  - Collectively remain engage in your profession, the decision-making process and the Society

THINK END-TO-END AND CRITICALLY EVERYDAY. Our freedom, security and safety is at stake!

Oracle Corporation

Steve Cooperman
Vice President
Homeland Security Solutions

ORACLE

We Cannot Become Complacent

"The Threat Is Real, and Pervasive,..
The Want To Destroy The
American Way Of Life"
Lt. General Keith Kellogg
June 17th, 2003

ORACLE

Information Technology and Homeland Security

"Information contributes to every aspect of homeland security and is a vital foundation for the homeland security effort"

The National Strategy for Homeland Security
Office of Homeland Security--July, 2002

ORACLE

Data Is The Asset

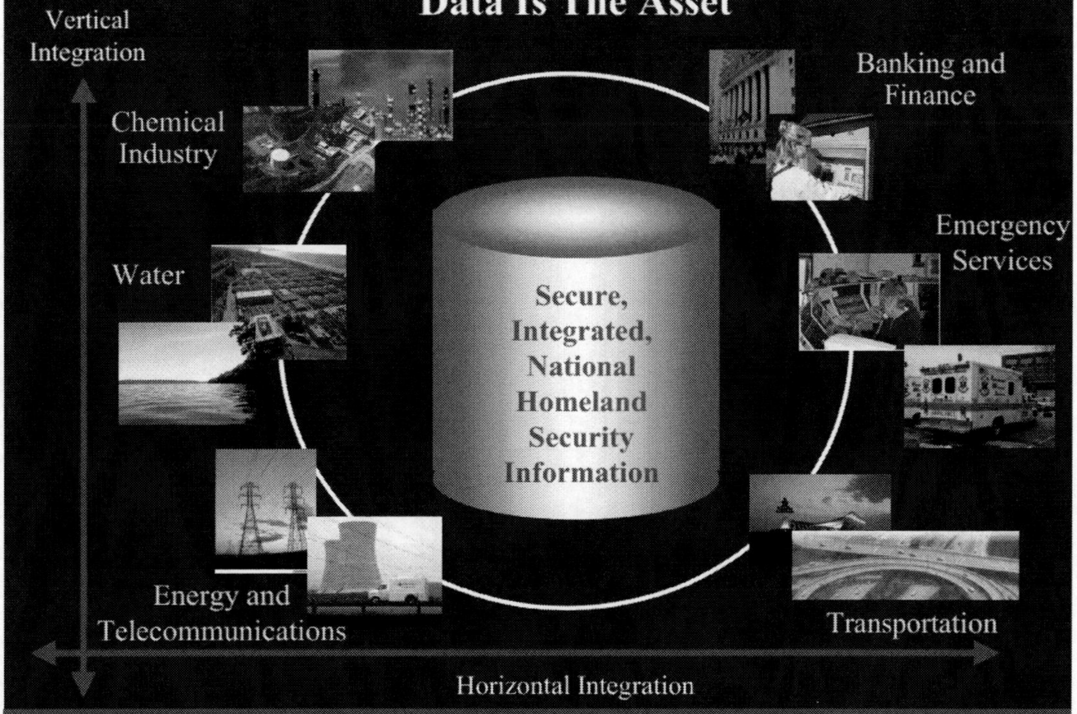

ORACLE

Information Security

- **There Is Direct Relationship Between Cyber and Physical Security**
- Systems Must Be Prepared to Counter Not Only Threats Posed by Physical Access to Infrastructure but Also Access to Information
  - Ex. Unauthorized Access to Information Used by a Port in the Conduct of Its Business Can Be Exploited Just As Effectively As Access to the Port Itself
    - Inadequately Protected Databases Containing:
      - Contents of Containers
      - Detailed Cargo Tracking Information
      - Purchasing Data
- Solutions Must Use Technology That Ensures Information Security
- IT Must Be Involved In Decision Process

ORACLE

Goal: Put The Highest Level Of Security On Our Most Critical Assets

ORACLE

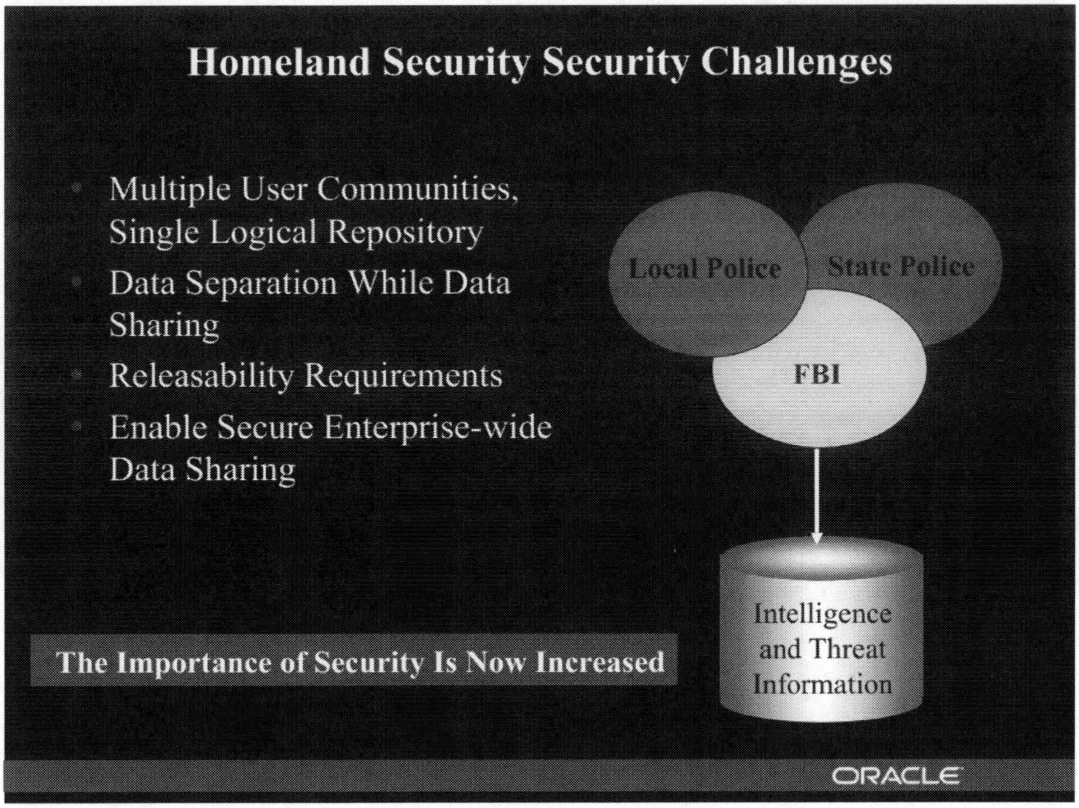
Homeland Security Security Challenges
Multiple User Communities, Single Logical Repository
Data Separation While Data Sharing
Releasability Requirements
Enable Secure Enterprise-wide Data Sharing
Local Police
State Police
FBI
Intelligence and Threat Information
The Importance of Security Is Now Increased
ORACLE

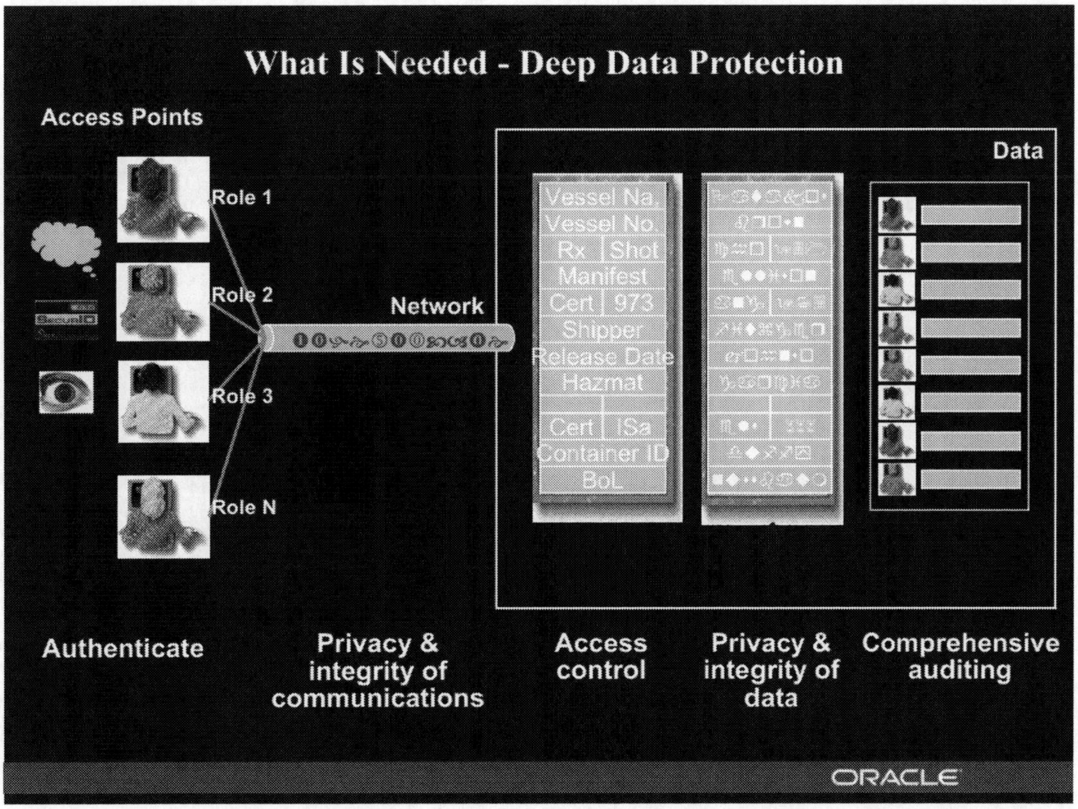
What Is Needed - Deep Data Protection
Access Points
Role 1
Role 2
Role 3
Role N
Network
Data
Vessel Na.
Vessel No.
Rx
Shot
Manifest
Cert
973
Shipper
Release Date
Hazmat
Cert
ISa
Container ID
BoL
Authenticate
Privacy & integrity of communications
Access control
Privacy & integrity of data
Comprehensive auditing
ORACLE

How Do You Know If Your Database Is Secure?

- The International Standard - Common Criteria-ISO/IEC 15408
  - The Common Criteria represents the outcome of a series of efforts to develop criteria for evaluation of IT security that are broadly useful within the international community

ORACLE

IAC Solutions Lab

Oracle Information Assurance Center

- Physical and virtual center
- Focus on customer education
- Test bed for leading-edge security solutions

ORACLE

H S Solution Success
A Solid IT Foundation Is Critical

- Foundation
  - an underlying base or support; *especially* : the whole masonry substructure of a building

ORACLE

Establishing a HS Technology Foundation

ORACLE e-businesssuite

ORACLE COLLABORATIONsuite

DEVELOPER 9i SUITE

APPLICATION 9i SERVER

ORACLE 9i UNBREAKABLE

- The Platform Needs To Addresses Key HS Requirements:
  - Access Heterogeneous Data
  - Integrate a Variety of Data Types
  - Manage Vast Quantities of Data
  - Find Patterns and Insights
  - Collaborate Securely

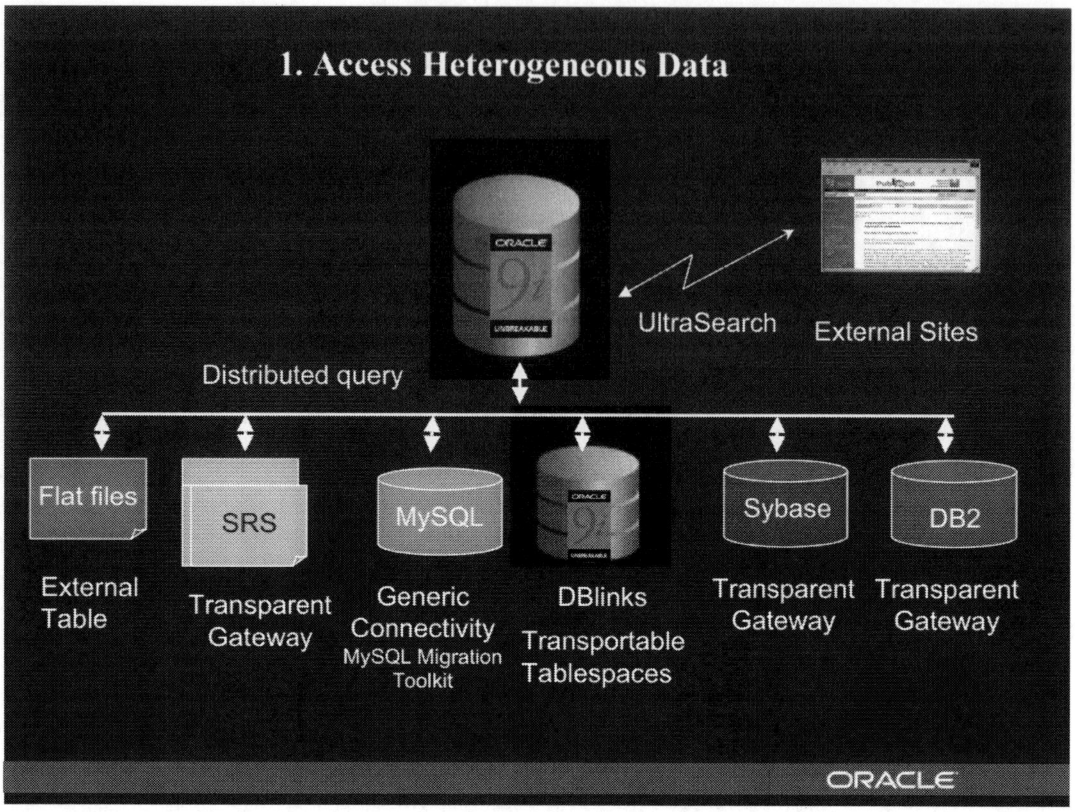
1. Access Heterogeneous Data
UltraSearch
External Sites
Distributed query
Flat files
SRS
MySQL
Sybase
DB2
External Table
Transparent Gateway
Generic Connectivity
MySQL Migration Toolkit
DBlinks
Transportable Tablespaces
Transparent Gateway
Transparent Gateway
ORACLE

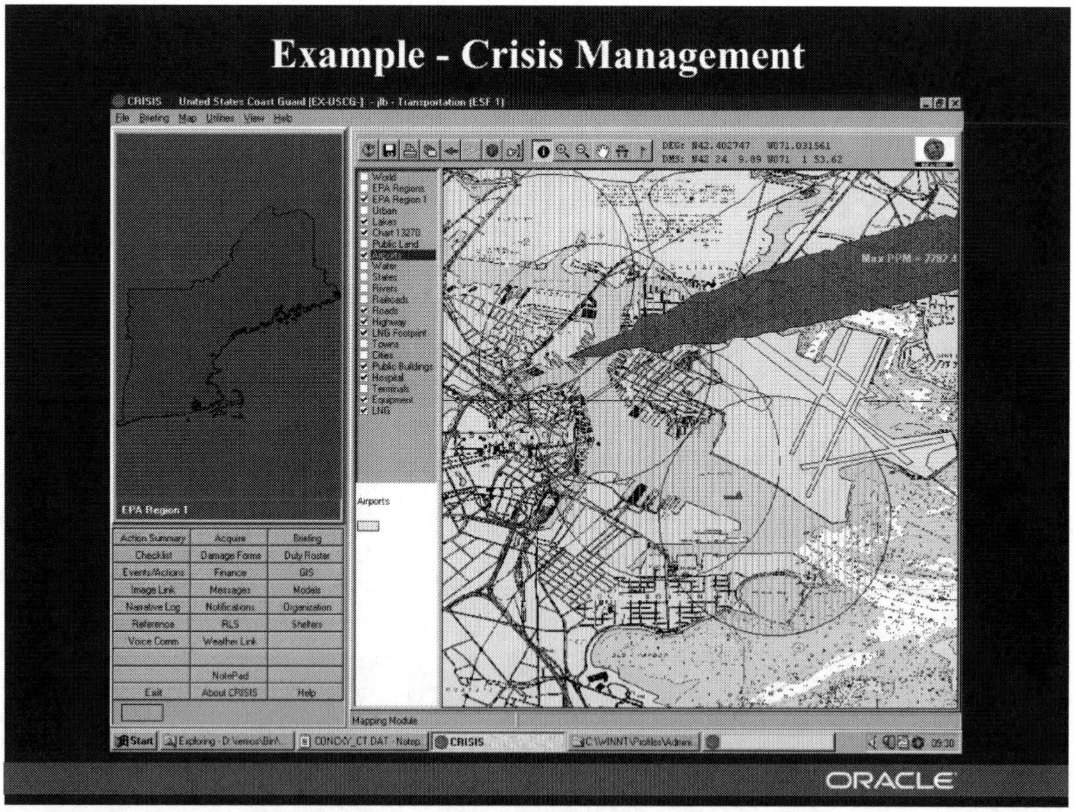
Example - Crisis Management
EPA Region 1
Action Summary
Acquire
Briefing
Checklist
Damage Forms
Duty Roster
Events/Actions
Finance
GIS
Image Link
Messages
Models
Narrative Log
Notifications
Organization
Reference
RLS
Shelters
Voice Comm
Weather Link
NotePad
Exit
About CRISIS
Help
Mapping Module
Airports
ORACLE

2. Integrate a Variety of Data Types

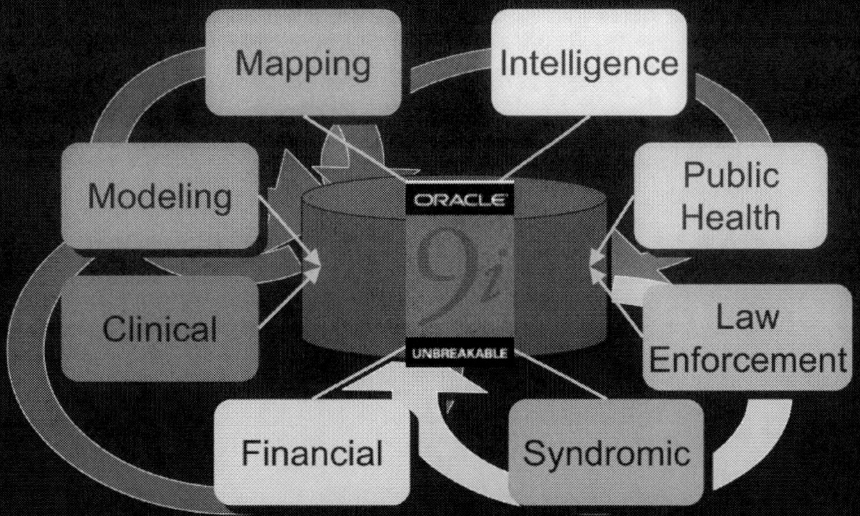

ORACLE

Example – NYC DoITT

- Case Study - New York City
  - Developed standardized digital basemap for all agencies
    - 6,000 miles of underground pipes
    - 1 million water/sewer connections
    - 32,000 sq. miles of Infrastructure Data
    - 7,500 digital photographs
- The Office of Emergency Management created a public site for emergency preparedness
  - **Extensively Used To Support 9/11 Response and Recovery**

ORACLE

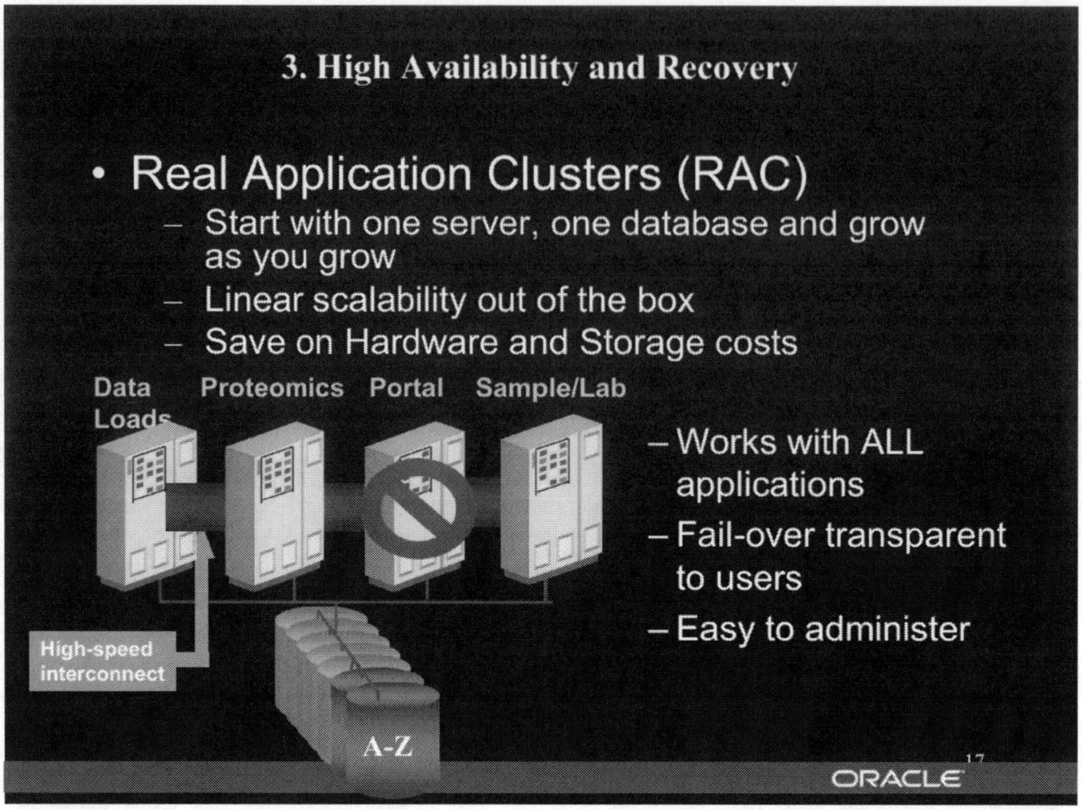
3. High Availability and Recovery
• Real Application Clusters (RAC)
– Start with one server, one database and grow as you grow
– Linear scalability out of the box
– Save on Hardware and Storage costs
Data Loads
Proteomics
Portal
Sample/Lab
High-speed interconnect
A-Z
– Works with ALL applications
– Fail-over transparent to users
– Easy to administer
17
ORACLE

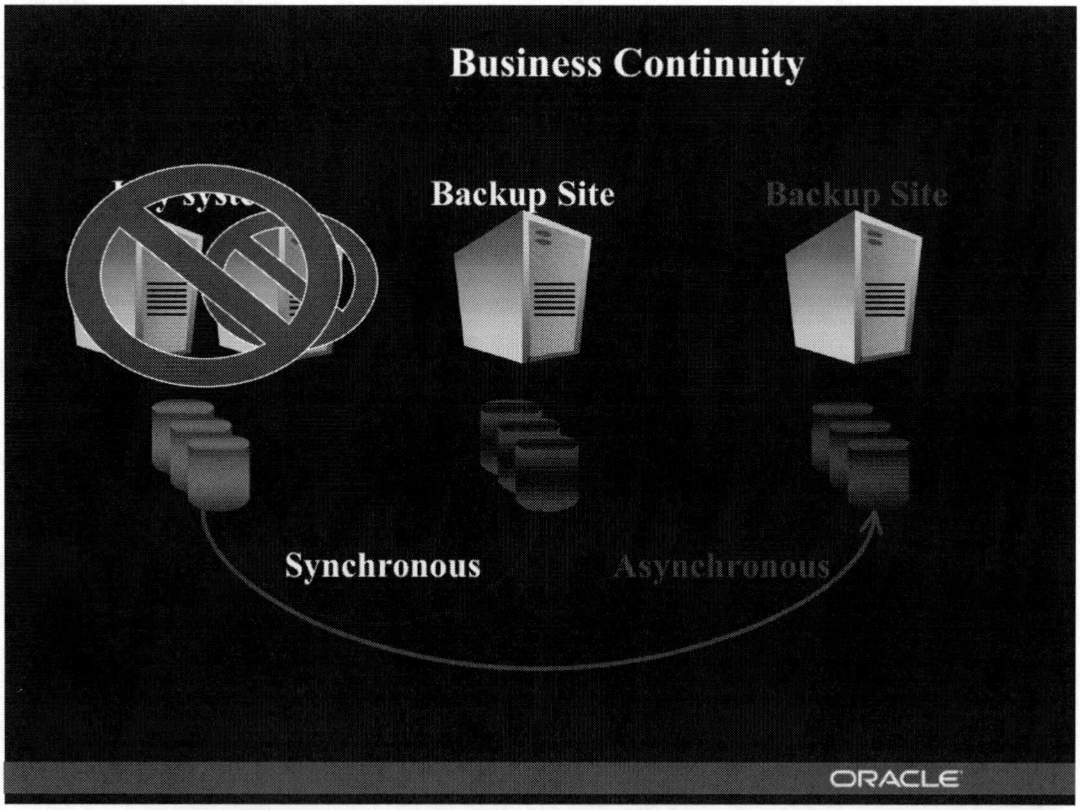
Business Continuity
Backup Site
Backup Site
Synchronous
Asynchronous
ORACLE

Business Continuity

COMMERZBANK

- Developed high availability solution prior to Sept. 11th
  - Oracle HA and data warehouse technologies
  - Global data warehouse
  - Provided critical redundancy/data backup
  - Scalable to support 300 employees
- On September 11th
  - Required fail over to backup facility in Rye, NY
  - Recovered to alternate facility in hours
  - Fulfilled business obligations same day
- Commerzbank was prepared
  - 100% data backup & recovery
  - Minimal downtime

ORACLE

4. Find Patterns and Insights

Homeland Security Data

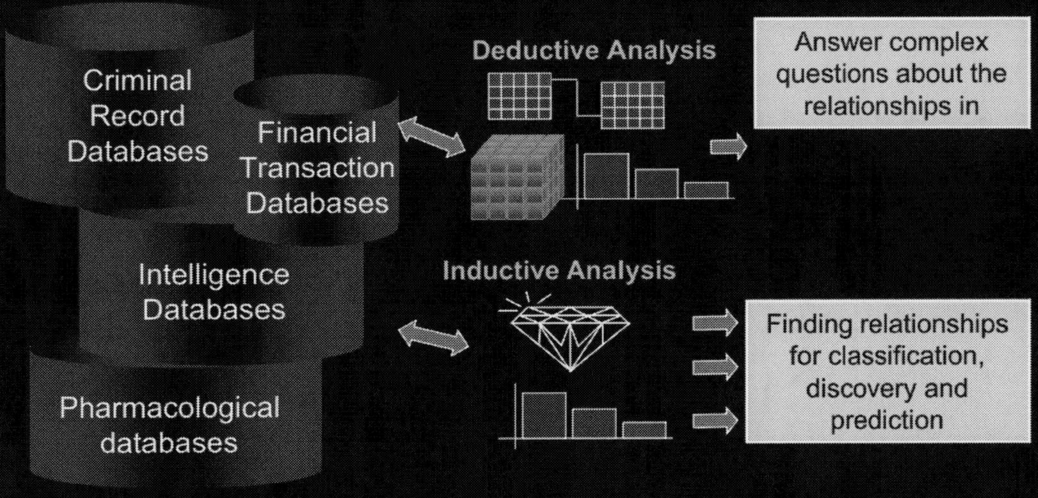

ORACLE

Deliver Daily Business Intelligence

Real-Time Access to Complete Business Information

Manage By…

- ***Objective***: Set corporate and personal targets
- ***Fact***: Provide performance-based metrics
- ***Exception***: Continuously evaluate performance

…For Better Decision Making

- What is the project schedule and budget impact of design changes?
- How can I best adjust to planning exceptions?
- How are supplier deliveries impacting my on-time delivery capability?
- How should I allocate production resources to meet variable demand?
- Which carrier can accommodate last-minute volume and destination changes?

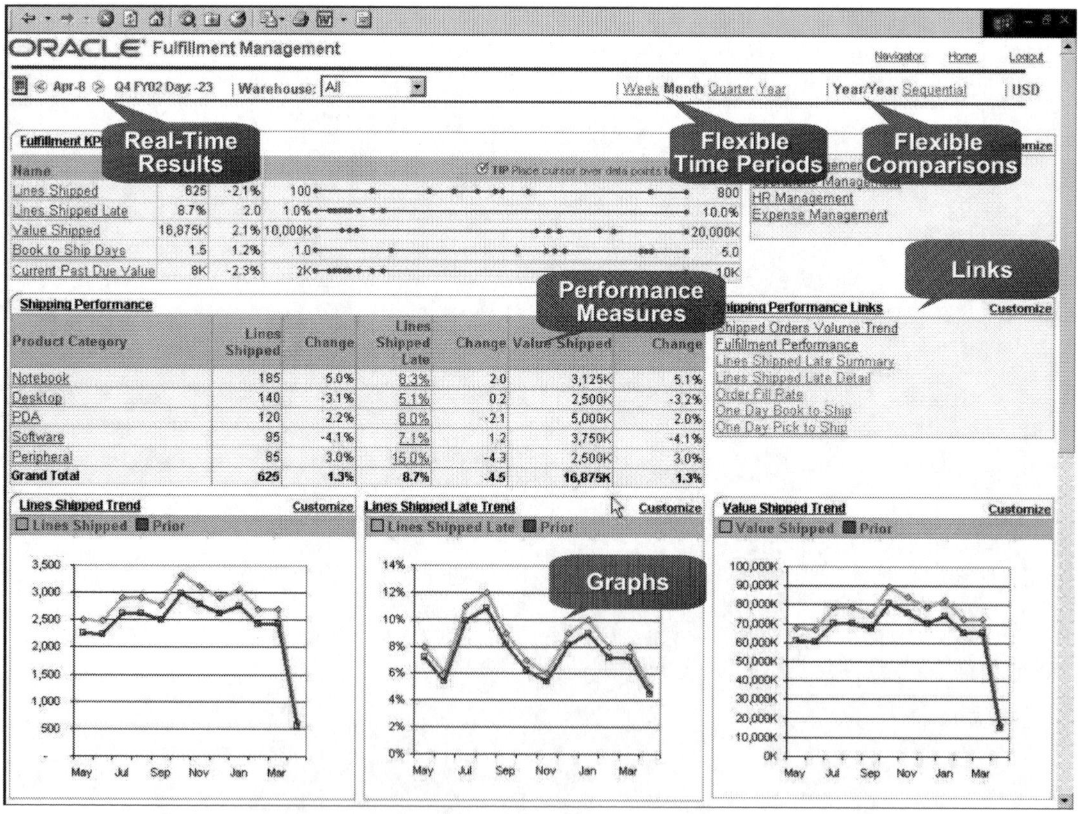

5. Collaborate Securely

- **Oracle Collaboration Suite**
  - Integrated Communications
  - Single Enterprise Search Across All Repositories
    - Internal & External
  - Flexible Access
    - Web, Desktop
    - Wireless and Telephone

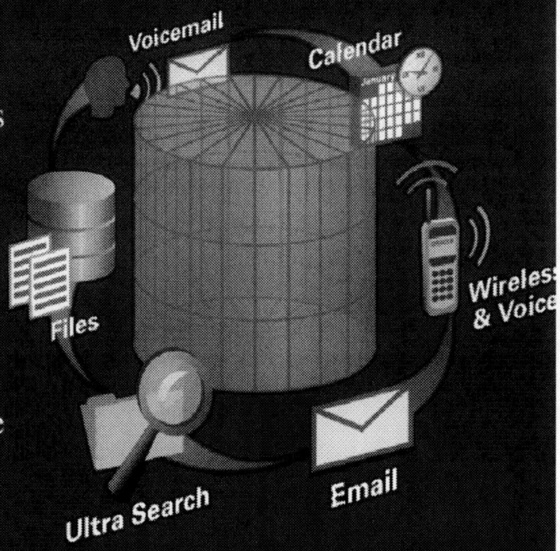

ORACLE

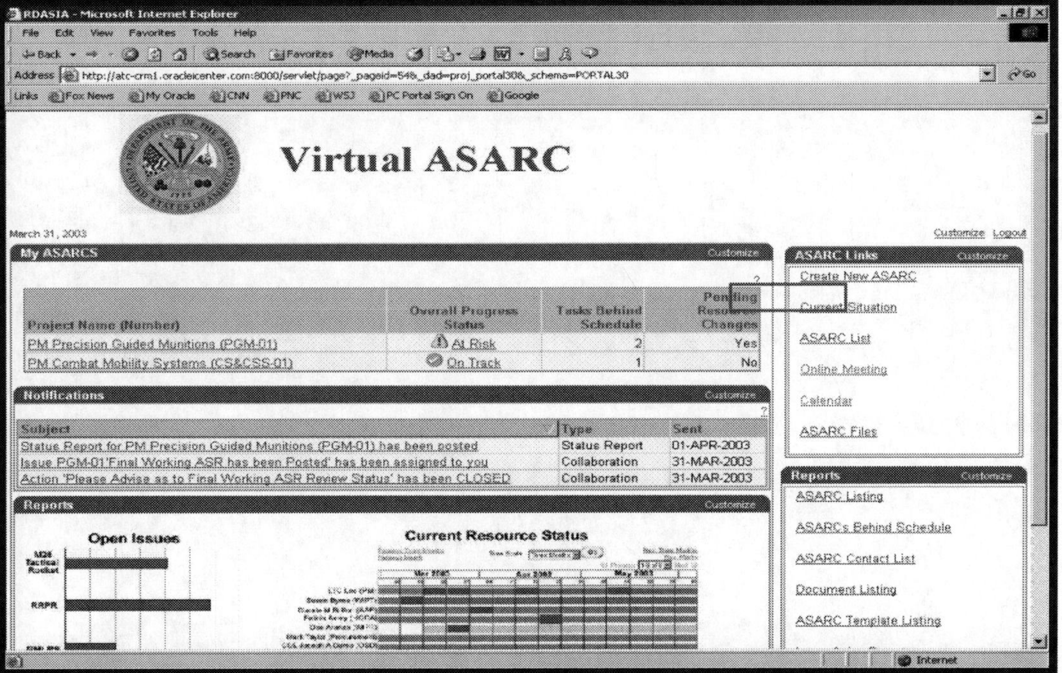

ORACLE

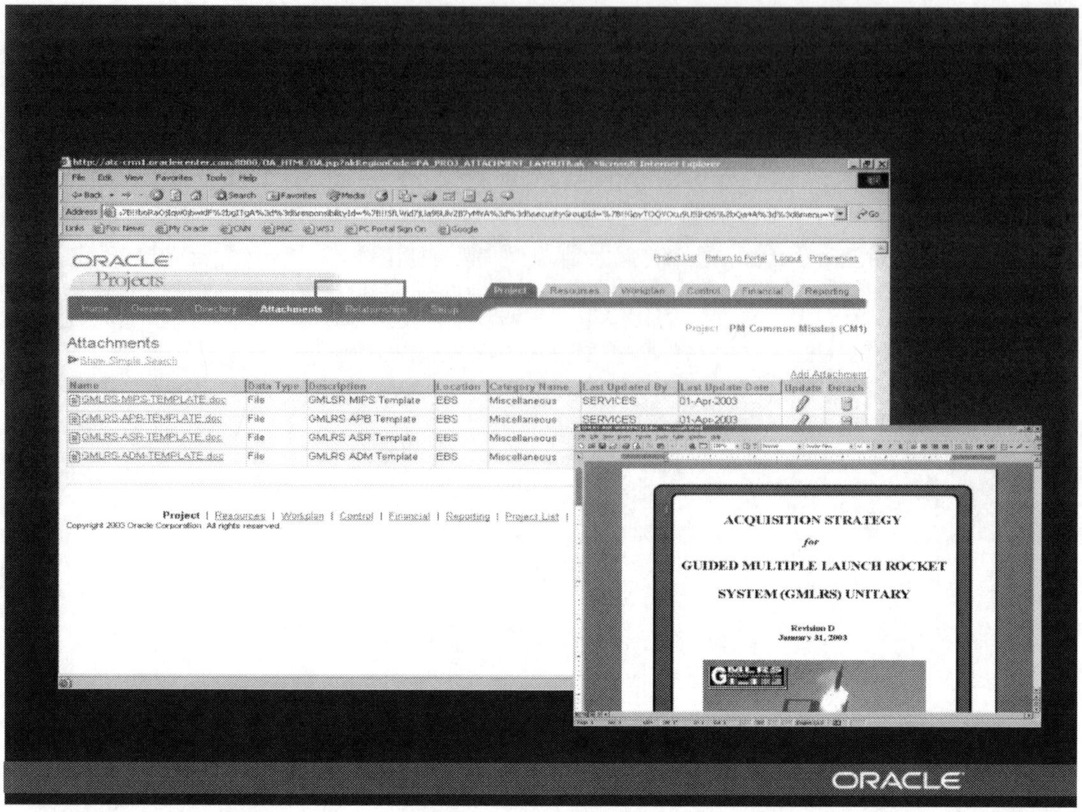
ORACLE
Projects
Attachments
Project PM Common Missles (CM1)
Add Attachment
Name
Data Type
Description
Location
Category Name
Last Updated By
Last Update Date
Update
Detach
GMLRS-MIPS-TEMPLATE.doc File GMLSR MIPS Template EBS Miscellaneous SERVICES 01-Apr-2003
GMLRS-APB-TEMPLATE.doc File GMLRS APB Template EBS Miscellaneous SERVICES 01-Apr-2003
GMLRS-ASR-TEMPLATE.doc File GMLRS ASR Template EBS Miscellaneous
GMLRS-ADM-TEMPLATE.doc File GMLRS ADM Template EBS Miscellaneous
Project | Resources | Workplan | Control | Financial | Reporting | Project List |
Copyright 2003 Oracle Corporation. All rights reserved.
ACQUISITION STRATEGY
for
GUIDED MULTIPLE LAUNCH ROCKET
SYSTEM (GMLRS) UNITARY
Revision D
January 31, 2003
ORACLE

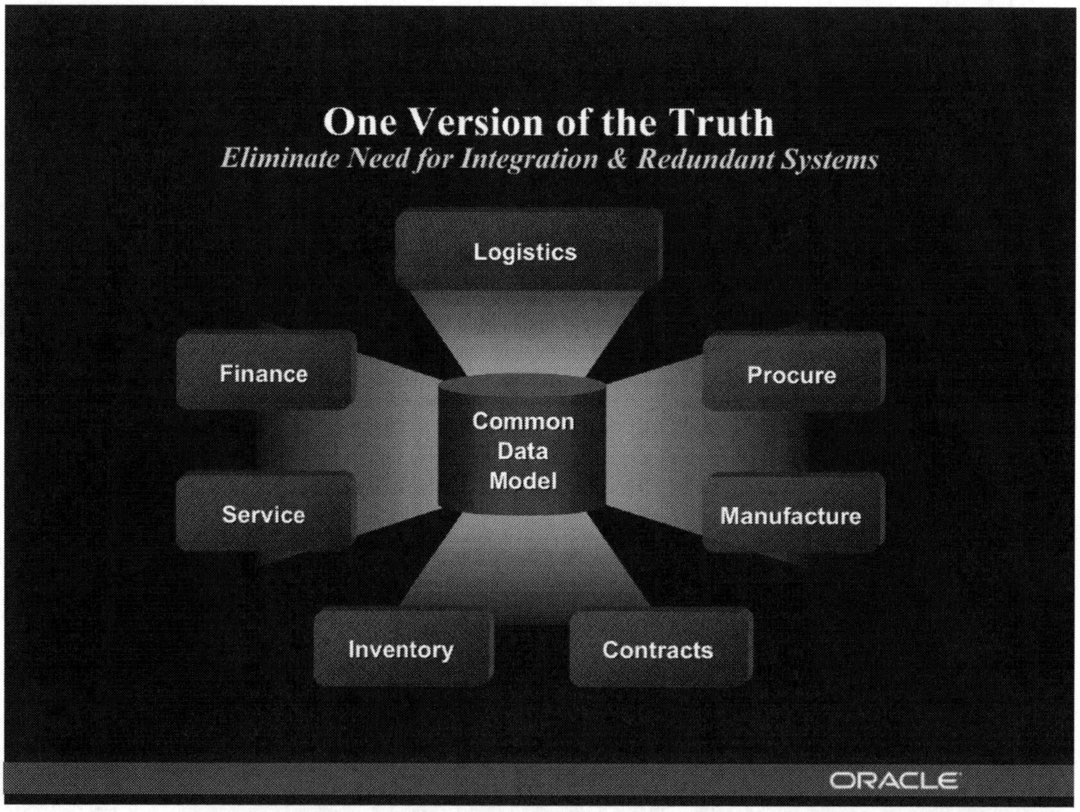
One Version of the Truth
Eliminate Need for Integration & Redundant Systems
Logistics
Finance
Procure
Common Data Model
Service
Manufacture
Inventory
Contracts
ORACLE

Oracle Corporation

Steve Cooperman
Vice President
Homeland Security Solutions

steven.cooperman@oracle.com

703.364.2310

ORACLE

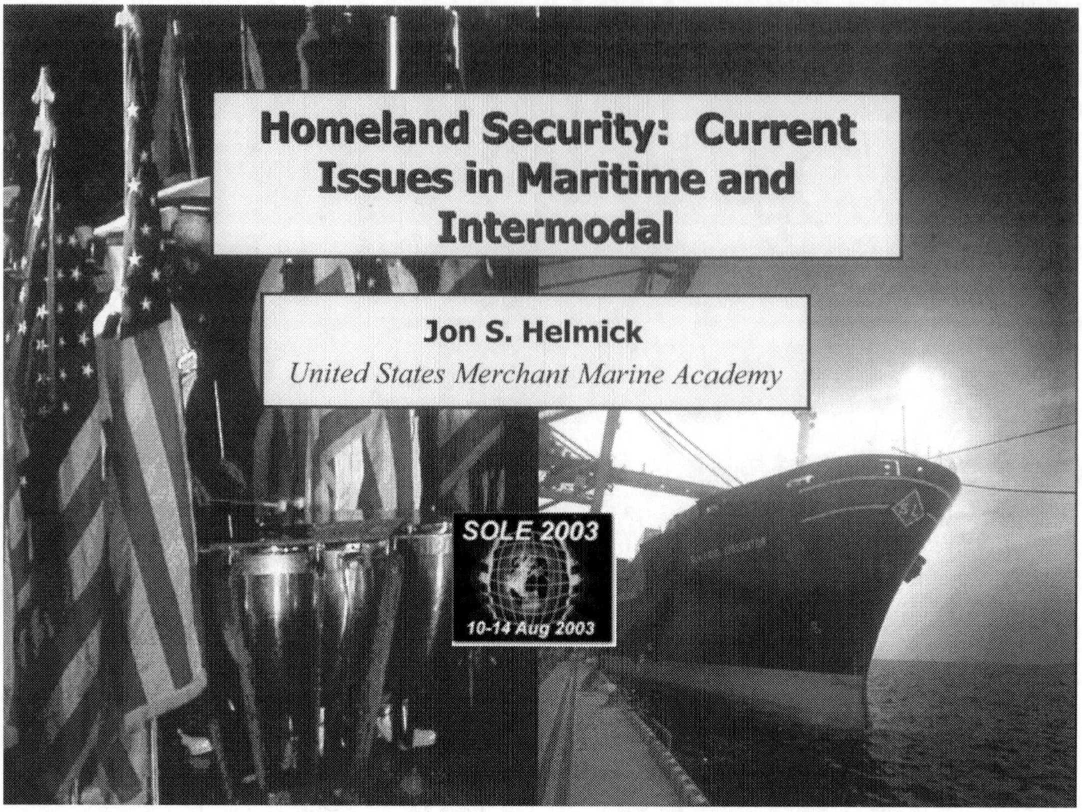

Session Objectives

- *Highlight nature of challenge*
- *Summarize key requirements*
- *Describe DOT & IMO responses*

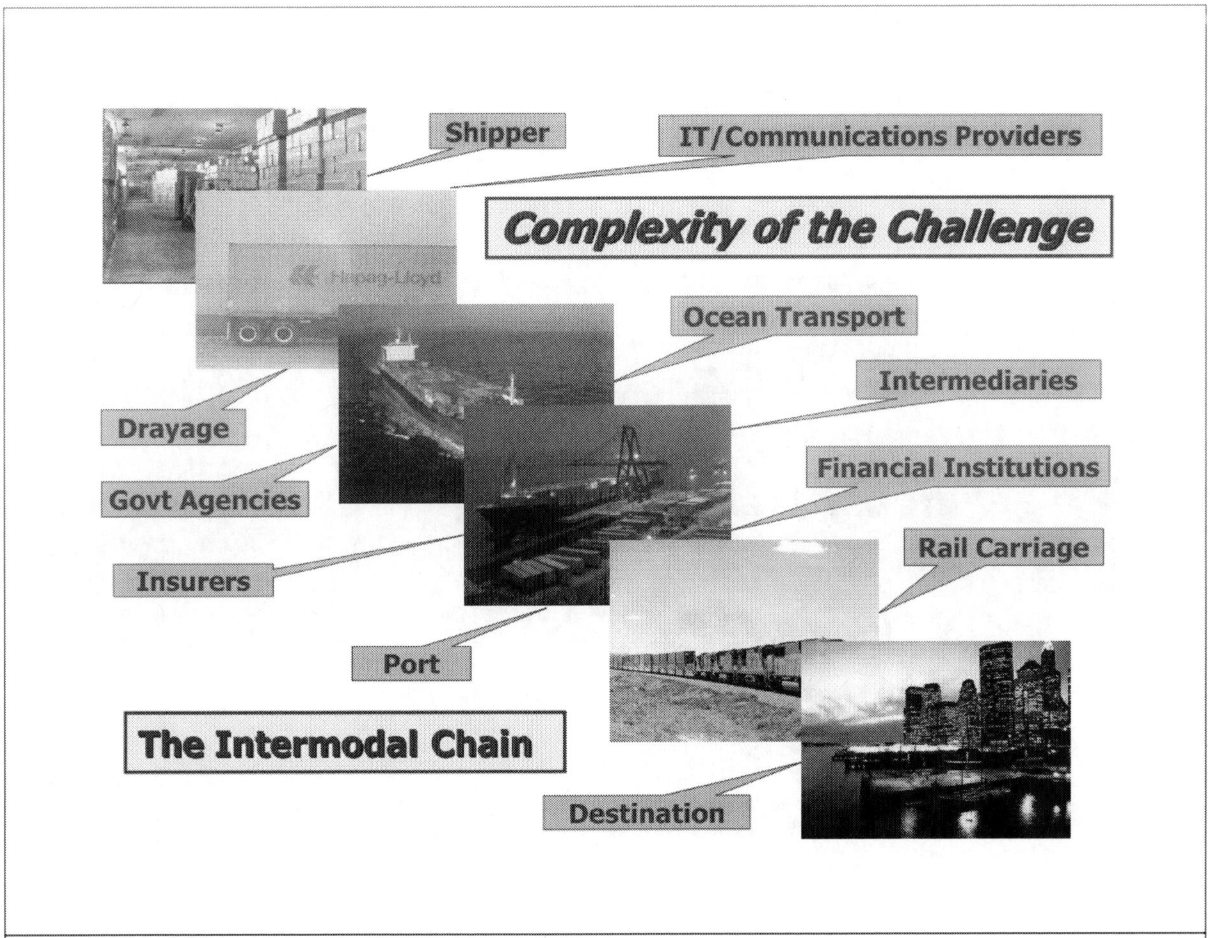
Complexity of the Challenge
Shipper
IT/Communications Providers
Ocean Transport
Intermediaries
Drayage
Govt Agencies
Financial Institutions
Rail Carriage
Insurers
Port
The Intermodal Chain
Destination

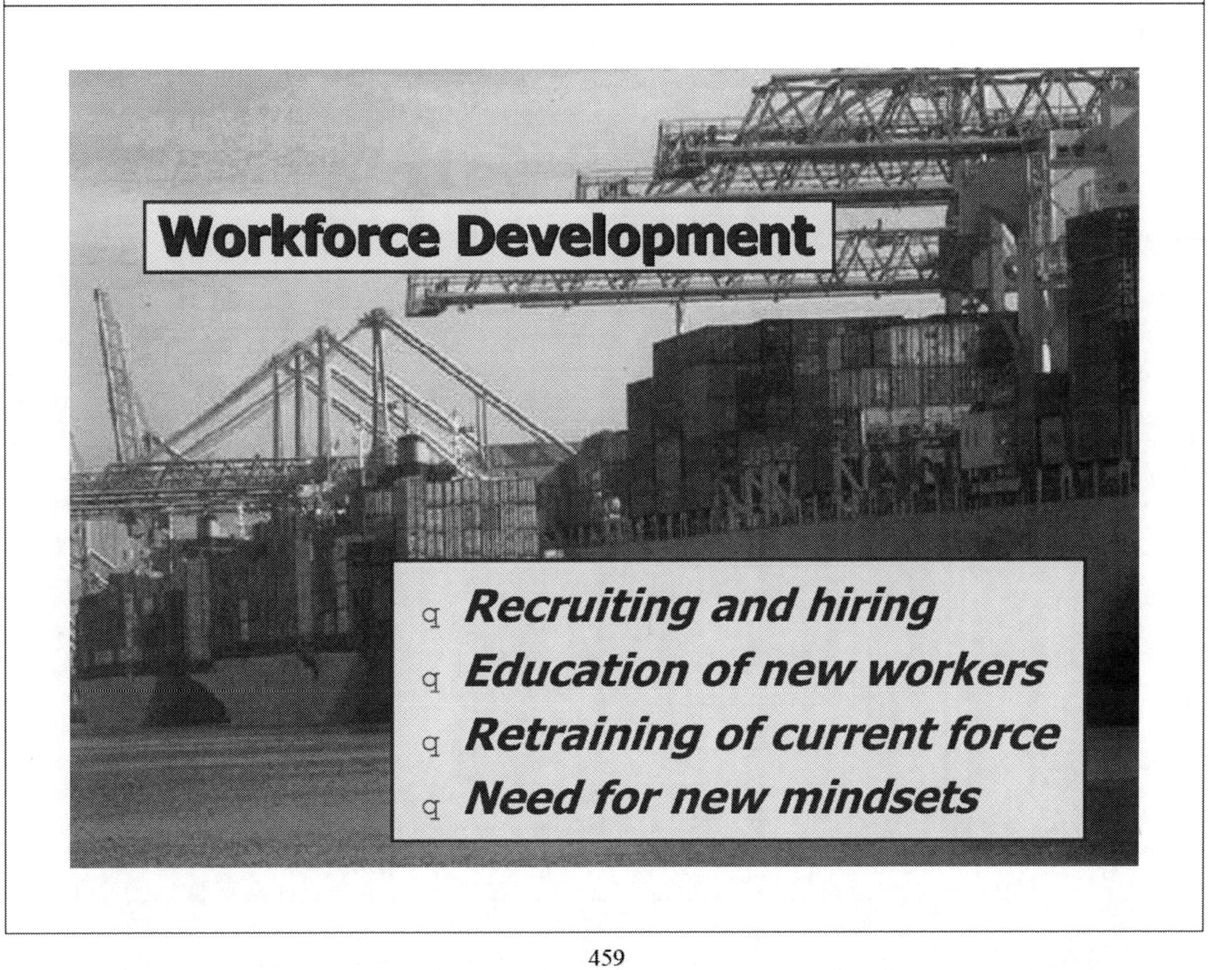
Workforce Development
q Recruiting and hiring
q Education of new workers
q Retraining of current force
q Need for new mindsets

MTSA 2002
Vulnerability assessments
National & area plans
TSCs for personnel
AIS system
Intermodal system security
Section 109

MTSA Sec. 109 Project
Legislative charge
Objectives
History
HANJIN

MTSA Project, cont'd
Interagency collaboration
International implications
Public outreach

Report to Congress
Curriculum
Standards
Certification
Transcript

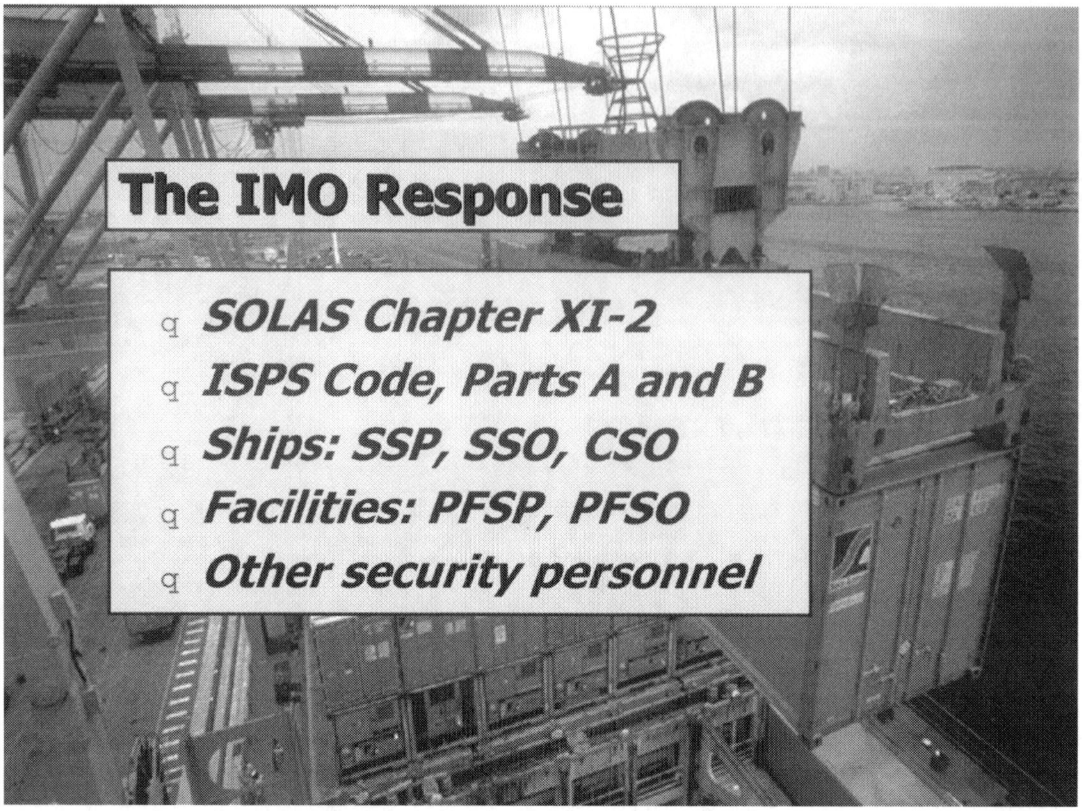
The IMO Response
SOLAS Chapter XI-2
ISPS Code, Parts A and B
Ships: SSP, SSO, CSO
Facilities: PFSP, PFSO
Other security personnel

IMO SSO Duties
V/L inspections
Ship Security Plan
Ensure trained crew
Report incidents
Coordinate with CSO, PFSO
Security equipment

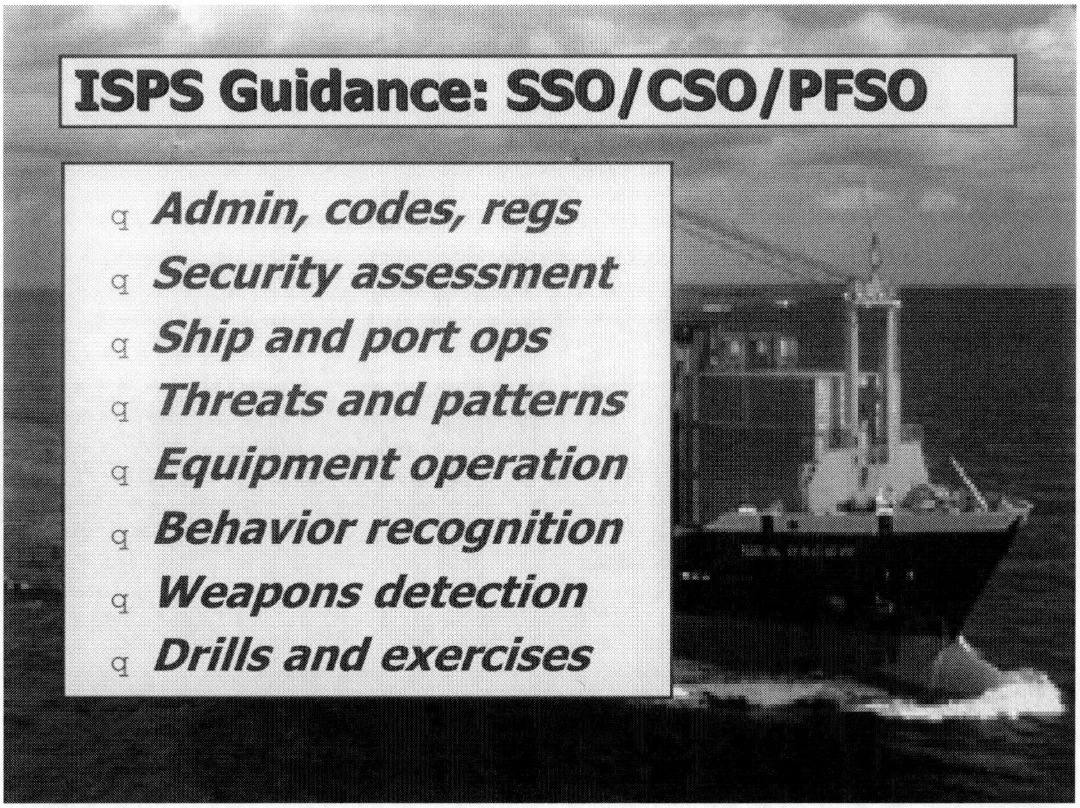
ISPS Guidance: SSO/CSO/PFSO
q Admin, codes, regs
q Security assessment
q Ship and port ops
q Threats and patterns
q Equipment operation
q Behavior recognition
q Weapons detection
q Drills and exercises

Issues
q Who will be the SSO?
q Who will train him/her?
q What can we expect?

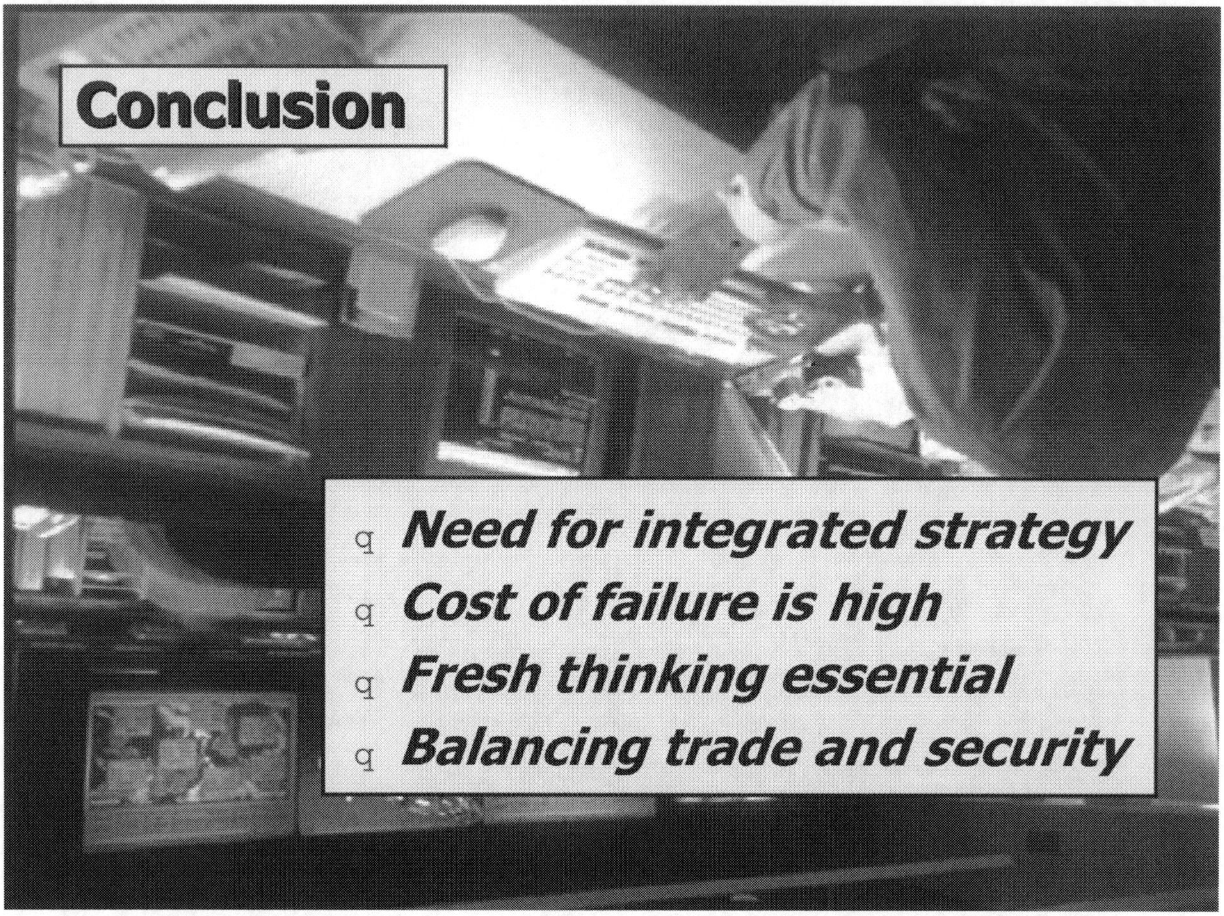
Conclusion
q Need for integrated strategy
q Cost of failure is high
q Fresh thinking essential
q Balancing trade and security

simplexity

INNOLOG

INNOVATIVE LOGISTICS TECHNIQUES, INC.

SOLE 2003

August 14, 2003

---

simplexity

- **Who We Are**
- **Reflections On The Strategic Airport Security Rollout (SASR)**
- **Moving Out On Supply Chain Security**
- **Complexities Of Our Environment**

4/17/2017 Innovative Logistics Techniques, Inc. P. 2

INNOLOG at a Glance

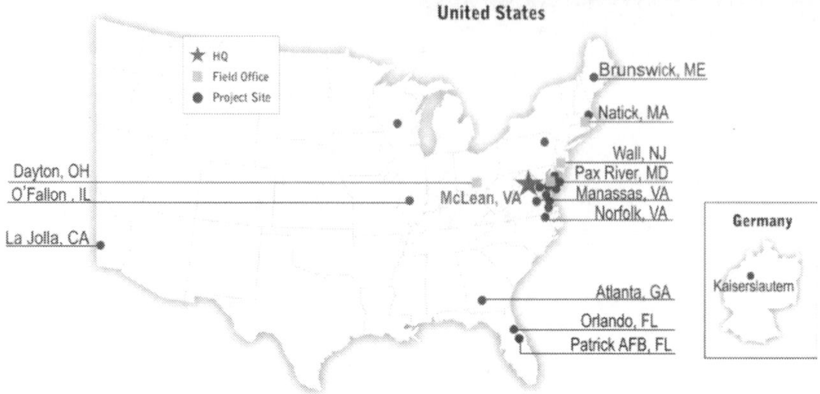

- ✓ 28 on-site and regional offices
- ✓ Locations in the United States, Europe
- ✓ Headquartered in McLean, Virginia
- ✓ Logistics solutions experts for public and private sectors
- ✓ Privately held, minority–owned since 1989
- ✓ Efficient, effective supply chain logistics solutions
- ✓ Customer success focused
- ✓ Outstanding performance record

Core Business Areas

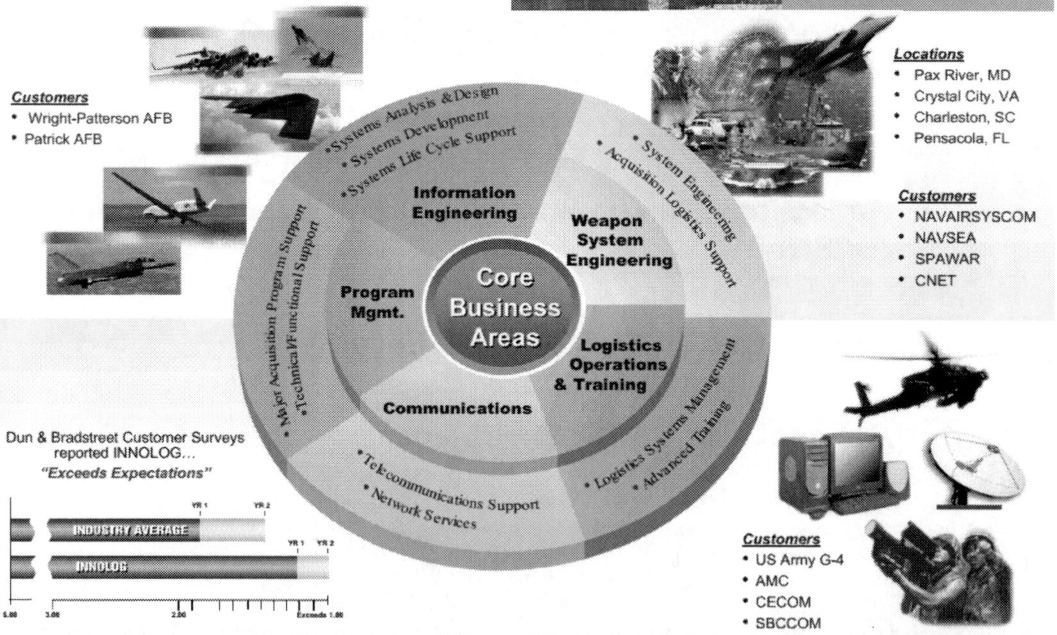

Old Paradigm vs New Paradigm

Traditional Logistics:

Transportation, Distribution, Warehousing, Inventory, Stockage, Maintenance, Supply, Servicing, Fuel, Food, Parts, Repair, Trucking, etc.

21st Century Logistics:

✓ End-to-end view and understanding of the entire supply chain

✓ Technology enabled

✓ Linked, interlocking, secure

✓ Security now needs to be addressed

4/17/2017 Innovative Logistics Techniques, Inc. P. 5

Our Niche

INNOLOG's strategic intent is to be the

"Best in Class" in 3 areas:

- Integrated Logistics Support
- Asset Management/Tracking
- Supply Chain Security

4/17/2017 Innovative Logistics Techniques, Inc. P. 6

Background

The Strategic Airport Security Rollout (SASR) project was performed by INNOLOG as a subcontractor to Lockheed Martin from 28 June to 16 December 2002. INNOLOG was responsible for providing logistical support for 429 airports in support of the Transportation Security Administration's Strategic Airport Security Rollout program during the rollout and implementation phase of the SASR project.

Strategic Airport Security Rollout-SASR (5 1/2 Month Marathon)

- **429 Airports**
- **44,000 screeners trained and deployed**
- **40,000,000 individual schedules**
- **2,300 people hired by INNOLOG**
- **350 Hotels used**
- **44,000 packets prepared and shipped to more than 400 destinations**

"LUCK is when *opportunity* meets *preparation*"

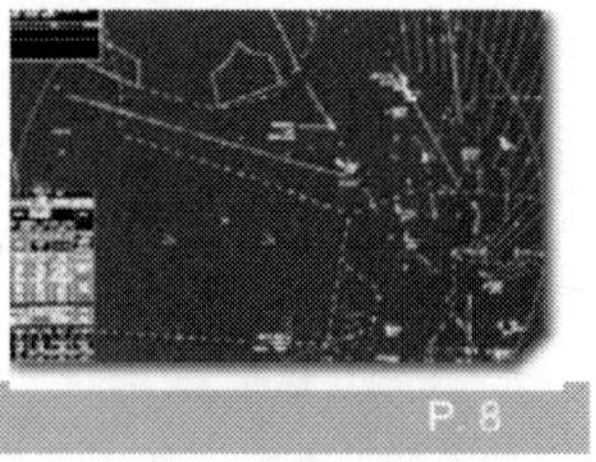

INNOLOG S.C.S. Activity

- **Over 14 years of government service and logistics systems engineering**
  - Supply Chain Management expertise
  - Assessment methodology
  - Integrated Logistics Support
  - Asset Management
- **Specific SASR qualification: large project, mission critical, met goals on time**
- **Two Operation Safe Commerce Awards**
- **Virginia Port Authority**

Supply Chain Security

Visibility – Security - Efficiency

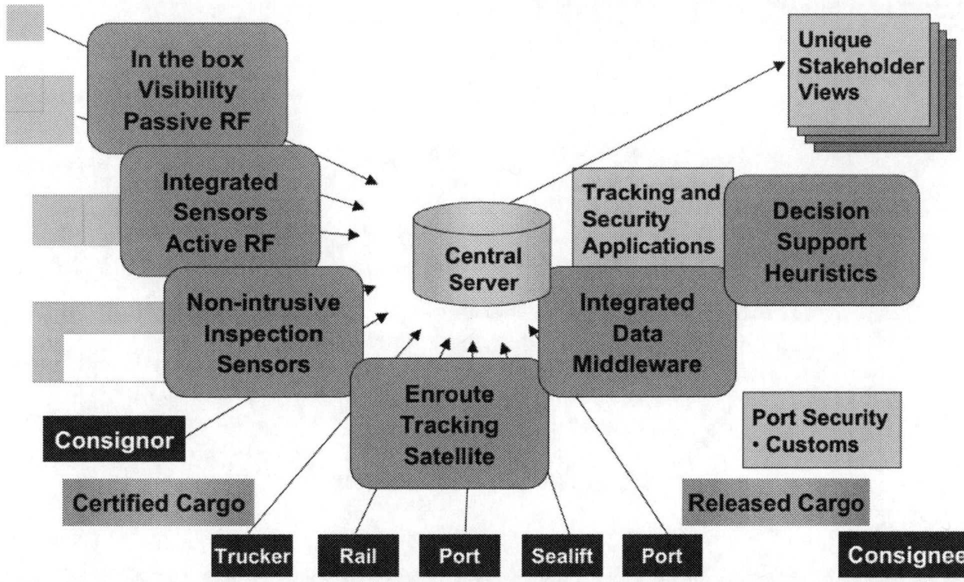

Key Stakeholders in Transportation Security

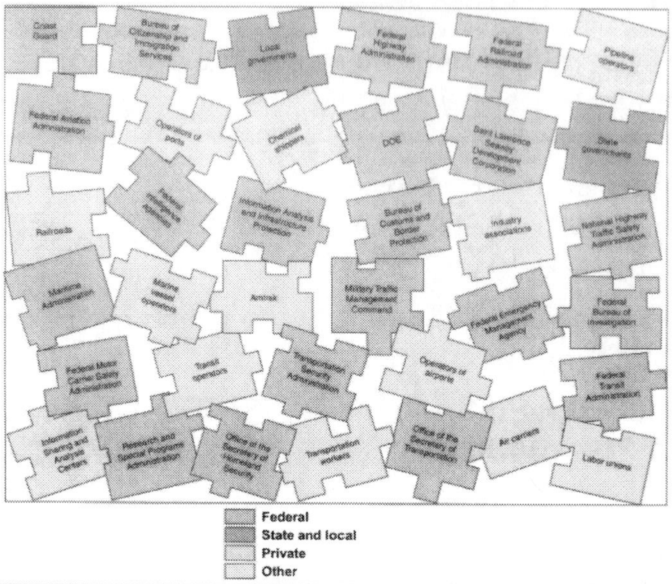

GAO-03-843

Illustration of How Risk Management Approach Can Guide Decision Making

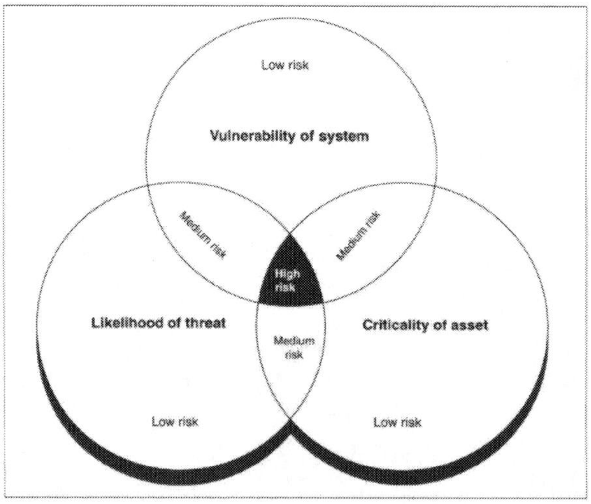

GAO-03-843

Going Forward

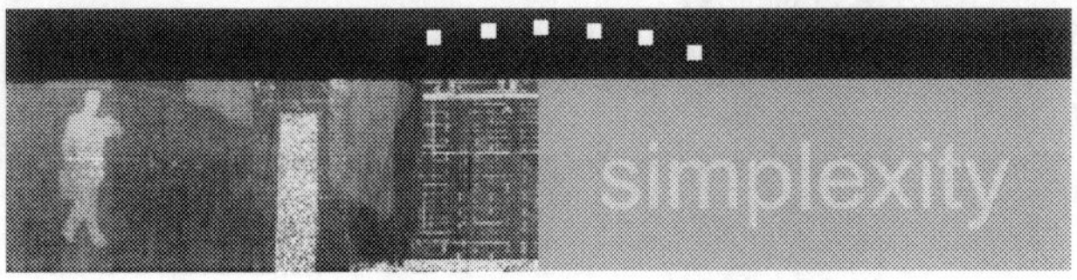

- Common Interest
- Complex Problem
- Cooperation and Compromise

The Logistics Services Department provides logistical, technical, and administrative support throughout the Center in the areas of transportation and supply and equipment management. The Logistics Services Department also participates in the Agencywide development of future logistics business management systems.

The Logistics Services strategy for FY 2003–2004 contains three fundamental goals:

Compliance–Ensuring compliance with all Government requirements and regulations while seeking efficiencies through proper channels when needed.

Reinvention–Challenging and changing traditional process methodologies for improvement in cost and efficiency by incorporating best practices of public and private sectors.

Teamwork–Fostering collaboration and consensus-building among contractors, employees, and customers to seek and improve our core products and services.

The Logistics Services Department's long-term vision is to exploit state-of-the-art technology and private sector management control initiatives in order to be the MSFC service provider of choice. Implementation of a new innovative asset management system as part of IFM will also be a key activity for the Logistics Services Department. The system will allow MSFC to manage assets acquisition-to-disposal; involve the customer to a larger degree in the management of their assets; eliminate redundant data entry points; provide up-to-date, fully descriptive asset information to the entire Agency; provide for life-cycle management; and assign full costs to assets.

Partnerships

The Logistics Services Office teams with the following partners:

- **Defense Contract Management Agency (DCMA)**–contract property administration and plant clearance.
- **Bionetics**–administrative aircraft operations and maintenance.
- **EG&G**–ground transportation, supply and equipment, flight hardware support, and physical inventories.
- **General Services Administration (GSA)**–general-purpose vehicles, excess property sales.
- **Signature Air**–aircraft hangar lease.

Logistics Services also has partnering arrangements with NASA Headquarters, Code J for IFM and Johnson Space Center for Space Station Program Critical Hardware (PCH) moves.

Functional Mission–*Provide Supply and Equipment Management Support to MSFC*

Relationship to President's Management Agenda	Relationship to NASA Strategic Plan and Implementing Strategies	Departmental Goals	Supporting Objectives	Representative Performance Measurements
Improved financial performance. Expanded electronic government.	**IS-1** Achieve management and institutional excellence comparable to NASA's technical excellence. **IS-4** Ensure that all NASA work environments, on Earth and in space, are safe, healthy, environmentally sound, and secure.	**Provide supply and equipment management support to MSFC organizations and stewardship of personal property assets.**	• Control inventory. • Receive and distribute materials and equipment. • Warehouse material and equipment. • Dispose of excess property. • Continue to pursue innovative solutions such as the JIT inventory management process. • Perform property administration for onsite contracts.	• Controlled Property Accountability–Ratio of lost items to total items maintained at less than or equal to the NASA average loss rate of 0.5%.
		Provide multimodal transportation services.	• Coordinate PCH moves. • Provide freight management. • Provide shipping services. • Maintain and repair special purpose vehicles/equipment. • Manage MSFC aircraft. • Special events transportation. • Provide flight hardware support operations.	• Establish and maintain a 10% per year or a 10-year replacement plan for special purpose equipment. • 100% of critical equipment in Reliability Centered Maintenance (RCM) program by the end of FY 2005.
		Provide Agencywide leadership in functional management of NASA legacy logistics business systems, and support development of IFM's Integrated Asset Management module.	• Serve as Agencywide functional manager for: – NASA Supply Management System. – NASA Equipment Management System. – NASA Property Disposal Management System.	Under development

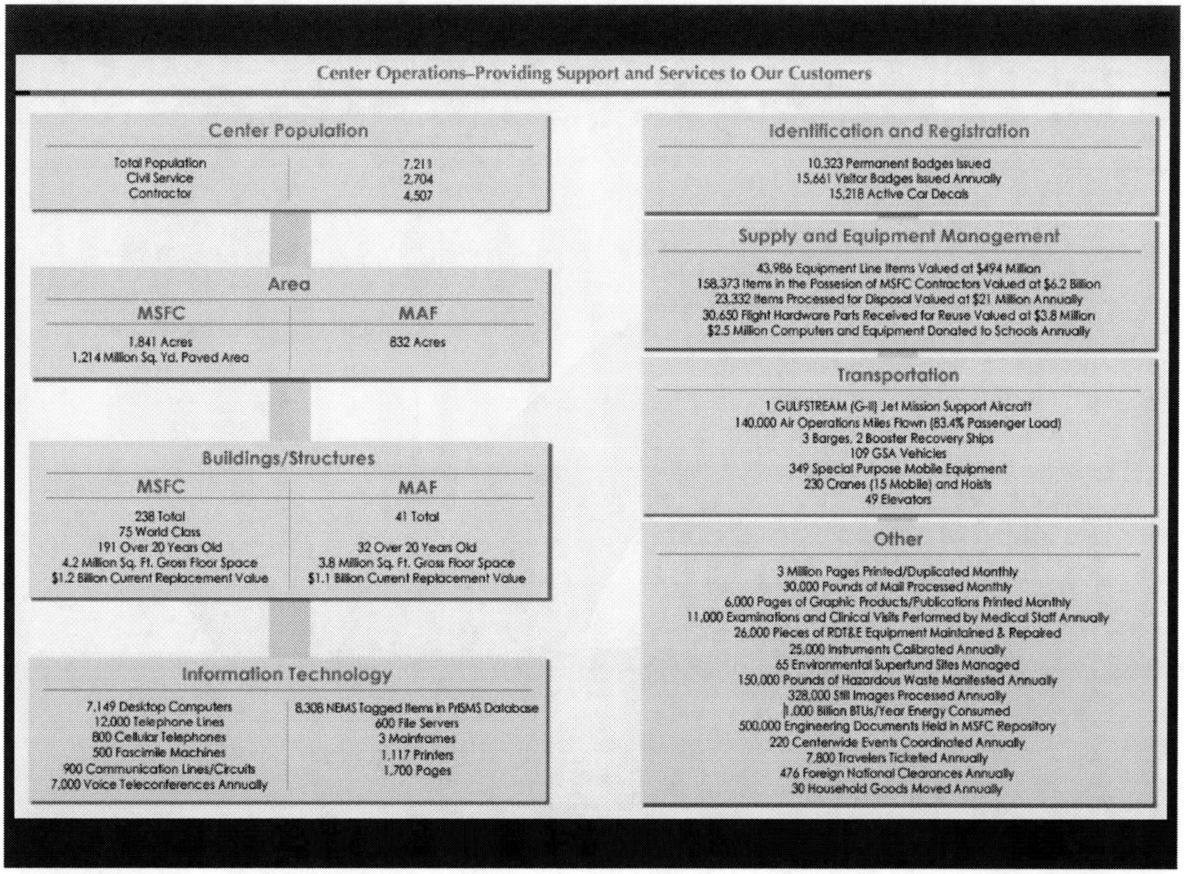

Center Operations–Providing Support and Services to Our Customers
Center Population
Total Population
Civil Service
Contractor
7,211
2,704
4,507
Area
MSFC
1,841 Acres
1,214 Million Sq. Yd. Paved Area
MAF
832 Acres
Buildings/Structures
MSFC
238 Total
75 World Class
191 Over 20 Years Old
4.2 Million Sq. Ft. Gross Floor Space
$1.2 Billion Current Replacement Value
MAF
41 Total
32 Over 20 Years Old
3.8 Million Sq. Ft. Gross Floor Space
$1.1 Billion Current Replacement Value
Information Technology
7,149 Desktop Computers
12,000 Telephone Lines
800 Cellular Telephones
500 Fascimile Machines
900 Communication Lines/Circuits
7,000 Voice Teleconferences Annually
8,308 NEMS Tagged Items in PrISMS Database
600 File Servers
3 Mainframes
1,117 Printers
1,700 Pages
Identification and Registration
10,323 Permanent Badges Issued
15,661 Visitor Badges Issued Annually
15,218 Active Car Decals
Supply and Equipment Management
43,986 Equipment Line Items Valued at $494 Million
158,373 Items in the Possesion of MSFC Contractors Valued at $6.2 Billion
23,332 Items Processed for Disposal Valued at $21 Million Annually
30,650 Flight Hardware Parts Received for Reuse Valued at $3.8 Million
$2.5 Million Computers and Equipment Donated to Schools Annually
Transportation
1 GULFSTREAM (G-II) Jet Mission Support Aircraft
140,000 Air Operations Miles Flown (83.4% Passenger Load)
3 Barges, 2 Booster Recovery Ships
109 GSA Vehicles
349 Special Purpose Mobile Equipment
230 Cranes (15 Mobile) and Hoists
49 Elevators
Other
3 Million Pages Printed/Duplicated Monthly
30,000 Pounds of Mail Processed Monthly
6,000 Pages of Graphic Products/Publications Printed Monthly
11,000 Examinations and Clinical Visits Performed by Medical Staff Annually
26,000 Pieces of RDT&E Equipment Maintained & Repaired
25,000 Instruments Calibrated Annually
65 Environmental Superfund Sites Managed
150,000 Pounds of Hazardous Waste Manifested Annually
328,000 Still Images Processed Annually
1,000 Billion BTUs/Year Energy Consumed
500,000 Engineering Documents Held in MSFC Repository
220 Centerwide Events Coordinated Annually
7,800 Travelers Ticketed Annually
476 Foreign National Clearances Annually
30 Household Goods Moved Annually

HOMELAND SECURITY

The Devil's in the Details

38TH Annual INTERNATIONAL Conference & Exhibition

Huntsville, Alabama

August 14, 2003

Dr. Russell A. Vacante

Director of Sector Leadership

Defense Acquisition University &

SOLE BOA Member

HOMELAND SECURITY

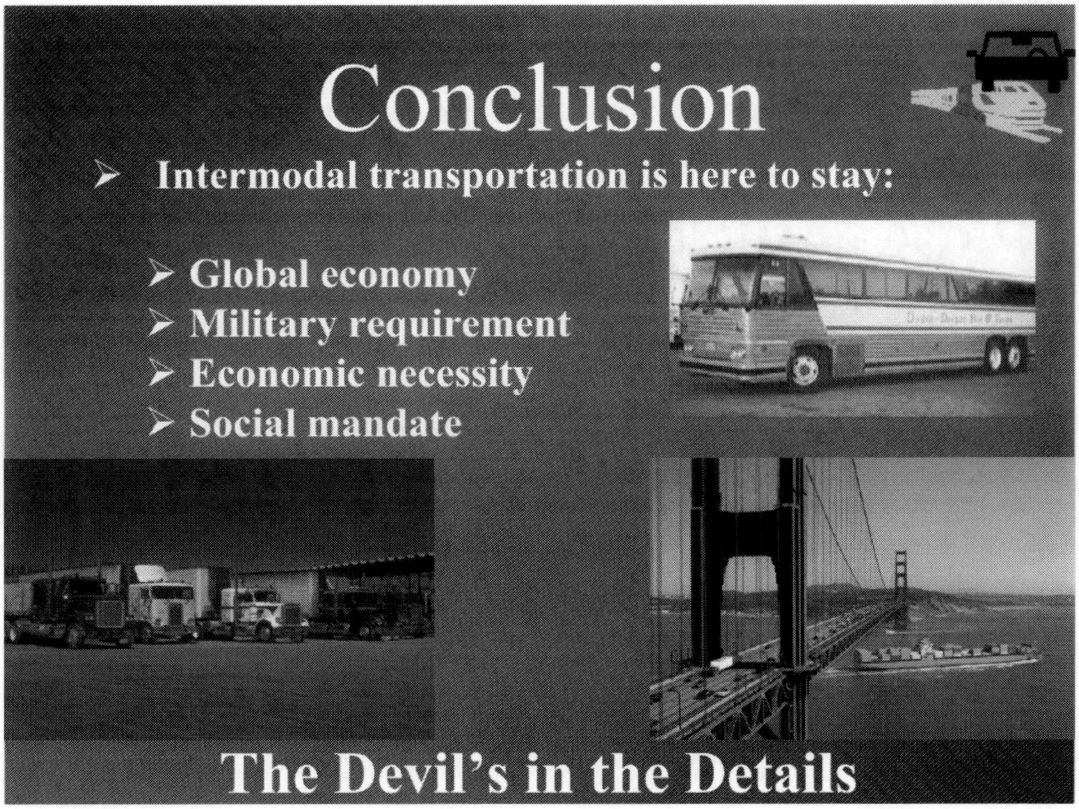
Conclusion
➢ Intermodal transportation is here to stay:
➢ Global economy
➢ Military requirement
➢ Economic necessity
➢ Social mandate
The Devil's in the Details

TRANSLOG
International
Website address:
http://www.translogintl.com
The Voyager
The TRANSLOG International News – Journal
RussV@erols.com

NATIONAL DEFENSE UNIVERSITY: PROGRAMS IN HOMELAND SECURITY

Linda Brandt, Ph.D.
Industrial College of the Armed Forces
National Defense University
(202) 685-4488
brandtl@ndu.edu
SOLE, 14 August 2003

National Defense University

- Established – 1976
- Mission: …educates military and civilian leaders through teaching, research, and outreach in national security strategy, and national resource strategy; joint and multinational operations: information strategies, operations and resource management; acquisition; regional defense and security studies."
- Premier joint military institution – "Chairman's school"
- Rapid growth in past decade: primary research and policy development institution for the DoD

Components

- **Schools:**
  - Industrial College of the Armed Forces (ICAF)
  - National War College (NWC)
  - Information Resources Management College (IRMC)
  - Joint Forces Staff College (JFSC)
  - School for National Security Executive Education (SNSEE)
- **Regional Centers**
- **Research:**
  - Institute for National Strategic Studies (INSS)
  - National Strategic Gaming Center (NSGC)
  - Center for Counterproliferation Research (CCR)
  - Center for Technology & National Security Policy (CTNSP)
- **Special Programs/Library**

NDU Interest in Homeland Security

"The events of September 11, 2001 have forever changed the way in which our nation will view and deal with the issues of homeland security. We recognize the need to ensure that our future military and civilian leaders are exposed to new HLS paradigms in our education curricula, as well as through our outreach efforts."

Vice Admiral Paul Gaffney
President, NDU
July 30, 2002

NDU Homeland Security Activities

- Conferences/Symposia/Outreach
- Education and Training
- Research
- Gaming

Component Activities

- INSS:
  - Outreach activities and conferences to inform/stimulate debate on HLS issues among a wide policy community
  - Conferences since 9/11/01 have HLS, counter terrorism, and civil military focus
  - Research focus

Component Activities, (con't)

- Strategic Gaming
  - Outreach to:
    - Senior Federal and State decision-makers – NSC, Congress/elected officials, appointees, Gov't/senior strategic officials
    - Interagency policy-makers – interagency, NSC staff, OSD/JCS, Combatant Commanders, NATO, EU, etc.
    - Educational institutions, think tanks, etc.
    - Future Senior military and civilian leadership – NDU programs

Component Activities (con't)

- **Senior Professional Military Education**
  - ICAF
  - NWC
- **Center for Technology & National Security Policy:**
  - Border and container security
  - Bioterrorism programs
  - Technology for HLS
  - Workshops and conferences
  - Courses on science and technology
- **Center for Counterproliferation Research**

Component Activities (con't)

- IRMC:
  - Information Assurance Certificate – HLS concentration
  - CIO Certificate
  - eGovernment Leadership Certificate
- SNSEE:
  - Curriculum built on national security strategy and policy including HLS strategy and evolving DoD policy
- Joint Forces Staff College
  - JPME
  - 40 hour HLS course – NDU certificate

Conclusions

- NDU integrates HLS into fabric of all programs
- DoD primary sponsor – interagency and intergovernmental outreach ongoing
- Advances Joint and DoD educational, research, and policy goals
  - Implementation of Goldwater-Nichols
- Department of Homeland Security
  - Has integration, interagency, culture issues
  - Education needs?

SOLE Conference, Huntsville, Alabama 14 August
Homeland Security
Dr. Michael Krause

TO SEE!!
The Art and Science of Seeing!

Preamble –

I want to expand the old saying that "seeing is believing." Seeing is knowing, knowing is thinking, thinking is understanding, understanding is the basis of decision-making. Seeing is the cognitive ability to imagine all sorts of solution. It is the imagination of the mind. So for logisticians interested in homeland defense "seeing" is both art and science. Logisticians have concentrated on science – scientific principle or as Mike McDuffie said "logistics is physics." But in my view logistics is not just physics – it is art, the cognitive ability to move from seeing, to knowing to thinking, to understanding to decision – in short it is art!

My friends and colleagues, Chuck Mahan, Tom Edwards, Roy Beauchamp, Mike McDuffie, and others have suggested the right solutions. Their thoughts and deeds should be applied. Further, the scenario, which Tom Burlin presented yesterday, which showed the powerful synergism of information sharing to successfully prevent a potential disaster, illustrates what needs to be done in Homeland Defense.

Outline

- At War
- Define "to see" Visibility
- Example from the Desert
- War games, simulation and operation centers
- What is industry doing?
    - Deter, Defend, React, Recover
- Conclusion

At War

I submit that Homeland Security is about protecting the Nation. Before 9/11 I used to quip, "We are at war, only we don't know it." After 9/11 we know we are at war. It will be a long war – against terrorism; some say thirty years in duration. We are successful in the initial campaigns – Afghanistan and Iraq. I believe our enemies have attacked our way of life. They have as an objective to threaten our "life, liberty, and the pursuit of happiness." In short the mean us harm. They mean to attack the very fiber of our life and liberty – our financial and economic health.

Logistics is in the forefront of this attack, because logistics – the supply and transportation chain – is the very foundation of our economic strength. In our mid-century, logistics – including transportation – accounted for 18% of our GNP; now 50 years later it is only 8% of GNP. But this is a huge number. While the % has actually gone down, logistics in its global reach has actually increased. You have heard about our dependence on imports and the number of ships and container coming into our country – some says about 17,000 per day. This is only through sea and airports. The actual number if rail and truck from our NAFTA partners are included goes even larger. Our logisticians have emphasized speed, efficiency and effectiveness. The functional element, which is missing and needs to be factored in, is security.

First we need to be able to learn "to see." Seeing is visibility – real time asset visibility, real time situational awareness, seeing, is knowing. Seeing is the first part of the ability to observe, orient, decide, act, the OODA Loop!

The Desert

When we went into the Desert for the first time, I was privileged to be the logistics planner for Operation Desert Shield and Storm. We planned for the reception and onward movement of a lot of stuff: 117,000 vehicles, 10,000 tracks; enough stuff to feed, house, fuel, ammunition and sustain 540,000 soldiers, sailors, airmen and marines in the conduct of the campaign we used 516 ship and 10,000 air freighter sorties to move and supply the force. But we could not see "the stuff," or know that it was coming, or decide to re-allocate the stuff in transit, or communicate it to those who controlled and moved it. In short we were blind.

Where are we now?

Well we've come a long way – we can now see – observe Iraqi Freedom and Afghanistan Enduring Freedom - where we have total asset visibility, we have in transit visibility, we can communicate the movement to those who need to see it move and prepare for its arrival, and we can network all concerned. We have tagged, we have enabled the logistician – both in the commercial and military world - "to see." In short, we both military and commercial, now have the systemic means to enable us to see the logistic supply chain in its global dimension.

Why is this useful in Homeland Security? If we are enabled "to see" where a product, and item, a commodity comes from – from point of origin to point of loading – within the global supply chain – then it can be documented, known, categorized, data sorted, shippers, carriers, customs all can share these data points. Anomalies in this process can sort out potential dangerous shipments of cargo – either by air or sea – which means to destroy the very basis of our economic liberty – free and unencumbered trade and commercial intercourse. By attacking the seams in our logistics supply chain – electronically or physically – a thinking opponent can do us grave damage. This damage is not only physical – causing death and destruction, but also psychological, financial and thereby economic. Look at the statistics from 9/11. Indeed look at the disruption of west coast ports caused by a single – peaceful event – the west coast dock strike.

War Games

In this effort to broaden our ability "to see" – war games, simulations are being conducted. Much like the scenario that Tom Burlin presented to us yesterday. These scenario war games – simulations - enable us to see not only in a physical sense but to use our thinking abilities – to use our imagination: These war games stretch the planning horizon so that we will see the possible affect of traumatic events. You've probably read about the simulation which Booze, Allen, Hamilton conducted in late fall of last year, as reported in the Wall Street Journal. In summary, a series of attacks against our ports and transportation infrastructure cost over $2.5 trillion dollars.

Now, the National Defense University recently conducted several simulations, which accented our vulnerabilities in our logistics system.

At our SOLE opening session, 38 years ago, Werner von Braun used breakfast as an example of the art of logistics – bringing diverse food products together without fail, every time. Not unexpectedly, the NDU war game focused on the vulnerability of our food supply. The simulation was called "Silent Prairie." The focus was our food supply vulnerability. The scenario showed how quickly hoof and mouth disease – caused either by natural or terrorist acts – could affect the very fiber of our being – and our breakfast and dinner tables! Spread rapidly from a local start in North Carolina, to over 40 states, the disease caused over 60 million cattle and sheep to be killed; created an environmental disposal disaster, a control management problem, and cost the country a significant dip in GNP. Military forces were to be used to contain and control the quarantined areas. This action occurred during a heavy – real time – commitment in the global war against terrorism naturally stretching our military - particularly the reserve – forces even further.

The second NDU war game "Impending Storm" centered on the vulnerability of our logistic transportation system. The scenario began during our real time deployment to Iraq with an oil tanker explosion, which closed to the port of Galveston. The magnitude of the resultant oil spill – on the order of the Exxon Valdez – was initially the focus of effort. After the fact intelligence reports seemed to indicate the proximate cause as terrorist boat rammed the tanker and caused the explosion, fire and spill. Shortly thereafter, a tractor-trailer exploded en route to Macon, Georgia. Fast work in identification traced the container to an Egyptian vessel delivering cargo into the port of Charleston. Before this ship could be re-inspected, it blew up in the shipping lanes by the port of Charleston. At this stage, intelligence work traced the ships ports of call, cargo and containers to South American ports of call, where intelligence previously reported Al Qaeda en roads. There was no question that this was a terrorist attack. This act was followed closely by a cruise ship fire and explosion – with a heavy loss of life – in San Juan, Puerto Rico. Reports indicated a boat like ramming, although there were conflicting reports of a fire being started on board the ship itself. As if this were not enough, reports from the port of LA, Long Beach from an eyewitness who "saw a 55 gallon drum like object" being dumped into the water provided the backdrop for a self imposed "lock-in/out" of the port until minesweeping could be accomplished. The Coast Guard and Navy reported that their minesweepers and trained dolphins would take "at least a week" to arrive. As these events unfolded decision makers – Members of Congress and high-ranking principals – debated whether to close the ports. One team did, whereas the other did not. The team that choose not to close the ports explained their decision rational as insuring continued economic activity while under attack, thereby not allowing the enemy to gain his presumed objective of maximizing economic disaster resultant from the attacks. Play was stopped after forty-five days with an assessment of multi-trillion dollar impact. Intelligence revealed that these were targeted attacks to ports of embarkation for deploying forces, as well as sustaining supplies.

Next, this fall a war-game simulation by a different agency is planned which will look at the impact of a series of cyber attacks upon our financial, communications, logistics, transport, power and water infrastructure. The focus will look at how well we are doing in our critical infrastructure protection process. I'll let you know the results.

Communications Operations Centers

Back to the art and science of seeing. We now add joint operating centers to our abilities to see. Our nations capital – Washington, DC – has one of the best communication centers available – including our military. They have real-time digitized video of live feeds throughout the Capitol and surrounding community. The live feeds are communicated to designated on the ground commanders who then allocate forces – police, fire, first responders and military applicable to the situation. Three-dimensional models show ingress and egress routes to buildings and areas. Models and simulations will allow decision makers to determine the potential risk exposure from fire and potential harmful agents. It is likely that major metropolitan areas, potentially sea and airports will require similar joint operation centers, which allows them to see.

In the arena protecting military posts, camps and stations, a new agency Joint Program Executive Office for Chemical and Biological defense is developing chemical and biological defense mechanism, testing their best placement through simulation use and then placing these sensors around selected military installations. These new devices will require continuous monitorship through selected central organizations. Further, cognitive analytic methodologies will allow predictive human responses to an agent attack to be modeled and simulated for best response.

What is industry doing?

Many large companies have global supply chains. They recognize that preparations need to be made to deter, defend, react and recover from potential disruptions to their global supply chain. They have instituted many of the methodologies, which we have talked about here for the last three days: asset visibility, tracking methodologies, information sharing and integration. They have instituted information assurance programs, they have built communication operations centers; they have instituted consequence management training and exercises to prepare for interruptions of the supply chain.

Industry efforts must be coordinated with government initiatives. Customs initiatives now require point of origin and point of loading certification to be electronically filed 24 hours in advance of shipment. This moves our borders abroad. It allows us to see what is coming into our ports. Other initiatives – Operation Safe Commerce – Container tracking, hazardous material shipment tracking are methodologies of seeing.

Conclusion

So what's the point of all this "seeing?"

Well for one thing – logisticians have come a long way!
We were blinded – and you caused us to see!
When we could see, we began to know, to thinking and to understand and to decide, to integrate, to adopt, and to communicate and to become network centric: all to gain speed upon which our very economic survivability depends.

This is ability "to see" which allows security and us -logistical engineers - to gain efficiency, effectiveness! Which is essential for our survival.

But if you think we are there yet – you are wrong. There is a lot to be done.
Are we industry ready to share in this effort? What of IP and proprietary IT systems? What of standards in tracking and electronic data exchange? What about interface with the military? Who pays for the increased costs? What about the institutional relationships? What of privacy issues?
In short, we will need to overcome these obstacles.

SOLE 2003

August 14, 2003

SASR Rollout

- 5 ½ month marathon
- 429 airports
- 44,000 screeners
- 40,000,000 individual schedules
- 2,300 INNOLOG hires…most in 6 weeks
- 350 hotels
- 44,000 orientation packages to 400+ sites

SASR Approach

Concurrent Activity

- Discovery
- Information Architecture and Engineering
- Rapid Prototyping
- Consolidation and Hardening

SASR Features

- Local Data Capture
- Enterprise-wide Data Management
- Web-based Services

Lessons Learned/ Re-learned

- Never missed a rollout
- Stayed under our cost estimate
- Web-ex for training, on-line help desk, FAST all effective

But........

Lessons Learned/Re-learned (Cont.)

- HR and finance systems inadequate for surge..slow to hire
- Many employees hired sight unseen
- Daily comms between Ops and Support essential
- Need tight overtime controls
- Inadequate downsizing notice

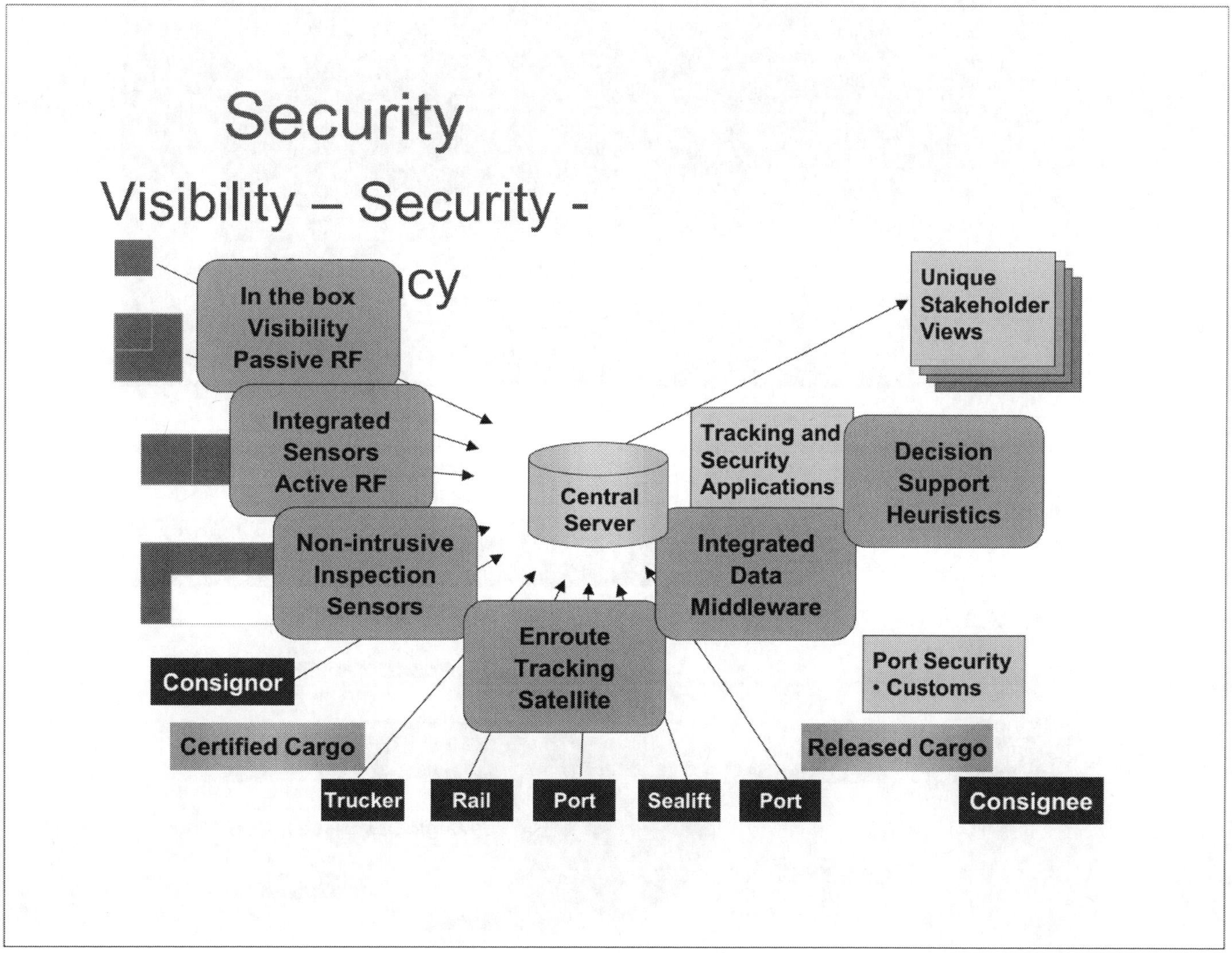
Security
Visibility – Security -
In the box Visibility Passive RF
Integrated Sensors Active RF
Non-intrusive Inspection Sensors
Central Server
Tracking and Security Applications
Decision Support Heuristics
Unique Stakeholder Views
Integrated Data Middleware
Enroute Tracking Satellite
Port Security
• Customs
Consignor
Certified Cargo
Released Cargo
Trucker
Rail
Port
Sealift
Port
Consignee

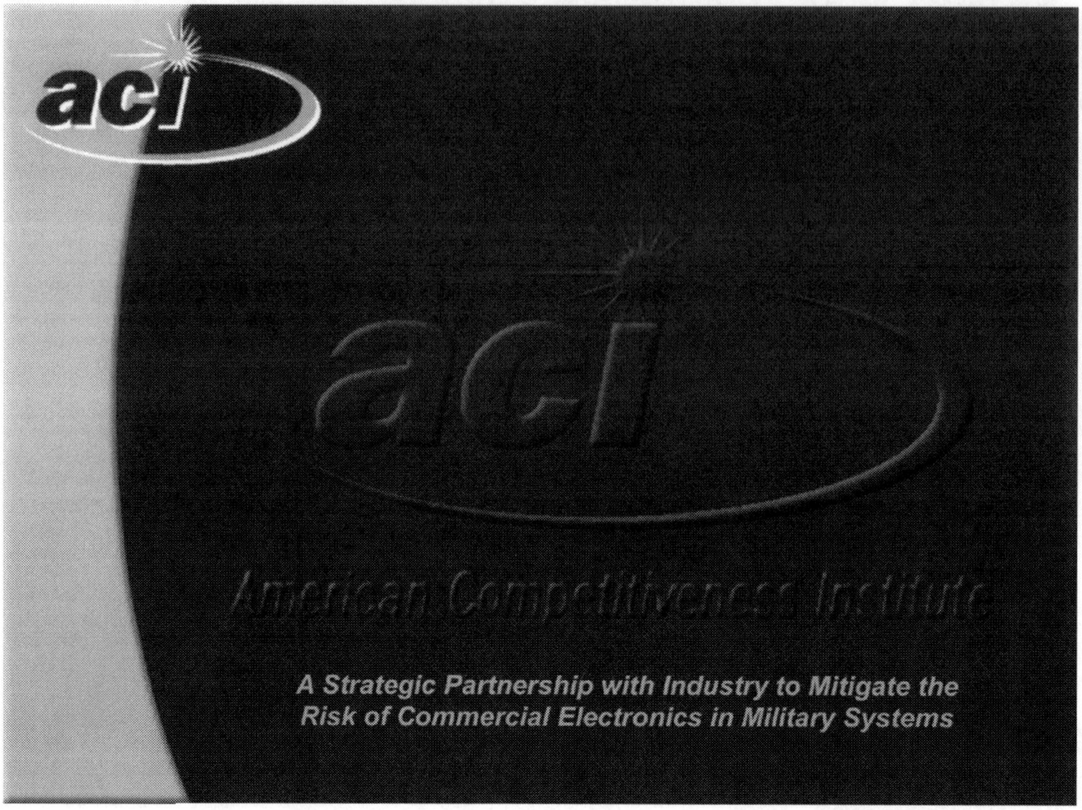
aci
aci
American Competitiveness Institute
A Strategic Partnership with Industry to Mitigate the
Risk of Commercial Electronics in Military Systems

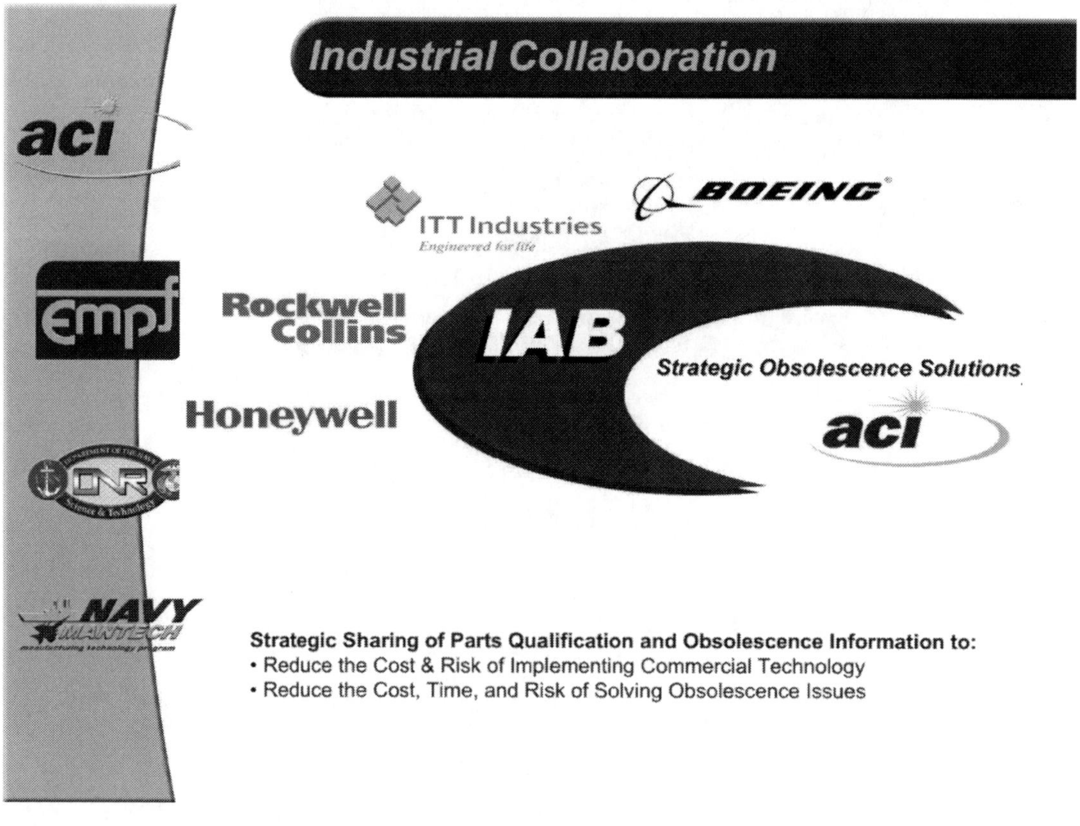
Industrial Collaboration
aci
ITT Industries
Engineered for life
BOEING
empf
Rockwell Collins
Honeywell
IAB
Strategic Obsolescence Solutions
aci
NAVY MANTECH
Strategic Sharing of Parts Qualification and Obsolescence Information to:
• Reduce the Cost & Risk of Implementing Commercial Technology
• Reduce the Cost, Time, and Risk of Solving Obsolescence Issues

Rapidly Changing Parts Supply Base

- **Aerospace Systems have Long Design-To-Acquisition Lead Times & Service**

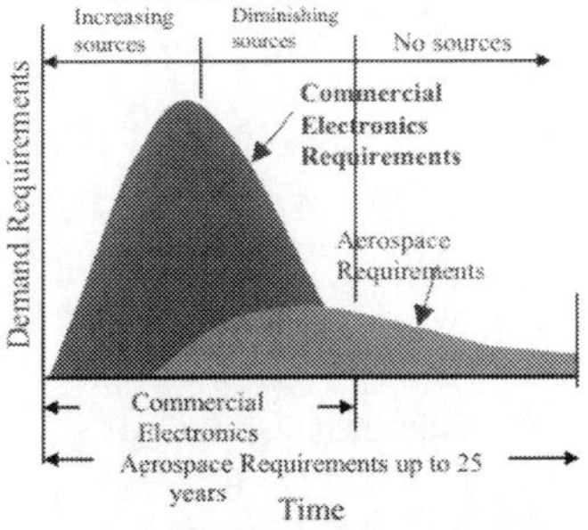

DoD/NASA Needs Are Not in Sync with the Commercial Electronics Marketplace

Military Share of Commercial Electronics Market Is <1% Today & Shrinking

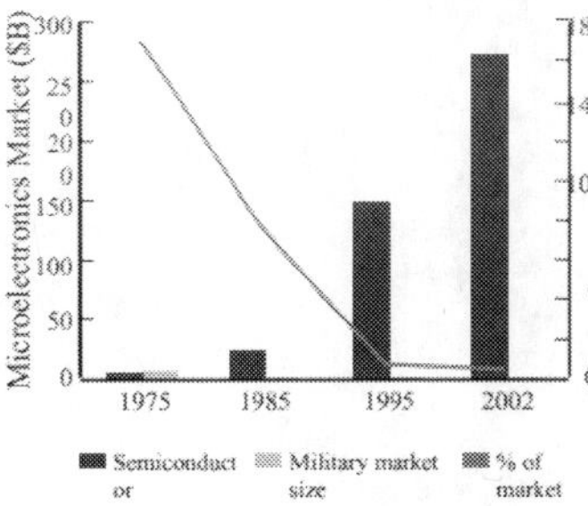

Now At All-Time Low

Industry Initiated, Industry Investment, Industry Commitment

Cost Impact of DMS Solutions

Increasing Program Risk ↓

Type	Possible Provider	Non-Recurring Engineering $(K)	Cost Multiplier per Part (x Times Original Cost)	
Alternate Source	Aftermarket vendor	None	4	Options available before a Lifetime Buy
Substitute	Other Service	None	8	
Lifetime Buy	DSCC or Part Manager	None	15	
Repackage	Aftermarket	10-50	20	Options remaining after Lifetime Buy
Remanufacture	Aftermarket or DMEA, HTT, DTC, etc.	30-100	30	
Emulation	GEM, DMEA, DTC	20-150	100	
Board Redesign	DMEA, HTT, DTC	100-500+	10,000	
COT Insertion	Commercial	1000-10000	Undetermined	

DSCC Defense Supply Center, Columbus
DMEA Defense Microelectronics Activity, Sacramento, CA
HTT Hardware Technology Center, Ogden, UT
DTC DMS Technology Center, Crane, In
GEM Generalized Emulation of Microcircuits, Sarnoff Research Center, Princeton, NJ
ITD Institute for Technology Development

Source: Joint Stars Program Office

Industry Initiated, Industry Investment, Industry Commitment

Objectives

➢Avoid duplicate efforts among industry to resolve DMS issues and qualify alternative components

➢Establish and implement **standard** part qualification test methodology that meets program requirements of all participants

➢Establish an infrastructure for all participants to share real-time,pre-competitive part-level data seamlessly

➢Establish a vehicle to notify participants of existing and impending obsolescence issues

Significant Cost Savings to DOD Through Information Sharing!

Industry Initiated, Industry Investment, Industry Commitment

Approach

Establish an Industry Team to leverage core competencies focused on replacement part qualification

➢Open to all Industry

Create a management system that enables industry collaboration to:

➢Capture identified replacement parts for declared obsolete parts

➢Capture qualification data of replacement parts

➢Notify participants of obsolescence issues

➢Capture instances in which parts are qualified/used outside of their designed operating range

➢Link to databases of other DoD agencies and subscribed services

Leverage Industry and Government partnership to address parts obsolescence issues

Industry Initiated, Industry Investment, Industry Commitment

Information/Communication Architecture

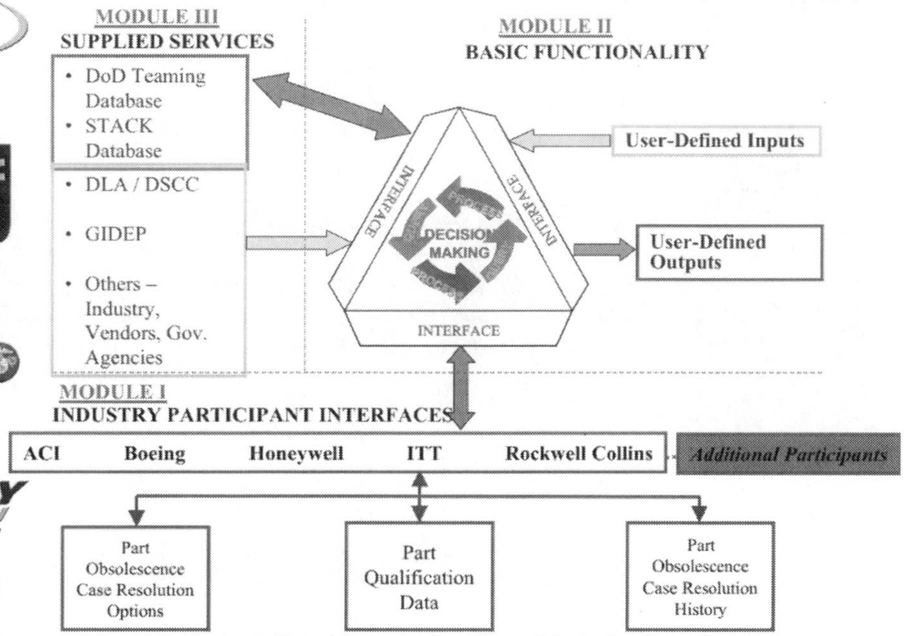

Industry Initiated, Industry Investment, Industry Commitment

Benefits

Reduced Cost, Schedule , and Technical Risk on Development, Production, and Sustainment Programs

- Collaboration will allow user to quickly access case resolution history by part number, thereby precluding redundant efforts for each participant to fix the same problem individually
- Collaboration will result in early notification of parts obsolescence issues, thereby reducing cost and risks associated with redesign efforts
- Collaboration with shared data on parts qualified to a common standard will reduce cost by precluding redundant efforts for each participant to qualify the same part individually
- Collaboration will serve as "One Stop Shop" for information contained in other DoD databases and common subscribed services
  - Leverage off existing MANTECH projects by facilitating data sharing

Industry Initiated, Industry Investment, Industry Commitment

Cost Avoidance - DMS Management

Resolution	Avoidance Method	NRE Cost Avoidance (Minor Redesign minus Avoidance Method)	Est. Cost Avoidance Per Case	
Case I	Substitute	($111,034 - $18,111)	~ $90,000	Lifetime Buy Still An Option
Case II	Repackage	($111,034 - $47,360)	~ $63,600	Lifetime Buy No Longer An Option
Case III	Emulation	($111,034 - $68,012)	~ $43,000	

Source: DMEA Cost Resolution Factors

Total savings ~ $90,000 per obsolete part occurrence if problem identified and resolved prior to End Of Life (EOL)

Industry Initiated, Industry Investment, Industry Commitment

Program Cost Avoidance

Increasing Program Risk ↓

Resolution	Low		Average		High		
	NRE	Recurring	NRE	Recurring	NRE	Recurring	
Existing Stock	$0	$629	$0	$1,884	$0	$3,249	Options available before a Lifetime Buy
Substitute	$15,000	$10,390	$19,000	$29,249	$24,000	$64,606	
Aftermarket	$41,000	$1,610	$50,000	$20,652	$59,000	$35,186	Options remaining after Lifetime Buy
Emulation	$55,000	$5,400	$72,000	$43,022	$89,000	$100,000	
Redesign – Minor	$82,000	$177,600	$117,000	$299,118	$153,000	$520,000	
Redesign - Major	$361,000	$0	$433,000	$0	$505,000	$0	

Source: DMEA Cost Resolution Factors (FY2002)

Industry Initiated, Industry Investment, Industry Commitment

Cost Savings - COTs Qualification

Scenarios with 4 Participating Companies

Scenario 1: Component Qualification using manufacturing data

- approx. 40 Hrs
- 40 Hrs * $100/hr = $4K
- 100 Components/yr * $4K/component = $400K
- ***Savings of $300K + per year***

Scenario 2: Component Qualification with physical testing

- 300 Hrs * $100/hr = $30K
- 100 Components/yr * $30K/component = $3,000K
- ***Savings of $2,250K per year***

Industry Initiated, Industry Investment, Industry Commitment

Discussions/Issues

aci

American Competitiveness Institute

SOLE – The International Society of Logistics
SOLE 2003

Integration of Commercial Technology into Boeing Systems/Platforms and the Effect on Life Cycle Cost

Strategy Requirements for Fulfilling the Objectives of Acquisition Reform

August 14th 2003

Jim Robles – Senior Technical Fellow
The Boeing Company
Phn: (206) 655-9062
Email: james.a.robles@boeing.com

BOEING

PHANTOM WORKS

Agenda

Advanced Platform Systems

Phantom Works — BOEING

- Context - Why It's Important
- The Challenge - Why it's Problematic
- The Effect on Life Cycle Cost (LCC)
- EIA-933 *A Standard for Preparing a COTS Assembly Management Plan*
- Company Internal Processes
- COTS Assembly Management
  - Useful Life Strategy
  - "Open" Environmental Assessment
  - Temperature
  - Requirements Tailoring
- Life Cycle Customer Support
- Conclusion

Assemblies are Following the Component Path ...

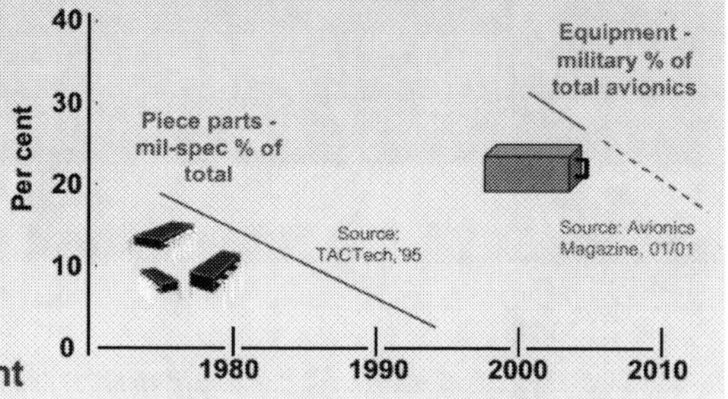

DOD Lack Of Impact On Electronics Industry Is Spreading To Assemblies.

BOEING

PHANTOM WORKS

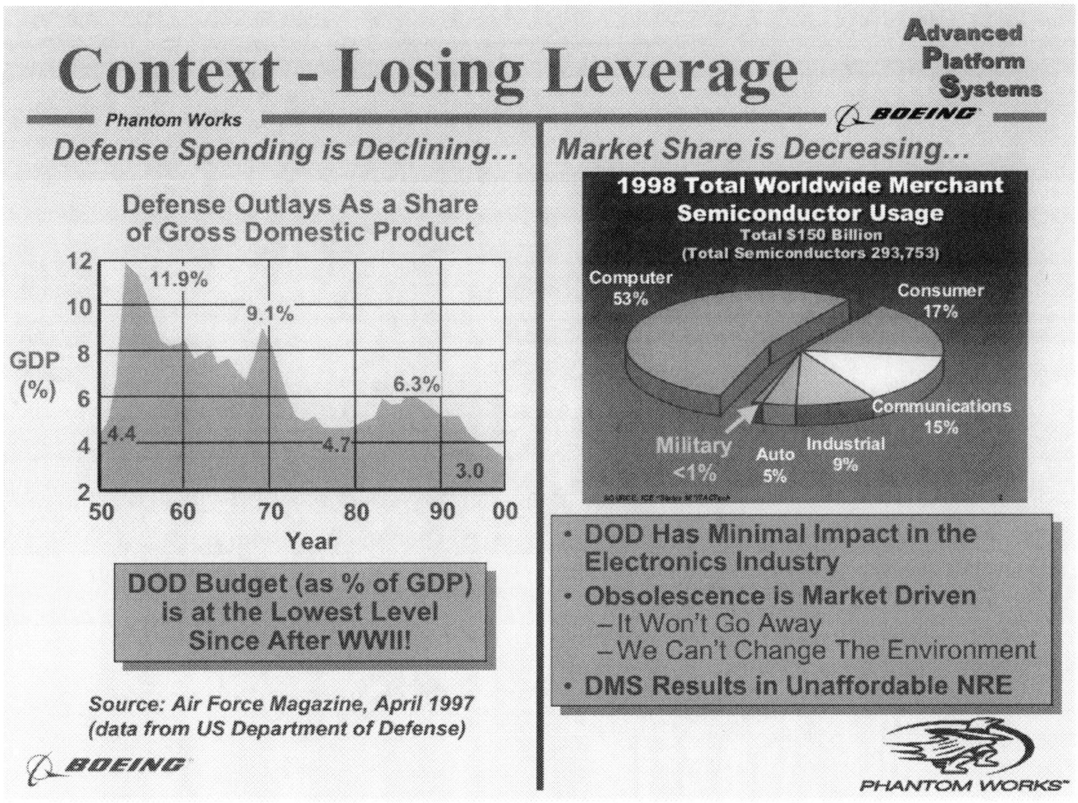

Context - Losing Leverage
Advanced Platform Systems
Phantom Works
BOEING
Defense Spending is Declining...
Defense Outlays As a Share of Gross Domestic Product
GDP (%)
11.9%
9.1%
6.3%
4.4
4.7
3.0
Year
DOD Budget (as % of GDP) is at the Lowest Level Since After WWII!
Source: Air Force Magazine, April 1997 (data from US Department of Defense)
BOEING
Market Share is Decreasing...
1998 Total Worldwide Merchant Semiconductor Usage
Total $150 Billion
(Total Semiconductors 293,753)
Computer 53%
Consumer 17%
Communications 15%
Industrial 9%
Auto 5%
Military <1%
• DOD Has Minimal Impact in the Electronics Industry
• Obsolescence is Market Driven
– It Won't Go Away
– We Can't Change The Environment
• DMS Results in Unaffordable NRE
PHANTOM WORKS

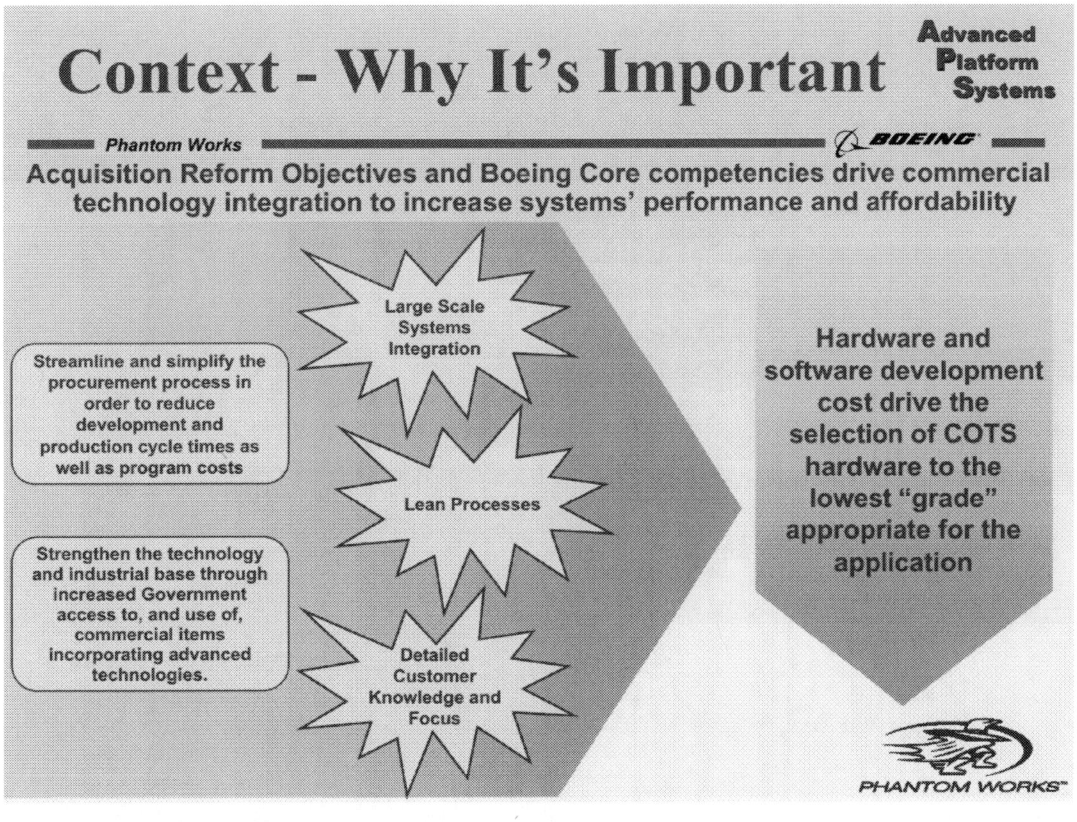

Context - Why It's Important
Advanced Platform Systems
Phantom Works
BOEING
Acquisition Reform Objectives and Boeing Core competencies drive commercial technology integration to increase systems' performance and affordability
Streamline and simplify the procurement process in order to reduce development and production cycle times as well as program costs
Strengthen the technology and industrial base through increased Government access to, and use of, commercial items incorporating advanced technologies.
Large Scale Systems Integration
Lean Processes
Detailed Customer Knowledge and Focus
Hardware and software development cost drive the selection of COTS hardware to the lowest "grade" appropriate for the application
PHANTOM WORKS

The Challenge - COTS Components Vs. Assemblies

Advanced Platform Systems

Phantom Works — BOEING

Design using COTS components	Design using COTS Assemblies
• Higher functional density & greater environmental capability	• Lower functional density & lower environmental capability
• Higher cost & lower availability	• Lower cost & higher availability
• Components & materials selected by program approved process	• Components & materials selected by COTS supplier
• Assembly processes understood by program	• COTS supplier assembly processes
• Configuration maintained per program plan	• COTS supplier configuration management plus ????
• **Weapon system integrator must understand environmental, safety, performance, etc. capability**	• **Weapon system integrator must understand environmental, safety, performance, etc. capability**

BOEING — PHANTOM WORKS™

COTS In Electronic Systems

Advanced Platform Systems

Phantom Works — BOEING

	Commercial Parts	Commercial Boards	Commercial Systems
Cost Savings	$	$	$
Military Application Integration Issues	• Thermal • Moisture	• Thermal • Moisture • Vibration	• Thermal • Moisture • Vibration • EMI/EMC

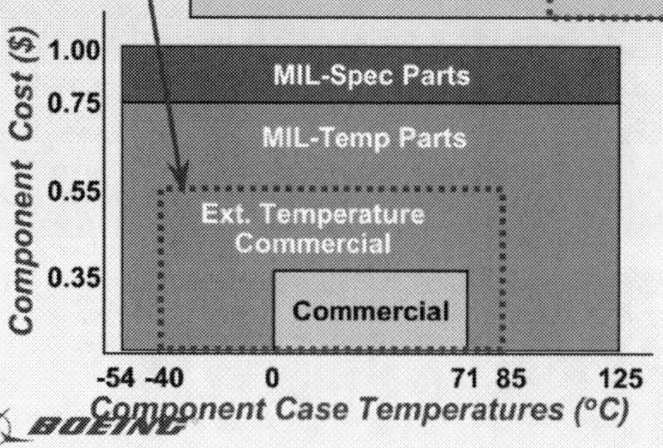

- **Thermal Issues**
- **Packaging Issues**
  - Moisture
  - Vibration / Shock
  - Nuclear Hardening
  - Chemical Hardening
- **Safety Issues**
- **Commercial Device Testability**

BOEING — PHANTOM WORKS™

The Effect on LCC

Advanced Platform Systems

Phantom Works — BOEING

Compared to what?
What is your definition of COTS?

- Design using less "commercial" COTS
- Development Cost
  - Higher hardware cost
  - Higher S/W cost
  - Lower integration cost
- Unit Recurring Flyaway Cost (URF)
  - Higher hardware cost
  - Higher S/W cost
- Operation and Support (O&S) Cost
  - Longer useful life – less frequent upgrades – Close the SIL?
  - Higher S/W maintenance cost
  - **Reliability/Failure Rate**
  - No special measures
- Obsolete technology in the field

- Design using more "commercial"COTS
- Development Cost
  - Lower hardware cost
  - Lower S/W cost
  - Higher integration cost
- Unit Recurring Flyaway Cost (URF)
  - Higher hardware cost
  - Lower S/W cost
- Operation and Support (O&S) Cost
  - Shorter useful life – more frequent upgrades – SIL operates forever
  - Lower S/W maintenance cost
  - **Reliability/Failure Rate**
  - Special measures
- Current technology in the field

BOEING — PHANTOM WORKS™

EIA-933

Advanced Platform Systems

Phantom Works — BOEING

- Requires establishment of engineering and business practices to assure COTS assemblies are:
  - Applied properly
  - Fully qualified for intended application
  - Compatible with integration process
  - Following processes to collect, store, retrieve, analyze and act on data
  - Selected, substituted and managed systematically
  - Maintain traceable path to qualified system through effective configuration management
  - Well understood and managed in terms of availability, obsolescence, reliability and impact on the application

COTS Boards

COTS Systems

BOEING — PHANTOM WORKS™

Levels of Integration

Advanced Platform Systems

Phantom Works — BOEING

- Platform Integrator
  - Integrates systems/Subsystems & lower
  - COTS Assembly Management Plan (CAMP) applies

- System/subsystem integrator
  - Integrates equipment & lower
  - CAMP applies

- Equipment Supplier
  - Integrates COTS assemblies
  - CAMP applies

- COTS Assembly Vendor
  - Integrates components
  - CAMP does not apply
  - Electronic Component Management Plan (ECMP) could apply?

- Component
  - Neither ECMP or CAMP apply

BOEING — PHANTOM WORKS

Why an Industry Standard?

Advanced Platform Systems

Phantom Works — BOEING

A Widely Accepted Standard

EIA-933 -- Standard Preparing a COTS Assembly Management Plan
•Tasks
•Objectives
•"Best Practice" guidance on widely accepted standards

• Participate in development of consensus standard • Know what customer expects • Know what to expect from supplier • Implement internal plans/ processes accordingly	**Government Customers (DoD, FAA, etc.)** Know what to expect in system/equipment integrator COTS Assembly Management Plans (CAMP's) **System/Equipment Integrators** Know what the government customer expects in system/equipment integrator CAMP's **Interested COTS Assembly Suppliers** Know what system/equipment integrators require to satisfy customers

Effective Utilization of COTS Assemblies
Minimization of Total Ownership Cost (TOC)
Optimization of Technology Insertion

BOEING — PHANTOM WORKS

Company Internal Processes The "How To"

Advanced Platform Systems

Phantom Works — BOEING

- Each company will define: For Boeing it's
  - D950-10651-1 Commercial-Off-The-Shelf (COTS) Assembly User's Guide
    - Maximum Utilization of existing "Command Media"
    - Provide guidance for individual program plans
  - Provide "how to" guidance to meet the objectives of EIA-933
    - Address subject matter expert (SME) areas of responsibility
  - Provide guidance, to programs, on requirements tailoring, environmental suitability, commercial standards, Etc.
  - Coordination through the COTS Hardware Technology Interest Group (TIG)
  - Initial version available since June 26th 2003

BOEING

PHANTOM WORKS™

Company Internal Processes

Advanced Platform Systems

Phantom Works — BOEING

Standard Process, and shared lessons learned, across the enterprise

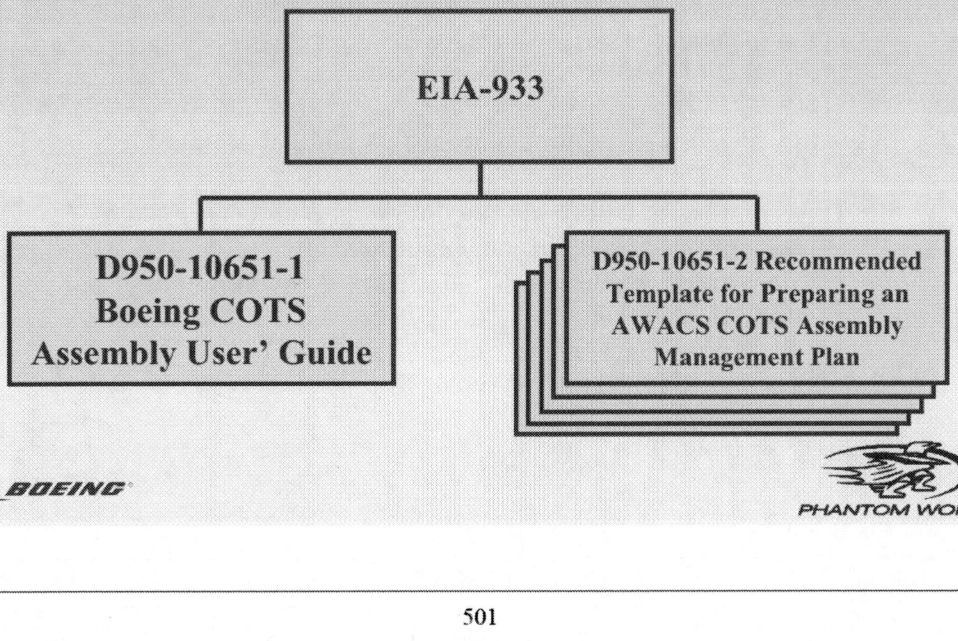

BOEING

PHANTOM WORKS™

COTS Assembly Management

Advanced Platform Systems

Phantom Works — BOEING

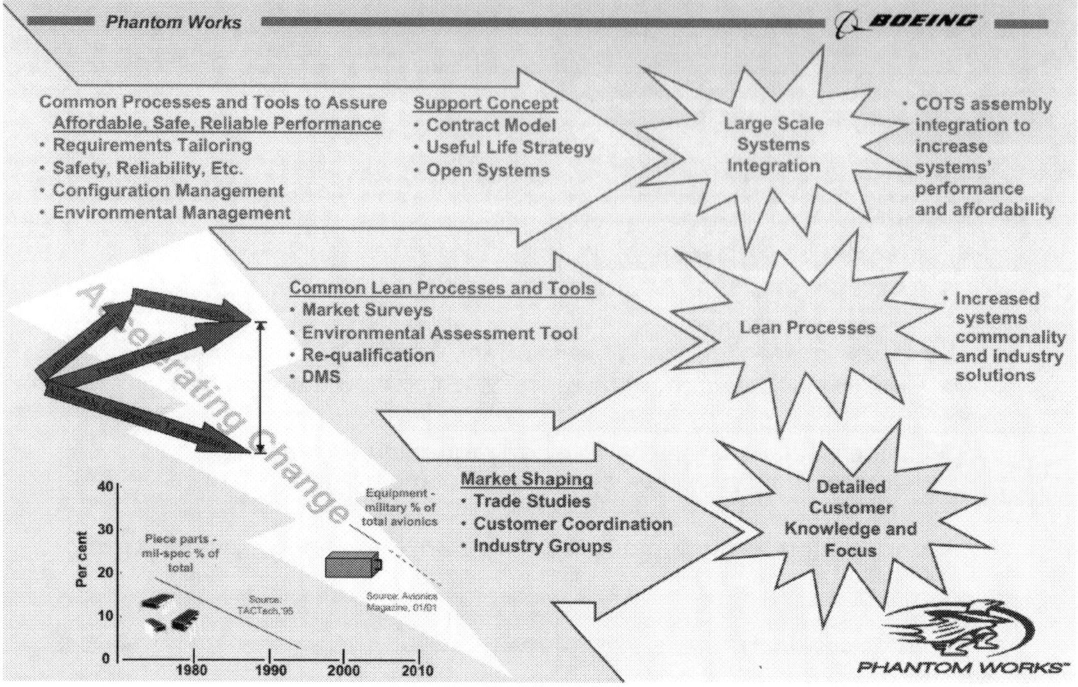

Useful Life Strategy

Advanced Platform Systems

Phantom Works — BOEING

- The "sine qua non" of strategy to minimize TOC while maximizing ease of technology insertion
  - Define program approach to manage the limited useful life of COTS hardware
  - In the absence, of a Useful Life Strategy, COTS will exacerbate the impact of DMS
- Essential element – Requires dialogue with the customer
  - Trade studies to determine the optimum useful life of each LRI
    - Weapon System Integrator responsibility
    - A driver for requirements tailoring and development of our support approach
- Comprehensive Life Cycle Customer Support (LCCS) Approach

BOEING — PHANTOM WORKS

"Open" Environmental Assessment

Advanced Platform Systems

Phantom Works — BOEING

- Application of open architecture principles is essential to minimize TOC.
  - The alternative is that COTS hardware shorter cycle times exacerbate the impact of DMS
- Open architecture principles are well understood by the "systems" community
  - Well supported commercial interface standards
  - Modular design concepts
  - Etc.
- "Openness" must address environmental ruggedness through the trade study process: TOC; performance; reliability; Etc.
  - COTS cycle times make "re-qualification" unaffordable
    - Configuration management issue
  - Risk associated with test/retest (lack of "openness") must be considered
  - Potential limitation on COTS hardware selection
- Assessment of "standards and processes" with test as prudent

BOEING — PHANTOM WORKS™

Temperature & Cost VME Example

Advanced Platform Systems

Phantom Works — BOEING

Part Temperature Grade	Part Temperature Range (Nominal)	Cost	Availability of Latest Product	Operating Cold Wall Temperature	Non-Operating Temperature
Commercial	0 C to 70C	1X	Highest	-20C to 55C	-50C to 100C
Industrial	-40C to 85C	3X	Lower	-40C to 65C	-50C to 100C
Military/ Premium	-55C to 125C	4X	Lowest	-55C to 85C	-62C to 105C

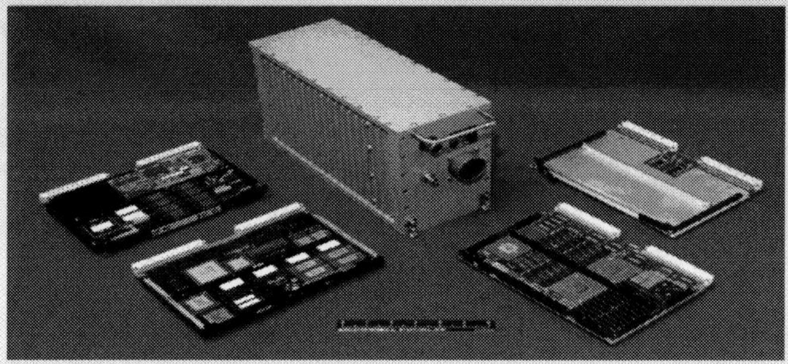

BOEING — PHANTOM WORKS™

Temperature Cycling - Background

Advanced Platform Systems

Phantom Works — BOEING

- A naturally occurring environment
- Increased electronics susceptibility with surface mount technology

- History – how we got where we are
- Embedded in military electronics supplier culture?
  - Should be part company design/manufacturing processes

- Generally <u>not</u> embedded in (office grade, Etc.) COTS hardware culture
  - Some COTS suppliers are capable
  - Address when driven by market

BOEING — PHANTOM WORKS™

Temperature Cycling – Background (Cont.)

Advanced Platform Systems

Phantom Works — BOEING

- We have "worked" the surface mount issue for military electronics
- Requires analysis/test, attention to detail and additional expense

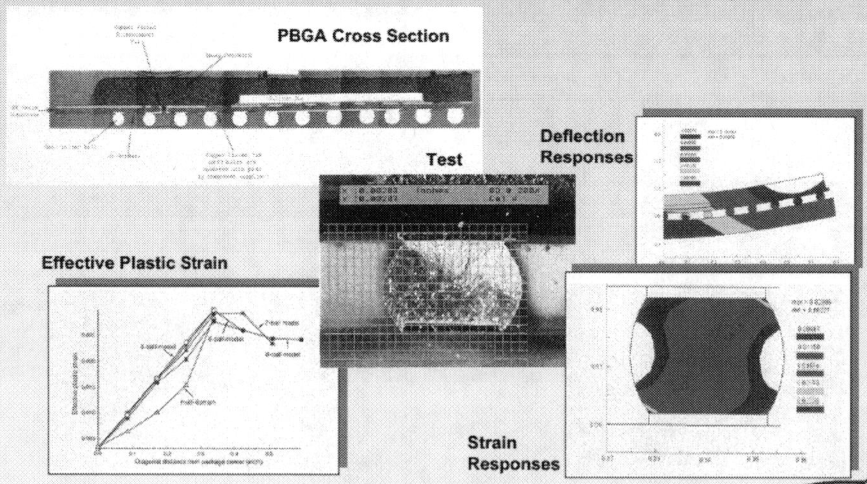

BOEING — PHANTOM WORKS™

Temperature Cycling – Commercial Practice

Advanced Platform Systems

Phantom Works — BOEING

- High Performance Internet Switch design (example) tested a board, from <u>-40C to 100C, 1160</u> cycles to first failure, and 1614 cycles to termination of test. (Cisco Systems @ ICAPS 2002)
- "Ruggedized (Defacto) Industry Standard" VME requires 3 cycles from minimum storage temperature to maximum storage temperature.
- IEEE 1101.2-1992 (Conduction Cooled VME) does not address temperature cycling.
- IEEE 1101.1-1991 (Convection Cooled VME) does not address temperature cycling.
- Intel Environmental Standards Handbook, June 1999 provides a Board Temperature Non-Operating Validation Test with, <u>-40C to 70C, 50 cycles</u>, no failures during functional test after exposure.
- The Intel Handbook also provides a System Temperature Non-Operating Validation Test with, -40C to 70C, 4 cycles, no failures during functional test after exposure.
- NEBS Requirements: Physical Protection, GR63-CORE, require Low Temperature Transition to Cold (Packaged) from 23C to -40C @ 30C/hour (1 transition), and a Low Temperature Transition to Room Temperature (Packaged) from -40C to 23C in less than 5 minutes (1 transition).

BOEING — PHANTOM WORKS

Temperature Cycling – Test Case

Advanced Platform Systems

Phantom Works — BOEING

- <u>Test Case</u> – Assume temperature cycling life of 50 cycles from –40C to 71C
  - Normal operation @ 50C component case temperature in a 35C ambient
  - Worst case operation @ 70C component case temperature in a 50C environment
- 56% Non-Operation, 34% Normal Operation, 10 % Worst Case Operation
  - <u>Life = 3.0 years</u>
- 56% Non-Operation, 0% Normal Operation, 44 % Worst Case Operation
  - <u>Life = 1.6 years</u>
- Temperature cycling must be a hardware assessment criterion

BOEING — PHANTOM WORKS

Requirements Tailoring

Advanced Platform Systems

Phantom Works — BOEING

- Detailed tailoring recommendation, and rational, must be developed for each application
- Environmental – may require cocooning and/or operational changes
  - Assure all relevant environments are included
  - Tailor as justified by systems engineering process
  - Eliminate as justified by systems engineering process
- M&P and Workmanship
  - By definition "how to" - should be deleted under Acquisition Reform - drives cost while degrading performance
  - Traditional "how to" requirements contain requirements that we can't meet with COTS hardware and that in some cases are not verifiable for any equipment
- Emphasize performance based systems engineering
  - Provide essential process guidance; PEM selection, Etc.
- Eliminate debate over "how to" requirements that we can't meet

BOEING

PHANTOM WORKS™

Life Cycle Customer Support

Advanced Platform Systems

Phantom Works — BOEING

- Boeing insight, rather than oversight, into supplier actions and equipment configuration
- Boeing approval of supplier processes, rather than specific selections/decisions, to fulfill our large scale system integrator responsibilities
- Contractual incentives (Lean Procurement, i.e. sharing of savings) to Boeing, and flown down to suppliers, to minimize TOC
- Contractor warranty fees based on total (by flight hour, Etc.) usage of hardware
- Contractor depot support
- Contractor Class 2 change configuration management authority to incorporate DMS solutions, reliability enhancements, Etc.
- Solution of DMS problems by the supplier, by developing a common solution across all programs that use the relevant hardware, rather than by program unique solutions developed by the customer, Boeing and the supplier
- Coordination with program block upgrade plans, and with supplier technology roadmaps, to minimize the impact of DMS occurrences

BOEING

PHANTOM WORKS™

Conclusion – We Have a Process/Strategy for COTS

Advanced Platform Systems

Phantom Works BOEING

Life Cycle Customer Support
- Minimize customer TOC
  - Predictable customer support cost
- Optimize system performance over time
  - Coordinated cost effective technology refresh
- Higher availability
  - Eliminate ageing avionics syndrome
- Grow Boeing Aerospace support business
  - Higher profits for Boeing and our suppliers

Requirements Tailoring
- Tailored Performance Based
- Tailored/deleted "how to"
- Customer insight rather than oversight

Selection/Implementation Process
- Performance
- Reliability
- Robustness
- Safety
- Configuration Management
- Etc.

Create customer trust to facilitate other two legs
- Assure optimum solution and required performance

BOEING

PHANTOM WORKS™

Backup

Advanced Platform Systems

Phantom Works BOEING

BOEING

PHANTOM WORKS™

Bad And Good News

Advanced Platform Systems

Phantom Works — BOEING

Assemblies are Following the Component Path ...

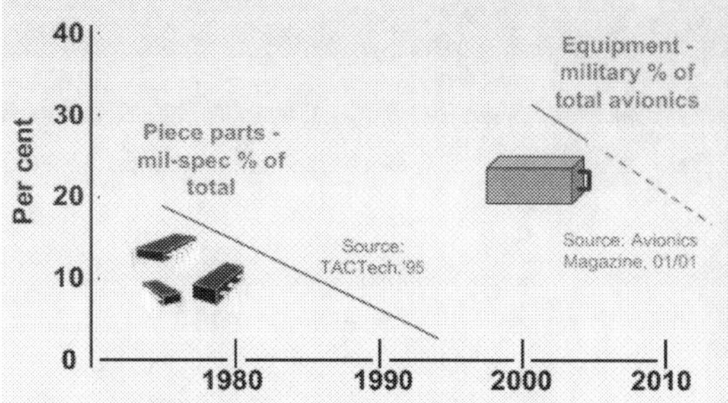

DOD Lack Of Impact On Electronics Industry Is Spreading To Assemblies.

COTS Components & Assemblies Are Getting Better ...

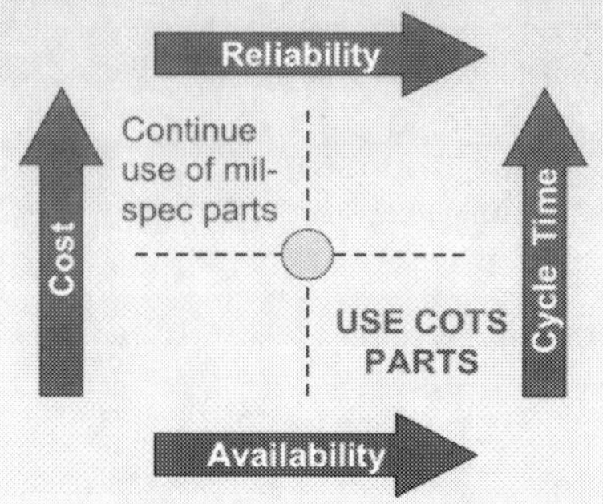

The Commercial Market Produces The Most Defect Free Products.

BOEING

PHANTOM WORKS™

EIA-933 Intent

Advanced Platform Systems

Phantom Works — BOEING

- Establish engineering and business practices to assure electronics assemblies are
  - Applied properly
  - Fully qualified for intended application
  - Compatible with integration process
  - Following processes to collect, store, retrieve, analyze and act on data
  - Selected, substituted and managed systematically
  - Maintain traceable path to qualified system through effective configuration management
  - Well understood and managed in terms of availability, obsolescence, reliability and impact on the application

BOEING

PHANTOM WORKS™

EIA-933 Intent

Advanced Platform Systems

Phantom Works — BOEING

- Development of a widely accepted industry standard for process management for the use of COTS assemblies in electronics systems
  - Support the twin goals of acquisition reform
  - Support industry, customer and regulatory agency needs
  - Maximize adoption and use of proven industry standards
- Applicable to commercial, civil and military applications
- Working group members include BAE Systems, Boeing, CMC Electronics, DY4, Honeywell, Lockheed Martin, L3 Communications, MITRE Corp., Northrop Grumman, Pole Zero Corp., Radstone Technology, Raytheon and Rockwell Collins

BOEING — PHANTOM WORKS

EIA-933 Background

Advanced Platform Systems

Phantom Works — BOEING

- A logical outgrowth of ongoing GEIA APMC efforts
  - Technical Advisory Group (TAG) to the International Electrotechnical Commission Technical Committee 107 (IEC TC 107) "Process Management For Avionics"
- IEC has published two documents for use by the suppliers of assemblies
  - IEC/PAS 62239, Edition 1.0, 2001-04, "Electronic Component Management Plans"
  - IEC/PAS 62240, Edition 1.0, 2001-04, "Use of Semiconductor Devices Outside Manufactures Specified Temperature Ranges"
  - "Third party certification" similar to ISO 9000
- GEIA APMC is currently addressing "effects of radiation" and "outsourcing of electronics manufacturing"

BOEING — PHANTOM WORKS

EIA-933 Content

Advanced Platform Systems

Phantom Works — BOEING

- Address processes identified in component level standards (IEC 62239/PAS & IEC 62240/PAS)
- Increased emphasis on systems engineering aspects (open systems, DMS Mitigation, etc.)
- "Extended range" to address all environments (vibration, temperature cycling, moisture/ corrosion, etc.)
- Higher level safety concerns
- Did not establish environmental grades

BOEING — PHANTOM WORKS™

EIA-933 Philosophy

Advanced Platform Systems

Phantom Works — BOEING

- It is unrealistic to try to define lists of assemblies that are always acceptable or, conversely, always unacceptable, in electronics applications.
- The important consideration in deciding whether or not a assembly can be used in a given application is the process used to assure its function, qualification, quality assurance, and reliability assurance.
- The process requirements should be based on industry consensus, and should be flexible enough to allow avionics OEMs to implement them in ways that are most efficient for them, and effective for the customer.

BOEING — PHANTOM WORKS™

EIA-933 Philosophy (Cont.)

Advanced Platform Systems

Phantom Works — BOEING

- The process, as implemented by a given avionics OEM, should be common for all programs and all customers, including aircraft integrators, regulatory agencies, defense agencies, etc. This will minimize cost and optimize quality and reliability.
- There should be effective and efficient verification that the above process is implemented and maintained correctly.

BOEING

PHANTOM WORKS™

SOW Requirement

Advanced Platform Systems

Phantom Works — BOEING

- The supplier shall develop a COTS Assembly Management Plan in accordance with EIA-933.

BOEING

PHANTOM WORKS™

D950-10651-1 & -2 Released June 26th 2003

Advanced Platform Systems

Phantom Works — BOEING

- D950-10651-1 *Commercial-Off-The-Shelf (COTS) User's Guide*
  - Clause by clause guidance "how" to implement EIA-933
  - Appendix A *Environmental Guidance*
  - Appendix B *Design and Construction Guidance*
  - Appendix C *Assessments*
  - Appendix D *RFI Questions* – mapped against:
    - FAA COTS Risk Mitigation Guide
    - NAVSEA Instruction 9083.1
  - Appendix E *Trade Studies (useful life)*
- D950-10651-2 *Recommended Template for Developing an AWACS COTS Assembly Management Plan* (Reflects AWACS 40/45)
  - Clause by clause implementation of EIA-933
  - Definition of how each specialty engineering function will implement each element of their program plan
- D950-10651-x and on to follow

BOEING — PHANTOM WORKS

Useful Life Trade Study

Advanced Platform Systems

Phantom Works — BOEING

- Affordability
  - Development Cost
    - What is the development cost impact of each option considered?
      - Hardware development
      - Software development
      - Integration
      - Environmental characterization (including the reduced cost of characterizing hardware for shorter Useful Lives)
  - Unit Recurring Flyaway Cost (URF)
    - Hardware cost for each shipset
    - Software cost for each shipset

BOEING — PHANTOM WORKS

Useful Life Trade Study (Continued)

Advanced Platform Systems

Phantom Works — BOEING

- Affordability (Continued)
  - O&S Cost
    - Removal and replacement costs for failed hardware
    - Other maintenance costs
      - Ground carts that would not otherwise be required
      - Maintenance personnel to maintain power on, etc. that would not otherwise be required
      - System Integration Lab (SIL) as required to maintain configuration compatibility.
    - Hardware cost for planned upgrades
    - Software costs for planned upgrades
    - Integration costs for planned upgrades

BOEING — PHANTOM WORKS

Useful Life Trade Study (Continued)

Advanced Platform Systems

Phantom Works — BOEING

- Lethality/Survivability
  - Performance
    - Performance of the hardware (processing speed, memory, etc.)
      - Does the planned upgrade rate (useful life) meet the user's ongoing demand for current technology?
  - Weight
    - Weight of the hardware
    - Installation weight effect (cocooning, shielding, etc.)
    - Aircraft system weight effect (ECS, power system, etc.)
  - Volume
    - Volume of the hardware
    - Installation volume effect (cocooning, etc.)
    - Aircraft system effect (ECS, power system, etc.)

BOEING — PHANTOM WORKS

Useful Life Trade Study (Continued)

Advanced Platform Systems

Phantom Works

BOEING

- Supportability
  - Integrity/Reliability
    - Integrity
      - Will the hardware withstand the required temperature cycling life?
      - Will the hardware withstand the required vibration/shock life?
      - Will the hardware withstand the required moisture/corrosion life?
    - Reliability
      - What will the installed reliability be?
      - Have Single Event Effects (SEE) been accounted for in the system architecture to provide the required mission success rate?

BOEING

PHANTOM WORKS™

Useful Life Trade Study (Continued)

Advanced Platform Systems

Phantom Works

BOEING

- Supportability (Continued)
  - Ease of Maintenance
    - Effect on remove and replace (R&R) time
    - Adequacy of build-in-test (BIT) capability
    - Effect on maintainer comfort and convenience
  - Ease of Technology Insertion
    - Does the selected hardware provide a scaleable, evolvable upgrade path?
    - Is the selected hardware build to environmental standards that will preclude the need for recharacterization?

BOEING

PHANTOM WORKS™

Single Event Effects (SEE) Microprocessor Complexity

Advanced Platform Systems

Phantom Works — BOEING

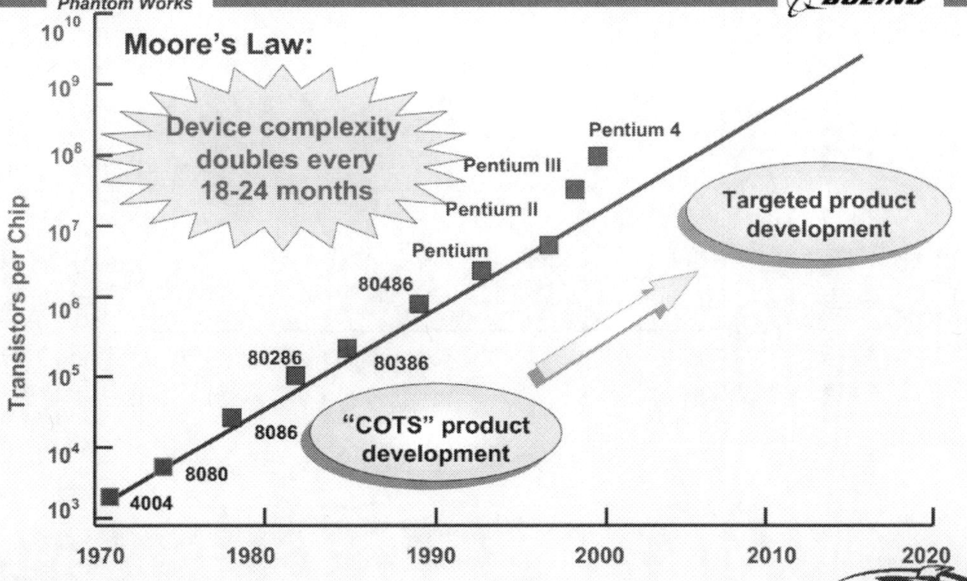

BOEING

PHANTOM WORKS™

Single Event Effects (SEE)

Advanced Platform Systems

Phantom Works — BOEING

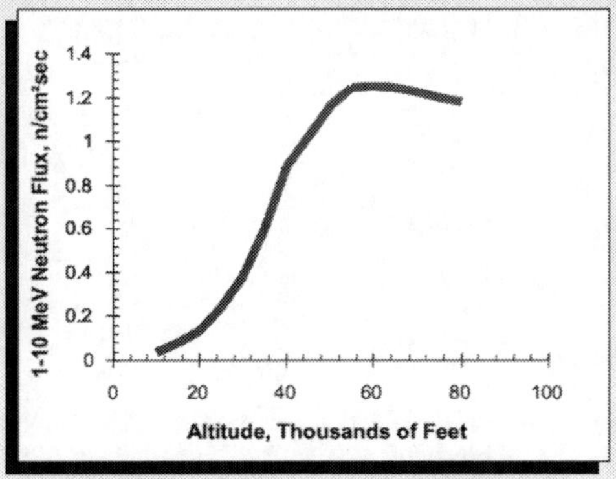

Main memory protected by error correcting code, but cache memory, which is increasing, is generally not protected

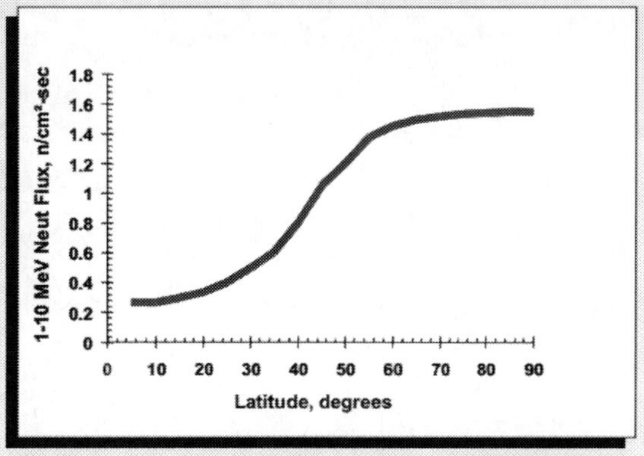

Smaller device geometries increase likelihood of multiple bit upsets, even in main memory

Higher radiation flux densities and lower threshold voltages ⇒ more single events

(Source: Dr. Eugene Normand)

BOEING

PHANTOM WORKS™

SEU Rate and Atmosphere Neutron Flux with Altitude

Advanced Platform Systems

Phantom Works — BOEING

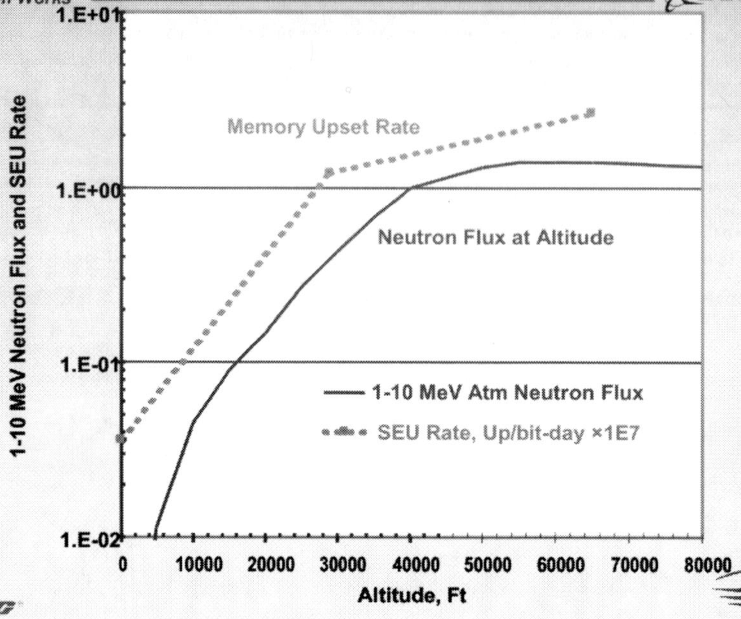

(Source: Dr. Eugene Normand)

BOEING — PHANTOM WORKS

Environmental Grades?

Advanced Platform Systems

Phantom Works — BOEING

- A concept to facilitate communication between COTS assembly suppliers, integrators and users
- De-facto standard environmental grades for VME assemblies provide a starting point
- Smart part numbering system?
- How many spaces to fill in?
- Is there interest?

BOEING — PHANTOM WORKS

Environmental Grades - Examples

Advanced Platform Systems

Phantom Works — BOEING

Temperature					
Environmental Grade	Non-Operating High Temperature	Non-Operating Low Temperature	Operating High Temperature	Operating Low Temperature	Temperature Cycling
0	Not Specified				
1 IEEE 1101.1-1991 Convection Cooled VME	70C 96 hours IEC 68-2-2 (1974)	-40C 72 hours IEC 68-2-1 (1990)			
"Ruggedized Industry Standard" Convection Cooled VME	100C or 105C depending on part grade	-50C or -62C depending on part grade	55C, 70C or 85C air depending on part grade and air velocity	0C, -40C or -55C air depending on part grade	3 cycles Minimum Storage Temperature to Maximum Storage Temperature
2 IEEE 1101.2-1992					
"Ruggedized Industry Standard" Conduction Cooled VME	100C or 105C depending on part grade	-50C or -62C depending on part grade	55C, 65C or 85C cold wall depending on part grade	-20C, -40C or -55C cold wall depending on part grade	3 cycles Minimum Storage Temperature to Maximum Storage Temperature
TBD More					

BOEING — PHANTOM WORKS™

Environmental Grades Smart Numbering System

Advanced Platform Systems

Phantom Works — BOEING

- How many numbers should be in the grade?
- Single environmental grade => Std - Grade A
- By Category => Std - Grade w-x-y-z
- By Environment => Std - Grade a-b-c-d-e-f-g-h-i-j-k-l-m-n-o
- What is beneficial to integrators & users?
- What is beneficial to suppliers?

Overall Environmental Grade																			
Temperature					Dynamic					Moisture/Corrosion/Altitude					Other				
Non-Operating High Temperature	Non-Operating Low Temperature	Operating High Temperature	Operating Low Temperature	Temperature Cycling	Operating Vibration	Operating Shock	Non-Operating Shock	Acceleration	Durability	Humidity	Salt Fog	Corrosive Gas	Operational Altitude	Storage Altitude	Flammability	Fungus	Toxic Materials	EMC	ESD

- Is there interest in developing such a standard?
  - EIA, VSO, AVSI, Etc.?

BOEING — PHANTOM WORKS™

PART OBSOLESCENCE STRATEGIES AT ROCKWELL COLLINS

Jack Harris

Rockwell Collins

August 14, 2002

Rockwell Collins Business

Rockwell Collins Military Products

Communication	*Navigation*	*Displays*
		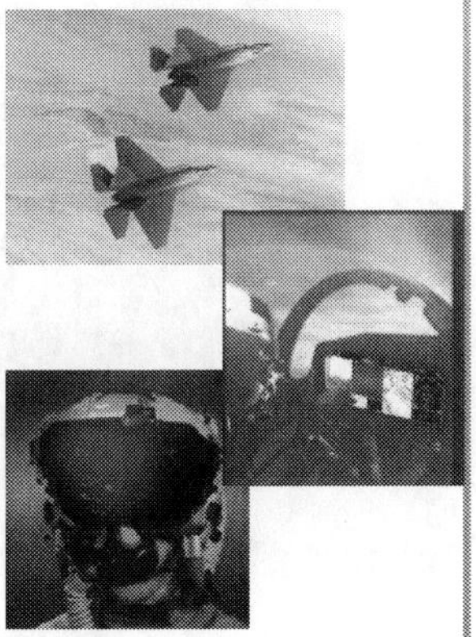
• Airborne Comm. Systems • Data Links • Satellite Communication • Secure Communication	• Airborne GPS Receivers • Radio Navigation • Ground Force Navigation • GPS for Missiles/Munitions	• Primary Flight Displays • Helmet Mounted Displays • Projection Displays

Industry Drivers

Aerospace Systems have Long Design-To-Acquisition Lead Times & Service

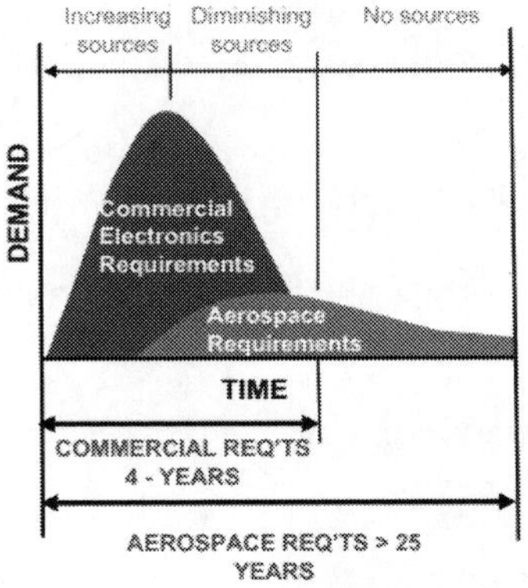

Military Share of Commercial Microelectronics Market Is <1% Today & Shrinking

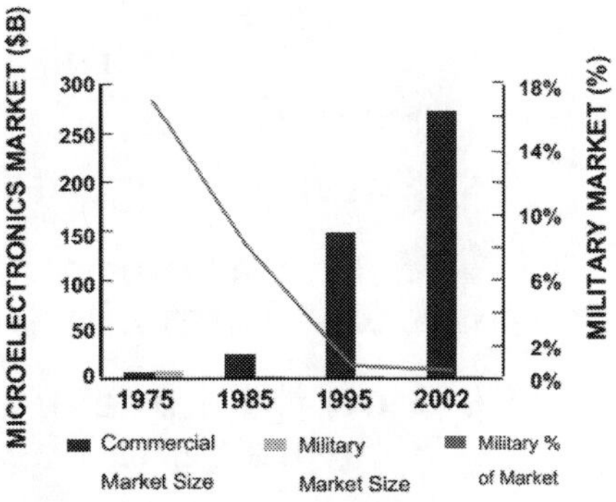

Highlights the dependence on commercial parts

COTS in Military Products

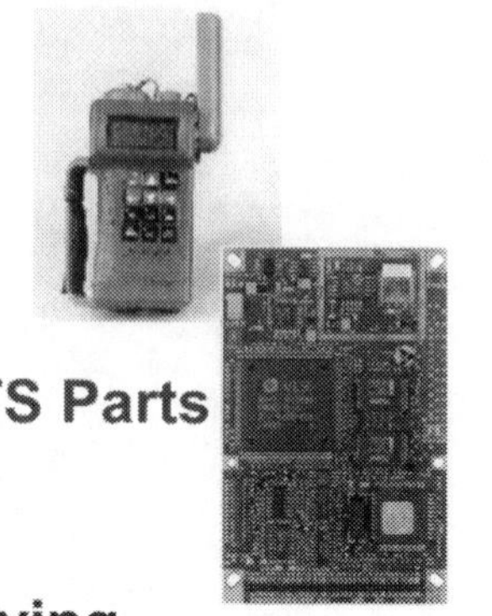

- Cost Reduction
- Wider Availability
- Lighter Weight, Smaller Size
- Latest Technology Available First as COTS Parts
- Lower Power Consumption
- COTS Quality & Reliability Steadily Improving
- Hermetic Choices are Rapidly Diminishing

COTS Implementation Requires Mitigation Strategies to Obsolescence

COTS Issues

- Limited Temperature Range (0 to 70C, or -40 to 85C); Unknown Performance and Reliability Outside of Data Sheet Temperature Range
- Unknown Durability in Harsh Vibration, Thermal Cycling
- Potential Legal Liability in high-rel use
- Eventual Vulnerability to Moisture, Unknown Long Term Life Characteristics
- New Die-Level Vulnerabilities with Smaller Features and Lower Voltages

COTS Issues

- Rapid Obsolescence vs. 20-year Products
- Unannounced Changes by COTS Vendors
- Thermal Issues (Poor thermal paths, self-heating popcorn failures)
- Competition with consumer products market
- Large Investment in Cost & time to Qualify Parts for use in harsh environments.

Many COTS Issues can be Designed around while obsolescence must be planned for

Overarching Obsolescence Strategy

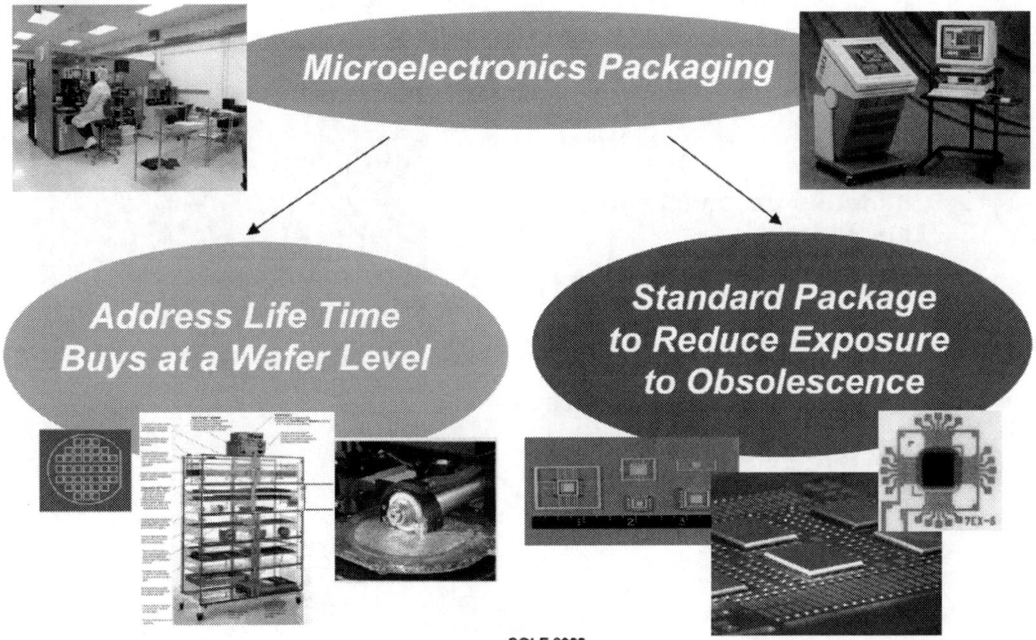

Last Time Buy at Wafer Level

- Allows for inventory to be held with lower associated costs
- Cost of conversion will be applied closer to the time of application
- This does not fit all, but would be justified on individual business cases
- A mix of last time/bridge buys at the component will also be part of the strategy

Standard Package

- Performs a specific, testable function
- Includes one or more bare die
- Includes passives and other elements
- Smaller than a credit card
- Has a single substrate that is critical to the delivery of the module's performance
- Used in a number of product applications

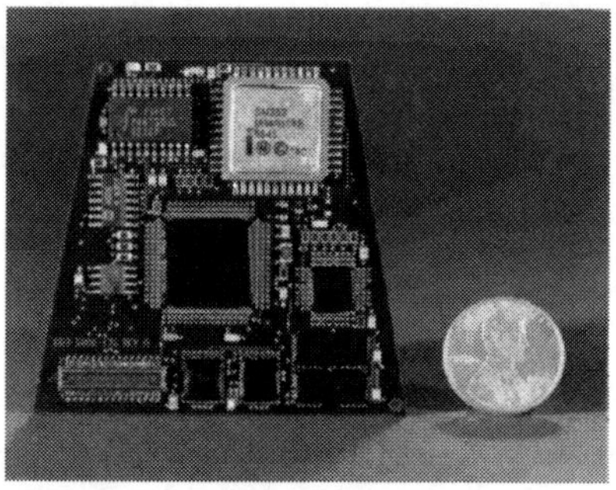

Summary

- **Part obsolescence will continue to be an issue for military suppliers**
- **Use of Standard package can improve time to market and reduce qualification costs**
- **Effective use of Die/Wafer versus component inventory has the opportunity to improve financial performance**

EMERGING OPPORTUNITIES

FOR

FOURTH-PARTY LOGISTICS ™ (4PL™)

SERVICE PROVIDERS

IN THE

UNITED STATES

DEFENSE

INDUSTRY

Michael D. Connor

-DISCLAIMER-

" This paper reflects only the personal views and opinions of the author and should not be construed to represent the official view of his employers (MPRI, Inc. and the Army Materiel Command) or any other organization."

TABLE OF CONTENTS

TABLE OF CONTENTS (continued)

TABLE OF CONTENTS (continued)

ACKNOWLEDGEMENTS

I wish to acknowledge the following institutions whose many logistics professionals provided me with much of the material for my research and have contributed immensely to the understanding of performance-based logistics, total life cycle systems management, and supply chain management in the United States (U.S.) defense industry:

- Jerry Cothran, Program Director, Performance-Based Logistics Department, Defense Acquisition University.
- Roger Hamerlinck, Senior Logistics Analyst, ILS Policy Division, Assistant Secretary of the Army (Acquisition, Logistics, and Technology).
- Louis Kratz, Director, Logistics Plans and Program, Office of the Assistant Deputy Under Secretary of Defense (Logistics and Materiel Readiness).
- Catherine Leach, Chief, ILS, Concepts and Requirements Analysis Division, Future Operations, G-3, Army Materiel Command.

Andersen Consulting trademarked the term 'Fourth-Party Logistics™' (4PL™) in 1998. For the sake of clarity throughout this document, all future references to 'Fourth-Party Logistics™' or '4PL™' will not carry the trademark 'TM' symbol.

ABSTRACT

Strategic analysis of the strengths, weaknesses, opportunities, and threats (SWOT) facing the U.S. industry and subsequent examination of alignment with fourth-party logistics (4PL) feasibility factors shows that some emerging opportunities do exist for fourth-party logistics service providers (4PLs) to form innovative, efficient, and effective supply chain management solutions for the defense industry. This comes especially to light under the Department of Defense's new Future Logistics Enterprise (FLE) and Performance-Based Logistics (PBL) initiatives. A plethora of articles in professional and management journals and edited books repeatedly proclaim performance bases logistics and supply chain management, especially in the defense sector, as the envy and model of supply chain efficiency and effectiveness. The major defense contractors have all attended PBL implementation briefings and are keen to collaborate with DoD to drive costs out of the supply chain through shrewd cost containment, fixed cost outsourcing, and vertical integration and control of the primary and secondary distribution chains. Effectively and necessarily, however, the supply chain and life cycle management of weapon systems remains segmented and "stove-piped" with almost complete control from the top (Program Executive Officers/Program Managers (PEOs/PMs)) end of the chain with no competition or collaboration from within to generate true supply chain competitive advantage.

Without continued mergers or expansion, the U.S. defense industry market share is set to stagnate with no real gains possible short of a significant evolution in supply chain management. In this environment, the 4PL, or supply chain integrator, provides one of the most synergistic ways forward for the U.S. defense industry to increase enterprise value. This paper addresses how 4PL offers the defense industry the ability to increase value through fixed capital reduction, increased revenue, operations cost reduction, and increased working capital. The 4PL relationship, in essence, leverages the combined parties' technology, economies of scale, core competencies and expert management of the entire supply chain to maximise enterprise value. This paper will also elaborate further on some of the functional ways that the 4PL can do this, which includes the following:

- Asset transfer
- Asset utilization
- Product quality
- Customer service
- Operational efficiency
- Procurement savings
- Process enhancement
- Inventory reduction
- Reduced cycle times

In closing, because different 4PL operating models leverage different expertise and efficiencies, availability of specific solutions to specific client requirements makes the 4PL relationship a flexible one for all supply chain and "corporate" defense team members.

1. INTRODUCTION

The objective of this project is to analyse available data and professional input to determine whether or not emerging opportunities exist for 4PLs to help provide integrated management for the supply chains and total life cycle systems management (TLCSM) of U.S. DoD weapon systems. In the following paper, an elaboration of the 4PL concept that explains what a 4PL can provide an organization or PEO/PM, especially those in the U.S. defense industry.

Later chapters include a summary of structured interviews with U.S. logistics association and DoD institutional professionals. The discussion includes critical analysis of available defense data and research (notably supply chain and life cycle management journal articles) and addresses the connectivity, or alignment, with requirements of the U.S. defense industry and the solutions offered by potential 4PLs. In the end, strategic SWOT analysis will show where the 4PL can maximize defense industry strengths and opportunities and minimize weaknesses and threats.

As the need for management of the entire supply chain and the integrated logistics enterprise emerges across defense industries, corporations are repositioning themselves to take advantage of competitive advantage that they can garner from within the supply chain. Since the defense contracting industry is becoming so concentrated in the U.S., the need for further competitive advantage necessitates the most efficient and effective management of the logistics enterprise solution. Through enterprise value-added, 4PLs purport to reduce fixed capital, increase revenue, reduce operational costs, and unburden working capital for their clients.

So what is fourth-party logistics (4PL) and what does a 4PL service provider do? In essence, the 4PL is a supply chain integrator that assembles and manages the resources, capabilities, and technology of its own organization with those of complementary service providers to deliver a comprehensive supply chain solution. Supply chain evolution has occurred, with organizations moving from in-sourcing to outsourcing to 4PL arrangements (Gattorna, 1998). Gattorna continues by saying that while outsourcing logistics is now accepted business practice, 'Fourth-Party Logistics' is emerging as a breakthrough solution to modern supply chain challenges...to provide maximum overall benefit.

Central to the 4PL's success is the "best of breed" approach to providing services to a client. The development of 4PL solutions leverages the capabilities of 3PLs, technology service providers, and business process managers to provide the client organization with greater cross-functional integration and broader operational autonomy. Two key distinctions make the concept of 4PL unique and set it apart from other supply chain and logistics enterprise outsourcing options available to the market today. First, a 4PL delivers a comprehensive supply chain solution, and secondly, a 4PL delivers value through the ability to influence the entire logistics chain (Bauknight, 2000). This paper will provide extensive discussion of what the 4PL can deliver to the US defense industry.

2. METHODOLOGY

This project followed the flowchart at Appendix A from conception to presentation. Within the framework of using a life-cycle approach – concept, baseline or benchmark, transition, solution, application – secondary and primary sources were used to establish whether a feasible alignment between the current state of the U.S. defense industry and the value offered by a 4PL ultimately exists or not. This is done in the context of offering enterprise value to the defense industry.

Due to the very modern nature of the 4PL concept and lack of knowledge and application, precise analytical techniques usually offered by primary research such as surveys was not realistic for this project. The large number potential contributors to such a new management concept made it unpractical to survey every major player involved in the defense industry supply chain.

However, this paper can and did benefit from the input and judgement of logistics professionals and this was done by informal discussions with academic and institutional professionals to include those acknowledged at the beginning of this paper. Results of these interviews are summarized later in this paper and the discussion questions are appended at Appendix D. Lastly, most of the logistics and supply chain variables examined are not open to mathematical modelling or statistical relevance so none was attempted.

3. RESULTS

As elaborated upon throughout this paper, research results across the board point to support and need for an evolving managerial and structural supply chain scheme within the Department of Defense (DoD) and defense industry. Recognizing that supply chain and distribution channels have many costs that can be reduced substantially has added to the imperative for management and professionalism (Sparks, 1998). Defense contractors have extended their influence back into logistics management and concepts such as integrated distribution, just-in-time distribution, electronic data interchange (EDI), quick response and efficient consumer response (ECR) which are all becoming increasingly important, reflecting the scope and power of the contractors and the drive to service and integration. The old inefficient, supplier-led practices have been swept away by the modern, technology rich, retailer-led and customer focused ways of ensuring product availability.

Perhaps most importantly, contractors are now attempting to engender a more co-operative and collaborative stance in many supply channels, recognizing that there are still gains to be made on standards and efficiency. In this context, McKinnon (1996) identifies six trends in logistics that can also be applied to the defense industry. These include:

- Increased control over secondary distribution
- Logistics system restructuring
- Quick response adoption
- Streamlined primary distribution

- Introduction of collaborative supply chain management
- Reverse logistics

This simplification of the channel structure has been accompanied by the complication of many of activities within the supply chain and the demands of, and pressure on, the various organizations has increased. The logistics transformation, relates Sparks, (1998) has not always been easy or constant, but the basic position has moved away from transactional to the associative with an emerging focus on integration. Responsiveness to customer demand and performance have become the key factors along with product availability. In this light, as the pressure for collaborative relationships continue to increase, the types of supply links and flows have had to change. The changes now focus on the following four areas:

- Technology
- Internationalisation
- Alliances
- Management

Sparks (1998) says that the integration within and between companies is now essential and increasingly the replacement of product flows by information flows enabled by investment is being enhanced by finance and risk flows. At the same time, contractors are increasingly operating on an international scale whether in terms of sourcing of products or operation of support organizations. In essence, the flows among the groupings are complicated by the inter-service dimensions and therefore require closer management. Lastly, the type and calibre of management required for the new methods of operating are very different to previous management requirements in terms of skills required and the roles to be played. At issue is, however, whether physical activities and information management needs to be carried out by the contractor or the supplier at all. Others can undertake many of the flow issues, although controlled by the key participants. All said, this transformation of defense logistics, specifically PBL, and the issues that surround the progression lend it to the efficiencies that 4PLs can offer. This alignment will be addressed later in this paper, but first a look at the baseline requirement for outsourcing logistics or supply chain functions and processes in the U.S. defense industry.

4. FOURTH-PARTY LOGISTICS (4PL) - A FEASIBLE SOLUTION

For a 4PL to respond effectively to the broad, complicated needs of today's organizations, the 4PL needs to deliver comprehensive supply chain solutions focused on all elements of supply chain management tailored to specific client needs. According to Accenture (1998), one of the world's leading 4PL management consultancies, a 4PL supply chain solution includes four phases of work:

- Reinvention
- Transformation
- Implementation
- Execution

These offerings are explained and discussed in more detail in the following paragraphs.

4.1 Supply Chain Solutions

4.1.1 Reinvention. At the highest level of the 4PL solution is *Reinvention*. The most likely source of enhancements is through synchronization of supply chain planning and execution activities across supply chain participants, or collaboration between independent supply chain participants. *Reinvention* leverages traditional supply chain management consulting skills, aligning business strategy with supply chain strategy, to creatively redesign and integrate the supply chains of the participants. Figure 4.1 shows a typical 4PL relationship graphically.

Figure 4.1 Typical 4PL Service Provider Relationship

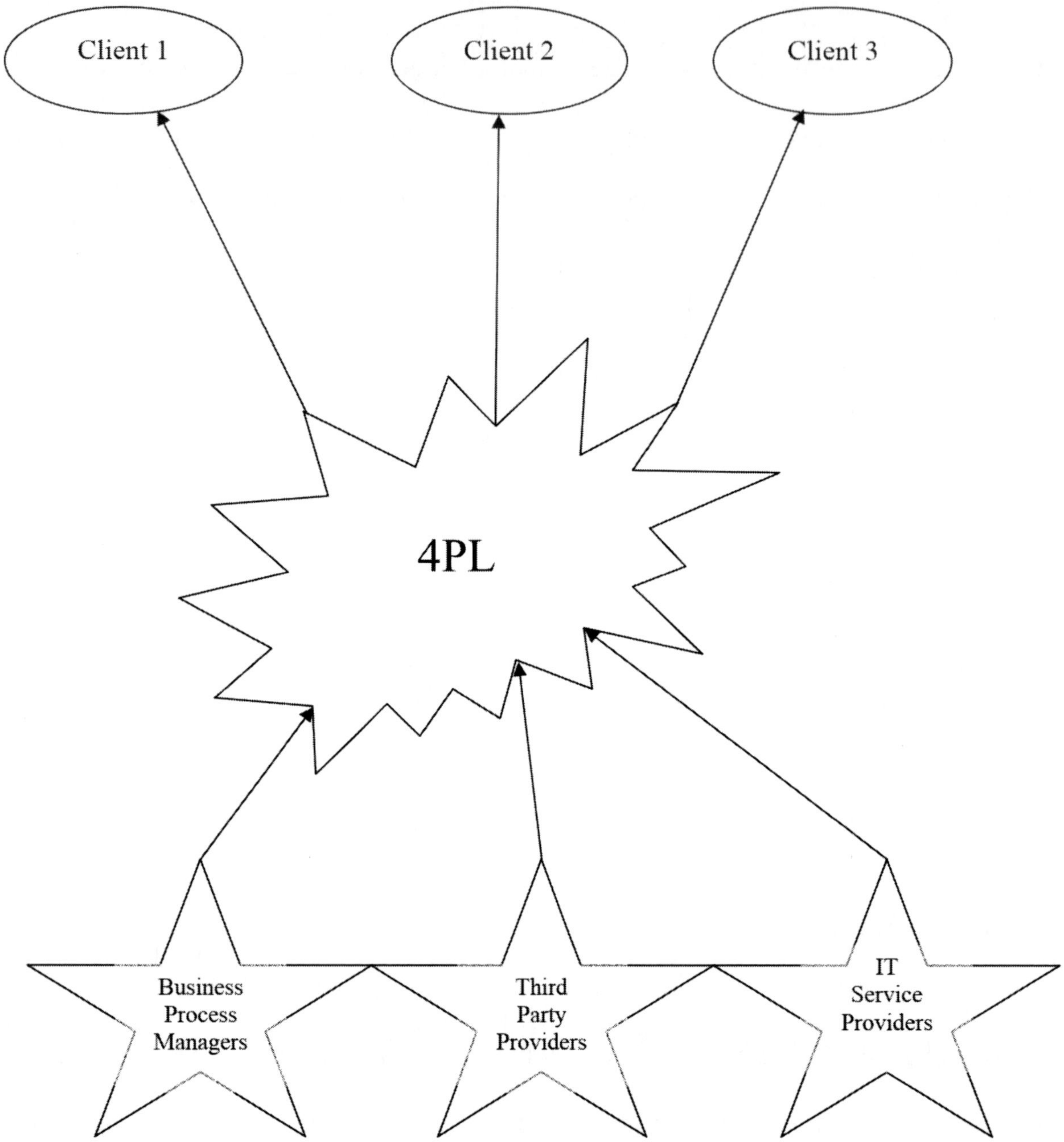

[Adopted from Bauknight, 1998]

4.1.2 Transformation. The next phase of the 4PL solution is *Transformation. Transformation* efforts focus on specific supply chain functions including sales and operations planning, distribution management, procurement strategy, customer support, and supply chain technology. *Transformation* leverages strategic thought, deep analysis, process redesign, organizational change management, and technology to integrate the supply chain activities and processes within the client.

4.1.3 Implementation. The third phase is *Implementation.* A 4PL implements recommendations including business process realignment, systems integration of technology across the client organizations and service providers, and transition of operations to the 4PL delivery team. Careful attention is paid to organizational change, recognizing that the "people" factor is a critical driver of success in the transition to the 4PL arrangement. The goal is to avoid the fall to common, ineffective implementation of well-designed strategies and business processes that have limited the effectiveness of consulting solutions and the delivery of projected results.

4.1.4 Execution. The fourth and final phase is *Execution.* A 4PL provider takes on operational responsibility for multiple supply chain functions and processes. The scope goes well beyond traditional transportation management and warehouse operations logistics outsourcing. An organization can outsource the entire range of its supply chain activities to a 4PL provider; however, a 4PL solution will likely be a subset of supply chain functions or processes drawn from the full "menu" of execution offerings.

4.2 Operating Models

While 4PL solutions will likely be customized to suit the needs of a particular client or situation, the following operating models conceptually portray how 4PL relationships are normally configured.

4.2.1 <u>Synergy Plus</u>. The **Synergy Plus** operating model relies on a working relationship between the 4PL organization and a third-party service provider. In this model, a 4PL and 3PL partner to market supply chain solutions that capitalize on the capabilities and market reach of both organizations. The 4PL could provide a broad range of services to the third-party logistics provider including: technology, supply chain strategy skills, capability to go to market, and program management expertise. The 4PL would work inside the 3PL organization, as depicted in Figure 4.2. The 4PL-3PL relationship may be contractually binding or structured in the form of a marketing alliance.

Figure 4.2 Synergy Plus Model

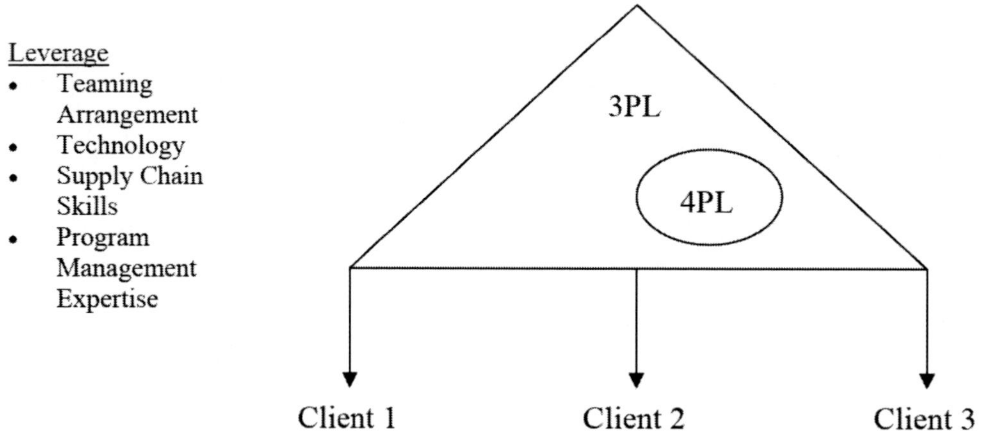

[Adopted from Bauknight, 1998]

4.2.2 Solution Integrator. The core 4PL model is known as **Solution Integrator**. In this operating model, the 4PL operates – and manages a comprehensive supply chain solution for a single client. The Solution Integrator arrangement will encompass the resources, capabilities, and technology of the 4PL with complementary service providers to provide a comprehensive integrated supply chain solution that delivers value throughout the client organization's supply chain components. The 4PL can integrate the capabilities of multiple service providers with the client organization. Figure 4.3 shows this model.

Figure 4.3 Solution Integrator Model

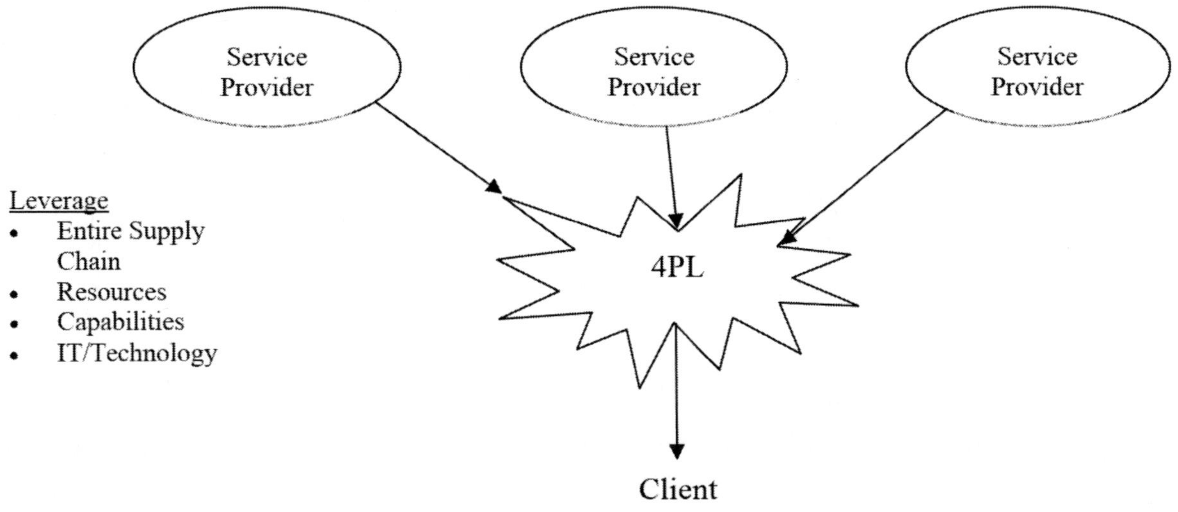

[Adopted from Bauknight, 1998]

4.2.3 Industry Innovator. The final and most complex operating model is termed **Industry Innovator**. Within this model, a 4PL organization develops and runs a supply chain solution for multiple industry players with a focus on synchronization and collaboration. The formation of industry solutions can provide the greatest benefits. However, it is complex and will challenge the most competent organizations. The 4PL will seek industry efficiencies through superior operational strategies, technology, and operational execution across the supply chain. This arrangement type will more than likely be an outgrowth of an initial Solution Integrator relationship. Figure 4.4 portrays this model.

Figure 4.4 Industry Integrator Model

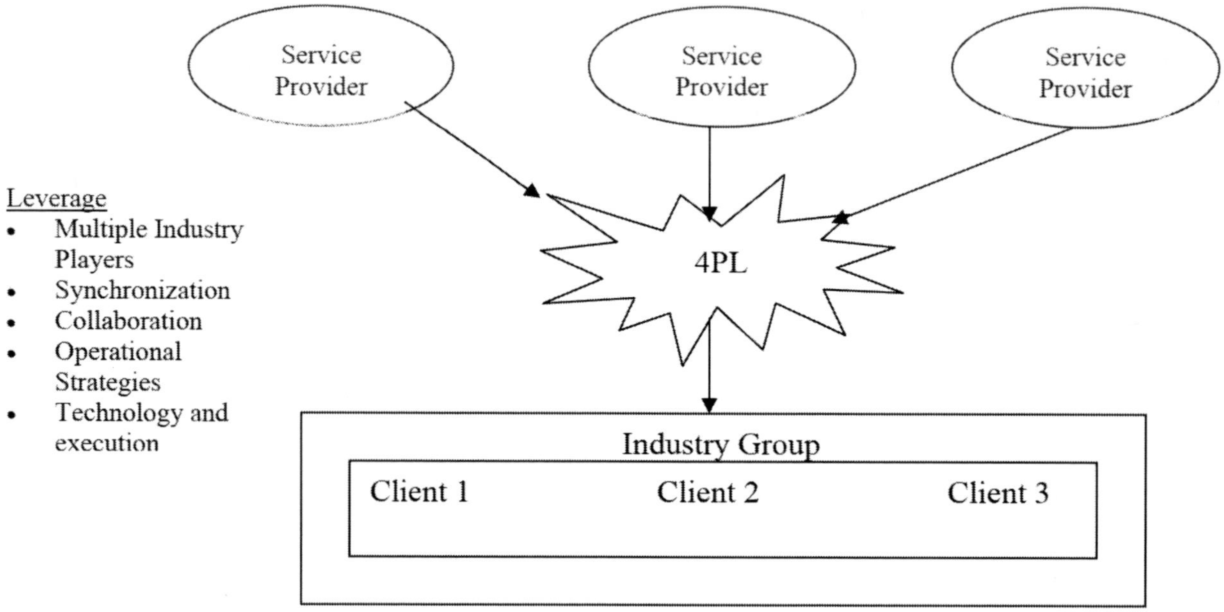

[Adopted from Bauknight, 1998]

4.3 Enterprise Value

To be successful, however, a 4PL leverages a full range of service providers (3PLs, IT providers, contract logistics providers, call centers, etc.) along with the capabilities of the client and its supply chain partners. The 4PL acts as a single point of interface with the client organization and provides the management of multiple service providers through a teaming partnership or an alliance. The 4PL solution can align the capabilities of the 4PL and the "best of breed" logistics service providers to deliver supply chain solutions.

The second key distinction between 4PL and current approaches to supply chain outsourcing is a unique ability to deliver value to client organizations over the entire supply chain. The 4PL approaches the concept of supply chain integration through four key drivers of shareholder value:

- Increased revenue
- Operating Cost Reduction
- Working Capital Reduction
- Fixed Capital Reduction.

An organization should note the key functional activities that the 4PL brings to an organization along with the ability to leverage both the 4PL strengths and those of the client. These are needed to consummate the strategic goals of any firm. Traditional approaches have tended to focus only on operating cost reduction and asset transfer. Figure 4.5 on the following page shows the 4PL enterprise value process graphically followed by discussion of each key driver.

Figure 4.5 Enterprise Value

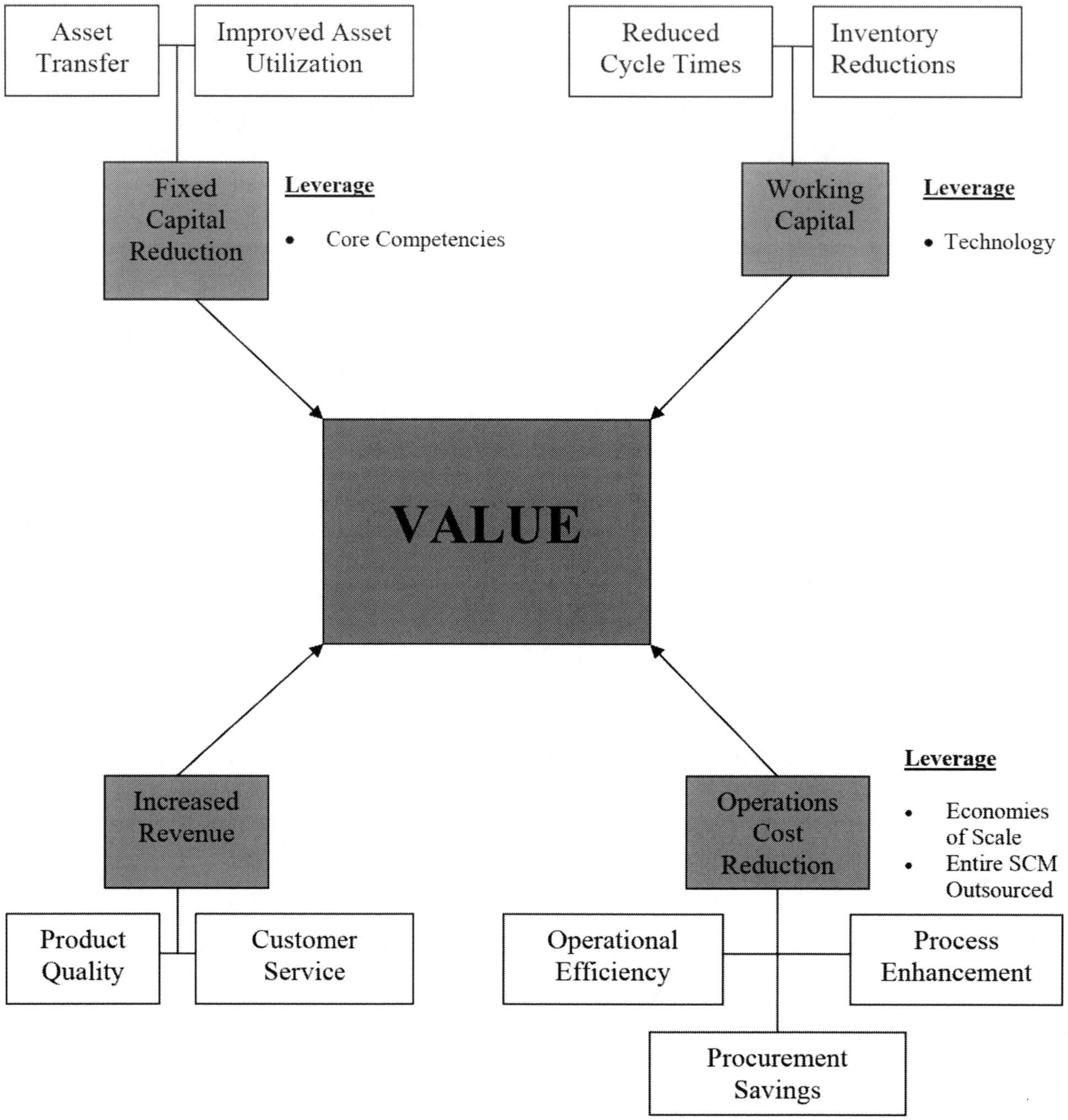

[Adopted from Bauknight, 1998]

4.3.1 Increased Revenue

Revenue growth can be driven by enhanced product quality, product availability, and improved customer service. Experience has shown that customer service measures, such as stock outs and ship complete, can be improved significantly. With the 4PL focusing on the entire supply chain - not just the efficiency associated with warehousing or lowest cost transportation - dramatic customer service improvements can be attained.

4.3.2 Operating Cost Reduction

Operating cost reductions of up to 15% can be driven through operational efficiencies, process enhancements, and procurement savings. Savings can be achieved through the complete outsourcing of the supply chain function – not just components – and economies of scale. Synchronization of supply chain activities across supply chain participants can lead to operating cost reductions and a lower cost of goods sold due to integration of processes, improved planning and execution of supply chain activities.

4.3.3 Working Capital

Working capital reductions up to 30% can be realized through inventory reductions and reduced "order to cash" cycle times. The proactive use of technology to manage order and unit movement throughout the pipeline can minimize the amount of inventory required, as well as increase item availability to reduce the cycle times.

4.3.4 Fixed Capital Reduction

Capital reductions can result from capital asset transfer and enhanced utilization. The 4PLs can take ownership of physical assets, thus freeing up assets. This allows the client organization to invest in its core competencies, i.e., research and design, product development, sales, marketing – not in bricks and mortar – impacting the balance sheet and broad level change.

4.4 Supply Chain Metrics

So, what key factors make a 4PL relationship feasible in an industry such as defense? Bauknight (2000) maintains that the following factors must be present.

4.4.1 Is the supply chain key to the success of the enterprise but not every supply chain process a core competency?

4.4.2 Does the organization struggle to manage increasing levels of supply chain complexity?

4.4.3 Do customers' supply chain demands exceed organization's ability to deliver?

4.4.4 Does the organization have IT/technology to integrate supply chain processes and 3PLs?

4.4.5 Can the enterprise make better use of capital now dedicated to supply chain assets?

Each of these feasibility factors will be looked at later vis-à-vis a SWOT analysis of the defense industry and form the key alignment factors to consider in looking at the defense logistics and supply chain.

4.5 Summary of Discussions

Before completing a critical analysis of secondary sources, however, a look at primary research is necessary. A series of questions were discussed with logistics professionals from the following organizations:

- Performance- Based Logistics Department, Defense Acquisition University.
- ILS Policy Division, Assistant Secretary of the Army (Acquisition, Logistics, and Technology).
- Logistics Plans and Program, Office of the Assistant Deputy Under Secretary of Defense (Logistics and Materiel Readiness).
- ILS Section, Concepts and Requirements Analysis Division, Future Operations, G-3, Army Materiel Command.

The questions commented upon were used to ascertain whether the professionals felt that the U.S. defense industry could, given the current environment, embrace a new supply chain management arrangement (4PL) to the effect of competitive advantage. The questions used – see Appendix D - made clear the future competitive environment envisioned with TLCSM and PBL.

What follows is a summary of their comments. The general consensus was that until the processes and enterprise integration challenge aspects of TLCSM and PBL were addressed and institutionalized, that TLCSM would move slowly. Although attempts to fund weapon systems PBL pilot tests have really never gotten off the ground, the PEO/PM and sustainment communities have reservations about what they are expected to do under PBL. Add to this the contractual, legal, and funding barriers to enabling PBL DoD wide and the advantages that a 4PL could bring to the table are diminished. Ultimately, until a 'culture change' takes place in the DoD and defense contractor industry, where collaboration and partnering becomes the norm, than warfighter, PEO/PM, and product support organizations will all rely on their own bottom line. Still, the need for the services and management expertise that 4PL offers both the PEO/PM and the warfighter can eventually be realized once a major weapon systems proves the premise that DoD gets product support more cheaply, more quickly, and with a smaller foot print. That is the DoD goal.

5. TLCSM AND PBL ALIGNMENT WITH 4PL

5.1 Industry Strengths, Weaknesses, Opportunities, and Threats (SWOT) Analysis

SWOT analysis of the U.S. defense industry as a whole in the U.S. is necessary to see whether a logical and subsequent alignment of the 4PL feasibility factors envisioned is present. The following SWOT analysis summarizes the key issues facing the industry (Clarke, 2000).

5.1.1 Strengths

- Mandated Logistics Management Information (LMI) use leverages the information technology capabilities of 4PLs.
- Automated Identification Technology (AIT) and Embedded Diagnostics/Prognostics allow contractor faster remote data collection and reporting while the temporary waiver of Contractor on the Battlefield policy allows forward contractors to repair/replace more quickly and cheaply.
- TLCSMs move toward Long Term Contracts and Performance-Based Agreements (PBAs) policy minimize risk assumed by the contractor and especially the PEO/PM community while maximizing profits.
- The Integrated Data Environment allows programs such as Joint Computer-Aided Acquisition and Logistics System (JCALS), Joint Engineering Data Management information Control System (JEDMICS), and Global Combat Support Systems – Army (GCSS-A) interact in real time and standardize information across the services

and subordinate units.

5.1.2 Weaknesses

- Current TLCSM Funding is lagging behind operational implementation/ application of TLCSM and PBL.
- Capturing needed data using the current cost accounting system is burdensome and not totally compatible with those required by TLCSM and PBL.
- PBL is a "must pay" contract that reduces commander's flexibility in changing priorities.
- Since many organizations depend on taxing of appropriated dollars and working capital funds to cover expenses (especially logistics headquarters), TLCSM and PBL surface several concerns for instability of operational funds.
- Cultural barriers to change make identifying performance specifications considering other than organic logistics systems make moving towards a drastically new management structure are challenging.
- Statutory limitations (e.g., Title 10, Uniformed Services Code) and A-76 study requirements tie the hands of the PEO/PM and contractor community as far as working options.

5.1.3 Opportunities (OADUS/LSM and ChainLink Research, 2002)

- The Future Logistics Enterprise (FLE) embodies the best practices and strategies from both industry and the DOD.

- The FLE's proposed policies and practices comprise extremely high payback initiatives with low risk. The concepts and practices at the heart of these initiatives have been successfully implemented previously in both DOD and industry.
- The scale of change, though massive, also has precedent in global industrial transformations. These industries have not only gone through major transformations in how the entire industry operates, but are exemplified by cross-enterprise cooperation between industry competitors and cross-enterprise integration between supply chain partners.
- The collaborative approaches advocated by the FLE programs can have major benefits to the US economy by creating new revenue opportunities for industry. The infrastructure, technology, and services required to support FLE, will take logistics capabilities to a new level that will enable expanded business opportunities for the private sector above and beyond their business with the DOD.
- Sharing information with the private sector through a TLCSM approach will net gains in research and development, reduced cost in procurement and maintenance, and improved service responsiveness.

5.1.4 Threats

- Inadequate attention to sustainment requirements during specification phase for weapon systems.
- Break in responsibility between acquisition and sustainment phases.
- Focus on functional optimization versus customer service.

- TLCSM and PBL objectives cannot be accomplished without cross-enterprise integration that cuts across silos within DoD and reached out to industry partners.
- Lack of collaborative agreements and confidentiality issues for the private sector.
- Significant change management issues within DoD personnel as process change and knowledge transfer occurs.
- The graying of the DoD workforce gives urgency to the need for cross-fertilization with private-sector trading partners.
- Supply chain management is getting more complex as sourcing, distribution, and transportation gets more complex.

5.2 Feasibility Factor Alignment

As described in the last chapter, alignment of feasibility factors between what the 4PL can provide a client and the current state of the U.S. defense industry within that context reveals the following key matches.

5.2.1 Supply Chain Success. The defense industry supply chain in the U.S. is unequivocally the champion success story of the entire industry as illustrated in most all texts and professional considerations, especially those considered for this project. However, not all supply chain processes are a core competency of the major defense contractors. This can be seen in the heavy outsourcing of their warehousing, transportation, and distribution functions.

Obviously, making sure product support is available to the customer (war-fighter), and in the right amount and at the right time depends predominantly on the supply chain. It is without a doubt the key to success of all defense organizations, but especially the major defense contractors. Any deficiency in the supply chain in delivering 'the right product, to the right location, at the right time, to the right consumer' is tantamount to losing a customer to the competition in marketing terms. The contractors cannot afford to get the supply chain wrong.

No matter how robust their internal ICT is, the multiples cannot be expected to consider every supply chain process a core competency.

5.2.2 Supply Chain Complexity. Again, virtually all logistics professionals within and outside the industry agree that defense supply chain streamlining has led to one of the most complex supply chains of any industry in the world. Management of this immense complexity begs a new and wider set of management skills only offered by a world-class set of management skills. (See Appendix C for a list of such skills).

The multiple's dependence on composite relationships with IT providers, business process managers, warehousing, transportation, distribution, inventory management, and customer support organisations inherently increases the level of supply chain complexity. Current logistics systems within the U.S. defense industry are so sophisticated that delays of more than a few hours on a delivery produces an exception report. This sophistication, says Seth and Randall (1999), has two implications – investment and robustness. But SWOT analysis has shown that the defense industry has already invested heavily, hundreds of millions of dollars as a matter of fact, in the control of their supply chain and even more on the assets within the supply chain.

5.2.3 Customer's Supply Chain Demands. In light of the recent conflicts and timely re-supply challenges that continue to plaque the defense industry, it becomes evident that sometimes, and probably increasingly, the warfighter's demand will exceed the core organization's ability to deliver. Although, current practice for the defense contractors is to blame the suppliers and wholesalers for inadequate supply, it is the primary support integrator that interfaces with the customer and the party that must answer to problems within the supply chain independently.

Although manufacturers and suppliers have been content to obtain sales volume wherever they can get it and done so at the power of the major defense contractors, relationships within the supply chain are being pursued with growing unease in the public eye. However, even for organizations with strong logistics teams that participate in supply negotiations with the multiples, the pressure for business remains irresistible. Sooner or later, as noted for many 3PL 'fixed-cost' distributors, breakdowns in the supply chain will lead to customer's physical, service, and performance demands not being met.

5.2.4 Supply Chain Integration using Information Technology and 3PLs. This is an area that U.S. defense companies outright lead the world overall in – namely in applying IT innovation to their supply chain and logistics. The defense industry's integration of their supply chain utilizing IT is probably only surpassed by the automotive industry. Additionally, its heavy reliance on

3PLs to run their centralized warehouses and distribution is growing exponentially. Outsourcing only entreats a continued and increased presence within the industry.

5.2.5 Supply Chain Assets and Capital. As mentioned several times in this paper, the major defense contractors and PEOs/PMs do not want to have to invest heavily in capital assets and especially supply chain assets. The contractors realize that they earn larger profit margins by investing in retail activities rather than storage or distribution space. This situation alludes to the fact that the contractors want to better utilize and minimize their capital expenditures on supply chain assets. .

Also, high investment in IT systems to run such a diversity of stores, items, suppliers, and supply chain variables has added to the amount of capital U.S. contractors have invested – now hundreds of millions of dollars. All said, the higher capital investments made in the U.S. need servicing by higher profit margins.

Discussion on the factors above could continue on ad infinitum with minor agreements and disagreements. The bottom line is that SWOT analysis and the alignment/connectivity analysis of feasibility factors against the current operating environments present within the U.S. defense industry reveals a potential for further exploration and consideration.

6. CONCLUSION/RECOMMENDATION

As shown time and again above, the multiples in their current environment, match up factor for factor with the metrics necessary for considering the feasibility of a 4PL management relationship. The key alignment matches addressed above and in several earlier discussions and analyses show that it is feasible that a 4PL relationship using one or more of the mentioned models could aid the defense industry players in further streamlining their supply chain functions even further. Most of the earlier discussion on outsourcing and 3PLs centred on the myriad advantages that such supply chain processes could provide the industry and the organizations embracing of this fact, conceptually and physically. A 4PL arrangement is simply the next step forward to managing the supply chain efficiently and effectively with an eye on enterprise value, competitive advantage, and core competencies.

In support of this consideration, the Delphi survey (McKinnon and Foster (2000) of 129 logistics specialists throughout the European Commission (EC) forecast that by 2005 the "majority of large companies will deal with one lead logistics service provider". The report also stresses that the following factors will exert a reasonably strong influence on the outsourcing decision:

- Need for greater operational flexibility
- Geographical expansion
- Pressure to cut operating costs
- Desire to improve service quality
- Access to wider IT experience

- Access to greater logistics expertise
- More innovative logistics solutions
- Avoiding the need for capital investment

On the other hand, the report (2000) also suggests that many logistics trends will continue through 2005, namely that large contractors will further extend their control over the supply chain and companies will outsource an increasing share of logistics expenditure. A key forecasted issue is that of outsourcing of higher value-adding logistics services, particularly information management and product customisation.

Obviously, the most relevant projection for the purpose of this project is that most logistics professionals agree strongly that a majority of large companies and government organization will want to deal with a 'single' or 'lead' or 'primary 'service provider in the future. Coupled with the earlier alignment analysis of 4PL factors with a SWOT analysis of the defense industry, this suggests that opportunities do exist conceptually and functionally for such service provider relationships.

Most logistic and acquisition professional do not see an abrupt acceptance or adaptation of new supply chain management relationships, perhaps only in a more collaborative approach within the supply chain. While this may appear unfortunate, it is understandable until 4PLs repeatedly prove themselves in more relevant industries and more importantly, within the U.S. The ultimate recommendation of this project, especially in light of current defense industry TLCSM and PBL issues, is that the major defense contractors in the UK consider strongly how they can progress their strategic supply chain management within the industry. This consideration of new management relationships will necessarily include looking at enterprise value as discussed in this paper and gives them a chance at improved competitive advantage and ultimately bigger market share and higher profit.

In closing, it is necessary to reiterate the fact that without future consolidation, internationalisation, and/or collaboration within the U.S. defense industry and its supply chain, there exists a limit to growth and progress. These issues are left for someone else's investigation or to a future paper/project.

Appendix A

Project Methodology and Flowchart

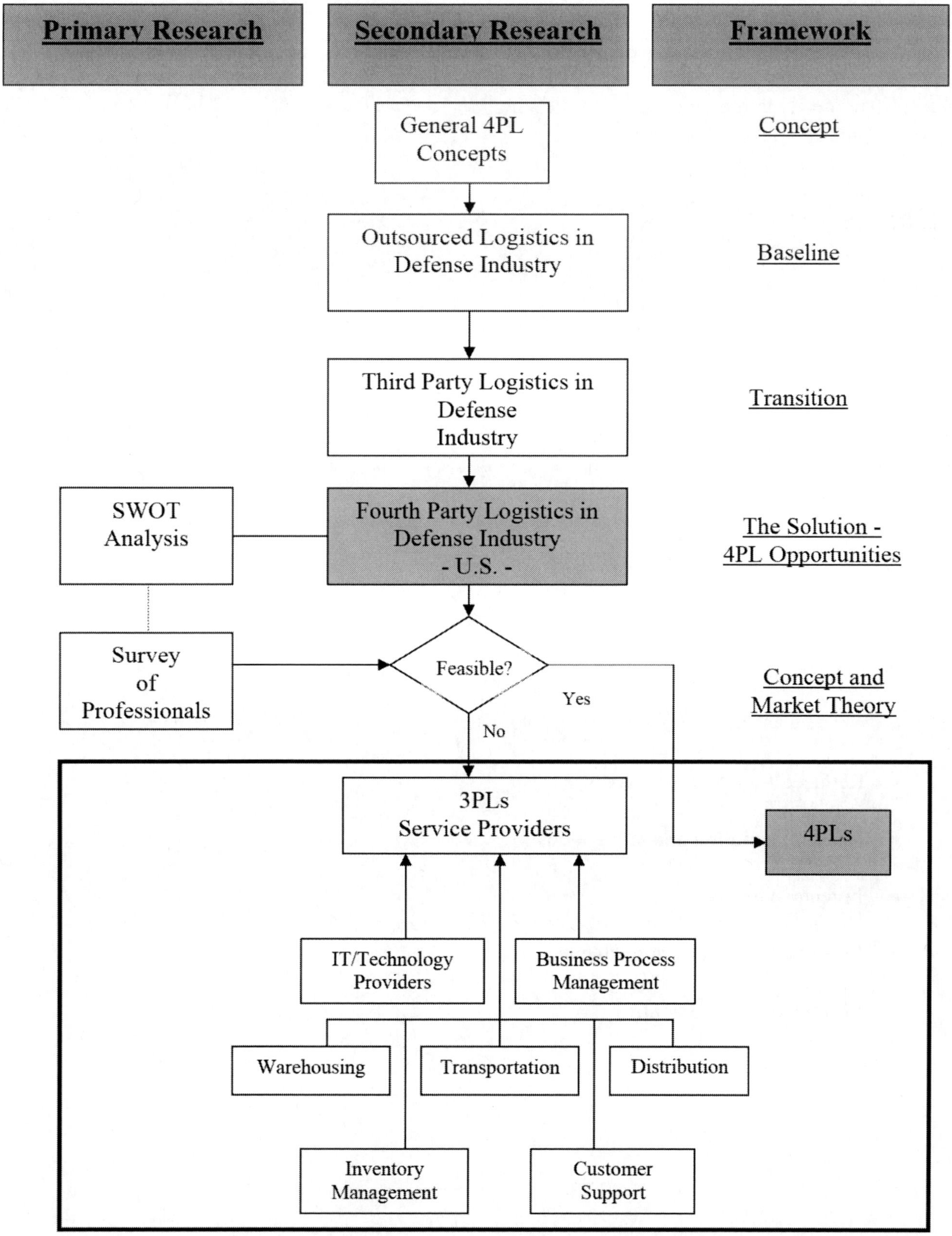

Appendix B

The Outsourcing Decision

Christopher (1998) recently stated that a typical self-evaluation checklist concerning the outsourcing issue/decision may include the following:

Shipper's needs

- Acquisitions/divestitures within last 5 years,
- Expanding/contracting markets and products,
- Capital/headcount constraints,
- Customer/completive requirements, and
- Logistics management information systems enhancements;

Expected benefits from outsourcing

- Reduced transportation costs,
- Material handling and storage costs,
- Inventory levels,
- Improved channel responsiveness, and
- Improved channel control;

Supplier credibility

- Scope of services offered,
- Contract logistics experience and capability,
- Industry experience,
- Proven ability,
- Supplier financial strength, and
- Completive pricing;

Outsourcing experiencing

- Contract trucking,
- Contract warehousing,
- Integrated logistics,
- Channel management outsourcing,
- Performance based contracting

Management commitment

- Credible sponsor,
- Corporate culture for innovation and change,
- Reward/motivation systems, and
- Ability to benchmark current costs

Appendix C

The 4PL Skill Set

The 4PL provider needs to possess a comprehensive set of skills to effectively deliver a 4PL solution. The depth of skills and knowledge will be critical to the success of the arrangement. A 4PL should possess the following criteria:

- Delivery of world-class supply chain strategy formulation, business process redesign, technology integration and people management capabilities

- Leader in integrating supply chain technologies and outsourcing capabilities

- Experience in Business Process Management and Outsourcing Availability of a large body of trained supply chain professionals

- Global capabilities, reach and resources

- Ability to manage multiple service providers

- Strong relationship and teaming skills

- Understanding of organizational change issues

(Bauknight, 1998)

Appendix D

Discussion Questions

1. The copywriter of the term 'Fourth-Party Logistics'' Accenture (formerly known as Andersen Consulting), has formed 4PL relationships with several large firms especially overseas. Accenture spoke at the recent European Defence Logistics 2003 Conference noting that there is no doubt a change taking place in a way that defense logistics operations are run and that collaborating with best-practice partners is a win-win solution.

Question #1: Do you see any other functional outsourced areas within the U.S. defense industry (e.g., business process management, warehousing, transportation, distribution, inventory management, and/or customer support) lending themselves to 4PL relationships in the foreseeable future and why/why not?

2. The defense industry in the U.S. is very complex and concentrated and the leading defense contractors have invested large amounts of capital trying to cut costs, maintain market share, or expand where possible. In theory, 4PLs capitalise on and leverage their management skills, expertise, capabilities, resources, and possible cross-industry collaboration in order to help maximise the value of their client's business through fixed capital reduction, freeing up of working capital, increased revenue, and operating costs reduction. This ultimately allows their client to focus on their core competencies.

Question# 2: Given this environment, do you see an increased opportunity for 4PLs and the DoD to form new relationships within the U.s. defense industry? If so, how?

3. Question #3: Lastly, what is your general outlook for the U.S. Defense Industry as far as supply chain management and performance-based logistics arrangements, particularly outsourcing of logistics functions (3PLs and 4PLs)?

REFERENCES

Bauknight, D. (1998). "Fourth Party Logistics – Breakthrough Performance in Supply Chain Outsourcing", *Supply Chain Management Review,* Global Supplement, Accenture.

Christopher, M. (1992). *Logistics – The Strategic Issues*. London: Chapman & Hall.

Christopher, M. (1998). *Logistics and Supply Chain Management: Strategies for Reducing Costs and Improving Service*. London: The Financial Times.

Cooper, J. (1994). *Logistics and Distribution Planning – Strategies for Management.* London: Kogan Page.

Coyle, J., Bardi, E., and Langley, C. (1992). *The Management of Business Logistics*. New York: West Publishing Company.

Cummings, L. (1992). *Logistics Goes Global: The Role of Service Providers and Users.* Cranfield: Cranfield University Press.

Fawcett, P., McLeish, R., and Ogden, I. (1992). *Logistics Management.* Essex: Prentice Hall.

Fernie, J. and Sparks, L. (1998). *Logistics and Retail Management: Insights into Current Practices and Trends from Leading Experts*. London: Kogan Page.

Gattorna, J. and Walters, D. (1996). *Managing the Supply Chain – A Strategic Perspective.* London: MacMillan Press, LTD.

Gattorna, J. (1998). *Strategic Supply Chain Alignment: Best Practice in Supply Chain Management*. London: Macmillan Press, LTD.

Gourdin, K. (2000). *Global Logistics Management: A Competitive Advantage for the New Millennium.* Oxford: Blackwell.

Hoffman, K. (2000). "Just What Is a 4PL Anyway?", *Global Logistics & Supply Chain Strategies*, Volume 4, Number 7, August, pp. 48-54.

Kakabudse, N. and Kakabudse, A (2000). "Outsourcing: a paradigm shift", *Journal of Management Development,* MCB University Press, Volume 19, pp. 670-728.

Kopczak, L., (1999). *"Trends in Third-party Logistics",* White Paper, Stanford Global Supply Chain Management Forum/Montgomery Research, pp 1-6.

Leib, R. and Randall, H. (1996). "A Comparison of the Use of Third-party Logistics Services by Large American Manufacturers, 1991, 1994, 1995", *Journal of Business Logistics,* Volume 17, Number 1, p. 310.

McIvor, R. (2000). "A practical framework for understanding the outsourcing process", *Supply Chain Management: An International Journal*, Volume 5, Number 1, pp. 122-136.

Office of the Assistant Deputy Under Secretary of Defense for Logistics Systems Management and ChainLink Research (2002). *The Future Logistics Enterprise – Roadmap to Transformation*. Cambridge, MA: OADUS/LSM.

Robeson, J., Copacino, W., and Howe, R. (1994). *The Logistics Handbook*. New York: Maxwell Macmillan International.

Slater, A. (2000). "Should Third-party Logistics Service Providers Compete or Cooperate?", *Logistics and Transport Focus, Journal of Institute of Logistics and Transport*, Volume 2, Number 9, November.

Smith, D. (1998). "Logistics in Tesco." In: *Logistics and Retail Management: Insights into Current Practices and Trends from Leading Experts*, ed. Fernie, J. and Sparks, L. (1998). London: Kogan Page.

Sparks, L. (1998). "The Retail Logistics Transformation." In: *Logistics and Retail Management: Insights into Current Practices and Trends from Leading Experts*, ed. Fernie, J. and Sparks, L. (1998). London: Kogan Page.

BIOGRAPHY

Mr. Connor has over 22 years of logistics experience in both the military and military contracting arena. Mike spent 12 years on active duty as an Armor Army Officer. This took him to The Federal Republic of Germany from 1982-1989 and Fort Devens, MA from 1989-1992.

After leaving active duty, Mr. Connor moved to Washington, DC. There he began work as a logistics analyst with Logicon. This included travel to Germany, the Republic of South Korea along with several locations in the U.S. At Logicon, Mike provided systems engineering and technical assistance to the All Source Analysis System (ASAS) Program Office.

In 1996, Mike accepted a position with MPRI and left for Bosnia-Herzegovina (BiH) under the auspices of the "Train and Equip" mission. He spent three years in BiH where he oversaw the arrival, transshipment, and storage of materiel donated to BiH. He also assisted in the subsequent distribution of same equipment to units of the BiH military. Lastly, he spearheaded a comprehensive inspection of all logistics organizations in the BiH military.

Currently, Mr. Connor works at the Headquarters, Army Materiel Command as a Senior Logistics Analyst specializing in Performance-Based Logistics, Total Life Cycle Systems Management, and Future Operations.

Performance Based Logistics
What It Takes

by
Charles O. Coogan, C.P.L., Fellow

Abstract

Performance Based Logistics (PBL) has been established by the Office of the Secretary of Defense as the new way to acquire and operate support for systems. It is expected to improve operational capability while reducing cost and deployment footprint. To meet its full potential, the PBL approach requires significant adjustments to the way we think about systems, and the roles of both the government and industry. This paper examines the new orientation, and the skills and tools necessary to implement it successfully. The paper draws on the experience of the author in establishing PBL programs in the US and overseas, and the unique approaches used. It describes the challenges encountered in defining the performance criteria, designing the system and its related support, and implementing the performance agreements. This paper relates to the symposium theme by demonstrating how the challenges of government/industry partnership can be satisfied in a cost-effective manner. The paper will be of interest to logisticians, engineers, and program managers.

Performance Based Logistics (PBL), the current Department of Defense approach to improving warfighter capability, reducing deployment footprint, and reducing cost of ownership, offers new opportunities and challenges. Opportunities for the government include more direct access to commercial practices for providing logistic support, additional incentives for industry performance, potential reductions in cost, and potential increases in system effectiveness. For industry, opportunities include potential to increase business scope and duration on a given program, potential for entering new business areas, and greater freedom to apply innovative approaches to product development and support. With these opportunities there are new risks and new capabilities required by both government and industry. This paper will explore some of these opportunities and risks with a view toward explaining what it takes to be successful in this new environment.

Before addressing what it takes to be successful let's establish a common understanding of what PBL is and what it means to both the DoD and industry. This is considered necessary because the author frequently finds misconceptions of PBL in both industry and the government. These misconceptions lead to miss application and, frequently, lost opportunities.

PBL, as used in this paper, is based on the DoD Interim Guidance provided February 12, 2003. That guidance provides the following definition of PBL:

A strategy for weapon system product support that employs the purchase of support as an integrated, affordable performance package designed to optimize system readiness. It meets performance goals for a weapon system through a support structure based on long-term performance agreements with clear lines of authority and responsibility

Jerry Beck, AIAA RMS and Logistics Workshop 30 May 2002, Merging Logistics & Acquisition at the OSD Level

Key words in this definition are:

- Long-term arrangements
- Partnerships between government and industry

The intent of PBL is to form a long-term partnership between industry and the government early in the development of a system or product that is focused on enhancing warfighter capability over the life of the system or product. The belief is that if industries' long-term profitability is in play, then industry will use its special talents to optimize profit while meeting the government's performance objectives. This will be done by improving Reliability and Maintainability in design, and designing and operating highly efficient support systems.

The concept of PBL calls for establishment of a Performance Based Agreement (PBA) between the warfighter and the Program Manager for the system early in the system's life cycle. The PBA establishes the performance objectives and the resources necessary to achieve that performance over a significant portion of the system life. A Performance System Integrator (PSI) is selected by the Program Manager and assigned responsibility for integrating the efforts of industry and government support providers responsible for meeting the performance objectives. Memorandum of Agreements are established with government providers and contracts are established with industry providers with clear definition of performance requirements and the means of measuring performance. A key part of the process is the understanding that high performance will be rewarded and poor performance will be penalized.

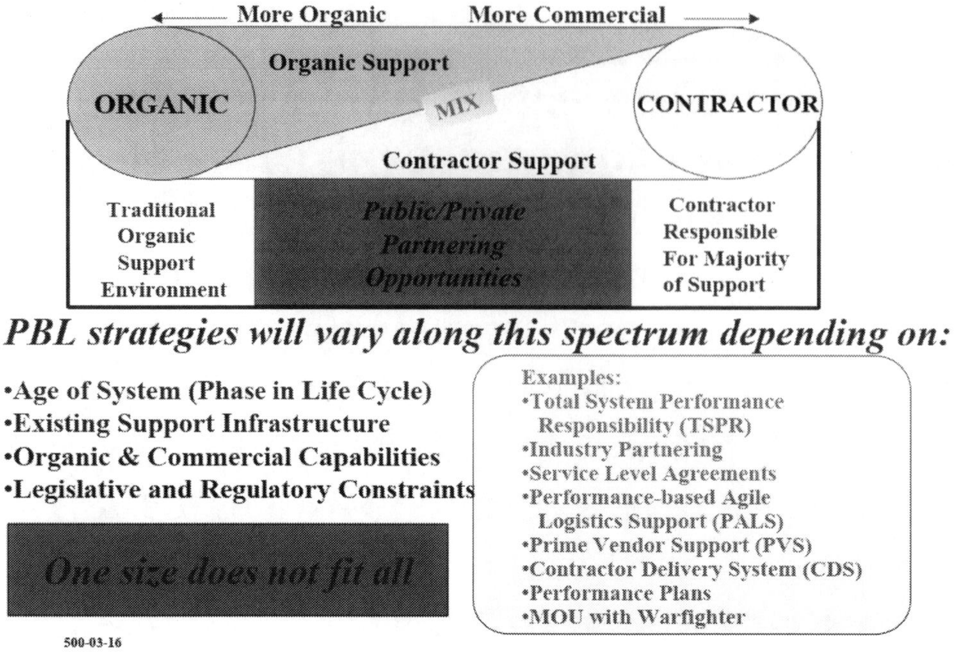

Jerry Beck, AIAA RMS and Logistics Workshop 30 May 2002,
Merging Logistics & Acquisition at the OSD Level

Figure 1. Spectrum of PBL Strategies

Figure 1 shows the range of potential distribution of support providers under PBL. Determination of what the mix should be for any given product or service is based on several factors. One is public law. There are a series of public laws that were designed to control assignment of workloads related to military systems to commercial entities. These must be complied with. Another important factor is the Business Case Analysis (BCA). The BCA is used to compare alternative sources for support on a best value basis. The BCA serves as a formal record of the evaluation of alternatives and as the basis of recommended solutions.

Because of recent emphasis on Contractor Logistic Support (CLS), many people in both government and industry incorrectly believe that PBL is simply another name for CLS or contracting out maintenance and supply functions. This leads to questions like "Do we really want to apply PBL to this program?" PBL should be applied to all programs. The correct question is "How can we get the best overall system performance at the lowest cost?"

Enough about what PBL is, what does it take to be successful? The answer depends in part on where the program is in its life cycle. Let's start with an operational system that is at or near the end of production. The system and its support have been fielded and we are past most of the initial fielding challenges. We have a fairly solid experience base. We know what the current system performance is and what it is costing to operate. Can we apply PBL to this program? Of course we can. Should we? Of course we should. Can we get as much benefit as if we applied PBL in the earlier phases? Probably not.

So, what do we need to apply PBL? First we need a factual assessment of current performance in measurable terms. We need a definition of overall performance in terms such as Operational Availability or some other expression of readiness and a measure of Operations and Support (O&S) cost. We need to be able to decompose those overall performance metrics to lower level metrics such as reliability and supply delay or wait times. Next, we need a correspondingly clear definition of the performance required by the warfighter or system/product user. Ideally this definition would be in the same terms as the definition of current performance. This definition of performance along with any constraints such as funding availability is included in a PBA. The skills and tools needed to do these first steps are very similar to the skills needed to properly define requirements for new systems. These skills are currently in short supply in both government and industry.

After establishing the PBA, we need some innovative business types and logistic analysts to define ways of moving performance from where it is to where it is required to be by the warfighter or user. The business types must be capable of evaluating a wide range of business options. They must be capable of defining a wide range of innovative support options and determining the cost and risk associated with each option. The logistics engineers must be capable of evaluating the support performance of each option. Options will involve providing all elements of support such as maintenance supply support, training, in-service engineering, and technical documentation management.

Once the preferred solution is selected and implemented, the PSI must be capable of measuring performance of the full range of support and making adjustments as necessary to achieve performance goals.

In government support activities, failure to meet performance criteria can result in embarrassing letters and criticism from senior managers. In the commercial sector, failure to meet performance objectives can mean loss of award fee, lost contracts and, in extreme cases, business failure. Achieving or exceeding performance criteria can mean millions or even billions of additional income. In short, you can not afford to fail so you need a good business plan, effective support management, and innovative and aggressive logistic engineering.

Now let's move earlier in the acquisition process to the beginning of production. Assume that we have designed the system and its support, but have not yet produced either. Under this condition there is limited opportunity to improve the deliverable product. An exception would be minor changes that produce significant performance or cost improvements. There usually is greater opportunity to improve support performance by improving the support arrangement. All of the capabilities described in the operational phase above are needed. In addition, you will need the ability to predict system and support performance before the system is fielded. Unlike the support analysis of yesteryear where the objective was mountains of documentation, the successful logistic engineer of tomorrow will be a keen business manager who understands logistics. The future contractor will be asked to commit to a long-term fixed price contract to produce and support his or her products.

It is the earlier phases of product development that offer the greatest potential for achieving the improvements desired. It is in the early phases that requirements are formulated, specifications are developed, and designs are initiated. During this period, government and contractors have the greatest opportunity for innovation and initiative. This early period also offers the greatest challenge in the need for adequately skilled logistic engineers, systems engineers, and designers. It takes more than logisticians with experience supporting operational systems or design engineers accustomed to designing to a defined requirement or specification. The need is for design engineers and logistic engineers who are capable of developing effective requirements and specifications. This requires expanded education in systems analysis, economics, and systems engineering. It requires specialized training in the new skill areas and organizational arrangements that are conducive to and reward innovation.

So how do we acquire or develop the required skills and tools? It is not by attending a two or three day seminar or reading a few published papers. The process starts at the top. Senior leadership must recognize the real need and make a long-term commitment to developing the required capability. Existing staff members must be screened for inherent capabilities. Selected candidates must be provided concentrated training, guidance, and experience. This usually requires a concerted effort over a 6 to 8 month period. In addition to specialized training, a commitment to acquiring the tools of the trade and making the required organizational adjustments if needed. It usually involves developing an effective Systems Engineering activity and including a Logistic Engineering capability within Systems Engineering.

To meet the requirement over the longer term, there is a need for engineering schools to establish and operate logistic engineering programs leading to an engineering degree in logistic engineering.

The challenges of PBL are significant, but so are the potential benefits. For those who understand and take action to meet the challenges, the rewards are significantly improved combat capability for the warfighter, increased profitability for industry, and reduced cost for the taxpayers. For those who attempt business as usual, the prospects are not nearly so bright. Let's work together to reap the benefits of PBL.

CHARLES O. COOGAN

Mr. Charles Coogan is director and founder of Acquisition Logistics Engineering, a specialty engineering firm emphasizing the integration of specialty engineering at the front end of the development process. Mr. Coogan's extensive background in DoD, NASA, and commercial systems analysis provides the basis for development and application of innovative approaches for dealing with needs of future systems. He is directly responsible for developing practical methods for implementing specialty engineering for both large and small systems and has taught these methods to government and industry analysts.

Mr. Coogan has a wide range of experience in the fields of Systems Engineering, Design, and Logistics. He has a bachelor's and master's degree in mechanical engineering from Oklahoma State University, is a graduate of the Defense Systems Management College, and is a Certified Professional Logistician. He is a Fellow of The International Society of Logistics (SOLE).

His military experiences include pilot, advanced systems development engineer, aircraft modification engineer, system manager, and deputy program manager for logistics, Director of Acquisition Plans and Analysis for the Air Force Acquisition Logistics Division, and participant in the early studies for the formation of the Space Command.

His civilian assignments include Director of Logistics Research for Battelle Columbus Laboratories, and President of Acquisition Logistics Engineering. He has spent the last seventeen years specializing in developing and applying methods to influence the design of systems to reduce operating and support burdens. He is the author of the draft U.S. Army Handbook, "Guide to LSA During Concept Exploration."

He served as Chairman of The International Society of Logistics (SOLE) Ad Hoc Committee on Re-Engineering Supportability, an international effort to streamline application of Supportability in the Government and commercial sectors. That Committee developed methods for accomplishing and metrics for measuring, Performance Based Supportability. He has successfully used Performance Based Supportability methods on several programs and is developing documentation of the Performance Based Supportability process. Mr. Coogan developed the Front End Analysis process and has applied it to more programs to gain insights to major cost drivers. He has also lead the Total Ownership Cost (TOC) analysis efforts for several major programs resulting in over $250 Billion in cost reductions.

Mr. Coogan's systems engineering approach to acquisition logistics has been successfully applied to systems of all sizes and degrees of complexity with consistently good results. His practical methods form the foundation of ALE's success.

Commercial Off the Shelf (COTS) Fixed Wing Aircraft and Life Cycle Contractor Support (LCCS)

The U.S. Army Fixed Wing Program Management Office (FWPMO) is the primary manager for the majority of the Army's fixed wing aircraft fleet and presently manages a total of 258 aircraft of nine types[i] on six separate Life Cycle Contractor Support (LCCS) contracts[ii]. The FWPMO is aligned under the Program Executive Office (PEO) for Aviation, Aviation Systems Program Manager (PM).

The LCCS contracts that the FWPMO manages fall under the Army Materiel Command's (AMC) Aviation and Missile Command's (AMCOM) Acquisition Center. The FWPMO's charter is the management of the Army's fixed wing fleet for its total life cycle; from basic need documents through acquisition strategies and programs to production and procurement, maintenance and sustainment, modifications, retirement and disposal. The majority of the aircraft in the fixed wing fleet are commercial in nature and have counterparts serving the commercial private and public sectors. The rationale for procuring commercially available aircraft was to take advantage of the cost savings inherent in acquiring already developed and fielded systems. The commercial infrastructure provides a logistics / engineering system without the need for the military services to duplicate the same support structures. Type certification is maintained by the LCCS contractors, using the Federal Aviation Administration regulatory requirements. Even the Special Electronic Mission Aircraft (SEMA) have their origins in converted commercial aircraft or in designs based on commercial aircraft.

As a result of the U.S. Army's entry into commercial aircraft acquisition, the U.S. Air Force used the Army C-12/U-21 acquisition as a template for their initial commercial aircraft acquisition entry during the procurement phase of the KC-10 Aircraft. From that experience base, the Air Force went on to acquire numerous commercial derivative systems, to include the C-12 J (Beech 1900)[iii]. This commercial background has led the Army to pursue the LCCS concept for the life cycle care of its various fleet aircraft. The LCCS concept used by the Army is another form of performance based logistics, or PBL.

Army Fixed Wing Aviation Structure and Contracts

PEO (Program Executive Office) – Aviation
Program Manager Aviation Systems

Fixed Wing Product Manager

C-23	C-12/RC-12/UC-35	C-12/RC-12/UC-35	C-12/RC-12/UC-35
Duncan Aviation	DynCorp International	DynCorp International	DynCorp International

C-20	C-26	C-37	RC-7
Sabreliner	Fairchild	Gulfstream	Avtel

The Fixed Wing Product Manager's Office manages fixed wing aircraft in support of the Active Army, Army Reserve and Army National Guard. Its mission is to develop, procure, sustain, modify and dispose of fixed-wing aircraft to include delivering new aircraft, maintaining fielded aircraft on an LCCS basis, modifying fielded aircraft, and retiring older aircraft. The Army's operational missions include executive transportation; special electronic mission aircraft; theater aviation companies (TACs); operational support airlift (OSA); research, development, test and evaluation; the training base; regional flight centers and state flight detachments. The Army OSA program provides cost avoidance of approximately $45-million each year for TDY and commercial air travel expenses. As a resource multiplier, Army OSA aircraft, both in CONUS[iv] and OCONUS[v], preserve costly rotary wing flying hours, save TDY funds and optimize time for our combat leaders, managers and soldiers. The NON-OSA mission includes the RC-12 and DHC-7 aircraft, which provides various electronic intelligence gathering and special operations systems.

Aircraft dedicated to the OSA mission are operated by three military organizations. They are the Active Army (United States Army Europe - USAREUR, Eighth United States Army - EUSA, United States Army Japan - USARJ), the Army National Guard (Operational Support Airlift Agency, OSAA via State Flight Detachments and Regional Flight Centers) and the Army Reserve (United States Army Reserve Command, USARC). OSA mission aircraft utilized under this LCCS contract are the C-12 and the UC-35. SEMA missions are all under the Active Army commands with assigned units under the Intelligence and Security Command (INSCOM), Forces

Command (FORSCOM) and USAREUR with locations at various CONUS and OCONUS sites. SEMA aircraft under these contracts are the RC-12 variants of the Raytheon Beech A200CT aircraft. Other fixed wing aircraft missions include the training base (flight training and transitions, military test pilot training), test and evaluation aircraft (research, test support, navigational aid monitoring) and special mission support aircraft. For example, the Army CECOM (Communications Electronics Command) Flight Activity at Fort Monmouth, NJ is using a modified RC-12D aircraft for its Foliage Penetration (FOPEN) project. In addition to OSA missions, fixed wing aircraft have been and are regularly employed in support of contingency operations and deployments in areas that include the Central Command area of operations, Bosnia and the Balkans, Africa, East Timor, Honduras and Colombia. If the Army has a unit or units deployed to any worldwide location you can safely assume there are fixed wing aircraft in the support structure.

The Army's fixed wing aircraft have not always been under the care of LCCS contractors. Early aircraft were primarily maintained by soldier mechanics and supported by the Army's logistical system in conjunction with their Original Equipment Manufacturers (OEM) support systems. The LCCS contracts reviewed in this article are responsible for C-12 (Raytheon Beech King Air Twin Turbo Prop), RC-12 (Raytheon Beech King Air SEMA variants), C-23C (Shorts SD3 and SD-360) and UC-35 (Cessna Citation V Ultra Fan Jet) aircraft. The C-12 was the Army's first aircraft maintained under an LCCS contract. It began its service in August 1975 following the 1973 acquisition selection and purchase of the C-12 from Beech Aircraft (now Raytheon Aircraft). Beech Aerospace Support Inc (BASI), a subsidiary of Beech Aircraft, was the first LCCS contractor used by the Army. The Army's U-21 aircraft (Beech Queen Air Twin Turbo Prop) converted to LCCS in March 1987 but all have subsequently all retired with the exception of one U-21 aircraft that is no longer on LCCS coverage. The C-12 and RC-12 contract support was held by BASI (then renamed Raytheon Aerospace Corporation) until 1996 when the contract was awarded to AGES and up to the present LCCS contractor, DynCorp International LLC (DI, a CSC Company) headquartered in Fort Worth, Texas. The DI basic contract was awarded in August 2000 (start date 28 August 2000) with a total of nine possible yearly renewable options and includes LCCS for the C-12, the RC-12 and the UC-35. This is the first Army LCCS contract to span more than the heretofore five year periods and offers many advantages for a cooperative and mutually beneficial contract between the Army and DI. The C-23 LCCS contract was formerly held by Bombardier Aerospace (1990-1994), then by Duncan Aviation (1995-1999) and the present basic contract was awarded to Duncan Aviation of Lincoln, Nebraska in September 1999 (start date 16 January 2000) with a total of four yearly renewable options.

In addition to the C-12/RC-12/UC-35 contract with DynCorp, the FWPMO (PEO Aviation) and AMCOM also have LCCS contracts (not the subject of this article but similar in many ways) for support of the C-20 Gulfstream III and IV (USAF contract with Sabreliner), the C-26 Metroliner (USAF contract with Fairchild), the C-37 Gulfstream V (USAF contract with Gulfstream) and the Dehavilland RC-7 (Army contract with AVTEL). In addition, some other Army fixed wing aircraft of various types and very low densities (C-182 Cessna, C-31 Fokker, UV-18 DeHavilland, UV-20 Pilatus, others) are managed by separate commands (U.S. Army Parachute Team, U.S. Army Military Academy) and may be rolled under the management of the FWPMO at a future date.

Duncan is a defense contractor supporting the government and private industry with a workforce of 1800 employees in 39 locations and has a total of 68 employees at 19 sites providing LCCS under the C-23 contract. DynCorp (now a CSC company) is a defense contractor supporting the government and private industry with a workforce of 23,000 employees in 550 locations worldwide. DynCorp has a total of 373 employees providing LCCS under its contract at 74 sites. With the CSC acquisition of DynCorp, the Corporation has a total worldwide workforce of 90,000 employees.[vi] As the prime contractors, both Duncan and DynCorp have formed teams and relationships with various other aviation support organizations in order to offer the Army the support required for its aircraft systems. These other support sub-contractor team members include Pratt & Whitney (C-12/C-23/RC-12/UC-35A engines), Bombardier (C-23 site operations support), Cessna (UC-35 OEM), Raytheon Aircraft (C-12/RC-12 OEM), Short Brothers Ltd (C-23 OEM), Stevens Aviation (C-12/RC-12 Depot operations), Professional Aviation (C-12/RC-12 Landing gear), AAR (C-12/RC-12 Propellers), Global Eagle (DynCorp warehouse operations, parts shipments worldwide), Messier Services (C-23 Landing Gear) and Duncan Aviation (C-23 Propellers).

Society of Logistics Engineers
Tennessee Valley Chapter

U.S. Army COTS Fixed Wing Aircraft & LCCS

Primes & Their Subs

Duncan Aviation

- •OEM – Shorts
- •Site Personnel – Bombardier
- •Depot
  - •Duncan Aviation -Kalamazoo
- •Engines – Pratt & Whitney Canada
  - •PT6A-65AR
- •Landing Gear - Messier
- •Props – Duncan Aviation
- •Warehouse/Shipping - Bombardier

DynCorp International

- •Aircraft OEM
  - •Cessna
  - •Raytheon Beech
- •Site Personnel – DynCorp
- •Depot
  - •Stevens Aviation/Service Center/RUAG
- •Engines
  - •Pratt & Whitney Canada
    - •PT6A-41/42/65B/67/67D
    - •JT15D-5D/PW535A
- •Landing Gear – Professional Aviation
- •Props – AAR Aviation Services
- •Warehouse/Shipping – Circle Aviation

The missions of the Army's 235 fixed wing aircraft managed under these LCCS contracts cover a number of varying areas from straightforward transportation of VIP passengers and cargo and maintenance of lines of communication under the OSA mission to direct wartime-level SEMA support. Duncan is contracted to provide a yearly total of 420 hours for each C-23 aircraft (35 flight hours per month). DynCorp is contracted to provide a yearly total of 600 hours for each C-12/RC-12 aircraft (50 flight hours per month) and 800 hours for each UC-35 aircraft (67 flight hours per month). Flying hours (141,182 annual flying hour program) are funded under CLIN X002, which will be explained later in this article.

The LCCS contracts are managed by the FWPMO, a Lieutenant Colonel (LTC) with a staff consisting of military personnel, Department of the Army Civilians (DAC) and support contractors. They interface daily with the Aviation PEO, Duncan, DynCorp, Government acquisition support personnel (to include the Procuring Contracting Officer, the PCO) at AMCOM and the Defense Contract Management Agency (DCMA), the user military commands, user units at site level and associated offices at Headquarters, Department of the Army (HQDA) (operations, funding, logistics, force structure).

The C-12/RC-12/C-23/UC-35 FWPMO support team provides daily support to all beddown base user sites and their associated military commands. Its personnel maintain a website for information dissemination, POCs and information downloads (contract, air worthiness releases, safety bulletins, briefings, and photos). They develop, fund, and manage modification programs in conjunction with Federal Aviation Administration (FAA), Global Air Traffic Management (GATM), International Civil Aviation Organization (ICAO) and other guidelines (e.g., Instrument Landing System (ILS) protection, GATM, 8.33 MHz separation, Terminal Collision Avoidance System (TCAS) II, Enhanced Ground Proximity Warning System (EGPWS)). They work with the Contractor to provide technical approval and funding with the PCO for over and above repairs and related programs and projects and to manage and fund time before overhaul (TBO) programs for components such as engines, landing gear and propellers. They coordinate with units, the contractor and the engineer support matrix team from the Aviation and Missile Research and Development Engineering Center (AMRDEC) to assist in data for and issuance of airworthiness releases for particular items of equipment. They provide ongoing technical interpretation and updates of the LCCS contracts in conjunction with the assigned contract PCO.

Primary funding for the contracts comes as Operations and Maintenance funds from HQDA via three primary sources (Army – OMA, National Guard – OMNG, USAR – OMAR) and is applied to differing contract line item numbers (CLINs) to support the various maintenance actions of the LCCS contracts. Funding is obligated against the CLINs with the normal financial methods of funding source documents and contract modifications and authorizations by the assigned PCO. A breakout of the primary CLINs is discussed later in this article.

Primary Funding Sources (within the Army)

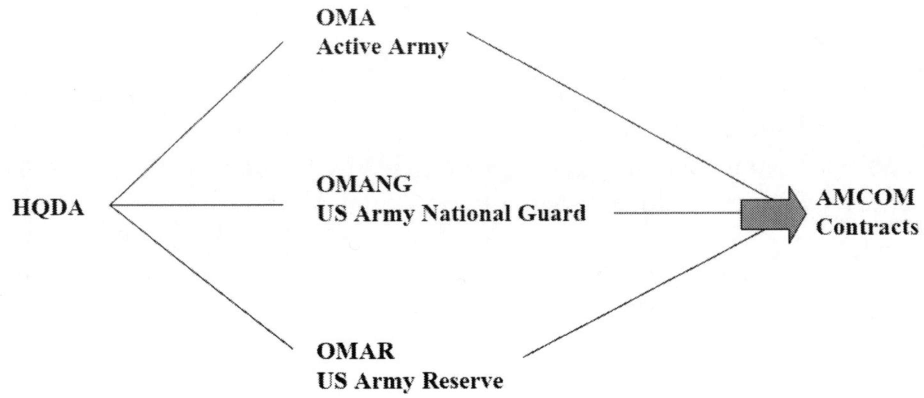

The Duncan and DynCorp basic LCCS contracts are firm fixed type contracts with CLINs structured to provide support in various areas. The basic unit of support for these contracts is the fixed wing beddown base/site that is aligned with an Army unit-level organization. These sites fall under varied Army, Army National Guard and Army Reserve commands at ninety-four worldwide locations.

The contract CLINs (with specificity to contract) cover:

CLIN X001 - Base Operations Support – Same on both LCCS contracts.
CLIN X002 - Aircraft Material - Flying Hour Program - same on both LCCS contracts.
CLIN X003 - Data (LCCS) - Duncan
CLIN X003 - Scheduled Maintenance - DynCorp
CLIN X004 - Propeller Overhaul - Duncan
CLIN X004 - Over and Above Maintenance - DynCorp
CLIN X005 - Strip and Repaint - Duncan
CLIN X005 - Cost Reimbursable/ Travel and Per Diem - DynCorp
CLIN X006 - Over and Above Maintenance – Duncan
CLIN X006 - Data, Not Separately Priced - DynCorp
CLIN X007 - Over and Above – Elective Improvements - Duncan
CLIN X007 - Transition Phase In - DynCorp
CLIN X008 - Facilities - Duncan
CLIN X008 - Not used - DynCorp
CLIN X009 - Phase in/Phase Out - Duncan

CLIN X009 - Not used - DynCorp
CLIN X010 - Engine Overhaul - Duncan
CLIN X010 - Transition Phase Out - DynCorp
CLIN X011 - Engine Repair - Duncan
CLIN X011 - Not used - DynCorp
CLIN X012 - Engine Parts and Materials and O&A Labor - Duncan
CLIN X012 - Not used - DynCorp
CLIN X013 - Travel and Per Diem and Deployments - Duncan
CLIN X013 - Not used - DynCorp

These CLINs enable the FWPMO and Acquisition Center to effectively manage the aircraft fleet and make timely payments to Duncan and DynCorp for regular firm-fixed price support actions and for those over and above actions that vary in their scope of involvement, cost and intensity. A breakout of how each CLIN normally functions is further defined below:

CLIN X001-Base Operations Support. The "X" represents the contract option year; the initial (base) option period (28 Sep 00 – 31 Jan 01) was zero (0) and the next, or first option (1 Feb 01 – 31 Jan 02), is 1. The full contract, if the Government exercises the contract options each year, includes five (Duncan) or nine (DynCorp) option years. For example, actions under this CLIN in the first option year are numbered 1001. Actions for CLIN X002 for option period 1 would be 1002. CLIN X001 includes basic beddown base support at a total of 93 sites in the Continental U.S. (CONUS) and overseas (OCONUS). Sites range from one aircraft up to 15 aircraft. Our minimum manning level is two mechanics and goes as high as 21 mechanics and maintenance personnel at our largest site (Wiesbaden Army Airfield, Wiesbaden, Germany). All site personnel are contractually required to have an Airframe and Powerplant (A&P) FAA license rating or its equivalent for other technical specialties (e.g., Avionics FCC license). In addition, the site personnel are also contractually required to have a secret DoD clearance.

These are performance-based contracts and both Duncan and DynCorp are required to maintain the aircraft in their LCCS contract at a Mission Capable (MC) rate of at least 80 percent per aircraft calculated over a monthly period (from the first day in the month through the last day in the month) with allowances for conditions and circumstances that are out of the Contractor's control. These allowances are termed Non Reporting Time (NRT) and are spelled out for most normal contractual LCCS situations. Situations not specified in the contract or SOW are decided by the Contracting Officer with the assistance of the FWPMO and the contractor. A few of the normal NRT areas include C-12/RC-12 TBO engine and propeller change out (not to exceed 2 calendar days per engine), C-23 engine change out (not to exceed 1.5 days per engine), C-23 propeller change out (not to exceed 1 day per propeller), UC-35 TBO engine change out (24 hours per engine), C-12/RC-12 100 hour inspection (labor not to exceed 4 hours), C-23 C-Check (not to exceed 5 days), C-23-D Check (not to exceed 6 days), UC-35 single hot section inspection (HSI) (not to exceed 29 hours), C-12/RC-12 complete set landing gear TBO (not to exceed 4 calendar days) and C-23 landing gear removed and replaced at time of overhaul (3 calendar days). Additional NRT conditions are listed in the contract and SOW. These NRT allowances give the Contractor assistance in managing these specified circumstances but are not necessarily the actual amount of time it may take to complete the action. For instance, NRT for a C-12 engine change is 1.5 days but it may take a maintenance crew 2 days to perform the action.

The Contractor (DynCorp in this case) assumes the NMC time for the additional half day and should have covered that additional maintenance time in his proposal. If either contractor does not maintain at least 80 percent MC on the aircraft for a specific month then that contractor receives reduced CLIN X001 payment for that particular aircraft.

A few additional performance-based measures are a part of both contracts. If DynCorp does not clear specifically SOW-identified aircraft faults (e.g. Flight Management Systems, Global Positioning Systems, Primary Navigation Systems, others) within 5 days (10 days OCONUS) then the aircraft is considered contractually non-mission-capable (NMC). If DynCorp does not clear non-grounding aircraft faults (written in the fault portion of the aircraft logbook) within 45 days, each write-up accrues a weekly reduction of CLIN X001 payment until the fault is cleared or the PCO allows relief. If Duncan does not clear non-grounding aircraft logbook faults within 30 days the aircraft is considered contractually NMC. In both contracts, if aircraft are considered NMC their MC rate begins decreasing until it results in decreased CLIN X001 payments or the aircraft is repaired.

NRT affects both the supported military unit and the Contractor. For example, an aircraft may be non-available for missions due to shipment of an engine resulting from an unanticipated engine replacement (DynCorp NRT not to exceed 3 calendar days CONUS and 6 calendar days OCONUS) brought about by an ingestion of FOD (foreign object damage) or some unanticipated engine failure before its normal TBO. As long as the shipment time is within the NRT limits it does not count against the aircraft's monthly MC rate. The military unit's Army reporting system (DA Form 1352 and associated rules) does not allow for the NRT and the unit's DA Form 1352 computed MC rate will be lower (all other reporting items equal) than the Contractor's MC rate. This difference in reporting (two separate systems, different rules and reporting periods) requires understanding on the Government's (military unit chain of command) part. The Contractor could (if the subsequent MC rate falls below 80 percent for that month) receive reduced payments under CLIN X001 if the NRT, for a condition not under his control, was not a provision of the contract. If the MC rate falls below 80 percent, and NRT is not a factor, then the Contractor receives reduced CLIN X 001 payment for that month.

Site support personnel normally work a 40-hour workweek and utilize "flex" time in order to meet the mission requirements of the Army fixed wing unit at that site. Flexible, or flextime, is the contractor's method to manage his support personnel to meet the needs of each individual site's missions while remaining within a 40-hour workweek. This requires close coordination between the individual site lead and the contracting officer representative (COR) at each site. For example, an A&P mechanic at a single aircraft site may work early morning hours to provide coverage for morning missions and end his/her workday in the early afternoon. The other site mechanic (remember, 2 minimum at single sites) may start his/her normal workday mid to late morning and stay until the aircraft returns in the evening to provide recovery and maintenance support preceding the next day's missions. Both mechanics will have to adjust their schedules periodically to provide scheduled, or unscheduled aircraft maintenance best performed with two mechanics (i.e., landing gear change, engine change, phase maintenance inspections, C or D checks). These schedule adjustments are most successfully accomplished when close coordination and working relationships exist between the site COR and contractor site personnel. Overtime is an additional expense and is only used as needed by the contractors to fill in-company needs or as authorized by the Contracting Officer after careful review. Overtime is a good example of an over and above cost that is above the basic cost of the site. It is sometimes authorized to cover additional man-hours needed for unit deployments or surge periods. In all cases of Government-funded overtime, the overtime must be approved before the fact via a technical process between the user unit, the FWPMO, the Contractor and the Contracting Officer. Payment for overtime is normally assessed to the user unit or its Major Command (MACOM) and is made via the FWPMO and Contracting Officer to the contractor.

Contractor CLIN X001 site maintenance includes the maintenance of Government Furnished/Supplied Equipment (GFE/GSE) and the contractor furnished equipment (CFE). It also includes hazardous waste management and disposal, which is contractually the responsibility of the individual contractors, and must be done in conjunction with local waste management policies and support programs. Each site, depending on the level of available Government support, is responsible for the effective, correct and timely disposal of hazardous waste generated by its LCCS activities.

Facilities such as hanger, office and storage areas are the responsibility of the Government and vary from site to site depending on local requirements. Many hangers and related support facilities are Government-owned but a number are leased or rented by the Government (normally at state flight detachments) and may even be co-use facilities with other commercial activities. The Contractor is responsible to secure, clean and maintain all assigned spaces and to repair any damages caused by its personnel.

Other types of support included under CLIN X001 include aircraft weighing in accordance with (IAW) OEM and Army publications and manuals, crew systems maintenance to include preventative and corrective maintenance and/or replacement/inspection/storage of items issued with/for the aircraft (first aid kits, over water survival kits), long range navigation updates (KLN-90B Global Positioning System (GPS), Flight Management System (FMS) 800, FMS 3000, GNS/XLS, other systems), aircraft survivability equipment maintenance to line replacement unit (LRU) level, maintenance of unit technical libraries and maintenance and calibration of CFE and GFE test, measurement and diagnostic equipment (TMDE). This does not include all items of CLIN X001 support but should give the reader an idea of how encompassing a good LCCS support program can and should be. The idea is for the LCCS contractor to take care of the aircraft from cradle to grave.

Another important LCCS coverage under the provisions of CLIN X001 is the Contractor's recovery of fixed wing aircraft when they become non-mission capable (NMC) at off-site (non beddown base) locations. This area differs significantly between the Duncan LCCS contract and the DynCorp LCCS contracts. Duncan is only responsible for aircraft recoveries once it has been authorized payment to perform the recovery action. The speed at which the Government (FWPMO and Acquisition Center) is notified and provided a Duncan recovery estimate is critical to the effective start of recovery operations by Duncan. Only after the repair effort plan (normally under CLIN X006 and CLIN X013) is reviewed and authorized by the PCO will the repair efforts begin. This is, in the author's opinion, a major shortcoming in the Duncan LCCS contract. Provisions in the DynCorp LCCS contract designate DynCorp as responsible to initiate recovery operations no later than (NLT) 24 hours from notification of a requirement. Unless the recovery requirement is out of the Contractor's (DynCorp) control (for instance a lightning strike, or some other fault not considered covered under CLIN X001 and CLIN X002) the recovery does not have to wait on the Government's authorization. Per the DynCorp contract, "Recovery operations shall include the required test equipment parts and personnel." We have had aircraft recoveries due to NMC shortcomings related to avionics, blown/deflated tires, bird strikes, lightning strikes and many other circumstances. Some of the off-site recovery locations to date include Iceland, Adak Island, Africa, Sarajevo, Greece, Wake Island and many non-site locations in CONUS. These recovery efforts, if under the Duncan contract, would have taken additional time at increased costs.

Some examples:

A C-23C sustains a blown main landing gear tire upon landing (crew responsible in this case) at a location other than a Duncan support site. The flight crew notifies the unit COR (unless he/she is on the crew) who then fills out a work request to Duncan (submitted via site personnel via fax to Duncan). Duncan works up a recovery plan and submits it to the FWPMO. The plan is technically reviewed, funds are allocated for wheel and tire assembly and its shipment to the site and for the travel and perdiem of the Duncan mechanics to the site. The plan is submitted to the PCO for approval/authorization. If approved, the plan is forwarded to Duncan who then begins the recovery.

The C-23 Over and Above Process

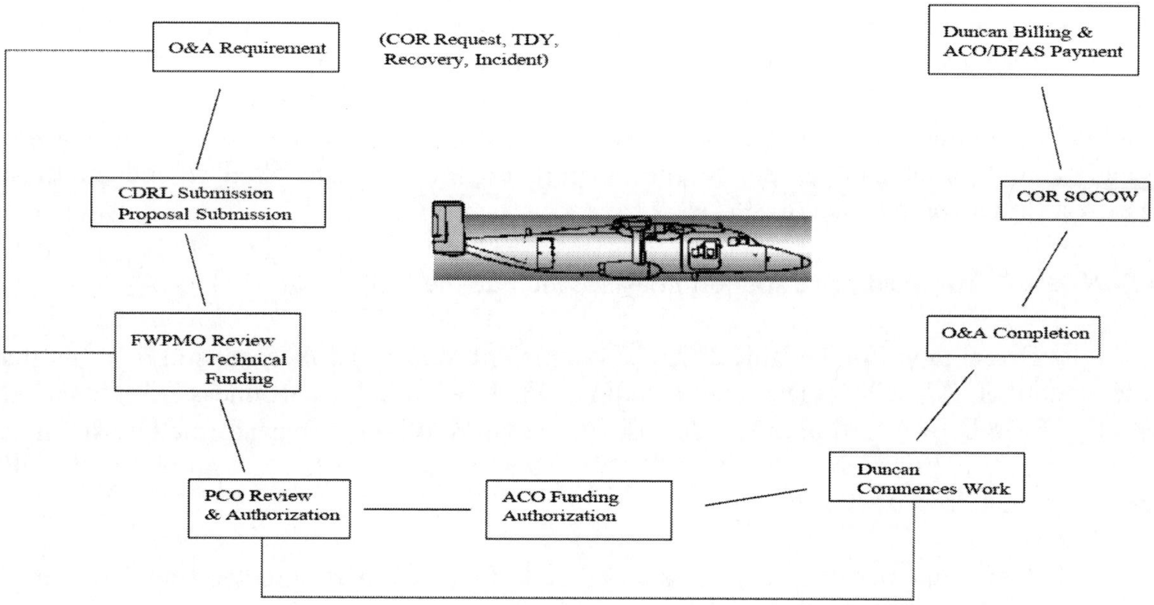

An RC-12D returning to Korea, following completion of an ACI (depot – level airframe condition inspection) with strip and repaint, is at 25,000 feet after traveling 800 miles of 1022 miles on the sixth leg of its flight (Midway Island to Wake Island, Pacific) when it gets a Master Caution light with a bleed air failure segment light. The crew continues its flight to Wake Island but cannot continue its flight until the problem is fixed. Wake Island has no regularly scheduled commercial flights so DynCorp coordinates with the military to send a mechanic with tools and parts on the military aircraft that goes from Hawaii to Wake Island and other Pacific locations once per week. An A&P mechanic from the Hawaii beddown base flies to Wake Island, repairs the aircraft (bleed air leak in the de-ice bleed air line) and catches the military transport flight back to Hawaii. The RC-12D and crew continue on to their home station in Korea.

A C-12F develops an engine problem while on a mission in the European Command (EUCOM) area of operations. It lands safely at an airport in a foreign country and a maintenance recovery is initiated by DynCorp following notification by the Army flight crew. A DynCorp mechanic with a replacement engine fuel control unit (a CLIN X002 part), associated installation hardware and tools is flown commercially by DynCorp to the aircraft's location. The mechanic removes the faulty fuel control, installs and rigs its replacement, performs ground runs on the aircraft and transfers it to the Army crew for a maintenance test flight. Following successful completion of the test flight the aircraft is returned to service and the mechanic returns to Wiesbaden, Germany (the aircraft home support site) on the next available commercial flight. This recovery was accomplished under the provisions of CLIN X001 (manning) and CLIN X002 (flying hour support) without any contractual actions.

A UC-35 aircraft had a single engine failure while on a mission in Germany and landed at a civilian airport. DynCorp submitted its initial and follow-up notification and repair contract data requirement lines (CDRLs) and the repair was reviewed by the FWPMO and approved by the PCO. A replacement rental engine was shipped to Germany, the failed engine was replaced, the aircraft was rigged and test flown and then returned to mission capable status. The failed engine was returned to the OEM for teardown analysis (internal bearing failure), repaired (to include any warranty considerations) and returned to its aircraft. The rental engine was removed and sent back to join the OEM rental pool, the regular engine was reinstalled, rigged and the aircraft was test flown and returned to service.

CLIN X001 firm fixed price support does not include the following:

- Direct labor for Technical Directives (TD's) requiring incorporation by other than on-site personnel. Most TD's (Service Bulletins, OEM or FAA Airworthiness Directives, AMCOM Safety of Flight or Aviation Safety Advisory Messages, others) are performed by site mechanics using firm fixed price labor support, but some may require expertise not normal to the site. This category includes that type of support.

- Travel and per diem expenses as a result of Government directed travel and/or Government directed relocation of employees and dependents. This type of support is not normal to the firm fixed price portion of CLIN X001 and is covered under CLIN X005 (Cost Reimbursable - DynCorp) or CLIN X013 (Travel cost reimbursable – Duncan), which will be discussed later in this article. Government (unit) directed deployments requiring mechanics' support are a good example of this type of expense. The assigned unit's MACOM will often pay these additional expenses via AMCOM and the contract.

- Transportation, packaging and shipping of beddown base parts inventory and support equipment associated with aircraft reassignments and/or base closures. An example of this type of non-CLIN X001 firm fixed price support was the closure of the DynCorp site at Cigli AFB, Turkey and the subsequent movement of aircraft, mechanics and site support equipment to other locations. These type costs would be borne under CLIN X004 (Over and Above Maintenance) and CLIN X005.

CLIN X002 - Aircraft Material. This portion of the contract provides for maintenance, replenishment, repair of spares, support equipment, and airframe. The pricing structure is based upon a flying hour rate per hour of aircraft flight operation. These functions are funded by specific flying hour costs accrued by user units each month. For example, as stated earlier, the projected average flying hours for the C-12/RC-12 aircraft is 50 flying hours per month (600 hours per year), those for the C-23 are 35 hours per month (420 hours per year) and for the UC-35 are 67 per month (800 per year). Duncan and DynCorp bill the Government (via the FWPMO and the Acquisition Center and Administrative Contracting Officer - ACO) a contractually specified rate (developed during the source selection stage of the procurement) for every flying hour that a C-12/RC-12, C-23 or UC-35 flew during the preceding month. If the aircraft flew 35 hours then the amount billed is 35 times the hourly rate for the related option year. If the aircraft flew 100 hours, which can and does happen during surge periods, then the Contractor bills for 100 times the hourly rate. The overall fleet average for flying hours is billed monthly and authorized for payment by the ACO. The operations tempo (Optempo) for aircraft may vary depending on location and time of year

Duncan and DynCorp are responsible for all parts and tools (less that furnished by the Government as GFE/GSE and specific SEMA prescribed load list (PLL)/authorized stockage list (AQL) parts) needed to maintain the aircraft. This includes all direct and indirect parts and materials for the aircraft. One exception is specific parts and systems that are part of the mission gear on the RC-12 SEMA aircraft. They are the responsibility of the Army unit and any associated contractors or military support commands. In most instances, the Contractor must replace, at his expense, any PLL/AQL used in support of the SEMA fleet and all GFE/GSE must be returned in operational condition following completion of the contract. The Contractor provides all petroleum supplies (less aviation fuel and deice fluid).

Duncan and DynCorp are contractually obligated to provide the same level of LCCS support in contingency or wartime operations as during normal peacetime operations. This support is contingent upon the availability of commercial transportation for parts and movement of support personnel. If that commercial support is not available due to geographical or political reasons, the Army (MACOMs, units, PM) is responsible to coordinate or provide the needed support. Commercial transportation is, in most cases, available in contingency areas and is faster and more streamlined that military support if both exist side by side. DynCorp relies heavily on just-in-time (JIT) delivery of needed parts and equipment to its sites worldwide and this method has not proven effective in contingency/wartime situations.

CLIN X003 – Data (LCCS) – Duncan
CLIN X003 - Scheduled Maintenance - DynCorp. Scheduled aircraft maintenance includes propeller overhauls, aircraft strip and repainting, airframe condition inspections, hot section inspections and engine overhauls. Originally, these types of fixed maintenance events were rolled up into the flying hour programs. But the Services recognized that it was more cost effective to separate these maintenance activities out of the flying hour program and track them separately. These maintenance actions are tracked via the Contractor's CITIS (Contractor Integrated Technical Information Service) and updated daily. The FWPMO (via internet terminal access), and user units (via their local lead mechanic's internet terminal), have full-time access to the DynCorp CITIS. The CITIS will be explained in more detail later.

Propellers are removed by site mechanics and sent to the DynCorp subcontractor, AAR (Allen Aircraft Radio Aviation Services), for overhaul and return to use. During a normally scheduled propeller TBO change sequence, a replacement propeller will arrive at the user site a minimum of 20 hours prior to the projected TBO time. The propeller that has reached its TBO is removed, the new/overhauled propeller is installed (plus rigged and test flown) and DynCorp bills against the CLIN X003 price for that action. Propeller repairs and overhauls for C-23 aircraft are handled by Duncan in much the same way as DynCorp although their FFP is covered under CLIN X004 and their subcontractor is a subsidiary of Duncan Aviation. If a propeller requires premature replacement due to internal failure or an incident of some type, then the repair will be handled as a regular CLIN X002 (internal failure, warranty issue) or as an over and above action (incident related or unscheduled) via CLIN X004 if DynCorp or CLIN X006 if Duncan. In all cases, the FWPMO and the PCO are involved in the technical evaluation and the subsequent funding of the item. This sequence is essentially the same on all scheduled maintenance through these CLINs.

Aircraft strip and repainting is primarily accomplished on C-12/RC-12 aircraft on a 5-year interval in conjunction with airframe condition and inspection (ACI) schedules. C-23 strip and repaint actions are based on a paint condition evaluation procedure and are essentially completed as needed unless delayed due to budget constraints. Duncan FFP strip and repaints of C-23 aircraft are accomplished at their facility in Kalamazoo, Michigan under FFP (firm fixed price) CLIN X005. C-12/RC-12 ACIs (with strip and repaints) are accomplished at the DynCorp subcontractor facilities at Stevens Aviation in Greenville, South Carolina and FFP strip and repaints of UC-35 aircraft are done at The Service Center in Oklahoma City, Oklahoma or RUAG in the Federal Republic of Germany.

Aircraft hot section inspections (HSI) are accomplished at the user locations by site personnel. The CLIN X003 funds (DynCorp) cover the normal replacement items in an HSI and any over and above items are covered via additional technical reviews and associated funding by the FWPMO and PCO utilizing CLIN X004 (DynCorp). HSIs are a cost reimbursable action (over and above) under the Duncan contract and are funded via CLIN X006. The over and above review and funding process is normally accomplished within a matter of hours or a few days due to innovative and streamlined procedures at the Acquisition Center, the FWPMO and DynCorp.

Engine overhauls work in somewhat the same manner as propeller overhauls. Scheduled engine changes are projected and closely tracked via the Duncan and DynCorp CITIS and site and

FWPMO personnel. Rental engines are used on C-23 (Duncan) aircraft if sufficient engines are not available in the GFE engine pool and are normally furnished on C-12/RC-12/UC-35 (DynCorp) aircraft approximately 21 days or 20 flight hours before the TBO is due. Rental engines, furnished via firm fixed price per flying hour by DynCorp, are used on the aircraft while their normal engine is being overhauled or repaired. FWPMO policy on C-12/RC-12/UC-35 engines is to keep the same engine with the same aircraft throughout its life. Engine overhauls normally take about 2 to 3 months to accomplish. When the overhaul is completed the engine comes back to the site, is reinstalled, rigged and test flown and the rental engine goes back to the DynCorp engine subcontractor (Pratt & Whitney). If an engine fails prematurely due to internal or incident related actions the change is handled much the same way as far as the use of the rental engine and the return of the original engine once repaired. The funding for the engine repair is handled as a warranty issue if it fails prematurely due to an internal fault and as an over and above action under CLIN X004 (Duncan CLIN X011) if due to FOD, sudden stoppage or some other abnormal reason. As with all equipment failures, if the failure is related to a manufacturer defect or shortcoming then warranty considerations will be applied in the form of credits to the Government. The FWPMO owns some GFE C-12 engines that are used in ways similar to rental engines if they are the correct aircraft type engines for the aircraft needing the repair. If a GFE engine is mounted in lieu of a rental engine then no rent is required and the Contractor does not incur any costs for any possible failures or shortcomings (unless Contractor induced) of the GFE engines. In the case of C-23 GFE engines, the GFE is normally used for the TBO action (or repair action) and then the TBO or NMC engine is overhauled or repaired and returned to the GFE inventory.

CLIN X004 – Over and Above Maintenance – DynCorp, CLIN X006 – Duncan. Aircraft over and above maintenance under includes depot and non-depot level repairs, parts and materials not considered CLIN X002 and elective improvements and TD's (Technical Directives).

Repairs and maintenance actions must occasionally be accomplished to correct unscheduled maintenance actions that are not covered within the normal CLIN X002 maintenance area. These actions are part of CLIN X004 (CLIN X006 under the Duncan LCCS contract). Engine repairs that fall outside the normal scheduled maintenance guidelines (e.g., Technical Bulletin modifications done internally to engines while at Pratt & Whitney) are one type of depot level repair. Another type action is the repair of wing delamination areas on C-12 and RC-12 aircraft or depot-level incident damage of any of the aircraft covered under these LCCS contracts.

Elective improvements are often required to keep the fixed wing fleet up to date and to comply with safety and operational improvements such as TCAS II (terminal collision avoidance system), GATM (global air traffic management) features, and other modifications and updates are presently underway at Raytheon E-Systems, Rockwell Collins and Stevens Aviation and the Army Aviation Test Center and are funded via CLIN X004 or other related funding. An upcoming elective improvement to the DynCorp LCCS fleet is the installation of next-generation GPS ELT (Electronic Locator Transmitters – C-12/RC-12/UC-35)), dual door cables (C-12/RC-12) and cockpit vent windows (C-12F3/T/U) on designated aircraft.

For example:

A C-12D assigned to the Air Traffic Control unit at Fort Rucker, AL for navigational aid flight tests needed a stormscope to increase the safety performance its in-flight tests and to bring it into configuration with the rest of the fixed wing fleet. The FWPMO drafted a request for proposal, which was then reviewed and forwarded by the PCO to DynCorp for response. The DynCorp proposal, when received, was reviewed, funded, approved and authorized by the FWPMO/PCO team. The installation was scheduled at the Stevens Aviation depot facility, completed as planned and the aircraft returned to service with an increased capability.

CLIN X005 – Cost Reimbursable – DynCorp, CLIN X013 Travel and Per Diem and Deployments - Duncan. The cost reimbursable CLIN gets a lot of use when aviation units need to deploy their aircraft to locations separate from their normal sites. These types of trips are separate from regular RON (remain overnight) missions and most often involve the movement of aircraft and support mechanics and equipment to locations for specific missions. The Army fixed wing fleet nearly always has aircraft and mechanics on deployment operations. The deployments may vary from one mechanic and one aircraft for 7 days to 6 mechanics and 4 aircraft for a year. Per diem costs for deployments are funded at Joint Travel Regulations (JTR) and U.S. State Department (depending on location) rates and include additional costs for commercial airfare (when the contractor is not allowed or able to use the military aircraft), rental vehicles or equipment transportation and communications, overtime and other associated costs are borne by the unit or its MACOM, via the FWPMO. Deployment costs are based on best estimates of the costs and PCO funding authorizations utilize a not to exceed (NTE) limit. If the Contractor reaches the 85 percent level of the NTE, he then notifies the FWPMO and PCO of a possible need for additional funding authorization. All deployment costs are cost reimbursable and actual billing documents and procedures are required prior to payment by the ACO. The FWPMO, the PCO and both contractors have streamlined these procedures to allow for deployment authorizations within hours if funding is available on the appropriate funding CLIN for each contract. A large measure of rapid response on these CLINs, and others, is the ability of the FWPMO and MACOMs to think ahead and make sure they have adequately funded upcoming actions or have adequate funding reserves to handle unforeseen circumstances.

How do Duncan and DynCorp manage their part of the contract? Both contractors work closely with the Government through the PCO, the ACO and the FWPMO to keep the right personnel using the correct procedures for the LCCS contract operations and funding. Duncan is headquartered in Lincoln, NE with primary subcontractor Bombardier offices in Bridgeport, WV. The DynCorp LCCS headquarters is in Fort Worth, TX with regional managers in Europe, Asia, the Eastern United States and the Western United States and subcontractors in various U.S. states (e.g. OK, KS, TX, SC) and foreign countries (e.g. Canada, Germany).

The critical contractual reports, or CDRLs (Contract Data Requirement List) associated with both contracts are stated under the contract SOWs and are used to monitor worldwide maintenance, reporting and funding actions. Most of the CDRLs are required by the Government in electronic form via the Contractor CITIS or via email.

CDRLs

Duncan		DynCorp
Daily/Monthly Flying Hour Report	A001	Data Accession List
Semi-Annual GFP Inventory	A002	Monthly Contract Funds Status Report (CFSR)
Engine Condition Trend Report	A003	Monthly Program Status
FOD Report	A004	Accident/Incident Report
Spares/Standards Report	A005	Monthly Depot Cost Report
Annual TBO Report	A006	Quarterly TBO Report
Quality Assurance Report	A007	Daily/Monthly Flying Hour Report
Engine/Prop/Gear Overhaul Report	A008	AD/AB Advisory Report
Overage/Shortage/Damage GFP Report	A009	Quarterly Engine Trend Monitoring Report
Compliance w SB/AD	A010	Contingency Plan
GFP/Quality Assurance Report	A011	Annual Spare Parts Usage
Semi-annual Spare Parts Usage	A012	Annual GFP Inventory
Man-hour Estimate, Technical Cost Proposals	A013	Semi-annual Warranty Mgt
Monthly CFSR	A014	Weekly Depot Status Report
Management Plan	A015	Overhaul/Repair Report
Data Accession List	A016	Premature Failure Report
Quarterly Configuration Mgt	A017	Annual Airworthiness Report
Man-hour Technical Cost Proposal	A018	Quality Deficiency Report
Quality Assurance Teardown Report	A019	Teardown Deficiency Report

Annual Depot Maintenance Cost Report	A020	Quarterly Aircraft Configuration Report
Not Utilized	A021	Phase-Out Plan
Not Utilized	A022	Elective Improvements Study/Services
Not Utilized	A023	Elective Improvements Test Plan
Not Utilized	A024	Elective Improvements Test/Inspection Report
Not Utilized	A025	Elective Improvements Electromagnetic Environ Effects Verification
Not Utilized	A026	Elective Improvements Verification Procedures
Not Utilized	A027	Elective Improvements Commercial Drawings and Associated Lists

One of the Contractor's key systems for managing this contract is his CITIS. The Duncan CITIS is called Dash and the DynCorp CITIS is called Maintenix. DynCorp has been implementing a new CITIS called AeroDyne, which will replace Maintenix within the next year.

DASH[vii] is a DOS-based maintenance program that Duncan utilizes to track TBOs on time-change items, historical aircraft data, other related maintenance data and for CDRL reports. It is primarily utilized at their subcontractor level with Bombardier and is not web based. Duncan sites do not have Duncan-furnished computers or web access.

Maintenix[viii] is an automated maintenance program that is used to manage all aircraft scheduled actions (phases, TBOs), unscheduled actions, repair parts orders and tracking, contract reports and data to and from all 74 sites. Nearly all of the AMCOM electronic CDRLs are generated by or captured on Maintenix, the DynCorp restricted website or via email. The Maintenix server is based at the DynCorp Fort Worth, TX location and has terminals and access at the headquarters, all 74 sites and depot locations and with the FWPMO at AMCOM. Additional links are established with DynCorp support companies.

DynCorp has chosen to replace Maintenix and most, if not all, of its functions with AeroDyn. The AeroDyn software is a web-based aviation management system designed to automate aviation organizations business processes and provide timely access to aircraft critical information and reporting capabilities[ix].

Duncan beddown base mechanics (called field service representatives; FSRs) provide daily input on aircraft status and related data, aircraft faults, parts requests and other information to Bombardier on a daily basis via a combination of faxed forms and telephone calls. DynCorp beddown base mechanics enter aircraft status and related aircraft data, aircraft faults, parts requests and personnel status into Maintenix on a daily basis. That data is used to activate parts requests and returns and to track all TBO and scheduled inspections and actions.

Both contractor parts systems include the management of bench stock and required parts at all sites, GFE PLL parts at RC-12 SEMA and selected overseas-deployed sites and the Government furnished equipment located at Duncan's Clarksburg, WV and DynCorp's Fort Worth warehouses. Duncan's warehouse is operated by Bombardier and DynCorp's by Eagle Global. Other parts needed for the LCCS contract are provided via suppliers (Volvo Aero Services, Aviall, Bombardier, Cessna, Raytheon Rapid, Tulsa Air, United Fasteners) via the Duncan and DynCorp purchasing departments using best commercial practices.

Duncan site requisition are submitted to Bombardier via telephone, facsimile, and email and processed according to their priority of need. DynCorp site requisitions are submitted via AeroDyn (formerly by Maintenix) or via phone and email if necessary, received in the DynCorp Logistics Support Center (LSC) and worked according to their priority of need. DynCorp utilizes 5 priorities: AOG (aircraft on ground) is the highest, PR 01 MESL (72 hour response), PR 02 aircraft faults (30 days), PR 03 TBOs (delivery prior to TBO time or date) and PR 04 Stock and Support Equipment.

When the DynCorp LSC receives a requisition it searches for the parts in the following order of priority: the DynCorp warehouse, DynCorp sites, consigned inventory and subcontract inventory. The LSC fills from those sources whenever possible but if they do not have the part then the LSC searches the following parts suppliers: Avial, TulsaAir and Elliot Beech. If the order is over $2,500 then it is passed to the Purchasing section.

Purchasing at both Duncan and DynCorp queries vendors and fills the requisitions. Parts are purchased and then shipped via established accounts for the best method of shipment per the requisition urgency of need and the site location. Shippers for both contractors include FedEx, UPS, Emery Worldwide, DHL and Eagle Global Logistics. Although both contractor's state that AOG's receive 24/7 coverage, if the repair part or component is not available in the contractors' warehouse it is very likely that it will not be purchased or shipped until the next available business day of the providing manufacturer or parts vendors. Transportation forwarders utilized by Duncan and DynCorp arrange shipments from warehouses and drop shipments from vendors (vendors directly to the needed site) whenever possible to avoid shipping delays.

Non-business day parts requirements are worked via telephonic communications to the maintenance managers, or their off-hours duty personnel on call for after hours/weekend/holiday contingencies. If the part is an AOG part and available it ships immediately, if not available then the purchase action is processed the next workday.

The parts return sequence is critical for all core returns (landing gear, generators, avionics equipment, servos, and many items), repair and return items and cross-leveled parts between sites. The logistics support center personnel of both contractors coordinate all these actions.

Summary. Life Cycle Contractor Support for aircraft has been around for many years and is a very viable option if the contract is written to give the customer, the Army in this case, what it wants and needs. The present Army LCCS contracts with Duncan and DynCorp are delivering the best support possible (within contractual and funding limitations) to the Army's FWPMO - managed C-12, RC-12, C-23 and UC-35 fixed wing fleets. This combination of visionary LCCS contracts, capable and diligent Government oversight and management and capable and competent contractors is working well for all parties concerned and continues to improve with time.

Joseph J. Vins, C.P.L.

The author is an on-site support contractor working for Science Applications International Corporation (SAIC) and provides technical and logistical support to the Army's Fixed Wing Program Management Office at Redstone Arsenal, Alabama. He holds degrees from Grand Valley University (B.S.) and the University of Michigan (M.S.) and is a graduate of the Army Transportation Officers Basic and Advanced Courses, the Rotary Wing Pilot Flight Course, the Aviation Maintenance Test Pilot Course and the Command and General Staff College. He retired from the U.S. Army in 1995 following a 23 year career within enlisted and officer ranks in intelligence, transportation, personnel, supply and aviation logistics fields. He joined the Tennessee Valley Chapter of S.O.L.E. in 2000 and was designated a C.P.L in January 2001. He is the present Chapter Historian and is also a member of the C.P.L. Certification Training Team.

---

[i] U.S. Army Fixed Wing PMO
C-12
C-20
C-23
C-26
C-37
EO5B
RC-7
RC-12
UC-35
[ii] U.S. Army Fixed Wing PMO
Duncan – U.S. Army DAAH23-00-C-0030
DynCorp – U.S. Army DAAH23-00-C-0226
Avtel – U.S. Army DAAH23-00-C-0029
Fairchild – USAF F34601-97-C-0032
Gulfstream – USAF F33657-02-D-2011
Sabreliner – USAF F34601-95-C-0538
[iii] Helen Tirone, DynCorp International LLC
[iv] CONUS – Continental United States
[v] OCONUS – Outside CONUS - Overseas
[vi] Helen Tirone, DynCorp International LLC
[vii] DASH – Proprietary to Bombardier Services America Corporation
[viii] Maintenix – Proprietary to Volvo Aerospace
[ix] AeroDyn Product Overview, page 2

Agenda

- Overview
- Performance Based Logistics (PBL)
- Key PBL Characteristics
- Potential Impact of PBL
- PBL Strategies
- Total System Performance Responsibility (TSPR)
- Incentives
- Partnering
- Business Case Analysis
- TSPR Program Development Cycle
- Summary – Important Considerations

38th Annual SOLE Conference: August 12-14, 2003 *Dr. William T. Baylis* *Slide 2*

Overview

- The procurement lull in new system acquisition, and the increasing reliance on aging platforms far past their original planned life cycle, is expanding the need for a concerted effort to upgrade and update defense systems.
  - This applies to legacy systems, as well as the limited number of new systems that DoD will acquire in the future, as a means to create savings.
- Innovative approaches to support of legacy systems, and the integration of logistics support concepts into the acquisition process for new weapons platforms, can be used to produce life cycle savings, reduce cycle times and improve performance.

One approach to reducing costs while maintaining or improving performance is through Performance Based Logistics.

Performance Based Logistics

- **Definition**: A multi-year arrangement (commercial or organic) where the provider is held to customer-oriented performance requirements such as reliability improvement, availability improvement, and reduced delivery times with the end goal of improving logistics support to the fleet...may result in part or all of the Supply Chain being managed by the contractor.

PBL Suppliers provide...
- Warehousing / Transportation
- Consumable Piece Parts
- Configuration Management
- Obsolescence Management
- Repair / Overhaul / Replace
- Guaranteed Availability
- Guaranteed Reliability

Goals/Objectives
- To provide Warfighters increased Operational Readiness
- To enhance the Logistics Response Times
- To enhance Deployment
- To Reduce the Logistics Footprint
- To Reduce Logistics Cost

General Business Approach:
- PBL must provide increased Reliability and/or Availability at the same or a reduced cost.
- PBL must pass a Business Case Analysis.

Buying Performance

Managing Suppliers not Supplies!

Spectrum of PBL Strategies

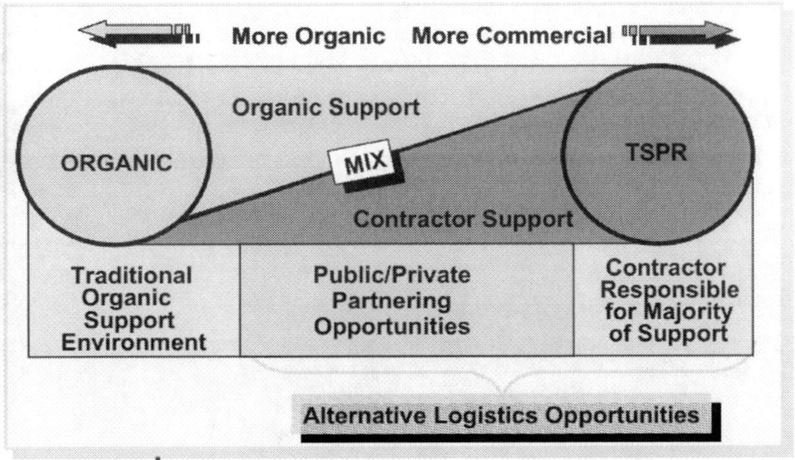

Strategies vary along spectrum depending on: →

- Age of System (Phase in Life Cycle)
- Existing Support Infrastructure
- Organic & Commercial Capabilities
- Legislative and Regulatory Constraints

Key PBL Characteristics

➢ PBL is a key enabler to achieving improved logistics capability through Alternative Logistics Support (ALS) strategies over the total life cycle of the system

- **Structure business relationships that will meet performance goals**
- **Facilitates Life-Cycle Management**
- **Ensure lines of authority are clearly assigned**
- **Reduces Total Ownership costs and future obsolescence risks**
- **Improve reliability, maintainability and supportability**
- **Stabilizes budget planning and execution**
- **Integrate systems development with logistics sustainment processes into performance based product support capability**
- **Can be provided from either the organic or commercial sources of Government-Industry partnerships**

PBL Supplier Roles

Warehousing
Requirements Determination
Engineering/Tech Services
Repair/Overhaul/ Replace Decision
Transportation
Guaranteed Availability
Consumable Piece Parts
Warranties
Configuration Control
Obsolescence Management
Technology Insertion

Results

- Lower Response Time
- Improved Reliability
- Lower Cost of Ownership

Potential "Beneficial" Impact of PBL

- Potential "Beneficial" Impact [Beneficial] of Performance Based Logistics (PBL):
  - Reduce life cycle costs of systems
  - Maintain affordable superior combat capability
  - Upgrade systems using new technology with less complexity in shorter cycle
  - Be resilient to changes in technology throughout the life of systems
  - Mitigate obsolescence problems caused by shortened technology life cycles

38th Annual SOLE Conference: August 12-14, 2003 *Dr. William T. Baylis* *Slide 7*

Government and Commercial Benefits

Government Benefits

- Availability of **Competitive Commercial** sources and **Best Commercial Practices** enables:
  - **Increased Readiness**
    - Higher reliability, supportability and availability
    - More consistent maintenance
    - Timely product engineering improvements
  - **Reduced Life-Cycle-Costs**
    - Less infrastructure and spares inventory
    - Faster and more efficient re-supply lines
    - Shared sustainment costs
    - Access to commercial pricing
  - **Reduced future Risk**
    - Obsolescence
    - Diminished Manufacturing Sources
    - Increased O&S costs
    - Budget instability

Commercial Provider Benefits

- Increased **Profit** opportunity **Self Motivates** industry to continuously:
  - Increase performance
  - Reduce costs
- **Long-Term** contracts encourage investment in product/process improvement
- Provides for greater **Self-Determination** and **Opportunity**
  - Expands aftermarket activities
  - Ties the Government to the provider
  - Avoids parts break-out by the Government
  - Permits retention of design control
  - Eliminates redundant practices

38th Annual SOLE Conference: August 12-14, 2003 *Dr. William T. Baylis* *Slide 8*

PBL Strategies

Alternative Logistics Support (ALS)

Logistics support concept that diverges from the traditional support methods reflected by three-level maintenance and DoD provided material support.

Virtual Prime Vendor (VPV) – Consumable Parts Support

Government arranges with a contractor to provide support to a depot for a specific platform.

Third Party Logistics (3PL) – Service Providers

Government arrangements with commercial companies who offer multiple logistics services such as direct customer ordering, transportation and integrated distribution services

Contractor Logistics Support (CLS) – Maintenance and Material

Cradle-to-grave life cycle support similar to Prime Vendor and DVD, but also having responsibility for in-service engineering, updates and modernization, configuration management and technical data, viability to industrial base sources.

PBL Strategies

Direct Vendor Delivery (DVD) – Material Management

Contractor is prime point of stock issue (material management including: provisioning, repair and return, ICP/stock point management, demand forecasting.

Total System Performance Responsibility (TSPR) – System Performance

TSPR is a support and sustainment strategy where the contractor assumes responsibility for system modifications, performance, integration tasks, sustainment tasks and cost management throughout the program's life cycle. The contractor usually maintains Government Furnished Property (GFP) as a part of full service partnering. The government remains accountable for the program's execution and provides incentives for the contractor to continuously improve reliability, insert improved technology, ensure supportability and reduce weapon system TOC.

Private-Public Partnership (PPP) – Performance Based Arrangement

Allows service to establish organic maintenance while contractors provide business management practices, materials, and engineering. This is not a type of PBL but is an enabler to arrive at a performance based solution.

Total System Performance Responsibility (TSPR) Definition

- The Total System Performance Responsibility (TSPR) program is a product support strategy for major weapon system platforms, whereby one or a limited number of contractors are responsible for system modifications, integration tasks and sustainment tasks to meet warfighter requirements.
- The Government remains accountable for program execution.

- The benefits of a TSPR arrangement include, but are not limited to:
  - Decreased product delivery time
  - Reduced costs and data
  - Reduced program office manpower
  - Fewer Engineering Change Proposals (ECPs)
  - Reduced Total Ownership Cost (TOC)
  - Increased product quality and readiness

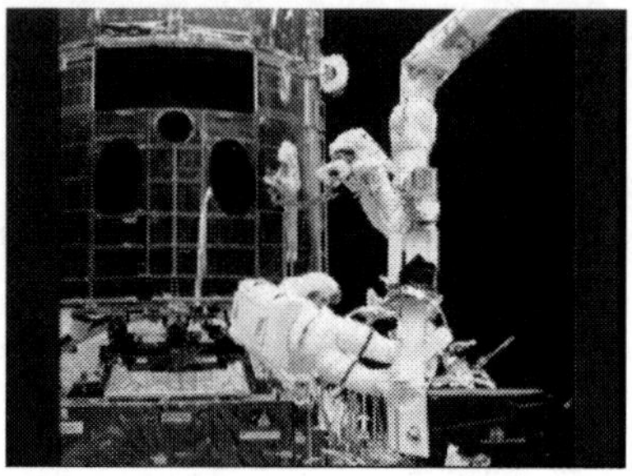

Objectives of TSPR Type Contract

- Under a Total System Performance Responsibility (TSPR) contract, the contractor assumes responsibility for system life-cycle management.
- TSPR transfers performance responsibility and risk to the contractor
  - Gives the contractor more discretion over design, configuration, and requirements solutions. The contractor is also given performance responsibility over the fielded system.
- For an effective TSPR type contract to be effective, it needs to incorporate:
  - Contractor innovation
  - Change management
  - Successful long-term partnerships based on mutually aligned goals and consensus among government and contractor personnel.

Major Themes of TSPR Type Contracts

- System Integration - Support of the system is to be consistent with the End Item
  - DoD Directive 5000.1 [effective May 12, 2003]states in reference to performance-based logistics
    - PMs shall develop and implement performance-based logistics strategies that optimize total system availability while minimizing cost and logistics footprint. ...... Sustainment strategies shall include the best use of public and private sector capabilities through government/industry partnering initiatives, in accordance with statutory requirements.
- System Management - Manage the system instead of the individual commodities
  - TSPR Type Contracts emphasize a system management approach to ensure achievement of an effective and efficient sustainment program at the least possible cost.

Essential Elements for TSPR Type Contracts

- TSPR type contracts are structured into two slightly overlapping segments:
  - Program development
  - Contract structure.

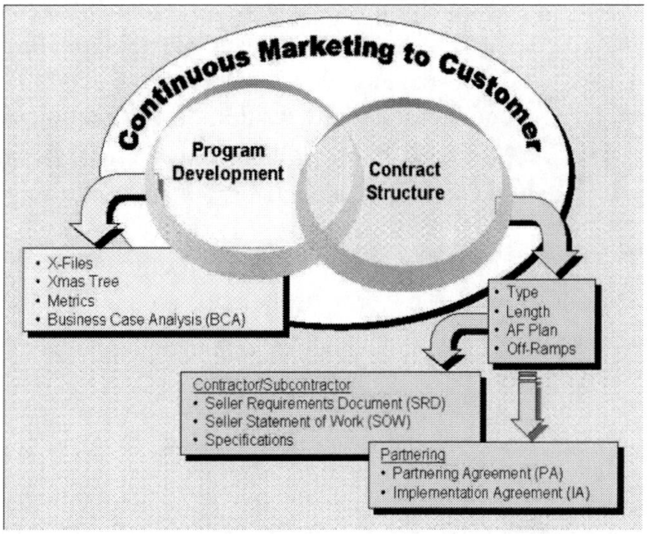

TSPR Incentives

- The TSPR type program makes use of an award fee that is tied to performance by the contractor in various areas such as management, operational and support. Measurement of the contractor's performance that, in turn affects their award fee amount, is tied to agreement upon metrics.
- The Government and Contractor jointly develop contract specific Performance Areas and Associated metrics. For each performance area, metrics are developed and agreed upon in advance. At the end of the evaluation period these metrics will be used to determine the Award-Term allocation or payout.
- The award term component is a dynamic process allowing refocus from year to year. The Award-Term arrangement continues by using the yearly evaluation period during any additional years awarded under the contract. This arrangement allows the flexibility to the government, (agreed upon by both govt. and contractor), to change the evaluation criteria year to year if required by circumstances such as threat, mission, environment, etc.

Metrics

- Metrics are used to answer the question – How good do I have to do it? This being the case, metrics are tied directly to and developed in conjunction with incentives and award fees. It is imperative that all metrics that are to be used to measure contractor performance in a TSPR (or any type) contract are agreed to by the Government, user and contractor and are written down unambiguously.
- Feedback Loop - A very important aspect of good metrics is the design of a feedback loop. Metrics measure things and tells one what is going on. Feedback loops provide for making positive changes to the metrics and informs one if the changes that were made improved the product.

Control & Flexibility Award Term Contract

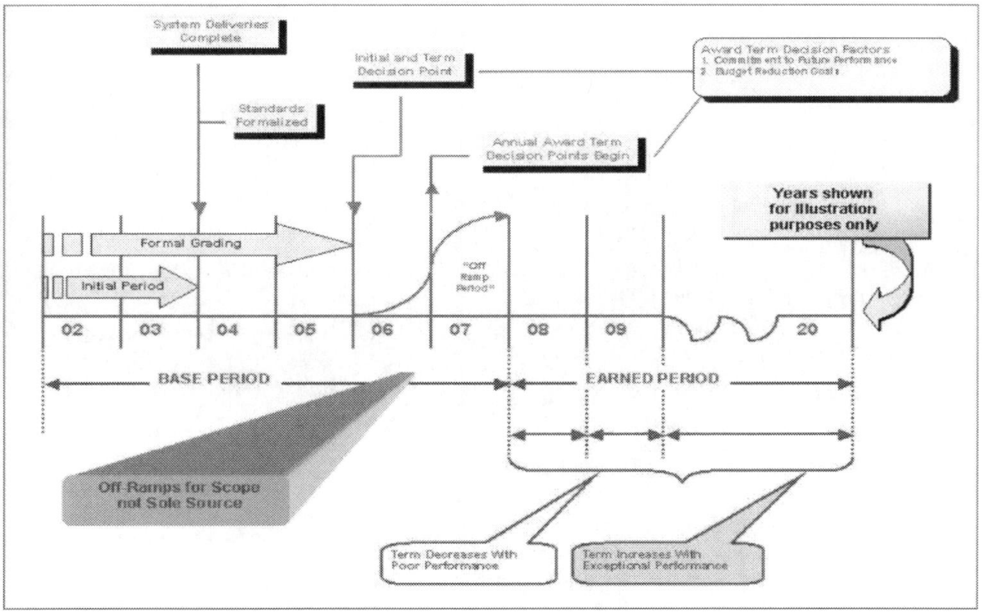

Partnering

- Because TSPR contracts are usually struck early in a system's life, long-term government contractor partnerships are formed. Being an important aspect of TSPR contracts, initial partnering roles and relationships should be set up during the early stages of the program. It is hoped that these partnerships with mutual goals will lead to lower total ownership costs for the government.
- It is also important that the following are kept in mind during the contract process:
  - Partnering Policy, Special Programs and the Law
  - Competing With Your Customer
  - Partnering Components
    - Partnering Agreement (PA)
    - Implementation Agreement (IA)
    - Project Order
    - Temporary Work Requests (TWR)

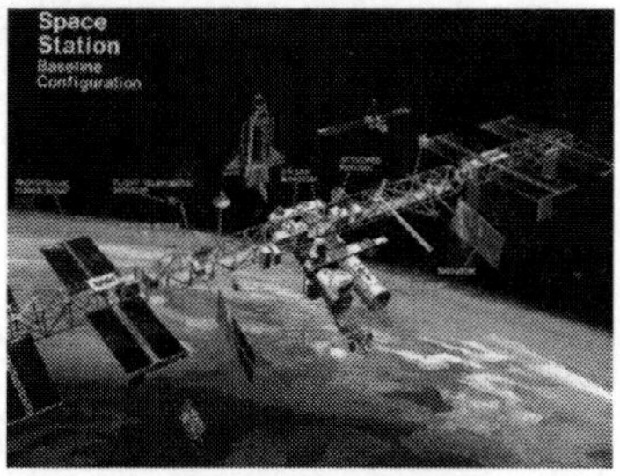

Partnering Components

Partnering Agreement (PA)

- Overarching agreement covering the contract period
- Defines roles & responsibilities among the players
- Provides for CORE and non-CORE workloads
- Defines terms & conditions that apply to all Implementation Agreements (IAs) and Temporary Work Requests (TWRs)
- Describes the IA, Project Order, and TWR processes
- Pricing methods
- Funding
- Tasking by Contractor
- Acceptance by Contractor and payment by Government
- Signed by responsible Government and Contractor management

Implementation Agreement (IA)

- Specifies summary level work content for a fiscal year, with planning IAs for five years
- IA(s) to be appended to the Partnering Agreement for each major work area
- Software maintenance & PME repair IAs included initially
- TRD and top level flow charts
- Firm costing of fixed work packages and hourly rates for other work
- Relies on Project Order issued by Government to reserve funds for estimated TWR activity -- issued periodically
- Developed by Government and Contractor
- Approved by Government and Contractor management

Partnering Components

Project Order (PO)

- Execution enabling document
- Incorporates negotiated PA & IA by reference
- Enables TWR issuance and performance
- Provides funding for estimated workload for stated period
- Provides authorization, subject to issuance of TWRs
- Issued by Government

Temporary Work Requests (TWR)

- Contractor workload ordering vehicle
- Unilateral Contractor document to Government for firm cost workloads
- Bilateral Contractor and Government document for other orders

Business Case Analyses Approach

Determine high cost driver & potential high cost driver systems with significant improvement potential

Define a "solution set" that meets the requirements for at least equivalent performance at equivalent or lower cost

Review reliability and maintenance cost change trends over time

Assess key logistics cost driving issues such as false failure indications, premature failures after repair and turn around time

Identify technology or repair Process changes that could provide solutions to reliability or impending obsolescence problems

38th Annual SOLE Conference: August 12-14, 2003 *Dr. William T. Baylis* *Slide 21*

PBL - New Programs

PBL New Programs

PBL strategies should start during the concept exploration phase and evolve as an integral part of the weapons systems development and procurement

Payoff New Programs

- Contractor can develop Tech Data to support the program concept
- Explore Commercial Off the Shelf (COTS) and Commercial commonality investment
- Explore Obsolescence avoidanc
- No significant investments in infrastructure

38th Annual SOLE Conference: August 12-14, 2003 *Dr. William T. Baylis* *Slide 22*

PBL - Legacy Programs

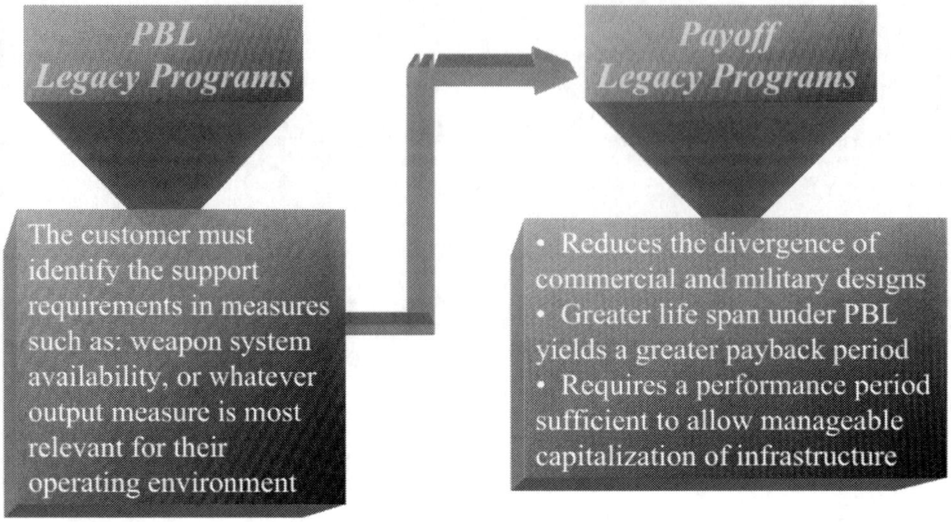

38th Annual SOLE Conference: August 12-14, 2003 *Dr. William T. Baylis* *Slide 23*

TSPR Process

- **Common questions**
  - **Legacy**
  - **New Acquisition**
  - **What tasks are to be done**
  - **Who should do it**
  - **Cost improvements**
  - **Performance improvements**

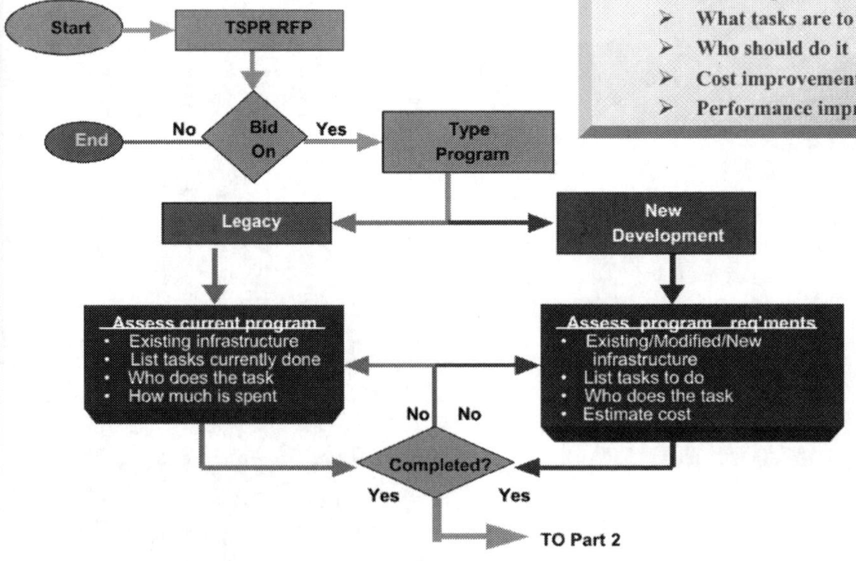

38th Annual SOLE Conference: August 12-14, 2003 *Dr. William T. Baylis* *Slide 24*

TSPR Process

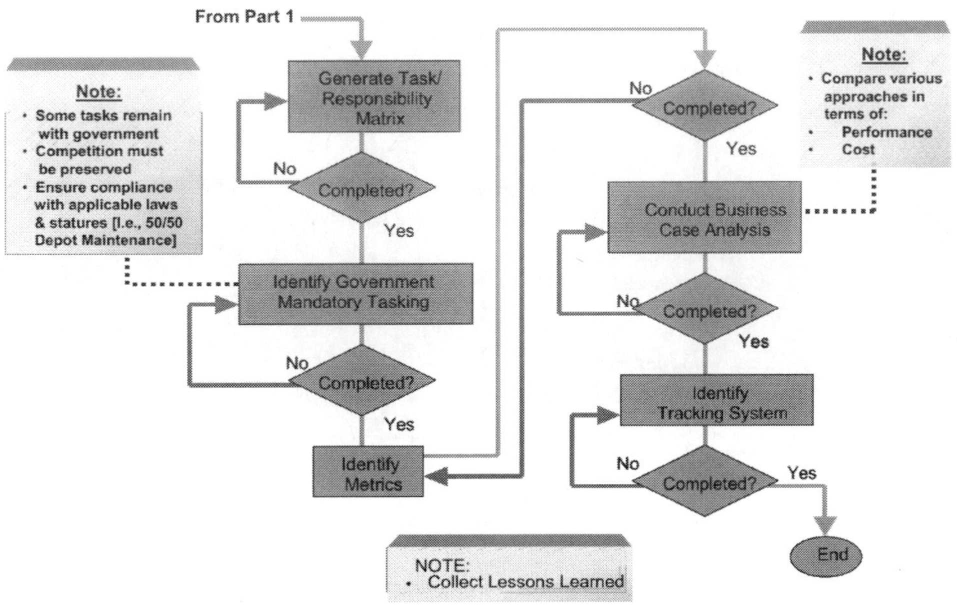

38th Annual SOLE Conference: August 12-14, 2003 Dr. William T. Baylis Slide 25

Partnering Work Breakdown

TASK	PRIME TASK	SUBCONT. TO GOV'T	LEGACY CONTRACT	NEW CONTRACT	REMARKS
PRIME MISSION EQUIPMENT (PME)					
Repairs:	X				
Communications Subsystem		X	X		
Operations and Control Subsystem	X	X	X		
Radar Subsystem	X	X	X		
Data Subsystem		X			
COTS	X				
Field Service Representative (FSR) Support	X				
Deployment Support	X				
PME Depot Screening	X				
TPS Screening		X			
Back-shop Screening	X				
Retrofit/Upgrades	X				
COMBS	X				

38th Annual SOLE Conference: August 12-14, 2003 Dr. William T. Baylis Slide 26

Responsibility Matrix

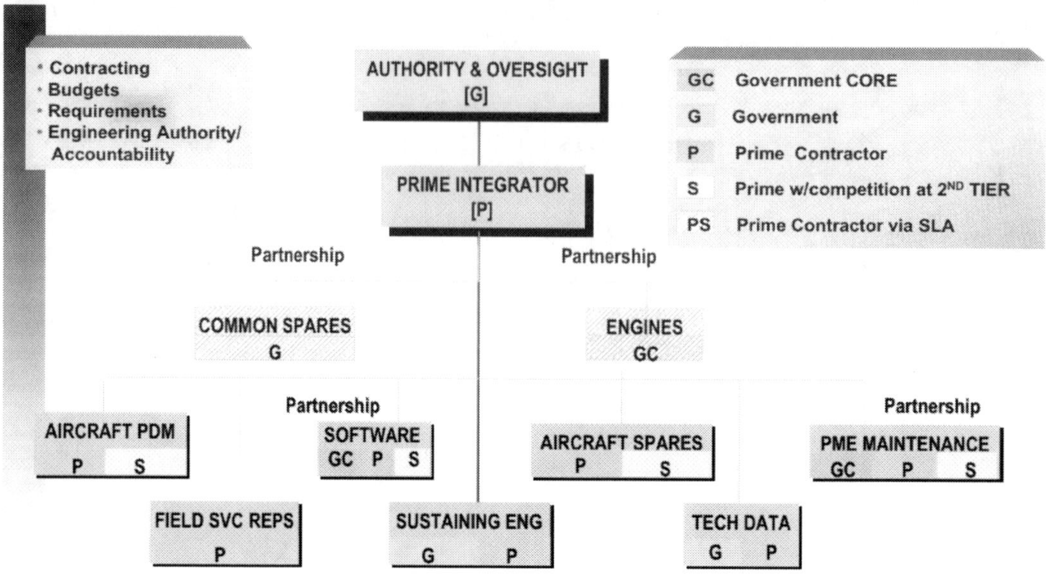

38th Annual SOLE Conference: August 12-14, 2003 *Dr. William T. Baylis* *Slide 27*

Summary - Important Considerations

- Avoid Being Drawn into Endless Budget Drills
- Forming a Good Relationship with Team is Essential
  - Professional Relationship, Confidence in Your Team, Non Threatening
  - Long Range Agreement, Partnering Agreement, Implementation Agreement, Service Level Agreements (SLAs), are the Result, Not the Beginning
  - Strong Team Including Outside Support is Essential
- New Approach to Award Fee and Award Term Concept Need to Be Documented
- Attention to Detail and Exhaustive "What Ifs" Lead to Visionary Contract Clauses
- Best Value Wins – But Only if Broad Support is Achieved

38th Annual SOLE Conference: August 12-14, 2003 *Dr. William T. Baylis* *Slide 28*

Maritime Security Legislation/Initiatives: How are they affecting the Supply Chain

MIDN Aaron Lewis
MIDN John Melogy
MIDN Brendan Smith

Executive Summary:

After September 11th, Congress implemented three major programs in order to respond to terrorist threats worldwide. These programs/initiatives are designed to make the global supply chain safer, without compromising efficiency. This goal has been achieved with varying degrees of success. The effectiveness of these programs/initiatives and their effect of the overall global supply chain and the global business environment will be discussed.

The three programs that will be discussed are the Maritime Transportation Security Act of 2002, the Container Security Initiative, and the Customs Trade Partnership against Terrorism, and their impact on the freight supply chain. These three programs are interrelated, and their purposes are to ensure the safety and security of cargo that enters the U.S. from overseas. It is clear that for successful homeland security, both the United States and foreign governments will have to work closely together implementing these initiatives. This paper will explain the background of each program, its goals, and how it affects the supply chain.

Introduction

In the wake of the 9/11 terrorist attacks our lawmakers and policymakers have been passing legislation and instituting programs that are intended to make our ports and our supply chain safer. This is due to only 2% of all containers being inspected upon arrival within the United States. It was realized that there was no way to truly track what was entering the United States. Originally security was focused on piracy, drugs, contraband, and other smuggling activities. With the realization that weapons of mass destruction could be shipped into a major city within containers, security measures were refocused. Many initiatives and proposals were quickly conceived in response to this new threat. At this time neither the practicability, feasibility nor the potential effect on global commerce of these diverse proposals can be taken into account due to the programs still being in the infancy stage. Three major initiatives, C-TPAT, CSI, and the Maritime Security Act of 2002, will be discussed, focusing on their intentions, goals, and the effects that they are having on the global supply chain, as well as the way that they may shape the future direction of port, container, and supply-chain security.

C-TPAT

In order to achieve an environment where security and efficiency are paramount, you have to start with the government forming an alliance with industry. This is what C-TPAT provides, a more secure internal port environment. C-TPAT stands for the "Customs Trade Partnership against Terrorism." C-TPAT is a program developed by the U.S. Department of Homeland Security's Customs & Border Protection Division (CBP). The program is a joint government-business initiative that is intended to build cooperative relationships between the Customs Bureau and private companies that will strengthen overall supply chain and border security.

The Customs Bureau has come to the realization that the only way to effectively secure the supply chain and our borders is by working more closely with the private sector. According to the U.S. CBP:

C-TPAT recognizes that US Customs can provide the highest level of security only through close cooperation with the ultimate owners of the supply chain, importers, carriers, brokers, warehouse operators and manufacturers. Through this initiative, Customs is asking businesses to ensure the integrity of their security practices and communicate their security guidelines to their business partners within the supply chain.[1]

The Customs Bureau is encouraging all companies to register as C-TPAT members. There is a detailed and lengthy process for registering, but Customs promises a set of benefits for members. The registration process involves first conducting a "comprehensive self-assessment of supply chain security using the C-TPAT security guidelines." These guidelines were jointly developed by Customs and individuals from the private sector. These guidelines encompass the areas of:

- procedural security
- physical security
- personnel security
- education and training
- access controls
- manifest procedures
- conveyance security.[2]

After the self-assessment is completed, the company must submit a supply chain security profile questionnaire to Customs. This will allow Customs identify problems with the company's security measures. After the questionnaire is analyzed, Customs works with the company to "develop and implement a program to enhance security throughout the supply chain in accordance with C-TPAT guidelines."[3]

This program is voluntary, so in order to get companies to participate, Customs must show the companies that there are benefits to being in the program. Customs lists several benefits to participating companies. Among these are:

- reduced number of inspections (reduced border times)
- assigned account manager at Customs
- access to the C-TPAT membership list
- eligibility for account-based processes (bimonthly/monthly payments)
- emphasis on self-policing, not Customs verifications.

There are certainly some potential drawbacks for companies. According to the Journal of Commerce, more than 1,500 importers have signed a "memorandum of understanding" to secure their internal supply chains under C-TPAT. The journal quotes Christopher D. Perry, an attorney who specializes in customs matters, as advising shippers "not to rush into C-TPAT without a formal plan in place." He said that it takes an average importer six months to perform a risk analysis of its supply chain and to develop an action plan. He warned that importers who don't have a well thought out plan when they sign up for C-TPAT are inviting Customs to impose a plan on them. He says: "You are assuming obligations Customs wouldn't impose on you otherwise." This means that if the company doesn't sign up for C-TPAT, Customs can't force them to have a security plan imposed on them, but after they do it is likely that they will. He also

---

[1] http://www.customs.ustreas.gov/xp/cgov/import/commercial_enforcement/ctpat/fact_sheet.xml

[2] Journal of Commerce. May 19, 2003. "Exel in C-TPAT Program."

[3] http://www.customs.ustreas.gov/xp/cgov/import/commercial_enforcement/ctpat

questions the benefits of being a C-TPAT member, especially for low-risk importers. He asks, "If you are a low-risk importer already, do you become low-low risk under C-TPAT?"[4] Companies need to evaluate the pros and cons of joining this program, and not just sign up for it without analyzing what it will mean for their business. If a company already has a good relationship with Customs, and is subject to few searches, what incentive does it really have to join? The fear is that Customs may begin harassing companies that are not members of C-TPAT, just because of that fact. This also raises the question of the costs of implementation. Why would a business want to change its business practices if it has to foot the entire cost? The question is who is really benefiting from C-TPAT? The consumer, government, and the business itself all benefit in some degree, so where the cost lies is an issue that needs to be discussed.

Fortunately there is a brighter side to C-TPAT. According to the Under Secretary of BTS, C-TPAT will tighten the borders without impeding the legitimate flow of commerce. There are also hidden benefits to the internal security of ports. By complying with the new program, the port site becomes more secure, therefore making it an undesirable target for theft. It becomes more difficult for thieves who prefer easy targets. The personnel security assures person having access to cargo are not terrorists. If persons with questionable backgrounds know of the hiring process and security check, they are less likely to apply. Illegal aliens will not be inadvertently hired, therby reducing INS sanctions. With the new integrity of the work force, lower turnover rates will occur, saving money on training. C-TPAT also streamlines the paperwork process, making the system more efficient. These are just a few of the benefits. Yes, there is an initial capital investment, but the return in the long run greatly outweighs the costs.

Because of the United States' position and power in the world economy, this program is bound to have wide ranging effects on the global supply chain. Because of the fact that Customs has little direct influence over foreign companies, Customs has decided to seek the participation of the largest U.S. importers and Exporters in C-TPAT. The reason for this is that "It's easier and quicker for Customs to ask major U.S. importer to certify that its overseas suppliers are loading containers in a secure environment to negotiate for that assurance with a foreign government, which may not want to make U.S. concerns a priority."[5]

Customs is eventually going expect foreign companies who do business in the U.S. to become members of C-TPAT (A British firm, Exel, recently signed up after being asked by Customs). The key to making the system work is going to be cooperation, and above all trust between Customs, foreign companies, and foreign governments. The Journal of Commerce says of cooperation and trust: "None of this is going to happen unless everyone begins trusting each other more. How many foreign nations will allow the U.S. free rein to validate factory sites on their soil? Practically speaking, there are too many factories to validate. Customs will have to trust its foreign partners to certify the security of outbound cargo...."[6] This program is going to take a great deal of diplomatic skill and tact to develop overseas, but the rewards in terms of increased U.S. security at home could be worth the effort.

---

[4] Journal of Commerce. June 2, 2003. "Radar Screen."
[5] Journal of Commerce. April 29, 2003. "Pushing out the Borders."
[6] Journal of Commerce. May 21, 2003. "Washington View: Who do you trust?"

CSI

As C-TPAT is an alliance with industry, CSI is more focused on forming an alliance with ports. CSI mainly focuses on a containers port of origin. Container Security Initiative, CSI, is a program designated to strengthen port and maritime security without interrupting trade flows. Homeland security is a major concern since September 11th. Due to this, container security has become a major issue in the United States Congress. Containerization is an indispensable, but very vulnerable link in the global supply chain. Ensuring security of the containerization/intermodal system is essential due to the fact that 90% of the world's cargo moves by ship. Approximately 75% of all general cargo is containerized. Each day 16,000 containers enter the United States, with on 2%, 320 containers per day being checked. Therefore CSI expands the territorial borders of the United States in order to reduce the risks of a container threat. What will be the effects of this new program on the supply chain, and will it cause a slowdown in port operations in both loading and discharging ports?

The Container Security Initiative consists of four core elements. The first element is establishing security criteria to identify high-risk containers. Customs is not able to inspect every single container that moves through our ports. At the present time only about 2% of containers are inspected. As an alternative, Customs must determine which containers are coming from higher risk countries where security is known to be poor. Element number two is pre-screening containers before they arrive at U.S. ports; also known at the 24-hour rule. This is done overseas in cooperation with foreign governments to ensure that most, if not all containers have been properly checked for weapons, drugs, and other contraband that would be detrimental to the security of the United States. The third element is using technology to pre-screen high-risk containers. Technologies such as X-ray and gamma-ray scanners are new tools being used to screen containers for illegal weapons. Unfortunately, these methods are very expensive and can slow down the trade process overall. The final element of the CSI is developing and using smart and secure containers. A smart container is one that can tell you if the lock has been tampered with and if it's been opened since the last loading or discharge port. These four elements are essential to the CSI program and our overall security as a nation.[7] These elements have been implemented in the 20 Mega-ports around the world, as well as other minor ports who are active participants in the program.

CSI was launched in January 2002, and 18 of the top 20 megaports have agreed to join CSI and are at various stages of implementation. These megaports are points of passage for approximately two-thirds of containers shipped to the United States. They include: Hong Kong, Shanghai, Singapore, Rotterdam, Pusan, Bremerhaven, Tokyo, Genoa, Yantian, Antwerp, Nagoya, Le Havre, Hamburg, La Spezia, Felixstowe, Algeciras, Kobe, and Yokohama. Having CSI implemented in these ports should make the movement of cargo containers much more secure.

Since February 2002, the 24 hour rule has gone into effect. Typically, cargo sits on the pier for several days waiting to be exported. With this down time CSI requires NVOCC's (Non-Vessel Operating Cargo Carrier) and VOCC's (Vessel Operating Cargo Carrier), who are not already, to register with the FMC. The vessels will enter their container's cargos into AMS (Automated Manifest System), 24-hours prior to the container boarding a vessel, inbound to the United States. This allows the waiting time at

---

[7] http://usinfo.state.gov/topical/pol/terror/02022505.htm

the port of export to be used for inspecting, so when the container arrives in the U.S. it can be immediately released. The containers deemed high risk will be targeted. It is impracticable to search all containers, so only containers deemed high risk will be checked before leaving the departure port.[8] One of the many questions that arise in implementing this system in foreign ports is who will pay for the costs of implementing and running the CSI program.

In the United States, the importer may have to pay the cost of moving, inspecting, and unloading the containers. Because of the tremendous volume of containers that arrive in the U.S. every year, it isn't practical for the US government to cover the entire costs of securing our intermodal system. The government simply cannot, or is not willing to, subsidize the private sector in order to meet all of the requirements.[9] The private sector will have to "absorb" many of these costs. Companies will grudgingly pay for this, but CSI may eventually bring benefits, such as greater efficiency and faster operations. This is perhaps a long way down the road. As with any new system it is not yet determined who will pay the costs for sure. The costs should be divided amongst those who reap the benefits of the system. So who benefits the most?

Overseas, the host country will determine who pays the direct cost of screening and unloading the containers, while improving security.[10] This directly leads to the cost of X-ray and high technological equipment. Many of the countries already have large container screening machines. In fact, some ports already have extremely sophisticated detection technology in operation. Customs is even providing names manufacturers for the CSI host country to pursue procuring equipment.[11] The cost of this will lie in how that country's government determines it necessary. All these factors of CSI tie together in improving the global supply chain and security.

CSI will affect the global supply chain and security by increasing the ability to intercept terrorist weapons smuggled in containers. Also, it will provide more efficient flow of cargo between ports and will make it easier for US customs to only check high risk containers by pre-determining high risk containers at the port of origin. This allows low-risk containers to move out of the discharge port quickly. This program heavily affects the supply chain because it begins at the loading port. This is in sync with Customs' mission of "pushing out our borders." CSI is truly a global program, and it will not only affect the U.S., but also the rest of the world. Right now we are in the early stages of CSI, but we feel that in 5-10 years from now, the program will be in full operation in 50 ports worldwide and will be an effective tool in fighting terrorism. It will also increase the flow of containers across all borders of participating nations. CSI is seen as a key part to vastly improving global trade security in the near future.

Maritime Security Act of 2002

The Maritime Security Act of 2002, also known as the Hollings Bill, provides for a national system for securing the Marine Transportation System for the first time. The Act calls for the Secretary of Transportation (SOT) to conduct an assessment of all

[8] http://www.customs.ustreas.gov/xp/cgov/newsroom/press_releases/03122003.xml
[9] The Journal of commerce: "Make current Box security Work." 21 May 2003. p.22
[10] http://www.customs.ustreas.gov/xp/cgov/newsroom/press_releases/03122003.xml
[11] The Journal of commerce: "Make current Box security Work." 21 May 2003. p.23

vessels and facilities on or near the water to identify those at high risk of involvement in a security incident.[12] This means an incident resulting in a significant loss of life, environmental damage, transportation system disruption, or economic disruption. Once the vulnerable infrastructure is identified, and interim security measures have been adopted, the Coast Guard will conduct a more detailed vulnerability assessment of vessels and facilities.

Objective

The bill also mandates a National Maritime Transportation Security Plan and regional Area Maritime Transportation Security Plans to be developed by the Coast Guard to deter a transportation security incident. Area plans will also be produced to encompass contingency responses to potential terrorist attacks.[13]

Recently the IMO released the ISPS Code which now takes precedence over the aforementioned Act. MTSA has requirements above and beyond the ISPS Code, however lacks funding. Therefore the MTSA has implemented the ISPS Code which will:

- enable the detection and deterrence of security threats within an international framework
- establish roles and responsibilities
- enable collection and exchange for assessing security
- provides a methodology for assessing security
- ensure that adequate security measures are in place.

This will also require the ship and port facility staffs to do the following:

- gather and assess information
- maintain communication protocols
- restrict access; prevent the introduction of unauthorized weapons, etc
- provide the means to raise alarms
- put in place vessel and port security plans; and ensure training and drills are conducted.[14]

For the first time ever, all ports, facilities, and vessels must have comprehensive security plans and incident response plans based on detailed Coast Guard vulnerability assessments and security recommendations.[15] The plans will be submitted in conjunction with the Coast Guard's review of them. They must be IMO approved and all facilities will operate under the approved security plans.

Because of these plans, local port security committees will be able to better coordinate the efforts of federal, state, local, and private law enforcement agencies, including intelligence, FBI, Customs, Immigration, and the Coast Guard.

The US Coast Guard will develop secure areas in ports as part of their security plans and limit access to these areas through background checks and a transportation security identification card. Firearms and other weapons will be restricted. Background checks will be conducted for employees working in security-sensitive areas and seafarers

---

[12] http://www.netlobby.com/s1214_summary.htm
[13] http://www.blankrome.com
[14] http://www.lr.org/market_sector/marine/maritime-security/what_is_ISPS_code.htm
[15] http://www.littleriverbooks.com/entry-0.htm

will be required by to carry internationally acceptable identification.[16]

Funding

A grant program for fair and equitable allocations to port authorities, waterfront facility operators, and State and local agencies to provide security infrastructure and services will be established by direction of Congress. Grants for various types of security upgrades have been made since September 11, 2001. This also authorizes grants necessary to help recipients comply with the federal security requirements. The legislation requires the Administration to propose funding levels for seaport security programs and mandates annual reports outlining compliance with the security mandates.

$90 million in grants for research and development will be awarded to develop methods to increase the ability of the U.S. Customs Service to inspect merchandise carried on any vessel arriving in the US; develop nuclear detection equipment, and improve tags and seals used on shipping containers, including smart sensors. $33 million for the development of security training and certification of federal, state, and private security personnel will be granted.[17] The program for training will be mandated by the SOT. Training will be provided at each of the six state maritime academies, The United States Merchant Marine Academy, and other security training schools.

A maritime intelligence system will be developed to collect and analyze information concerning vessels operating in US waters. This system will work with other agencies to collect and analyze crew, passengers, and cargo information. The reporting of crew members, passengers, and imported cargo to better track suspicious activity is expected to improve. All commercial vessels will be equipped with AIS, Automatic Identification System, when navigating on US waters, although this has not been implemented and probably won't be for at least several years.[18] AI is a system that identifies a vessel, their location, cargo, and displays this information on a radar screen. This is much like aviation radars that are used today. A long range vessel tracking system for vessels on international voyages that include US waters are also being implemented to track vessel movements.

A secure system of trade is forecasted by allowing for secure maritime borders and an efficient cargo transportation system. The United States and the users of the Marine Transportation System will benefit by having their vessels and cargoes screened, inspected, and cleared sooner and more efficiently.[19] The Transportation Oversight Board will establish a program to enhance the physical security of cargo containers, including container seals and locks.

Antiterrorism measures maintained by foreign ports will be analyzed. Those ports that do not maintain effective antiterrorism measures will find their ships denied access to U.S. ports since they may be a security risk to international maritime commerce. By not conforming to these new measures, there will be a decreased and more inefficient supply chain. The act will ensure a safer and more productive world trade system.
Initially the effects of the Maritime Security Act will may raise costs and slow down cargo movement as the bugs in the system are worked out. It is hoped that with all the

---

[16] http://www.iss-riomar.com/Maritime%20Security%20Act%20of%202002.htm
[17] http://www.ussailing.org/offshore/MTSA%20summary.pdf
[18] http://www.netlobby.com/s1214_summary.htm
[19] http://www.intercargo.org/news/pages/180.htm

provisions provided in the Act, facilities on board will begin to take precedent over facilities not onboard for cargo movements. Eventually most cargoes will be identified before they reach the United States, minimizing the terrorist threat.

Conclusions

In order for success in implementing these security initiatives worldwide, The US government and private sectors will have to work closely and diplomatically with foreign governments and companies. To do this, the owners of the supply chain must adopt technology such as x-ray machines, smart containers, RFID systems, and freely share information. This will give us a better way to understand what is actually in these containers that are passing through US borders. Many people have envisioned a seamless, streamlined global environment, where all traffic is monitored and communications are transparent to ensure the safety of all. A large, overarching international cargo monitoring system may or may not be realistic. The cost for a system like this would be high. Governments are reluctant to provide the billions and billions of dollars, and enact the mountains of legislation that it would take to implement such a system. Because of this, the solutions to our security problems must be cost-effective, because they will most likely be absorbed by the private sector. Private industry may have to take more responsibility on security to prevent the government from enacting harsher security laws. The downside to security is that it may restrict trade, cost more money, and slow down cargo movement. That is why the private companies must work with the US and foreign governments for these programs to be successful.

<u>**Works Cited**</u>

"Exel in C-TPAT Program." Journal of Commerce. May 19, 2003.

"Make Current Box Security Work." The Journal of Commerce: May 21, 2003.

"Pushing out the Borders." Journal of Commerce. April 29, 2003.

"Radar Screen." Journal of Commerce. June 2, 2003.

"Washington View: Who do you trust?" Journal of Commerce. May 21, 2003.

Internet Sources

Customs & Border Protection. **"Commercial Enforcement." Online Posting.**
http://www.customs.ustreas.gov/xp/cgov/import/commercial_enforcement/ctpat

Customs Headquarters, "Fact Sheet: Container Security Initiative Guards America, Global Commerce from Terrorist Threat." Online Posting.
http://www.customs.ustreas.gov/xp/cgov/newsroom/press_releases/03122003.xml

Hansen, Steve. "Port & Maritime Security Legislation Approved by U.S. House." Online Posting. http://www.house.gov/transportation/press/press2002/release386.html

Holland, Haight. "U.S. Maritime Transportation Security Act of 2002." Online Posting
http://www.littleriverbooks.com/entry-0.htm

Intercargo. "U.S. Maritime Transportation Security Act of 2002." Online Posting.
http://www.intercargo.org/news/pages/180.htm

ISS-RioMar, "Maritime Security Act of 2002 (from SALA)." Online Posting.
http://www.iss-riomar.com/Maritime%20Security%20Act%20of%202002.htm

Lloyd's Register Americas, Inc. "Maritime Security – What is the ISPS Code?" Online Posting.
http://www.lr.org/market_sector/marine/maritime-security/what_is_ISPS_code.htm

Marlowe & Company, "Legislative Summary: Maritime Transportation Security Act of 2002 (S. 1214)." Online Posting.
http://www.netlobby.com/s1214_summary.htm

Nolan, Dan. "Maritime Transportation Security Act." Online Posting.
http://www.ussailing.org/offshore/MTSA%20summary.pdf

U.S. Customs Service, "Fact Sheet: U.S. Customs Service's Container Security Initiative." Online Posting. http://usinfo.state.gov/topical/pol/terror/02022505.htm

TECHNICAL DATA KNOWLEDGE MANAGEMENT (TDKM)
Transforming the Delivery and Use of Logistic Technical Data

William J. Rumschlag

Annually, thirty thousand individual CD-ROMs are distributed to seven hundred sites, both afloat and ashore, in support of U. S. Navy submarines. While an improvement over hard copy products, experience has shown that instead of the end users being buried in reams of paper, they are now buried in piles of CD-ROM's. The creation, testing, distribution, and installation of CD-ROM's delays receipt of new data, consumes resources, and requires labor at the receiving end. CD-ROM's have been found on a ship tucked away in a corner - the same way paper used to be found tucked away. The average 'time-to-market' for a change to a technical manual on CD-ROM can be as long as ninety days. TDKM represents a major change in how the Navy manages and distributes its technical data, reducing the time-to-market by as much as ninety percent. The objective of the TDKM Project is to deploy a technical data knowledge management system to deliver, maintain and dynamically tailor via the Internet the deployed digital technical data for both operational units and individual users. The focus of the TDKM Project is the entire supplier chain for technical data from the original supplier to the actual fleet end user.

1. INTRODUCTION. The objective of this project is to deploy a field implementation of a technical data knowledge management system to dynamically tailor and maintain the deployed digital technical data for both operational units and individual users. The Technical Data Knowledge Management TDKM System is built upon an Integrated Data Environment (IDE) designed with the potential to provide a uniform content management and knowledge distribution environment for the entire Navy and other Department of Defense (DoD) agencies. The TDKM System features an advanced content management and control system architecture allowing for the management, versioning, distribution, and control of electronic documents at the sub-document, information object level. Central to the TDKM System is a Warfare Community Knowledge Management System built upon commercially available enterprise management software, serving as a knowledge broker between the fleet end user digital library and the various content repositories maintained by and for the Navy shore establishment. The user interface to the data in the library is managed and controlled by web-based management software and the user's selected portal. TDKM "snaps-in" to existing user portals through a portlet and conforms to the selected portal's presentation standards. The web-based management software permits the warfare community manager in the field (e.g., Fleet Type Commander), who best knows the users needs, to update the user presentation on a daily basis and to refine and customize the user profile based on what the user needs to know.

The focus of the overall TDKM project is the entire supplier chain for technical data knowledge from the original document and other technical data supplier to the actual fleet site. It solves the problems associated with CD-ROM distribution, i.e., the cost and time of creating, testing, distributing, and installing CD's. In addition, by managing data at a more granular level, the TDKM System lends itself to the integration of technical data and training product development by better supporting data re-use and repurposing. There are three primary environments that make up the TDKM System – the Wholesaler, the Broker, and the Retailer. The interfaces between these environments have been automated to effect seamless access and information flow from one to the other.

- **Wholesaler Environment / Document Operations Center (DOC).** A central technical data repository, featuring an advanced content management and control system architecture allowing for the management, versioning, and control of electronic documents at the sub-document, information object level.

- **Broker Environment / Warfare Community Knowledge Manager.** Provides the core knowledge management functions, access to the technical data in a shore-based environment and distribution services for the fleet environment. The Broker builds, stores, and maintains profiles describing the technical data requirements for users and also constructs and maintains the map (or indices) to the content data stores. It pulls the necessary data objects from the distributed content management systems, assembles a user digital technical data library (or update to the existing library,) and pushes this library or update to the user site.

- **Retailer Environment / Shipboard Knowledge Manager.** Provides the fleet end user seamless, on-line access to the technical data in both connected and disconnected modes, as well as administrative management functions.

2. <u>WHOLESALER ENVIRONMENT.</u> (See Figure 1.) The Wholesaler Environment is made up of several individual services that function together to manage and store the system technical data. These services can be considered separate entities, but they must communicate between each other to provide the warfare community with properly formatted and maintained integrated technical data. A general description of the Document Operations Center (DOC) is discussed in the following paragraphs.

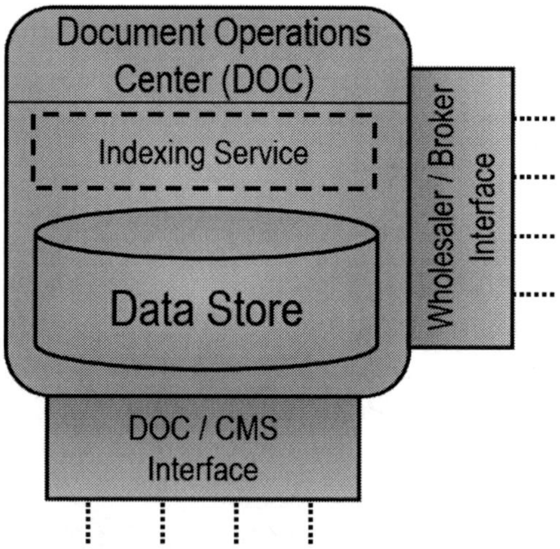

Figure 1 - Wholesaler

NOTE: While outside of the TDKM System, a typical state-of-the-art Content Management System (CMS) provides for a standardized document management and authoring/development solution, covering various data formats, supporting re-purposing of the data to deliver multiple products, and supporting changes and updates to technical manuals at the content component levels. General requirements for the CMS are not within the scope of this document; however, since the technical data being created, edited and approved within the CMS is subsequently provided to the TDKM System as published data, it will need to meet certain requirements prior to being distributed through the TDKM System. Those specific requirements that the TDKM System require of the CMS are addressed here. The underlying data structure and metadata requirements are described in Sections 2.1.1 and 2.1.2 below.

2.1. Document Operations Center (DOC). The DOC is the primary repository for the documents needed to populate the end-user digital libraries. This data is made up of the completed and rendered technical data after approval and publishing. The specific design of the DOC is outside the scope of this document. Communications with the DOC is accomplished using Hyper Text Transfer Protocol (HTTP) or Hyper Text Transfer Protocol Secure sockets (HTTPS) over an Internet Protocol (IP) based network. Key parts of the DOC are described in more detail below.

2.1.1. Data Structure. A Content Management System or equivalent will supply the documents used by the TDKM System. This section discusses how the documents and various levels of information will be handled by the system. Refer to Figure 2 below.

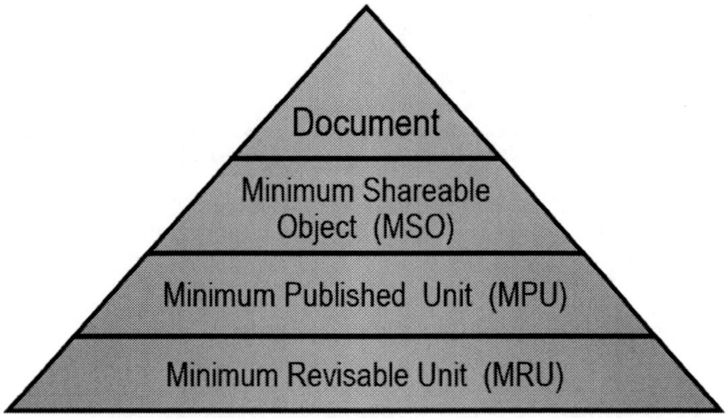

Figure 2 – Document Object Hierarchy

- **Document / Technical Manual Identification Number (TMIN) Level.** Typically tracked in an external configuration management system such as the Technical Data Management Information System or Configuration Data Managers Database - Open Architecture. (TDMIS is the technical manual life-cycle tracking system used by the Navy. CDMD-OA, formerly SCLSIS, is the Navy's configuration management system for ships.) Documents are made up of one or more MSOs.

- **Minimum Sharable Object (MSO) Level.** Defined by Subject Matter Expert (SME). Use the persistent identifier contained within the delivered document to identify the individual MSOs. The TDKM configuration file details the MSOs that make up the document and the files that comprise each MSO. The concept of the MSO is new to technical manuals, the basis of which was the Shareable Content Object Reference Model (SCORM) requirements defined by the training community. An MSO is comprised of one or more MPUs.

- **Minimum Published Unit (MPU) Level.** These are the individual files that make up the published document. The files can be in various formats such as HTML, XML, PDF, JPG, MPEG, etc. The MPU is comprised of one or more MRUs.

- **Minimum Revisable Unit (MRU) Level.** These are the pieces of the document that are maintained in the CMS and are the lowest/smallest object used in the authoring environment. There currently is not a requirement to manage at this level in the TDKM System since it is oriented around publishing and distribution rather than the actual creation of the source data.

2.1.2 Metadata Requirements. The below eXtensible Markup Language (XML) Document Type Definition (DTD) lists the metadata used by the TDKM System. (This is a partial DTD in that is does not list elements that are not exposed to the TDKM System – i.e., those only used in a Content Management System (CMS) or by the training community.) These fields form the foundation of the TDKM Configuration File that is used to move MPUs throughout the system.

```
<!-- <!DOCTYPE tdkm_meta_data_fields [ -->

<!-- Publication Status. Values are Under Development, Final Issue, Superseded, Cancelled,
Foreign Vessel and Other. -->
<!ELEMENT td_pub_status EMPTY>
<!ATTLIST td_pub_status status (ud|fi|su|ca|fv|other) #REQUIRED other_status CDATA #IMPLIED>

<!-- Technical Data Applicability. Identifies the applicability to a class, hull, etc. -->
<!ELEMENT  td_applicability (#PCDATA)>

<!-- Technical Data Publication Number. Field may be broken down to populate other fields. -->
<!ELEMENT td_pubno   (#PCDATA)>

<!-- Technical Data Stock Number. -->
<!ELEMENT td_stockno (#PCDATA)>

<!-- Technical Data Former (Previous) Publication Number. -->
<!ELEMENT td_fmr_pubno (#PCDATA)>

<!-- Date the Technical Data was originally issued. -->
<!ELEMENT td_original_pub_dt (#PCDATA)>

<!-- Technical Data Revision Number. -->
<!ELEMENT rev_no (#PCDATA)>

<!-- Technical Data Change Level. -->
<!ELEMENT change_level (#PCDATA)>

<!-- Number assigned to an alteration.  Types can be a ECP, Ship Alt, Work Package. -->
<!ELEMENT  assign_alter EMPTY>
<!ATTLIST assign_alter no CDATA #REQUIRED type CDATA #IMPLIED>

<!-- A number assigned for each alteration.  Used to drive applicability. -->
<!ELEMENT  assign_alter_ric_no EMPTY>
<!ATTLIST assign_alter_ric_no no CDATA #REQUIRED>

<!-- Title. Indicates the subject of the data or published unit. -->
<!ELEMENT td_title (#PCDATA)>

<!-- Type. Indicates type of data or published unit - Description, Operations, Maintenance.-->
<!ELEMENT pub_type (#PCDATA)>

<!-- Expanded Ship Work Authorization Breakdown Structure. -->
<!ELEMENT eswbs_cd  (#PCDATA)>
```

```
<!-- System Designator. Used to identify system/component as text. -->
<!ELEMENT sys_designator (#PCDATA)>

<!-- Contains the 4-character Standard Subject Classification Code (SSCC) for the system. -->
<!ELEMENT  sssc EMPTY>
<!ATTLIST sssc four-digit-code CDATA #REQUIRED>

<!-- Effectivity Information. Used to narrow effectivity searches such as by Model Number,
Serial Number, etc. -->
<!ELEMENT  effectivity_info (single | boundedrange | unboundedrange)+ >
<!ATTLIST effectivity_info effectivity_type CDATA #REQUIRED>

<!-- Single effectivity number such as "Tail Number X" -->
<!ELEMENT single   EMPTY>
<!ATTLIST single number CDATA #REQUIRED>

<!-- Range of effectivity numbers such as "Tail Number X through Y" -->
<!ELEMENT boundedrange   EMPTY>
<!ATTLIST boundedrange lowrange CDATA #REQUIRED highrange CDATA #REQUIRED>

<!-- Unbounded range of effectivity numbers such as "Tail Number X and Up" -->
<!ELEMENT unboundedrange  EMPTY>
<!ATTLIST unboundedrange lowrange CDATA #REQUIRED>

<!-- Security Code. Used to indicate Unclassified, Classified, Secret, and Top Secret. -->
<!ELEMENT  sc_cd EMPTY>
<!ATTLIST sc_cd code (u | c | s | ts) 'u'>

<!-- Technical Data Special Handling Information. -->
<!ELEMENT  special_handling (#PCDATA)>
<!ATTLIST special_handling
        COMSEC                       (YES|NO) "NO"     NATO          (YES|NO) "NO"
        SCI                          (YES|NO) "NO"     SAPs          (YES|NO) "NO"
        SIOP                         (YES|NO) "NO"     SIOP_ESI      (YES|NO) "NO"
        NNPI                         (YES|NO) "NO"     RD            (YES|NO) "NO"
        CNWDI                        (YES|NO) "NO"     FRD           (YES|NO) "NO"
        FOUO                         (YES|NO) "NO"     SBU           (YES|NO) "NO"
        DEA_SENSITIVE_INFORMATION    (YES|NO) "NO"     DoD_UCNI      (YES|NO) "NO"
        SENSITIVE_INFORMATION        (YES|NO) "NO"     FGI           (YES|NO) "NO"
        NOFORN                       (YES|NO) "NO"     ORCON         (YES|NO) "NO"
        PROPIN                       (YES|NO) "NO"     REL_TO        (YES|NO) "NO" >

<!-- Distribution Statement to indicate the type as A, B, C, D, E, F, or X. -->
<!ELEMENT  distr_statement  (#PCDATA)>
<!ATTLIST distr_statement type (A | B | C | D | E | F | X) #REQUIRED >
```

2.2. Wholesaler / CMS Interface. The internet (or an intranet) provides a single point of access for the data providers. The interface provides a means to efficiently update the DOC from a remote location by a data provider. The data provider update feature takes into account updates by the local content manager. Updates are accomplished with a common uniform resource locator (URL) addressing scheme and uses the HTTP or HTTPS protocol. The update manager provides the necessary tools for the updating activity to properly configuration control the documents that are being added, modified or deleted.

2.3. Wholesaler / Broker Interface. The Secure Internet Protocol Router Network (SIPRNET) or Non-Secure Internet Protocol Router Network (NIPRNET) provides a single Internet Protocol (IP) point of access to the DOC for the downstream Broker Environment. This interface communicates via HTTP or HTTPS and returns self-describing eXtensible Markup Language (XML) data sets as a result of processing Simple Object Access Protocol (SOAP) messages from external applications.

NOTE: All TDKM System interfaces are built as web services based on SOAP, Web Services Definition Language (WSDL) and Transmission Control Protocol/Internet Protocol (TCP/IP) for data control and transmission.

2.4. Indexing Service. The Indexing Service provides a predefined XML-based indexing schema so the downstream Broker Environment can query and identify the available documents in the DOC. These queries are based on the available metadata contained in the TDKM Configuration file as described in Section 2.1.2 above.

3. BROKER ENVIRONMENT. (See Figure 3 below.) In order to perform its primary function, the Broker Environment builds, stores and maintains profiles describing the technical data requirements for users and also constructs and maintains the map (or indices) to the Wholesaler/Document Operations Center (DOC). Employing these instruments, it pulls the necessary data objects from the distributed Wholesaler/DOC; assembles a user digital technical data library collection (or update to the existing library) according to the needs identified by the user profile(s); and pushes this collection of technical data and/or incremental updates to the user site. The Broker Environment is made up of several individual services that function together to create the overall knowledge management function. These functions can be considered separate entities, but they must communicate between each other to provide the overall goal of providing the warfare community with an integrated technical data knowledge management function. They include the following:

- An overall Warfare Community Knowledge Manager and Administrator Service that identifies the user and knows where the applicable data that the user needs is located.

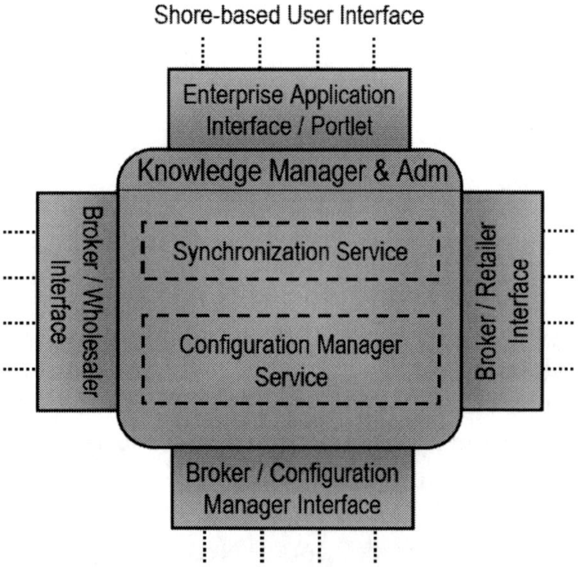

Figure 3 - Broker

- A Synchronization Service that updates the shipboard data sets with the most current data available.
- A Configuration Manager Service that provides the Knowledge Manager with the ability to identify which data is applicable to a specific user.
- A Shore-based User Interface portlet that communicates the appropriate information to and from the Warfare Community Knowledge Manager.
- Knowledge Manager Enterprise Application Interface (EAI)/Portlet

3.1. Warfare Community Knowledge Manager. The overall Warfare Community Knowledge Management System has two major implementations working in conjunction with each other. Typically, the Warfare Community Knowledge Manager is installed at a shore location and is administrated by the shore-based command; however, it is envisioned that these shore commands will be very close organizationally and physically to the operational units. The Warfare Community Knowledge Manager is considered the parent node for the Shipboard Knowledge Manager and each shipboard installation is considered a child node that can operate independently (disconnected) from the parent node but still relies on the parent node to determine the latest data available for the ship.

3.1.1. Knowledge Manager Administrator. The Knowledge Manager Administrator interface is web enabled to accommodate remote administration. The following administration functions are included.

- Synchronization Service Setup
- Configuration Manager Setup
- Database Update
- Enterprise Application Interface (EAI)/Portlet

3.3. Synchronization Service. The Synchronization Service performs data synchronization between the Wholesaler and Retailer Environments. The Synchronization Service identifies the Shipboard Knowledge Manager by the ship's profile. Based on the profile, the Synchronization Service identifies the applicable data necessary to make a complete digital library for the specific Shipboard Knowledge Manager. The Synchronization Service identifies the applicable updates by communicating with the Configuration Manager Service and Warfare Community Knowledge Manager, then doing a comparison of the identified updates with the current data set being controlled by the Shipboard Knowledge Manager. The Synchronization Service then compares all the identified updates to those available on the Wholesaler. The Synchronization Service locates and transfers all necessary and available data to the Shipboard Knowledge Manager and then performs the appropriate add, modify or delete actions necessary to completely synchronize the Shipboard Knowledge Manager's data library. Only the data applicable to the identified profiles is synchronized. Additionally, only the out-of-synch data will be transferred between the Warfare Community Knowledge Manager and the Shipboard Knowledge Manager, i.e., incremental update technology will be employed using byte level synchronization to mitigate bandwidth limitations for the units. If the Warfare Community Knowledge Manager's identified data already matches the Shipboard Knowledge Manager's data, the Synchronization Service does not transfer the data. The Synchronization Service also reports all actions to both the Warfare Community Knowledge Manager Administrator and Shipboard Knowledge Manager Administrator.

The Synchronization Service is able to operate in continuous mode with synchronization actions being performed on a predefined schedule based on system settings controlled by either the Shipboard or Warfare Community Knowledge Manager Administrators. Once data has been updated at the Wholesaler, the data becomes available for the Synchronization Service to update the Shipboard Knowledge Manager's data library. The Synchronization Service is also able to operate in both "push" and "pull" mode. Either the Shipboard Knowledge Manager or Warfare Community Knowledge Manager Administrator has the ability to initiate the manual execution of the Synchronization Service.

3.4. Configuration Manager Service. The Configuration Manager Service obtains information from various external configuration management systems such as the Technical Data Management Information System (TDMIS) or Configuration Data Managers Database - Open Architecture (CDMD-OA). The Configuration Manager Service uses this input to determine which data is applicable to a specific command, ship or user. (It is assumed that other services have similar configuration databases that could be tapped into to act as an input to this service.) Based on the level of granularity in which the data is tracked, the Configuration Manager Service identifies which MPUs, MSOs and documents are applicable to a specific profile based on input from the Warfare Community Knowledge Manager.

The Configuration Manager Service employs a web-based service and is able to identify and return data to an external application describing the technical documentation applicable to an individual class of ship, multiple classes of ships, and individual ship or multiple ships. The data contains the appropriate revisions/changes applicable to the requested unit. The Configuration Manager Service is able to return data sets that include large amounts of configuration data such as all of the technical manuals and drawings applicable to a specific ship or return the change/revision of a specific drawing or technical manual based on the technical document number and its applicable unit.

3.5. Shore-based User Interface. A web-based interface is included, which is used to provide the shore-based users the ability to communicate with the Warfare Community Knowledge Manager. All data accessed through the Shore-based User Interface is located in the appropriate Wholesaler or command-specific information located locally at the Warfare Community Knowledge Manager's site.

The Shore-based User Interface allows the use of predefined profiles or allows the end-users to customize their profile to gain access to all or a portion of the data being managed by the Warfare Community Knowledge Manager. This allows the users access to filtered or unfiltered data based on their specific needs. A good example is a shipyard worker who is only interested in data related to a specific submarine. The user selects a predefined profile for that submarine. However, the next day the shipyard worker needs information about high-pressure air compressors and needs to search the entire knowledge store for the information. The Shore-based User Interface allows an unfiltered search for the data to find the largest data set available. Additionally, the shipyard worker might want to create a custom profile to narrow the amount of data to a specific area of interest but still provide access to a larger portion of the data store when compared to a predefined profile.

The Shore-based User Interface is not intended to be a primary user interface portal but to provide a service that a primary portal can use to locate and manage technical documents. The Shore-based User Interface is able to "snap-in" to existing systems and relies on those system's user management functions, such as profiles, to filter the information for a specific topic or user. The portal provides a web-based interface that presents information in a format to which users are already accustomed and allows users at all levels to simultaneously access the system using nothing more than a standard web browser.

Communication to and from the Shore-based User Interface via the portal is accomplished via the Broker's Enterprise Application Interface (EAI)/Portlet, described below.

3.6. Enterprise Application Interface (EAI)/Portlet. The EAI is a web services interface that provides a common interface structure so other programs can access the functionality of the Broker Environment and the Warfare Community Knowledge Manager. The EAI interface mechanisms will be published in Web Services Definition Language (WSDL) for the ease of use by third party applications and will describe the legal methods and attributes to access the Warfare Community Knowledge Manager.

4. RETAILER ENVIRONMENT. (See Figure 4.) The retailer, or shipboard environment, is able to operate in two basic modes as described below.

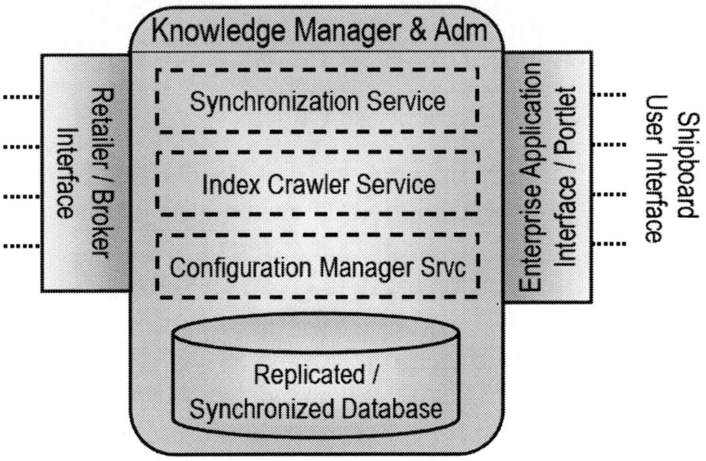

Figure 4 - Retailer

- **Connected Mode.** The first mode is considered the connected mode when the Shipboard Knowledge Manager component of the digital library is connected to the shore-based network (such as when the ship is in port) and in communication with the Warfare Community Knowledge Manager. During this period, the shipboard digital library is placed in a state of synchronization between the Shipboard Knowledge Manager and Warfare Community Knowledge Manager. Shipboard users still access the required data from the shipboard data store. It is the responsibility of the synchronization service to ensure that the shipboard users have the ability to view the most up-to-date data available. When in this mode, the shipboard users are able to access information directly through the Warfare Community Knowledge Manager interface to the supplier network. This situation may occur when a shipboard user has the need to view data not directly applicable to their ship.

- **Disconnected Mode.** The second mode is the disconnected mode when the ship is at sea and does not have the means to communicate with the Warfare Community Knowledge Manager. While in this mode, all data is accessed via the ships local data store. This data should be updated based on the last synchronization session with the Warfare Community Knowledge Manager or via CD updates while in disconnected mode.

4.1. Shipboard Knowledge Manager. The Shipboard Knowledge Manager component is installed on the ship and administrated by the shipboard command. In general, the functionality available in the Broker Environment is duplicated at the Retailer Environment, since the Retailer Environment will have the capability to operate in disconnected mode. While in the connected mode, the Warfare Community Knowledge Manager is considered the parent node for the Shipboard Knowledge Manager and each Shipboard Knowledge Manager installation is considered a child node. The Shipboard Knowledge Manager relies upon the Warfare Community Knowledge Manager to determine the latest data available for the ship.

4.1.1. Shipboard Knowledge Manager Administrator. The shipboard component of the Knowledge Manager Administrator's interface is available to the local managers to accommodate remote administration. The following administration functions are included:

- Warfare Community Synchronization Setup (connected mode)
- Shipboard Synchronization Setup (disconnected mode)
- Shipboard Index Crawler Setup (disconnected mode)
- Shipboard Configuration Manager Setup
- Shipboard Database Update
- Profile Management – The Shipboard Administrator will provide profile management to personnel onboard based on the profile templates created by the TDKM System. It is still the Administrator's responsibility to ensure proper access and to provide the template necessary to create the profile.

4.2. Shipboard Synchronization Service. The Shipboard Synchronization Service is available to the Shipboard Knowledge Manager Administrator while the ship is in the disconnected or standalone mode. (This service should not be confused with the Warfare Community Knowledge Manager Synchronization Service that operates in connected mode.) The Shipboard Synchronization Service may be utilized when the ship is not connected to the pier but still receives data from an outside organization through one of the official distribution channels. A likely scenario for the use of this service will be during a long deployment when the ship is unable to connect to the Warfare Community Knowledge Manager and perform an online synchronization. While in manual mode, the Shipboard Administrator places the newly provided data in a predefined location on the local shipboard network and the Shipboard Synchronization Service, with the help of the Shipboard Index Crawler and Shipboard Configuration Manager, identifies the necessary data in the update and synchronizes the new data with the existing shipboard data set.

4.3. Shipboard Configuration Manager Service. This service identifies which data is applicable to a specific command, ship or user. This may not be necessary if the Warfare Community Knowledge Manager has done its job correctly, because only the data applicable to the local ship will be on the shipboard data store. Therefore, everything that can be accessed by a user on the ship is applicable to that ship.

4.4. Shipboard User Interface. A web-based interface is used to provide the shipboard users the ability to communicate with the Shipboard Knowledge Manager. In most cases, all data accessed through the Shipboard User Interface is located on the shipboard network. However, the Shipboard User Interface still allows the users to access information related to other ships or classes while in connected mode.

Similar to the Shore-based User Interface, the Shipboard User Interface is also not intended to be a primary user interface portal but to provide a service that a primary portal can use to locate and manage technical documents. Communication to/from the Shipboard User Interface via the portal is be accomplished via the Retailer's Enterprise Application Interface (EAI)/Portlet, similar to the Broker's EAI/Portlet.

4.5. Shipboard Index Crawler Service. The Shipboard Index Crawler Service is available to the Shipboard Knowledge Manager and can be used to create access lists and predefined search spaces while the ship is in disconnected mode. The Shipboard Knowledge Manager Administrator should only use the Shipboard Index Crawler Service when the ship is unable to connect to the Warfare Community Knowledge Manager for extended periods, and it becomes necessary to update the shipboard data set via manual means. The Shipboard Index Crawler Service parses data based on the same indexing schema designed for the Warfare Community Knowledge Manager. This implies that either the data has to arrive with appropriate indexing schema or the Shipboard Knowledge Manager is able to convert legacy-indexing schemes into the Warfare Community Knowledge Manager's compatible indexing schema.

5. SUMMARY. Figure 5 below illustrates all the components of the TDKM System tied together, along with the external interfaces to a Content Management System (CMS) and a Configuration Management System.

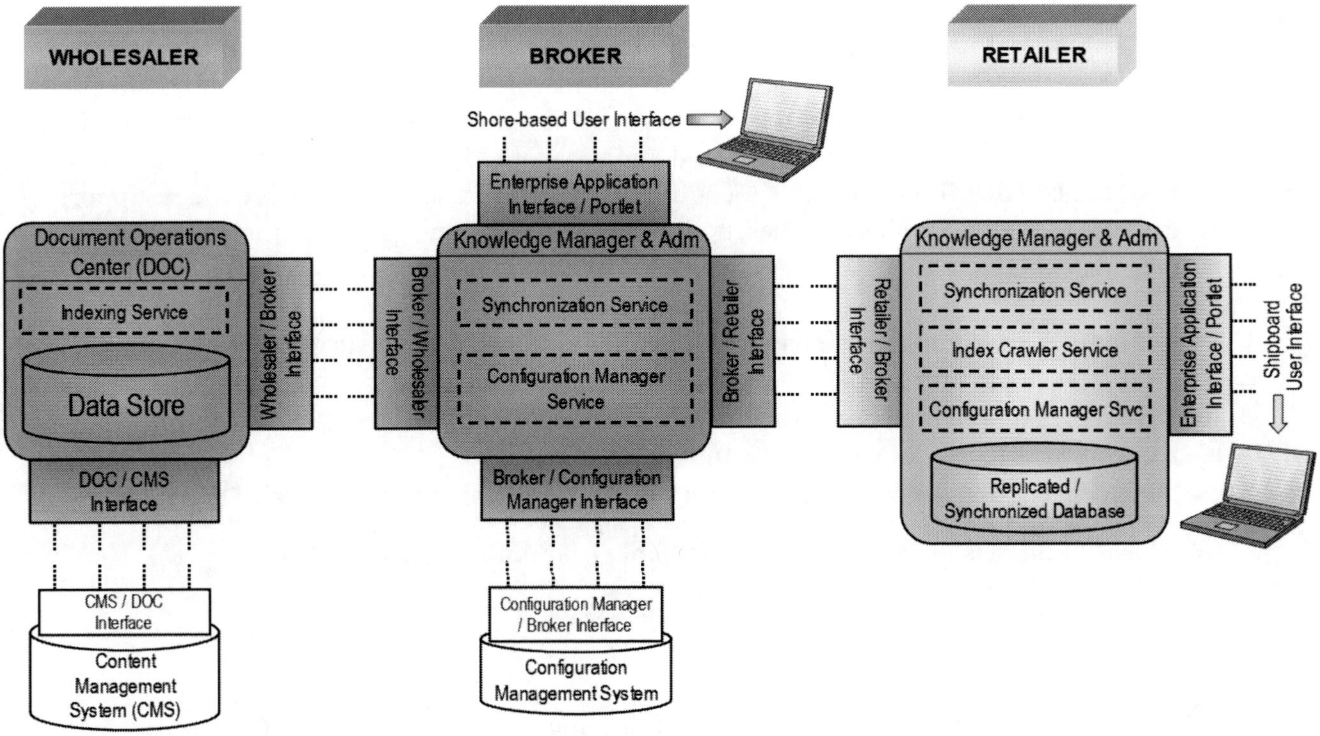

Figure 5 – Complete TDKM System

Figure 6 below illustrates the overall TDKM System notional concept.

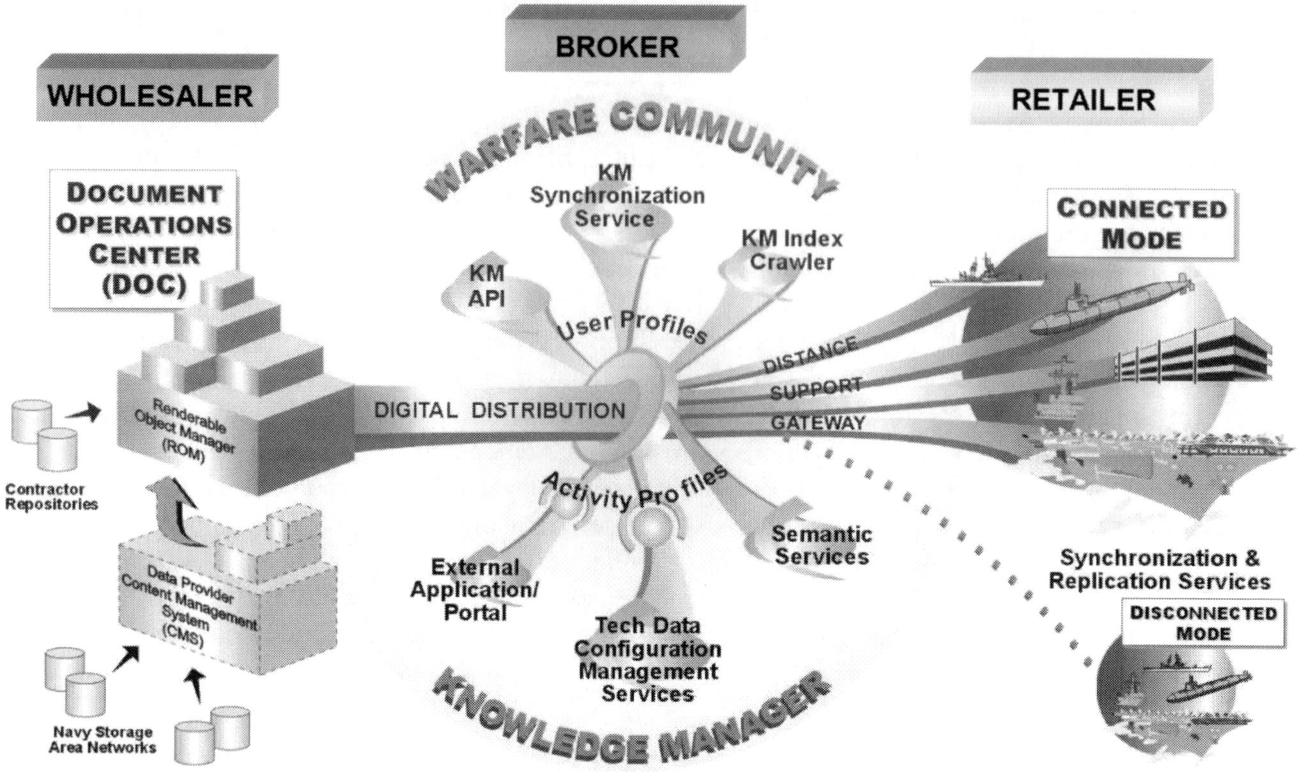

Figure 6 – Notional TDKM System Concept

A TDKM System proof-of-concept prototype, sponsored by Deputy Chief of Naval Operations for Fleet Readiness & Logistics and Deputy Under Secretary of Defense for Logistics & Material Readiness, was installed at the Naval Surface Warfare Center - Carderock Division (NSWC-CD), Commander, Submarine Forces Pacific (COMSUBPAC,) USS COLUMBUS (SSN 762), and Naval Submarine School in Groton, CT. The purpose of this supplier-to-warfighter prototype was to demonstrate the feasibility of TDKM as an end-to-end digital data distribution environment over SIPRNET to serve both shore Fleet support infrastructure as well as deploying operational units. The following list summarizes TDKM benefits:

- Improves configuration management and distribution time/costs of technical data
- By increasing overall data granularity and thereby improving data accessibility, encourages technical data re-use and repurposing
- Provides a robust electronic repository that is responsive to user queries and needs
- Uses industry standards such as eXtensible Markup Language (XML)
- Plugs into any enterprise portal as a web service 'portlet'
- Reduces manpower at the library site
- Gets the right data to the right user at right time

TDKM represents a major change in how the Department of Navy manages and distributes its technical data, reducing the time-to-market for technical data by as much as ninety percent. The TDKM concept can easily be exported and applied to all services in the Department of Defense.

Acknowledgements

The author would like to acknowledge the support of the following people, without whose support the TDKM Project, and this resulting paper, would not have come to fruition:

- Mr. L. McGowan, Naval Sea Systems Command, NAVSEA07
- Mr. E. Jorgensen, Naval Surface Warfare Center - Carderock Division
- Mr. D. Streett, AMSEC LLC
- Mr. D. McKnight, AMSEC LLC
- Mr. B. McGarrigle, AMSEC LLC
- Mr. C. Nosil, AMSEC LLC

Author's Biography

Mr. Rumschlag, Logistics Technology Services Division Manager at AMSEC LLC in Hampton, VA, has worked in the electronic publishing arena for a large defense contractor for the last 14 years. He oversaw his company's migration from a page-oriented publishing system to Standard Generalized Markup Language (SGML) beginning in the early 1990's. His organization publishes 30,000 military technical manual and engineering drawing CD-ROMs per year and distributes them to 700 activities – both ashore and afloat. He currently is working on eliminating those CD-ROMs in favor of an internet-based push/pull system to deliver dynamically tailored technical data to remotely deployed sites around the world – the Technical Data Knowledge Management (TDKM) System. He has a Bachelor of Science in Computer Science degree, cum laude, from Old Dominion University, Norfolk, VA.

Logistics Data Integration

Lou Sciaroni, CPL

Abstract:

Due to the transformation efforts taking place in today's Army, existing logistics data systems are changing dramatically. These changes will have a tremendous impact on logistics data deliveries for the Legacy, Interim, and Objective Force weapon systems. The US Army Materiel Command Logistics Support Activity's (LOGSA) powerLOG application can ease the pains of this transition. PowerLOG will minimize the contract modifications and system interface issues on Legacy and Interim Force systems, integrate logistics data during system development of the Interim and Objective Force systems, improve and standardize Original Equipment Manufacturer (OEM) data delivery formats, and to expand data interoperability with the other Services. This presentation will provide an overview of powerLOG and its capabilities to support DOD's modernization efforts.

Paper:

LMP, GCSS-A, CCSS, SDS, ERP, SAP, LMI, IETM,... You might be asking yourself, "What do these mean? And how do they affect me?" If you have any dealings with the Army at all you are probably familiar with many of them. The Logistics Modernization Program (LMP) and the Global Combat Support System Army (GCSS-A) are modernization efforts to replace the Army's outdated wholesale and retail logistics systems utilizing Enterprise Resource Planning (ERP) software such as SAP. While the GCSS-A implementation may be years away, transition to the LMP system has already begun. The LMP system is replacing many systems, the largest being the Commodity Command Standard System (CCSS) wholesale logistics system. It will provide enhanced decision support and integrated logistics management.

Up until LMP fielding, the Original Equipment Manufacturer (OEM) had standardized ways to deliver data to the government. Specifically, in terms of provisioning/parts data to the CCSS, deliveries were limited to a few 80-card column formats. Governing these formats were the MIL-STD-1388-2B, Logistics Support Analysis Record (LSAR), before that it was MIL-STD-1388-2A, LSAR, and prior to that it was the MIL-STD-1552, Provisioning. These formats were mandated prior to 1996, in the Army's System Acquisition Directive and Instruction (DOD 5000.1 and 5000.2), and therefore, all system acquisitions delivered the data in these formats.

In the mid-90's, that all changed when the LSAR standard was eliminated and was replaced by a performance specification. It has been more than 6 years since the MIL-PRF-49506, Logistics Management Information (LMI) performance specification was implemented in an attempt to acquire properly formatted logistics data, in performance terms. While the LMI provided for a contract vehicle to acquire the data, it lacked a data format. Based on support that we have provided since the LMI was published, and survey results on the use of the LMI, it is our assessment that PMs and OEMs are currently using both the LMI and the LSAR simultaneously to contract for and produce logistics data.

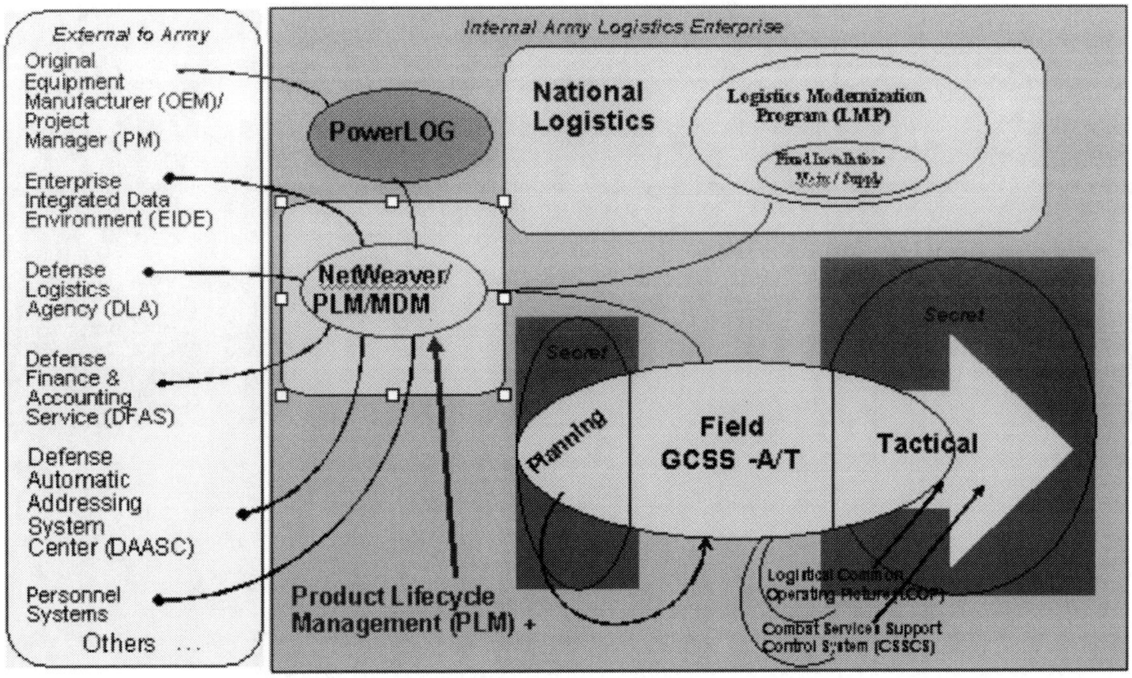

Used and modified with permission from Enterprise Integration, Inc.

Figure 1: PowerLOG and the Army's Logistics Architecture

The LMI states in the first paragraph, *"The contractor may, and is encouraged to, suggest alternative means of satisfying requirements of this specification to make information more readily available and to utilize more efficient business practices."* This statement gives the contractor freedom to choose from many different systems and formats to deliver the LMI data, but they have typically continued to provide the data to the government via the LSAR software programs. They continue to use them because they have an investment in LSAR software, their personnel are trained on these systems and are familiar with their formats. Also, they know that likewise, the government systems (at least legacy systems such as CCSS) can load them and will be satisfied with the output data and report formats.

Sometimes, however, under LMI contracts the OEM does not use the LSAR format, and the interchange formats are not clearly spelled out in the contract. Since each LMI contract can be tailored with a different set of data elements, having unique formats, and their own data relationships, data interchange problems can occur. When the time comes to deliver the data to systems such as CCSS, and the data is not in a standard format, an expensive and time-consuming effort is required to convert all of this data to a usable format.

To alleviate these types of problems, we are working with the DOD community to develop a data interface standard using eXtensible Markup Language (XML) as the mode of data transfer. The government is not interested in how the contractor stores the logistics data, but rather how the data is able to load into their systems. If the government is going to continue to maintain logistics data, there must be a document that clearly identifies what that format must look like. In the short-term, we are working with the LMP program to help them tailor the LMI and create appropriate guidance for LMP users. This document will contain a complete list of LMP data elements and the appropriate formats for delivery.

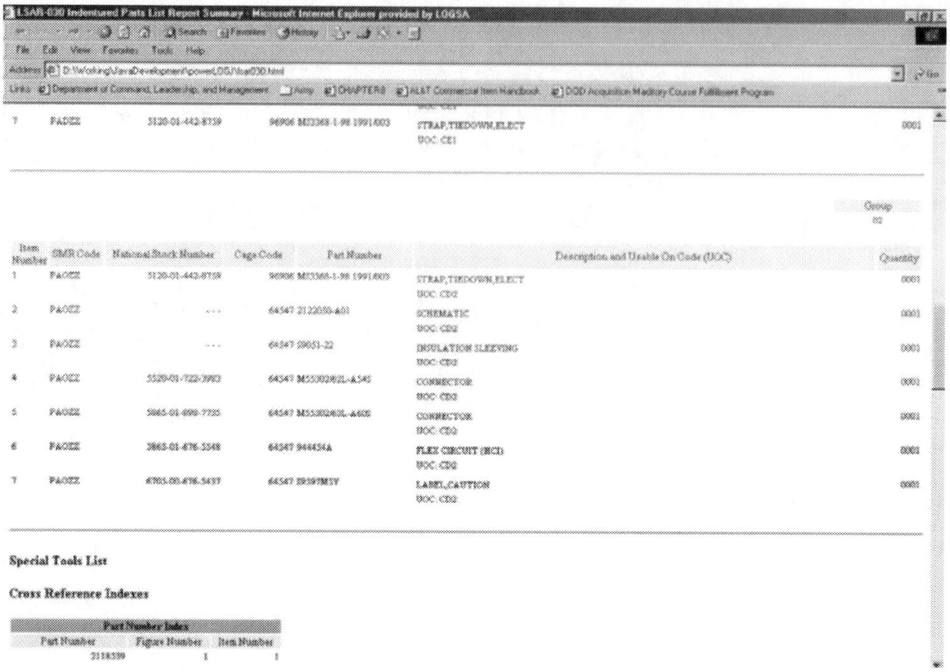

Figure 2. PowerLOG Repair Parts and Special Tools List Output

Another solution to the data interchange problem arising from the elimination of the LSAR, is to provide an application that the OEMs can use, free of charge, that is capable of producing a standard format. This application would be of great benefit to the OEM that does not already have a system capable of producing formats able to load seamlessly into the government's data systems.

LOGSA's powerLOG software is our attempt to do just that. PowerLOG can import the LSAR format as well as a variety of other legacy data formats. This allows the government to accept data from existing contracts thereby avoiding costly contract modifications for those deliveries. It can also produce more than 30 standard reports such as the Maintenance Allocation Chart, Maintenance Plan, Provisioning Technical Documentation, Repair Parts and Special Tools Lists, and Bill of Materials. By using powerLOG, OEMs now have a tool to satisfy LMI requirements without increased software costs, and the government has a tool to accept and validate the contractor's deliverables. Best of all, the powerLOG outputs are in XML format to make it easier to interface with other databases. The LMP program is reviewing the powerLOG's XML outputs as a potential OEM-LMP interface format.

Because powerLOG is based on standard formats, the outputs can readily interface with other DOD applications. In addition to CCSS and LMP as mentioned earlier, the outputs will interface with systems such as the Navy's ICAPS, the Air Force's D220, PFSA, Visual Sesame, CASA, IADS, etc. The focus of the data interfaces mentioned initially centered on the provisioning/parts data. We are working with other communities such as the Environment

Health and Safety, Packaging, Freight, Cataloging, and Manpower areas to ensure their data will transition properly from the OEM to the government systems. Along these lines, we are working with the Interactive Electronic Technical Manual (IETM) community to enable our reports to satisfy MIL-STD-40051, Standard Practice for the Preparation of Digital Technical Information for Technical Manuals, formats and our XML outputs meet MIL-STD-236, Interface Standard on Digital Publication Development, requirements. As a report is selected, the data from the application is tagged by the application based on the user's report selections. The output is an HTML document viewable in the user's browser, with an underlying XML document that can be used to transfer and manipulate the data.

Allowing each weapon system program to create their own data set creates a variety of problems when passing data from one system to another. The powerLOG application can help standardize the way the OEM passes data to the government, provides standard outputs, provides an interface to the LMP and other government systems, and gives PMs and other government agencies a tool to accept and verify OEM data deliveries. The powerLOG application is helping the Army to transform from the Legacy Force to the Objective Force and the other Services to transform their processes as well.

Bio

Mr. Sciaroni is currently the Chief of the Logistics Engineering Division at LOGSA. He has worked in the area of engineering logistics for 14 years at the USAMC Logistics Support Activity and the Materiel Readiness Support Activity. During this time, he aided in the development of MIL-PRF-49506 and MIL-STD-1388-2B, validated logistics software systems, and led the powerLOG development effort. Lou graduated with honors from the Army's Maintainability Engineering Intern Program, has the Army's Level III Certification in Acquisition Logistics, and is a Certified Professional Logistician. He has a Bachelor of Science degree in Electrical Engineering from the University of Missouri-Rolla and a Master of Science degree in Industrial Engineering from Texas A&M University.

Logistical Analysis for Critical Infrastructure Protection (CIP) "Factory to Foxhole"

Larry W Ground, CPL
Raytheon
Arlington, VA
703 413-1220
larryground@earthlink.net

Robert L Smith, PMP
Raytheon
Arlington, VA
703 413-5339
Robert_L_Smith@Raytheon.com

Abstract

The CIP Vision is to assure that the critical infrastructure assets DOD depends upon are available to mobilize, deploy and sustain military operations. All critical bases and installations throughout the world must identify their critical assets and commercial and defense infrastructure required to support their missions, plans, and operations. By identifying vulnerabilities, eliminating single-point failures, by adding redundant capabilities, by mitigating risk, and by identifying and exercising workarounds or other options, we can identify ways to strengthen their respective infrastructures. This analysis, using the Logistics Joint Analysis Method (LogJAM) tool, assessed networks and links and nodes supporting military logistics operations, uncovered vulnerabilities, and identified failure sets that, if not protected, could result in severe consequences for a military tasked with a rapid deployment. This paper gives a summary of this analysis and outlines some of the further uses the tool could have and how it has been used in the commercial arena. This is truly a melding of Defense and Commercial Logistics.

The first step, and arguably the most important one, in the Critical Infrastructure Protection program (CIP) is to **analyze and assess** commercial and defense infrastructure worldwide to determine its criticality to national security, its vulnerabilities and the risks to those assets. Subsequent steps address other aspects of protecting the infrastructure, including remediation, mitigation and reconstitution, to name just a few.[1]

The analysis and assessment phase provides a significant challenge to the Combatant Commanders. US Pacific Command (PACOM), designated by the Joint Chiefs of Staff as the first combatant command to perform a detailed CIP analysis, expects to devote the largest portion of its CIP resources to performance of the analysis and assessment phase. The vast size of the PACOM area of responsibility results in what staff planners refer to as the *tyranny of distance* in describing logistics support to ground and air combat forces. Operating far from the commercial/industrial base, military units are highly dependent on a steady and predictable distribution flow. The thousands of intervening miles increase reaction times and limit the number of available options when infrastructure is threatened.[2]

Several factors led to the selection of the Logistics Joint Analysis Method (LogJAM) to support CIP at PACOM. Originally developed as a corps-level logistics staff planner for Army ground forces, the knowledge base for LogJAM has been extended to include air force, navy and marine units. The underlying algorithms for calculating combat demand requirements and modeling material distribution are based in artificial intelligence, using a constraint-directed heuristic search algorithm developed by Mark Fox while at Carnegie Mellon University.[3] Originally designed under the name of Knowledge Based Logistics Planning Shell (KBLPS),[4] the capabilities of LogJAM were significantly enhanced through the addition of infrastructure-based reasoning to the distribution planning module. LogJAM incorporates time, distance and capacity considerations when determining the end-to-end material flow capability of the logistics system. The adaptability of the knowledge base, the tremendous detail, and the global stretch make it possible for LogJAM to model from factory-to-foxhole. Finally, LogJAM has been applied successfully to the analysis of major, non-conventional military logistics support operations by other organizations.[5]

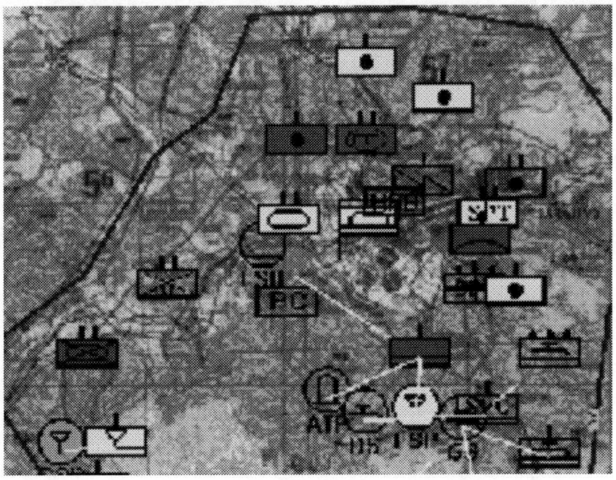

Figure 1 LogJAM provides a striking visual of how well logistic requirements are being satisfied.

For discussion purposes, the modeling of logistics distribution in LogJAM, and the associated CIP analysis, can be illustrated by examining three general areas.

- **Factory-to-foxhole**, with a focus on operations *within the fence*, including warehouse operations, staging operations and shipment via road, rail or air.
- Distribution in a **bare base environment**, where the available infrastructure is extremely limited and the demand for material requires the movement of large quantities.
- Distribution in a **robust environment**, where infrastructure provides numerous options for routing material flow under normal circumstances, but which is susceptible to major disruption by system-wide interruptions, e.g. an ice storm.

Factory to foxhole

Not too many years ago, combatant commanders and their staffs could safely limit their analysis of logistics support to things under their direct control. Logistics support at the national and strategic level were assumed to be a *given*. The services, working with commands such as USTRANSCOM and DLA, were responsible for getting the support **to** the combatant commander, leaving him to focus on warfighting. Ideally, the combatant commander would never need to concern himself with logistics operations outside his area of responsibility.

A number of things have changed to expand the combatant commander's area of interest.

- Strategic transportation is more global in its reach than ever before. The introduction of the C-17 aircraft permits US TRANSCOM to routinely deliver

Figure 2 With its ability to land at forward logistics bases, the C-17 blurs the line between inter-theater and intra-theater transportation.

loads from the CONUS sustaining base directly to forward tactical locations. The lines of responsibility that previously separated inter-theater transportation and intra-theater transportation have been blurred, and in some cases removed completely.

  - There is recognition of a higher likelihood of multiple, simultaneous or near-simultaneous regional conflicts. Combatant commanders are faced with the possibility of competing for scarce resources with other combatant commanders or even between multiple regions within their area of responsibility.

- Terrorists have demonstrated the ability to conduct actions within the continental United States. Whereas before the homeland could be safely assumed to be immune to enemy action, today it must be considered just as open to attack as any other place in the world.
- The basic philosophy of defense logisticians has evolved. Gone are the *iron mountains* of yesteryear, replaced with mobile pre-positioned stocks and an increased emphasis on rapid, on-demand distribution. While this has solved many of the earlier problems associated with immobile stockpiles, it has increased the dependence of the combatant commander on reliable flow of material to support his operations.

In modeling operations at the factory level, we focused on an example where inventory stocks are held in a centrally located warehouse until a need is identified. The stocks are withdrawn from the warehouse and staged for movement, under the control of the warehouser, to a transportation entry point. Multiple modes of transportation were examined, including road, rail and air.

We examined each element of the system in isolation, to determine its impact on the system operation. If the staging area was degraded in operation while all other aspects were not affected, how much would overall efficiency be impacted? Each element of the system was examined in turn. Then the elements were grouped and examined in pairs and larger sets.

In this example, the connection to the railhead proved to be the most significant asset. When warehousing or staging capability were constrained in isolation, the system was able to regulate the flow to keep stocks flowing, albeit at a reduced rate. When the functionality at the railhead was reduced, the system encountered significant problems. The upstream functions (warehousing and pre-staging) were unable to compensate for the bottleneck at the railhead. Further investigation led to a closer examination of the relationship between road transportation as an alternative to rail transport.

Bare base environment

For the bare base environment, the scenario considered a force with high demand for fuel, operating in a region where the delivery of fuel to the theater was restricted to movement by rail. Movement by air, while feasible, was ruled out due to the high requirements for fuel and the lack of available aircraft to bring fuel in. In this instance, we employed an unclassified database with information on rail and road networks along the East Coast from mid-Pennsylvania to South Carolina, with extensions into Georgia.

The rail network is categorized by a robust network in the north and central region, with multiple nodes and links. These eventually meet in two legs that link the rest of the network with the theater of operations. The two legs meet at a single node in the northeastern portion of the theater, before splitting again. From this single node, movement to the consuming units could be handled by rail or by road movement. Rail movement was preferred, to avoid transferring between modes and to minimize the requirements for truck transport units in theater.

The rail infrastructure is relatively fixed, i.e. it can not be improved or modified in the amount of time available, with the resources available. Storage in-theater is relatively low, making it impossible to stockpile more than 1-2 days of inventory for a reserve.

The analysis involved a systematic examination of the rail legs connecting the various nodes. The various nodes, particularly the single node that dominates the northeast corner of the theater of operations, could be considered areas for concern. In general, though, these nodes are located in populous areas with moderate to high levels of security and are under constant surveillance. The links, on the other hand, traverse remote regions, through terrain where surveillance is spotty and continuous security is infeasible. The focus of the analysis was directed toward the links and away from the nodes themselves.

LogJAM allows the analyst to set the characteristics of each segment of the infrastructure individually. The rate of movement along a particular segment can be set in kilometers per hour and the segment can be declared to be *open* or *closed*. The information for the infrastructure segments comes initially from the download of data from outside sources.

LogJAM will model road, rail, inland waterway and pipeline, as well as air movement. The analyst can add more infrastructure data by drawing in segments on the map-based user interface. The analyst can also sub-divide segments and give different characteristics to each segment. For instance, if a bridge or tunnel has a restricted speed that is different from the rest of the road, the analysis can *break* the route at each end of the restricted area and assign the lower speed to that segment of the route.

In calculating the time to transport material through the network, LogJAM examines each shipment separately. If earlier shipments cause congestion along particular routes, LogJAM will attempt to move subsequent shipments along less congested routes. The underlying algorithms rely on the resource constraints to guide the quest for more efficient overall operation.

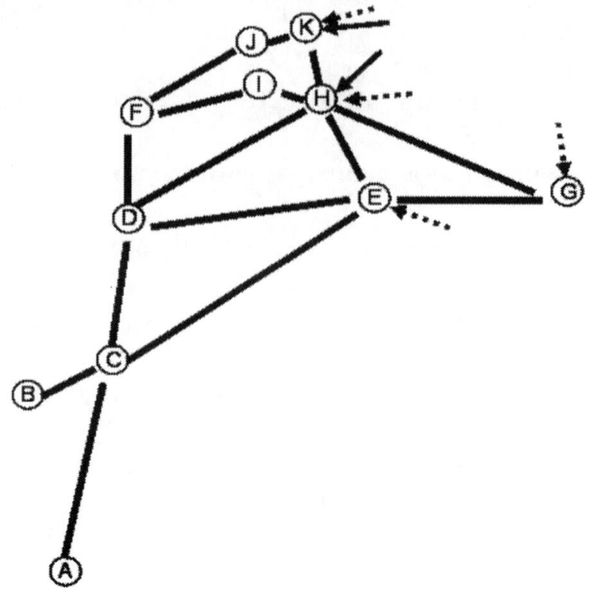

Figure 4 The network funnels down to a single point at Node C before branching off to the customers at Nodes A and B

The analysis began at the consuming units and worked backward through the network. The network is most sparse at the consuming end, with more robustness as one travels upward toward the distribution sources.

A total of 18 different cases were analyzed. The results serve to focus the attention of decision-makers on the individual links and the sets of links that cause the greatest potential for disruption of fuel distribution flow.

The setup of the model took about 1 ½ days. The analysis of the first case took about 2 hours. The setup and analysis of subsequent cases took less than 2 minutes for each case.

Robust environment

For the robust environment, we examined a scenario with very robust road transportation network and a high demand for ammunition. We were particularly interested in examining the road network for hidden weaknesses. A secondary issue concerned distribution of high priority items within a system focused on high-demand, high-volume items. Would these critical items *get lost in the shuffle*?

The initial analysis focused on closing individual legs of the network to determine the impact. Almost universally this proved to have little or no impact. The robustness of the network offset the loss of a single leg.

The second level of analysis involved closing multiple legs to determine the impact. For the most part, closing only two legs, even if they were parallel or connecting the same node, had little impact. The speed of the network was sufficient to allow alternate routings that resulted in degradations of no more than 2-3% overall.

The third level of analysis involved isolating key nodes. Key nodes were identified by physical examined and every link into or out of the node was closed, in turn. This resulted in some minor localized disruptions, but the overall system performance was never degraded by more than 8%. The local disruptions ran as high as 70%, but some stocks always made it through the system, sometimes traveling by very circuitous routes. The local disruptions would have severely hampered local operations, but overall, the system was minimally impacted.

Having demonstrated that the system was relatively safe from hidden weaknesses, we turned our attention to the distribution of high priority items. An overall degradation of the system was imposed on the network by creating an ice storm. The ice storm significantly reduced movement rates along the network and made movement outside of the network nearly impossible. The immediate result was to reduce the flow of material to a fraction of its normal levels.

Analysis was then focused on the movement of the high-priority stocks. It was not surprising to discover that the high-priority stocks were moving at a higher rate than the lower priority items. The satisfaction of high-priority requirements was commensurate with their specific priority.

Success on the issue of high-priority satisfaction led to another avenue of analysis. What would it take in terms of external resources to meet the full demand for high-priority items? Since the road networks were closed, could heavy-lift helicopters be used as an alternative means to move the high-priority munitions? The CH-47D Chinook helicopter was used as the candidate because of its large lift capability and its availability to support the mission.

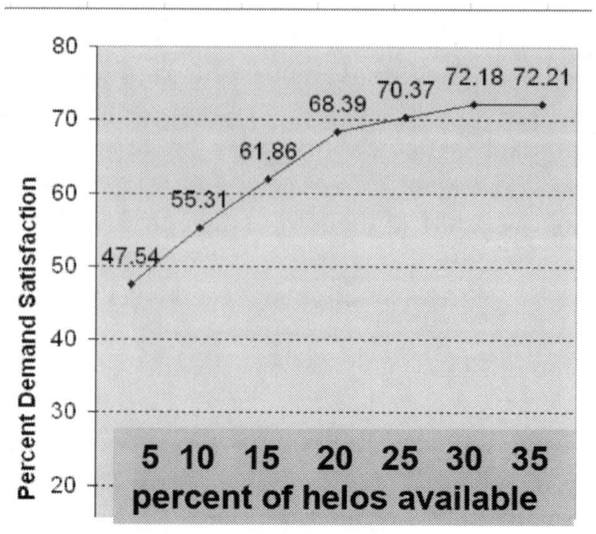

Figure 5 There is a linear relationship when using between 5% and 20% of the helicopters. Above 30%, there is no significant gain.

LogJAM made it possible to analyze the situation employing various numbers of helicopters. It revealed a linear relationship between the number of helicopters and the amount of ammunition moved, but only up to a certain point. Beyond that level, the number of helicopters did not significantly increase the movement of ammunition. Other factors besides the number of helicopters, including refueling and maintenance, crew rest, and availability of support equipment, conspired to prevent the system from making the best use of the additional assets. In a resource-constrained environment, this provides critical information for consideration in allocating resources.

Future Uses

LogJAM has proven its worth for modeling logistics distribution from the commercial sector to the battlefield, from *factory to foxhole*. Future efforts will likely expand the types and number of military units being modeled, to include all allied and coalition nations. The ability to model end-to-end, with a single integrated picture of the logistics distribution network, will be exploited to determine the impact of disruptions in one sector of the network on elements in the far distant reaches of the network. The trend toward distribution-based logistics support and just-in-time deliveries makes it more important than ever before that we understand the health and condition of the distribution network.

Accurately gauging the impact of logistics on military operations is the ultimate challenge for military logistics analysis. In the coming months we will be exploring the best means to integrate the logistics modeling of LogJAM with a simulation for theater operations, such as the Joint Conflict and Tactical Simulation, or JCATS. Our goal is to create a comprehensive picture of the logistical situation in the context of its support to the warfighter. Very shortly we expect to be in a position to offer decision makers a detailed, quantifiable analysis of the impact of losses to the logistics infrastructure. LogJAM has given us a tremendous step forward in the right direction.

Biographies

Larry Ground, CPL is an analyst with Raytheon Intelligence and Information Systems. He has over 25 years of experience in logistics and for the past seven years has focused on the development, deployment and support of logistics decision support tools. He currently leads the Modeling and Simulation Cell within the Joint Program Office for Special Technology Countermeasures in Dahlgren, VA, supporting combatant commander staffs in the area of Critical Infrastructure Protection. Retired from the US Army as a Lieutenant Colonel, he served in logistics planning and operations positions at all levels from platoon to Army staff, and taught at the US Army Command and General Staff College. Contact him at Raytheon, Arlington, VA; larryground@earthlink.net.

Robert Smith, PMP is a program manager with Raytheon Intelligence and Information Systems. He has over 15 years of experience in logistics and for the past seven years has focused on the deployment and support of logistics decision support tools. His research interests include development of tools for analysis and decision support of logistics planning, including the Logistics Joint Analysis Method (LogJAM). His team was awarded the Defense Modeling and Simulation Office Analysis Award for 1999 for the innovative use of LogJAM. He is presently working to support combatant commander staffs in the area of Critical Infrastructure Protection. Retired from the US Army, he served in command and operations positions at all levels from platoon to Combatant Commander staff. Contact him at Raytheon, Arlington, VA; Robert_L_Smith@Raytheon.com

[1] Details of the process cannot be fully discussed in this forum. Interested parties should contact the authors directly for further information.
[2] USPACOM Critical Infrastructure Protection (CIP) Conference and Combatant Commanders' Workshop, Honolulu, HI, January 27-31, 2003.
[3] "Variable and Value Ordering Heuristics for the Job Shop Scheduling Constraint Satisfaction Problem," by Norman M. Sadeh, Carnegie Mellon University, and Mark S. Fox, University of Toronto, *Artificial Intelligence*, October, 1988. .
[4]. Knowledge Based Logistics Planning Shell End User Manual, Carnegie Group Inc, 1996.
[5] "Answering the Right Question – Logistics Network Analysis" by Doug Hoffman, Joint Warfare Analysis Center, June 2002, 70th MORSS.

The Life Cycle Costing Methodology: Lessons Learned from the Examination into the Procurement Process of Two Military Systems[1]

By

Kongkiti Phusavat, Ph.D
Department of Industrial Engineering
Faculty of Engineering
Kasetsart University

Abstract:
The paper stems from the research effort to examine the life cycle cost behavior (actual and committed categories) of the two systems used in the Thai military. The primary objective of this research is to study the life cycle costing behavior from the perspective of a buyer. It is also the research's objective that a comparison will be made between the life cycle costing curve of a designer/producer and of a buyer. This research is based on the question whether the conclusion stated in regard to the cost consideration during the design is applicable for the procurement (or acquisition). Fabrycky and Blanchard (1991), from the designer/producer's point of view, suggest that the actual cost that takes place up to the design phase is 30% of the life cycle cost. While at this phase, an organization commits up to 80% of the total life cycle cost of the system (i.e., products). Based on this research finding, it is discovered that between 42-49 % of the total costs of the systems over the useful lives actually occurred when the purchasing decisions were made. Further, almost 100% of the life cycle cost of the systems under study was committed at the selection. This is because 98.31-99.61% of the entire life cycle costs, that have been recorded, are the results of the system acquisitions. This implies that, after the acquisition, the flexibility in regard to cost management is greatly diminished.

The life-cycle costing methodology (Fabrycky and Blanchard, 1991) has been widely applied to help guide design activities for the designer/producer perspective. The methodology advocates that the customer must be integrated into the design process throughout the system's life cycle. To help understand its importance, it is necessary to explain the life cycle concept of the system (Blanchard, 1998). The system begins with customer needs. Then, the system will be designed, developed, tested, produced, utilized/ maintained, and retired/ disposed.

For the identification of customer needs phase, there are several activities and tools included such as classification of customer demography, product deficiency, Quality Function Deployment, and statement of needs. There are three major activities embedded in design and development. The first activity is called conceptual design (identification of operational requirements— mission profile, effectiveness requirement, deployment and distribution, expected useful life, operating conditions, and maintenance/support policy). The second activity is known as preliminary design (operational flow and maintenance flow diagrams). Finally, the last activity is described as detailed design (design for reliability, maintainability, supportability,

[1] This paper is based on the thesis at the master-degree level completed by Capt. Anuwat Luengvilai. Capt. Luengvilai graduated from the Department of Industrial Engineering at Kasetsart University in June 2000.

human factors, economic feasibility, and environmental friendliness). After the design and development, the next phase is referred to as testing. Testing usually includes prototyping, preparation of a test site, data collection, and design revision.

After having successfully tested the design of the system, the next step of the life cycle phase is production/construction. Then, the intended user will use the system. In this phase, there are also other activities involved such as maintenance and support to ensure customer satisfaction. When the system reaches its useful life, the system will proceed to its last phase of its life cycle, known as retirement and disposal. Figure 1 demonstrates all phases in the system's life cycle.

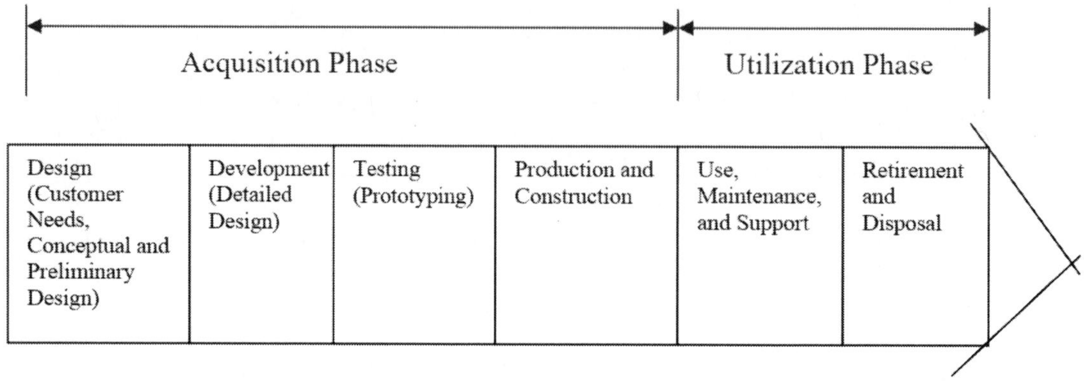

Figure 1: Life Cycle Phases from the Designer/Producer's Point of View (Adapted from Fabrycky and Blanchard, 1991)

The importance of design for life cycle of the system is not confined to maximizing customer satisfaction. Fabrycky and Blanchard (1991) argue that the design activity can significantly influence the cost behavior of the system. Such scenarios resulted from a poorly- designed system include the following.

- System (product) recall, repair and replacement
- Urgent technical assistance and handling after useful life
- Search for new suppliers of raw materials
- New production set-up
- Cost overrun from product warranty
- Logistic delay for consumers during maintenance
- Large inventory asset in comparison with sale revenue
- Poor on-time delivery due to packaging size

Given the financial consequence at the production and operation stages of the system's life cycle, Fabrycky and Blanchard (1991) advocate the greatest potential area for cost saving and prevention is at the design phase. This is because changes in system design (packaging, characteristics, size, useful life, maintenance support activity, disposal methods, etc.) at the production and operation stages are much more costly relatively to changes during design activities. Cost competitiveness for new system can take place when no such unnecessary cost incurs.

Fabrycky and Blanchard (1991) conclude that, for the organization involving with design, development, and production/construction of the system for consumer use, approximately 80% of the life cycle cost of the system is committed when the design activity is completed. At the same time, the actual cost up to a completion of design activities is estimated to incur around 30% of the system's life cycle cost. These findings indicate that the greatest impact on the system's life cycle cost occurs at the design phase. This is because the production is made according to design specification. The after-sale-service plan is based on the maintenance/support policy determined at the design phase. The difficulty and safety during the retirement/ disposal phase is resulted from materials selected during the design phase. Figure 2 demonstrates the cost behavior of the life cycle cost committed and the actual life cycle cost incurred.

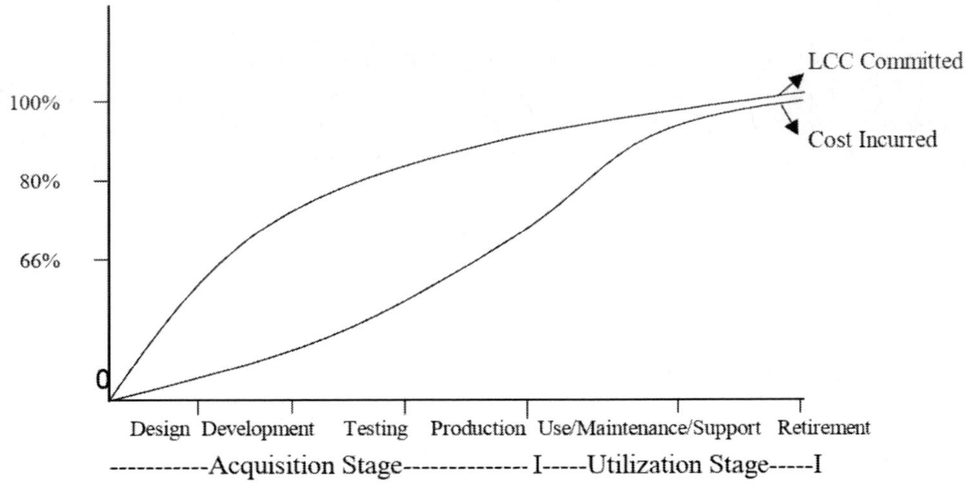

Figure 2: Life Cost Behavior for Committed and Actual Cost Incurred (Fabrycky and Blanchard, 1991)

For this research, some revision may have to be made in regard to the life-cycle concept. This is because this research focuses on the study of the behavior of the life cycle cost committed from the perspective of the buyer (instead of the designer/producer). First of all, the phases in the system's life cycle may be somewhat different. From the buyer's perspective, there are probably five primary stages in the system life cycle. They are current deficiency assessment/need identification, feasibility study and alternative analysis, selection/ purchasing, utilization/ maintenance/ support, and retirement/ disposal.

The deficiency assessment/need identification stage includes an examination and verification of needs, and a determination of operational requirements. The feasibility study and alternative analysis phase includes data collection according to operational requirements, an economic evaluation of alternatives, after-sale service options on installation, maintenance, and support, and etc. The purchasing/selection phase includes the selection made at the "best" possible alternative. The utilization/ maintenance/ support include labor for operator and maintenance personnel, parts, materials, transportation, inventory, documentation, and so on. Finally, the retirement/ disposal phase includes transportation, movement, handling, and so on. Figure 3 demonstrates the phases and stages in the system's life cycle from the buyer's point of view.

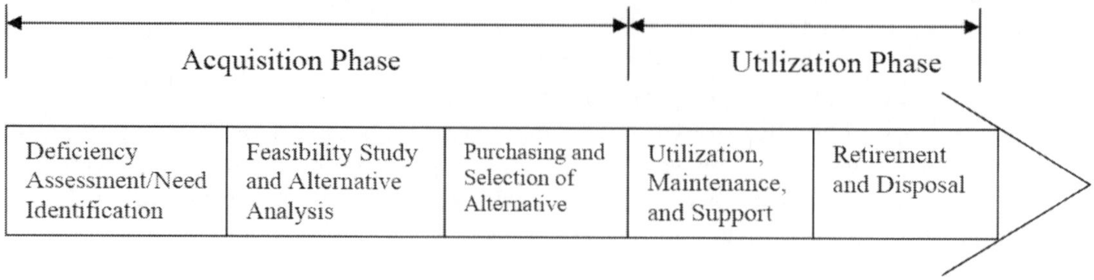

Figure 3: Life Cycle Phases from the Buyer's Point of View

In this research, the acquisition of two military systems by a public organization (small missile-defense systems from two different countries) was to be examined. It should be noted that the agency that provided data on the systems' life cycle costs requests that its name and system types remain anonymous. Hereafter, the two systems will be referred to as System A and B respectively. These two acquisitions under study were made ten years ago. The useful life of each system was anticipated at that time to be about 5 years (although the actual use has taken a few years longer). This was due to rapid change in weapon technology.

For this investigation, the actual costs that had taken place over the useful lives of Systems A and B are to be collected. All the values of the cost are to be converted to the same time horizon, at the "present." The interest rate used is the Minimum Lending Rate (or risk-free rate) at the time of the acquisition. The conversion is necessary since, in some cost categories, the expenditures had occurred at the different periods during the 5-year horizon.

The cost, included in the acquisition phase, is the purchase. At the same time, the cost associated with the utilization phase includes operating cost, spare/repair parts, support and maintenance cost, and utilities. Data of these cost categories has been traced over the period of 5 years. It should be noted that some of cost data shown in the utilization phase had to be estimated by systems' users. They are, for example, upkeep maintenance of facilities for storage and testing, and utilities. Table 1 illustrates the actual cost of the system's life cycle at their present values. (The data on retirement and disposal cost is not available for this study. Since both Systems A and B and their spares contain no known chemical and hazardous materials, the cost at this stage probably has no impact on the research conclusion.)

Given careful analysis, many of the costs, occurred at the utilization phase, were based on the decision to acquire the system. In other words, without the purchase, these costs would not have taken place. The expenditures regard to preparing facilities for system use, obtaining supporting/handling equipment for system operation and readiness, and facilitating and conducting special training for system's operators and maintenance personnel would not have taken place (without this procurement). The primary reason for these costs to take place was to support the utilization of the system.

Table 1: System Life Cycle Cost for Systems A and B

Description	Present Value of System A, in Thai Baht	Present Value of System B, in Thai Baht
ACQUISITION PHASE		
1. Purchasing	**398,309,420**	**103,004,084**
• System	346,605,338	103,004,083
• System modification	46,250,234	-
• Technical data	5,453,848	-
UTILIZATION PHASE[2]		
2. Operation (mainly operators)	**2,133,443**	**1,854,751**
3. Maintenance	**641,906**	**644,386**
• System	439,890	441,590
• Facilities	202,016	202,796
4. Support (facility preparation for system use)	**165,895,924**	**72,243,300**
• Land	10,000,000	-
• Building	135,019,820	-
• Accommodation	20,876,104	-
5. Supporting/handling equipment	**252,848,431**	**31,808,070**
6. Training	**16,475,506**	**1,135,661**
• Operator	4,270,837	811,187
• Maintenance personnel	12,204,669	324,474
7. Spare and repair parts	**102,759,677**	-
8. Utilities	**2,188,153**	**2,196,107**

At the same time, the only cost category that is necessary (the military would have to pay regardless of the procurement) is operation. Based on the results from the above computation, for System A, the military initially paid 42.32% of the total expenditures throughout its useful life while committed up to 99.61% of its life-cycle cost. Similarly, the acquisition of System B represents almost one- half (48.38%) of the total life cycle cost. However, when the acquisition was made, the military would have already committed to all of the system's life-cycle cost (or exactly at 98.31%).

A further analysis shows that, for System A, the cost associating with logistic support makes up 57.16% of the entire life cycle cost. Moreover, this logistic support cost represents 99.09% of the life cycle cost that was committed when System A was acquired for services. These results are also similar to that of System B. The logistic support represents 49.41% of the actual life cycle cost while the life cycle cost committed attributing to logistic support stands for 95.73% (when the selection is made to purchase System B). Table 2 demonstrates the complete analysis of the life cycle cost of both Systems A and B.

[2] The life-cycle cost committed is to be computed from the % of unnecessary cost (i.e., it is based on a comparison between the cost from purchasing plus unnecessary cost at the utilization stage relative to the total life-cycle cost at the present. For this study, the unnecessary cost implies that without an acquisition, it will not take place. This cost may take place at the same time when the acquisition is made. On the other hand, the necessary cost indicates that an organization will have to disburse with or without an acquisition.

Table 2: Life Cycle Costing Analysis for Systems A and B

Description	System A	System B
1. Cost associated with the acquisition phase	398,309,420	103,004,084
2. Cost associated with the utilization phase	542,943,040	109,882,275
3. Total life cycle cost	941,252,460	212,886,359
4. % of actual life cycle cost for acquisition	42.32	48.38
5. % of actual life cycle cost for utilization	57.68	51.62
6. % of actual life cycle cost for logistics	57.16	49.41
7. % of life cycle cost committed when the system selection is made (except for operation)	99.61	98.31
8. % of life cycle cost committed that can be attributed to logistic support when the system selection is made(except for operation, maintenance, and utilities)	99.09	95.73

There are several aspects of the life cycle cost that have been learned. First of all, at the utilization phase of the system, almost all the costs associated with this category were resulted from the purchasing decision. Simply put, these costs would not have been taken place without the purchase of the two systems. Secondly, even though there are two perspectives in this investigation, the research finding is consistent with the premise suggested by Fabrycky and Blanchard (1991). From the buyer's point of view, the analysis prior to the selection is very critical since almost or all life cycle cost associated with the system to be purchased will be committed at this phase. From the designer/producer's point of view, the design phase is critical since the majority of the life cycle cost of the system to be produced will be committed at this phase. Table 3 provides this comparison.

Table 3: Comparison between Design and Purchasing Decisions from the Life Cycle Costing Perspective

Comparison	% of Cost Actually Incurred at the Acquisition Phase	% of Life Cycle Cost Committed at the Acquisition Phase
Design Decisions	≈ 30%	≈ 80%
Purchasing Decisions	≈ 42-49%	≈ 98-100%

In conclusion, given this knowledge, the careful review of the current procurement or acquisition process should be made so that the life cycle cost of the system is an integral part of an overall system feasibility analysis. Identification of operational requirement (such as number of hours in one day under operation, operating environment, skills for system operator, useful life, and reliability of the system) should be made to ensure the prevention of unnecessary cost. In addition, an assessment of maintenance capability or prospect of sharing maintenance personnel, ability to interchange parts, or share database and facility, cooperate on using similar supporting and handling equipment during system operation must be part of the system evaluation and analysis.

References:

1. ANSI/SAE ARP 4293. 1992. Life Cycle Cost-Techniques and Applications American Society, Milwaukee, Wisconsin.
2. Benson, S. 1998. "Life Cycle Costs and the Disc Pump" Discflo Corporation. Available at http://www.discflo.com.
3. Blanchard, Benjamin S. 1998 "Systems Engineering and Management" John Wiley: Singapore.
4. Blanchard, Benjamin S. 1998 "Logistics Engineering and Management" Prentice-Hall International: Singapore.
5. Blanchard, B. S. and Fabrycky, W. 1991. "Life-Cycle Cost and Economic Analysis" Prentice-Hall, Englewood Cliffs: NJ.
6. Bullinger, H. J., Warschat J., and Boop, R. 1994. Methods and Tools to Support Design for Recycling. 2nd International CIRP Seminar on Life Cycle Engineering RECY'94 (Erlangen, Germany, Oct. 10-11). CIRP, Bamberg. :
7. Burringer. 1998. "Life Cycle Cost" Berringer & Associates, Inc. Available at http://www.burringer1.com/lcc.html.
8. Bussey, L. E. 1978. "The Economics Analysis of Industrial Projects" Prentice-Hall, Englewood Cliffs: NJ
9. Coenenbery, A., Fisher T., and Schmits J. 1994. Target Costing and Product Life Cycle Costing Instrument, Zeitschrift for Planning 16 (1) : 20-26
10. Coullahan and Siegfried. 1996. Life Cycle Costing, Zeitschrift for Planning 18 (4): 38-45.
11. Defense System Management College, 1991. System Engineering Management Guide. Ft. Belvoir VA. DSMC. 10 (1): 72-79.
12. Juran and Gryna. 1993. "Quality Planning and Analysis" John Wiley & Sons: NY
13. Luengvilai, Anuwat. 2000 "Study of Life-Cycle Costing Behavior" Thesis Submitted to the Department of Industrial Engineering, Kasetsart University
14. Stiglitz, J.S. 1990. "Economics of the Public Sector" W.W. Norton & Company: NY
15. Tarquin, A. J. and Blank, L. T. 1989. "Engineering Economy" McGraw-Hill: Singapore
16. Vesey, J. T. 1991. The New Competitors: They Think in terms of Speed of the Market. Executive 5 (5): 27-33.

Abstract for the SOLE Annual Conference 2003
Topic Area: How do you deal with unplanned obsolescence in a military environment?
Classification: Unclassified
Title: "Fighting The War On Unanticipated Obsolescence"
Author: Laura E. King
Abstract: Obsolescence has become a critical problem for the acquisition community in recent years. Weapon Systems are remaining in the field past their original projected useful life. Technology continues to go forward at a staggering pace, particularly in the area of computing. This further compounds the obsolescence problem. As soon as a change takes place that extends the life of a fielded system, action is required to assess the impact of the change and budget for any unforeseen requirements vital to ensure system sustainment. Anticipated and unanticipated obsolescence must be addressed to ensure readiness rates are maintained. Today very few resources are available to guide acquisition personnel in solving the obsolescence issues facing them. There is no definitive regulation or publication that addresses the problem and provides a "plan of attack". The absence of doctrinal guidance emphasizes the need for the acquisition community to share information and assist each other in the fight against unanticipated obsolescence. This paper will provide resources that can assist the acquisition community in addressing the problem. It will also provide some first hand experience on a system that is currently experiencing obsolescence issues.

Fighting The War On Unanticipated Obsolescence

"Obsolete – To go out of use:" Websters New World Dictionary.

Claude Shannon, the acclaimed mathematician of the 1930s, once described information as the reduction of uncertainty". In the rapidly changing commercial off-the-shelf (COTS) technology environment, obtaining information to combat obsolescence is critical. As acquisition professionals procure the latest technology for insertion into weapon systems, uncertainty cannot be tolerated. This paper is the true-life story of one Project Managers journey into the realm of uncertainty. The lessons learned as well as the resources that can help other Project Managers will be of interest to anyone who is dealing with technological obsolescence.

Obsolescence has become in recent years, a critical problem for the acquisition community. Weapon systems are remaining in the field past the original projected useful life for a variety of reasons. Some of these include schedule slips, emerging aging aircraft issues, competing priorities for funding, and funding constraints for new systems and modifications imposed by the downscaling of the military infrastructure. Technology continues to go forward at a staggering pace, particularly in the area of electronics and computing.

To better understand how unanticipated obsolescence can occur, and what might be done to off set the problem, I will use the example of the Joint Tactical Ground Station (JTAGS) Product Office. As the Logistics Chief, I have first hand knowledge of the events I am about to describe.

The JTAGS was developed to be a transportable information processing system that provides theater Combatant Commanders the capability to receive and process satellite threat data on tactical ballistic missile launches. JTAGS disseminates warning, alerting, and cueing to the war fighter in real time. JTAGS was a joint interest program developed between the Army and Navy and managed by the JTAGS Product Office, Headquartered by the Program Executive Office (PEO) for Air and Missile Defense located in Huntsville, Alabama.

As JTAGS was being designed, thought was already given to future product improvements that would take advantage of changing technologies and doctrine. The current JTAGS works with the Defense Support Program (DSP) Satellite Infrared sensors. The Multi-Mission Mobile Processor (M3P), the follow-on to JTAGS, will take advantage of the Space Based Infrared System (SBIRS) satellite constellation when deployed. The M3P will be used by the Air Force for strategic mission operations. The M3P will provide improved launch point predictions, trajectory/cueing information and predicted ground impacts.

Delays in the overall SBIRS program caused the fielding of the M3P to be delayed by over 2 years from the date originally projected. This delay had the cumulative effect of creating obsolescence issues affecting the sustainment of JTAGS. This forced the JTAGS Product Office and it's contractor for depot level Contractor Logistics Support (CLS), Northrop Grumman, to analyze and determine what actions were necessary to ensure readiness levels at each JTAGS location were not adversely impacted.

In a series of meetings, the Product Office met with the Northrop Grumman CLS personnel to determine what approach would be taken to resolve issues that were likely to occur as a result of the schedule slip. The COTS processors were identified as the most likely problem items. In addition to the COTS processors some equipment was JTAGS system unique commercial adaptations. Some of these items had not been purchased or built since the fielding of JTAGS in 1997.

Failure and usage data was sought to do prognostic analysis. A survey was also done to determine what companies could still produce spare parts that might be purchased, what suitable substitutes might be available for items no longer produced or sold, and determination as to which items might be best re-engineered or reverse engineered. The Product Office also requested spare equipment from the Attack and Launch Early Reporting To Theater (ALERT) program that was deactivated in 2002. This analysis based on the resulting information, formed the basis for what would be a two-pronged approach to solving the obsolescence issues being realized by JTAGS.

Two approaches were developed to deal with the increasing obsolescence problem. Both solutions would be dollars driven, dependent on the Operations and Maintenance (OMA) funding availability. The best and more costly solution (referred to in our office as the "optimal solution") would be to replace all of the COTS equipment with the latest technology. This approach would insure the ability of the JTAGS Product Office to sustain the new equipment out into the future. If another slip in the SBIRS program should again impact the delivery of the M3P, the "optimal solution" could insure continued JTAGS operational capability and readiness levels beyond the current known slip of 2 years.

The second approach (referred to by our office as the "bare bones solution") would attempt to maintain JTAGS. This approach with the degree of uncertainty of vendor support and the unpredictability of certain failures resulting from extended operations of the JTAGS was assumed to have large risk implications to readiness levels.

Unfunded Requirements (UFRs) were identified, then projected and requested through the budget process for O & M. We pushed hard for our funding and settled in to see how quickly the obsolescence issues would begin appearing.

We didn't have long to wait. The mid plane is a COTS JTAGS system unique item. The mid plane functions similar to a back plane found in most computer systems. It is the top level in a hierarchical network. During the summer of 2001, a mid plane failure occurred. A spare mid plane had been initially procured at the same time the mid planes destined for the JTAGS had been bought. The spare was installed and the unserviceable mid plane returned to the JTAGS CLS Depot. The Depot sent the unserviceable mid plane to Computerized Rugidization Inc (CRI) for repair. In the interim, from the time of purchase of the mid plane until the first request for repair, the original manufacturer had been bought out by another company and not only the drawing package was missing but also the test fixture. Then in March 2002, a second mid plane failed, with the potential for lower unit readiness. There were no spares to replace it.

A Tiger Team was formed to address the mid plane issue with CRI. The team consisted of Product Office and Northrop Grumman personnel. The issue was elevated to MG Urias, PEO for Air and Missile Defense. He quickly came on board with his support both for the UFRs and in insuring that CRI recognized the sense of urgency required to ensure JTAGS systems are at the highest readiness rates. The drawings for the test fixture were located shortly thereafter. Northrop Grumman went into action and contracted the building of the test fixture, repair of the two mid planes, and the building of two spares to supplement JTAGS in the out years.

The value of the tiger team cannot be over estimated. In today's environment, government and contractors must work effectively toward the same goals. No longer can we view each other as adversaries but must come together to develop the best solutions to our common problems. The tiger team formed to solve the mid plane issue did just that. All members of the tiger team put the readiness of JTAGS as their collective goal and worked tirelessly to achieve the solution. This same group continues to work toward solving all of JTAGS obsolescence problems today. The tiger team is a key asset in the fight to beat obsolescence.

Budget Process

One of the major problems when dealing with obsolescence is that the Program Objective Memorandum (POM) process is not very robust in responding to last minute requirements, like unanticipated obsolescence. A thorough knowledge of the Planning, Programming and Budgeting System (PPBS) process is essential for anyone involved in the submission of UFRs to the POM. "PPBS is a biennial process used to acquire, allocate, account for and analyze personnel and financial resources for the DoD." A tutorial on the PPBS process is available at www.acq.osd.mil.

Buy in from the user community is essential to the success of getting UFRs funded. JTAGS successfully lobbied for, and received support, from the user community in the form of letters at the General Officer level and phone calls and email to the funding boards in Washington DC. This was in addition to the support from MG Urias and AMCOM community. JTAGS is currently in the process of doing a technology refreshment of its COTS processors.

Technology Refreshment

Technology refreshment was defined in one article I read as "The periodic replacement of COTS components, e.g. processors, displays, computer operating systems, commercially available software (CAS) within larger DoD systems to assure continued supportability of that system through an indefinite service life." 2 What is needed is policy, regulations, and a general consensus of understanding as to what technology refreshment is, and how and when, it should be implemented.

Although COTS usage represents many advantages, not the smallest of which is an overall savings in Operating and Support costs, it also contains risks. Some of the ways to mitigate those risks using technology refreshment are:

- "purchase commercial model upgrades as they evolve
- a one-time or life of type spares purchase, or
- data rights escrow purchasing sufficient technical data to solicit follow-on supply support concurrent with the manufacturer's end of production." 2

Resources That Can Help

During the course of the JTAGS excursion into obsolescence, several resources were discovered to be available that can assist with obsolescence problems. The remainder of this paper will be devoted to those resources. This is by no means a comprehensive list. There may well be other avenues for assistance. Hopefully one or more will be useful to the audience in dealing with their own obsolescence issues. At a minimum, should unexpected obsolescence become a problem, you will now know where to begin.

The Electronics Analysis and Prototyping (EAP) Laboratory within the Aviation and Missile Research Development and Engineering Center (RDEC) has been designated to be the Aviation and Missile Command's (AMCOM) leader and center of technical expertise on obsolescence management issues. The goal of the EAP is to respond to and mitigate obsolescence. The EAP's capabilities include:

-"Acquisition contract Scope of Work preparation, proposal evaluation/negotiations: The timely, correct wording in a contract can benefit in making the contractor proactive in dealing with obsolescence.

-Comprehensive obsolescence management risk assessments: What are the tradeoffs? How much risk and when will it occur? This information is essential to planning for and defeating obsolescence.

-Component availability projections: The RDEC maintains data bases that can look at a company and its products and determine when that company will no longer support the part and what the replacement will be.

-Projected obsolescence resolution sustainment costs for out-year budgeting: Extremely important. As already mentioned the POM process does not respond well to last minute changes in the budget.

-Solution recommendations, costs analysis, and implementation plans: An overall plan to guide the acquisition professional using all available tools.

-Redesign and testing of obsolete hardware: Some parts may be worked locally in the EAP lab. Cost savings are an obvious advantage here.

-Obsolescence notice alert monitoring and notification: Can't keep up with that myriad of parts you are responsible for managing? Let EAP do it for you.

-Program parts selection: Which parts do we target now as candidates for Continuous Technology Refreshment (CTR)?

-CTR Analysis"3

CTR is the replacement to the Modernization Through Spares program. CTR is funded with O & M and is based on technology and insertion and use of commercial products, processes, and practices that will extend a system's useful life.

The guidelines for use of O & M funds for CTR are clear and include projects that:

- "Spares/components that must have demonstrated acceptability and military utility
- Spares/components that are replaced through the course of normal maintenance processes (no planned overhauls of all systems)
- Spares/components that are distributed through the normal supply system
- Spares/components must meet the criteria for being two way interchangeable with the existing interfacing equipment.
- Any revisions to technical documentation at the field and depot level must conform to the form, fit, and function."4

CTR is considered a procurement strategy. It is not funded separately but takes advantage of funding initiatives currently available. When using OMA funding for CTR remember that the goal is to sustain the system, not to increase the performance envelope. To contact the EAP at RDEC for assistance contact Mr. Bob Gibbs at 256-313-0590 or email: obsolescence@rdec.redstone.army.mil.

Letterkenny Army Depot (LEAD) can also offer assistance with electronic systems integration, wiring harnesses, fiber optic cables, military standard soldering, repair and test of multiple layer circuit boards down through three layers. They can reverse engineer these types of electronic spares and produce them in quantities required. This is especially useful when a part has gone obsolete and the original manufacturer no longer makes the part. The liaison for LEAD at AMCOM is Mr. James Goins. He can be contacted at (256) 876-0410.

Tobyhanna Army Depot (TYAD) offers the capability to reverse engineer printed wiring assemblies (PWAs), both double sided and multilayer boards. If requested a full technical data package (TDP) can be developed from the effort. Once developed the TDP can be used to procure PWAs from commercial sources or be produced at TYAD. Due to system obsolescence and downsizing, production quantities for most systems are going down. Inventory levels for spares are decreasing to accommodate the upgrade to the newest technology. Just-in-time manufacturing environments in use at TYAD for low production runs eliminate the burden of having to keep excess obsolete, or soon to be obsolete, parts sitting on the shelf. To do business with TYAD, contact Mr. Frank Estock at 570-895-7089 or email Frank.Estock@tobyhanna.army.mil.

The JTAGS example provided a real life success story and, I hope, some encouragement to those that may be facing similar struggles with their respective systems. The key to the success was the cooperation and support of all parties who were stakeholders in JTAGS. As with most things, no one person can do it alone.

This paper has provided some alternate approaches as to how to deal with unanticipated obsolescence. The various agencies identified as resources are ready to help the acquisition community in finding answers to the ongoing struggle with technological obsolescence. I hope that I have succeeded in provoking thought and providing a useful forum and resources that will better arm the acquisition community in the future as we continue "Fighting The War On Unanticipated Obsolescence".

Bibliography

1. Baillie, Billman, Coogan, Meeker, Spangler, Steely, "Successful POM Submittals to Resource Sponsors", 23 August 2002.

2. Haines, Linda, "Technology Refreshment Within the DoD", Program Management, March-April 2001, PG 22-27.

3. AMSAM-RD-SE, MEMORANDUM FOR DISTRIBUTION, Subject: Obsolescence Management, 1 Aug 02.

4. www.monmouth.army.mil/cecom/lrc/specstd/ve/defhtml, Definitions, pg 1.

Mini bio:
Laura E. King, Acquisition Corp Member, is the current Logistics Chief in the JTAGS/M3P Product Office, Aviation and Missile Command. She is responsible for the sustainment of the fielded JTAGS and the development of sustainment policy for the emerging M3P. JTAGS is currently deployed in three mission critical OCONUS theaters and provides theater combatant commanders the capability to receive and process satellite threat data on tactical ballistic missile launchers. Ms. King is the 1995 recipient of the Integrated Logistics Support Department of the Army Achievement Award for Logistics Support Improvement for Materiel/Information Systems. She is the author of 5 published articles on various topics dealing with logistics that include "Winning the War on Obsolescence" "Telemaintenance", "Force Projection Logistics", and "Modeling and Simulation".

MIMOSA AND ARMY METROLOGY

Dr. Carl M. Powe, Jr.

ABSTRACT

The U. S. Army is committed to the utilization of commercially developed off-the-shelf open systems to ensure interoperability and reduce the costs associated with implementing changes. MIMOSA (Machinery Information Management Open Systems Alliance) is a non-profit industry trade association that has developed open interface standards for the transfer of maintenance, repair, diagnostics, prognostics, and operations data. This paper expresses the concept of utilizing the MIMOSA commercial open standards to develop the interfaces needed to integrate the planned Calibration Management Information System (CALMIS) with the Army Standard Management Information System (STAMIS) and the Global Combat Support System-Army/Tactical (GCSS-A/T).

INTRODUCTION

For the past ten years, the U. S. Army has been undergoing a major transformation from a heavy force that was developed to address cold war threats to a light, more mobile force designed to fight and win smaller conflicts anywhere in the world on short notice. One of the key enabling technologies supporting the transformation is management information systems. This paper briefly describes the Army Vision 2010, The Standard Army Management Information System (STAMIS), the Global Combat Support System - Army/Tactical (GCSS-A/T), the Army Metrology System and information requirements, the Management Information Open Systems Alliance (MIMOSA), and some of the issues associated with utilizing MIMOSA open system interfaces to transfer Army metrology data from one location to another.

ARMY VISION 2010

Army Vision 2010 provides the roadmap for the Army's contribution to the concepts presented in Joint Vision 2010. Following the conclusion of the cold war, there was a perception that a conventional Army was no longer needed. History, however contradicted the myth. During the period 1950 - 1989, the Army conducted ten major deployments. Surprisingly, during the next six years, twenty-five deployments were executed. Currently, the Army must be prepared to fight and win the nation's wars, provide a range of military operations other than war (MOOTW), and to deter aggression. These operations require commitment to support and be supported by allies and coalition partners that translates to management information systems interoperability. The changing geostrategic environment has resulted in a mission structure that may be categorized in seven areas: Defending or Liberating Territory, Punitive Intrusion, Conflict Containment, Leverage, Reassurance, Core Security, and Humanitarian. Army Vision 2010 states that these missions require the "full spectrum" of Army capabilities. To achieve the full spectrum of capabilities, certain operational patterns focus the tasks needed to achieve the military objectives. The operational patterns are: Project the Force, Protect the Force, Shape the Battlespace, Decisive Operations, Sustain the Force, and Gain Information Dominance. The first five align with the Joint Vision 2010 operational concepts of Dominant Maneuver, Precision Engagement, Focused Logistics, and Full Dimensional Protection. The latter, Gain Information Dominance, is fully integrated and supportive of the other patterns of operation and the operational concepts of Joint Vision 2010

The operational concept of primary interest for this paper is Focused Logistics. Current doctrine requires the capability to transport a combat brigade (approximately 5,000 warfighters and more than 300 light weight armored vehicles anywhere in the world in 96 hours from lift off. Further, the requirement exists to emplace in combat a division (12,000 - 15,000 troops with equipment) in 120 hours, and five divisions in 30 days. In addition, it is planned that the forces will immediately engage the enemy without the traditional staging. Rehearsal and final planning will be accomplished enroute by utilization of simulation techniques and other information systems. Commanders are expected to engage the enemy immediately upon exiting the aircraft. This change in mission requirements is driving a major transformation of the Army in terms of personnel, training, equipment, tactics, and most importantly, management information systems that will affect every operation of the new transformed Army. Focused Logistics is central to the new concepts. At least for the past fifty years, there has been a determined effort to reduce the "tooth to tail" ratio. That is, reduce the logistics footprint in terms of the number of combat service support personnel and support related equipment and supplies required to keep the combat forces in effective fighting condition. With the new rapid tempo of battle, there is not time to supply and maintain equipment in conventional ways. Conditioned Based Maintenance (CBM), embedded diagnostics, and prognostics will enable the selection of equipment that is predicted to not fail for some specified period of time (typically the projected period of the planned engagement). In addition, CBM enables a reduction in the size of the logistical footprint. Since management information systems pervade all of the patterns of operation, they are being revised into a system of systems as well.

Global Combat Support System-Army/Tactical (GCSS-A/T)

A Joint Chief of Staff publication describes logistics as the science of planning and carrying out the movement and maintenance of forces. It includes the development, manufacture, fielding, use, maintenance, and final disposition of the resources needed to wage war. Combat service support (CSS) includes providing the means of manning, arming, fixing, fueling, moving, and sustaining warfighters and their equipment in a combat environment. Another way of expressing the concept is to consider the life cycle of a weapons system. A perceived need establishes a requirement, which is evolved into hardware, and software that is eventually manufactured, tested, and distributed to the solders who have been trained on its use and maintenance. At the end of the system's life cycle, it is demilitarized and disposed of. At one time this concept was known colloquially as the "womb to tomb" cycle. Modern warfare techniques define a need for a single, integrated, and interactive CSS automation and communications system that constitutes a management information system that enables the functions of CSS.

The Global Combat Support System-Army (GCSS-A) is the Army effort toward the development of an integrated multi-service Global Combat Support System (GCSS). There are two versions: (1) GCSS-A/Sustainment addressing Army Wholesale Logistics (the depot system) and (2) GCSS-A/Tactical addressing the Army Retail Logistics System (unit level logistics). The GCSS-A/Sustainment is being developed to replace and/or interface with existing legacy Wholesale systems while GCSS-A/Tactical is being developed to replace and/or interface with existing legacy Retail systems. In addition, it will include personnel, financial, medical, and other non-logistics combat support system functions. Ultimately, the wholesale and retail systems will be integrated. The key word with the GCSS-A systems is "integrated". Legacy systems are mostly stand-alone "stove-pipe" systems that are not integrated and do not support communication between systems.

Legacy Management Information Systems

The Standard Army Management Information System (STAMIS) is a series of largely stand-alone software systems developed over the past 35 years to perform varied functions. More than twenty systems assist in the performance of acquisition, logistics, transportation, identification, recruiting management, personnel, supply, ammunition, distance learning, medical, maintenance, global messaging, property book, and sustaining base. The systems that are of particular importance to the theme of this paper are:

- Maintenance
    - The Unit Level Logistics System-Ground (ULLS-G)
    - Unit Level Logistics System-Air (ULLS-A)
    - Standard Army Maintenance System-1 (SAMS-1)
    - Standard Army Maintenance System-Installation/Table of Distribution and Allowance (SAMS-I/TDA)
- Supply Property
    - Standard Property Book-Redesign (SPBS-R)
    - Unit Level Logistics System-S4 (ULLS-S4)
- Supply Support Activity
    - Standard Army Retail Supply System-1 (SARSS-1)
    - Standard Army Retail Supply System-2AD (SARSS-2AD)(partial)
- Ammunition
    - Standard Army Ammunition System Modernization Ammunition Transfer Point/Division Ammunition Office (SAAS-MOD ATP/DAO)
- Management
    - Integrated Logistics Analysis Program (ILAP)
    - Standard Army Retail Supply System-2AD (SARSS-2AD)(Partial)
    - Standard Army Maintenance System-2 (SAMS-2)
    - Standard Army Retail Supply System-2AC (Partial)(SARSS-2AC)
    - Standard Army Retail Supply System-2 Gateway (DSTDD-3GW)(Partial)

- Integrated Materiel Management
  - Standard Army Retail Supply System-2AD (SARSS-2AD)
  - Standard Army Retail Supply System-2AC/B (SARSS-2AC/B)
  - Standard Army Retail Supply System-2Gateway (SARSS-2GW)
  - Standard Army Ammunition System-Materiel Management Center Ammunition Supply Point (SAAS-MMC-ASP)

These systems are the key legacy systems that are being integrated with or replaced by the GCSS-A/T.

Army Metrology

The design of weapon systems and communications equipment requires utilization of known and standardized values for electrical (alternating current and direct current), frequency, time, and physical measures such as torque values. To assure that a "volt is a volt" anywhere in the Army at any location in the world, an Army Test, Measurement, and Diagnostic Equipment (TMDE) Calibration and Repair Support (C&RS) Program was established. The program assures that measurements are traceable to the national standards held by the National Institute of Standards and Technology (NIST), the U. S. Naval Observatory (time and frequency standards), and consensus standards. The traceability is achieved by an unbroken chain of comparison with higher-level standards, the use of physical constants and construction, derivation from other basic standards, ratio measurements, or combinations of these techniques. There are three levels of calibration standards: secondary transfer, secondary reference, and primary reference. User equipment is calibrated by calibration technicians utilizing secondary transfer equipment standards. The secondary transfer standards are calibrated by the secondary reference laboratories and the secondary reference standards are calibrated by the primary reference standards. The primary reference standards are calibrated through the use of national standards.

The organizational responsibilities for the Army TMDE C&RS program are assigned by Headquarters, Department of the Army (DA) to the U. S. Army Materiel Command (AMC). The Commander, AMC further designated the U. S. Army Test, Measurement, and Diagnostic Equipment Activity (USATA), an element of the U. S. Army Aviation and Missile Command, the responsibility of executing the DA TMDE C&RS program.

A comprehensive management information system is required to assist in managing the calibration of all Army equipment worldwide. The current management information system is the Test, Measurement, and Diagnostic Equipment (TMDE) Integrated Materiel Management System (TIMMS). It is a stand-alone system that was designed independent of STAMIS. The system enables the collection and reporting of scheduling, workload, man-hour expenditure, cost accounting, and supply data. There are three major sections of TIMMS: Production Control, Supply, and Utilities. The Production Control section provides the functions needed to schedule the customer equipment, process items through the calibration and repair process, and produce needed management reports. The Supply module provides for requisition, stock, receipt, and issue of repair parts and self-service supplies. The capability to provide supply related management reports is also provided. The Utilities section provides the tools needed to support the TIMMS system.

Machinery Information Management Open Systems Alliance (MIMOSA)

MIMOSA is a non-profit trade association with sponsorship and membership by industrial and military asset management system providers and end-users. The association develops information integration specifications to enable open, integrated solutions for managing complex data and information relative to asset condition. Current sponsors are: Siemens, Indus International, DLI Engineering Corporation, The DEI Group, Science Applications International Corporation, and CSI Emerson Process Management. There are more than fifty members worldwide as shown at Figure 1.0.

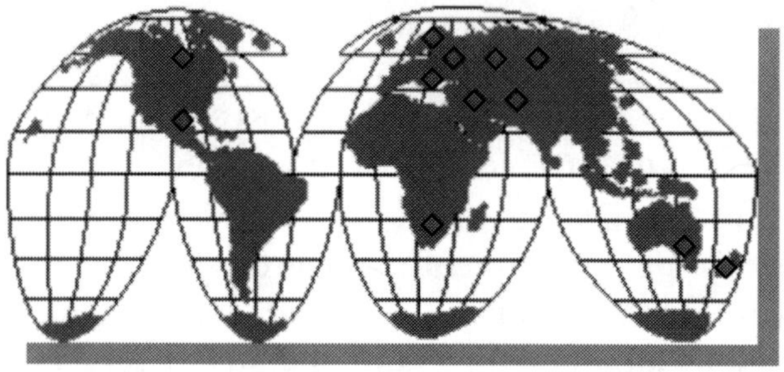

Figure 1.0 MIMOSA Membership Distribution

All iterations of the DOD Joint Vision and the Army Vision emphasize the importance of using open systems to assist in achieving interoperability of weapons systems and command, control, communications, computing, intelligence, and surveillance (C4ISR) systems. To further these objectives, the DOD established the Open Systems Joint Task Force (OSJTF) as a cooperative effort of the Army, Navy, Air Force and the Office of the Under Secretary of Defense (Acquisition and Technology) with the following mission:

- Make Open Systems Architecture an integral part of the acquisition process,
- Provide assistance in implementing open systems, and
- Promote acceptance of open systems.

Clearly, utilization of open systems architecture within the DOD is mandatory.

MIMOSA members from around the world have spent more than five years developing the Open System Architecture for Enterprise Application Integration (OSA-EAI) specification. Recently, the MIMOSA worked with the OPC Foundation to announce OpenMRO™ thus packaging Tech-Web and CRIS (Common Relational Information Schema) XML (Extensible Markup Language) data structures inside OPC's XML-DA (XML data access) Complex Data specifications. This allows any OPC-compliant plant automation with need for complex data such as asset registry information, diagnostic/prognostic information, maintenance work tracking/operator action tracking, reliability, and complex data (vibration, image, video, etc.) to retrieve or post this information in an open manner. The resulting MIMOSA OSA-EAI Architecture Summary is depicted at Figure 2.0.

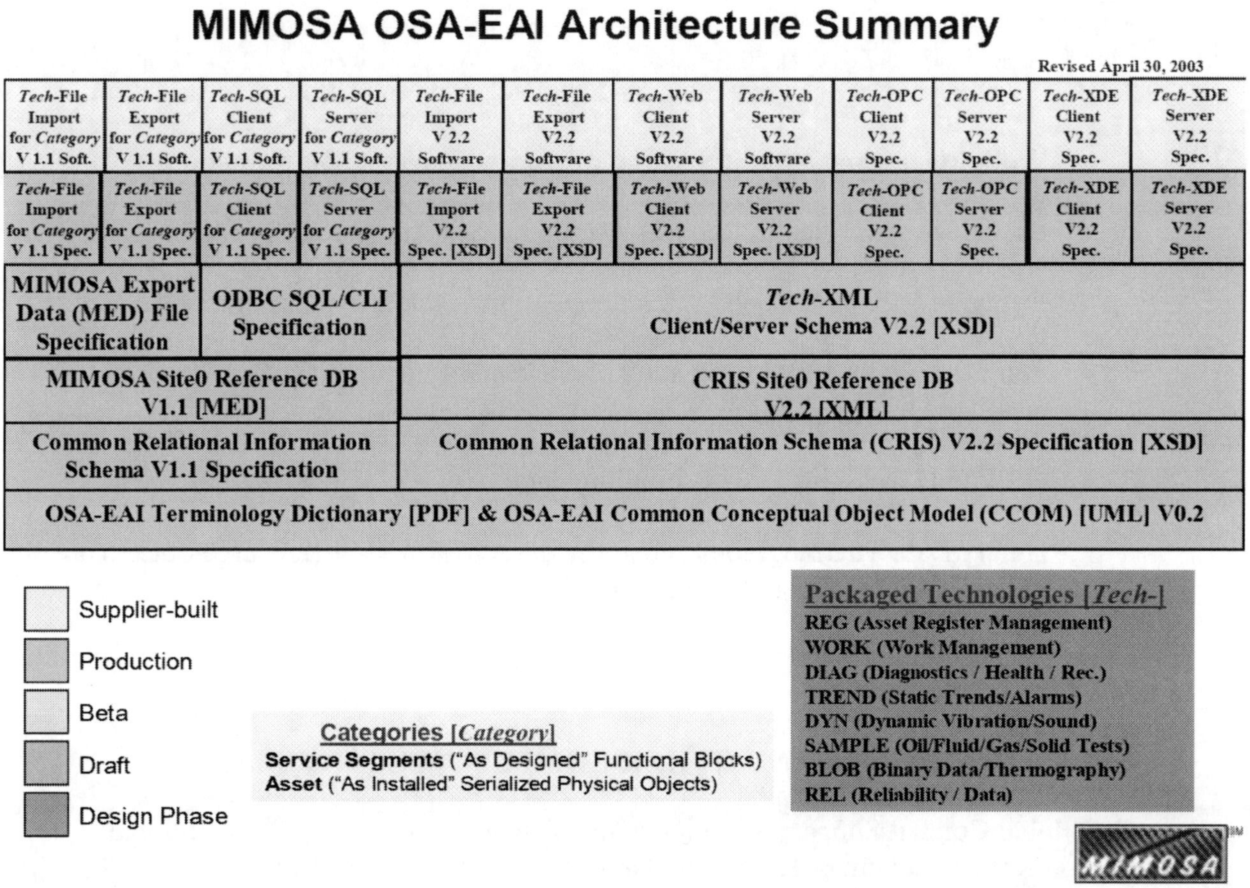

Figure 2.0 Architecture Summary

The CRIS schema contains more than 300 tables depicting various types of asset condition data. Unlike proprietary stovepipe systems, systems developed in accordance with the CRIS enable communication of data and information from many different systems thus enabling interoperability.

The MIMOSA specifications define five types of interfaces that can be utilized for the transfer of data in both directions: (1) Tech-File for transferring data in a file format, (2) Tech-SQL (structured query language) for use with an ODBC (open database connectivity) data server, (3) Tech-Web for use with an HTTP (hypertext transfer protocol) XML (extensible markup language) data server, (4) Tech-OPC for XML OPC exchange of wrapped MIMOSA query and response information, and (5) Tech-XDE (XML document exchange) for XML exchange by any document exchange mechanism. HTTP or HTTPS (secure) protocols using XML messages are used for Tech-Web communications.

To facilitate customizing an interface integration, each interface type is further divided into Application Technology Packages generally addressing the following data characteristics:

- Asset Register Management - "as designed" and "as installed" information
- Work Managemnt - audit tracking of work management information
- Diagnostics and Health Records - equipment health state information
- Dynamic Vibration/Sound - creation and retrieval of dynamic measurements
- Static Trends/Alarms - creation and retrieval of historical scalar measurements and alarms
- Oil/Fluid/Gas/Solid Tests - sampling data
- Binary Data/Thermography -creation and retrieval of binary large objects used with thermography and imaging monitoring

These specifications are used for communicating data and information between condition monitoring, diagnostic, asset management, and work management systems.

MIMOSA AND OTHER COMPLIANCE DOCUMENTS

The Global Combat Support System - Army/Transition (GCSS-A/T) operational requirements document (ORD) draft change proposal specifies the utilization of open systems interface architecture such as the CRIS. The next change proposed to MIL-STD 3008 (TM), Interactive Electronic Technical Manual (IETM) Technical Data Requirements to support the Global Combat Support System - Army specifies the complementary use of the MIMOSA standards. The International Standards Organization (ISO) Technical Committee 108, Sub-committee 5 works toward developing standards for monitoring and evaluating machines. The MIMOSA Technical Director, Ken Bever, chairs Working Group 6 of a sub-committee focusing on standards related to data processing and analysis procedures for conditioning monitoring and diagnostics. Although not a member of the ISO, the MIMOSA standards are mentioned in and compliant with ISO 13374. The result of the inclusion of MIMOSA in these documents is widespread acceptance and support by the international asset condition assessment and analysis community.

CALIBRATION MANAGEMENT INFORMATION SYSTEM (CALMIS)

The PM-TMDE Integrated Management System (TIMMS) described in the Army Metrology section, above, was developed as a DOS (disk operating system) system and has been upgraded to function in a Windows environment. Since it is a stand-alone system, it is cost prohibitive to upgrade to satisfy current requirements to support engineering data as well as integration with STAMIS and GCSS-A/T. SAIC presented a proposal to develop a new system entitled CALMIS that would satisfy operational and engineering data requirements for worldwide calibration support. In addition, the system would, through the use of MIMOSA standards, have an open interface to STAMIS and GCSS-A/T as it becomes available.

SUMMARY

As a result of Army Vision 2010 guidance, the Army is being transformed into a highly mobile and responsive force that will utilize digitization for command, control, communication, computing, intelligence, and reconnaissance (C4ISR) as well as combat service support. The requirement for interoperability is mandatory. Open computer systems architecture assures and enhances interoperability. Central to the proper operation of weapon systems is calibration that is traceable to national standards. The current PM-TMDE Integrated Materiel Management System (TIMMS) supporting Army metrology is a stand-alone system that is not integrated into the Standard Army Management Information Systems (STAMIS) or the Global Combat Support System - Army/Tactical (GCSS-A/T). The Calibration Management Information System proposed by SAIC will utilize MIMOSA open interface standards to assure interoperability with STAMIS and GCSS-A/T.

BIBLIOGRAPHY

1. Army Regulation 750-43, Army Test, Measurement, and Diagnostic Equipment Program
2. Department of Defense Joint Vision 2010
3. Department of Defense Directive 5000.1, The Defense Acquisition System
4. Department of Defense Directive 5000.2, Operation of the Defense Acquisition System
5. Deputy Program Executive Officer, Business Information Systems, United States Army Program Executive Office, Enterprise Systems
6. MIL-STD-3008 (TM), Department of Defense Standard Practice, Interactive Electronic Manual (IETM) Technical Data Requirements to Support the Global Combat Support System (GCSS-A), 30 September 2000
7. MIMOSA Open System Architecture for Enterprise Application Integration (OSA-EAI) Specification
8. Product Manager, Automated Logistics and Integrated Systems (http://www.gcss-army.lee.army.mil/), United States Army Program Executive Office, Enterprise Systems

9. Project Manager, Logistics Information Systems (http://www.gcss-army.lee.army.mil/), United States Army Program Executive Office, Enterprise Systems
10. United States Army Combined Arms Support Command, Global Combat Support System - Army High Level Functional Description
11. United States Army Combined Arms Support Command, Operational Requirements Document (ORD) for Global Combat Support System - Army (GCSS-A)
12. United States Army Program Executive Office (http://www.eis.army.mil/), Enterprise Information Systems
13. U. S. Army Test, Measurement, and Diagnostics Activity, Test, Measurement, and Diagnostic Equipment (TMDE) Integrated Materiel Management System (TIMMS) Users Guide
14. United States Army Vision 2010

CARL M. POWE, JR
BIOGRAPHY

Dr. Powe is a retired Regular Army Ordnance Officer with specialties in the integrated logistical support of missiles, nuclear weapons, and conventional munitions. He is currently employed as a Senior Scientist/Engineer with Science Applications International Corporation in support of the Software Engineering Directorate, Aviation and Missile Research Development and Engineering Center, U. S. Army Aviation and Missile Command, Redstone Arsenal, AL. He has developed and taught courses on information technology for the Deputy Chief of Staff for Command, Control, Communications, Computing, and Intelligence, Headquarters, Department of the Army and Faulkner University and developed management information systems for United Technologies and Thiokol Corporation. He holds BS, MBA, and D.Mgt. degrees and is a graduate of the U. S. Army Command and General Staff College and the "Economics of National Security" course from the Industrial College of the Armed Forces. Military awards include: Legion of Merit, Bronze Star Medal, Meritorious Service Medal with Oak Leaf Cluster, and Vietnamese Gallantry Cross.

THE LOGISTICS OF AIRCRAFT SURVIVABILITY - PROTECTION AGAINST HOSTILE THREATS, CRITICAL TO MISSION SUCCESS/BATTLE SPACE SURPREMACY

By
Kenneth H. Brockel
Harry G. Ivory, Jr.
Cliff S.Vermont

The purpose of Aircraft Survivability Equipment (ASE) is to protect the host platform against hostile battle space threats, thus allowing for mission accomplishment. As the U.S. Army expands it's theater of operations due to changing world politics, our soldiers and aviators face constantly increasing threats which are more complex and technologically advanced than ever before. This is especially true with the recent war on terrorism, whereby even our homeland has potential for battle space activity. The Army's current inventory of legacy ASE was fielded within the 1980 through 1990 timeframe. The equipment in it's current configuration has either reached, or is rapidly approaching, life expectancy. Parts obsolescence; optical, mechanical, and structural component deterioration; and increased maintenance requirements; all tend to escalate Operational and Supportability (O&S) costs, and reduce system Readiness. With the next generation of ASE slated for out year fielding, and the anticipated quantities being very restricted, it is inevitable that the current legacy ASE will continue to be a major player in the Objective Force Structure for many years to come. The paper will review the emerging issues of how to maintain an affordable effective bridge to the objective system utilizing a mix of legacy with Mission Reliability focused performance level upgrades and integration of new technology into the process of ASE systems support.

Increasing Profitability Through Warranty Assessment

by

G. Stephen Brunner

Abstract

Warranties are an essential part of the current business environment. Effective warranty program management improves competitive edge and provides dramatic opportunities to increase the bottom line. Effective warranty assessment uses a Life Cycle Engineering approach to gain insights into warranty programs and the associated costs to government and industry.

This paper focuses on the "fixed price per operating hour" warranty program prevalent in industry today and cost reduction prospects in the operation and support environment. The paper explores the methodology, tools, and model that provide an organized process for gaining visibility into the life cycle costs of a warranted product. Armed with an effective warranty assessment, the program manager can select the warranty that is most competitive in the marketplace and then aggressively address the cost drivers of implementing that warranty. The paper provides insights that will result in more reliable products, increased customer satisfaction, reduced cost and increased profit. The paper relates to the SOLE Symposium theme by demonstrating how government and industry can collaborate to establish working programs that benefit both participants.

This paper would be of particular interest to program managers, proposal/marketing managers and chief operating officers in government and industry.

Warranty Advantages

Warranties are an essential part of the current business environment and can provide significant benefits to a program. Effective warranty program management improves the contractor's competitive edge and provides dramatic opportunities to increase his bottom line. From the government perspective, warranties allow program managers to do better budgetary planning, free up program funds for other opportunities, and reduce risk. During the warranty implementation period, the government program manager also has time to assess the operational and support costs of fielded hardware before committing to organic capability.

There are significant differences between the characteristics of a public (government) warranty and a private (commercial) warranty program. A commercial warranty consists of a statement from the manufacturer regarding what should be expected from the product or service. This statement is little more than an insurance policy against initial quality discrepancies with no input from the customer. When we address systems on the order of ships and aircraft, warranties can be much more complex. But there can be some overlap between the government and commercial warranty programs. Currently, there is a thrust in government acquisitions toward the purchase of Commercial Off-the-Shelf

(COTS) items. Along with the commercially available hardware or service, the program manager is encouraged to obtain the same warranty terms offered to the general public.

Warranty Program Definition

The type of warranty program that we will focus on is more than a one-sided offering of an insurance policy. Government program warranties offer the opportunity for the contractor and the customer to benefit by providing input to the program structure through effective negotiations that balance the risks and incentives for both participants. The Air Force Materiel Command defines a warranty as "a promise or affirmation given by a contractor regarding the natures, usefulness, or condition of the supplies or the performance of the services furnished under contract."[1] A well written warranty delineates the rights and obligations of the contractor and the government with the objective of motivating the contractor to design, produce, deliver, and, in this case, support quality products while making a profit.

There are many different types of warranty programs in use today, but the one that seems to be gaining popularity is a version of the Reliability Improvement Warranty (RIW) known as the "fixed price per operating hour" warranty or, as trademarked by Rolls-Royce, "Power-by-the-Hour". In this type of warranty, the contractor is usually responsible for all the system maintenance for the duration of the warranty period. The RIW, as the name implies, focuses on achieving an acceptable reliability of the mature system. Reliability is most often measured in Mean Time Between Failure (MTBF). One of the objectives of the RIW is to motivate the contractor to increase system reliability. The contractor's motivation is increased profit potential realized if MTBF can be improved above the warranty program pricing basis. By improving the fielded hardware MTBF above that which was negotiated in the warranty, the contractor gets to keep more of the warranty program payments because of the reduced number of repair actions. The contractor expends less resources maintaining the system while the warranty program income remains constant.

A "fixed price per operating hour" warranty is structured by projecting a failure rate and cost of repair of the contractor's system. Then the government applies a usage rate to determine a fair cost to maintain the system. This is the cost to the government of the warranty program. The revenue to the contractor is in the form of a fixed amount based on operation of the system. The government benefits from this type of warranty by avoiding the cost of depot and intermediate support, spares, maintenance parts, maintenance training, and technical data. Life Cycle Cost (LCC) is monitored and controlled for the system, and budgetary planning is more predictable for the government program manager. For the cost of the warranty program, the contractor assumes all the cost of maintenance for the system. Understanding and reducing the cost to perform this maintenance provides opportunity for the contractor to increase profit. The government also benefits from improved reliability through increased operational availability of the system.

Figure 1 shows the opportunity the contractor has to increase profit given a fixed income warranty program. As the plot shows, the contractor will lose profit dollars (and

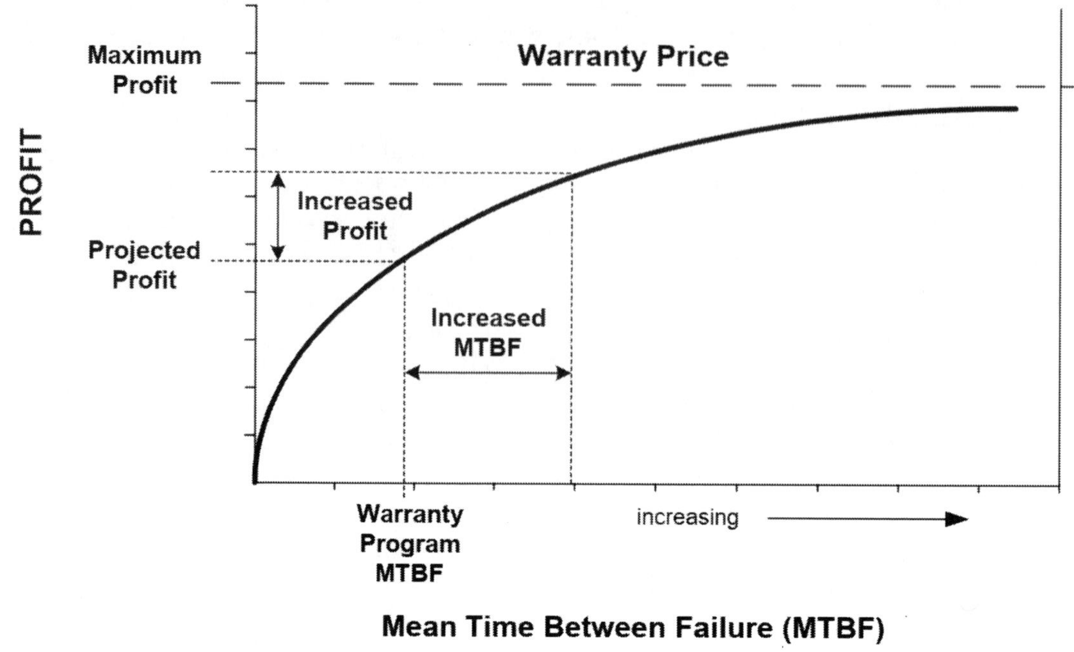

Figure 1. Notional Representation of Warranty Program Profitability

eventually lose money) if the achieved MTBF for the fielded hardware is less than the warranty program value. However, if the MTBF for the fielded hardware exceeds the warranty program value, profit continues to rise with increasing MTBF until it approaches the warranty price. The profit curve flattens out as MTBF increases; approaching a value where essentially all the warranty price would be profit (except for some small fixed administration costs). If the contractor is able to improve the system MTBF, there is a direct increase in warranty program profit. When thought of in this manner, the opportunity for increased profitability of a warranty program becomes clear.

Warranty Assessment Model

Contractors who have traditionally worried about lowering the cost to produce the system to increase profits may lack the ability to discover the areas of cost that should be addressed in a warranty program. A warranty assessment model is under development to provide the methodology and tools needed by the contractor to gain visibility into these cost reduction opportunities. The objective of the model is to accurately reflect the relationship between design and support system issues and operational warranty costs. By applying the model early in the warranty program definition, we have a better idea of the opportunities that exist to influence the hardware and support system design. The inputs to the warranty assessment model include length of warranty, number of units produced, maintenance concept, complexity of the system, projected system usage, MTTR, and a realistic MTBF goal. There will be other parameters used by the model to identify warranty program cost centers, but the major influences are listed. These parameters are used to comprehensively reflect the costs to both the contractor and the government of warranty program implementation. These costs include spares, training, labor, support equipment, technical manuals, system tracking and transportation, and repair parts. Using the "fixed price per operating hour" warranty program, the contractor takes responsibility for most of these costs in exchange for fair compensation for providing this level of support. In prior procurement contracts with the government that did not include a warranty, the contractor's responsibility ended when the equipment was accepted by the government.

Using a Life Cycle Engineering approach, the warranty assessment model will give the contractor's warranty program manager insights to the cost associated with the different phases of system life. This model meets the need for improved visibility of reliability and maintainability beyond the production phase to the fielded product. In particular, cost centers in the Operating and Support (O&S) environment are highlighted, which may not have been a contractor concern previously. More and more manufacturers are embracing this new business opportunity upon realizing that O&S costs for a system can be two-thirds of the total cost of ownership. Providing the life cycle maintenance and support services for their product offers a significant revenue source. In some cases, it represents greater income potential than the initial sale of the product.

The important part comes when evaluating the cost of providing support on a fixed income per operating hour, since that represents the contractor's profitability. But, for many of the contractors that have traditionally focused on reducing production costs, getting into a brand new business means assessing totally different cost drivers. Since system reliability is the focus of a RIW and can be one of the biggest drivers of O&S costs, the model accurately reflects the ripple effect a change in reliability can mean to warranty program costs. The impact of increased reliability on other O&S parameters is not lost on the government customer. The contractor can increase profitability by reducing LCC for the system and at the same time positively impact the system's ability to meet government Essential Performance Requirements (EPRs). The model is set up to distinguish between contractor and government warranty program costs. It is particularly sensitive to factors that are under the control of the participating parties. Therefore, as cost centers are highlighted, they can be further investigated to determine cost drivers. The cost centers are presented by the model in Pareto hierarchy. This gives visibility to the opportunities that make the biggest impact on program costs. The model can use expert estimates or data ratioed from a current system to assess the total LCC associated with the warranty program being analyzed. The information provided to the program manager gives insight to program costs broken out by the development, production, and operational phases. It also shows total cost incurred by year of the program for both contractor and government for budgetary planning purposes.

As a program manager, one of the most important factors in a warranty program is exposure to program changes. You may say "that model is great if program parameters that I input remain constant". Well, the model has the capability to assess program risk, including length of program, number of systems produced and maintenance concept. By simply inputting a reasonable range of possible risk, the model will use expected value to provide risk exposure visibility for this warranty program. The model can project the changes in program costs to both the contractor and government by cost category. Using these projections, a manager can make a determination of warranty program value on a business case basis.

Warranty Assessment Benefits

Warranty program definition and assessment truly requires a Life Cycle Engineering approach. Each phase of the life of a system represents its own challenges and opportunities. Input to the program by both contractor and government benefits both parties through influence of the warranty program design. The warranty becomes more than a one-sided insurance offering. It is a performance-based agreement. An effective warranty integrates reliability, maintainability, supportability, availability, and cost to optimize system performance. The earlier in the development program these Essential Performance Requirements are addressed, the bigger the impact the warranty program can have on system effectiveness and program profitability to the contractor.

The visibility that the warranty assessment model gives to the total life cycle cost results in many more possibilities to impact system and support definition to reduce cost and increase profit. The contractor can effectively focus his program efforts by concentrating on the cost areas that have the least burden of cost reduction implementation and possess the highest potential for major impact to warranty program costs, as identified by the model. Armed with a thorough warranty program assessment, the contractor can aggressively address the cost drivers of implementing the warranty and increase profit. President and CEO of Rolls-Royce, John Cheffins, summarized the contractor's warranty program view by stating "Now this (power-by-the-hour guaranteed cost maintenance contract) aligns our upside with airline (or customer) upside. If the product is durable and reliable, we both have an upside. It allows us to be more profitable if we have a better product…"[2]

The government has asked its program managers to assess the benefits of a warranty on all new acquisition programs. By offering a comprehensive warranty program, contractors are very competitive in today's marketplace. The "fixed cost per operating hour" warranty program offers the government fixed costs for budgetary planning with no surprises and the motivation for the contractor to improve reliability. Accomplishment of a warranty program assessment early in system development offers the greatest opportunity for warranty program improvement both to the contractor and the government. The cost reduction insights provided by the warranty assessment model can result in improvements in reliability and maintainability that directly contribute to contractor profitability and customer satisfaction.

[1]Quoted from Air Force Material Command, System Warranty Guide, February 2003.

[2]Taken from AviationNow.com from an interview with John Cheffins at the 2001 Paris Air Show

G. STEPHEN BRUNNER

Mr. Brunner is a Systems Analyst with the System Analysis team at Acquisition Logistics Engineering (ALE). His duties include analyses in the areas of logistics engineering, supportability in product design and Reliability & Maintainability.

Education

Masters of Science, Mechanical Engineering, University of Florida
Bachelor of Science, Mechanical Engineering, University of Tennessee

Specialized Training

Systems Engineering, Program Management, LSA Orientation

Qualifications

Mr. Brunner has had ten years of experience with a Department of Defense contractor for gas turbine engines. He has been a leader in the implementation of logistics and supportability considerations in the design process, working with design engineers and subcontractor personnel to meet maintainability goals. He has extensive practical experience from flight test support and operational readiness assignments. He is well acquainted with the many aspects of logistics support from his experience managing a DoD development program Supportability IPT that coordinated the diverse perspectives of logistics engineering.

As a system analyst, Mr. Brunner can bring his design and field experience to bear on ALE clients' specialty engineering and logistics support projects.

Melding Defense and Civilian Logistics: The Just-In-Time Process and the Objective Force: A Perfect Match?

Clifton Officer Jr.

Abstract

The United States Army is using its Legacy systems for current sustainment. It is using the Interim Force to experiment with different strategies and tactics that can be implemented in the Objective Force. All this is taking place in an environment of small to medium conflicts worldwide as well as terrorist threats both abroad and inside the United States.

The Army's Just-In-Time system is called Distribution Management (DM) (previously known as Velocity Management (VM)) and will be used to transport equipment and supplies to the forward units without using a lot of organic equipment or large storage areas within the theater. The question is whether the implementation will insure mission accomplishment while continuing to preserve the lives of the soldiers.

While budget necessity has driven the planning community to use JIT, we must also realize the effects that a pure JIT system will have on the soldier. When we implement a JIT system, we must insure the safety of both the soldiers involved and the non-combatants. There will be missions that occur in peacetime that could cost lives in surprising ways.

Military leaders discuss collateral damage, but when that damage becomes more than a mote in the public's collective eye, the reality of the damage sets in and causes a backlash that will cost the military in the long run. Neither the American public (nor most other civilized nations) will abide that cost.

TH-C-5-OFFICER

Background

The US Army and the Department of Defense is in the position of having to do more with less. Budgets were reduced, while the operational tempo has increased. The last taste of war that the American public had, seemed easy to swallow but expensive to buy, so there is an outcry for the warriors to cut back on their needs.

As a part of this cut back, the costs of doing business logistically have been analyzed and found wanting. Therefore, the leadership of this country deemed it necessary to find new ways to afford the conflicts of the future.

Joint Visions 2010 (JV2010) and 2020 (JV2020) have both articulated the need for a more focused logistics backbone for the new Objective Force as well as a reduced logistical footprint in the theater of conflict. The focus will be attained using better information technologies and near real-time data updates before, during, and after the conflict.

Focused logistics is going to rely on Distribution Management (DM), another term for Just-In-Time, which will use the transportation system to hold 'inventory' while items move to the using unit. This way inventories will be reduced to the bare minimum and allow compliance with the Joint Vision tenet of a reduced logistical footprint.

In order for the Objective Force to be adaptable, flexible, and highly mobile, the amount of logistical support must be reduced. No longer can we afford to have a high ratio of support versus combat personnel, units, and equipment.

The problem with this idea is that the American public seems to have become averse to seeing or hearing about casualties, whether they are our own or whether they are the civilians of another country. The conflict-incurred pain, injury, and death of non-combatants of the enemy country stir the heartstrings of Americans and cause twelfth hour revaluation of plans, strategic, operational, and tactical.

Certainly, the public is correct to feel some empathy towards the innocents abroad, but the fact remains that the military is still required to answer when the nation calls. Moreover, it does not matter whether the conflict involves all out war, humanitarian assistance, or some other matter that falls along the continuum of conflict.

The White Paper: Concepts for the Objective Force (US Army, 2001) states:

> Innovative, multi-modal distribution concepts, exploitation of more reliable systems, systems commonality … will reduce maintenance and supply requirements, while improving readiness and enhancing strategic deployability.

It will be vitally important for the national leadership to remember that, while JIT is an exceptional way to cut costs in the civilian sector, the costs for the military are quite different.

As an analogy, if a post commander gets weather reports stating that freezing temperatures and rain-slicked highways are very possible the next day, the commander may decide to have the post's personnel come in two hours later than normal. This would give the ground a chance to warm up and melt the ice. It would also allow the post's personnel to avoid traffic in an area not known for its cold weather driving skills.

What happens if the freeze does not come? The major costs involved were those applied to the administrative leave incurred.

TH-C-5-OFFICER

Now, replace the post with a unit in combat and replace the personnel with supplies in the JIT network. How far off can the timing be?

In addition, remember that the capabilities of the weather computers are, in many ways, comparable to those of the military logistics system.

While it is not within the purview of this paper to cover every detail of the future of American military logistics, it will point out some of the studies that have taken place and discuss their meaning within the context of the Objective Force. The paper then reaches some conclusions about whether a JIT system is applicable to the type of support needed during the expected conflicts.

Discussion

As Peters (1998) said, "Today, information mastery is the enabler of both war and policy." There is no way that a planner can have a 100% guarantee about what is going to occur in the future. However, with historical information and up-to-date situational awareness, that planner will have a better idea about upcoming events.

Current information systems have a great capacity for data collection and conversion of the acquired data into useable information for decision- making. "We are the sum of that which we are allowed to know, and American citizens and soldiers are allowed to know more than any human beings in history." (Peters, 1998)

"On tomorrow's distributed asymmetric battlefield … time and distance will drive sustainment operations. … Combat operations will cover a vast area encompassing widely dispersed combat elements engaged at different intensities and in different battle rhythms, with unsecured lines of communication (LOCs) spread throughout the battlespace inside an area of operations. … In Vietnam, unlike the Gulf War, resupply by air routinely sustained units up to battalion level for weeks at a time. … As in Vietnam, air delivery and evacuation will be essential to sustainment continuity." (Solomon, 2002)

While the Objective Force White Paper states that the use of "new strategic platforms" would "complement use of prepositioned stocks", the Velocity Management Training Support Package (1997) notes the decreased reliance on them due to the "difficulty in predicting where the next operation will occur". The system used for the JIT environment in the Army (and in other services) has to take the differences in operational environment into consideration.

TH-C-5-OFFICER

In a study of JIT at several CONUS Army posts, deliveries were simplified using pre-planned routes and stops, just as they currently occur in the field during tactical training. "On post, routes were set up to eliminate wasted driving time between customer drop-off points, and cargo in the truck was staged to match the delivery route. Drop-off times were set at each location, where a crew of soldiers stood ready to unload truck cargo with the efficiency of a race car's 'pit crew'." (Wang & Champy, 2000)

The problem is that if we understand the Joint Vision (and common military sense) correctly, we do not want to use the same routes or stops repeatedly. Planning has to consider the movement of the unit and not underestimate the intelligence of the people who would strive to keep the unit from accomplishing its mission.

Lenzini (2002), while discussing Anticipatory Logistics, states, "Knowing on-hand supply levels will help logistics leaders to better configure 'pulsed' logistics resupplies, typically consisting of 3 to 7 days' worth of supplies." The question is how to carry those supplies.

The military planners are in the midst of trying to reduce the amount of 'stuff' that the soldier will carry and, at the same time, reduce the logistical footprint in theater. The unit will still be obliged to carry some of those supplies for the soldier so that the individual unit can remain highly mobile.

"Objective Force units will arrive in theater capable of self-sustainment for 3-7 days and have a system of potable water generation and replenishment at every echelon." (Riggs, 2002) Even with the advent of water generating capabilities that can be carried on a small trailer and foodstuffs that can be placed in a soldier's pocket for reconstitution at some later time, there are limits as to the amount of food that any small combat unit can carry.

If we are talking about having a unit that is highly mobile, flexible, and adaptable, then we cannot expect them to be weighed down with 3-7 days of supplies. Those supplies must come from somewhere else, and arrive in a timely manner.

As we discuss a reduced footprint, we also must consider the increased operational tempo that is currently taking place in military units. This tempo probably will not drop any time soon. “Reduced sustainment demand is critical to achieving a smaller theater sustainment footprint. However, the requirement to sustain increased velocity and tempo offsets some of the benefits of demand reduction.” (USAWC, 2001)

“The ideal operating environment for JIT is one where-

- All systems work efficiently.
- There is limited fluctuation in supply and demand, such as in a scheduled manufacturing process.
- The supplier is geographically close and close cooperation and communication are characteristic…
- A zero balance is unlikely but not extremely undesirable.
- Safety stock is considered excess.” (Vanairsdale, 1992)

Does this set of characteristics match the requirements placed on JIT in a military, tactical environment? “A review of doctrine, literature, and experience reveals that the Army procurement, distribution, and consumption environment has the following characteristics-

- Systems operate at less than 100 percent efficiency.

- Demands are unpredictable due to variable mean-time-between-failure and operational tempo.

- Proximity and identity of the supplier may change each year or with each new contract.

- The penalty for zero balances is mission failure.

- Safety stock is required for lead time and deployment readiness requirements." (Vanairsdale, 1992)

Therefore, if we consider the differences between the ideal manufacturing environment and the military environment, it is easy to see that we cannot directly apply JIT if we are to have successful military missions. At least, not without some modifications allowing a buffer at the using unit level as well as one at the supporting unit. "A comparison of the operating environment for successful JIT implementation and the operating environment of the Army spares inventory management program indicates that the two simply are not compatible." (Vanairsdale, 1992)

The problem, of course, is the tendency for units to overemphasize the need for additional or supplementary stocks to carry the unit through periods of non-receipt of materiel. "Units within a battalion or larger unit with similar equipment tend to stock the same items on their individual PLLs (Prescribed Load Lists). This redundancy causes separate units to transport the same items, unit-level PLL clerks to manage the same items, and generally requires units to stock more of the same items than necessary for maintaining the unit's equipment. This results in excess stockage." (Haynes, et. al., 1997)

The user does have the right idea, though, and should be supported not only from a purely logistical point of view, but from a morale view as well. If we know that we are going into a fight with a limited amount of materiel and that any additional supplies are ‘in the mail’, can we honestly say that we would feel relatively at ease about putting our lives on the line? “The future management of logistics policy… must rely on velocity and responsiveness to get the repair part from the depot to the customer on an accelerated OST (Order-Ship-Time) while remaining efficient and affordable… This places new demands on logisticians who must continue to accurately estimate needs before the needs become critical requirements.” (Haynes, et. al., 1997)

When discussing a TACOM program that began prior to the official VM undertakings, Kucyk (1997) stated, “Under [the] initiative (direct vendor delivery/electronic data interchange (DVD/EDI)), commodities are purchased directly from a major vendor using EDI purchase orders, thus bypassing the traditional acquisition process. In addition, the vendor ships the requisitioned materiel directly to the end user instead of to a central receiving point.”

The aforementioned program is fine within its limits, but just how many vendors can we expect to ship directly to the using unit in wartime? With all that materiel arriving from different vendors, there has to be someone on the ground near the using unit to anticipate the arrival of and receive the items. Those items then need to move forward to the using unit in a timely and efficient manner. Unless, of course, we expect ‘mail call’ to replace a consolidated receiving point.

Taylor (1998) explained that, “Velocity management is founded on three basic

tenets-
TH-C-5-OFFICER

- Improved flow of materiel in terms of both speed and accuracy
- Substitution of velocity for mass
- Elimination of functions that do not add value"

Writing in September 1997, Eger noted that, "Currently, VM is being implemented through the work of four process improvement teams (PITs): order and ship time, repair cycle (RC), stockage determination, and financial management. Each PIT works to improve its processes by first defining the process, then measuring the process, and finally improving the process by implementing the lessons learned in the first two steps."

"[T]he goal of the PITs is to identify and eliminate sources not only of delays but also of errors and waste. Focusing on time, quality, and cost will deliver a logistics system that is faster, better, and cheaper." (RAND, 1998)

The logistical planners rely on the 80-20 rule that states that 80% of the cost of inventories can be blamed on a mere 20% of the individual items in that inventory. "Heavy items account for only a small percent of the total requisitions shipped by air, but over 80% of the total weight, generating a staggering air freight bill. By forward positioning enough of these 'big and' heavy' items in USAREUR, USTRANSCOM can switch to surface mode for replenishment to DLA and AMC forward storage locations, who can then resupply USAREUR units from stocks in theater." (VM, 2001a)

Joint Vision states that we want to reduce the logistical footprint in theater, and then the planners state that the way to get around the cost of transportation is to place some percentage of materiel forward in a prepositioned location. The stocks are a part of the footprint and someone has to go get those stocks. The unit can go get them, but when the unit hits the ground in a conflict, we have to decide if we want the warfighters using their valuable time receiving supplies or utilizing that time to fight.

Using OST as a metric allows the planners to get a picture of the cost, in time, of not having a part. However, OST as used previously in the military, only applied to travel from and return to the Supply Support Activity (SSA) by the original order and the received item, respectively.

"The efforts of the Order-Ship Time (OST) PIT (Process Improvement Team) over the past 3 years have reduced the OST for the Active Army in the continental United States (CONUS) by 54 percent. This improvement is a direct result of the use of scheduled, dedicated trucks. These trucks bypass central receiving points whenever possible and deliver supplies … directly from the depot to the SSA." (Walden, 1999)

In a statement in the Velocity Management newsletter (Summer 2000), the Chief of the VM team announced that Customer Wait Time (CWT) had been approved as a key Army metric. Implementing the use of CWT means improving access to the unit-level ordering process and insuring that the information relevant to CWT that needs to be put into the system actually gets put in. "CWT [Customer Wait Time] is an 'end-to-end' metric that measures the actual performance of the Army supply chain. It thus provides a holistic view of the entire Army supply chain process." (VM, 2001b)

Understanding the need for rapid movement and receipt of goods is important as is realizing the cost of carrying inventory. Careful planning needs to take place to insure that we do not limit the using unit (through contracting) to only one or two vendors who may not be able to fulfill their part of the deal due to external circumstances (i.e., transport vehicle destroyed).

"Prime Vendor eliminates the layering of supplies at multiple echelons and shifts inventory, inventory management, transportation, and personnel costs from the Government to commercial firms. Prime Vendor programs take advantage of the experience of commercial vendors, whose profit-based business practices demand lean inventories and rapid deliveries. Prime Vendor is Velocity Management in action." (VM, 1998)

Conclusion

In 1994, Halliday and Moore stated, "DoD should study industry distribution models carefully and selectively use or adapt them. Initial steps would include putting one agency in charge of the DOD elements involved with distribution, from requisition to receipt, and altering their goals so that they are system wide and they focus on satisfying warfighter needs. Then the process would require rigorous review to ensure that all subordinate elements and procedures worked toward achieving that goal."

They did not advocate taking JIT at face value and applying it without any effort to adapt it to the military situation. The leadership has to make decisions (and good ones) about what JIT should mean in a tactical atmosphere.

"Like the 19th-century's military-technological entrepreneurs, today's technology salesmen predict that future units will have at least three to five times the firepower of current ones, and thus can afford to be smaller in size and fewer in number." (Echevarria, 1998) While we are moving toward this new frontier of smaller means better, we have to insure that we do not reduce our military units below a level that can accomplish the required missions as well as meet the operational tempo.

"If JIT is adopted across the board, the probability of mission failure will be significant. Possible gains in inventory management efficiency do not outweigh the consequences of mission failure." (Vanairsdale, 1992) Consider the benefit of having needed materiel in the pipeline against the cost of a soldier's life.

In its January 2002 report to the Senate Armed Services Committee, the GAO noted that, "DOD has not developed a strategic plan to coordinate these initiatives or to provide a road map for identifying or prioritizing future activities. However, DOD may find that a 'one-size-fits-all' approach will not work for all services and that it will need to tailor its approach to meet its specific needs and requirements." (GAO, 2002) Even the DOD comments responding to the report did not specifically address the need for a strategic plan. It only addressed "implementing plans to upgrade the Federal Procurement Data System to provide more detail on service acquisitions" and "developing an oversight process for the acquisition of services."

As DOD implements JIT, they also have to measure the ability of the system to accomplish the mission. Rather than a piecemeal set of metrics, it would be more effective to have an overall performance measurement system that covers the entire supply chain, as opposed to measuring separate and disparate facets of the chain.

Laitinen (2002) presented "an integrated performance measurement system (IPMS) based on a managerial view." He was attempting to develop "an appropriate managerial tool for measuring and improving performance." Although the tool is designed especially for the small company, the DOD could adapt it for use. "The principal idea is to follow resource use from the point when the very first (elementary) allocation is made, to the point when the results of the allocation are realized in the shape of revenues [as in reductions in taxpayer cost]. The dimensions at any point along the chain are regarded as determinants of the dimensions that succeed them."

Laitinen's (2002) approach "focuses strongly on improving performance, rather than simply measuring it." Everyone along the supply chain has a role in total quality management, which is essentially, what this approach provides.

Tying the IPMS to future technological advances and to the equipment currently available enhances the military ability to perform at a high optempo with reliability. "With the advent of Radio Frequency Identification (RFID), real-time global supply chain visibility is possible. However, true supply chain visibility will only be achieved once we marry this mobile asset-tracking technology with supply chain and logistics event management systems." (Dugan, 2002)

Martha and Subbakrishna (2002) address safeguards that corporations take which may also be feasible for use by the US government. In their article for Supply Chain Management Review, they discuss the following steps:

- Insure the risk – if you can
    - Hedge using options or futures (mainly a corporate type of insurance, but there may be future situations that can take advantage of this)
    - Plain old insurance
- Cultivate alternate sourcing arrangements
    - Relying heavily on a single source for a product or for critical components leaves a company highly vulnerable to prolonged and expensive supply gaps
- Line up alternate transportation
    - Smart sourcing strategies include backup plans for transportation tie-ups as well.
- Help the customer decide what to choose

- Don't work in a vacuum. Talk with the customer about choices that have to be made during emergencies.

- Build in quick response to shifts in demand
- Manage inventory to the "right" level
- Prepare for the new realities

The greatest of the new realities is asymmetric warfare. This warfare does not only involve flying airliners into buildings. It can be as simple as a shoulder-fired weapon used to bring down the aircraft that is bringing your overseas unit their JIT supplies.

Suddenly, there are no supplies.

The military could use a form of JIT to insure that a buffer is available at the using unit. (Bonvik, et. al., 1996) This goes against what some leaders think of when they say Just-In-Time, but is more realistic in terms of the reliability of the supply chain in a wartime situation.

Roach, writing in a monograph in 1997, concluded, "JIT improvement provides the asset visibility, flexibility, and cost effectiveness needed to support future class IX repair parts supply and distribution. However, without vision and total support by the US Army leadership, JIT systems and methods even if implemented will not dramatically improve…operations."

Using JIT will vastly improve the ability of the US military to accomplish its many varied missions. The Objective Force design allows the National Command Authority to continue the task of leading the world through trying times. As we design and improve the functionality of the units within the Objective Force, the national leadership must continue to consider the cost of losing soldiers due to an over-reliance on a strictly JIT process without building in a buffer that allows soldiers to have a fall-back position.

Harvey, writing in 2001, stated, “The goal is to reengineer and improve support functions by establishing baselines, identifying sources of inefficiencies, setting goals for corrective actions taken, and measuring performance.” An over-reaction to budget necessities could cause lives to be lost somewhere along the continuum of conflict. Therefore, it is also true that the goal must be to protect lives, American and otherwise.

Bibliography

Bonvik, Asbjoern M., Couch, Christopher, Gershwin, Stanley B. *A Comparison of Production-Line Control Mechanisms.* Accepted for publication in the International Journal of Production research. April 1996.

Coyle, John J., Bardi, Edward J., Langley, C. John, Jr. *The Management of Business Logistics: A Supply Chain Perspective.* 7th Ed. South-Western Thomson Learning. Canada. 2003.

Dugan, Joseph H. *Using Radio Frequency Identification to Drive Real-time Supply Chain Management.* Internet World website. Retrieved October 21, 2002. http://www.internetworld.com/news.php?/inc=vc/10092002a.html. October 2002.

Echevarria, Antulio J. II. *Tomorrow's Army: The Challenge of Nonlinear Change.* Parameters. Autumn, 1998.

Eger, Andrew C. CPT. *Reducing Repair Cycle Time.* Army Logistician. Sep 1997.

Fuller, Tony LTC. *Velocity Management newsletter.* http://www.cascom.army.mil/vm. Volume 1, Issue 3, Summer 2000.

General Accounting Office. *Best Practices: Taking a Strategic Approach Could Improve DOD's Acquisition of Services.* Report to the Chairman and Ranking Minority Member, Subcommittee on Readiness and Management Support, Committee on Armed Services. U.S. Senate. January 2002.

Halliday, John M. and Moore, Nancy Y. *Materiel Distribution: Improving Support to Army Operations in Peace and War.* RAND Issue Paper IP-128. March 1994.

Harvey, Aaron C. III, LTC (P). *The Road to Focused Logistics.* Strategy Research Project, US Army War College. Carlisle Barracks, PA. 2001.

Haynes, Gregory A. CPT, Holguin, George CPT, Martin, Michael B. CPT, Matuskevich, Cynthia A. CPT, McLaughlin, Scott D. LT, and Nelson, James A. LT. *PLL Policy: Changing at the Speed of Velocity Management.* Quartermaster Professional Bulletin. Spring 1997.

Hernandez, Arnaldo. *Just-In-Time Manufacturing: A Practical Approach.* Prentice Hall. NJ. 1989.

Kucyk, Douglas P. *Velocity Management-Ahead of Its Time at TACOM.* Army Logistician magazine. Sep 1997.

Laitinen, Erkki K. *A dynamic performance measurement system: evidence from small Finnish technology companies.* Scandinavian Journal of Management, Number 18. 2002.

Lenzini, Joshua M., MAJ. *Anticipatory Logistics: The Army's Answer to Supply Chain Management.* Army Logistician magazine. Sep-Oct 2002.

Martha, Joseph and Subbakrishna, Sunil. *Targeting a Just-In-Case Supply Chain for the Inevitable Next Disaster.* Supply Chain Management Review website. Retrieved October 9, 2002. http://www.manufacturing.net/scm. Sep. 2002.

Peters, Ralph. *The New Strategic Trinity*. Parameters. Winter 1998.

RAND. Speeding the Flow: How the Army Cut Order-and-Ship Time. RAND Arroyo Center Army Research Division. 1998.

Riggs, John M. Testimony on Ground Force Modernization. Statement before the House Committee on Armed Services Subcommittees on Military Procurement and Military Research and Development, US House of Representatives. April 11, 2002.

Roach, Franklin D. Just-In-Case or Just-In-Time: Total Asset Visibility and Just-In-Time Distribution's Impact on Future Class IX Repair Parts Operations in US Army COSCOMs and DISCOMs. Monograph for the School of Advanced Military Studies, US Army Command and General Staff College. Fort Leavenworth, KS. 1998.

Solomon, Billy K., LTG. Improving Maneuver Sustainment for the Objective Force. Army Logistician magazine. Nov-Dec 2002.

Taylor, Curtis D. CPT. Knowledge-Based Logistics. Army Logistician. Nov-Dec 1998.

United States Army. White Paper: Concepts for the Objective Force. 2001.

United States Army Combined Arms Support Command (CASCOM). Velocity Management Training Support Package. 1 July 1997

United States Army War College. Army Transformation Wargame 2001. April 2001. Carlisle Barracks, PA.

Vanairsdale, Michael J., COL. Just-In-Time Inventory: Trading Efficiency for Effectiveness. Army Logistician magazine. Mar-Apr 1992.

Velocity Management Team. Prime Vendor: Velocity Management at DLA. Army Logistician. Jan-Feb 1998.
TH-C-5-OFFICER

Velocity Management Team. *Dollar Cost Banding – A First Look.* Velocity Management newsletter. Volume 1, Issue 1, Winter 2000.

Velocity Management Team (a). *Army Transitions to Customer Wait Time (CWT) for Better View of Supply Chain.* Velocity Management newsletter. Volume 2, Issue 1, Spring 2001.

Velocity Management Team (b). *Changing the Airlift-Sealift Mix for Better Support to USAREUR.* Velocity Management newsletter. Volume 2, Issue 1, Winter 2001.

Viale, J. David. *JIT Forecasting and Master Scheduling: Not an Oxymoron.* Crisp Publications, Inc. Menlo Park, CA. 1996.

Walden, Joseph L. LTC. *A Velocity Management Update.* Army Logistician. March-April 1999.

Wang, Mark Y.D., & Champy, James A. *Accelerated Logistics: Streamlining the Army's Supply Chain.* RAND Pub MR-1140-A. 2000.

Clifton Officer Jr. is a US Army Materiel Command Fellow, with the Close Combat Division, Close Combat/Medium Range Directorate at AMCOM-IMMC. He received his B.S. in Business Administration from Upper Iowa University, Ft. Polk, Louisiana in 1996. After graduation, he worked for BDM and TRW at Ft. Polk, LA for about seven years as the Technical Leader for the Combat Service Support Tactical Analysis Feedback Facility in the Joint Readiness Training Center (JRTC).

Clif received his M.S. in Business Administration with a concentration in Health Services Administration from Central Michigan University at Ft. Polk, LA in 1997. He joined the Federal Service in 2001 when he was selected as an AMC Fellow by the Headquarters, US Army Materiel Command, Alexandria, VA. As a Fellow, Clif received training in various Army Career Fields, such as Logistics, Contracting, Quality, and Reliability and

TH-C-5-OFFICER

Maintainability. He also received an M.S. in Business Administration from the Florida Institute of Technology in 2002. Clif served twenty years in the US Army in the logistics arena with experience in distribution, customer support, system management, system design, and acquisition.

Clif is currently training as an Item Manager with the Bradley section of the Close Combat/Medium Range Directorate. He will continue through a series of positions at HQAMC, AMCOM, CECOM, and TACOM as well as other major commands over the next three years that will allow him the opportunity to gain the operational and technical experience necessary to move into leadership positions. These positions will replace the losses from the anticipated retirements of management personnel. That is the stated goal of the AMC Fellows program.

TH-C-5-OFFICER

TITLE

THE TEAMING TOOLSET:
An Effective Merging of Government and Commercial Project Team Practices

AUTHORS

Dr. Conna Condon conna_condon@uiuonline.org
Dr. Elizabeth Rivers rivers@nova.edu
Dr. James Skertich james_skertich@uiuonline.org

ABSTRACT

Military, government, and commercial project teams can use the same project management tools with comparable success. A recently completed study evaluated the effectiveness of the *teaming toolset,* a comprehensive package of project task and process management tools, with a "procedurally just" reward system. This toolset resulted from merging project task management tools, developed in the defense industry and standardized by the Project Management Institute, with project process management tools, developed through academic and commercial research on team development activities and performance. The process management performance assessment tool, originally used in the health care industry, was validated for multidiscipline application as part of this research study of project teams efficacy. Results supported the position that use of the teaming toolset significantly impacted the perceptions of goals clarity, internal team feedback, and team conflict awareness. No significant performance difference was found for participants with defense industry or military backgrounds.

Introduction and Overview

In a study of 600 teams, Barnard (1999) found that today's teams require better preparation for teaming. This training results in a sense of empowerment by management that believes in the team development process. Clearly teaming skills are a critical issue for today's businesses. Therefore, business has called upon the academic community to prepare students to work in teams (Gardner & Korth, 1998; Wheelan, Murphy, Tsumura, & Fried Kline, 1998). Academia's response has been to modify course curricula to include team projects (Bolton, 2000; Condon 2003). However, simply forming study groups and assigning group projects is not sufficient to create effective teams or provide effective teaming experience. Preparing students for real world team success requires much more structured guidance. (Condon, 2003) Real teams use research-based team process development tools and task management tools developed in industry and based upon The Project Management Institute's PMBoK (1996).

A recently completed study evaluated the effectiveness of a comprehensive package, called the *teaming toolset.* It represents the merger of defense industry developed project task management tools, standardized by the Project Management Institute in the PMBoK, combined with project process management tools developed in academic and commercial research on team development (Scholtes, Joiner & Streibel, 1998; Drexler, Sibbet & Forrester, 1988; Janz, Colquitt, & Noe, 1997; Parker, 1994a; Parker, McAdams & Zielinksi, 2000). The performance assessment tool was originally used in the health care industry and validated as part of a study of project teams. (Deeter-Schmelz & Ramsey, 1998) Perhaps the most significant component in the *teaming toolset.* is a "procedurally just" reward system.

The literature related to external leader interventions in team development (Spreitzer 1995a, 1995b & 1996; Bolton, 1999; Kirkman & Rosen 1999 & 2000), team design (Cohen & Bailey, 1997; Gardner, 1998; Barnard, 1999; Potthast, 1999; VanDerVegt, Emans & VanDeVliert, 2000) was reviewed to develop the *teaming toolset*, Gladstein's 1984 model of task group effectiveness was linked to the phases of team development identified in Tuckman's model (1965) as the basis for the *teaming toolset* model (Figure 1). Recent findings related to establishing a team vision, project task and process approaches will be briefly discussed. Preference to team, including the impact of the presence of a social loafer on a team and the mitigating influence of a procedurally just reward system were examined.

The Teaming Toolset Model

Teams have been modeled based upon two general approaches: (1) the team as a variable in the organizational design; and (2) the developmental phase variables within the team. The team level analysis treats the team as an entity that can be measured and analyzed. The organizational level analysis develops the equation at the organizational level of design. Gladstein's model of task group effectiveness is an organizational-based model. Gladstein identifies the elements of group composition and structure. It is the organization's responsibility to create teams with effective composition, structure, and resources, including training and rewards. In this research, this is identified as the external leader empowerment requirement for effective teaming.

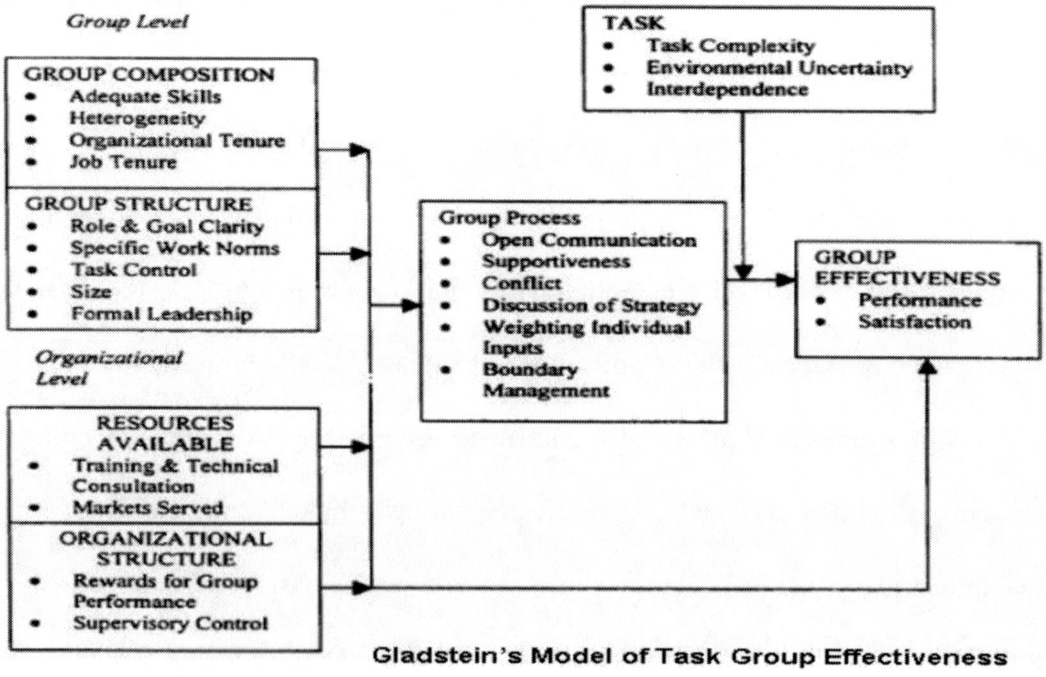

Figure 1 Gladstein's Model of Task Group Effectiveness

A consistent thread across team development literature is the phased concept of team development. Most researchers have developed a four or five phase model of team development. (Tuckman, 1965; Drexler, Sibbet, & Forrester, 1988; Katzenbach and Smith, 1993; Parker, 1994; Wheelan, 1996) They have recognized that groups of individuals willing to work together as a team, are inspired to accomplish clearly identified goals and acknowledge and appreciate their team members. This personal identification with the team is a prerequisite for working together effectively and key to achieving high quality work results. Coaching has been identified by some as he skill most needed by external leaders. However, Wagerman (1997), in a study of self managed teams, unexpectedly determined that external leader team design factors were more important to the success of teams than coaching. Consistent with the findings of other organizational model researchers, she found that: (a) simple, clear, engaging direction, which specifies the end but not the means, was critical to success. (b) Teams require a significant *real team task* that requires interdependent work to succeed. (c) Teams need a place, technology and other resources "that make it possible for the team to work in a timely, proactive, and effective fashion" (Wagerman, 1997, p. 49). Team goals and group norms that support strategic thinking, the authority to manage their work, and team-based rewards for achieving their goals are essential for a successful teaming experience. Of particular significance was Wagerman's finding that, if all other factors were effectively addressed in design of the teams, and development of norms was encouraged, the teams would develop effective norms naturally. "This finding implies that given the other six critical success factors for effective teaming are provided, norms that supported active problem-solving and strategic thinking tend to emerge and be maintained more carefully by team members. "Tackling the other six factors first greatly increased the chances that a leader was successful in building appropriate team norms." (Wagerman, 1997, p. 49). This recommendation, was substantiated by findings of other recent studies (Deeter-Schmelz & Ramsey, 1998; O'Connor, 2001) of external leader empowerment of project team.

Methods

The efficacy of the *teaming toolset* was demonstrated most recently in March - April, 2003. The sample in this study was a group of graduate and undergraduate students attending an online university based in the mid-west. All courses in the university require a team project. In some courses, such as information systems management, the team project is reality based focused on improving an existing process in a team member's company. Other courses use team reports of real-world case analyses. The target population includes a significant number of U.S. Military and former military members in addition to adult learners currently employed in the commercial sector (Condon, 2003).

Designed as an *ex-post-facto, quasi*-experimental study using descriptive correlation analysis, it adhered to Simon & Francis' (2001) recommendation to use this methodology when investigating "one or more characteristic of a group to discover the extent to which the characteristics vary together." (p. 27) A treatment group of courses included the *Teaming Toolset,* while the control group of courses specifically did not contain teambuilding tools. Student's assignment to courses was random based upon term registrations.

The study represented a cross-sectional as opposed to longitudinal survey since data collection occurred in a single term. Since correlation studies only establish association between variables, prediction of future results based on these findings is not possible. Data consisted of reported self-perceptions and teammates' perceptions of team process performance.

The courses using the *teaming toolset* also included an instructional guide and a template to assist in developing a vision, team name, and project name for either a feasibility study or current trends research study. The template provides task breakdown (a.k.a. work breakdown structure) as well as status reporting guidance. The feasibility study template includes specific guidance for identification of alternatives and determination of the reliability, sustainability, and maintainability of each alternative for comparison. Guidance is provided in establishing a communication plan and developing rules and norms for handling conflict within the team.

A pretest-posttest assessment of the perceived efficacy of the *teaming toolset* was measured for the treatment courses. Peer evaluation of each member's contributions to both the team tasks and the teaming process were reported to faculty and averaged for use in weighting the team rewards (grade sharing).

The Population

A total of 282 students completed the term, with 117 consenting to participate in the research study. Of these students, 95 submitted the demographic questionnaire. A total of 35 were from control group courses and 60 were from the treatment group courses. Since no control group teams were fully represented, analysis at the team level was not possible. The subsequently reported profile is based on aggregate analyses.

There was no appreciable difference between the profiles of treatment and control groups and the aggregate profile. The following summary is the aggregate sample demographic profile. The usable responses represented 34 percent of the population frame, with 36.8 percent male and 63.2 percent female. Age ranged from 21 to 56 and were equally distributed around a mean age of 36.4 years; three students left the age field blank. Prior military or defense industry experience was reported by 25.3 percent. Regarding prior team experience, 3.2 percent reported none, while 18.9 percent reported 1-3 experiences, 31.6 percent reported 4-6 experiences, and 46.3 percent reported 7 or more experiences. Regarding prior team training, 28.4 percent reported none, while 31.6 percent reported 1-3 trainings, 11.6 percent reported 4-6 experiences, and 27.4 percent reported 7 or more trainings. It is noteworthy that more students with defense backgrounds had more than 7 prior experiences than students without defense experience. A total of 61.1 percent of the students indicated they were enthusiastic about teaming.

The Results

The primary research question sought to determine if provision of a toolset, embedded into the requirements for the course would impact the self-reported experience of teaming. A statistically significant difference was found on the overall scores for a two- tail .05 alpha. Comparisons based on individual evaluation criteria were mixed and are reported in Table 1. Inspection of individual responses suggested the possibility of "halo effect" which skewed some ratings towards the maximum allowable score. Another observation seemed to reflect a greater propensity to rank a peer lower than self recognizing this would impact the grade earned for the team project. Significant differences were noted for setting goals, receiving feedback, and handling conflict.

There was no significant difference between participants' performance with and without defense backgrounds. It was noteworthy that unlike the general population, the assessment results for those with defense backgrounds were positively skewed.

Table 1. Results of Test of Significance Difference

	Items	Significance Level
	OVERALL: Average of all items	@ 2 tail .05 alpha
1.	Works toward the understood goals of the team	@ 2 tail .05 alpha
2.	Contributes to an informal, comfortable, and tension-free work environment	@ 1 tail .10 alpha
3.	Is enthusiastic about working with the team and exhibits high morale	Fail to rejected
4.	Follows through on commitment	@ 1 tail .10 alpha
5.	Takes pride in the team's work	@ 1 tail .10 alpha
6.	Shows interest in other team members' achievements	Fail to rejected
7.	Readily accepts feedback on performance	@ 2 tail .05 alpha
8.	Encourages others to achieve at high levels	Fail to rejected
9.	Is able to stay focused on team tasks	@ 1 tail .10 alpha
10.	Exhibits open lines of communication with other students	Fail to rejected
11.	Is sensitive to the feelings of others	Fail to rejected
12.	Is able to resolve conflict effectively	@ 2 tail .05 alpha
13.	Is eager to try new approaches	Fail to rejected

In addition to the empirical measurements reported above, anecdotal comments posted in the online study group communications were analyzed. Although students were required to prepare a schedule during Week 2 of the term as part of the Project Approach grade, not all used the optional status/schedule update form to track their progress. This was true even for those who had taken prior courses which used earlier versions of the *Teaming Toolset*. The only tools used consistently were those specifically associated with grade points. This observation was not surprising and substantiates the earlier observation that simply forming study groups and assigning group projects is not sufficient to create effective teams or provide effective teaming experience. Since the schedule update tool was not being used, a few days before a group milestone assignment was due the study group discussion rooms typically included posted messages asking what "we're supposed to be doing?"

Conclusions and Recommendations

This research provided a valuable initial field test of the *Teaming Toolset* and identified a number of areas for continued improvements and future research. The results were significantly impacted by the "halo effect." Future research should consider using a 10 points Likert scale. This would be expected to spotlight the few severe "social loafers " team members usually reported in the 1 and 2 points range. However, the magnitude to the revised scoring range would separate them from the team members who participated, but still required skills development. Furthermore, providing narrative behavioral descriptions defining each value should discourage the ubiquitous use of a score of 10 except as an unusual case. Emphasis on the importance of the factually based peer review activity's role in grade determination should be made early in any course using the *teaming toolset* package.

Since students only used those tools with rewards (grade points) associated with them, the value of using the schedule update tool should be presented clearly and mandatory use should be considered. External leaders of teams should encourage, reward, and facilitate team incremental progress through assignment of incremental deliverables, progress reports and reviews. Furthermore, sufficient time must be provided from assignment to deliverable allowing the team to analyze, develop and implement the plan. Interdependent performance requires time to develop methods for effective communication and work allocation across the team.

Use of the *teaming toolset* can empower project teams to define their goals, allocate assignments, and establish norms and communication protocols more effectively. Leaders must encourage and facilitate the use of the project management tools through some form of perceived reward weighting and procedural justice. When this happens, teams have a more effective teaming experience.

Bibliography

Barnard, Janet (1999). The empowerment of problem-solving teams: is it an effective management tool? [Electronic version] *Journal of Applied Management Studies,* 8, 73.

Bolton, Michele Kremen (1999). The role of coaching in student teams: A "just-in-time" approach to learning. [Electronic version] *Journal of Management Education,* 23, 233.

Cohen, Susan G., & Bailey, Diane E. (1997). What makes teams work: group effectiveness research from the shop floor to the executive suite. *Journal of Management,* 23, 239.

Condon, C. N. (2003) A Dissertation: The antecedents and consequences of external leader empowerment of small group teams. In publication process with ProQuest

Deeter-Schmelz, Dawn R., & Ramsey, Rosemary. (2000). Student team performance: A method for classroom assessment. [Electronic version] *Journal of Marketing Education,* 20, 85.

Drexler, A., Sibbet, D., & Forrester, K. (1988). The team performance model. In W. B. Reddy & K. Jamison (Eds.), *Team building: Blueprints for productivity and satisfaction.* San Diego, CA: University Associates.

Gardner, Brenda S., & Korth, Sharon J. (1998). A Framework for Learning to Work in Teams. [Electronic version] *Journal of Education for Business,* 74, 28.

Janz, Brian D., Colquitt, Jason A., & Noe, Raymond A. (1997). Knowledge worker team effectiveness: the role of autonomy, interdependence, team development, and contextual support variables. [Electronic version] *Personnel Psychology,* 50, 877.

Katzenbach, J.R., & Smith, D.K. (1993). *The wisdom of teams: Creating the high performance organization.* Boston, MA: Harvard Business School Press.

Kirkman, Bradley L., & Rosen, Benson. (1999). Beyond self-management: Antecedents and consequences of team empowerment. *Academy of Management Journal,* 42, 58.

Kirkman, Bradley L., & Rosen, Benson. (2000). Power Up Teams. [Electronic version] *Organizational Dynamics,* 28, 48.

O'Connor, Sheila Ann. (2000). Facilitating team process skills in engineering student design teams using a web-based coaching system. (Doctoral dissertation, Wichita State University, 2000). Retrieved December 21, 2001, from Source: ProQuest Information and Learning, UMI, Digital Dissertations.

Parker, Glenn, McAdams, Jerry, & Zielinski, David. (2000). Full team ahead. [Electronic version]. *Security Management ,* 44, 24.

Parker, Glenn. (1994a). Top 10 ways to guarantee team failure. [Electronic version] *Personnel Journal,* 73, 69.

Parker, Glenn. (1994b). Cross-functional teams. [Electronic version] *Small Business Reports,* 19, 58.

Potthast, Margaret J. (1999). Outcomes of using small-group cooperative learning experiences in introductory statistics courses. [Electronic Version] *College Student Journal*, 33, 1, 34

Scholtes, Joiner, & Streibel. (1996). *The team building handbook* Madison, WI: Oriel, Inc.

Simon, M. & Francis, J. (2001) *The dissertation and research cookbook from soup to nuts: A practial guide to help you start and complete your dissertation or research project.* (3rd Ed.) USA: Kendall/Hunt Publishing

Spreitzer, Gretchen M. (1996). Social structural characteristics of psychological empowerment*Academy of Management Journal*, 39, 2, 483

Spreitzer, Gretchen M. (1995). An empirical test of a comprehensive model of intrapersonal empowerment in the workplace. [Electronic Version] *American Journal of Community Psychology*, 23, 5, 601

Spreitzer, Gretchen M. (1995). Psychological empowerment in the workplace: dimensions, measurement, and validation*Academy of Management Journal*, 38, 5, 1442

Tuckman, B. W. (1965). Development sequence in small groups. [Electronic version] *Psychological Bulletin,* 384-99.

Van Der Vegt, Gerben, Emans, Ben & Van De Vliert, Evert (2000). Team Members' Affective Responses to Patterns of Intragroup Interdependence and Job Complexity. [Electronic Version] *Journal of Management*, 26, 4, 633

Wagerman, Ruth (1997). Critical success factors for creating superb self-managing teams.. [Electronic Version] *Organizational Dynamics*, 26, 1, 49

Wheelan, Susan A. & Hochberger, Judith M. (1996). Validation studies of the group development questionnaire . [Electronic Version] *Small Group Research*, 27, 1, 143

Wheelan, S., Murphy, D., Tsumura, E., & Fried Kline, S. (1998). Member perceptions of internal group dynamics and productivity. [Electronic version] *Small Group Research,* 29, 371-393.

Authors' Biography

Dr. Condon is a process consultant with over 25 years experience in the defense industry and over 5 years experience as an online educator. She currently is a member of the Upper Iowa University Online Program faculty. It is a direct result of this combination of backgrounds that her dissertation focused on external leader empowerment of small group teams.

Dr. Rivers is a process consultant specializing in application of Six Sigma and Lean thinking to support a systems logistics integrated management approach yielding innovative solutions to complex enterprise problems. As dissertation chair, her specific interests are reflected in the approach taken in this applied research project.

Dr. Skertich is a graduate student advisor and online educator retired from a career in the retail jewelry industry. His participation in the dissertation research was pivotal in the effectiveness of the outcome.

INTEGRATED LOGISTICS SUPPORT (ILS) AS A CONDUCTOR

Name :Mehmet Hilmi Ozdemir
Address :Inventory Control Center (EKM K.lıgı),Turkish Navy Golcuk Kocaeli Turkey 41650
E-mail :mhozdemi@ekm.tsk.mil.tr

ABSTRACT

Logistics' definition varies according to the education, title, rank, or position of the one who makes the definition. To me, logistics can be defined as an art of management of all processes in real life. Technically, logistics is a science dealing with the acquisition of reliable, maintainable, and supportable systems with the best value. These systems may vary from a simple component to a complex platform. There are some logistics disciplines (Maintenance plan, Supply support etc.) to be taken into consideration to provide supportable system designs to the ultimate users. To implement logistics disciplines, we have to accomplish some scientific and engineering analysis efforts. The method of accomplishing these efforts can be called as Logistics Support Analysis (LSA). LSA is integral part of the systems engineering processes. An effective LSA process is a key to the logistics success. ILS is an art of management, which makes all logistics disciplines be implemented concurrently by LSA process centric. The goal of the ILS is harmonizing all logistics processes in the acquisition programs. ILS also brings all different perceptions of parties (user, buyer, contractor etc.) to a common base. ILS is like conducting an orchestra and ILS manager is like an orchestra conductor.

When we type "*Definition of Logistics*" and hit the search button on a search engine on the Internet, we will probably get thousands of related pages. Among them we can extract hundreds of different definitions made by people with different perspectives.

We often encounter the key word "logistics" in our daily life. Be it on trucks on the highway, magazines, web sites, and on television or at the beginning of company names and everywhere. There must be a good reason for that. But what does the term actually mean?

If we want to look at the linguistic roots of the term logistics, they lie in the Greek "*logos*" (intellect, arithmetic), and in the Franco-Germanic root "*loger*" (to supply, to support). We also see the implementation of transportation and provisioning disciplines of logistics back to about 2700 B.C.

Today, bellows are commonly used definitions for the term logistics:

"A business planning framework for the management of material, service, information, and capital flows."

"The science of planning and carrying out the movement and maintenance of forces."

"The procurement, maintenance, distribution, and replacement of personnel and material."

"The process of planning, implementing, and controlling the efficient, effective flow and storage of goods, services, and related information from the point of origin to the point of consumption in order to meet customers' requirements."

The definition of Logistics varies according to the education, title, rank, or position of the one who makes the definition. Most of the definitions are a sign of military issues, because the origin of the logistics term comes from military environment.

I think that most of the definitions made for the term logistics are not adequate to cover its broader meaning. It is an essential issue to make the term logistics' broader meaning clear to be able to fully understand its coverage. Logistics is not just transportation, provisioning, engineering, supply support, or a technical tool. Beyond all these, logistics is from "cradle-to grave". To me, "*logistics can be defined as an art of management of all processes in real life.*" Because, all logistics phases are to be experienced through even a simple process. There must always be a trigger (definition of need) at the beginning of each process, an effort to reach best value during the process and a recoverability phase at the end just like logistics process flow.

As a technical definition, logistics is a science dealing with the acquisition of the reliable, maintainable, and supportable systems throughout the life cycle with the best value. These systems may vary from a simple component to a complex platform (a pump, a ship, or a space station etc.).

A system's life cycle begins with the definition of need, continues with operational phase and ends with the recoverability phase. From definition of need to the beginning of operational phase, acquisition logistics processes take place. During the operational phase including recoverability phase, operational logistics processes take place.

Acquisition logistics deals with all support activities between the time that a need is identified and the beginning of the operational phase to be able to deliver a supportable system to the user. The acquisition logistics incorporates concept, feasibility, project definition, full-scale development, and production processes. The answer to the question "what are the right requirements for operational logistics?" should be found during acquisition logistics phases. It will be too late to answer the same question at the end of the acquisition logistics. And the result would be a non-supportable system design.

The main goals of the acquisition logistics are influencing design decisions to improve supportability, achieving lowest cost of ownership, and meeting support needs. To be able to fully understand the spectrum of acquisition logistics, the processes can be divided into activities done before and after the completion of the design. Within this distinction, influencing design and identifying significant cost issues are to be done before the completion of the design, identifying adequate support resources is to be after the completion of the design. In summary, acquisition logistics aim to eliminate waste and to get "best value" by trying to set a balance between performance, support, and cost. Acquisition logistics activities can be likened to the activities done within a brain of the human body.

Operational logistics deals with all activities, which sustain a system when it is in the possession of the user to perform the mission. The operational logistics activities are day-to-day activities provided by organizations such as: maintenance, supply, training, transport, inventory control, and engineering. The goal of the operational logistics is sustaining systems with available support resources. Operational logistics is arms and legs of the human body mentioned above.

Logistics provides support to the user by implementing its technical disciplines such as:

- Maintenance plan
- Supply support
- Packaging, handling, storage and transportability (PHS&T)
- Technical documentation
- Manpower, Personnel, and Training
- Special tools and support equipment

The most critical logistics discipline is maintenance planning since it is the trigger for all processes in other logistics disciplines. Maintenance planning is the process, which coordinates the development and refinement of the preferred method of supporting a system to keep it in a serviceable condition. Maintenance planning also proposes solutions as to who will do required maintenance actions and where and how it will be done. Maintenance planning has three steps:

- Maintenance Philosophy
- Maintenance Concept
- Maintenance Policy

Each unit has different missions, different support systems for accomplishing maintenance, and varying levels of capability within their own organizational structure. The maintenance plan for an item of equipment must be tailored to fit the maintenance structure of its ultimate user. This individual maintenance structure reflects each organization's philosophical approach to maintenance, or the maintenance philosophy. Maintenance philosophy is a statement of the overall architecture of the user's support infrastructure. Maintenance philosophy can be applied to all projects and systems. Deciding to implement performance-based maintenance on the contrary to operating hours based maintenance in the entire Navy is a good example for the philosophical approach to the maintenance.

To be able to perform maintenance tasks effectively and efficiently, you need to make an extensive planning and preparation that starts at the very beginning of the concept phase. The maintenance planning process begins with development of a maintenance concept based on the maintenance philosophy. The maintenance concept is a statement of general guidelines to be used in developing the detailed maintenance plan for a system. Maintenance concept is the foundation for maintenance plan. Maintenance concept can be applied specific projects.

Maintenance policy is the final detailed maintenance plan itself. It documents exactly how maintenance will be accomplished for the system. It also identifies the physical (real) resource package to be provided to the user. The difference between maintenance concept and maintenance policy is that maintenance policy deals with each part in detail while maintenance concept does not.

In most cases, Government identifies maintenance philosophy and maintenance concept (functional processes) before the completion of the design, and Contractor identifies maintenance policy (physical process) after the design completed.

Maintenance plan should be cost effective, must support the mission of the unit, must consider all other logistics technical disciplines, is bounded by resource limitations and is the *challenge*.

Spare parts are required to support both preventive and corrective maintenance tasks. The availability of spare parts directly affects the overall operational availability (being operable at any random time) of a system. Below is the generic formula for operational availability of a system.

$$\text{Operational Availability (Ao)} = \frac{\text{Uptime}}{\text{Uptime+Downtime}}$$

As seen in this equation, the less down time results the higher operational availability figure. The factors affecting Ao figure are Turn Around Time and availability of spares. If you have the right spares, at the right place with the right quantity, as the downtime decreases the operational availability increases.

Supply support is a technical discipline that identifies, documents, procures, manages, and controls materials (spare parts, repair parts, and consumables) required to support the system. Supply support incorporates provisioning, spares management, and NATO codification processes. All these processes are linked to each other.

Within supply support process, it is really important to clearly understand spares terminology used in spares pipeline. A typical spares pipeline that shows the difference between terms related to spares is shown in the Figure 1. The reason of giving that much importance on the spares terminology is that the management of the spare part, repair part, consumable items, and bulk items should be different.

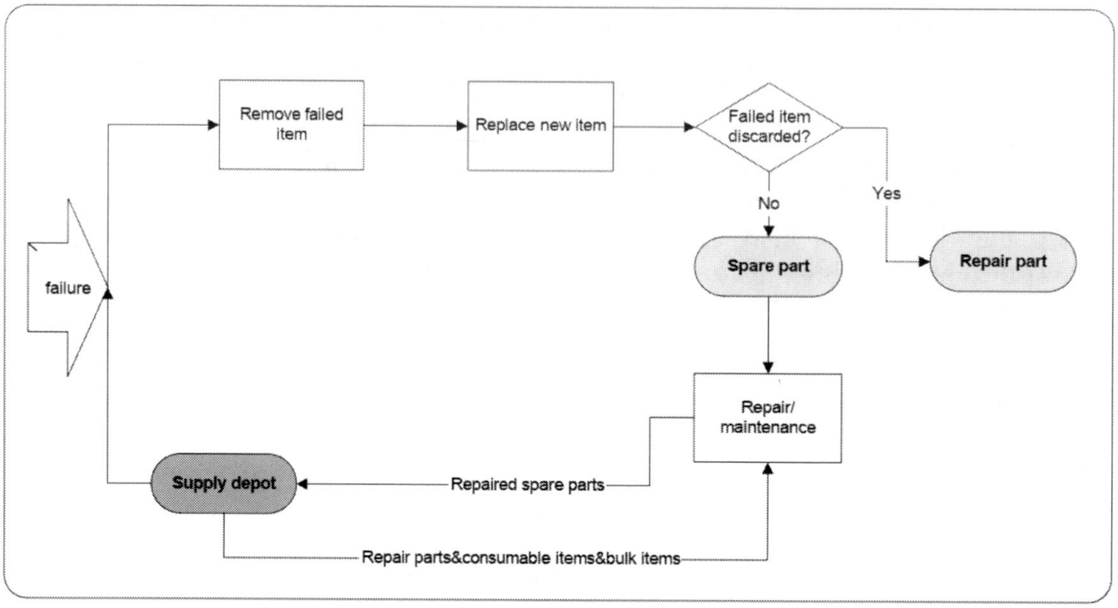

Figure 1, Spares Pipeline

Provisioning is determination of the *range* (number of different items) and *depth* (quantity of each item) of spares to be procured and stocked to support maintenance activities. The maintenance plan is the main input for provisioning process, because you have to select adequate spare parts for each maintenance level (Depot or Intermediate or Organizational) to be able to achieve operational availability. But it is not that easy to predict the future and use a standard spares model in an environment with this much fluctuation. Creating statistical projections for the future using historical consumption data or past experience may make the most accurate prediction.

Packaging Handling Storage and Transportability (PHS&T) is the overall characteristics of an item, which enable efficient packaging (physical protection), handling (physical indoor movement), storage, and transport (physical outdoor movement). In most cases, PHS&T issue is given limited importance whereas it may have a significant impact on the availability of a system. Therefore, PHS&T must be considered as an integral part of the design process. During the operational logistics, the user's perception is always to get operable equipment at any time he needs. To meet user's needs, the transportability of equipment becomes a critical issue, because it doesn't matter how well equipment is designed or how well it operates if the user can't use, move or deploy it. The main goal of PHS&T is to plan, develop, and manage the activities necessary to ensure that equipment is operable when the ultimate user owns and moves it over its operational life.

The ultimate user mostly cares about operational PHS&T, while the buyer cares about acquisition PHS&T. The acquisition PHS&T takes place for the items starting at procurement from manufacturer until delivery to the ultimate user. This part of PHS&T is the easy part.

The operational PHS&T takes place for the items that must be stored or moved by the ultimate user. This is the challenge part of the PHS&T.

The technical manual is the only documentation that is received by the ultimate user. Therefore, it is one of the most important documents that the equipment producer prepares. The ultimate user can install, operate, maintain, and support the equipment only by using technical manuals. Technical manuals provide detailed information such as pictorial descriptions of operation and maintenance procedures, necessary support and test equipment, identification of spare and repair part, or configuration structure of the equipment to the ultimate user. The lack of proper technical manuals will significantly degrade the ability of the user to operate and maintain the equipment.

Proper technical manuals does not mean tons of thick books used as a means of weight on the ships to set the balance on the though seas. When we say technical manuals, we talk about the manuals having proper, acceptable and adequate content and format. We have to look for minimum information to be provided (i.e. it is said that 262 English words are enough to define all maintenance actions.), technical accuracy, comfortable language, readability, and understandability within the content of the manuals. At the same time, the manuals should be provided by considering presentation, organization, usability, and standardization issues about the format.

The biggest cost driver within a life cycle of equipment is manpower, personnel, and training. For example, they say that seventy percent of the total cost of a car is manpower and personnel cost. In most cases, we take into consideration only manpower issues in the operation and maintenance processes. Manpower means a measure of total number of human resources. But more important issue to be considered here is personnel. Personnel mean physical attributes, skills, grades, and qualifications to perform specific activities. We have to consider both issues together to be able to get manpower and personnel integration (MANPRINT).

The critical issue is to define number of people (dedicated, shared, or indirect) to be required and training needs for operation, support, and training processes. To do that we have to identify which tasks must be accomplished to operate and support the equipment. These tasks can only be identified based on the information that is generated by other logistics disciplines or engineering activities. At the same time we have to determine our existing manpower and personnel (skills and knowledge) assets in detail. For example, maintenance concept is the key input to develop requirements for maintenance personnel at any maintenance level.

Another big cost driver within a life cycle of equipment is Support and Test Equipment (STE). STE is an extra cost since it needs extra personnel and training and requires support itself. STE can be classified as special STE (only used to operate and support a single system) and common STE (used to operate and support more systems). During the acquisition logistics, one of the main goals should be to minimize the need for special support equipments, maximize the need for common support equipments and automatic test equipments. The design of the equipment has impacts on the level of needs for STE. Therefore, during the design phase, we have to give necessary importance on the use of STE to operate and maintain the equipment. For example, if equipment is designed with self-test capability to track a failure in a module within the equipment, the operator can easily remove and replace the defective module using common tools and there would be no need for sophisticated fault isolation support equipment. Then, we can concentrate on the repair of modules rather than having to track defective module.

I guess giving a broader meaning to term logistics is not a wrong approach after taking a brief look at the logistics disciplines. Within the content of all these disciplines, we have to accomplish a lot of scientific and engineering analysis efforts. The method of accomplishing these efforts can be technically called as Logistics Support Analysis (LSA). LSA is used by logistics organizations to meet their objectives. LSA is integral part of the systems engineering process. LSA incorporates all engineering processes such as Reliability, Maintainability, Availability, Supportability, Testability, Failure Mode Effect Criticality Analysis (FMECA), Economic/Non-Economic Level of Repair Analysis (LORA), Human Factors Engineering, System Safety Engineering, and Total Life Cycle Cost Analysis.

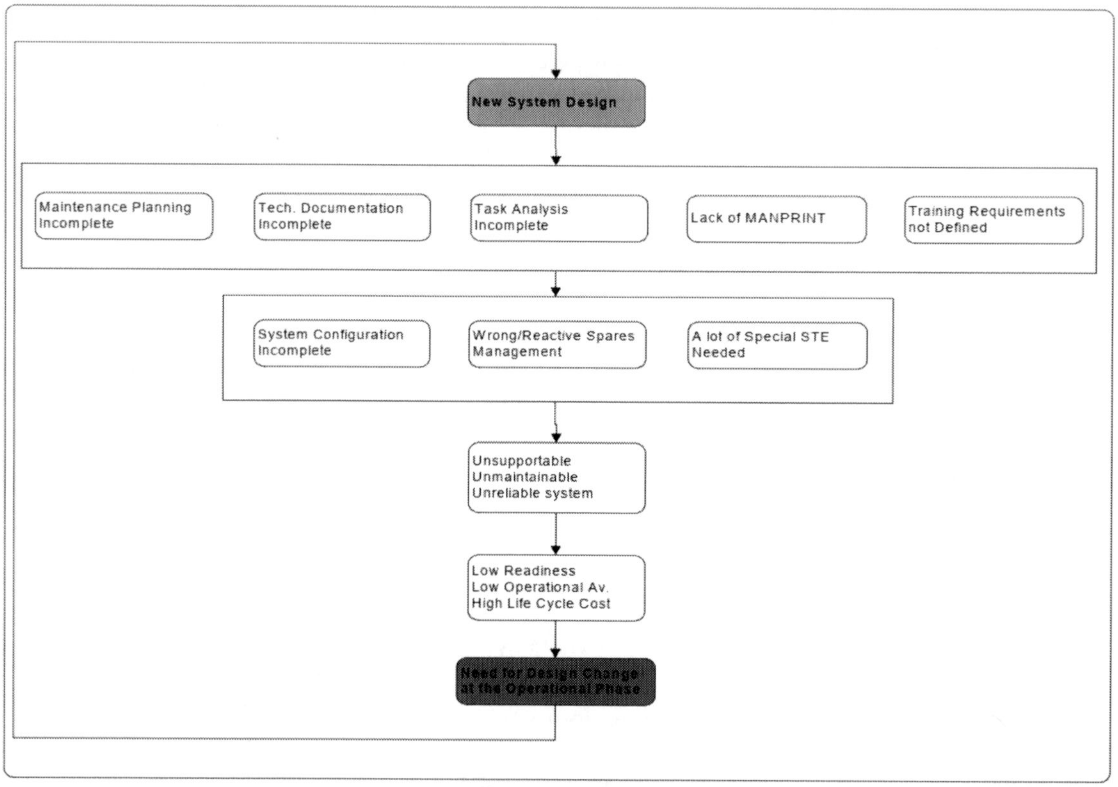

Figure 2, Need for LSA

The LSA process requires simple models to address all logistics issues during design phase at the acquisition logistics. The key issue within LSA is to be able to influence design to get supportable and cost effective systems at the end. LSA is to be implemented not to face with all possible negative impacts of a new design project shown in Figure 2. It is clearly understood that we need LSA to be able to reach our ultimate objectives such as high readiness, high operational availability, and low life cycle cost. The LSA process is a must to break the closed loop in the above figure and minimize the need for design change after the initial design. The LSA process must also have the capability to give quick and easy answers. Therefore, the best approach should be "*Least is Best*" within LSA.

LSA can be reviewed within two phases as functional LSA and Physical LSA. Functional LSA deals with the implementation system-engineering processes to create supportable designs. Physical LSA deals with the planning of resource packages to support the systems.

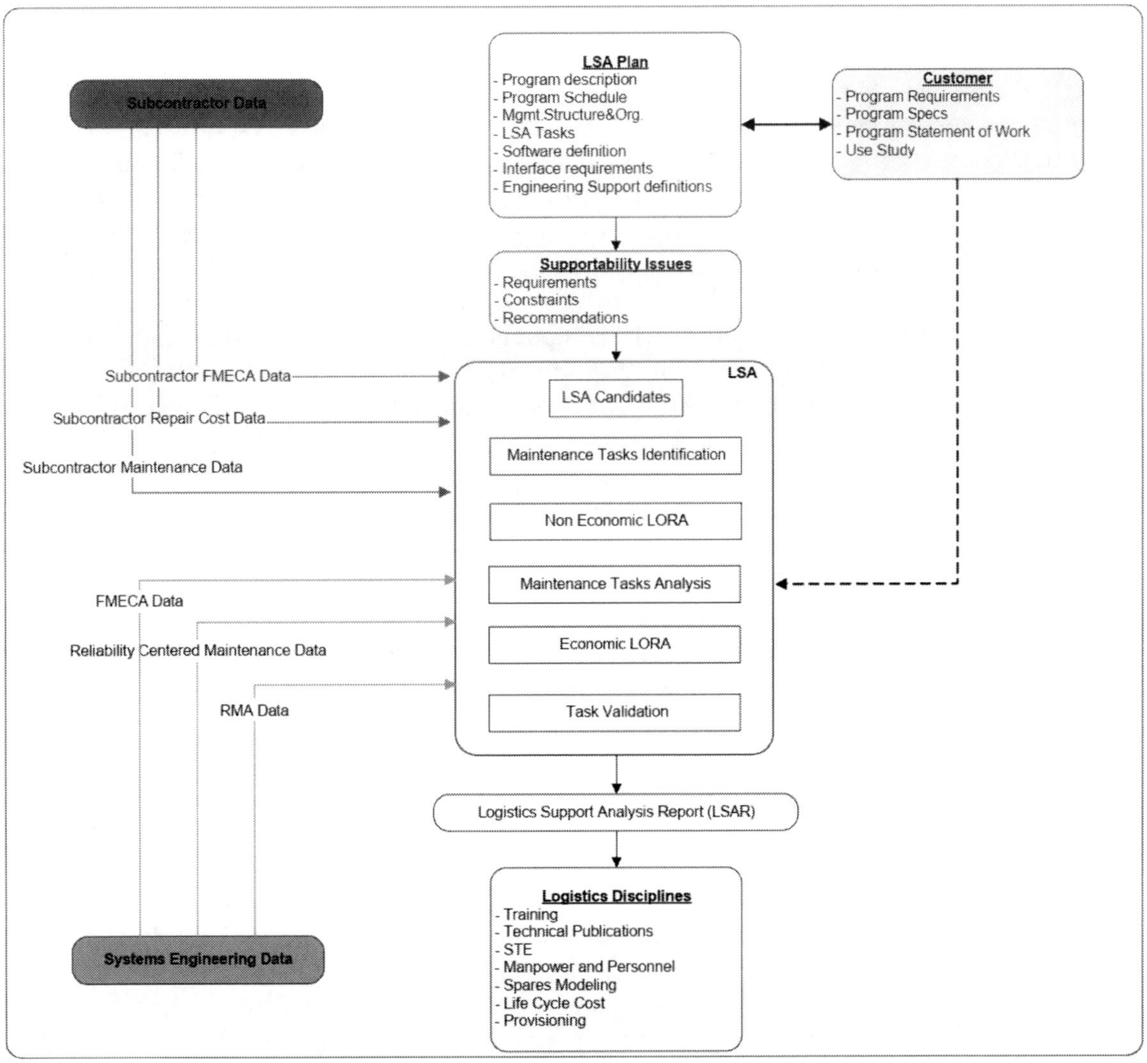

Figure 3, LSA Process

Figure 3 illustrates a generic LSA process that is normally conducted. The LSA process requires inputs from subcontractors, engineering, and customer. The LSA process commences with a plan incorporating program organization, schedule, and specifications derived from the customer's detailed program description. By using all inputs many analysis are accomplished within the LSA process, and the output will be LSAR. LSAR is a meaningless data warehouse by itself until we create useful reports using this warehouse for the logistics disciplines such as training, manpower and personnel, and spares modeling.

An effective LSA process is a key to the logistics success. The main objectives of the LSA process should be decreasing Total Life Cycle Cost, increasing effectiveness, acquiring supportable systems, and providing solutions to the integration problems.

Up to here I did not mention about Integrated Logistics Support (ILS) at all. I prefer to emphasize, "what ILS is not" to clearly define what it is. ILS is not a thing that you can grab by your hand, is not a process that you can draw its flow chart, or is not one of the sections of a contract. ILS is the integration of all logistics efforts within an acquisition program. This integration is not an interface, connectivity, or coordination.

During a system's life cycle a lot of logistics efforts are planned and accomplished by different organizations. If we want to talk about integration for all these efforts, we have to take into consideration all other perceptions, requirements, and needs of different parties in the first place. For example, a contractor has designed a system for a submarine with high performance and low cost, but it requires taking apart a lot of components with a lot of different special tools and skills to reach a part on which it would be just done a remove and replace task at the Organizational level. In this situation, contractor has finished the design according to the buyer's (Government) perception. Two parties, contractor and buyer, are happy with the design. But, where is the ultimate user's perception in this design? It is missing, because the following questions were not asked in the first place:

- In which environment will be the system operated?
- Who is going to maintain the system at the Organizational level?
- Which skills needed for the system maintenance at the Organizational level?
- Can I keep required people and skills on a submarine throughout the system's life cycle?
- Do I have enough space to do the maintenance tasks and store required special tools and parts on a submarine?
- What if another component fails during a remove and replace task?
- Do I have to keep spare for failed component during a remove and replace task?

It is possible to find more questions to be asked. The meaning of integration is to ask these types of questions at the very beginning of the logistics efforts and make a design having answers to these questions.

This type of integration is extremely important within today's environment, since Governments are cutting budgets while support requirements and support, manpower and personnel costs are increasing.

ILS is an art of management, which makes all logistics disciplines be implemented concurrently by LSA process centric. The goal of the ILS is harmonizing all logistics processes in the acquisition programs. ILS also brings all different perceptions of parties (user, buyer, contractor etc.) to a common base. ILS is like conducting an orchestra and ILS manager is like an orchestra conductor.

LIST OF REFERANCES

1. "Logistics", http://www.investorwords.com
2. "Definition of Logistics", http://www.crossintl.com
3. "A brief History of Logistics", http://www.dpwn.com
4. "Definition of Logistics", http://www.clm1.org
5. "What is Logistics?", http://www.logisticsworld.com
6. "Logistics Support Analysis", http://www.mtain.com
7. "Integrated Logistics Support", http://www.educesoft.com
8. "Logistics Support Analysis", http://www.aspirecl.com
9. "Core Logistics Definition", http://www.ndia.org
10. "Logistics and Logistics Support Analysis", http://www.jamesvjones.com
11. "Logistics and Administration", http://www.un.org
12. "Acquisition Logistics", MIL-HDBK-502
13. "Logistics Support Analysis", Defense Acquisition Deskbook
14. "Integrated Logistics Support", http://www.roc.noaa.gov
15. "Logistics Engineering and Management", Blanchard, B.S. (1998)

BIOGRAPHY

Born in Izmir, Turkey in December 5th, 1972. Following middle school, I attended Naval High School in İstanbul, Turkey for four years and graduated from high school in 1990.

After receiving B.S. degree in Operation Research at Turkish Naval Academy, commissioned as an ensign in August 1994. Served on three different ships as department head and Executive Officer. During this period, received various appreciation letters from commanders to whom I reported.

Awarded to serve and teach as an exemplary officer at Turkish Naval Academy and assigned to a training ship as a first Commanding Officer among peers. During my command, selected as an excellent ship and awarded by a Vice Admiral.

After receiving M.S. degree in Material Logistics Support Management at Naval Postgraduate School in Monterey, CA, assigned to Turkish Inventory Control Center as project officer. Working on configuration management, COSAL/COSBAL preparation for the ships, provisioning processes, preparing ILSP and logistics related parts of RFPs in the acquisition programs. Making presentations about ILS management and teaching short ILS courses. Participant of ILS courses both in Turkey and Europe. Also participant of 2002 SOLE Annual Conference.

I am married and have a three-year old daughter.

NORWEGIAN DEFENCE CASE STUDY:

MAINTENANCE IN THE NORWEGIAN ARMED FORCES – Norwegian Defence Industry's Role (1995-2000)

This report is unique and it is the first time such thorough analyses of operating and maintenance spending in the Norwegian Armed Forces and Norwegian Defence Industry's role (1995-2000) has been done.

1) Breakdown of Operating and Maintenance Spending
The methodology used is firstly, to present a holistic view by determining the size and volume of the Norwegian Armed Forces budget and spending on maintenance. Secondly, breaking this down into direct costs for maintenance of weapons systems and platforms, and thereafter breaking this further down to each respective service (Army, Navy and Air Force), including NODECA.
2) The Many Suppliers
Thirdly, breaking this down into suppliers categorized by size of income, country of origin, industry categories and presenting certain representative Norwegian companies/suppliers in the defence industry.
3) Possibilities for Norwegian Defence Industry
A brief look at NAMSA and more.

Observations & Conclusions
The average total estimated annual direct maintenance cost of all weapons systems and platforms in stock and use, is estimated to be approximately 1.7 billion NOK, and this represents on average a 22 % share of the total annual peacetime costs for goods and services of the Norwegian Armed Forces. 12 % of this total annual peacetime cost share is made up exclusively of ammunition purchases.

Recommendations
In addition, the report presents a number of recommendations, both to the Norwegian Ministry of Defence (MoD) and to the Norwegian Defence Industry (NHO/NFL) regarding the interdependency between Defence Capabilities Management and Strategic Logistics Management.

1) Armed Forces Future Strategy

a) Extended long-term committed national industrial materiel cooperation
b) Supply Chain Management:
   i) Outsourcing
   ii) New cost-effective interaction routines with suppliers.

Kjeller, January 15th, 2003.

Thomas L Halvorssen
Senior Adviser
Group for Industrial Strategy
Norwegian Defence Research Establishment (FFI)
POBox 25, N-2027 KJELLER, Norway.

ARL
Penn State

Asset Health Monitoring of Combat Assault Vehicles for Enhanced Logistics Command and Control

Ed Crow, Head
S&OA Division
814/863-9887
ecc1@psu.edu

Les Johnson, Dept. Head
Adv. Sensors & Controls
814/865-3913
ldj1@psu.edu

Karl Reichard, Dept. Head
Condition-Based Maintenance
814/863-7681
kmr5@psu.edu

ARL
Penn State

Relevant Issues In Asset Health Monitoring

- Definitions and Terms
- Technology of Diagnostics and Prognostics
- Application to Ground Combat Vehicles
  - Camp Pendleton Exercise in Simulation
  - Ground Vehicle Health Monitoring Demonstration
- RCM, FMECA & Cost Benefits Analysis
- Open Systems Architecture for Sensor Systems Interface
- Prognostics for Electrical Power Systems

ARL Penn State — Diagnostics and Prognostics- Spectrum of Use

Time Based Maintenance >> Diagnostics >>> Prognostics

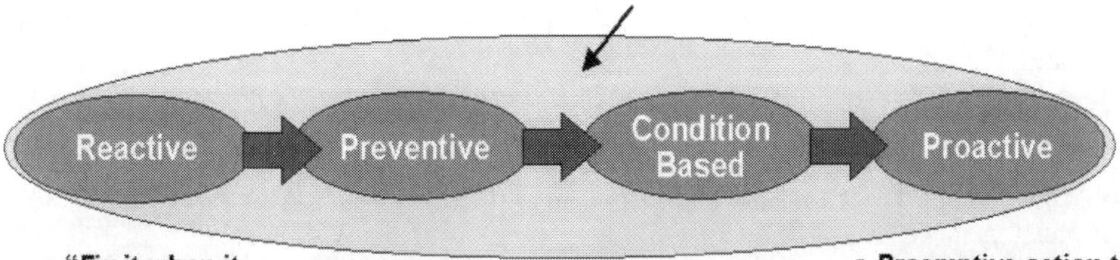

- "Fix it when it breaks"
  - Costly
  - Risky
- Scheduled
  - Reduce failures
  - Costly
  - May cause damage
- Determined by an objective measure of need
  - More effective
  - Reduces failures
  - Safely eliminates PM
  - Reduces capital
- Preemptive action to optimize reliability, eliminate defects, & avoid failure
  - Most effective
  - Minimizes failures
  - Reduces capital

Ref: Handbook – *"Operating Equipment Asset Management – Your 21st Century Competitive Necessity"* First Edition

ARL Penn State — Systems Health Monitoring

Apply appropriate sensors (data), analysis (knowledge), and reasoning (interpretation) to estimate the health and track the degradation of equipment.

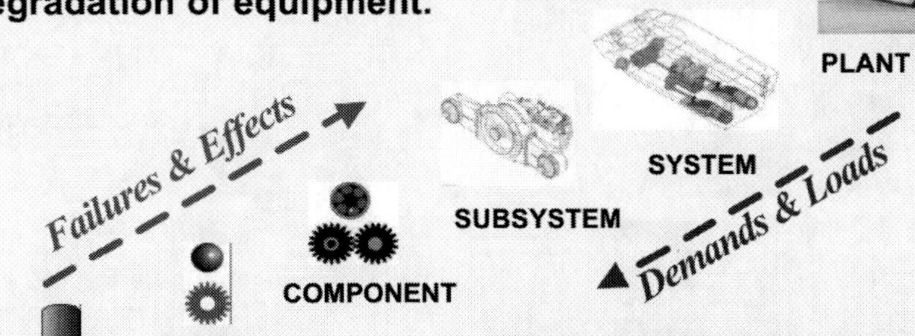

- **Detect and isolate component degradation and impending failure**
- **Give appropriate alerts to operator, maintainer and asset manager**

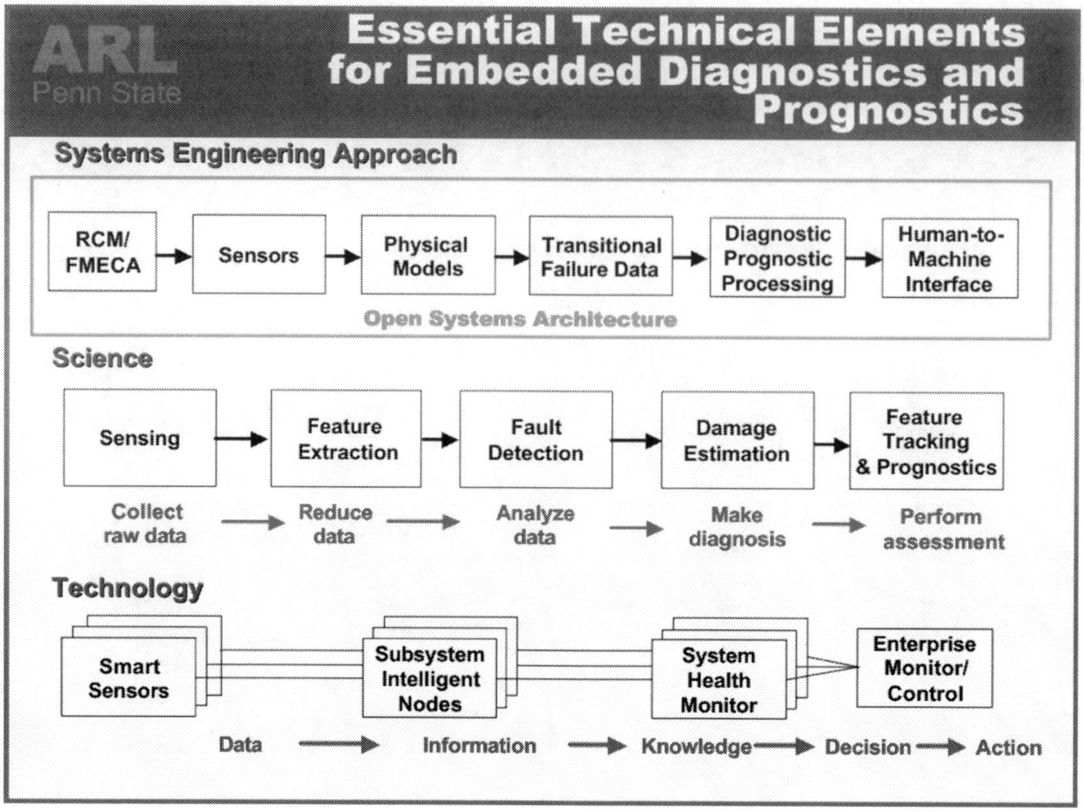
ARL
Penn State
Essential Technical Elements for Embedded Diagnostics and Prognostics
Systems Engineering Approach
RCM/ FMECA
Sensors
Physical Models
Transitional Failure Data
Diagnostic Prognostic Processing
Human-to-Machine Interface
Open Systems Architecture
Science
Sensing
Feature Extraction
Fault Detection
Damage Estimation
Feature Tracking & Prognostics
Collect raw data
Reduce data
Analyze data
Make diagnosis
Perform assessment
Technology
Smart Sensors
Subsystem Intelligent Nodes
System Health Monitor
Enterprise Monitor/ Control
Data
Information
Knowledge
Decision
Action

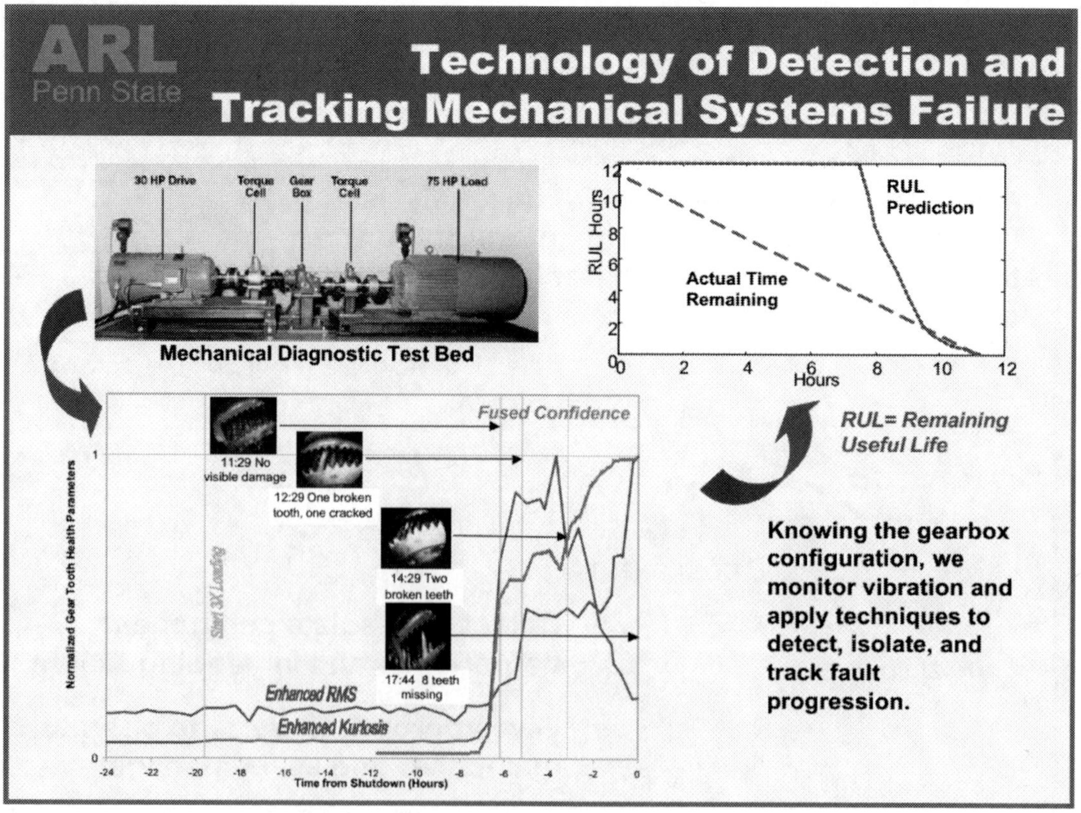
ARL
Penn State
Technology of Detection and Tracking Mechanical Systems Failure
30 HP Drive
Torque Cell
Gear Box
Torque Cell
75 HP Load
Mechanical Diagnostic Test Bed
RUL Hours
RUL Prediction
Actual Time Remaining
Hours
Fused Confidence
11:29 No visible damage
12:29 One broken tooth, one cracked
14:29 Two broken teeth
17:44 8 teeth missing
Start 3X Loading
Enhanced RMS
Enhanced Kurtosis
Normalized Gear Tooth Health Parameters
Time from Shutdown (Hours)
RUL= Remaining Useful Life
Knowing the gearbox configuration, we monitor vibration and apply techniques to detect, isolate, and track fault progression.

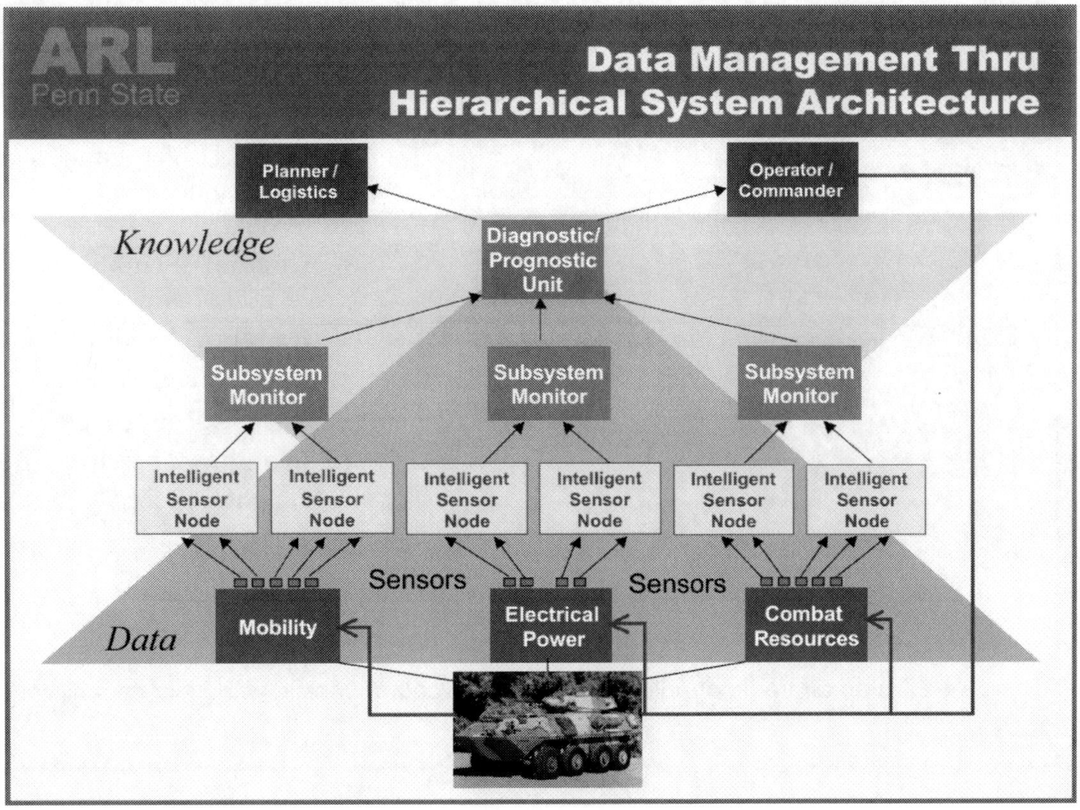
ARL
Penn State
Data Management Thru
Hierarchical System Architecture
Planner / Logistics
Operator / Commander
Knowledge
Diagnostic/ Prognostic Unit
Subsystem Monitor
Subsystem Monitor
Subsystem Monitor
Intelligent Sensor Node
Intelligent Sensor Node
Intelligent Sensor Node
Intelligent Sensor Node
Intelligent Sensor Node
Intelligent Sensor Node
Sensors
Sensors
Data
Mobility
Electrical Power
Combat Resources

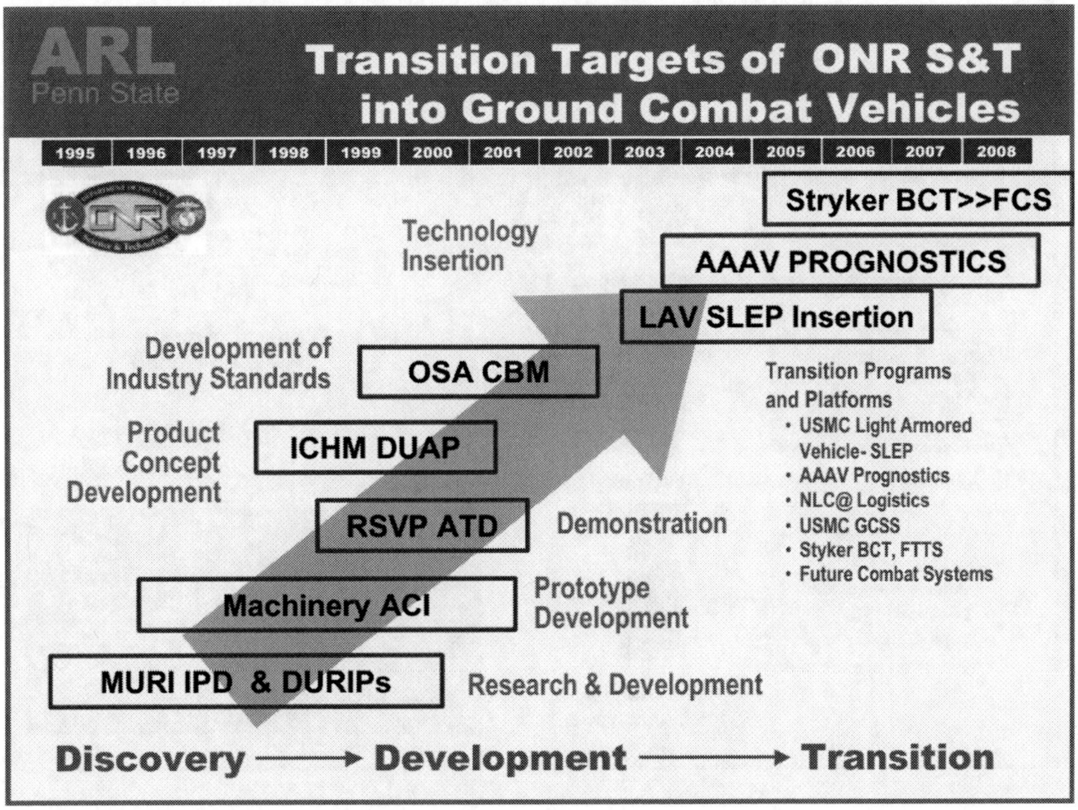
ARL
Penn State
Transition Targets of ONR S&T
into Ground Combat Vehicles
1995 1996 1997 1998 1999 2000 2001 2002 2003 2004 2005 2006 2007 2008
Stryker BCT>>FCS
Technology Insertion
AAAV PROGNOSTICS
LAV SLEP Insertion
Development of Industry Standards
OSA CBM
Transition Programs and Platforms
• USMC Light Armored Vehicle- SLEP
• AAAV Prognostics
• NLC@ Logistics
• USMC GCSS
• Styker BCT, FTTS
• Future Combat Systems
Product Concept Development
ICHM DUAP
RSVP ATD
Demonstration
Machinery ACI
Prototype Development
MURI IPD & DURIPs
Research & Development
Discovery → Development → Transition

Combat Assault Vehicle Test Bed Light Armored Vehicle (LAV-25)

ARL Penn State

- **Crew**: Driver, gunner, commander and 6 troops
- **Combat Weight**: 28,200 pounds
- **Range**: 410 miles
- **Land Speed**: 62 mph
- **Swim Speed**: 6 mph
- **Length**: ~ 21 feet
- **Height**: ~ 9 feet

The LAV-25 is an air transportable, all-terrain, all-weather vehicle with night capabilities.

LAV Monitoring System Layout (Demonstration Hardware)

ARL Penn State

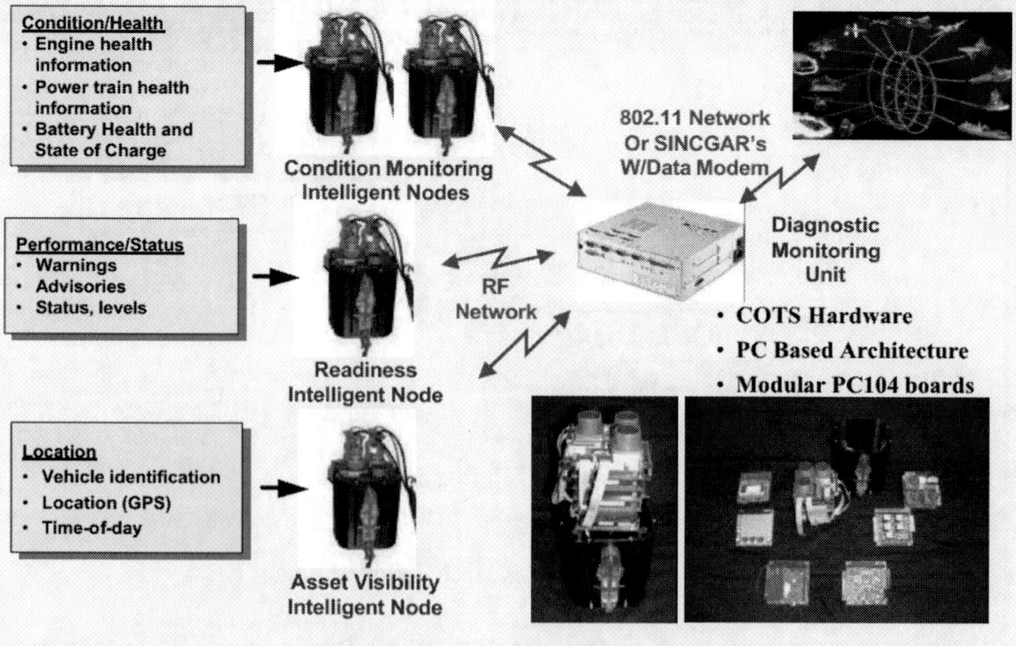

ARL
Penn State
LAV Test Bed At Penn State ARL
Click here for video

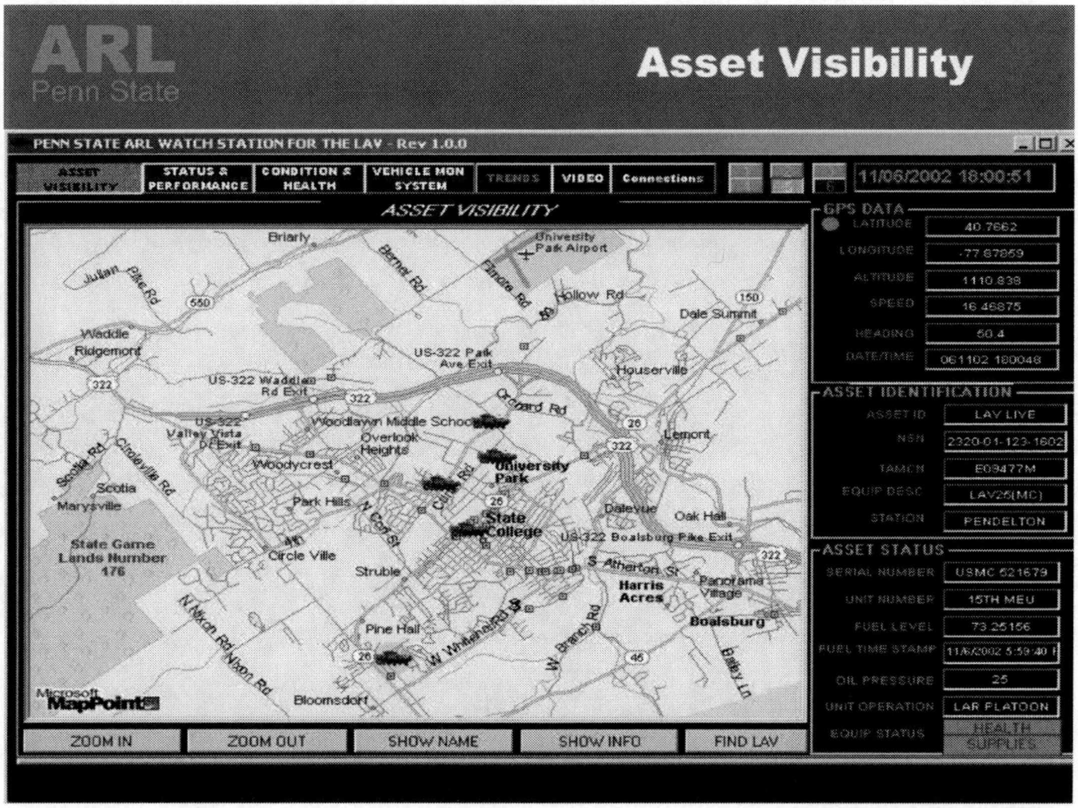
ARL
Penn State
Asset Visibility
PENN STATE ARL WATCH STATION FOR THE LAV - Rev 1.0.0
ASSET VISIBILITY
STATUS & PERFORMANCE
CONDITION & HEALTH
VEHICLE MON SYSTEM
TRENDS
VIDEO
Connections
11/06/2002 18:00:51
ASSET VISIBILITY
GPS DATA
LATITUDE 40.7662
LONGITUDE -77.87859
ALTITUDE 1110.838
SPEED 16.46875
HEADING 50.4
DATE/TIME 061102 180048
ASSET IDENTIFICATION
ASSET ID LAV LIVE
NSN 2320-01-123-1602
TAMCN E09477M
EQUIP DESC LAV25(MC)
STATION PENDELTON
ASSET STATUS
SERIAL NUMBER USMC 521679
UNIT NUMBER 15TH MEU
FUEL LEVEL 73.25156
FUEL TIME STAMP 11/6/2002 5:59:40
OIL PRESSURE 25
UNIT OPERATION LAR PLATOON
EQUIP STATUS HEALTH SUPPLIES
ZOOM IN
ZOOM OUT
SHOW NAME
SHOW INFO
FIND LAV
Microsoft MapPoint
University Park
State College
Boalsburg
Lemont
Houserville
Dale Summit
Park Hills
Pine Hall
Bloomsdorf
Harris Acres
Struble
Scotia
Marysville
State Game Lands Number 176

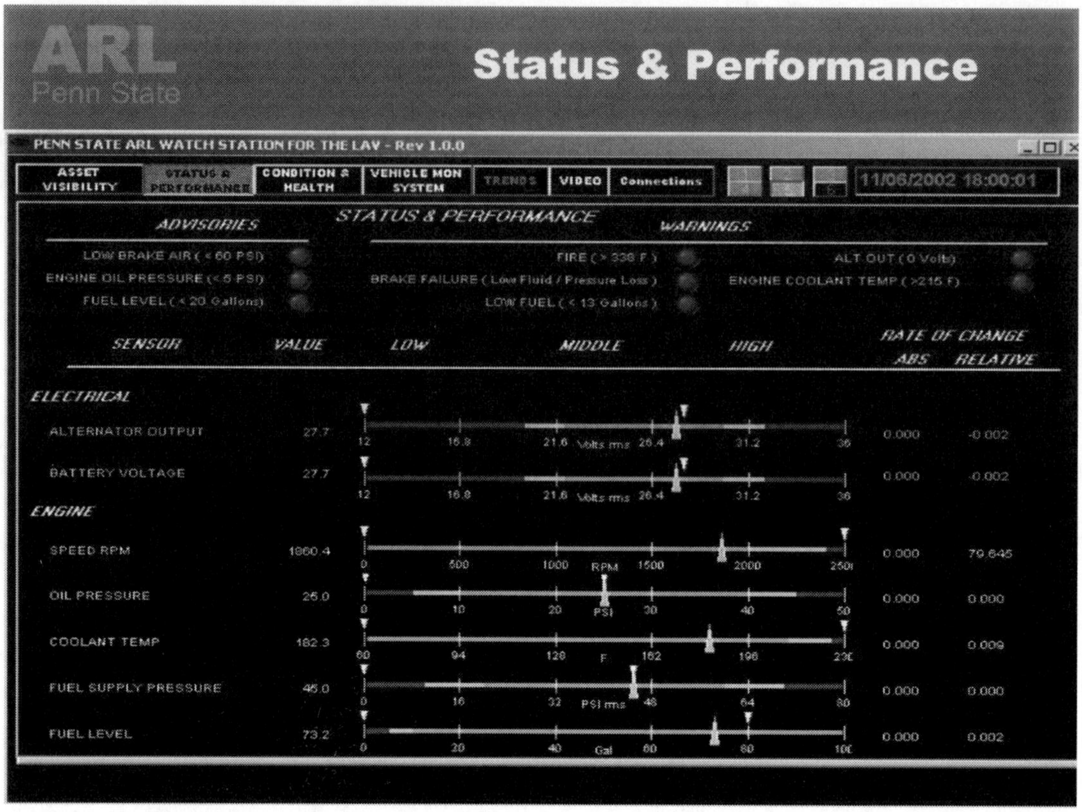
ARL
Penn State
Status & Performance
PENN STATE ARL WATCH STATION FOR THE LAV - Rev 1.0.0
ASSET VISIBILITY
STATUS & PERFORMANCE
CONDITION & HEALTH
VEHICLE MON SYSTEM
TRENDS
VIDEO
Connections
11/06/2002 18:00:01
STATUS & PERFORMANCE
ADVISORIES
WARNINGS
LOW BRAKE AIR (< 60 PSI)
ENGINE OIL PRESSURE (< 5 PSI)
FUEL LEVEL (< 20 Gallons)
FIRE (> 338 F)
BRAKE FAILURE (Low Fluid / Pressure Loss)
LOW FUEL (< 13 Gallons)
ALT OUT (0 Volts)
ENGINE COOLANT TEMP (>215 F)
SENSOR
VALUE
LOW
MIDDLE
HIGH
RATE OF CHANGE
ABS
RELATIVE
ELECTRICAL
ALTERNATOR OUTPUT
27.7
0.000
-0.002
BATTERY VOLTAGE
27.7
0.000
-0.002
ENGINE
SPEED RPM
1860.4
0.000
79.645
OIL PRESSURE
26.0
0.000
0.000
COOLANT TEMP
182.3
0.000
0.009
FUEL SUPPLY PRESSURE
46.0
0.000
0.000
FUEL LEVEL
73.2
0.000
0.002

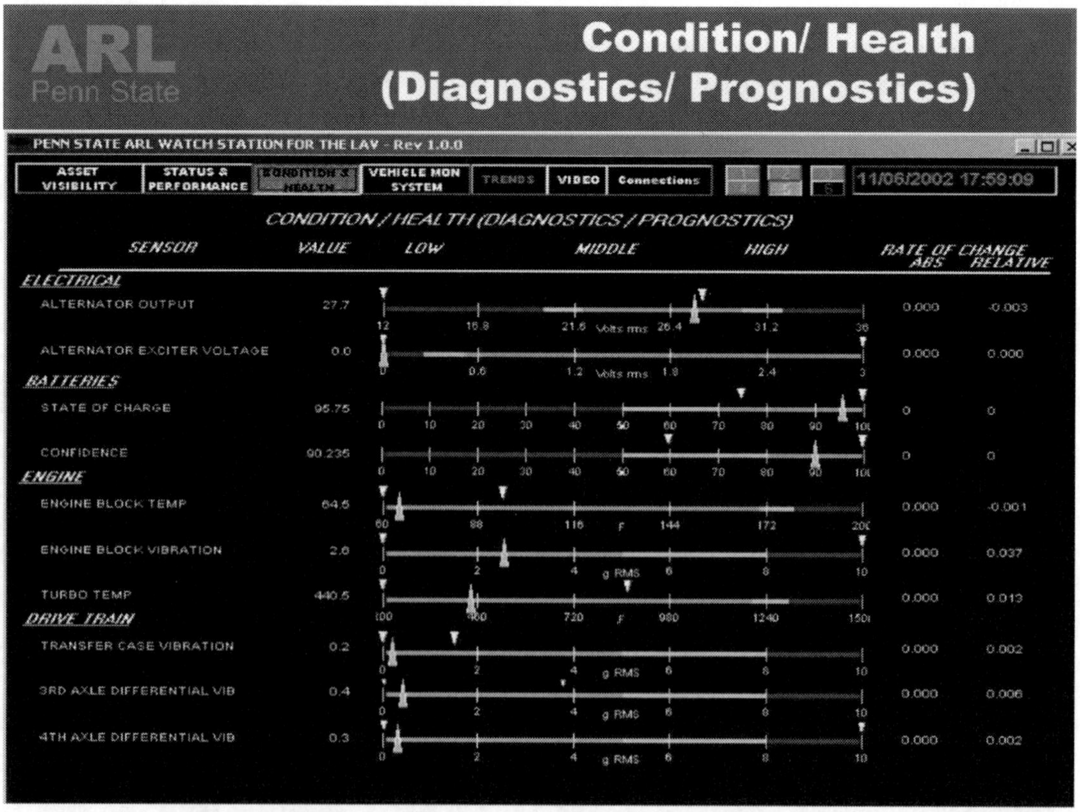
ARL
Penn State
Condition/ Health
(Diagnostics/ Prognostics)
PENN STATE ARL WATCH STATION FOR THE LAV - Rev 1.0.0
ASSET VISIBILITY
STATUS & PERFORMANCE
CONDITION & HEALTH
VEHICLE MON SYSTEM
TRENDS
VIDEO
Connections
11/06/2002 17:59:09
CONDITION / HEALTH (DIAGNOSTICS / PROGNOSTICS)
SENSOR
VALUE
LOW
MIDDLE
HIGH
RATE OF CHANGE
ABS
RELATIVE
ELECTRICAL
ALTERNATOR OUTPUT
27.7
0.000
-0.003
ALTERNATOR EXCITER VOLTAGE
0.0
0.000
0.000
BATTERIES
STATE OF CHARGE
95.75
0
0
CONFIDENCE
90.235
0
0
ENGINE
ENGINE BLOCK TEMP
64.5
0.000
-0.001
ENGINE BLOCK VIBRATION
2.6
0.000
0.037
TURBO TEMP
440.5
0.000
0.013
DRIVE TRAIN
TRANSFER CASE VIBRATION
0.2
0.000
0.002
3RD AXLE DIFFERENTIAL VIB
0.4
0.000
0.006
4TH AXLE DIFFERENTIAL VIB
0.3
0.000
0.002

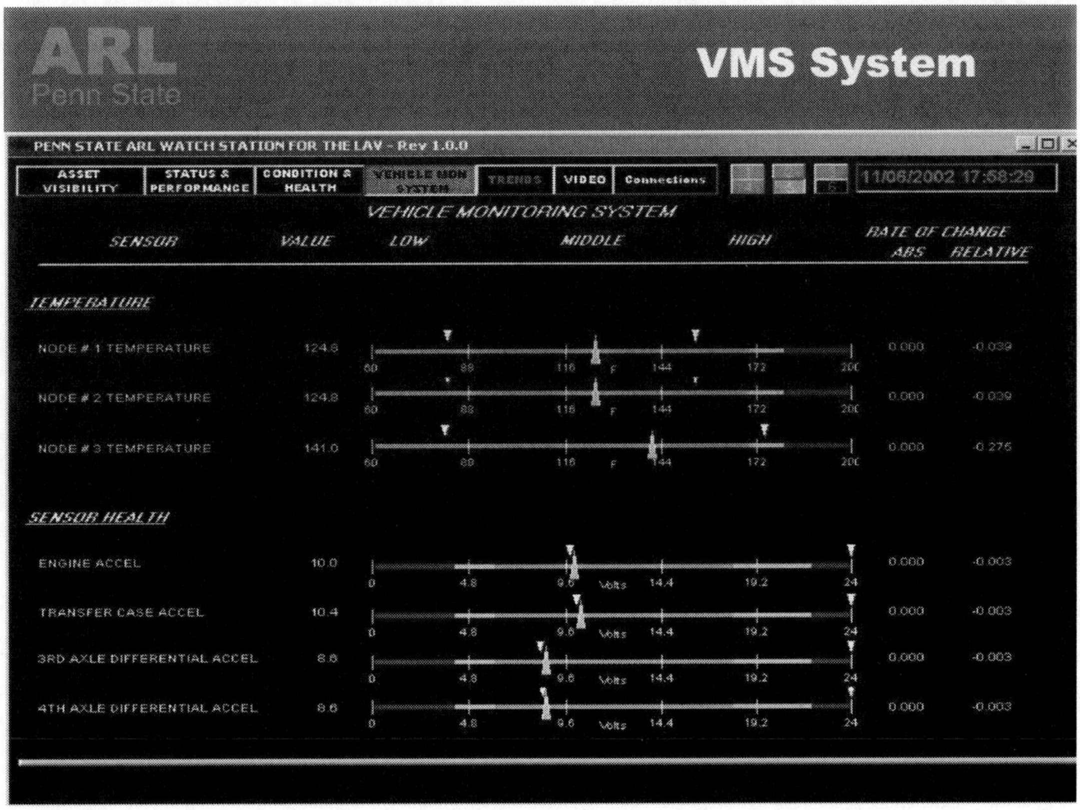
ARL
Penn State
VMS System
PENN STATE ARL WATCH STATION FOR THE LAV - Rev 1.0.0
ASSET VISIBILITY
STATUS & PERFORMANCE
CONDITION & HEALTH
VEHICLE MON SYSTEM
TRENDS
VIDEO
Connections
11/06/2002 17:58:29
VEHICLE MONITORING SYSTEM
SENSOR
VALUE
LOW
MIDDLE
HIGH
RATE OF CHANGE
ABS
RELATIVE
TEMPERATURE
NODE # 1 TEMPERATURE 124.8 0.000 -0.039
NODE # 2 TEMPERATURE 124.8 0.000 -0.039
NODE # 3 TEMPERATURE 141.0 0.000 -0.275
SENSOR HEALTH
ENGINE ACCEL 10.0 0.000 -0.003
TRANSFER CASE ACCEL 10.4 0.000 -0.003
3RD AXLE DIFFERENTIAL ACCEL 8.8 0.000 -0.003
4TH AXLE DIFFERENTIAL ACCEL 8.6 0.000 -0.003

ARL
Penn State
Live Video
PENN STATE ARL WATCH STATION FOR THE LAV - Rev 1.0.0
ASSET VISIBILITY
STATUS & PERFORMANCE
CONDITION & HEALTH
VEHICLE MON SYSTEM
TRENDS
VIDEO
Connections
11/06/2002 17:57:14
OUTSIDE LAV 12:56:09 6-NOV-
INSIDE LAV 12:56:07 6-NOV-

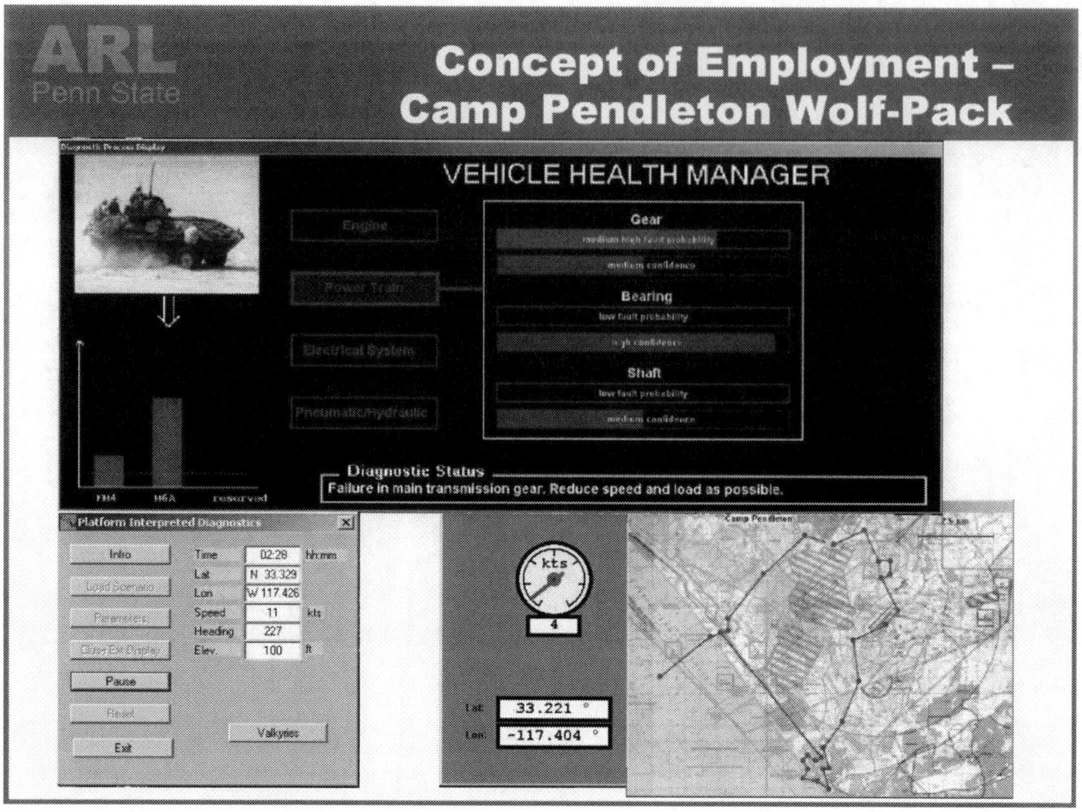
ARL
Penn State
Concept of Employment –
Camp Pendleton Wolf-Pack
VEHICLE HEALTH MANAGER
Engine
Power Train
Electrical System
Pneumatic/hydraulic
Gear
medium high fault probability
medium confidence
Bearing
low fault probability
high confidence
Shaft
low fault probability
medium confidence
Diagnostic Status
Failure in main transmission gear. Reduce speed and load as possible.
Platform Interpreted Diagnostics
Info
Load Scenario
Parameters
Close Ext Display
Pause
Reset
Exit
Time 02:28 hh:mm
Lat N 33.329
Lon W 117.426
Speed 11 kts
Heading 227
Elev. 100 ft
Valkyries
kts
4
Lat 33.221 °
Lon -117.404 °
Camp Pendleton

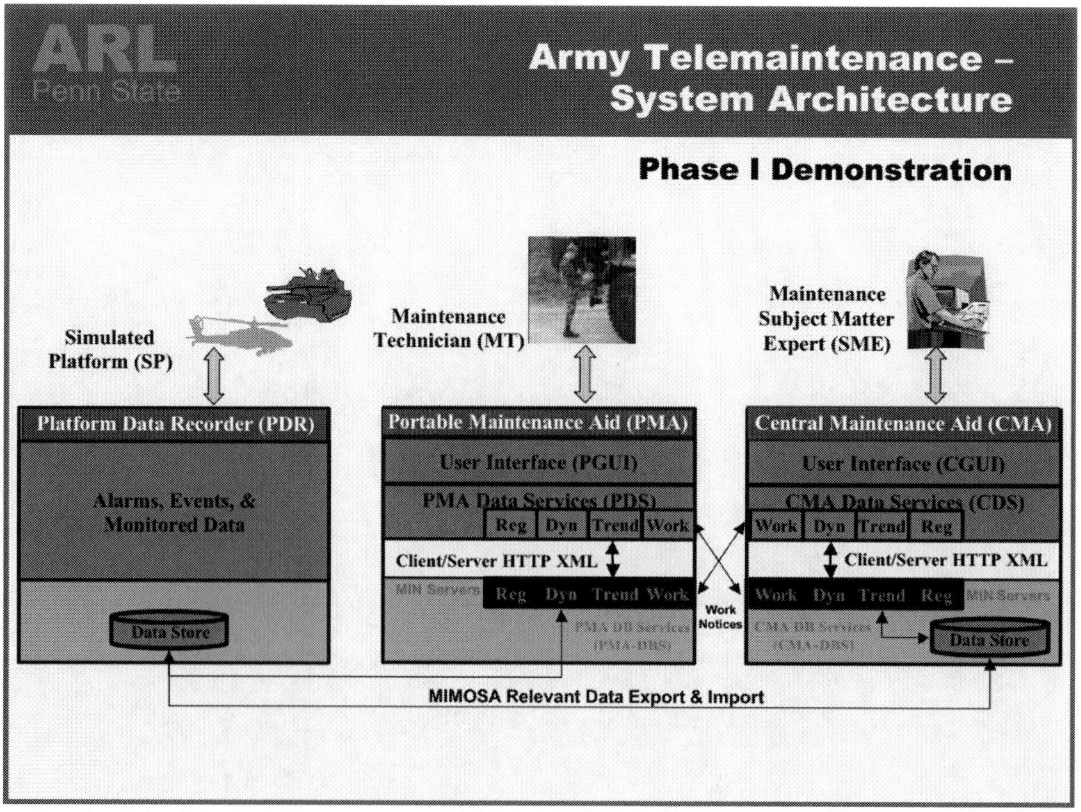
ARL
Penn State
Army Telemaintenance –
System Architecture
Phase I Demonstration
Simulated Platform (SP)
Maintenance Technician (MT)
Maintenance Subject Matter Expert (SME)
Platform Data Recorder (PDR)
Alarms, Events, & Monitored Data
Data Store
Portable Maintenance Aid (PMA)
User Interface (PGUI)
PMA Data Services (PDS)
Reg Dyn Trend Work
Client/Server HTTP XML
MIN Servers
Reg Dyn Trend Work
PMA DB Services (PMA-DBS)
Work Notices
Central Maintenance Aid (CMA)
User Interface (CGUI)
CMA Data Services (CDS)
Work Dyn Trend Reg
Client/Server HTTP XML
Work Dyn Trend Reg
MIN Servers
CMA DB Services (CMA-DBS)
Data Store
MIMOSA Relevant Data Export & Import

ARL
Penn State

Army Telemaintenance – Data Access

Both the maintenance technician and the SME see the same data collected during the mission

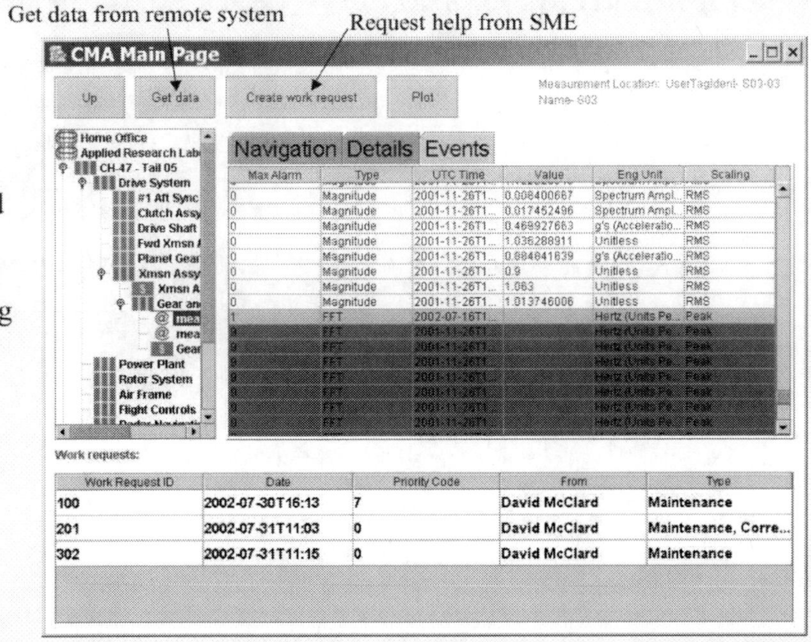

ARL
Penn State

Operational Availability vs. Maintenance Actions

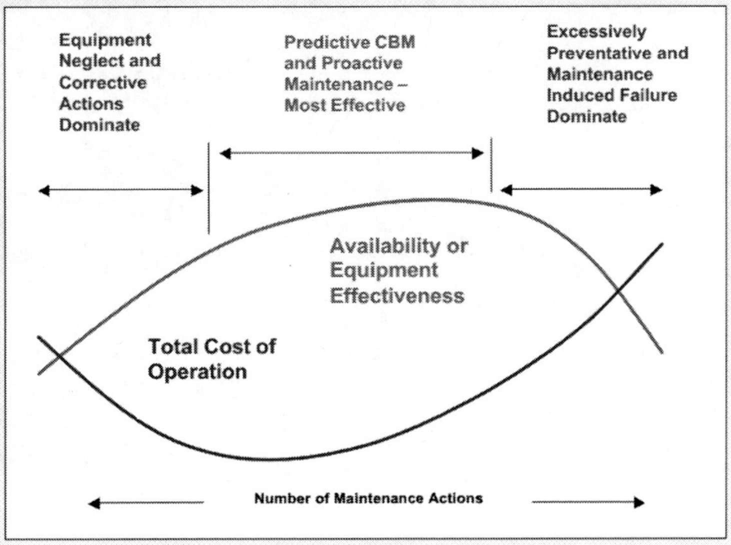

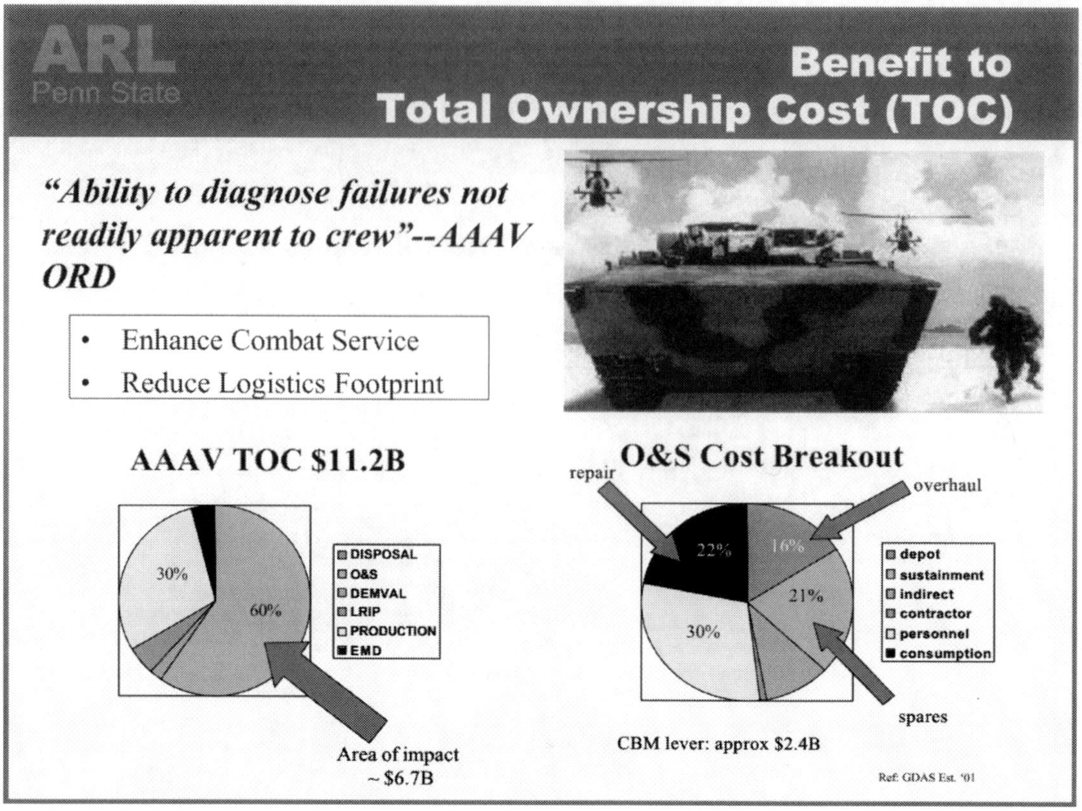
ARL
Penn State
Benefit to
Total Ownership Cost (TOC)
"Ability to diagnose failures not readily apparent to crew"--AAAV ORD
• Enhance Combat Service
• Reduce Logistics Footprint
AAAV TOC $11.2B
30%
60%
DISPOSAL
O&S
DEMVAL
LRIP
PRODUCTION
EMD
Area of impact
~ $6.7B
O&S Cost Breakout
repair
overhaul
22%
16%
21%
30%
depot
sustainment
indirect
contractor
personnel
consumption
spares
CBM lever: approx $2.4B
Ref: GDAS Est. '01

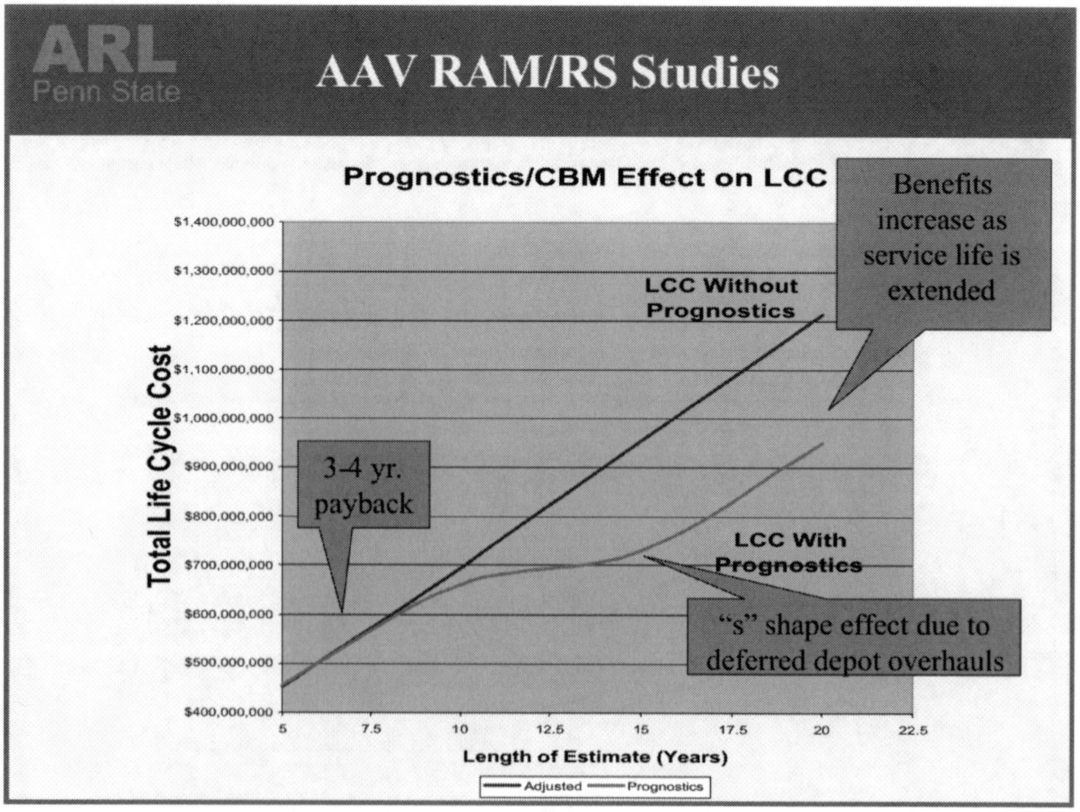
ARL
Penn State
AAV RAM/RS Studies
Prognostics/CBM Effect on LCC
Benefits increase as service life is extended
$1,400,000,000
$1,300,000,000
$1,200,000,000
$1,100,000,000
$1,000,000,000
$900,000,000
$800,000,000
$700,000,000
$600,000,000
$500,000,000
$400,000,000
Total Life Cycle Cost
LCC Without Prognostics
3-4 yr. payback
LCC With Prognostics
"s" shape effect due to deferred depot overhauls
5
7.5
10
12.5
15
17.5
20
22.5
Length of Estimate (Years)
Adjusted
Prognostics

Increased Operational Availability

ARL Penn State

AAV RAM/RS Data (Hours)	W/O Prog	W/Prog
Mean Time Between Failures	64	73.6
Mean Time To Repair	0.87	0.87
Mean Logistics Delay Time	5.4	2.7675

AAV RAM/RS Calculations	W/O Prog	W/Prog
Forecasted Op Availability	91.08%	95.29%
Increase in Op Avail w/Prog		4.21%
Increased AAVs Mission Capable w/Prog		29
Total LCC Costs per AAV w/Prog		$973,504
Operational Availability Opportunity Benefit of Prognostics		**$27,890,754**

Benefits can either be: increased Ao; decreased life cycle cost or reduced number of assets for same total operational availability

Qualitative Advantages

ARL Penn State

- Command and Control (decision-making)
- Reduction in Maintenance-Induced Errors
- Increased Effectiveness and Responsiveness of logistics in USMC
- Reduction in Transportation and Inventory Costs for repair parts
- Reduction in shipboard space requirement for repair parts
- Positively impact material life which reduces the end item fielding requirement and contributes to military transformation
- Increased safety of operators and passengers

Qualitative Assessment

ARL Penn State

- (-) False Alarms
- (-) Defense contractor resistance to to reduction in after-market parts sales and those responsible for day-to-day status of machinery.
- Far Reaching impact on future maintenance infrastructure
  - Less Maintenance Actions and Errors
  - Less Manpower (Technicians)
  - Less Facilities and Test/Support Equipment
  - "Transformation" of Maintenance

Open System Architecture for Condition Based Maintenance

ARL Penn State

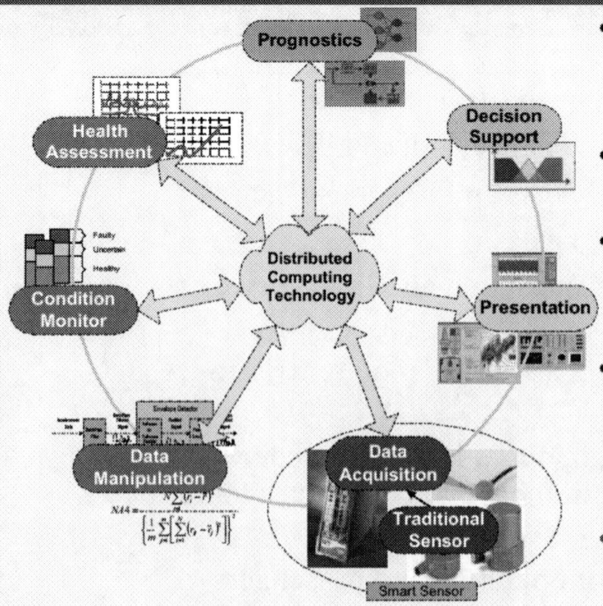

- Standardized architecture for autonomous control and system monitoring
- Breaks monitoring system into functional layers
- OSA-CBM standard defines inputs and outputs required for each layer
- Autonomous controller interface will depend on level of abstraction at controller input.
- www.osacbm.org

ARL Penn State

OSA CBM Architecture

1 – Data Acquisition: Collects analog data from traditional sensors or interfaces to a smart sensor and acts as data server to system.
2 – Data Manipulation: May perform single and/or multi-channel signal transformations along with specialized feature extraction algorithms.
3 – Condition Monitor: Compares features against expected values or operational limits and output enumerated condition indicators (e.g. low, normal, high).
4 – Health Assessment: Determines if the health of a monitored system or subsystem is degraded. This layer may generate a diagnostic record that proposes one or more possible fault conditions with an associated confidence.
5 – Prognostics: Project the current health state into the future, accounting for estimates of future usage profiles. Reports health status at a future time, or may estimate the remaining useful life (RUL) of an asset given its projected usage.
6 – Decision Support: Provide recommended actions and alternatives. Recommendations include maintenance action schedules, modifying the operational configuration, or modifying mission profiles.
7 – Human Interface (Presentation Layer): Displays high-level status (health assessments, prognosis, or support recommendations) to human user.

ARL Penn State

The Case for Battery Health Monitoring

Causes

•Aging: dry-out,dendrites; passivation; corrosion
•Charging: overcharge; low electrolyte charging
• Mechanical/Vibration: case cracks; broken plates

Problems

-Damaged or faulty battery not detected until attempted engine start
-Remaining time not accurately known while using only battery power
-Remaining engine starts using the vehicle batteries not known
-Impending battery faults not detected

Present Solutions

-Carry backup or reserve batteries
-Over-design batteries to reduce use and time between failures
-Heavy, costly

Impact to the Service

$36M Possible Cost Avoidance *
-$17.5M M&S for Secondary Battery Maintenance
-$ 7.2M Primary Battery Procurement & Disposal
-$ 8.8M Secondary Battery Procurement & Disposal
-$ 2.5M ILS Reduction and Training Costs
Realized if Battery Health Monitoring is implemented

* Battery Charger/Analyzer Review, August 2000.

Battery Prognostics Application to Combat Assault Vehicle

ARL Penn State

ONR Funded Battery Prognostics S&T

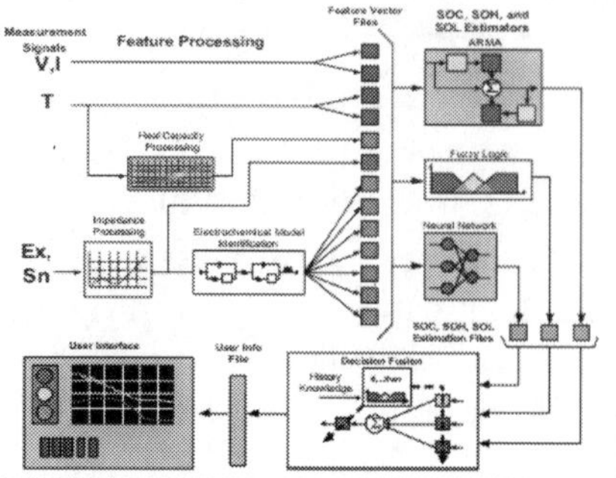

- Fast, reliable predictions of SOC, SOH, and SOL with performance errors <5%
- A low power system (<1/2 watt) that could be embedded in a battery, equipment using the battery, or hand-held meter

to AAAV CANbus

TOC FNC Funded Application to AAAV

Patent #6,307,378 ***[Grant N00014-98-1-0795]***

PENNSTATE ARL

Systems Approach

Mission Information Requirements

Mission Readiness – Operational Readiness for Mission Planning

Safety/Platform Status operator alert of pending, critical system / component fault

Combat Systems and Life Cycle Support – inputs to an optimized maintenance activity

System Cost

Cost/Benefit	Threshold	Objective	Current
Design to Unit Prod'n Cost	$X.XXM	$X.XXM	$X.XXM
Total Ownership Cost	$XX.XB	$XX.XB	$XX.XB

Mission Critical Components and Their Failure Modes

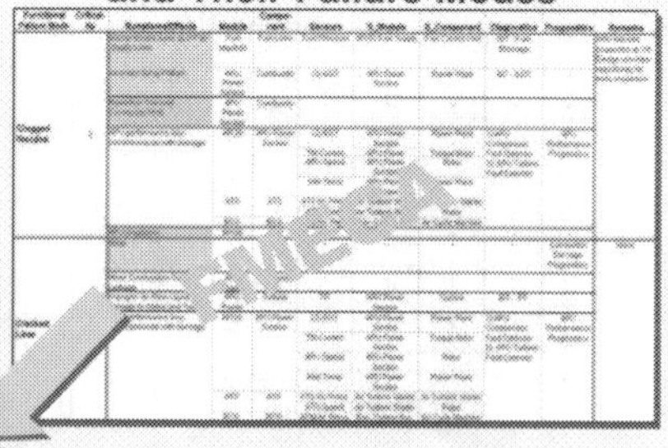

AAAV/SS4CBM Critical Item Product Development Specification SB-AAAV-20001

Sensors, Signals Monitoring and Diagnostics

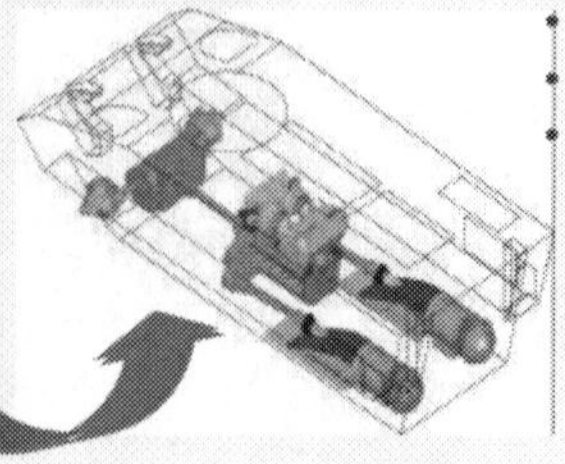

Tiered Design -
- Information layer
- Network layer
- Hardware layer
- Software layer

ARL Penn State

Considerations for Deployment

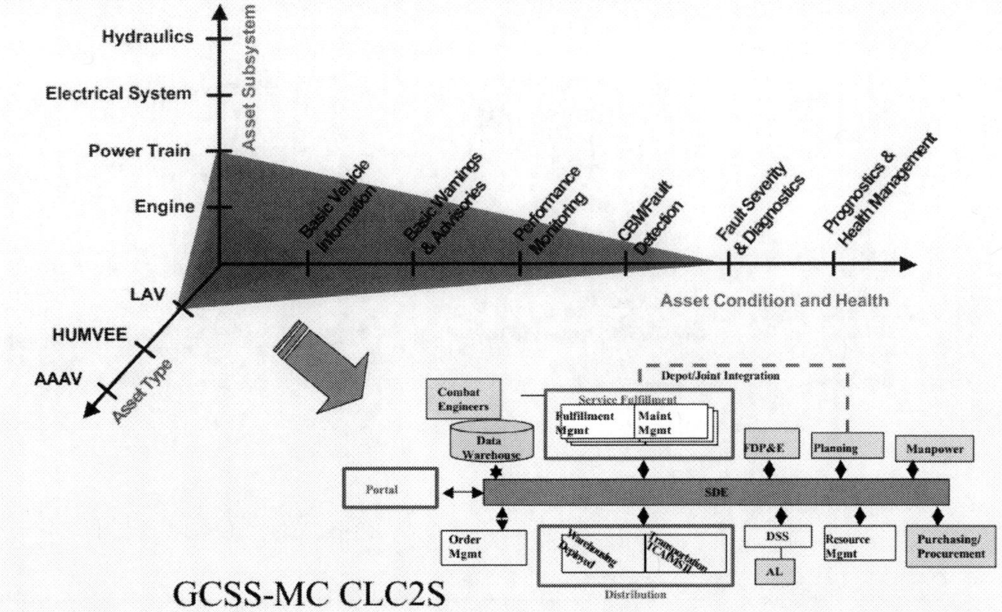

ARL Penn State

Path Forward: Asset Health Management for Command and Control

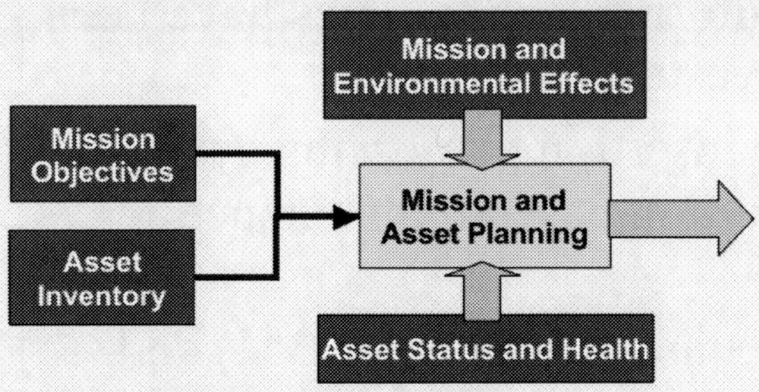

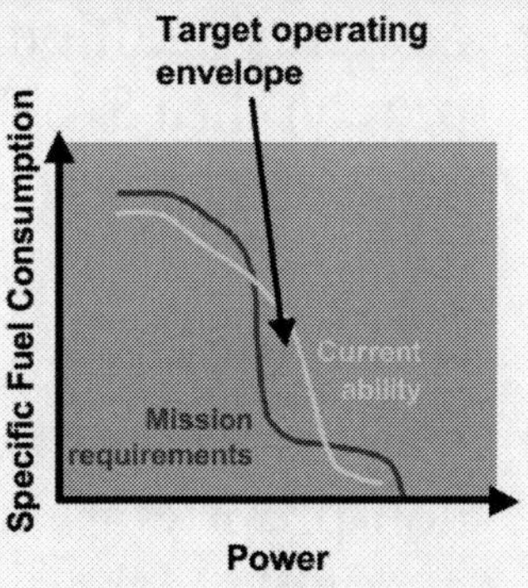

<u>Intelligent Mission Planning:</u>

- Incorporates asset condition
- Tailors mission tasks to specific capabilities
- Considers mission effects on asset condition

<u>Result:</u>

- More effective match of capabilities to needs
- Increased probability of mission success
- Decreased maintenance and logistics costs

How do I match remaining useful life and asset capability with particular mission elements?

ARL Penn State

Enabling Tactical Force Management

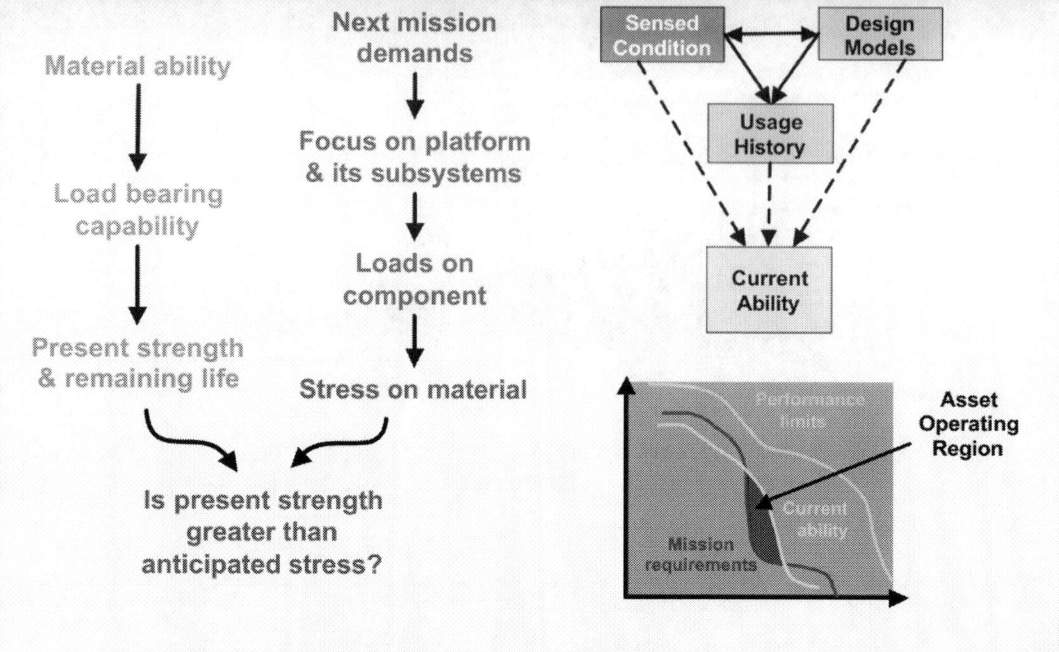

ARL Penn State

Conclusion

- Systems health monitoring technologies have been proven thru S&T investments
- There is a benefit to insertion of systems health monitoring and condition based maintenance technology
- Use of open system standards (OSA-CBM) and non-proprietary solutions will allow “best available technologies of the times” to be used
- Intelligently monitoring systems are safer, more reliable, better assure the mission and reduce total ownership cost.

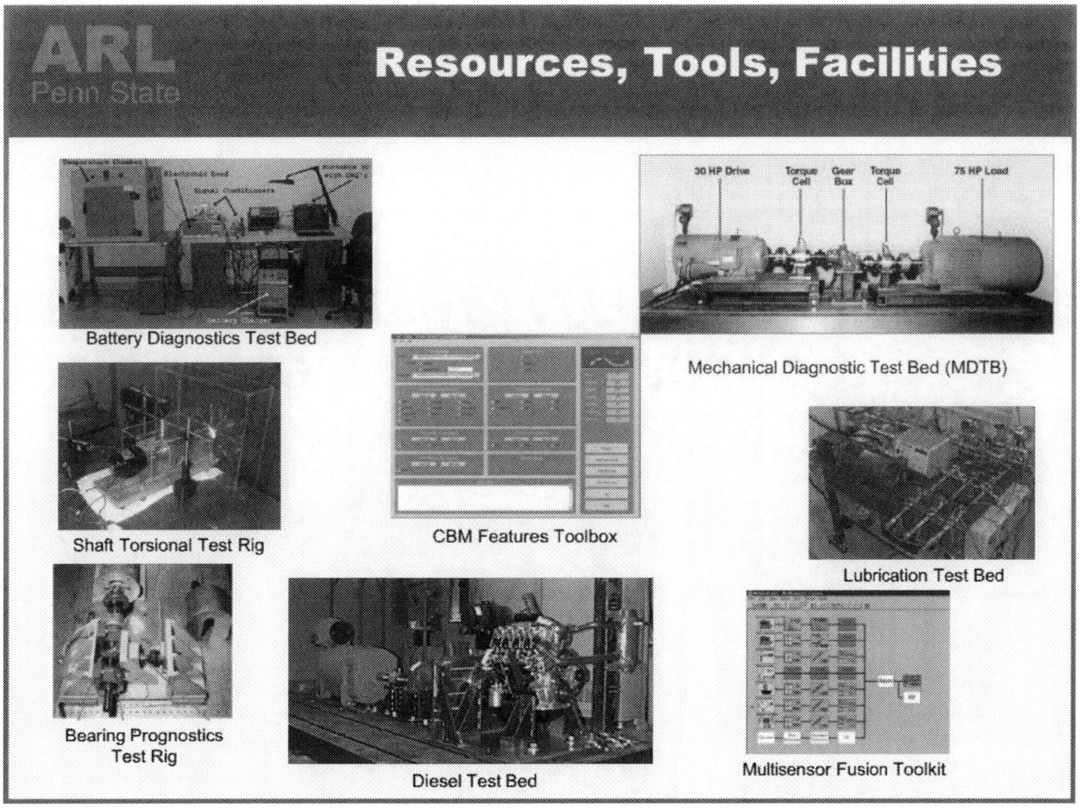
ARL
Penn State
Resources, Tools, Facilities
Battery Diagnostics Test Bed
30 HP Drive
Torque Cell
Gear Box
Torque Cell
75 HP Load
Mechanical Diagnostic Test Bed (MDTB)
Shaft Torsional Test Rig
CBM Features Toolbox
Lubrication Test Bed
Bearing Prognostics Test Rig
Diesel Test Bed
Multisensor Fusion Toolkit

The Applied Research Laboratory
The Pennsylvania State University
www.arl.psu.edu/areas/soa/soabiz.html
WELCOME TO ARL
ARL Penn State
P.O. Box 30
State College, Pennsylvania 16804
www.arl.psu.edu
(814) 865-6343

MARINE CORPS EQUIPMENT READINESS INFORMATION TOOL (MERIT)

By

Mr. Michael A. Williamson, CPL

United States Marine Corps
Marine Corps Logistics Command

ABSTRACT

Marine Corps Logistics Command has developed a Materiel Readiness Decision Support Tool which graphically depicts the materiel readiness and detailed supply and maintenance information for all Marine Corps readiness reportable Weapon Systems. Marine Corps Equipment Readiness Information Tool (MERIT) transforms data into "intelligence". This situational awareness tool allows Commanders at all levels throughout the Marine Corps to make informed decisions that ensure that we are maintaining our combat readiness at the highest state possible while investing our scarce resources wisely. This paper provides a sneak preview of a tool that is revolutionalizing how the Marine Corps manages readiness.

I. Introduction.

The Marine Corps Equipment Readiness Information Tool (MERIT) is the first of its kind Equipment Readiness management tool developed by capitalizing on existing Marine Corps efforts! MERIT is a powerful, web-enabled tool which graphically depicts the current readiness posture and detailed supply and maintenance information for all Marine Corps readiness reportable TAMCNs. Versatile, scalable, and intuitive, MERIT taps into legacy data from Marine Corps Systems and also will be able to import from planned future Marine Corps logistics systems as well as non-Marine Corps automated information systems.

II. Background.

In Nov 2000, the Materiel Command formed the Materiel Readiness Integrated Product Team (MRIPT), which brought together a cross-functional team that focused on materiel readiness policy, calculations, displays, reporting and procedures. Among other changes and improvements in Marine Corps materiel readiness, the MRIPT identified and began development of an information tool which would allow us to not only display readiness data but would also provide a "drill down analysis" capability that could be used throughout the Marine Corps Enterprise.

HQMATCOM chartered the MRIPT to move the Marine Corps toward a single materiel readiness capability. This "one watch" for materiel readiness will allow us to move from reactive to proactive total life cycle systems management. Some of the challenges associated with achieving that "one watch" for materiel readiness have been: visibility and reporting of materiel readiness data and information, lack of standardization and lack of supply and maintenance integration.

III. Discussion.

MERIT transforms data into valuable information that provides a dynamic adaptable view of Equipment Readiness by Commodity and Functional Area. An automatic graphics generator feature provides customized information of current and historical readiness and is ideal for developing readiness related briefing charts at all levels within the Marine Corps. Using a drilldown approach, MERIT takes you from the top level of Marine Corps Readiness posture to the supply status of specific parts. By drastically reducing the readiness information data gathering effort, MERIT enables users to solve and prevent readiness problems.

MERIT provides a total view of the Marine Corps Readiness picture. It's scope, versatility, and user-friendly operation makes MERIT a "need to have" for everyone associated with ensuring the readiness of Marine Corp equipment. MERIT gives Force Commanders visibility of their Readiness trends, problems and associated causes. It also provides detailed information required by maintainers, Logistics Management Specialist (LMS's), Program Managers (PM's), and analysts.

MERIT is an enterprise level initiative that achieved Phase I, Initial Operating Capability on 20 December 2002, with Full Operational Capability achieved on 28 Mar 2003.

IV. Conclusion.

MERIT is the tool that will move the Marine Corps toward a single materiel readiness capability. Through our Rapid Prototype Development efforts, MERIT will provide the Marine Corps with Total Life Cycle Systems Management enhancement capabilities. This enterprise level function should continue to be performed by the Albany Command in the future.

AUTHOR'S BIOGRAPHY

Michael A. Williamson, CPL

Serving his 20th year with the Marine Corps, he is currently the Director, Studies and Analysis Department, Marine Corps Logistics Command. Previous positions include, Principal Director, Storage and Distribution Directorate; Deputy Director Fleet Support Division; Director Operations, Materiel Division; Director, Maintenance Data Analysis Center; and Logistics Management Analyst. Graduate of the Navy's Logistics Intern Program. Currently enrolled in the Senior Executive MBA program at the University of Tennessee. Holds a BBA from Georgia Southwestern University. Member of the Defense Leadership and Management Program. Married to the former Debra Presley and they have two girls, Michelle and Micah.

AUTHOR INDEX

SOLE – The International Society of Logistics
14625 Baltimore Avenue, Suite 303
Laurel, Maryland 20707-4902
USA

ISBN 978-1-5108-3839-0

CURRAN ASSOCIATES INC.
proceedings.com